780 2

Encyclopedia of BIBLE DIFFICULTIES

Encyclopedia of BIBLE DIFFICULTIES

Gleason L. Archer

Foreword by
KENNETH S. KANTZER

Regency
Reference Library
Zondervan Publishing House
Grand Rapids, Michigan

ENCYCLOPEDIA OF BIBLE DIFFICULTIES
Copyright © 1982 by The Zondervan Corporation
Grand Rapids, Michigan

Regency Reference Library is an imprint of Zondervan
Publishing House, 1415 Lake Drive, S.E.,
Grand Rapids, Michigan 49506

Library of Congress Cataloging in Publication Data

Archer, Gleason Leonard, 1916–
    An encyclopedia of Bible difficulties.

    Bibliography: p.
    Includes index.
    1. Bible—Examinations, questions, etc.
I. Title.
BS612.A73   220.6   82-1964
ISBN 0-310-43570-6   AACR2

Edited by Richard P. Polcyn
Designed by Martha Bentley

Printed in the United States of America

90 91 92 93 94 / AF / 17 16 15 14 13

Contents

7 Foreword
11 Preface
13 Acknowledgments
14 How to Use This Encyclopedia
15 Recommended Procedures in Dealing With Bible Difficulties
19 Introduction: The Importance of Biblical Inerrancy
45 The Pentateuch
55 Genesis
109 Exodus
126 Leviticus
129 Numbers
146 Deuteronomy
155 Joshua
163 Judges
167 Ruth
169 1 Samuel
183 2 Samuel
191 1 Kings
204 2 Kings
216 1 Chronicles
225 2 Chronicles
229 Ezra
233 Nehemiah
234 Esther
235 Job
242 Psalms
250 Proverbs

254 Ecclesiastes
261 Song of Solomon
263 Isaiah
272 Jeremiah
276 Ezekiel
282 Daniel
294 Hosea
296 Joel
297 Amos
298 Obadiah
300 Jonah
303 Zechariah
305 Malachi
307 The New Testament and the Old Testament
311 The Synoptic Gospels
316 Matthew
362 Mark
365 Luke
369 John
377 Acts
385 Romans
396 1 Corinthians
403 Galatians
404 Ephesians
406 Colossians
410 2 Thessalonians
411 1 Timothy
416 2 Timothy
418 Hebrews
423 1 Peter
425 2 Peter

428   1 John
430   Jude
431   Revelation
435   Bibliography

437   Index of Persons
450   Index of Subjects
464   Index of Scripture
       References

Foreword

Dr. Gleason Archer has written this encyclopedia to show that there is nothing in the Bible inconsistent with the claim that it is the inerrant Word of God. In the last century this doctrine has increasingly come under sharp criticism. Unfortunately Christians who oppose the doctrine of biblical inerrancy usually misunderstand it. In most cases they gleaned their view of what it means from an uninstructed Sunday school teacher or an overenthusiastic radio preacher. Perhaps they have never had the occasion to consult the work of a serious-minded scholar. Readers will soon discover that the view of inerrancy set forth by Dr. Archer is the historical position of the church in all of its major branches. Behind it stand the illustrious names of Augustine, Aquinas, John of Damascus, Luther, Calvin, Wesley, and a host of others. Put quite simply, this view of inerrancy holds that the Bible tells us truth and never says what is not so.

It might be helpful to begin by dispelling some of the most common misunderstandings of biblical inerrancy. Evangelicals do not try to prove that the Bible has no mistakes so that they can be sure the Bible is the Word of God. One might prove that a newspaper article is free from all mistakes, but that would not prove that the newspaper article is the Word of God. Christians hold the Bible to be the Word of God (and inerrant) because they are convinced that Jesus, the Lord of the church, believed it and taught His disciples to believe it. And ultimately their conviction of its truth rests on the witness of the Holy Spirit.

Likewise evangelicals do not hold that inerrant inspiration eliminates the human element in the production of the Bible. True, evangelicals have stressed the divine authorship of Scripture because this is most frequently denied and it is this that gives Scripture its unique importance. But informed evangelicals have always insisted on a truly human authorship of Scripture. Even those who were willing to use the word *dictation* (as did Calvin and the Tridentine Council of the Roman Catholic church) always made very clear that they were not referring to the model of a boss dictating to a stenographer. Rather, they meant to stress the divine (as well as human) responsibility for the words of Scripture and that the inscripturated words are just as truly God's authoritative words as though He had dictated them.

One could argue (illogically) that God could prevent the biblical writers from error only by eliminating their freedom and their humanity, but evangelicals have not so argued. Rather, the Bible is both a thoroughly human and a thoroughly divine product. As a divine product it possesses absolute authority over the minds and hearts of believers. As a human product it displays within itself all of the essential marks of its human writing. No doubt God could have given us a Bible in the perfect language of heaven, but then who of us would have understood it? He chose to communicate his will to us through the imperfect medium of human language with all its possibilities for misinterpretation and misunderstanding. On the other hand the gift of language is one of our most trustworthy means of communicating our wishes and our ideas to one another. God, therefore, chose to communicate to us through this imperfect instrument of human language.

In writing the Bible, its authors used figures of speech, allegory, symbolic language, and the various genre of literature employed by other human authors. Moreover, because they wrote in the language of the common man of two or more millennia ago, they frequently chose not to provide specific technical data where that was not important to their purpose. Never do they speak in the vocabulary of modern science. They felt no more obligation to be precise and exact in many of their statements than we do in our ordinary conversation. Divine inspiration guaranteed only the truth of what they wrote. God preserved them from error both of ignorance and of deception. But He did not prevent them from speaking as humans. And only if we take the ridiculous and self-contradictory position that error is essential to all human speaking and writing, can we insist that the true humanity of Scripture necessarily carries with it false statements. While preserving their full humanity, with all that implies for the character of their writing, the Holy Spirit kept the writers of the Bible from making erroneous statements. As a result we do not need to pick and choose what is taught in Scripture. All of it is God's truth.

The attempt, like Dr. Archer's, to show that there are no mistakes or false statements in the Bible is frequently objected to from opposite viewpoints. One asks, "Why bother to defend the Bible? You do not defend a roaring lion from a mouse. Nor should we place ourselves in the false position of defending the Scripture. We need only to unleash it. It will conquer by its own power without our feeble endeavors to support it."

But the faith of some troubled souls is hindered by misunderstanding the Scripture. They are confused by what seems to them to be false statements or self-contradiction. We need, therefore, to clear away such false obstacles to faith. If there remains any obstacle to faith, it should be the stumbling block of the cross or the cost of discipleship rather than an imaginary obstacle that could easily be eliminated. In spite of what we sometimes hear, God never asks us to crucify our intellects in order to believe.

A second objection to dealing seriously with alleged discrepancies and mistakes in the Bible comes from the opposite position that it is not worthwhile to do so because it is perfectly obvious that the Bible is full of errors. There is no uniformity in the way in which this second type of judgment comes, but all forms of it stem basically from too little faith in the Bible. World-famous theologian, Karl Barth, for example, declares that the Bible shouts from the housetop that it is a human book and that an essential part of its humanity is to err. Others hold that the Bible is a book God inspired in order to give us religious truth but not precise facts of science and history. To waste time defending the Bible in these latter areas is to do it a disservice, they say. It diverts attention away from the real purpose of the Bible, which is rather to instruct us in spiritual and moral matters. A variant of this position is that the purpose of the Bible is to lead us to the personal truth of Christ. The Bible may be wrong on many points, but it points to the Savior; and to focus attention on points of geography, history, astronomy, and biology is only to divert it from its true goal—personal faith in Christ.

Of course, there are also others who hold that the Bible is full of errors because its authors were simply children of their times. Miller Burrows, former professor of New Testament at Yale University, accurately summarizes this rather typical modern viewpoint: "The Bible is full of things which to an intelligent educated person of today are either quite incredible or at best highly questionable. . . . The protracted struggle of theology to defend the inerrancy of the Bible (i.e. its complete truth) against the findings of astronomy, geology, and biology has been a series of retreats ending in a defeat which has led all wise theologians to move to a better position." (*Outline of Biblical Theology* [Philadelphia: Westminster, 1946], pp. 9, 44)

Common to all of these objections is the conviction that any defense of biblical inerrancy is at best a waste of time and at worst positively harmful because it leads one away from the true purpose of the Bible, which is to bring us to God.

The inerrantist's response is quite simple. For him the basic issue is: Who is Jesus Christ? If the Bible is so far from the truth that it is all wrong as to who Jesus Christ is, then there can be no question about it: the Bible is full of erroneous statements. It is nonsense to discuss whether or not the Bible tells us only the truth in all it teaches if, in fact, it is really dead wrong on the main thrust of its teaching. In short, evangelical inerrantists have no quarrel with radicals who reject Jesus Christ as their religious guide. But for those who accept Jesus Christ as their divine Lord, the teaching of Jesus Christ must be taken with dreadful seriousness. It is consistent to deny Jesus Christ as Lord and also to reject the full authority of the Bible, but it is inconsistent to confess Him as Lord and then reject His teaching. On this matter, the evangelical seeks only to be consistent. Jesus is Lord, and the evangelical believes what He taught about the full truthfulness of the Old Testament. By the Holy Spirit He also promised to give similar authority to His disciples for their guidance of the church after He had completed His own earthly ministry.

The evangelical, moreover, does not feel the overwhelming force of the discrepancies and errors alleged by some to be profusely scattered throughout the Bible. He finds that most such problems dissolve the moment one sees clearly that the Bible is a human book written in the ordinary language of two thousand and more years ago. It is only when we try to make the Bible into a book written in the exact, precise style that we have become accustomed to in a modern laboratory report that we run into difficulty.

For the same reason the evangelical considers it unreasonable for anyone to demand that he must be able to demonstrate the complete harmony of all Bible passages before he can reasonably accept them as true. The Bible was written millennia ago by independent authors drawn from various cultures and scattered over many centuries. In view of the nature of the Bible, it is much more reasonable that we should *not* be able to demonstrate on the basis of our limited knowledge a neat harmony of all biblical data. Quite to the contrary, the evangelical is amazed that there are as few apparently insoluble problems as there are. Inerrancy is not unbelievable nor does it require a sacrifice of the intellect. Rather, the actual situation with respect to biblical problems is precisely what we should expect in view of the fact that the Bible is a book of inerrant truth coming to us from across many centuries and alien cultures.

Finally, just a word needs to be said about Dr. Archer and his special qualifications for this task. Few scholars are so uniquely equipped in their command of ancient languages and of the tools of biblical scholarship as is Dr. Archer. In addition to his own integrity as a scholar, he is a dedicated student of Scripture and a trustworthy guide for those who wish to understand Scripture better. His book will be a rich gold mine for those who hold to the inerrancy of Scripture and who need help in seeking to bring that conviction into harmony both with what they read in the Bible and the facts of the empirical world about them. I believe this book will prove immensely valuable to many earnest Christians and I heartily commend it to the church and to all serious Bible students.

Kenneth S. Kantzer

Preface

The idea for this book first occurred to me in October 1978, in connection with the Summit Conference of the International Council on Biblical Inerrancy, held in Chicago. At that time it was apparent that a chief objection to inerrancy was that the extant copies of Scripture contain substantial errors, some of which defy even the most ingenious use of textual criticism. In my opinion this charge can be refuted and its falsity exposed by an objective study done in a consistent, evangelical perspective. Nothing less than the full inerrancy of the original manuscripts of Scripture can serve as the basis for the infallibility of the Holy Bible as the true Word of God.

The earnest debate current within Evangelicalism (as well as that within neoorthodoxy and liberalism) has impressed on me the urgent need for this book. Undoubtedly, a panel of scholars would have produced a superior piece of work; but in consideration of the time element, it seemed best to handle this as a one-man work.

For several years I have been engaged in apologetics for *Decision* magazine, produced by the Billy Graham Evangelistic Association in Minneapolis. Many of the articles that appear in this encyclopedia were previously prepared for *Decision*, and all such are identified with (D*). The longer discussions, however, have been especially prepared for this book.

The problems and questions dealt with in this volume have been directed to me during the past thirty years of teaching on the graduate seminary level in the field of biblical criticism. As an undergraduate at Harvard, I was fascinated by apologetics and biblical evidences; so I labored to obtain a knowledge of the languages and cultures that have any bearing on biblical scholarship. As a classics major in college, I received training in Latin and Greek, also in French and German. At seminary I majored in Hebrew, Aramaic, and Arabic; and in post-graduate years I became involved in Syriac and Akkadian, to the extent of teaching elective courses in each of these subjects. Earlier, during my final two years of high school, I had acquired a special interest in Middle Kingdom Egyptian studies, which was furthered as I later taught courses in this field. At the Oriental Institute in Chicago, I did specialized study in Eighteenth Dynasty historical records and also studied Coptic and Sumerian. Combined with this work in ancient languages was a full course of training at law school, after which I was admitted to the Massachusetts Bar in 1939. This gave me a thorough grounding in the field of legal evidences. Additionally, I spent three months in Beirut, Lebanon, in specialized study of modern literary Arabic. This was followed by a month in the Holy Land, where I visited most of the important archaeological sites.

This extensive training, combined with the classroom challenge of thousands of seminarians I have been privileged to teach, has especially prepared me for an undertaking of this sort. I candidly believe I have been confronted with just about all the biblical difficulties under discussion in theological circles today—especially those pertaining to the interpretation and defense of Scripture. It may be that some readers of this book will be disappointed to find that some of their personal difficulties have not been covered. If so, please send your problem in written form to the publisher. If there is sufficient response, a supplemental volume may be produced.

I have attempted to present the material in the average layman's language—that is, all but the technical terminology. Yet at the same time I have occasionally transliterated the Greek, Hebrew, Aramaic, or related languages for the benefit of those acquainted with them. Less frequently the actual characters are used for the benefit of those who are technically trained.

As I have dealt with one apparent discrepancy after another and have studied the alleged contradictions between the biblical record and the evidence of linguistics, archaeology, or science, my confidence in the trustworthiness of Scripture has been repeatedly verified and strengthened by the discovery that almost every problem in Scripture that has ever been discovered by man, from ancient times until now, has been dealt with in a completely satisfactory manner by the biblical text itself—or else by objective archaeological information. The deductions that may be validly drawn from ancient Egyptian, Sumerian, or Akkadian documents all harmonize with the biblical record; and no properly trained evangelical scholar has anything to fear from the hostile arguments and challenges of humanistic rationalists or detractors of any and every persuasion. There is a good and sufficient answer in Scripture itself to refute every charge that has ever been leveled against it. But this is only to be expected from the kind of book the Bible asserts itself to be, the inscripturation of the infallible, inerrant Word of the Living God.

In regard to the Bible versions used in the discussion of biblical texts, I have often translated directly from the Hebrew or Greek, especially where some technical point of wording was involved. When I have used recent English versions, the New American Standard Bible (NASB) has been most frequently cited, followed by the New International Version (NIV). Less frequently I have used the King James Version (KJV) or the American Standard Version (ASV). Occasionally the name of God, Yahweh, has been substituted for LORD in quoting a verse from a particular version. (Only the Jerusalem Bible [JB] among the more recent versions uses the original name Yahweh.) I feel that it would be far better to use this name wherever the Hebrew original does.

Acknowledgments

I would like to express my appreciation to my colleagues and friends of the International Council on Biblical Inerrancy and to its board of directors, under the leadership of James Montgomery Boice and Jay Grimstead, who have warmly encouraged me to pursue this project and have afforded me all possible assistance in carrying it through. I am grateful to the president and the board of Trinity Evangelical Divinity School for granting me a sabbatical term and a reduced load during this last academic year so that I might bring this book to completion. My warmest gratitude goes also to Zondervan Publishing House for its generous help in enabling me to pursue my work on an accelerated schedule and for covering all extra expenses arising from it.

A special tribute is due my former colleague and faithful friend Harold Lindsell, who through his recent writings has exercised such a decisive influence in bringing this vital issue of Biblical inerrancy to the attention of our evangelical constituency throughout the English-speaking world. Nor should I fail to mention the debt I owe to my former pastor Harold John Ockenga of Park Street Church, Boston, whose powerful defense of the complete trustworthiness and divine authority of Holy Scripture exerted such a decisive influence on my convictions as a college student and sent me into the ministry of the gospel rather than into the legal career I had chosen for myself.

I think also of my gifted and faithful former colleagues Wilbur Smith and Carl F.H. Henry, my esteemed theology professor John Kuizenga of Princeton, and Oswald T. Allis of Westminster. Each has had a real influence on my understanding of the trustworthiness of Scripture. The same is true of Francis A. Schaeffer, whose deeply perceptive mind sends forth such a timely prophetic call to our confused generation on both sides of the Atlantic. Nor should I forget gifted scholars of a former generation, like William Henry Green and Robert Dick Wilson of Princeton and J. Gresham Machen of Westminster, whose writings contributed so much to my understanding of God's Word and my confidence in its infallible authority.

Above and beyond all the enrichment and strength I have ever received from these faithful servants of Christ, I wish to offer my thanks and praise to my incomparable Redeemer and King, the Lord Jesus Christ, who by His blessed Spirit reached down to me in my darkness and sin, drew me to Himself in redeeming love and sanctifying grace, and made me a child of the King. "To me, who am less than the least of all saints, is this grace given, that I should preach among the Gentiles the unsearchable riches of Christ" (Eph. 3:8).

How to Use This Encyclopedia

The Bible passages dealt with in this volume are given in the order of their appearance in the Bible. This makes it easy for the readers to find the verse or verses that present a problem to them. If a certain passage is not treated in the place expected, it is possible that it is discussed under some other reference. The index of Scripture references will be helpful for finding such verses. In addition, the index of subjects and persons will help the readers locate specific topics, even if the exact Scripture references are unknown to them. Most of the Synoptic problems are found under Matthew, but those that appear in the other two Synoptics are easily located in the Scripture index, as well as under the subject listing.

A bibliography has been prepared for those who wish to make more complete studies of certain texts or topics.

Recommended Procedures
in Dealing With Bible Difficulties

In dealing with Bible problems of any kind, whether in factual or in doctrinal matters, it is well to follow appropriate guidelines in determining the solution. This is most easily done by those who have carefully and prayerfully studied the Bible over a number of years and have consistently and faithfully memorized Scripture. Some guidelines are as follows:

1. Be fully persuaded in your own mind that an adequate explanation exists, even though you have not yet found it. The aerodynamic engineer may not understand how a bumble bee can fly; yet he trusts that there must be an adequate explanation for its fine performance since, as a matter of fact, it does fly! Even so we may have complete confidence that the divine Author preserved the human author of each book of the Bible from error or mistake as he wrote down the original manuscript of the sacred text.

2. Avoid the fallacy of shifting from one a priori to its opposite every time an apparent problem arises. The Bible is either the inerrant Word of God or else it is an imperfect record by fallible men. Once we have come into agreement with Jesus that the Scripture is completely trustworthy and authoritative, then it is out of the question for us to shift over to the opposite assumption, that the Bible is only the errant record of fallible men as they wrote about God. If the Bible is truly the Word of God, as Jesus said, then it must be treated with respect, trust, and complete obedience. Unlike all other books known to man, the Scriptures come to us from God; and in them we confront the ever-living, ever-present God (2 Tim. 3:16–17). When we are unable to understand God's ways or are unable to comprehend His words, we must bow before Him in humility and patiently wait for Him to clear up the difficulty or to deliver us from our trials as He sees fit. There is very little that God will long withhold from the surrendered heart and mind of a true believer.

3. Carefully study the context and framework of the verse in which the problem arises until you gain some idea of what the verse is intended to mean within its own setting. It may be necessary to study the entire book in which the verse occurs, carefully noting how each key term is used in other passages. Compare Scripture with Scripture, especially all those passages in other parts of the Bible that deal with the same subject or doctrine.

4. Remember, no interpretation of Scripture is valid that is not based on careful exegesis, that is, on wholehearted commitment to determining what the ancient author meant by the words he used. This is accomplished by a painstaking study of the key words, as defined in the dictionaries (Hebrew and Greek) and as used in parallel passages. Research also the specific meaning of these words in idiomatic phrases as observed in other parts of the Bible.

15

Consider how confused a foreigner must be when he reads in a daily American newspaper: "The prospectors made a *strike* yesterday up in the mountains." "The union went on *strike* this morning." "The batter made his third *strike* and was called out by the umpire." "*Strike* up with the Star Spangled Banner." "The fisherman got a good *strike* in the middle of the lake." Presumably each of these completely different uses of the same word go back to the same parent and have the same etymology. But complete confusion may result from misunderstanding how the speaker meant the word to be used. Bear in mind that inerrancy involves acceptance of and belief in whatever the biblical author meant by the words he used. If he meant what he said in a literal way, it is wrong to take it figuratively; but if he meant what he said in a figurative way, it is wrong to take it literally. So we must engage in careful exegesis in order to find out what he meant in the light of contemporary conditions and usage. That takes hard work. Intuition or snap judgment may catch one up in a web of fallacy and subjective bias. This often results in heresy that hinders the cause of the Lord one professes to serve.

5. In the case of parallel passages, the only method that can be justified is harmonization. That is to say, all the testimonies of the various witnesses are to be taken as trustworthy reports of what was said and done in their presence, even though they may have viewed the transaction from a slightly different perspective. When we sort them out, line them up, and put them together, we gain a fuller understanding of the event than we would obtain from any one testimony taken individually. But as with any properly conducted inquiry in a court of law, the judge and jury are expected to receive each witness's testimony as true when viewed from his own perspective—unless, of course, he is exposed as an untrustworthy liar. Only injustice would be served by any other assumption—as, for example, that each witness is assumed to be untruthful unless his testimony is corroborated from outside sources. (This, of course, is the assumption made by opponents of the inerrancy of Scripture, and it leads them to totally false results.)

6. Consult the best commentaries available, especially those written by Evangelical scholars who believe in the integrity of Scripture. A good 90 percent of the problems will be dealt with in good commentaries (see Bibliography). Good Bible dictionaries and encyclopedias may clear up many perplexities. An analytical concordance will help establish word usage (e.g., Strong's, Young's).

7. Many Bible difficulties result from a minor error on the part of a copyist in the transmission of the text. In the Old Testament such transmissional errors may have resulted from a poor reading of the vowels; Hebrew was originally written in consonants only, and the vowel signs were not added until a thousand years after the completion of the Old Testament canon. But there are also some consonants that are easily confused because they look so much alike (e.g., ד [*d*, daleth] and ר [*r*, resh] or י [*y*, yod] and ו [*w*, waw]). Besides that, some words are preserved in a very old spelling susceptible of misunderstanding by later Hebrew copyists. In other words, only a resort to textual criticism and its analysis of the most frequent types of confusion and mistake can clear up the difficulty (for bibliography on this, cf. Introduction). This takes in confusion of numerals also, where statistical errors are found in our present text of Scripture (e.g., 2 Kings 18:13).

8. Whenever historical accounts of the Bible are called in question on the basis of alleged disagreement with the findings of archaeology or the testimony of ancient non-Hebrew documents, always remember that the Bible is itself an

archaeological document of the highest caliber. It is simply crass bias for critics to hold that whenever a pagan record disagrees with the biblical account, it must be the Hebrew author that was in error. Pagan kings practiced self-laudatory propaganda, just as their modern counterparts do; and it is incredibly naive to suppose that simply because a statement was written in Assyrian cuneiform or Egyptian hieroglyphics it was more trustworthy and factual than the Word of God composed in Hebrew. No other ancient document in the B.C. period affords so many clear proofs of accuracy and integrity as does the Old Testament; so it is a violation of the rules of evidence to assume that the Bible statement is wrong every time it disagrees with a secular inscription or manuscript of some sort. Of all the documents known to man, only the Hebrew-Greek Scriptures have certified their accuracy and divine authority by a pattern of prediction and fulfillment completely beyond the capabilities of man and possible only for God.

Introduction: The Importance of Biblical Inerrancy

Throughout the history of the Christian church, it has been clearly understood that the Bible as originally given by God was free from error. Except for heretical groups that broke away from the church, it was always assumed that Scripture was completely authoritative and trustworthy in all that it asserts as factual, whether in matters of theology, history, or science. In the days of the Protestant Reformation, Luther affirmed, "When the Scripture speaks, God speaks." Even his Roman Catholic opponents held to that conviction, though they tended to put church tradition on almost the same level of authority as the Bible. From the days of the earliest Gnostics, whom Paul had to contend with, until the rise of deism in the eighteenth century, no doubts were expressed concerning the inerrancy of Scripture. Even Unitarians like Socinus and Michael Servetus argued their position on the basis of the infallibility of Scripture.

The rise of rationalism and the deistic movement in the eighteenth century led to a drastic modification of the inerrant status of the Bible. The lines were soon drawn quite clearly between the deists and the orthodox defenders of the historic Christian faith. An increasing aversion toward the supernatural dominated the intellectual leadership of the Protestant world during the nineteenth century, and this spirit gave rise to "historical criticism" both in Europe and America. The Bible was assumed to be a collection of religious sentiments composed by human authors completely apart from inspiration by God. If there was any such power as a Supreme Being, He was either an impersonal Force that pervaded the created universe (the pantheistic view), or else He was so far removed from man as to be Wholly Other and, as such, almost completely unknowable (the Kierkegaardian alternative). At best, Scripture could only offer some sort of unverifiable testimony that pointed toward the living Word of God, a reality that could never be adequately captured or formulated as propositional truth.

In the first half of the present century, the lines were clearly drawn between orthodox Evangelicals and the opponents of scriptural inerrancy. The Crisis theologians (whose views on revelation trace back to Kierkegaard) and the liberals or modernists (who subordinated the authority of Scripture to the authority of human reason and modern science) forthrightly rejected the doctrine of inerrancy. Whether or not they avowed themselves to be "Fundamentalists," all those who laid claim to being Evangelicals stood shoulder to shoulder in their insistence that the Old and New Testaments, as originally given, were free from error of any kind.

During the second half of this century, however, a new school of revisionists has risen to prominence, and this school poses a vigorous challenge to biblical inerrancy and yet lays claim to being truly and fully evangelical. The increasing popularity of this approach has resulted in the detachment of a large number of

19

formerly evangelical seminaries from the historic position on Scripture, even here in America. As Harold Lindsell has documented this trend in his *Battle for the Bible* (Grand Rapids: Zondervan, 1976), virtually all the theological training centers that have embraced (or even tolerated as allowable) this modified concept of biblical authority exhibit a characteristic pattern of doctrinal erosion. They resemble ships that have slipped their moorings and are slowly drifting out to sea.

There is always a transitional period, however, during which these defecting schools maintain—especially to their rank-and-file constituency from whom they derive their financial support—that they are still completely evangelical in their theology, that they still adhere to the cardinal doctrines of the historic Christian church. They have simply shifted to firmer ground in their defense of the truth of Scripture. As one of their advocates has put it: "I believe that the Bible is without error, but I refuse to let someone else define what that means, in such a way that I have to go to ridiculous extremes to defend my faith."[1] Proponents of this approach invariably argue that they alone are the honest and credible defenders of scriptural authority because the "phenomena of Scripture" include demonstrable errors (in matters of history and science, at least), and therefore full inerrancy cannot be sustained with any kind of intellectual integrity. The evidential data simply will not permit a successful defense of the historic Christian position on Scripture. Even as originally composed in Hebrew, Aramaic, and Greek, we may be certain that the autographa themselves contained factual errors (except, perhaps, in matters of doctrine).

In answer to this claim, it is incumbent on consistent Evangelicals to show two things: (1) the infallible authority of Scripture is rendered logically untenable if the original manuscripts contained any such errors and (2) no specific charge of falsehood or mistake can be successfully maintained in the light of all the relevant data. For this reason the appeal to the phenomena of Scripture leads not to a demonstration of its fallibility but to added confirmation of its divine inspiration and supernatural origin. In other words, we must first show that the alternative of infallibility without inerrancy is not a viable option at all, for it cannot be maintained without logical self-contradiction. And, second, we must show that every asserted proof of mistake in the original manuscripts of Scripture is without foundation when examined in the light of the established rules of evidence.

Without Inerrancy the Scriptures Cannot Be Infallible

To all professing Christians, the authority of the Lord Jesus Christ is final and supreme. If in any of His views or teachings as set forth in the New Testament He was guilty of error or mistake, He cannot be our divine Savior; and all Christianity is a delusion and a hoax. It therefore follows that any view of Scripture that is contrary to Christ's must be unqualifiedly rejected. If the New Testament means anything at all, it testifies to the deity of our Lord and Savior—all the way from Matthew to Revelation. All who claim to be Evangelicals are completely agreed on this point. If this is so, then it follows that whatever Jesus Christ believed about the trustworthiness of Scripture must be accepted as true and binding on the conscience of every true believer. If Christ believed in the complete accuracy of the Hebrew Bible in all matters of scientific or historical fact, we must acknowledge His view in these matters to be correct and trustworthy in every respect. Moreover, in view of the impossibility of God's being guilty of error, we must recognize

---

[1]William S. LaSor in "Theology News and Notes," p. 26 of the 1976 Special Issue entitled "Life under Tension—Fuller Theological Seminary and 'The Battle for the Bible.'"

that even matters of history and science, though not per se theological, assume the importance of basic doctrine. Why is this so? Because Christ is God, and God cannot be mistaken. That is a theological proposition that is absolutely essential to Christian doctrine.

A careful examination of Christ's references to the Old Testament makes it unmistakably evident that He fully accepted as factual even the most controversial statements in the Hebrew Bible pertaining to history and science. Here are a few examples.

1. In speaking of His approaching death and resurrection, Jesus affirmed in Matthew 12:40: "For as Jonah was three days and three nights in the belly of a huge fish, so the Son of Man will be three days and three nights in the heart of the earth" (NIV). Apart from a theory-protecting bias, it is impossible to draw from this statement any other conclusion than that Jesus regarded the experience of Jonah as a type (or at the very least, a clear analogy) pointing to His own approaching experience between the hour of His death on the cross and His bodily resurrection from the tomb on Easter morning. If the Resurrection was to be historically factual, and if it was to be antitypical of Jonah's three-day sojourn in the stomach of the huge fish, then it follows that the type itself must have been historically factual—regardless of modern skepticism on this point. The facticity of the Jonah narrative is further confirmed by Matthew 12:41: "The men of Nineveh will stand up at the judgment with this generation and condemn it; for they repented at the preaching of Jonah, and now one greater than Jonah is here" (NIV)—namely, Jesus Himself. Jesus implies that the inhabitants of Nineveh actually did respond to Jonah's stern warning and denunciation with self-abasing humility and fear—precisely as recorded in Jonah 3. Jesus declares that those raw, untaught pagans were less guilty before God than the Christ-rejecting Jews of His own generation. Such a judgment clearly presupposes that the Ninevites did precisely what Jonah says they did. This means that Jesus did not take that book to be a mere piece of fiction or allegory, as some would-be Evangelicals have suggested. Adherence to such a view is tantamount to a rejection of Christ's inerrancy and therefore of His deity.

2. Another account in Scripture that is often considered scientifically and historically untenable is that of Noah's ark and the great Flood found in Genesis 6–8. But Jesus in His Olivet Discourse clearly affirmed that "as in those days that were before the Flood they were eating and drinking, marrying and giving in marriage, until the day when Noah entered the ark, and they did not know it until the flood came and took them all away, so shall the coming [parousia] of the Son of Man be." Here again Jesus is predicting that a future historical event will take place as an antitype to an event recorded in the Old Testament. He must therefore have regarded the Flood as literal history, just as it was recorded in Genesis.

3. The Exodus account of the feeding of the two-million-plus Israelites by the miracle of manna for forty years in the Sinai desert is rejected by some self-styled Evangelicals as legendary. But Jesus Himself accepted it as completely historical when He said, "Your forefathers ate the manna in the desert, yet they died" (John 6:49). Then in the following verse He presented Himself to the multitude as the antitype, as the true and living Bread sent down from the Father in heaven.

4. It is safe to say that in no recorded utterance of Jesus Himself, or any of His inspired apostles, is there the slightest suggestion that inaccuracy in matters of

history or science ever occurs in the Old Testament. To the scientific or rationalistic skepticism of the Sadducees, Jesus cited the precise wording of Exodus 3:6, where Moses is addressed by God from the burning bush (the bush that burned miraculously without being consumed) in the following terms: "I am the God of Abraham, the God of Isaac, and the God of Jacob" (Matt. 22:32). From the present tense implied by the Hebrew verbless clause, our Lord drew the deduction that God would not have described Himself as the God of mere lifeless corpses moldering in the grave but only of living, enduring personalities enjoying fellowship with Him in glory. Therefore the Old Testament taught the resurrection of the dead.

5. So far as the historicity of Adam and Eve is concerned, Christ implied the validity of the account in Genesis 2:24, where it is said of Adam and Eve: "For this reason a man will leave his father and mother and be united to his wife, and the two will become one flesh" (Matt. 19:5). In the preceding verse He referred to Genesis 1:27, which states that God specially created mankind as male and female—at the beginning of human history. Regardless of modern scientific theory, the Lord Jesus believed that Adam and Eve were literal, historical personalities. Similar confirmation is found in the Epistles of Paul (who testified that he received his doctrine directly from the risen Christ [Gal. 1:12]), especially in 1 Timothy 2:13–14: "For Adam was formed [*eplasthē*, "molded," "fashioned"] first, then Eve. And Adam was not the one deceived; it was the woman who was deceived and became a sinner" (NIV). The point at issue in this passage is the historical background for the man's leadership responsibility in the home and in the church; the historicity of Genesis 3 is presupposed. In this connection it should be noted that in Romans 5:12–21 the contrast is drawn between the disobedience of Adam, who plunged the human race into a state of sin, and the obedience of Christ, who by His atoning death brought redemption to all who believe. In v.14 Adam is stated to be a *typos* ("type") of Him (Christ) who was to come. If therefore Christ was a historical personage, being the antitype of Adam, it inevitably follows that Adam himself was a historical personage as well. No one can lay honest claim to loyal adherence to the doctrinal infallibility of Scripture and leave open the possibility of a mythical or legendary Adam, as the single ancestor of the human race. This highly doctrinal passage in Romans 5 (which serves as the basis for the doctrine of original sin) presupposes that Genesis 2–3 contains literal, factual history.

Without Inerrancy the Bible Cannot Be Infallible

In recent years there has been a strenuous effort made by the revisionist movement within American Evangelicalism to defend the legitimacy of maintaining a kind of infallible authority or trustworthiness of Scripture that allows for the appearance of factual errors in matters of history and science—even in the original manuscripts of Scripture. It is urged that the Bible was never intended to be a textbook of science or history, only of theology and doctrine. There may have been occasional mistakes in the area of astronomy or biology, and misunderstandings reflecting the backward views of a prescientific age may be reflected in the Hebrew text; but surely these mistakes cannot be regarded as endangering or compromising the validity of the theological teachings that constitute the main thrust of those ancient books. And if perchance now and then there may be contradictions between one statement of historical fact and another in some other passage, these errors may be freely and frankly admitted without damage to the status of the Bible as an infallible textbook in matters of metaphysics and theology.

A flexible defense such as this makes it much easier to maintain an evangelical commitment to biblical authority without appearing ridiculous to professional historians and scientists who question the truth status of the Scriptures on the ground of its many factual errors.

In response to this eloquent and plausible argument for infallibility without inerrancy, we must point out several serious weaknesses and fallacies that render it a basically untenable position to maintain. Its many self-contradictions render it hopeless as a viable option for the responsible Christian who has come to terms with the truth claims of Jesus Christ. Such a serious charge against a position held by so many outstanding leaders in the modern evangelical world must be supported by very strong and compelling arguments, and so we shall set forth these arguments for the consideration of every open-minded reader of this book.

To evade the charge that proven factual errors in Scripture are an evidence of its false status as a revelation from God is a maneuver that cannot succeed. Skeptics and detractors of the Bible have always resorted to this type of attack in order to prove their point, that the sixty-six books are basically human documents, devoid of any special inspiration from God. Despite the neoorthodox contention that the error-filled Hebrew and Greek documents of Scripture somehow point the questing soul of a true believer to some kind of suprahistorical, suprascientific level of metaphysical truth, intellectual and moral integrity demands that we face up to the validity of the attacks of these skeptics. This *via media* offered by the revisionist Evangelicals and neoorthodox theologians cannot be successfully maintained. There can be no infallibility without inerrancy—even in matters of history and science—and sooner or later the schools or denominations that accept this *via media* slip away from their original evangelical posture and shift into substantial departures from the historic Christian faith. There are some good and solid reasons for this doctrinal decline.

In any court of law, whether in a civil or criminal case, the trustworthiness of a witness on a stand is necessarily an important point at issue if his testimony is to be received. Therefore, the attorney for the opposing side will make every effort in his cross-examination of the witness to demonstrate that he is not a consistently truthful person. If the attorney can trap the opposing witness into statements that contradict what he has said previously or furnish evidence that in his own community the man has a reputation for untruthfulness, then the jury may be led to doubt the accuracy of the witness's testimony that bears directly on the case itself. This is true even though such untruthfulness relates to other matters having no relationship to the present litigation. While the witness on the stand may indeed be giving a true report on this particular case, the judge and jury have no way of being sure. Therefore, they are logically compelled to discount this man's testimony.

The same is true of Holy Scripture. If the statements it contains concerning matters of history and science can be proven by extrabiblical records, by ancient documents recovered through archaeological digs, or by the established facts of modern science to be contrary to the truth, then there is grave doubt as to its trustworthiness in matters of religion. In other words, if the biblical record can be proved fallible in areas of fact that can be verified, then it is hardly to be trusted in areas where it cannot be tested. As a witness for God, the Bible would be discredited as untrustworthy. What solid truth it may contain would be left as a matter of mere conjecture, subject to the intuition or canons of likelihood of each individual. An attitude of sentimental attachment to traditional religion may incline one person to accept nearly all the substantive teachings of Scripture as probably true. But someone else with equal justification may pick and choose whatever teachings in the Bible happen to appeal to him and lay equal claim to legitimacy. One opinion is as good as another. All things are possible, but nothing is certain if indeed the Bible contains mistakes or errors of any kind.

Those who allow for inaccuracies or self-contradictions in the original manuscripts of the Bible usually take refuge in the teaching ministry of the Holy Spirit, which they receive through some sort of existential encounter with God, an encounter that takes place in the context of Bible study—fallible though that Bible may be! They trust that the Holy Spirit leads them so that they can get at the Living Word of God and enjoy all the solid benefits of redemption and fellowship with God that old-fashioned Evangelicals suppose these freethinkers have lost through their discarding biblical inerrancy. But these revisionists have nevertheless —perhaps unwittingly—set in motion a dialectical process of degeneration and spiritual decline that impels them in the direction of increasing skepticism or eclecticism. They tend to exploit their self-given freedom of choice in such a way as to conform to the prevailing opinions of the circles in which they move. Their consciences are no longer bound, as Luther put it, by the authority of the written Word of God.

The second basic difficulty with the revisionist position (i.e., infallibility without inerrancy) is that it sets up a basis of distinction that is totally rejected by the authors of Scripture and by Christ Himself. No support whatever can be found for the distinction between historical, scientific truth and doctrinal, metaphysical truth—according to which "minor, inconsequential error" may be allowed for the former but be excluded from the latter.

As we examine the Old Testament, we look in vain for any distinction between abstract theological doctrine and the miraculous events that marked the history of redemption. In Psalm 105, for example, composed at least five centuries after the Exodus, we are met with a joyous symphony of praise to Yahweh for the ten plagues He inflicted on Egypt to compel the release of Israel by Pharaoh. These miraculous events, impinging on matters of history and science, are clearly treated as factual, as real episodes in Israel's past. In the following poem, Psalm 106, the name of the Lord is exalted for His mighty deliverance in parting the waters of the Red Sea to allow the safe passage of the two-million-plus congregation of the Hebrews and in bringing the water back again just in time to drown their chariot-driving pursuers. God is here being thanked, not for some inspiring legend or myth, but for a solidly historical event—in every case an episode involving miracle, a striking departure from the usual laws of nature. The same psalm goes on to recall the sudden destruction of Dathan and Abiram as they tried to set aside Moses and his authoritative revelation from God. The very ground on which they stood opened up into great cracks as part of a seismic disturbance, and their families alone were swallowed up by the ground. Isaiah 28:21 refers to Joshua's historic victory over the Canaanite attackers of his Gibeonite allies, making it a base of comparison with a future military intervention of judgments against apostate Judah. "For Yahweh will rise up as at Mount Perazim, He will be stirred up as in the valley of Gibeon, to do His task, His unusual task, and to work His work, His unusual work." (It was at that Battle of Gibeon that more of the enemy were killed by hailstones from the sky than by the weapons of the Israelites.)

Thus we see that the later Old Testament authors were as sure of the Red Sea crossing and the other miracles as the apostles were sure of Christ's atoning death on Calvary. The apostles were also sure of the divine inspiration of the Davidic

24

Psalms. "Sovereign Lord," they prayed in Acts 4:24–26, "You spoke through the mouth of our father David, Your servant." Then they quoted Psalm 2:1–2. Peter affirmed that David composed Psalm 16:10: "Being therefore a prophet, and knowing that God had sworn with an oath to him that he would set one of his descendants upon his throne, he foresaw and spoke of the resurrection of Christ, that He was not abandoned to Hades, nor did His flesh see corruption" (Acts 2:30–31).

This full trustworthiness and authority of the Hebrew Scriptures was constantly recognized by the New Testament authors as they quoted the prophetic passages that point to Christ. Matthew particularly emphasized this authoritative status, saying, "All this took place to fulfill what the Lord said through the prophet" (see, e.g., Matt. 1:22; 2:5,15,23; 13:35; 21:4; 27:9). As L. Gaussen says, "Nowhere shall we find a single passage that permits us to detach one single part of it [i.e., the Old Testament] as less divine than all the rest" (*Theopneustia: the Bible, its Divine Origin and Inspiration,* trans. by D.D. Scott [Cincinnati: Blanchard, 1859], p. 67). Thus we see that the crucial distinction between the historical-scientific and the doctrinal-theological passages of the Old Testament is completely unknown either to the later Old Testament authors or to the apostolic writers of the New Testament in their treatment of the Hebrew Scriptures.

Most decisive against this division into historical-scientific and doctrinal-theological categories is the clear endorsement by our Lord Jesus Himself of even those passages in the Old Testament that speak of supernatural events most commonly rejected by rationalistic critics in our day. As we have already seen, Christ accepted as literally true (1) the historicity of Adam (Matt. 19:5), (2) the rescue of Noah and his family from the Flood by means of the ark (Matt. 24:38–39), (3) the literal accuracy of Moses' interview with God at the burning bush (Matt. 22:32), (4) the feeding of Moses' congregation by manna from heaven (John 6:49), (5) the historicity of Jonah's deliverance after three days in the belly of the whale (Matt. 12:40), and (6) the repentance of the pagan population of Nineveh in response to Jonah's preaching (Matt. 12:41). Nothing could be clearer than that our divine Savior believed in the literal truthfulness of the entire Old Testament record, whether those accounts dealt with doctrinal matters, matters of science, or history. He who refuses to go along with the Lord in this judgment stands guilty of asserting that God can err (since Jesus is God as well as Man) and that the sovereign Creator (John 1:1–3) stands in need of instruction and correction by the finite wisdom of man. It is for this reason that we cannot possibly concede that the errancy of Scripture is reconcilable with true Evangelicalism or the historic Christian faith.

Third, the advocates of partial inerrancy (whether of the confessedly neoorthodox camp or the revisionist evangelical persuasion) fatally undermine the tenability of their theoretical position by their actual practice in the matter of teaching from the Bible. That is to say, when they preach to a congregation or teach at a Bible conference, they forsake their commitment to partial inerrancy altogether—at least insofar as they proclaim the authoritative message of Scripture itself. Whenever a preacher declares a truth from the Bible and calls on his audience to believe and act on that teaching, he thereby presupposes the total inerrancy of Scripture. In other words, he who affirms that a statement is true because the Bible affirms it, can do so with integrity only if he takes the position that whatever the Bible teaches is necessarily true. Otherwise he must always append to his proclamation of the biblical message the following additional corroboration: "In this particular case, we are warranted in believing what the Bible says—even though it may occasionally be mistaken in matters of history or science—because it does not appear to contravene the findings of modern scientific or historical knowledge." From the logical standpoint, therefore, it is a requirement of honesty that anyone who does not hold to the principle that whatever the Bible affirms is true simply because it affirms it, may not preach in such a way as to imply that no further corroboration is needed for its statements to be believed.

It is a matter of basic self-contradiction for a partial-inerrantist to hold that in matters of history and science the Bible may err and yet for him to expound any text from the Scripture as having authority in its own right. While he may perhaps preserve a greater measure of integrity if the text he is preaching happens to be purely doctrinal or theological, nevertheless he is false to his own position when he fails to justify his treating the text as inherently authoritative. Nearly all the cardinal doctrines of Scripture come in a historical framework, and very frequently in a supernatural setting. It is less than candid for a Christian spokesman to assure his audience that any such doctrinal affirmation in the Bible is to be received as factual unless he at the same time furnishes them with some sort of critical verification to the effect that "in this instance the Scripture speaks the truth." If the historical framework must be corroborated and critically sifted for error, then the doctrine it contains must be regarded as suspect. If, for example, the resurrection of the body from the grave is regarded by most professional scientists as impossible, then any advocate of partial inerrancy must carefully justify his acceptance of the bodily resurrection of Christ (if accept it he does) by adducing some other confirmation besides the mere statement in the Bible itself. Otherwise his proclamation that Jesus rose bodily from the grave because the Scripture says He did amounts to an assumption of complete inerrancy, even a matter of science involving the miraculous.

Fourth, a specially attractive appeal is often made by contemporary errantists to accept "the cold, hard facts" that the Bible text as we now have it does contain discrepancies of various kinds; and, in the absence of any infallible original manuscripts, we had better give up the effort to defend inerrant autographa that no longer exist. They urge that we should simply appreciate the Bible as it is and make the very best use we can of it in the form it has come down to us—marked with occasional mistakes of a minor sort, but still eminently usable as a guide to God and a saving knowledge of His will. Is it not much more honest, they urge, for us to be perfectly frank and admit the errors, wherever they appear, and simply go on from there, relying on the main and central teaching message and not vexing ourselves about troublesome minor details.

What the advocates of this stance toward Scripture fail to observe is that it is fundamentally dishonest to adopt the line of least resistance in the face of difficulty and say to the rationalistic skeptic, "Okay, in this instance you may be right. But I still have a right to hang on to my faith, no matter how many technical errors you may be able to discover in the text of the Bible." He who assumes such a position of intellectual surrender can only be classed as a weak-kneed irrationalist who has retreated into his own shell of subjectivity. He no longer has anything meaningful to contribute in the arena of debate and intelligent consideration, which all thinking men are responsible to engage in.

It is morally indefensible to put down the Bible—which presents itself as the uniquely authoritative Word of God—as the object of man's critical judgment so that one may decide (at least for himself personally) which parts of Scripture he may accept as binding on him and which parts he may safely disregard. To treat the Bible in this way is to trifle with God, and it can only result in a process of progressive stultification and a steady loss of theological certainty and moral conviction. Indeed, it can be reasonably argued that the plea to shy away from the defense of the accuracy and trustworthiness of Scripture whenever it is attacked on factual matters is hardly to be distinguished in principle from a policy of defending and adhering to the moral standards laid down in Scripture only when they do not conflict with modern standards of morality or when in one's personal life they do not conflict with what the professing Christian *wants* to do (whether or not it is the will of God).

Times of testing come into the life of every believer, when he has to choose between the hard, flesh-denying way of obedience, of integrity before God and man, and the way of self-indulgence, of giving in to the temptation to do what is easiest and pleasant from the standpoint of the self-seeking ego. He who does not put up a determined resistance against the seductively easy, flesh-pleasing way will find that he has lost his integrity, self-respect, and, indeed (apart from abject repentance and a complete reversal of direction), all hope of salvation. There is a clear analogy between this flabby response to the challenge of self-will to the moral integrity of a Christian believer and the response that he makes to a challenge to the inerrant authority and complete trustworthiness of the written Word of God. If he casts his lot with the easy way of bland concession, hoping to salvage his position as a Christian by retaining his faith in the fundamentals of Christian doctrine, he will find that in the long run this policy of giving in to the enemy will lead to the complete takeover of his homeland by the foe. His failure to put up a credible defense of Scripture will finally result in his loss of its assurance and comfort in the times of crisis and danger that await him.

The Importance of Inerrant Original Documents

Now that the inerrancy of the original manuscripts of Scripture has been established as essential to its inerrant authority, we must deal with the very real problem of the complete disappearance of the autographa themselves. Even the earliest and best manuscripts that we possess are not totally free of transmissional errors. Numbers are occasionally miscopied, the spelling of proper names is occasionally garbled, and there are examples of the same types of scribal error that appear in other ancient documents as well. In that sense—and only to that degree—can it be said that even the finest extant manuscripts of the Hebrew-Aramaic Old Testament and the Greek New Testament are not wholly without error. It is not that they contain actual mistakes or misinformation that cannot be rectified by the proper exercise of the science of textual criticism; but, in the sense that scribal mistakes do occur even in the best of them, it is technically true that there are no extant inerrant originals.

If, then, we have none of the error-free autographa that underlie the Bible text that has been transmitted to us, why not simply content ourselves with the less-than-inerrant copies and accept the plain fact that God did not find inerrancy so vital for inscripturated revelation that He preserved it to us in that form? What is the point of arguing about a collection of manuscripts that no longer exist? Is this not simply an academic question of a most abstruse kind, a question that surely should not divide the ranks of Evangelicals?

To put the question in this way is to misrepresent the basic issue at stake in a manner that is utterly misleading. We have already seen that Christ regarded the recorded statements and affirmations of the Old Testament authors as completely

27

accurate and trustworthy, whether they dealt with theology, history, or science. This is really what is at stake, and it is this level of truthfulness that is involved rather than technical infallibility in the art of scribal transmission. The copyist who inadvertently misspells some word in John 3:16 cannot be said to have introduced error in the sentiment or message of that salvation verse even though he may have slipped in his orthography. It is something far more essential than typographical errors that is under consideration when scriptural inerrancy comes up for discussion.

In answer to this challenge we offer the four following considerations.

1. The integrity of Scripture as the authoritative revelation of God is bound up with the issue of the inerrancy of its original inscripturation. It is impossible for a holy and righteous God to inspire any human author of the books of Scripture to write down that which is at any level misleading or false. He who sits in judgment on all wickedness and deceit will never stoop to the use or toleration of falsehood in the recording of His spoken revelation or of the historic or scientific facts chosen to compose the sixty-six books of His Bible. Nor is it conceivable that God in His perfection would allow any human agent whom He employs for the writing of Scripture to introduce elements of error or mistake simply on the ground of his humanness. The sovereign Lord who could use the wooden staff of Moses to bring down the ten plagues upon Egypt and part the waters of the Red Sea can surely use a fallible human prophet to communicate His will and His truth without blundering or confusion of any kind. The inerrancy of God's written Word as it was originally inspired is a necessary corollary to the inerrancy of God Himself. We must therefore condemn an attitude of indifference concerning the inerrancy of the original manuscripts of the Bible as a serious theological error.

2. It is wrong to affirm that the existence of a perfect original is a matter of no importance if that original is no longer available for examination. To take an analogy from the realm of engineering or of commerce, it makes a very great difference whether there is such a thing as a perfect measure for the meter, the foot, or the pound. It is questionable whether the yardsticks or scales used in business transactions or construction projects can be described as absolutely perfect. They may be almost completely conformable to the standard weights and measures preserved at the Bureau of Standards in our nation's capital but to the measure of their deviation from the official models in Washington, D.C., they are subject to error—however small. But how foolish it would be for any citizen to shrug his shoulders and say, "Neither you nor I have ever actually seen those standard measures in Washington; therefore we may as well disregard them—not be concerned about them at all—and simply settle realistically for the imperfect yardsticks and pound weights that we have available to us in everyday life. On the contrary, the existence of those measures in the Bureau of Standards is vital to the proper functioning of our entire economy. To the 220,000,000 Americans who have never seen them they are absolutely essential for the trustworthiness of all the standards of measurement that they resort to throughout their lifetime.

3. It may be true that we no longer possess any perfect copy of the inerrant original manuscripts of the Bible. But it is equally true that we have only imperfect copies of the Lord Jesus available to us today. Christ has ascended to His glorious throne at the right hand of the Father in heaven. All the observer has to look at now are imperfect representatives and agents of His, in the form of

sanctified and committed Christians. But shall we therefore affirm that because of His physical absence we need not concern ourselves about any standards of absolute love and moral excellence? No, but Hebrews 12:2 commands us to fix our eyes on Jesus (though He is beyond our physical reach or power to touch), as the Author and Perfecter of our faith. The spotless Lamb of God is still the inerrant model for our attitudes and manner of life, even though we are not privileged to behold Him with the eye of flesh as the apostles did prior to His ascension to glory. So also, we must cherish the inerrant originals of Holy Scripture as free from all mistake of any kind, even though we have never actually seen them.

4. If there was an admixture of error even in the original writings of the Bible, there is little point in textual criticism. The entire motivation behind this careful examination of the earliest manuscripts in Hebrew and Greek or in the ancient translations from them into other languages is based on the fundamental premise of original inerrancy. What useful purpose would be served by tracing back with painstaking care to the original reading if that reading may have contained falsehood or mistake? The Bible student would only become confused or injured by the misinformation contained by what has been described as the infallible Word of God. Thus we see that textual criticism, if it is to have any real meaning or validity, presupposes an original entirely free from deception or mistake.

The Remarkable Trustworthiness of the Received Text of Holy Scripture

Why do we not now possess infallible copies of those infallible originals? Because the production of even one perfect copy of one book is so far beyond the capacity of a human scribe as to render it necessary for God to perform a miracle in order to produce it. No reasonable person can expect even the most conscientious copyist to achieve technical infallibility in transcribing his original document into a fresh copy. No matter how earnest he may be to dot every *i* and cross every *t* and to avoid confusion of homonyms (such as "their" for "there" or "lead" for "led"), he will commit at least an occasional slip. It is for this reason that all writers have to check over whatever they have written and all publishers must employ skilled editors and proofreaders. Yet even the most attentive of these occasionally allow blunders to slip by. Such was the case of the "Immoral Bible" back in the sixteenth century, which went to press with the seventh commandment reading, "Thou shalt commit adultery." Although this edition was speedily recalled, the blunder got out to the public, much to the embarrassment of the publisher. These inadvertencies occur from time to time simply because of the imperfect quality of the attention of any human scribe. Nothing less than divine intervention could guarantee a completely errorless copy or set aside the human propensity to occasional slips in punctuation or spelling. But the important fact remains that accurate communication is possible despite technical mistakes in copying.

The real question at issue in regard to scribal error is whether an accumulation of minor slips has resulted in the obscuring or perversion of the message originally intended. Well-trained textual critics operating on the basis of sound methodology are able to rectify almost all the misunderstandings that might result from manuscript error. But in the case of documents in which scribal copying has been carried on with a view to deliberate alteration or the indulging of personal bias on the part of the copyist himself, it is quite possible that the original message has been irrecoverably altered. The question in regard to the text of the Bible centers on the data of textual criticism. Is there objective proof from the surviving manuscripts of Scripture that these sixty-six books have been transmitted to us with such a high degree of accuracy as to assure us that the information contained in the originals has been perfectly preserved? The answer is an unqualified yes.

In contrast to most other ancient documents that have survived in multiplied copies (such as the Egyptian *Tale of Sinuhe* or the Behistun Rock trilingual inscription of Darius I), collation of many hundreds of manuscript copies from the third century B.C. to the sixth century A.D. yields an amazingly limited range of variation in actual wording. In fact, it has long been recognized by the foremost specialists in textual criticism that if any decently attested variant were taken up from the apparatus at the bottom of the page and were substituted for the accepted reading of the standard text, there would in no case be a single, significant alteration in doctrine or message. This can only be explained as the result of a special measure of control exercised by the God who inspired the original manuscripts of Scripture so as to insure their preservation for the benefit of His people. A degree of deviation so serious as to affect the sense would issue in failure to achieve the purpose for which the revelation was originally given: that men might be assured of God's holiness and grace, and that they might know of His will for their salvation.

Readers interested in pursuing further the subject of textual criticism of the Old Testament or wanting information concerning the ancient copies of the Hebrew Scriptures discovered in the Qumran Caves near the Dead Sea are encouraged to consult Ernst Würthwein's *The Text of the Old Testament* (Oxford: Basil Blackwell, 1957) or my *Survey of Old Testament Introduction* (chaps. 3–4). For the text of the New Testament, consult A.T. Robertson, *An Introduction to the Textual Criticism of the New Testament*, 2d ed. (New York: Doubleday, 1928) or Vincent Taylor, *The Text of the New Testament* (London: Macmillan, 1961).

Scripture and Inerrancy

The foregoing discussion has demonstrated that the objective authority of Scripture requires inerrancy in the original autographa. Also, we have argued that infallibility necessarily requires inerrancy as its indispensable corollary. But as we have observed in the opening pages of this Introduction, revisionists have charged that the so-called phenomena of Scripture do not permit a credible defense of the claim that the Bible as originally given was free from error, even in matters of history and science. The contradictions and discrepancies in Scripture compel us to choose between which statement is right and which is wrong. Advocates of this approach invariably present lists of such alleged contradictions or statements that clash with findings of historical criticism and science. This challenge must not go unanswered; for if the revisionists' contention is correct, then inerrancy must indeed be surrendered—with all the devastating implications for the possibility of objective revelation. The main task of this present work is to demonstrate the unsoundness of this charge by examining the alleged discrepancies and in turn showing in each case that the charge is not well founded in fact, once all the relevant evidence has been considered.

The other chief line of evidence followed by these scholars pertains to the extensive use by New Testament authors of the Septuagint translation (Greek) of the Old Testament. It is argued that since the Septuagint often deviates substantially from the Masoretic Hebrew text, such employment of an inexact translation shows that to the New Testament authors the authority of the Old Testament was conceptual rather than verbal. And, of course, if the authoritative teaching of the

Hebrew Scriptures was to be found only in its concepts rather than in its wording, this virtually excludes any meaningful adherence to inerrancy. Particularly in those instances (rare though they may be) where the Septuagint passage is somewhat inexact in its treatment of the Hebrew original (at least as the Hebrew has been transmitted to us in the Masoretic text), it must be concluded that the New Testament writer did not consider the precise wording of the Old Testament a matter of real importance.

Logical though this deduction might seem at first glance, it fails to take into account several important considerations.

1. The very reason for using the Septuagint translation (which originated among the Jews of Alexandria, Egypt, in the third and second centuries B.C.) was rooted in the missionary outreach of the evangelists and apostles of the early church. Long before the first disciples of our Lord set out to spread the Good News, the Septuagint had found its way into nearly every Greek-speaking region of the Roman Empire. In fact, it was the only form of the Old Testament in circulation outside Palestine itself. As the apostles went from one Gentile city to another and brought the message of Christ to the Jews of the Dispersion, it was their primary purpose to show that Jesus of Nazareth had fulfilled the types and promises of the Old Testament, that holy record of God's saving truth that they already had in their hands. What other form of the Old Testament was available to them but the Septuagint? Only the rabbis and scholars had access to the Hebrew manuscripts, and no other Greek translation was available than the time-honored version from Alexandria. And so when the "noble Bereans" went home from their synagogue to check up on the teaching of Paul and Silas, what other Scriptures could they consult but their Septuagint?

   Suppose Paul had chosen to work out a new, more accurate translation into Greek directly from the Hebrew. Might not the Bereans have said in reply, "That's not the way we find it in *our* Bible. How do we know you have not slanted your different rendering here and there in order to favor your new teaching about Christ?" In order to avoid suspicion and misunderstanding, it was imperative for the apostles and evangelists to stay with the Septuagint in their preaching and teaching, both oral and written. On the other hand, we find in the case of Matthew and Hebrews that the Septuagint plays a much less important role. The frequent and copious quotations from the Old Testament found in these two books are often non-Septuagintal in wording and are perceptibly closer to the Hebrew original than the Septuagint itself. This is accounted for by the fact that both Matthew and the author of Hebrews were writing to a Palestinian Jewish readership, to whom the Masoretic or Sopherim text (as it is technically known) was close at hand.

2. In the overwhelming majority of cases where the Septuagint is quoted in the New Testament documents, the Greek rendering is beyond reproach in the matter of accuracy. The instances where a more paraphrastic rendering is quoted from the Septuagint are in the small minority—even though these few deviations have attracted much discussion on the part of critics. But even where there are noticeable differences in phraseology, there are virtually no examples of quotations from Hebrew passages that would not support the point that the New Testament author intends to make as he quotes from the Old Testament. Inasmuch as the Septuagint contains a good many sections

that substantially differ from the Hebrew of the Masoretic text, it can only be inferred that the apostolic authors purposely avoided any passages of the Septuagint that perverted the sense of the original.

3. The argument from the use of the Septuagint to the effect that the New Testament authors regarded the inspiration of the Old Testament as merely conceptual, not verbal, is completely belied by the example of Christ Himself. For instance, in Matthew 22:32 our Lord pointed out the implications of the exact wording of Exodus 3:6: "I am the God of Abraham, and the God of Isaac, and the God of Jacob." This particular quotation is verbally identical with the Septuagint, which supplies the word "am" (*eimi*) that is not actually expressed in the Hebrew original, even though it is clearly understood in a verbless clause such as this, according to the standard rules of Hebrew grammar. Jesus makes the point here that God would not have spoken of Himself as the God of mere corpses moldering in their graves for three or four centuries since their death. "He is not the God of the dead, but the God of the living," said Jesus. Therefore, Abraham, Isaac, and Jacob must have all been alive and well at the time Yahweh spoke to Moses from the burning bush in the early fifteenth century B.C.

Very similar attention to the exact wording of the Old Testament original text was involved in Christ's use of Psalm 110:1 [109:1 Septuagint] in his discussion with the Pharisees in Matthew 22:43–45. This quotation differs from the Septuagint by only one word (*hypopodion*, "footstool"). But the point of it was that the LORD (Yahweh) said to David's Lord—who was at the same time his messianic descendant—"Sit at My right hand until I make Your enemies Your footstool." By this remarkable passage Jesus demonstrated that the Messiah was to not only be a physical descendant of King David (tenth century B.C.) but was also David's divine Lord and Master.

4. The whole line of reasoning that says quoting Scripture from a less-than-perfect translation of the original necessarily implies a cavalier attitude toward inspired autographon is vitiated by an obvious fallacy. All of us, even the most highly qualified experts in biblical languages, customarily quote Scripture in the standard published translations available to our audiences or readers. But such use of the various translations, whether English, German, French, or Spanish, by no means proves that we have settled for a low view of scriptural inerrancy. We, like the first-century apostles, resort to these standard translations to teach our people in terms they can verify by resorting to their own Bibles. Yet, admittedly, none of these translations is completely free of faults. We use them, nevertheless, for the purposes of more effective communication than if we were to translate directly from the Hebrew or Greek. But this use of translations that fall short of perfection by no means implies the abandonment of conviction that the Scriptures as originally given were free from all error.

We must, therefore, conclude that the employment of the Septuagint in New Testament quotations from the Old Testament proves nothing whatever in favor of noninerrancy.

The Role of Textual Criticism in Correcting Transmissional Errors

In the preceding discussion we referred several times to the role of textual criticism in dealing with scribal errors in the transmission of the biblical text. So the reader may have some understanding of the methodology followed by scholars in handling such deviations, which appear in even the earliest and best extant manuscripts, we will indicate the guidelines to be followed in resolving such problems. The standard procedures for dealing with transmissional errors apply to all ancient documents, whether secular or sacred; but, of course, there are special features that relate to the biblical languages. These would include the shapes of the Hebrew letters as they evolved from the earlier period to later times, along with the gradual introduction of vowel-letters (i.e., consonants that indicate which vowel sounds or vowel quantities were to be used in words). In the case of the New Testament, composed in a language that used vowel characters as well as consonants (koine Greek), the changes in letter shape would also give rise to miscopying in the course of several generations of scribes.

A. *Types of Transmissional Errors*

Certain kinds of errors are apt to arise in copying any original document (*Vorlage*). We are all prone to substitute one homonym for another; i.e., "hole" for "whole" or "it's" for "its." English has a very difficult spelling system; the same sound may be written in a variety of ways: "way" or "weigh"; "to," "too," or "two." This problem was not so acute in ancient Hebrew or Greek; but there are occasional misspellings that occur even in the earliest copies of the biblical books, largely on the basis of similarity in sound. One of the most serious is the word *lō*. If it is written *l-'* (lamedh-aleph), it is the negative "not"; but if it is written *l-w* (lamedh-waw), it means "to him" or "for him." Usually the context gives a clear indication as to which of these *lō*s is intended; but occasionally either "not" or "for him" would be possible, and so a bit of confusion results.

One good example of the *lō* confusion is found in Isaiah 9:2 (9:3 in the English text). The Masoretic text (MT) reads *l-'*, making *lō* mean "not." KJV's translation is "Thou hast multiplied the nation, *and* [supplied in italics] not increased the joy; they joy before thee according to the joy in harvest." This rendering, however, introduces a strange reversal in the flow of the thought: God has increased the nation; yet He has not increased their joy, and yet they rejoice like those who gather in a bountiful harvest. But even the Masoretic Jewish scribes perceived this to be an inadvertent misspelling; so they put in the margin the correct spelling *l-w*. Then the verse means "Thou hast multiplied the nation [no "and"], Thou hast increased the joy for it; they joy before Thee according to the joy in harvest." The Syriac Peshitta so renders it, and likewise the Aramaic Targum of Jonathan and twenty medieval Hebrew manuscripts read it as *l-w* rather than *l-'*. Because it reads both aleph and waw, spelling *lō* as *l-w-'*, 1QIsa is not very helpful here. The Septuagint (LXX) is no help at all because the translator garbled the Hebrew completely and does not have either type of *lō* indicated in his rendering ("The majority of the people, which You have brought down in Your joy, they also will joy before You like those who rejoice in harvest." But it is at least 90 percent certain that NASB is correct in its translation: "Thou shalt multiply the nation, Thou shalt increase their gladness; they will be glad in Thy presence as with the gladness of harvest."

After considering this example of textual correction, let us survey eleven main kinds of transmissional errors known to the field of textual criticism.

1. *Haplography*

Essentially, haplography means writing once what should have been written twice. In student papers one often reads *occurence* instead of *occurrence*: the *r* has been written just once—which would make the word sound like *o-cure-ence*, according to our regular English spelling rules. In Hebrew it may be a single consonant that appears where there should have been two. Or it may be that two consonants are involved, or even two words. For example, in Isaiah 26:3—"You will keep in perfect peace him whose mind is steadfast, because he trusts in You" —the final words literally are "in you trusting," followed by "Trust in Yahweh" in v.4. In Hebrew the final word "trusting" is *bāṭûaḥ*, written *b-ṭ-w-ḥ*; the initial "trust" in v.4 is *biṭḥû*, written *b-ṭ-ḥ-w*. As they appear in the unpointed consonants, then, we have *b-ṭ-w-ḥ b-ṭ-ḥ-w*. These two words are therefore almost identical in appearance, even though the first is a masculine singular adjective and the second a plural imperative of the verb. Scroll 1QIsa has only *b-k b-ṭ-ḥ-w*, omitting the previous *b-ṭ-w-ḥ* altogether. Hence the Dead Sea Scrolls of Isaiah condense verses 3 and 4 to read thus: "A mind supported You will keep in real peace [lit., *šālôm šālôm*, 'peace peace']; because in you . . . they have trusted [or else a new sentence: 'Trust'] in Yahweh forever." The MT reads (correctly): "A mind supported You will keep in real peace, because it is trusting in You. Trust in Yahweh." It should be added that the word translated "trust" implies the vowel pointing *biṭḥû*; the 1QIsa context might imply a different pointing; i.e., *bāṭḥû*, which means "they have trusted." The LXX implies only a single *šālôm* and a single verb *bāṭḥû*, for it translates the whole section (including v.2) as follows: "Open the gates, let there enter in a people who observe righteousness and observe truth, laying hold of truth [apparently reading *yēṣer* ('mind') as the participle *nōṣēr* ('observing, keeping')] and keeping peace. For in You [v.4] they have hoped [or 'trusted'], O LORD [the regular substitution for *Yahweh*] forever [*ʿᵃ dê-ʿad*, lit., 'unto the age,' a rendering attested by both the MT and the corrected reading of 1QIsa]."

In other instances haplography may have occurred in the MT itself, as is probably the case in Judges 20:13. The regular Old Testament usage is to refer to the tribesmen of Benjamin as *bᵉnê-binyāmîn*, but the Sopherim consonantal text reads the tribal name *binyāmîn* alone (which also occasionally occurs). But LXX indicates the normal "the sons of Benjamin" reading (*hoi huioi Beniamin*) in both the A version and the B version (Judges in the LXX has two different Greek versions, both going back to the same Hebrew *Vorlage*, apparently). Interestingly enough, even the Masoretic scribes believed that the "sons of" should be in there, for they included the vowel points for *bᵉnê* ("sons of"), even though they did not feel free to put in the consonants of the word in such a way as to alter the Sopherim consonantal text that had been handed down to them.

2. Dittography

This common transcriptional error consists of writing twice what is to be written only once. A clear example of this in the MT is Ezekiel 48:16: *hᵃmēš hᵃmēš mēʾôt* ("five five hundreds"). Noting this mistake, the Masoretes left the second *hᵃmēš* without vowel pointing, indicating that the word should be omitted altogether in the reading. In 1QIsa, Isaiah 30:30 reads *hašmiaʿ hašmiaʿ* ("Hear, hear"), instead of the single *hašmiaʿ* that appears in the MT and is attested by the versions.

Another example of probable dittography occurs in Isaiah 9:5–6(6–7 Eng.), which reads at the end of v.5 *śar-šālôm* ("prince of peace") and at the beginning of v.6 *lᵉmarbēh hammiśrāh* ("of the increase of government"). Now this makes perfectly good sense in Hebrew as it stands, but there is one peculiar feature about the spelling of *lᵉmarbēh*. The *m* (mēm) is written in the special form that occurs at the end of a word. This clearly indicates that the Sopherim scribes found two different traditions concerning this reading: one that read only *šālôm* (at the end of v.5) and began v.6 with *r-b-h* (which should be vocalized as *rabbāh*, "great"; i.e., "Great shall be the government").

A final example of dittography is taken from the last verse of Psalm 23: "And I will dwell in the house of the LORD forever." As pointed by the Masoretes, the verb form *wᵉšabtî* would have to mean "And I will return [to the house]"—as if the psalmist had left the Lord's house and now expected to return to it permanently. But if the consonants are pointed *wᵉšibtî*, then we have the reading of the LXX: *kai to katoikein me* ("And my dwelling" [will be in the house]). This is rather unusual from the standpoint of Hebrew style, even though it is by no means impossible. Perhaps the most attractive option, however, is to understand this word as a case of haplography. With the introduction of the square Hebrew form of the alphabet after the return from Babylonian Exile, the shape of *w* (waw) greatly resembled that of *y* (yodh); and by the period of 1QIsa, it often happened that a long-tailed yodh looked precisely like a short-tailed waw. That being the case, it would be easy for haplography to occur whenever a yodh and a waw occurred together. The Greek copyist, then, might have seen what looked like two waw's together and figured that this was a mistake for a single waw, and hence left out the second one—which actually should have been a yodh. If this reconstruction is correct, then the original wording used by David was *wᵉyāšabtî*, meaning, "And I will dwell," expressed in the normal and customary Hebrew way.

3. *Metathesis*

This involves an inadvertent exchange in the proper order of letters or words. For example, 1QIsa has at the end of Isaiah 32:19 the phrase "the forest will fall" rather than MT's corrected reading "the city is leveled completely." It so happens that the word for "forest" (*ya'ar*) is written with the same consonants as the word for "city" (*'ir*). Since the verb *tišpal* ("is leveled completely") is in the feminine and *ya'ar* is masculine, the word for "city"—which is feminine—is the only possible reading. But the confusion of the Isaiah-scroll scribe is understandable since the word *ya'ar* does occur in the preceding clause of this verse: "though hail flattens the forest [*hayyā'ar*]."

In Ezekiel 42:16, however, it is obviously the MT that is in error, reading, "five cubits rods" (*ḥᵃmēš-'ēmôt qānîm*) instead of "five hundred rods" (*ḥᵃmēš mē'ôt qānîm*), which is the correction indicated by the Masoretes by having their vowel points go with the word for "hundreds" rather than with the word for "cubits." The LXX, the Latin Vulgate, and all the other versions read "five hundred" here rather than "five cubits."

4. *Fusion*

This consists of combining the last letter of the first word with the first letter of the following word, or else of combining two separate words into a single compound word. A probable example of the latter type is found in Amos 6:12, where the MT reads, "Do horses run on the rocky crags? Does one plow with oxen?" Obviously a farmer does plow with oxen, whereas horses do not run on rocky crags. Now it is possible to insert a "them" after the word "plow" (so NASB) or to insert an adverb "there" (so KJV, NIV). But actually there is no word in the Hebrew for either "them" or "there"; and it might therefore be better to split off the plural ending *-î(y)m* from the word *bᵉqārî(y)m* ("oxen") and understand it as the word *yām* ("sea"). Then the amended clause would read thus: "Does an ox plow the sea?"—an illustration of futile or senseless procedure, similar to horses running on bare rock. The only problem with this emendation, advocated by the critical apparatus of Kittel's *Biblia Hebraica,* is that no ancient version or surviving Hebrew manuscript so divides it.

Another textual problem of more far-reaching consequence is the apparent reference to a mysterious "Azazel" in Leviticus 16:8. In the procedure prescribed for the Day of Atonement, the high priest is to cast two lots for the two goats chosen for sacrifice. The NIV reads, "One lot for the Lord and the other for the scapegoat [*ᵃzā'zēl*]." The MT indicates some otherwise unknown proper name, Azazel, which was explained by the medieval rabbis as a designation of a hairy desert demon. Aaron, then, would be casting a lot for a demon. Now since there is no allowance made for the service or the worship of demons anywhere else in the Torah, it is most improbable that it should appear here (and in the following verses of the same chapter). The obvious solution to this enigma is found in separating the two parts of *ᵃzā'zēl* into *'ēz 'āzēl,* that is, the "goat of departure, or dismissal." In other words, as v.10 makes clear, this second goat is to be led off into the wilderness and there let go, thus symbolically bearing away the sins of all Israel from the camp of the Hebrew nation. Unquestionably the LXX so understood it, with its *tō apopompaiō* ("for the one to be sent off") and likewise the Vulgate with its *capro emissario* ("for the goat that is to be sent away"). So if we separate the two words that were improperly fused together in the Hebrew text, we have a reading that makes perfect sense in context, and which does not bring up an otherwise unexampled concession to demonology. In other words, "scapegoat" (KJV, NASB, NIV) is really the right rendering to follow, rather than "for Azazel" (ASV, RSV).

5. *Fission*

This refers to the improper separation of one word into two. For example, in Isaiah 61:1 the final word in Hebrew is *pᵉqaḥ-qāḥ,* according to the MT. Apart from this passage, there is no such separate *qôaḥ* known in the Old Testament, or, indeed, in all Hebrew literature. Even 1QIsa reads this word as one reduplicated stem, *pq2hqwḥ,* and so do many later Hebrew manuscripts. None of the versions indicate an awareness of two words here, but they all translate the Hebrew as "liberation" or "release" or even "recovery of sight"—relating *pqhqwḥ* to the root *pqh,* which refers to the opening of one's eyes in order to see clearly. Without doubt, therefore, the hyphen (or *maqqēf*) should be removed from the text and the word read as a single unit.

Another interesting example of fission is in Isaiah 2:20, where the MT reads *laḥpōr pērōt* ("to a hole of rats"). This is by no means a difficult reading, and it yields satisfactory sense as a proper place for discarding heathen idols. But on the other hand, the 1QIsa reading fuses the two into *lḥrprm* (with a masculine plural ending rather than feminine), which would probably mean "to the field mice." The Theodotion Greek does not know what to make of the word and so simply transcribes it into the meaningless *pharpharōth*; but at least it indicates that the Hebrew *Vorlage* read the two parts as a single word. The meaning would then be that the field mice would do a good job of gnawing to bits the heathen idols discarded in the field by their disillusioned worshipers. However, it must be admitted that the case for this emendation is not quite conclusive, and it should be regarded as merely a tentative correction.

6. *Homophony*

It often happens in every language that words of entirely different meaning may sound alike, like the English words "beat" and "beet"; or even the noun "well," the verb "well (up)," and the adverb "well." We have already alluded to a notable example in Isaiah 9, where *lô* ("for him") was incorrectly given in the MT as *lō'* ("not"). Another obvious example is Micah 1:15, where the MT reads *'aḇî lāḵ* ("my father to you") rather than *'āḇî lāḵ* ("I will bring to you"—the meaning obviously demanded by the context). The Masoretic notation in the margin favors the addition of an ' (aleph) to *'aḇî*. The LXX so translates it (*agagō soi*) and also the Vulgate (*adducam tibi*). As a matter of fact, it is conceivable that in Micah's day (eighth century B.C.) the imperfect of the verb "to bring" may have been optionally spelled without the aleph, owing to a greater brevity in the indication of sound.

7. *Misreading similar-appearing letters*

This type of error can actually be dated in history because at various stages of the alphabet development some letters, which later were written quite differently, resembled one another in shape. A notable example of this is the letter *y* (yodh), which greatly resembled the *w* (waw) from the postexilic period, when the square Hebrew form of the alphabet was introduced. In the Sermon on the Mount, Jesus spoke of the "jot" (yodh) as the smallest letter in the alphabet—"One jot or one tittle of the law shall not pass away until all be fulfilled" (Matt. 5:18). But up until the early sixth century B.C., yodh was as large a letter as many others in the alphabet and bore no resemblance whatever to the waw. Therefore we may confidently date all examples of confusion between yodh and waw to the third century B.C. or later.

Examples of misreading similar letters abound in 1QIsa. In Isaiah 33:13 it reads *yd'w* ("let them know") rather than MT's *wd'w* ("and know ye"). More significantly we find in the MT of Psalm 22:17 (16 Eng.) the strange phrase "like the lion my hands and my feet" (*kā'arî yāday wᵉraglāy*) in a context that reads "dogs have surrounded me; a band of evil men has encircled me—like the lion my hands and my feet!" This really makes no sense, for lions do not surround the feet of their victims. Rather, they pounce on them and bite them through with their teeth. Furthermore, this spelling of the word for "lion" (*'arî*) is rendered more than doubtful by the fact that in v.13 (14MT) the word "lion" appears in the normal way as *'aryēh*. It is most unlikely that the author would have used two different spellings of the same word within three verses of each other. Far more likely is the reading supported by most of the versions: *kā'rû* ("They [i.e., the dogs or evildoers] have pierced" my hands and my feet). This involves merely reading the final letter yodh as a waw, which would make it the past tense of a third person plural verb. This is apparently what the LXX read, for *ōryxan* ("they have bored through") reflects a *kārû* from the verb *kûr* ("pierce, dig through"). The Vulgate conforms to this with *foderunt* ("they have dug through"). The Syriac Peshitta has *baz'w*, which means "they have pierced through/penetrated." Probably the ' (aleph) in *kā'rû* represents a mere vowel lengthener that occasionally appears in the Hasmonean manuscripts such as 1QIsa and the sectarian literature of the second century B.C.

Another pair of easily confused letters is *d* (daleth) and *r* (resh). It so happens that at all stages of the Hebrew alphabet, both the old epigraphic and the later square Hebrew, these two always looked alike. Thus we find that the race referred to in Genesis 10:4 as the "Dodanim" appears in 1 Chronicles 1:7 as the "Rodanim." It is generally thought that Rodanim is the better reading because the reference seems to be to the Rhodians of the Asia Minor coastline. A rather bizarre aberration in the LXX rendering of Zechariah 12:10 is best accounted for by a confusion of r and d. The MT reads, "They shall look upon me whom they have pierced [dāqārû]." But the Greek version reads, "They shall look on me, because they will dance in triumph over [me]." The incongruous "dance" comes from misreading dāqārû as rāqādû, which involves reading the d as r and the r as d, all in the same word. But Theodotion preserves the correct reading by rendering exekentēsan ("they pierced through").

One of the most interesting and involved cases of letter confusion is found in the LXX rendition of the name of the pagan god mentioned in Amos 5:26. The MT spells this name as kywn ("Chiun," KJV), but the LXX gives it as Raiphan, implying rypn as their reading of their Vorlage. Now it so happens that in the period of the Elephantine Papyri (fifth century B.C.), k (kaph) was shaped very much like r (rēsh), and w (waw) greatly resembled p (pē). This meant that kywn could be mistaken as rypn. If the Vorlage read by the LXX looked like rypn, the translators had no way to correct it to the better reading because it was a foreign, heathen name. But we now know from the Akkadian spelling of the name of this god, associated with the planet Saturn and pronounced Kaiwanu, that kywn was the true, historical spelling of the name back in Amos's day. The interesting feature about Raiphan, however, is that it is so spelled in Stephen's quotation of Amos 5:26 appearing in Acts 7:43. As he addresses a mixed audience of Greek-speaking and Aramaic-speaking Jews, and representing as he does the Greek-speaking Dispersion of the Jews, he quotes from the LXX, rather than going back to the original Hebrew. For missionary purposes most of the apostles quoted from the LXX, simply because that was the only form of the Old Testament available to the Greek-speaking population of the Roman Empire. If they were to "search the Scriptures" to see whether Paul and the other Christian evangelists were treating the Old Testament fairly, they had to check in the LXX version to confirm the apostolic message as the truth of God.

On the other hand, there are some instances where the LXX seems to preserve a better reading than the MT, though this happens but rarely. In the Jerusalem church council narrated in Acts 15:17, James quotes a clinching argument for the divine warrant authorizing the addition of Gentile converts to the church without forcing them to become Jewish proselytes. He builds on the promise of Amos 9:11–12, which he quotes as "that the remnant of men may seek the Lord, and all the Gentiles [ethnē, "nations"] who bear My name." The received text reads as follows: "So that they may possess the remnant of Edom, and all the nations that bear My name." If that was the reading of the Hebrew text in the middle of the first century A.D., then James would have been rejected as grossly misquoting Scripture; for the whole point of the passage according to James was that the "remnant of men" were going to "seek the Lord." But if the only valid reading was yîrᵉšu ("possess"), rather than the yidrᵉšû implied by the LXX "(that they may seek"), then James' argument would have been totally beside the point. The progress of the textual corruption is easily reconstructed. If we assume that the original text read lᵉ ma'an yidrᵉ šû 'ōtô (w) šᵉ 'ērît 'ādām ("that the remnant of men may seek him"), then we can see that the word 'ādām ("men") might early have been misread as 'edôm ("Edom") since in the earlier orthography they would have been identical in appearance. The yidrešû may have looked like yirrešû, especially after d (daleth) acquired a short tail in the period of the Lachish Ostraca (Jeremiah's time); and the copyist may have thought he was looking at a dittograph that needed correction to yirešû—which in turn might well be construed as equivalent to yi(y)rᵉšû (from yāraš, "to possess"), inasmuch as the second y would hardly have appeared in writing according to the older orthography. The 'et of the MT, which is the sign of the direct object, may have been miscopied from an original *'ōtô(w)*, which failed to come through with the intended final *w* (waw). All this variation could have resulted from misreading only two letters: *r* for *d*, and a final *w* inadvertently dropped from *'ōtô(w)*. The mere fact that James's Jewish fellow elders, steeped as they were in the Hebrew Scriptures, offered no objection on the ground of misquotation is very powerful evidence that the LXX was true to the original Hebrew text at this point.

8. *Homoeoteleuton*

This Greek term means "having the same ending" and identifies the loss of text that can result when the eye of the copyist inadvertently passes over all the words preceding a final phrase that is identical with that which closes the sentence immediately preceding, or immediately following. Having taken his eyes off the *Vorlage* in order to copy down what he has just read, he turns back to it and sees the words he has just finished writing down. Supposing that he is ready to move on to the next sentence, he fails to observe that he has left out all the words preceding the second appearance of the repeated phrase. For example, in Isaiah 4:4–6 the copyist who wrote out 1QIsa encountered verses that had two occurrences of *yômām* ("by day"). The complete text should read as follows: "Then Yahweh will create over the whole area of Mount Zion and over her assemblies a cloud by day, even smoke and the brightness of a flaming fire by night; for overall the glory there will be a canopy. And there will be a shelter to give shade from the heat by day, and refuge and protection from the storm and rain." Now when the eye of the scribe jumped from the first "by day" to the second "by day," he left out fourteen Hebrew words in between. Unfortunately this could happen even in the more carefully preserved text-tradition of the MT itself. One notable instance occurs in Psalm 145, which is an alphabetic acrostic. Each successive verse begins with the next letter of the twenty-two-letter Hebrew alphabet. Now it so happens that the MT of v 13 begins with *m* (mem), that is, the first word is *malkûtᵉkā* ("your kingdom"). But then v.14 begins, not with *n* (nūn, the following letter in the alphabet), but with *s* (samekh, the letter following after nūn): *sômēk YHWH lᵉkol-hannōpᵉlîm* ("Yahweh upholds all those who fall down"). Where is the verse in between? Fortunately it has been preserved in the Greek of the LXX; and by translating this back to Hebrew, we come out with the probable original line: *neᵉmān YHWH bᵉkol-dᵉbārāyw wᵉḥāsîd bᵉkol-maᵃśāyw* ("Yahweh is faithful in all his words and gracious in all his works"). The recurrence of *YHWH bᵉkol* ("Yahweh in all") soon after *YHWH lᵉkol* ("Yaweh to all") was enough to throw the scribe off; and some time after the LXX translation of the Psalter had been completed, the verse beginning with *n* became entirely lost in the Masoretic text.

9. *Homoeoarkton*

This means "that which has a similar beginning" and involves a similar loss of intervening words, as the eye of the scribe jumps from one beginning to another. A striking example may be found in 1 Samuel 14:41, where the MT reads, "And Saul said to Yahweh, 'O God of Israel, grant a perfect one [i.e., a perfect lot].'" The situation demanded a discovery of God's leading in a time of national crisis. But according to the LXX version, Saul prefaced this request for a correct lot by a lengthy petition, saying, "Why have you not answered your servant today? If the fault is in me or my son Jonathan, respond with Urim; but if the men of Israel are at fault, respond with Thummim." The spelling of "a perfect one" (*tāmîm*) and "Thummim" (*tummîm*) would have been the same in the consonantal text of the

Hebrew *Vorlage*. (It should be explained that the Urim and Thummim were the two precious gems contained in a special compartment of the breastplate of the high priest and were to be used in ascertaining God's will when a choice was to be made between two alternatives.) Saul and his army, pursuing the defeated Philistines, needed to know whether God would have them continue the pursuit for another day; but God withheld giving them any clear guidance. Therefore Saul concluded that someone in his army must have transgressed against the Lord, and he was ready to resort to the casting of lots to find out who the culprit was. It so happened that Jonathan, unaware of Saul's vow invoked on anyone who would partake of food before the Philistines had been completely destroyed, had come across a comb of wild honey in the woods; and so he had quickly snatched up some of the honey to his mouth. Thus it came about that he who was the greatest hero of the hour—for he had started the rout of the Philistines against overwhelming odds—was about to be marked for death. But the eye of the Hebrew scribe unfortunately jumped from the first *ᵉlōhê yiśrā'ēl* ("O God of Israel") to the second one, passing over no less than twenty-six Hebrew words in between. But here again the LXX supplies us with all the missing words in Greek, and from these we can reconstruct them in Hebrew, as has been done in the critical apparatus of Kittel's edition.

10. *Accidental omission of words*

Homoeoteleuton and homoeoarkton account for the omission of substantial numbers of words. Here, however, we are considering the loss of an occasional word, where similar phrases are not the source of the difficulty, but where some ancient version, such as the LXX, furnishes us with a clue that a word has been lost in the received Hebrew text. Sometimes this omission occurred before the third century B.C., and so not even the LXX can retrieve it for us. Such an instance is 1 Samuel 13:1, which in the MT says, "Saul was . . . years old when he began to reign." The numeral has dropped out completely, and there is no way of ascertaining what it was. Many textual critics suggest other passages where a word has dropped out; but this falls into the class of mere conjecture and remains a matter of opinion, nothing more. We had best content ourselves with the objective data of the received text and the early versions. In the absence of special guidance from God, no such suggestion has any higher value than mere guesswork.

11. *Variants based on vowel points only*

As we have already seen, the Hebrew Scriptures existed only in the form of consonants all during the Old Testament period and indeed until well into the seventh or eighth century A.D. There is no clear evidence of the use of vowel indicators until the age of the Masoretes. A similar delay in the insertion of vowel points is demonstrable for Syriac and Arabic as well. But there was a very definite oral tradition preserved by the scribal order as to how the consonants were to be vocalized. From the LXX we can learn much as to the earlier pronunciation of Hebrew in the third and second centuries B.C., for there are many proper names spelled out with Greek vowels. As a matter of fact, a scholar named Origen in the third century A.D. prepared a vocalization of the Old Testament by the use of a Greek transliteration in column 2 of his *Hexapla*; but unfortunately rather little of that has been preserved.

The late origin of vowel points, which were not systematically inserted into the consonantal text until the Masoretic period, means that we must rely heavily on the oral tradition of the Jewish custodians of the Old Testament original. We can safely assume that in the vast majority of cases their voweling is true to the meaning of the original author. But there remain a small percentage of arguable passages where a slightly different pointing might significantly affect the meaning. In general, of course, Hebrew is perfectly understandable to those who regularly speak Hebrew, even though there are no vowel points indicated. Virtually all documents in Israel today are printed in consonants only, and there is never any dispute as to the sound or meaning of the words so written. (The same is true of Arabic and Syriac as well.) Nevertheless in dealing with literature written two thousand years ago, it remains true that speech patterns are far more varied—particularly in poetic genres—than would be true with modern Hebrew; and vowel points are a very necessary safeguard for accurate interpretation.

To illustrate some of the problems involving correct vowel pointing, let me discuss a few passages relating to the Lord Jesus. Each of these has been pointed differently by the Masoretes from what is indicated by the early versions or (in some cases) by the New Testament.

1. Isaiah 7:11 contains the invitation to King Ahaz to name any miraculous sign he wishes to confirm that Isaiah's message of deliverance for Judah by God is truly of the Lord. Isaiah then says (according to the MT): "Ask for a sign for yourself from Yahweh your God; make the request [š^e'ālāh] deep, or exalt it on high." This amounts to inviting him to name any kind of miracle in the heaven above or in the earth beneath. Interestingly enough, the Greek versions all point to a different voweling of š^e'ālāh, namely, š^e'lāh, meaning "to Sheol [Hades]." The LXX has *eis bathos* ("to the deep"); likewise Aquila, Symmachus, and Theodotion render it either *eis bathos* or *eis Hadēn* ("to Hades"). So also does Jerome in the Vulgate: *in profundum inferni* ("to the depth of Hades"). This adds up to considerable weight on the side of the emendation.

2. In Isaiah 9:5(6 Eng.) the MT reads, "And one [or 'he'] shall call" his name Wonderful. But the LXX (which is very sloppy in its rendering of this passage, to be sure) makes it the present passive *kaleitai*, which means "his name is called." The Vulgate *vocabitur* is likewise passive: "will be called"; the Syriac *ethqrī* is present passive, just like the LXX. All this adds up to a pretty strong case for repointing the MT *yiqrā'* to the passive *yiqqārē'* ("shall be called"). It makes a little better sense in the context and involves no change in the consonants.

3. In Micah 5:1(2 Eng.), the prophecy concerning Christ's birth in Bethlehem, the MT reads, "You are little to be among the thousands ['alpê] of Juidah," meaning "to be counted among the communities having a thousand families or more." But in Matthew 2:6 it is quoted thus: "You are very small among the leaders of Judah." The Greek word for "leaders" (*hēgemosin*) reflects a Hebrew *'allupê* instead of *'alpê*. This does not reflect the LXX, incidentally, for it supports the MT with *chiliasin* ("thousands"). Therefore it must come from some earlier, independent tradition.

4. Psalm 2:9, which is addressed by God the Father to His messianic Son, says (according to the MT), "You shall smash them with an iron rod," referring to hostile kings who will rebel against Him. This pointing of *t^erō'ēm* ("smash") seems to be confirmed by the second half of the verse: "You will dash them to pieces like pottery." On the other hand, the LXX reads *poimaneis* ("You will rule"), implying the vowel pointing *tir'ēm*. This is confirmed by the word for "rod," which is *šēbet*, the regular word for the staff of a shepherd or the scepter of a king. It is highly significant that this verse is quoted in Revelation 2:27: "He will rule [or 'pasture'] them with an iron scepter; he will dash them to pieces like pottery." Again, in Revelation 12:5 we read, "She gave birth to a son, a male child, who will rule

[*poimainein*] all the nations with an iron scepter." In both passages the emphasis is not so much on destruction or smashing as it is on shepherding or governing as a ruler over all the earth. The probabilities are, then, that we should repoint the MT's *t͟ʰrō'ēm* as *tir'ēm*. This latter reading is the one followed by the Vulgate (*regēs*) and the Syriac (*ter'e'*), for both mean "you will rule."

5. Psalm 22, the Psalm of the Crucifixion, reads in v.9 (according to the MT): "Trust thou [*gōl*] in Yahweh; He will rescue him [or, 'let Him rescue him'], deliver him [i.e., the psalmist in his suffering and humiliation], for He takes pleasure in him." This verse involves a rather awkward mixing of second person ("trust thou") and third person ("him"), referring to the same person in the same verse. But the LXX wording is "he trusted in the Lord; let Him deliver him." This implies repointing *gōl* as *gal*, the same consonants, but a different vowel. Not only is this supported by the Vulgate (*speravit*), but it is also supported by the Syriac ('*ettekel*). Most important of all, Matthew 27:43 makes it third person singular: "He trusts [*pepoithen*] in God. Let God rescue him." Considerations of context, the early versions, and the New Testament quotation all present a very good case for amending *gōl* to *gal*.

6. Psalm 90:2 in the MT reads, "Before the mountains were born or You did give birth [*watt͟ʰhōlēl*] to the earth or the world, . . . You are God." But in almost all the early versions, the verb "give birth" is read as a passive (*watt͟ʰhōlal*, "was given birth to"), thus making the second verb a passive, harmonizing with the first verb, "were born." The LXX, Aquila, Symmachus, Jerome, and even the Aramaic Targum (which usually conforms to the MT) unite in making the second verb passive. There is even one early Hebrew manuscript from the Cario Genizah (Ec1) that reads a passive instead of an active. We may, therefore, safely adopt this emendation and make it a passive—"were given birth to," which suggests writhing in pain, like a woman in labor.

B. *The Canons of Textual Criticism*

After sampling the eleven classes of textual error just described, in summary fashion we will list the seven "canons" or procedural rules textual critics use to come to an intelligent decision about divergent readings. These canons are arranged in the order of their priority or relative value.

Canon 1. Generally speaking, the older reading is to be preferred over a reading found in later manuscripts. There may be, however, less reliable readings in as old a manuscript as 1QIsa, simply because the latter was a rapidly made copy, intended for private use rather than for public worship or official instruction. But normally the older a manuscript is, the less likelihood there is of deviation from the reading of the autograph.

Canon 2. The more difficult reading (*lectio difficilior*) is to be preferred over the easier reading. This results from the greater likelihood on the part of a copyist to simplify a difficult word or phrase in his *Vorlage*, rather than to make a simple reading more difficult. But it should of course be added that when the more difficult reading seems to have resulted from confusion or inadvertence on the part of the scribe, this rule does not apply. The same is true if the reading is so difficult that it does not really make sense, or, again, if the more difficult reading expresses an idea or viewpoint quite contradictory to the sentiments expressed elsewhere in the book.

Canon 3. The shorter reading is generally to be preferred over the longer one. The reason for this is that copyists are more inclined to amplify or insert additional material for the purpose of clarification or embellishment than they are to leave out words already appearing in their *Vorlage*. But this rule does not apply if the shorter reading seems to result from haplography or homoeoteleuton, as described above.

Canon 4. The reading that best explains all the variants is most likely the original one. An excellent example of this was discussed above in connection with Psalm 22:16(17 Eng.), where we saw that a *kā'rú* ("they have pierced") misread as *kā''rí* (at a time when waw and yodh greatly resembled each other) most satisfactorily accounted for the MT reading; whereas it would be far less likely that "like the lion" would have been the original lying behind a *kā'rú*, which makes perfect sense in the context.

Canon 5. The reading with the widest geographical support is to be preferred over one that predominants only within a single region or a single manuscript family. Thus a reading attested by the LXX, the Old Latin, and the Coptic Egyptian versions does not have as much to commend it as one attested by the Vulgate and the LXX (outside of the Psalms, that is), or the LXX and the Samaritan. The reason for this is that both the Old Latin and the Coptic were translated originally from the LXX rather than from the Hebrew. For example, in Numbers 22:35 the Samaritan and the LXX agree on *tišmōr ̄dabbēr* ("you will be careful to speak"), as against MT's simple * t̄dabbēr* ("you will speak"). Even though some LXX manuscripts were found in the Qumran library, it is safe to say that the LXX and the Samaritan had very little influence on each other. Therefore if they unite on a reading divergent from that of the MT, it is quite possible they are correct.

Canon 6. The reading that more closely conforms to the style, diction, or viewpoint of the author in the rest of the book is to be preferred over a reading that seems markedly divergent. Of course this criterion must be applied with caution, for the author may be capable of a wider range of viewpoints and sentiments than modern liberals think admissible. We must firmly resist any emendation that merely reflects our own personal preference or opinion on a largely subjective basis.

Canon 7. A reading that reflects no doctrinal bias on the part of the copyist himself is to be preferred over one that betrays a partisan viewpoint. Thus we find in Isaiah 1:12 that the Masoretes have shied away from the alleged anthropomorphism of the MT's "When you enter to appear [*lērā'ōt*] before Me, who has required this from your hand, to trample my courts?" The obvious reading of the unpointed text would be, not the abbreviated form of a medio-passive infinitive (*lērā'ōt* for *t̄hērā'ōt*), but rather the active infinitive *lir̄'ōt* ("to behold"). The reason for reading it as medio-passive is a theological one. Since no man can ever see God, the prophet would not be foolish enough to forbid Israel to do something that the people could never do anyway. But the problem with the MT pointing is that "before" is normally written *t̄pānay* ("before me") rather than the simple *pānāy*, which means "my face," not "before." These two factors lead to the conclusion that the MT has resorted to an antianthropomorphic device, the false pointing of *lir̄'ōt* as the passive infinitive rather than the active. The Masoretes' high view of God as a transcendent spirit made them reluctant to allow the figurative expression "to behold my face," which was probably what Isaiah really intended to say. Yet it is quite possible that by Isaiah's time this had become an idiomatic expression for coming to the temple for worship and prayer. The word *pānîm* meant both "face" and "presence"; and since the presence of Yahweh rested over the ark of the covenant in the inner sanctum, the so-called table of shewbread was actually called in Hebrew "the table and the bread of the Presence" (*šulḥān w̄leem pānîm*). The twelve loaves were so designated because they were offered before the Presence of the Lord, concealed on the other side of the curtain separating the Holy Place from the innermost sanctum.

C. *Ground Rules for Competent Textual Correction*

Having gone through the general guidelines for choosing between alternative readings on the basis of the seven canons, we now come to a concluding summary that appears in Ernst Würthwein's excellent volume *The Text of the Old Testament* (New York: Macmillan, 1957), pp. 80–81. Würthwein is not an Evangelical scholar, but he does represent a very high level of German scholarship in the area of textual criticism; and his recommended procedures are beyond reproach—except perhaps on the part of critics who wish to alter the received text of Scripture in order to suit their own ideas of what it should have said. Here, then, is Würthwein's formula.

1. Where the MT and the other witnesses present the same reading, and it is sensible and intelligent, then let it stand without tampering. (It is inadmissible to reject this reading and resort to conjecture, as so many have ventured to do.)

2. Where there is a genuine deviation from the MT on the part of other witnesses, and both readings seem equally sensible, then the preference should clearly be given to the MT.

3. Where the text of the MT is for some reason doubtful or virtually impossible—whether from the standpoint of grammar or sense-in-context—and the reading offered by other witnesses offers a satisfactory sense, then the latter should be given careful consideration. This is especially true if it can be seen how the MT reading might have resulted through one of the familiar scribal errors (described above). But if, on the other hand, there is reason to believe that the ancient translator produced a clear reading only because he could not make out the meaning of the Hebrew text before him, and therefore guessed at what it might have intended to say, then we have a textual obscurity that can only be tentatively solved by resorting to conjecture.

4. Where neither the MT nor the other witnesses offer a plausible reading, then conjecture is the only course left to the critic. But he must do his best to reconstruct a reading that is as close as possible to the corrupted words in the received text, taking full cognizance of the standard types of scribal error and the various alternative readings that may most easily have developed from this original wording—if such it was.

5. In all his work with textual problems, the critic must pay due regard to the psychology of the scribe himself. How might he have fallen into this error, if error it was? How well does.it conform to his habit of mind or procedure observable in the rest of the book?

By means of this carefully worked-out formula, Würthwein has devised a sound method of scientific objectivity and systematic procedure that serves to eliminate much of the reckless and ill-considered emendation foisted on the public as bona fide textual criticism.

The Pentateuch

What solid evidence is there for the Mosaic authorship of the Pentateuch?

It is common in liberal or neoorthodox circles to deny that Moses had anything to do with the composition of the Pentateuch. Most critics of that persuasion feel that the so-called Books of Moses were written by several different, anonymous authors beginning in the ninth century and concluding with the final portion, the "Priestly Code," around 445 B.C.—just in time for Ezra to read it aloud at the Feast of Tabernacles (cf. Neh. 8). Still other scholars, especially those of the form-critical school, feel that rather little of the Pentateuch was actually written down until the time of Ezra, even though some portions of it may have existed as oral tradition for several centuries previous—perhaps even to the period of Moses himself. In view of the general consensus among non-Evangelical scholars that all claims to Mosaic authorship are spurious, it is well for us to review at least briefly the solid and compelling evidence, both internal and external, that the entire Pentateuch is the authentic work of Moses, under the inspiration of God the Holy Spirit.

Biblical Testimony to Mosaic Authorship

The Pentateuch often refers to Moses as its author, beginning with Exodus 17:14: "And Yahweh said to Moses, 'Write for me a memorial in a book . . . that I will utterly blot out the remembrance of Amalek.'" In Exodus 24:4 we read, "And Moses wrote all the words of Yahweh." In v.7 we are told, "And he took the book of the covenant, and read it in the hearing of the people." Other references to Moses' writing down the Pentateuch are found in Exodus 34:27, Numbers 33:1-2, and Deuteronomy 31:9, the last of which says, "And Moses wrote this law and delivered it to the priests." Two verses later it is made a standing requirement for the future that when "all Israel has come to appear before Yahweh, you shall read this law before all Israel in their hearing." This provision apparently comprises all of Exodus, Leviticus, Numbers, and most of Deuteronomy (at least through chap. 30).

Later on, after the death of Moses, the Lord gives these directions to Joshua, Moses' successor: "This book of the Law shall not depart from your mouth, but you are to meditate in it day and night, in order that you may be careful to do according to all that is written in it" (Josh. 1:8). The denial of Mosaic authorship would mean that every one of the above-cited verses is false and unworthy of acceptance. Joshua 8:32-34 records that with the congregation of Israel stationed outside the city of Shechem, on the slopes of Mount Ebal and Mount Gerizim, Joshua read aloud from the Law of Moses inscribed on stones the passages

45

in Leviticus and Deuteronomy referring to the blessings and curses, as Moses earlier had done (cf. Deut. 27–28). If the Documentary Hypothesis is correct, then this account must also be rejected as a sheer fabrication. Other Old Testament references to the Mosaic authorship of the Pentateuch are 1 Kings 2:3; 2 Kings 14:6; 21:8; Ezra 6:18; Nehemiah 13:1; Daniel 9:11–13; and Malachi 4:4. All these testimonies must also be rejected as totally in error.

Christ and the apostles likewise gave unequivocal witness that Moses was the author of the Torah (Law). In John 5:46–57, Jesus said, "If you believed Moses, you would believe me, for he wrote about me. But if you do not believe his writings, how can you believe my words?" How indeed! Likewise, in John 7:19, Jesus said, "Did not Moses give you the Law? And yet none of you does the Law." If Christ's confirmation of Moses as the real author of the Pentateuch is set aside—as it is by the modern critical theory—it inescapably follows that the authority of Christ Himself is denied. For if He was mistaken about a factual, historical matter like this, then He might be mistaken about any other belief He held or doctrines He taught. In Acts 3:22, Peter said to his countrymen, "Moses indeed said, 'A Prophet shall the Lord God raise up to you'" (cf. Deut. 18:15). Paul affirmed in Romans 10:5 that "Moses writes that the man who practices righteousness based on the law will live by that righteousness." But the JEDP theory of Wellhausen and the rationalistic modern critics deny that Moses ever wrote any of those things. This means that Christ and the apostles were totally mistaken in thinking that he did. Such an error as this, in matters of historical fact that can be verified, raises a serious question as to whether any of the theological teaching, dealing with metaphysical matters beyond our powers of verification, can be received as either trustworthy or authoritative. Thus we see that the question of Mosaic authenticity as the composer of the Pentateuch is a matter of utmost concern to the Christian. The authority of Christ Himself is involved in this issue.

Internal Evidences of Mosaic Composition

In addition to the direct testimonies of the Pentateuchal passages quoted above, we have the witness of the incidental allusions to contemporary events or current issues, to social or political conditions, or to matters of climate or geography. When all such factors are fairly and properly weighed, they lead to this conclusion: the author of these books and his readers must originally have lived in Egypt. Furthermore, these factors indicate that they had little or no firsthand acquaintance with Palestine and knew of it only by oral tradition from their forefathers. We cite the following evidences.

1. The climate and weather referred to in Exodus are typically Egyptian, not Palestinian (cf. the reference to crop sequence in connection with the plague of hail, Exod. 9:31–32).

2. The trees and animals referred to in Exodus through Deuteronomy are all indigenous to Egypt or the Sinai Peninsula, but none of them are peculiar to Palestine. The shittim or acacia tree is native to Egypt and the Sinai, but it is hardly found in Canaan except around the Dead Sea. This tree furnished the wood for much of the tabernacle furniture. The skins for its outer covering were the hide of the *taḥaš*, or dugong, which is foreign to Palestine but is found in the seas adjacent to Egypt and the Sinai. As for the lists of clean and unclean animals found in Leviticus 11 and Deuteronomy 14,

these include some that are peculiar to the Sinai Peninsula, such as the *dîśōn,* or pygarg (Deut. 14:5); the *ya'ᵃnāh,* or ostrich (Lev. 11:16); and the *tᵉ'ô,* or wild antelope (Deut. 14:5). It is difficult to imagine how a list of this sort could have been made up nine hundred years later, after the Hebrew people had been living in a country not possessing any of these beasts.

3. Even more conclusive are the geographical references that betray the perspective of one who is personally unfamiliar with Palestine but is well acquainted with Egypt. (1) In Genesis 13:10, where the author wishes to convey to his readers how verdant the vegetation of the Jordan Valley was, he compares it to a well-known locality in the eastern part of the Egyptian Delta region, lying near Mendes, between Busiris and Tanis. He states that the Jordan Valley was like "the land of Egypt, as you go toward Zoar" (Egyp. *T-;-r*). Nothing could be plainer from this casual reference than that the author was writing for a readership unfamiliar with the appearance of regions in Palestine but personally acquainted with the scenery of Lower Egypt. Such could only have grown up in Egypt, and this fits in only with a Mosaic date of composition for the Book of Genesis. (2) The founding of Kirjath-arba (the pre-Israelite name of Hebron in southern Judah) is stated in Numbers 13:22 to have taken place "seven years before Zoan in Egypt." This clearly implies that Moses' readers were well aware of the date of the founding of Zoan but unfamiliar with when Hebron—which became one of the foremost cities in Israel after the Conquest—was first founded. (3) In Genesis 33:18, there is a reference to "Salem, a city of Shechem in the land of Canaan." To a people who had been living in Palestine for over seven centuries since the Conquest (according to the date given this passage by the Wellhausen school), it seems rather strange that they would have to be told that so outstanding a city as Shechem was located "in the land of Canaan." But it would be perfectly appropriate to a people who had not yet settled there—as was true of the congregation of Moses.

4. The atmosphere and setting of the desert prevails all through the narrative, from Exodus 16 to the end of Deuteronomy (though there are some agricultural references looking forward to settled conditions in the land that they were soon to conquer). The prominence accorded to a large tent or tabernacle as the central place of worship and assembly would hardly be relevant to a readership living in Palestine for over seven centuries and familiar only with the temple of Solomon or Zerubbabel as their central sanctuary. The Wellhausen explanation for this, that the tabernacle was simply an artificial extrapolation from the temple, does not fit the facts; the temple was much different in size and furnishings from those described for the tabernacle in the Torah. But even this theory of historical fiction furnishes no exnation of why Ezra's contemporaries would have been so interested in a mere tent as to devote to it so many chapters in Exodus (25–40) and to refer to it in nearly three-fourths of Leviticus and very frequently also in Numbers and Deuteronomy. No other example can be found in all world literature for such absorbing attention to a structure that never

47

really existed and that had no bearing on the generation for which it was written.

5. There are many evidences of a technical, linguistic nature that could be adduced to support an Egyptian background for the text of the Torah. Detailed examples of this may be found in my *Survey of Old Testament Introduction* (pp. 111–14). Suffice it to say that a far greater number of Egyptian names and loan words are found in the Pentateuch than in any other section of Scripture. This is just what we would expect from an author who was brought up in Egypt, writing for a people who were reared in the same setting as he.

6. If the Pentateuch was composed between the ninth and fifth centuries B.C., as the Documentary school maintains, and if it extrapolated the religious practices and political perspectives of the fifth and sixth centuries back to the times of Moses (by way of a pious fraud), it is reasonable to expect that this spurious document, concocted long after Jerusalem had been taken over as the capital of the Israelite kingdom, would surely have referred to Jerusalem by name on many occasions. It would certainly have included some prophecy of the future conquest of that city and its coming status as the location of the permanent temple of Yahweh. But a careful examination of the entire text of Genesis through Deuteronomy comes up with the astonishing result that Jerusalem is never once mentioned by name. To be sure, Mount Moriah appears in Genesis 22 as the location of Abraham's attempted sacrifice of Isaac, but there is no suggestion that it was to be the future location of the temple.

In Genesis 14 there is a reference to Melchizedek as the "king of Salem"—not "Jeru-salem"—but again without any hint that it would later become the religious and political capital of the Hebrew Commonwealth. In Deuteronomy 12:5–18 there are references to a "place that Yahweh your God shall choose from all your tribes, to establish His name there for His dwelling." While these references are general enough to include such places as Shiloh and Gibeon, where the tabernacle was kept for extended periods of time before the erection of Solomon's temple, it is fair to assume that Deuteronomy 12:5 was mainly intended as a prediction of the establishment of the Jerusalem temple. Yet it is almost impossible to account for the failure of this allegedly late and spurious work of Moses to mention Jerusalem by name, when there was every incentive to do so. Only the supposition that the Torah was genuinely Mosaic, or at least composed well before the capture of Jerusalem in 1000 B.C., can account for its failure to mention the city at all by name.

7. In dating literary documents, it is of greatest importance to take stock of the key terms that are apparently current at the time the author did his work. In the case of a religious book, the titles by which God is characteristically referred to are of pivotal significance. During the period between 850–450 B.C., we find increasing prominence given to the title *YHWH ṣeḇā'ōṯ* (most frequently rendered in English versions by "the LORD of Hosts"). This appellation, which lays particular stress on the omnipotence of Israel's Covenant-God, occurs about sixty-seven times in Isaiah (late eighth cen-

48

tury), eighty-three times in Jeremiah (late seventh and early sixth centuries), thirteen times in the two chapters of Haggai (late sixth century), and fifty-one times in the fourteen chapters of Zechariah (late sixth to early fifth century). These prophets cover nearly the whole span of time during which the Pentateuchal corpus was being composed by Messrs. J, E, D, and P; yet amazingly enough, the title "Yahweh of Hosts" is never once to be found in the entire Pentateuch. From the standpoint of the science of comparative literature, this would be considered the strongest kind of evidence that the Torah was composed at a period when the title "Yahweh of Hosts" was not in use—therefore, all of it, even the so-called Priestly Code, must have been composed before the eighth century B.C. If this is a valid deduction, then the entire Documentary Hypothesis must be altogether abandoned.

8. If the Priestly Code portion of the Pentateuch was truly composed in the sixth and fifth centuries B.C., it would be expected that distinctively Levitical institutions and enrichments of public worship introduced from the time of David onward would find frequent mention in the Pentateuch. Such distinctives would surely include the guilds of temple singers, who were divided into twenty-four courses by King David (1 Chron. 25) and were often referred to in the titles of the Psalms. Yet no organized guilds of Levitical singers are ever once referred to in the Torah.

The order of scribes (*sōpērîm*) should certainly have received mention as the great chief of scribes, Ezra himself, was finalizing large portions of the Pentateuch in time for the 445 B.C.

celebration of the Feast of Tabernacles—according to the Wellhausen hypothesis. But for some strange reason there is no reference whatever to the scribal order or function, nor any prophetic hint that there will some day be such a class of guardians of the sacred text.

From the time of Solomon and onward, there was a very important class of temple servants known as the Nethinim ("those who have been given," i.e., to the service of the Lord in the temple). The number of Nethinim (392) who joined the 42,000 returnees from Babylon in 538 B.C. is included in the statistics of Ezra 2:58 and Nehemiah 7:60, along with the count of the Levites and priests. But there is no reference to them or prediction of them to be found in "Document P." Very strange!

From the time of David, "the sweet psalmist of Israel" (2 Sam. 23:1), liberal use was made of various musical instruments (stringed, wind, percussion—all three types) in connection with public worship before the Lord. Certainly a Mosaic sanction for this important feature of Levitical worship ought to have been included in the Torah if it had been composed as late as the tenth century or thereafter. But surprisingly enough, it fails to contain a single reference to musical accompaniment in connection with tabernacle worship. This is impossible to reconcile with a composition date in the fifth century B.C. It is beyond debate that a professional priestly group such as the Documentarians describe would have had the strongest motivation for including such cherished institutions as these among the ordinances of "Moses."

9. The Pentateuch, especially in Deuteronomy, contains several references to the future conquest of Canaan by the descendants of Abraham. The Deuteronomic speaker is filled with confidence that the Hebrew host will overwhelm all opposition within the land of Canaan, defeat every army, and storm every city they decide to attack. This is clearly reflected in the repeated exhortations to destroy every Canaanite temple or shrine with complete thoroughness (Deut. 7:5; 12:2–3; cf. Exod. 23:24; 34:13).

Since every nation defends its religious shrines with the utmost resistance of which it is capable, the assumption that Israel will be able to destroy every pagan sanctuary throughout the land assumes the military supremacy of Yahweh's people after their invasion of the land. At what other juncture in the career of the Hebrew nation could such a confidence have been entertained except in the days of Moses and Joshua? Here again, internal evidence points very strongly to a Mosaic date of composition. Nothing could be more unrealistic than to suppose that Josiah back in 621 B.C., when Judah was a tiny vassal state under the Assyrian Empire, could have expected to break down every idolatrous altar, destroy every pillar (*maṣṣēḇāh*) and cultic tree ('*ašērāh*), and smash every temple structure to rubble throughout the length and breadth of Palestine. Or how could the struggling little colony of post-Exilic fifth-century Judea expect to make a clean sweep of every heathen shrine from Dan to Beer-sheba?

The only conclusion to draw from these Pentateuchal commands to destroy all traces of idolatry is that it was within Israel's military capabilities to carry out this program throughout the whole region. But nothing could have been more inappropriate in the time of Zechariah, Ezra, and Nehemiah than to contemplate such a thorough extirpation of idol worship throughout Palestine. For them it was a battle just to survive, so repeated were their crop failures and so serious was the opposition of all the nations surrounding them. Neither "Document P" in the time of Ezra nor Deuteronomy in the days of Josiah could possibly be harmonized with such passages as these.

10. Deuteronomy 13:2–11 provides the penalty of death by stoning for any idolater or false prophet, even for a brother, wife, or child. Verses 12–17 go on to say that even if it is an entire city that has turned to idolatry, every inhabitant within it is to be put to death, all houses are to be reduced to rubble and ashes, and all property is to be put under the ban. This is no visionary theory but a serious ordinance with inbuilt investigative procedures, reflecting a program that is meant to be carried out within contemporary Israel. But as we examine the account of Judah's religious situation in the seventh century B.C. (or, indeed, in the eighth century from the time of Ahaz on), we find that idol worship was tolerated and practiced in almost every municipality throughout the kingdom—except during the reforms of Hezekiah and Josiah. This would have meant the destruction of every city and town throughout the realm, even including Jerusalem itself. No one devises laws that are completely impossible to carry out in the light of contemporary conditions. The only period in Israel's

history when such legislation could have been enacted and enforced was back in the days of Moses and Joshua—or possibly in the time of David. (Already by Solomon's time shrine worship on the "high places" was practiced.)

Moses' Qualifications for Authorship of the Pentateuch

From all the biblical references to Moses' background and training, it is apparent that he had just the right qualifications to compose just such a work as the Torah.

1. He had a fine education as a prince reared in the Egyptian court (Acts 7:22), in a land that was more literate than any other country in the Fertile Crescent. Even the mirror handles and toothbrushes were adorned with hieroglyphic inscriptions, as well as the walls of every public building.
2. From his Israelite ancestors, he must have received a knowledge of the oral law that was followed in Mesopotamia, where the patriarchs had come from.
3. From his mother and blood relations, Moses must have received a full knowledge of the experiences of the patriarchs, all the way from Adam to Joseph; and from this wealth of oral tradition, he would have been equipped with all the information contained in Genesis, being under the sure guidance of the Holy Spirit as he composed the inspired text of the Torah.
4. As a longtime resident of Egypt and also of the land of Midian in the Sinai, Moses would have acquired a personal knowledge of the climate, agricultural practices, and geographical peculiarities of both Egypt and the Sinai Peninsula, such as is obvious throughout the text of these four books (Exodus through Deuteronomy), which deal with the fifteenth-century world in the vicinity of the Red Sea and the Nile.
5. As the divinely appointed founder of a new nation to be governed by the revealed law of God, Moses would have had every incentive to compose this monumental work, including Genesis, with its full account of God's gracious dealings with Israel's ancestors before the migration of Jacob's family to Egypt. And since this young nation was to be governed by the law of God rather than by some royal despot like the pagan nations around them, it was incumbent on Moses to compose (under God's inspiration and guidance) a carefully detailed listing of all the laws God had given to guide His people in the ways of justice, godliness, and worship. Over the forty-year period of the wilderness wanderings, Moses had ample time and opportunity to lay out the entire system of civil and religious law that God had revealed to him to serve as the constitution for the new theocratic commonwealth.

Moses had, then, every incentive and every qualification to compose this remarkable production.

The Basic Fallacy Underlying the Documentary Hypothesis

The most serious of the false assumptions underlying the Documentary Hypothesis and the form-critical approach (the former assumes that no part of the Torah found in written form until the mid-ninth century B.C., the latter defers all writing down of the received Hebrew text of the Pentateuch until the time of the Exile) is that the Israelites waited until many centuries after the foundation of their commonwealth before committing any part of it to written form. Such an assumption flies in the face of all the archaeological discoveries of the last eighty years, that all of Israel's

51

neighbors kept written records relating to their history and religion from before the time of Moses. Perhaps the massive accumulation of inscriptions on stone, clay, and papyrus that have been exhumed in Mesopotamia and Egypt might have been questioned as necessarily proving the extensive use of writing in Palestine itself—until the 1887 discovery of the archive of Palestinian clay tablets in Tell el-Amarna, Egypt, dating from about 1420 to 1380 B.C. (the age of Moses and Joshua). This archive contained hundreds of tablets composed in Babylonian cuneiform (at that time the language of diplomatic correspondence in the Near East), which were communications to the Egyptian court from Palestinian officials and kings. Many of these letters contain reports of invasions and attacks by the Ḫa-bi-ru and the so-called SA.GAZ (the oral pronunciation of this logogram may well have been Habiru also) against the city-states of Canaan.

Wellhausen himself chose to ignore this evidence almost completely after the earliest publication of these Amarna Tablets came out in the 1890s. He refused to come to terms with the implications of the now-established fact that Canaan even before the Israelite conquest was completed contained a highly literate civilization (even though they wrote in Babylonian rather than their own native tongue). The later proponents of the Documentary Hypothesis have been equally closed-minded toward the implications of these discoveries.

The most serious blow of all, however, came with the deciphering of the alphabetic inscriptions from Serabit el-Khadim in the region of Sinai turquoise mines operated by the Egyptians during the second millennium B.C. These consisted of a new set of alphabetic symbols resembling Egyptian hieroglyphs but written in a dialect of Canaanite closely resembling Hebrew. They contained records of mining quotas and dedicatory inscriptions to the Phoenician goddess Baalat (who was apparently equated with the Egyptian Hathor). The irregular style of execution precludes all possibility of attributing these writings to a select group of professional scribes. There is only one possible conclusion to draw from this body of inscriptions (published by W.F. Albright in *The Proto-Sinaitic Inscriptions and Their Decipherment* [Cambridge: Harvard University, 1966]): Already back in the seventeenth or sixteenth centuries B.C., even the lowest social strata of the Canaanite population, slave-miners who labored under Egyptian foremen, were well able to read and write in their own language.

A third important discovery was the library of clay tablets discovered in the North Syrian site of Ras es-Shamra, anciently known as Ugarit, in which were many hundreds of tablets written around 1400 B.C. in an alphabetic cuneiform dialect of Canaanite, closely related to Hebrew. Along with business letters and government documents (some of which were written in Babylonian cuneiform), these tablets contained a great deal of religious literature. They related the loves and wars and exciting adventures of various deities of the Canaanite pantheon, such as El, Anath, Baal, Asherat, Mot, and many others, composed in a poetic form resembling parallelistic Hebrew poetry as found in the Pentateuch and in the Psalms of David. Here again we have indisputable proof that the Hebrew conquerors under Joshua, having emigrated from a highly literate culture down in Egypt, came into another civilization that made liberal use of writing. Furthermore, the high percentage of religious literature found at both Ras Shamra and Serabit el-Khadim utterly negate the supposition that, of all the ancient Near Eastern peoples, only the Hebrews did not contrive to put their religious records into written form until a thousand years later. Only the most unalterable form of bias in the minds of liberal scholars can account for their stubborn avoidance of the overwhelming mass of objective data that now support the proposition that Moses could have written, and in all probability did write, the books ascribed to him.

An even more fundamental fallacy underlies the modern Documentary approach, not only in regard to the authorship of the Pentateuch, but also to the composition of Isaiah 40–66 as an authentic work of the eighth-century Isaiah himself and the sixth-century date for the Book of Daniel. Basic to all these rationalist theories about the late and spurious nature of the composition of these Old Testament books is one firmly held assumption: the categorical impossibility of successful predictive prophecy. It is taken for granted that there is no authentic divine revelation to be found in Scripture and that all apparently fulfilled prophecies were really the result of pious fraud. In other words, the predictions were not written down until they had already been fulfilled—or were obviously about to be fulfilled. The result is a logical fallacy known as *petitio principii*, or reasoning in a circle. That is to say, the Bible offers testimony of the existence of a personal, miracle-working God, who revealed His future purposes to chosen prophets for the guidance and encouragement of His people. Through the abundance of fulfilled predictions, the Scripture furnishes the most compelling evidence of the supernatural, as exhibited by a personal God who cares for His people enough to reveal to them His will for their salvation. But the rationalist approaches all these evidences with a completely closed mind, assuming that there is no such thing as the supernatural and that fulfilled prophecy is per se impossible.

With this kind of bias, it is impossible to give honest consideration to evidence pertaining directly to the matter under investigation.

After a careful study of the history of the rise of modern higher criticism as practiced by the Documentarians and the form-criticism school, this writer is convinced that the basic reason for the refusal to face up to objective archaeological evidence hostile to the antisupernaturalist theories of the critics must be found in a self-defensive mentality that is essentially subjective. Thus it becomes absolutely essential for Documentarians to assign predictions of the Babylonian captivity and subsequent restoration (such as are found in Lev. 26 and Deut. 28) to a time after these events had already taken place. This is the real philosophical basis for assigning such portions (included in the "Priestly Code" or "Deuteronomic school") to the fifth century B.C., a thousand years later than the purported time of authorship. For, obviously, no mortal can successfully predict what lies even a few years in the future.

Since a fifteenth-century Moses would have to have foreseen what was going to happen in 587 and 537 B.C. in order to compose such chapters as these, he could never have composed them. But the Pentateuch says that Moses merely wrote down what almighty God revealed to him, rather than the product of his own unaided prophetic foresight. Hence, there is absolutely no logical difficulty in supposing that he could have predicted, under divine inspiration, events that far in the future—or that Isaiah in the early seventh century could have foreknown the Babylonian captivity and the subsequent return to Judah, or that Daniel could have predicted the major events of history between his own day (530 B.C.) and the coming of Antiochus Epiphanes in 170 B.C. In each case the prophecy comes from

God, the Lord of history, rather than from man; so there is no logical reason why God should be ignorant of the future that He Himself brings to pass.

Furthermore, the prophetic horizon of Daniel in Daniel 9:24–27 in actuality goes far beyond the Maccabean date assigned to it by rationalist scholars, for it pinpoints A.D. 27 as the exact year of Christ's appearing (Dan. 9:25–26). The same is true of the Deuteronomy 28:68 prediction of the aftermath of the Fall of Jerusalem in A.D. 70 and of the Isaiah 13:19–20 prediction of the total and permanent desolation of Babylon, which did not take place until after the Muslim conquest in the seventh century A.D. It is hopeless to attempt to account for such late fulfillments as these by alleging that the books that contained them were not written until after the predictions had actually come to pass. Thus we see that this guiding principle, which underlies the entire fabric of the Documentary Hypothesis, cannot be successfully maintained on objective or scientific grounds. It should, therefore, be abandoned in all our institutions of higher learning in which it is still being taught.

(As for the passages that are allegedly non-Mosaic on the basis of internal evidence, see the article on Exod. 6:26–27.)

Genesis

How can Genesis 1 be reconciled with theistic evolution?

In dealing with this question, we must carefully define our terms, for "evolution" is used in various senses by various people. We must distinguish between evolution as a philosophy and evolution as a descriptive mechanism for the development of species from the more primitive to the "higher" or more complex stages in the course of geological history. Furthermore, we must establish what is meant by *theistic* evolution. Then we will be in a better position to deal with its relationship to the creationism of Genesis 1.

Evolution as a Philosophy

Evolution as a philosophy seeks to explain the physical—and especially the biological—universe as a self-directed development from primeval matter, the origin of which is unknown but which may be regarded as eternally existing without ever having had a beginning. Philosophical evolution rules out any direction or intervention by a personal God and casts doubt on the existence of even an impersonal Higher Power. All reality is governed by unchangeable physical laws, and ultimately it is the product of mere chance. There is no reason for existence nor a real purpose for life. Man has to operate as an end in himself. He is his own ultimate lawgiver and has no moral accountability except to human society. The basis of law and ethics is basically utilitarian—that which produces the greatest good for the greatest number.

Not all these positions were advanced by Charles Darwin himself in his 1859 classic *The Origin of Species*. And yet the consistent atheism of philosophic evolution was a position he would not espouse, for he believed that a creating God was logically necessary to explain the prior existence of the original primordial ooze out of which the earliest forms of life emerged. It would be more accurate to call him a deist rather than an atheist, even though his system was taken over by those who denied the existence of God. But it should be pointed out that consistent atheism, which represents itself to be the most rational and logical of all approaches to reality, is in actuality completely self-defeating and incapable of logical defense. That is to say, if indeed all matter has combined by mere chance, unguided by any Higher Power or Transcendental Intelligence, then it necessarily follows that the molecules of the human brain are also the product of mere chance. In other words, we think the way we do simply because the atoms and molecules of our brain tissue happen to have combined in the way they have, totally without transcendental guidance or control. So then even the philosophies of men, their systems of logic, and all their approaches to reality are the result of mere fortuity. There is no absolute validity to any argument advanced by the atheist against the position of theism.

On the basis of his own presuppositions, the atheist completely cancels himself out, for on his own premises his arguments are without any absolute validity. By his own confession he thinks the way he does simply because because the atoms in his brain happen to combine the way they do. If this is so, he cannot honestly say that his view is any more valid than the contrary view of his opponent. His basic postulates are self-contradictory and self-defeating; for when he asserts that there are no absolutes, he thereby is asserting a very dogmatic absolute. Nor can he logically disprove the existence of God without resorting to a logic that depends on the existence of God for its validity. Apart from such a transcendent guarantor of the validity of logic, any attempts at logic or argumentation are simply manifestations of the behavior of the collocation of molecules that make up the thinker's brain.

Evolution as a Descriptive Mechanism

Evolution as a descriptive mechanism refers to that process by which less-advanced forms of life develop into higher forms of greater complexity. This is thought to be brought about by some sort of inner dynamic that, without any outside control or interference, operates according to its own pattern. In Darwin's day it was believed that this development resulted from the accumulation of chance characteristics and the retention of slight variations that arose during the earlier stages of the species' career and were genetically handed down to succeeding generations.

Since Darwin's time, however, this formulation of evolution as a mechanistic process, governed by the principle of the "survival of the fittest,"

has, for a variety of reasons, lost support in the twentieth century. G.J. Mendel's experiments in plant genetics demonstrated quite conclusively that the range of variation possible within a species was strictly limited and offered no possibility of development into a new and different species. After a large number of experiments as to the inheritability of acquired characteristics, it was finally determined by geneticists at the close of the century that there was absolutely no transmission of acquired traits because there was no way of coding them into the genes of the parent who developed those traits (cf. Robert E.D. Clark, *Darwin, Before and After* [Chicago: Moody, 1967]).

As for the continual series of transitional species that the Darwinian theory posited to mark the ascent from "lower" to "higher" orders on the ladder of biological development, the most extensive research possible has finally led scientists to the conclusion that there never were such "missing links." Thus Austin H. Clark (*The New Evolution* [New Haven: Yale, 1930], p. 189) confessed: "If we are willing to accept the facts, we must believe that there never were such intermediates, or in other words, that these major groups have from the very first borne the same relationship to each other that they bear today." Similarly, G.G. Simpson concluded that each of the thirty-two known orders of mammals appeared quite suddenly in the paleontological record. "The earliest and most primitive known members of every order already have the basic ordinal characters, and in no case is an approximately continuous sequence from one order to another known" (*Tempo and Mode in Evolution* [New York: Columbia, 1944], p. 106).

Therefore, it was necessary for Clark and Simpson to propose a completely non-Darwinian type of "evolution," which they called the "quantum theory" or "emergent evolution." It declares that dramatically new forms arise by mere chance, or else by some sort of creative response to new environmental factors. No suggestion was offered as to the origin for this capacity for "creative response." From the perspective of Darwinianism, this could hardly be considered evolution at all. As Carl F.H. Henry observed: "Supposition of abrupt emergence falls outside the field of scientific analysis just as fully as the appeal to supernatural creative forces" (R. Mixter, ed., *Evolution and Christian Thought Today* [Grand Rapids: Eerdmans, 1959], p. 211).

As for the developmental series customarily exhibited in textbooks and museums to show how evolution worked with horses and men from the earliest stages of Cenozoic until modern times, it should be understood that they prove absolutely nothing about the mechanism that engineered this development. A continuity of basic design furnishes no evidence whatever that any "lower" species phased into the next "higher" species by any sort of internal dynamic, as evolution demands. For if the museum visitor were to go to another part of that museum of science and industry, he would find a completely analogous series of automobiles, commencing with 1900 and extending up until the present decade. Stage by stage, phase by phase, he could trace the development of the Ford from its earliest Model T prototype to the large and luxurious LTD of the 1970s. Everyone knows that there was a continuity of basic design that altered in definite stages, sometimes with dramatically new features. But he would also be aware that it was the engineers at the Ford Motor Company plants who designed these changes and implemented them through craftsmen who followed their blueprints. The ascent from the eohippus to the modern racing horse can be accounted for in exactly the same way—except that in this case the architect and engineer was the Creator Himself.

Theistic Evolution

Theistic evolution posits the existence of God as Creator of all the material substance of the universe and Designer of all the processes to be followed by the various botanical and zoological orders in the development of His master plan. Unlike the philosophical evolutionist, the theistic evolutionist insists that matter was not eternal but was created by God out of nothing and was controlled in its development by the plan He had devised. In other words, the whole mechanism of the evolutionary process was and is devised and controlled by God rather than by some mysterious and unaccountable force for which there is no explanation.

As we weigh the question of whether theistic evolution can be reconciled with Genesis 1, we have to analyze very carefully whether we are dealing with a deistic or semi-deistic concept of a God who simply sets up the entire system, programming it in advance like some master computer, and then retires to the sidelines to watch the cosmic mechanism work itself out. Such a God is beyond the reach of prayer and takes no active, continuing interest in the needs of His creatures. There is no communication with Him and no salvation from Him; all is locked up in the framework of a rigid determinism.

Or else we may be dealing with a theistic evolution that allows for prayer and personal relationships between man and God, but which conceives of Him as bringing about the ascending biological orders by some kind of evolutionary mechanism that finds its dynamism and direction within itself. In view of the flimsy basis in scientific data for evolution as propounded by Darwin and its virtual rejection by "emergent" evolutionists (for these two bear as close a resemblance to each other as American democracy and the "democracy" of Iron Curtain nations today), there seems to be very little ground for even a scientifically minded theist to hang on to evolutionism at all. But if he accepts the implications of the integrity of species according to Mendelian limits, it could perhaps be argued that he keeps faith with the successive stages of creation of plant and animal orders and genera and species "after its kind," as emphasized in Genesis 1:11–12,21. If he understands the six creative days as intended by the Author to teach a succession of definite stages in the orderly development of the biological world up until the creation of man, then we should concede that this is reconcilable with the basic intent of that chapter.

All this, of course, depends on whether the theistic evolutionist accepts Adam and Eve as literal, historical, created individuals. Many of them do not, but they conceive of Homo sapiens as gradually developing from subhuman hominids and then finally developing a consciousness of God—at which moment, whenever it was, the ape-man became "Adam." Such, for example, was the view of Lecomte de Noüy in *Human Destiny* (New York: Longmans, Green & Co., 1947), who suggested that perhaps around 30,000 B.C. the Cro-Magnon became truly man by a sort of spiritual mutation that conferred on him the capacity of responsible moral choice. This type of approach can hardly be reconciled with the presentation of Adam and Eve as historical individuals with personal emotions and responses such as appears in Genesis 2 and 3 (and as certified by 1 Tim. 2:13–14). Any suprahistorical interpretation of Adam, such as is espoused by Neoorthodoxy, is definitely irreconcilable with Holy Scripture and the Evangelical faith.

Helpful Discussions of This General Topic

Anderson, J.K., and Coffin, H.G. *Fossils in Focus*. Grand Rapids: Zondervan, 1977.

Lammerts, W.E., ed. *Why Not Creation?* Grand Rapids: Baker, 1970.

Morris, H.M. *The Twilight of Evolution*. Grand Rapids: Baker, 1963.

Newman, R.C., and Eckelmann, H.J. *Genesis One and the Origin of the Earth*. Downers Grove, Ill.: InterVarsity, 1977.

Young, E.J. *Studies in Genesis One*. Philadelphia: Presbyterian and Reformed, 1973.

How can Genesis 1 be reconciled with the immense periods of time indicated by fossil strata?

One of the most frequently argued objections to the trustworthiness of Scripture is found in the apparent discrepancy between the account of creation given in Genesis 1 and the supposed evidence from the fossils and fissionable minerals in the geological strata that indicate Earth is billions of years old. Yet Genesis 1 allegedly teaches that creation took place in six twenty-four-hour days, at the end of which man was already on the earth. But this conflict between Genesis 1 and the factual data of science (in contradistinction to the theories of some scientists who draw inferences from their data that are capable of quite another interpretation by those equally proficient in geology) is only apparent, not real.

To be sure, if we were to understand Genesis 1 in a completely literal fashion—which some suppose to be the only proper principle of interpretation if the Bible is truly inerrant and completely trustworthy—then there would be no possibility of reconciliation between modern scientific theory and the Genesis account. But a true and proper belief in the inerrancy of Scripture involves neither a literal nor a figurative rule of interpretation. What it does require is a belief in whatever the biblical author (human and divine) actually meant by the words he used.

An absolute literalism would, for example, commit us to the proposition that in Matthew 19:24 (and parallel passages) Christ actually meant to teach that a camel could go through the eye of a needle. But it is abundantly clear that Christ was simply using the familiar rhetorical figure of hyperbole in order to emphasize how difficult it is spiritually for a rich man (because of his pride in his material wealth) to come to repentance and saving faith in God. To construe that passage literally would amount to blatant heresy, or at least a perversity that has nothing to do with orthodoxy. Or again, when Jesus said to the multitude that challenged Him to work some miracle, "Destroy this temple, and in three days I will raise it up" (John 2:19), they grievously erred when they interpreted His remarks literally. John 2:21 goes on to explain that Jesus did not mean this prediction literally but spiritually. "But He was speaking about the temple of His body. Therefore when He was raised from the dead, His disciples remembered that He said this, and they believed the Scripture." In this case, then, literal interpretation was dead wrong because that was not what Jesus meant by the language He used; He was actually referring to the far greater miracle of His bodily resurrection.

It thus becomes clear in this present case, as we study the text of Genesis 1, that we must not short-circuit our responsibility of careful exegesis in order to ascertain as clearly as possible what the divine author meant by the language His inspired prophet (in this case probably Moses) was guided to employ. Is the true purpose of Genesis 1 to teach that all creation began just six twenty-four-hour days before Adam was "born"? Or is this just a mistaken inference that overlooks other biblical data having a direct bearing on this passage? To answer this question we must take careful note of what is said in Genesis 1:27 concerning the creation of man as the closing act of the sixth creative day. There it is stated that on that sixth day (apparently toward the end of the day, after all the animals had been fashioned and placed on the earth—therefore not long before sundown at the end of that same day), "God created man in His own image; He created them male *and female*." This can only mean that Eve was created in the closing hour of Day Six, along with Adam.

As we turn to Genesis 2, however, we find that a considerable interval of time must have intervened between the creation of Adam and the creation of Eve. In 2:15 we are told that Yahweh Elohim (i.e., the LORD God) put Adam in the Garden of Eden as the ideal environment for his development, and there he was to cultivate and keep the enormous park, with all its goodly trees, abundant fruit crop, and four mighty rivers that flowed from Eden to other regions of the Near East. In 2:18 we read, "Then the LORD God said, 'It is not good for the man to be alone; I will make him a helper suitable for him.'" This statement clearly implies that Adam had been diligently occupied in his responsible task of pruning, harvesting fruit, and keeping the ground free of brush and undergrowth for a long enough period to lose his initial excitement and sense of thrill at this wonderful occupation in the beautiful paradise of Eden. He had begun to feel a certain lonesomeness and inward dissatisfaction.

In order to compensate for this lonesomeness, God then gave Adam a major assignment in natural history. He was to classify every species of animal and bird found in the preserve. With its five mighty rivers and broad expanse, the garden must have had hundreds of species of mammal, reptile, insect, and bird, to say nothing of the flying insects that also are indicated by the basic Hebrew term *'ôp* ("bird") (2:19). It took the Swedish scientist Linnaeus several decades to classify all the species known to European scientists in the eighteenth century. Doubtless there were considerably more by that time than in Adam's day; and, of course, the range of fauna in Eden may have been more limited than those available to Linnaeus. But at the same time it must have taken a good deal of study for Adam to examine each specimen and decide on an appropriate name for it, especially in view of the fact that he had absolutely no human tradition behind him, so far as nomenclature was concerned. It must have required some years, or, at the very least, a considerable number of months for him to complete this comprehensive inventory of all the birds, beasts, and insects that populated the Garden of Eden.

Finally, after this assignment with all its absorbing interest had been completed, Adam felt a renewed sense of emptiness. Genesis 2:20 ends with the words "but for Adam no suitable helper was found." After this long and unsatisfying experience as a lonely bachelor, God saw that Adam was emotionally prepared for a wife—a "suitable helper." God, therefore, subjected him to a deep sleep, removed from his body the bone that was closest to his heart, and from that physical core of man fashioned the first woman. Finally God presented woman to Adam in all her fresh, unspoiled beauty, and Adam was ecstatic with joy.

As we have compared Scripture with Scripture (Gen. 1:27 with 2:15–22), it has become very apparent that Genesis 1 was never intended to teach that the sixth creative day, when Adam and Eve were *both* created, lasted a mere twenty-four hours. In view of the long interval of time between these two, it would seem to border on sheer irrationality to insist that all of Adam's ex-

periences in Genesis 2:15–22 could have been crowded into the last hour or two of a literal twenty-four-hour day. The only reasonable conclusion to draw is that the purpose of Genesis 1 is not to tell how fast God performed His work of creation (though, of course, some of His acts, such as the creation of light on the first day, must have been instantaneous). Rather, its true purpose was to reveal that the Lord God who had revealed Himself to the Hebrew race and entered into personal covenant relationship with them was indeed the only true God, the Creator of all things that are. This stood in direct opposition to the religious notions of the heathen around them, who assumed the emergence of a pantheon of gods in successive stages out of preexistent matter of unknown origin, actuated by forces for which there was no accounting.

Genesis 1 is a sublime manifesto, totally rejecting all the cosmogonies of the pagan cultures of the ancient world as nothing but baseless superstition. The Lord God Almighty existed before all matter, and by His own word of command He brought the entire physical universe into existence, governing all the great forces of wind, rain, sun, and sea according to His sovereign will. This stood in stark contrast to the clashing, quarreling, capricious little deities and godlets spawned by the corrupt imagination of the heathen. The message and purpose of Genesis 1 is the revelation of the one true God who created all things out of nothing and ever keeps the universe under His sovereign control.

The second major aspect of Genesis 1 is the revelation that God brought forth His creation in an orderly and systematic manner. There were six major stages in this work of formation, and these stages are represented by successive days of a week. In this connection it is important to observe that none of the six creative days bears a definite article in the Hebrew text; the translations "*the* first day," "*the* second day," etc., are in error. The Hebrew says, "And the evening took place, and the morning took place, day one" (1:5). Hebrew expresses "the first day" by *hayyôm hāri'šôn,* but this text says simply *yôm 'eḥād* ("day one"). Again, in v.8 we read not *hayyôm haššēni* ("the second day") but *yôm šēni* ("a second day"). In Hebrew prose of this genre, the definite article was generally used where the noun was intended to be definite; only in poetic style could it be omitted. The same is true with the rest of the six days; they all lack the definite article. Thus they are well adapted to a sequential pattern, rather than to strictly delimited units of time.

Genesis 1:2–5 thus sets forth the first stage of creation: the formation of light. This must have meant primarily the light of the sun and the other heavenly bodies. Sunlight is a necessary precondition to the development of plant life and animal life, generally speaking (though there are some subterranean forms of life that manage to do without it).

Genesis 1:6–8 presents the second stage: the formation of an "expanse" (*rāqîa'*) that separated between moisture in suspension in the sky and moisture condensed enough to remain on the earth's surface. The term *raqîa'* does not mean a beaten-out metal canopy, as some writers have alleged—no ancient culture ever taught such a notion in its concept of the sky—but simply means "a stretched-out expanse." This is quite evident from Isaiah 42:5, where the cognate verb *rāqa'* is used: "Thus says the God Yahweh, the Creator of the heavens, and the one who *stretched* them *out* [from the verb *nāṭāh,* 'to extend' curtains or tent cords], the one who *extended* [*rōqa'*] the earth and that which it produces [the noun *ṣe'ěṣā'îm* refers always to plants and animals]." Obviously *rāqa'* could not here mean "beat out," "stamp out" (though it is often used that way in connection with metal working); the parallelism with *nāṭāh* (noted above) proves that here it has the force of extend or expand. Therefore, the noun *rāqîa'* can mean only "expanse," without any connotation of a hard metal plate.

Genesis 1:9–13 relates the third stage in God's creative work, the receding of the waters of the oceans, seas, and lakes to a lower altitude than the masses of land that emerged above them and thus were allowed to become dry. Doubtless the gradual cooling of the planet Earth led to the condensation of water necessary to bring about this result; seismic pressures producing mountains and hills doubtless contributed further to this separation between land and sea. Once this dry land (*hayyabbāšāh*) appeared, it became possible for plant life and trees to spring up on the earth's surface, aided by photosynthesis from the still beclouded sky.

Genesis 1:14–19 reveals that in the fourth creative stage God parted the cloud cover enough for direct sunlight to fall on the earth and for accurate observation of the movements of the sun, moon, and stars to take place. Verse 16 should not be understood as indicating the creation of the heavenly bodies for the first time on the fourth creative day; rather it informs us that the sun, moon, and stars created on Day One as the source of light had been placed in their appointed places by God with a view to their eventually functioning as indicators of time ("signs, seasons, days, years") to terrestrial observers. The Hebrew verb *wayya'aś* in v.16 should better be rendered "Now [God] *had made* the two great luminaries, etc.," rather than as simple past tense, "[God] *made*." (Hebrew has no special form for the pluperfect tense but uses the perfect tense, or the conversive imperfect as here, to express either the English past or the English pluperfect, depending on the context.)

Genesis 1:20–23 relates that on the fifth creative day God fully developed marine life, freshwater life, and introduced flying creatures (whether insects, lizards, or winged birds). It is interesting to observe that the fossil-bearing strata of the Paleozoic era contain the first evidence of invertebrate animal life with startling suddenness in the Cambrian period. There is no indication in the pre-Cambrian strata of how the five thousand species of marine and terrestrial animal life of the Paleozoic era may have developed, for there is no record of them whatever prior to the Cambrian levels (cf. D. Dewar, "The Earliest Known Animals," *Journal of the Transactions of the Victoria Institute* 80 [1948]: 22–29).

Genesis 1:24–26 records that in the sixth and final stage of the creative process, God brought forth all the land animals after their various species (*lemināh* in v.24 and *leminēhû* in v.25 mean "according to its kind," whether the antecedent was male or female in grammatical gender), culminating finally in the creation of man, as discussed more extensively above.

In this connection, a comment is in order concerning the recurring formula at the end of each creative day: "And it was/became evening, and it became/was morning, a second day" (or whatever ordinal it might be). The reason for this closing statement seems to have been twofold. First, it was necessary to make clear whether the *symbolic unit* involved was a mere sunrise-to-sundown day, or whether it was a twenty-four-hour day. The term *yôm* ("day") could mean either. In fact, the first time *yôm* occurs is in v.5: "And He called the light *day*, and the darkness He called night." Therefore, it was necessary to show that each of the creative days was symbolized by a complete twenty-four-hour cycle, beginning at sunset of the previous day

(according to our reckoning) and ending with the daylight portion, down to the setting of the sun, on the following day (as we would reckon it).

Second, the twenty-four-hour day serves as a better symbol than a mere daylight day in regard to the commencement and completion of one stage of creation before the next stage began. There were definite and distinct stages in God's creational procedure. If this be the true intention of the formula, then it serves as no real evidence for a literal twenty-four-hour-day concept on the part of the biblical author.

Some have argued that the reference in the Decalogue (commandment four) to God's resting on the seventh day as a basis for honoring the seventh day of each week strongly suggests the literal nature of "day" in Genesis 1. This is not at all compelling, however, in view of the fact that if there was to be any day of the week especially set aside from labor to center on the worship and service of the Lord, then it would have to be a twenty-four-hour day (Saturday) in any event. As a matter of fact, Scripture does not at all teach that Yahweh rested only one twenty-four-hour day at the conclusion of His creative work. No closing formula occurs at the close of the seventh day, referred to in Genesis 2:2–3. And, in fact, the New Testament teaches (in Heb. 4:1–11) that that seventh day, that "Sabbath rest," in a very definite sense has continued on right into the church age. If so, it would be quite impossible to line up the seventh-day Sabbath with the Seventh Day that concluded God's original work of creation!

One last observation concerning the word *yôm* as used in Genesis 2:4. Unlike some of the modern versions, KJV correctly renders this verse "These are the generations of the heavens and of the earth when they were created, in the *day* that the LORD God made the earth and the heavens." Since the previous chapter has indicated that there were at least six days involved in creating the heavens and the earth, it is abundantly evident that *yóm* in Genesis 2:4 cannot possibly be meant as a twenty-four-hour day—unless perchance the Scripture contradicts itself! (For a good discussion of this topic by a Christian professor of geology, see Davis A. Young, *Creation and the Flood and Theistic Evolution* [Grand Rapids: Baker, 1977]. Some details of his treatment are open to question, and he is not always precise in his terminology; but in the main his work furnishes a solid contribution to this area of debate.)

The Antiquity of the Human Race

Having presented the evidence for understanding the six creative days of Genesis 1 as distinct stages in the unfolding work of creation, we now proceed to the question of the antiquity of Adam and the commencement of the human race. This matter has been discussed at some length in my *Survey of Old Testament Introduction* (pp. 195–99). The great age assigned by paleanthropologists to the skeletons of various anthropoid species is a matter of considerable dispute. L.S.B. Leakey used potassium-argon analysis to arrive at the estimate of 1,750,000 years for the age of what he identified as the "Zinjanthropus" of Tanganykia ("Exploring 1,750,000 Years into Man's Past," *National Geographic* [October 1961]). Other specimens from the Olduvai Gorge area have been assigned even greater age than this.

The Neanderthal cave man is thought to have lived from 100,000 to 50,000 years ago, and he seems to have mastered such skills as the fashioning of stone arrowheads and axe-heads. The Neanderthal man also seems to have used fire for his cooking in the preparation of food. He may even have had some involvement in art as well, though the remarkable cave paintings in the caves of Altamira and elsewhere may well have been the product of the later race of Cro-Magnons.

At this point something should be said about some startling new geological discoveries that render the long-date estimates of conventional geological science nearly impossible to hold any longer. An extensive analysis of the evidence supplied by an exposed stratum on the bed of the Paluxy River, at Glen Rose, Texas, has been published by Cecil Dougherty of Temple, Texas, under the title *Valley of the Giants* (Minneapolis: Bible-Science Association, n.d.), which is now going into its sixth edition. In the *Bible-Science Newsletter* for April 1979 (p. 4), there is a report by Fred Beierle of Lyons, Kansas, concerning a 1978 field trip to this remarkable site. It exhibits on the very same stratum a good set of three-toed dinosaur tracks and then further upstream the characteristic tracks of Tyrannosaurus Rex and also of Brontosaurus. The low level of water during the summer drought made it especially easy to uncover and view areas where clear footprints of some early human species actually cross the tracks of those dinosaurs!

Furthermore, in an adjacent level on the same Cretaceous layer as these tracks, there was a long black streak that proved to be a fallen tree branch that had been reduced to charcoal by fire and was subsequently engulfed in the limey surface. It was about two inches in diameter and seven feet in length and was located about two hundred meters downstream from the human and dinosaur tracks. A section of this branch was removed and sent to R. Berger, a geophysicist at UCLA, for carbon-14 analysis. He later sent back his finding: the branch was 12,800 years old, ± 200 years. If this verdict is confirmed by other laboratories, it seems to indicate that the whole science of geochronology as practiced by traditional geologists is due for a complete overhaul. Here we have a late Mesozoic stratum containing evidence of early hominids contemporaneous with the most highly developed of the dinosaurs and dateable by the tree branch as being no more than 13,000 years ago!

An editorial on p.2 of this same issue of *Bible-Science Newsletter* furnishes an important clue as to the source of such gross error in the conventional geochronological methods of time computation. The careful analysis of fissionable minerals (such as the breakdown of uranium to lead or of argon 40 to argon 36) has operated on the simplistic assumption that all such deposits were originally composed of pure parent elements. Then after the magma cooled off, the parent element supposedly began to break down with the gradual loss of electrons and became the daughter element with a lower atomic count. But samples taken from the core of fairly recent volcanoes, one thousand years old or less, have specimens evidencing ages of many millions or even billions of years— judging by the proportion of daughter elements to the parent elements in the same sample. This inevitably yields the result that even in the initial stage of deposition, such fissionable formations already contained a high proportion of daughter elements. Therefore, they are almost valueless, or completely misleading, for the dating of the levels in which they are found. It will be interesting to see how conventional geology theorists will cope with this discovery. It cannot remain permanently ignored or suppressed from the public, no matter how defensive the long-date theorists may feel about the matter.

But however untrustworthy the dating methods may be that have led to such high estimates of the antiquity of these anthropoids, the fact remains that they can hardly be dated later than the creation of the Adam and Eve referred to in Genesis 1–3. However the statistics of Genesis 5 may be handled, they can hardly end up with a date for Adam much before 10,000 B.C. If these figures in Genesis are at all to be trusted, even granting the occurrence of occasional gaps in the genealogical chain, we are compelled to regard all these early anthropoids as pre-Adamic. In other words, all these species, from the Cro-Magnon back to the Zinjanthropus, must have been advanced apes or anthropoids possessed of considerable intelligence and resourcefulness—but who completely died off before Adam and Eve were created.

If we examine the biblical record carefully, we must recognize that when God created Adam and Eve in His own image (Gen. 1:27), He breathed something of His own Spirit into them (Gen. 2:7) in a way that He had not done to any previous order of creation. Did that divine image consist of some material form, some special kind of skeleton or anatomic structure? Certainly not, for God is spirit, not flesh (John 4:24). Therefore what made Adam of central importance was his inward makeup of soul (*nepeš*) and spirit (*rûah*), as well as his physical frame and bodily nature, with its animal passions and drives. From that first true human being, as a responsible moral agent, as a spirit-possessing person standing in covenant relationship with God, all the rest of the human race is descended (Rom. 5:12–21).

There may have been advanced and intelligent hominids who lived and died before Adam, but they were not created in the image of God. This is the line of distinction to which God's word commits us, and it is here that we must reject any interpretation of paleanthropological data that supposes that a skeletal resemblance establishes that pre-Adamic anthropoids were true human beings in the biblical sense of the term. Though these early cave dwellers may have developed certain skills in their pursuit of nourishment and engaged in war with one another—as other animals do—nevertheless there is no archaeological evidence of a true human soul as having animated their bodies.

Recent studies of the chimpanzee and the gorilla unquestionably show that subhuman species of ape are capable of tool making ("Chimpanzees use more objects as tools and for more purposes than any creatures except ourselves" [Jane Goodall, "Life and Death at Gombe," *National Geographic* (May 1979): 598]), holding hands, patting one another, embracing and kissing. They are also capable of heartless cruelty to one another, even to cannibalism of their own young. Gorillas can even talk in sign language with humans and tell lies to them, and they have actually learned how to use a camera (Francine Patterson, "Conversation With a Gorilla," *National Geographic* [October 1978]: 458–59). Therefore, evidences of similar intelligence in prehistoric "man" are no decisive proof of humanity in the Adamic sense, nor of moral and spiritual capacity. Hence no strain is put on biblical credibility by these non-Adamic, pre-Adamic races, whatever their antiquity.

In the Hebrew original, is the word "earth" used in Genesis 1:1 the same as "earth" in Genesis 1:10? (D*)

Yes, the word is *'ereṣ* in both cases. Whether it refers to earth in general or to a more restricted area is something to be determined from context—as is true with many of our English words. For example, John 3:16 uses "world" (Gr. *kosmos*) in the sense of all the human race, as objects of God's concern and redeeming love; but in 1 John 2:15 ("Love not the world") "world" is used in the sense of the organized system of rebellion, self-seeking and enmity toward God, which characterizes the human race in opposition to God.

So also *'ereṣ* may be used in the sense of the entire planet Earth in contrast to the heavens (Gen. 1:1). Or it may be the dry land in contrast to the oceans and seas (v.10). Or it may mean one particular country or geographical-political division, such as "the land of Israel" (2 Kings 5:2) or "the land of Egypt" (Exod. 20:2). In Genesis 2:5–9, *'ereṣ* refers to the area of Eden, where God prepared a perfect setting for Adam and Eve to dwell. In almost every case the context will lead us to the correct sense in which the word is meant by the author.

While it is reasonable to assume that God's creation referred to in Genesis 1:1 was "perfect," this fact is not actually so stated until after v.10. After the separation of water from dry land, it is mentioned that this work of creation was "good" (Heb. *ṭôḇ*, not the Hebrew word for "perfect," *tāmîm*, which does not occur until Gen. 6:9, where it refers to the "blamelessness" of Noah). The "goodness" of God's creative work is mentioned again in Genesis 1:12, 18,21,25, and 31 (the last of which states, "And God saw all that he had made, and, behold, it was very good," NASB). In the light of these citations, it would be difficult to maintain that God's creative work in Genesis 1:2 and thereafter was not really "good"; on the other hand, nowhere is it actually affirmed that it was "perfect"— though the term *ṭôḇ* may well have implied perfection.

As for the reference to the earth's being "waste and void" (Heb. *ṭōhû wāḇōhú*) in Genesis 1:2, it is not altogether clear whether this was a subsequent and resultant condition after a primeval catastrophe, as some scholars understand it (interpreting the verb *hāyᵉtāh* as "became" rather than "was"). It may simply have been that Genesis 1:1 serves as an introduction to the six-stage work of creation that is about to be described in the rest of chapter 1. In that case there is no intervening catastrophe to be accounted for; and the six creative days are to be understood as setting forth the orderly progressive stages in which God first completed his work of creating the planet Earth as we know it today.

Those who construe *hāyᵉṯāh* ("was") as "became" (a meaning more usually associated with this verb when it is followed by the preposition *lᵉ* occurring before the thing or condition into which the subject is turned) understand this to indicate a primeval catastrophe possibly associated with the rebellion of Satan against God, as suggested by Isaiah 14:10-14. That passage seems to imply that behind the arrogant defiance of the king of Babylon against the Lord there stands as his inspiration and support the prince of hell himself, who once said in his heart, "I will raise my throne above the stars of God; I will make myself like the Most High" (Isa. 14:14); this language would hardly have proceeded from the lips of any mortal king).

In 2 Peter 2:4 we read that "God did not spare angels when they sinned, but cast them into hell and committed them to pits of darkness, reserved for judgment." Those who espouse this interpretation suggest that a major disaster overtook the created heavens and earth mentioned in Genesis 1:1, as a result of which the earth needed to be restored—perhaps even recreated—in the six creative days detailed in the rest of Genesis 1.

It must be understood, however, that there is no explicit statement anywhere in Scripture that the primeval fall of Satan was accompanied by a total ruin of earth itself; it is simply an inference or conjecture, which may seem persuasive to some Bible students but be somewhat unconvincing to others. This, in brief, is the basis for the catastrophe theory.

Do the names for God in Genesis 1 and 2 show a difference in the authorship of the two chapters?

It is true that throughout the thirty-one verses of Genesis 1 the only name for God used is Elohim, and that the personal name for God, i.e., Yahweh, becomes prominent in chapter 2. Nevertheless this distinction of usage in the two chapters furnishes no solid evidence of difference in authorship. This theory was first brought into prominence by the French physician Jean Astruc back in 1753. He felt that Genesis 1 must have been taken from some earlier literary source produced by an author who knew of God only by the name Elohim, whereas Genesis 2 came from a different source that knew of God as Yahweh (or "Jehovah"). J. G. Eichhorn of Leipzig extended this Yahwist-Elohist source division to the rest of the chapters of Genesis all the way to Exodus 6:3, which was interpreted by him to mean that according to that "source" the name Yahweh was unknown until Moses' time. This implied that all the references to Yahweh occurring in Genesis must have come from a different source (J) that supposed that He was known by that name before Moses' time.

Exodus 6:3 says, "And I appeared to Abraham, Isaac, and Jacob as God Almighty [El Shaddai], but by My name Yahweh I did not make Myself known to them." This might seem to imply that the name itself was unknown before Moses' time, but such an interpretation goes against actual Hebrew usage. There is a very special significance to the phrase "to know the name of Yahweh" or "to know that I am Yahweh." This expression occurs at least twenty-six times in the Old Testament; and in every instance it signifies to learn by actual experience that God is Yahweh, the covenant-keeping

God who chastens, cares for, and delivers His covenant people from their foes. Thus we read in Exodus 6:7, "You shall know that I am Yahweh your God, who brings you out from under the burdens of the Egyptians." Even the Egyptians were to learn this from bitter experience, according to Exodus 14:4: "And the Egyptians shall know that I am Yahweh"—as a result of the ten plagues that were to fall on them.

Obviously Pharaoh knew that the name of the God of Moses was Yahweh, for he so referred to Him in Exodus 5:2: "Who is Yahweh that I should obey His voice to let Israel go?" Therefore we are to understand Exodus 6:3 as meaning "I showed Myself to Abraham, Isaac, and Jacob as the all-powerful Ruler of creation and Sovereign over all the forces of nature [i.e., as El Shaddai, God Almighty], but I did not show Myself to them as a covenant-keeping God in the miraculous, redemptive way that I am about to display in the deliverance of the entire nation of Israel from Egyptian bondage."

"Yahweh" connotes God's faithfulness and personal care of His covenant people—though this pertains to His dealings with individual believers as well. Thus in His relationships with Abraham and his family all through the Genesis account, God is referred to as Yahweh. But it was reserved for the generation of Moses to behold the wonder-working power of God on their behalf on an epoch-making scale. The Exodus record is marked by one redemptive miracle after another, with chastening judgments visited on Israel as well, in their times of rebellion and apostasy, until finally they were brought safely into the land of Canaan under Joshua, there to establish a new commonwealth under the guidance of the law of Moses. This, then, is the way we are to understand the true intent of Exodus 6:3, rather than in the simplistic way that Eichhorn and his followers of the Documentary (JEDP) school have construed it.

Going back, then, to the explanation for the difference in the name-usage followed in Genesis 2 as opposed to Genesis 1, the reason for this distinction is perfectly evident in the light of the previous discussion. "Elohim" was the only name of God appropriate in a narrative of God's work of creation as Ruler over all nature and the universe. But in chapter 2 He comes into a personal covenant with Adam and Eve; and therefore to them God (Elohim) displayed Himself as "Yahweh," the God of grace and covenant. Therefore, throughout the chapter, in all eleven occurrences, Yahweh occurs in combination with Elohim, never alone. This clearly implies that the same God who made the universe in six creative stages is the very same Lord who loved and cared for Adam as His son, created after His own image. The same is true throughout chapter 3: "Yahweh" is never used alone but only in combination with "Elohim." Not until we come to Eve's comment in Genesis 4:1 do we encounter the first occurrence of "Yahweh" (or LORD) alone, without Elohim.

In view of this consistent combination of the two names throughout chapters 2 and 3, it is difficult to imagine how Astruc, Eichhorn, or any other scholar could have come up with the theory that there ever was a prior source that knew of God only by the name Yahweh. In view of the constant joining of the two names together, one would have to suppose that some later redactor chose to glue together by dint of scissors and paste a snippet of "J" ending with "Yahweh" with a snippet of "E" or "P" that began with "Elohim." Such an artificial and bizarre process of combination extending through two entire chapters has never been discovered in the literature of any other nation or time. It calls for an extraordinary degree of naive credulity to suppose that it could have been so in the case of Genesis 2 and 3.

Before closing this discussion, it ought to be pointed out that, on the basis of comparative literature of the Ancient Near East, all of Israel's neighbors followed the practice of referring to their high gods by at least two different names—or even three or four. In Egypt Osiris (the lord of the netherworld and the judge of the dead) was also referred to as Wennefer (He who is Good), Khent-amentiu (Foremost of the Westerners), and Neb-abdu (Lord of Abydos); and all four titles occur in the Ikhernofei Stela in the Berlin Museum. In Babylonia the god Bel was also known by his Sumerian title of Enlil and by Nunamnir as well (cf. the Prologue of the Lipit-Ishtar Law Code). Similarly the Moon god was both Sin and Nanna, and the great goddess Ishtar was also known as Inanna or Telitum. In the pre-Mosaic Canaanite culture of Ugarit in North Syria, Baal was frequently called Aliyan (and that too in successive stichoi of parallelistic poetry, just as in the Hebrew Psalter), whereas the king-god El was also known as Latpan, and the artificer god Kothar-wa-Khasis was also called Hayyin (cf. Pritchard, ANET, p. 151, in connection with Aqhat).

In Greece the same practice held true: Zeus was also Kronion and Olympius; Athena was Pallas; Apollo was Phoebus and Pythius as well—all of which appear in parallelistic verses of Homer's epics. To insist that this same phenomenon in Hebrew literature must point to diverse prior sources is to ignore completely this abundant analogy from the literature of all of Israel's neighbors. It is difficult to see how source division on the basis of divine names can be accepted as intellectually respectable in the light of the known facts of comparative literature.

Doesn't Genesis 2 present a different creation order than Genesis 1?

Genesis 2 does not present a creation account at all but presupposes the completion of God's work of creation as set forth in chapter 1. The first three verses of Genesis 2 simply carry the narrative of chapter 1 to its final and logical conclusion, using the same vocabulary and style as employed in the previous chapter. It sets forth the completion of the whole primal work of creation and the special sanctity conferred on the seventh day as a symbol and memorial of God's creative work. Verse 4 then sums up the whole sequence that has just been surveyed by saying, "These are the generations of heaven and earth when they were created, in the day that Yahweh God made heaven and earth."

Having finished the overall survey of the subject, the author then develops in detail one important feature that has already been mentioned: the creation of man. Kenneth Kitchen says,

Genesis 1 mentions the creation of man as the last of a series, and without any details, whereas in Genesis 2 man is the center of interest and more specific details are given about him and his setting. Failure to recognize the complementary nature of the subject-distinction between a skeleton outline of *all* creation on the one hand, and the concentration in detail on man and his immediate environment on the other, borders on obscurantism (*Ancient Orient*, p. 117).

Kitchen then draws on the analogy of Egyptian inscriptions like the Karnak Poetical Stela of Thutmose III, the Gebel Barkal Stela, and those royal inscriptions from Urartu that ascribe the defeat of the nation's foes to their patron god, Haldi, and then repeat the same victories in detail as achieved by the reigning king of Urartu. Kitchen then adds,

> What is absurd when applied to monumental Near Eastern texts that had *no* prehistory of hands and redactors should not be imposed on Genesis 1 and 2, as is done by uncritical perpetuation of a nineteenth-century systematization of speculations by eighteenth-century dilettantes lacking, as they did, all knowledge of the forms and usages of Ancient Oriental literature (ibid.).

As we examine the remainder of Genesis 2, we find that it concerns itself with a description of the ideal setting that God prepared for Adam and Eve to begin their life in, walking in loving fellowship with Him as responsive and obedient children. Verses 5–6 describe the original condition of the "earth," or "land," in the general region of the Garden of Eden before it had sprouted verdure under the special watering system the Lord used for its development. Verse 7 introduces Adam as a newly fashioned occupant for whom Eden was prepared. Verse 8 records how he was placed there to observe and enjoy the beauty and richness of his surroundings. Verses 9–14 describe the various kinds of trees and the lush vegetation sustained by the abundant waters of the rivers that flowed out of Eden to the lower regions beyond its borders. Verse 15 indicates the absorbing activity that Adam had assigned to him as keeper and warden of this great natural preserve.

From the survey of the first fifteen verses of chapter 2, it becomes quite apparent that this was never intended to be a general creation narrative. Search all the cosmogonies of the ancient civilizations of the Near East, and you will never find among them a single creation account that omits all mention of the formation of sun, moon, and stars or ocean or seas— none of which are referred to in Genesis 2. It is therefore quite obvious that Genesis 1 is the only creation account to be found in the Hebrew Scripture and that it is already presupposed as the background of Genesis 2. Even the animals are not referred to until Adam is assigned the task of examining them carefully, one by one, in order to decide on an appropriate name for each species or bird and beast that was brought before him (vv.18–20). But before this phase of Adam's experience begins, he is brought into covenant relationship with God, who grants him permission to eat of the fruit of every tree in the garden except one: the tree of the knowledge of good and evil (vv.16–17). Verse 18 then shows how Yahweh proceeded to fill Adam's foreseen need of companionship—first by the fellowship with the animals and birds (vv. 19–20), then, after that proves to be unsatisfying, by the companionship of a wife, who is fashioned from the bone that was closest to Adam's heart (vv.21–22). The chapter closes with a vivid portrayal of Adam's joyous acceptance of his new helpmate and his unreserved commitment to her in love.

The structure of Genesis 2 stands in clear contrast to every creation account known to comparative literature. It was never intended to be a creation account at all, except insofar as it related the circumstances of man's creation as a child of God, fashioned in His image, infused with His breath of life, and brought into an intimate personal relationship with the Lord Himself. Quite clearly, then, chapter 2 is built on the foundation of chapter 1 and represents no different tradition than the first chapter or discrepant account of the order of creation.

Can the Garden of Eden be located on a map? (D*)

Genesis 2:10–14 furnishes some clues to the general location of Eden,

69

but it presupposes geological conditions that no longer hold. Hence it is hazardous to conjecture any site more precise than the headwaters of the Tigris and Euphrates rivers in the highlands of Armenia (i.e., the eastern border of modern Turkey).

The large river flowing from Eden subdivided into the Tigris and the Euphrates, as well as into two other long rivers (the Pishon, leading down to Havilah, along the southern coast of Arabia, and the Gihon, which went over to Cush—which may have been some Asiatic region lying to the east rather than the African Cush that was Ethiopia).

This indicates that the site was a high plateau or mountainous region (insuring a cool and comfortable temperature for Eden during the summer season), having copious headwaters to supply the four major river systems this passage describes. The Havilah, through which the Pishon flowed, was rich in gold, spices, and deposits of precious stones—which were found in abundance along the southern or southwestern coasts of Arabia. For the Cush, no such helpful clues are given; the name has been connected by some scholars with Kish in Sumeria or with the Kassites (who are thought to have originated in the Zagros mountain region).

The most plausible explanation for the later complete disappearance of the Pishon and Gihon rivers is the theory that mountain-building activity accompanying continental drift (for Arabia was originally connected with the Somalian and Ethiopian coast during prehistoric times) may have terminated those two river systems in the antediluvian period. This would be analogous to the uplift of the Mount Seir Range in Edom, which prevented the Jordan River from flowing all the way down to the Gulf of Aqaba, as it originally did.

Weren't the Israelites under the old covenant saved through obedience to God rather than because they looked forward in faith to a coming Savior? What passages indicate that such faith was necessary for their salvation? (D*)

From Genesis to Revelation the Bible makes it clear that no one was ever saved by his own good works but only by faith in the promises of God. Only in Eden was salvation put on the basis of obedience, with the accompanying warning of death for transgression of God's command: "But from the tree of the knowledge of good and evil you shall not eat, for in the day that you eat from it you shall surely die" (Gen. 2:17, NASB). In Genesis 3 this one command was broken by both Eve and Adam in response to Satan's temptation and deceit; and God confirmed their sentence of death by saying, "For you are dust, and to dust you shall return" (Gen. 3:19). From that time on, no human being has ever been saved by obedience—except the race of the redeemed, who are saved by faith in the atonement of Christ, whose deed of obedience paid the price of their salvation.

It is true that in both Testaments great emphasis is laid on obedience. In Exodus 19:5 (NASB) God promised Israel, "Now then, if you will indeed obey My voice and keep My covenant, then you shall be My own possession among all the peoples." But this by no means suggests an alternative way to heaven apart from faith; on the contrary, this promise was given to a company of believers who had already repented of sin and surrendered their hearts to the Lord in faith. Obedience was to be a necessary evidence or fruit of faith. It is not the apple that makes its parent tree an apple tree; it is the apple tree that makes its fruit an apple. Jesus said, "By their fruit you shall know them" (Matt. 7:16); in other words, grapes come only from vines, not thorn bushes, and figs only from fig trees, not thistles. Obedience is a necessary and natural consequence of faith, but it is never described as a substitute for faith anywhere in Scripture.

It should be noted that from the very beginning Adam and Eve taught their sons the necessity of sacrifice to the Lord for the sins they may have committed; thus Abel presented the acceptable blood sacrifice on his altar—as an act of faith that typically presented in advance the Atonement later to be offered on Calvary. Hebrews 11:4 makes this clear, "By *faith* Abel offered to God a better sacrifice than Cain.... And through faith, though he is dead, he still speaks." Genesis 15:6 records that when Abraham believed God, God reckoned it to him for righteousness. Romans 4:13 tells us that "the promise to Abraham and his descendants that he would be heir of the world was not through the law, but through the righteousness of faith."

As for the generation of Moses, to whom the promise of Exodus 19:5 was given, there could have been no misunderstanding whatever concerning the principle of salvation through faith alone. From the same chapter that contains the Ten Commandments comes the first of several references to sacrificial worship: "You shall make an altar of earth for Me, and you shall sacrifice on it your burnt offerings and your peace offerings, your sheep and your oxen" (Exod. 20:24, NASB). The underlying principle of each sacrifice was that the life of the innocent animal victim was substituted for the guilty, forfeited life of the believer. He received the forgiveness of God only through repentance and faith, not through obedience.

Hebrews 10:4, referring to the Old Testament dispensation, declares, "For it is impossible for the blood of bulls

and goats to take away sins" (NASB). Earlier, in 9:11–12, the Scripture states: "But when Christ appeared as a high priest of the good things to come, He entered through the greater and more perfect tabernacle, not made with hands,... and not through the blood of goats and calves, but through His own blood, He entered the holy place once for all, having obtained eternal redemption" (NASB).

How, then, is the benefit of this blood-bought atonement brought to sinners? It comes only through faith, not through deeds of obedience as works of merit—whether before the Cross or after. Scripture declares, "By grace you have been saved through faith; and that not of yourselves, it is the gift of God" (Eph. 2:8, NASB). But what kind of faith? The counterfeit faith that betrays itself by disobedience to the revealed will of God and by bondage to self and to sin? Certainly not! Salvation comes only through a true and living faith that takes seriously the absolute lordship of Christ and produces the fruit of a godly life—a life of true obedience, based on a genuine surrender of heart, mind, and body (Rom. 12:1).

It is from this perspective that we are to understand the earnest calls to obedience from the Old Testament prophets: "If you consent and obey, you will eat the best from the land; but if you refuse and rebel, you will be devoured with the sword" (Isa. 1:19–20). Similar is the requirement laid down by Jesus Himself: "And why do you call Me, 'Lord, Lord,' and do not do what I say?" (Luke 6:46, NASB). The apostles concur: "Even so consider yourselves to be dead to sin, but alive to God in Christ Jesus. Therefore do not let sin reign in your mortal body that you should obey its lusts.... But thanks be to God that though you were slaves of sin, you became obedient from the heart to that form of teaching to which you were committed, and having been freed from sin, you became slaves of righteousness" (Rom. 6:11–12,17–18, NASB).

Did Adam really die when he ate of the forbidden fruit?

In Genesis 2:17 God warned Adam, "But from the tree of the knowledge of good and evil you shall not eat, for in the day that you eat from it you shall surely die" (NASB). Later, in 3:4, Satan's serpent assured Eve, "Surely you will not die!" When Adam and Eve yielded to temptation and partook of the forbidden fruit, they certainly did not drop dead on that fateful day; but they lived on to face the rebuke of God (3:8–19). Was Satan right? Did God fail to carry out His promise? Certainly not! But the death that overtook the guilty pair that day was spiritual only; physical death did not come until centuries later (Gen. 5:5).

Scripture distinguishes three types of death. First, there is *physical* death, which involves separation of the soul from the body. The separated body undergoes chemical dissolution and reverts to the "dust of the ground" (i.e., the elements of which it was composed). The soul (*nepeš*) of subhuman creatures apparently ceases to exist (cf. Eccl. 3:21: "Who knows that the breath [*rûaḥ*, used here in the sense of the breath of life, metonymic of the nonmaterial personality of the human or subhuman animal] of man ascends upward and the breath of the beast descends downward to the earth?"). On the day Adam was disobedient, the sentence of physical death was imposed; but by God's grace the execution of that sentence was delayed.

The Old Testament people of God were fully aware that physical death did not entail the annihilation of the person who indwelt the body. Genesis 25:8 states that Abraham after his decease "was gathered to his people"—which implies a continuing consciousness of personal relationship with those who had preceded him in death. Job 19:25–26 quotes the suffering patriarch as saying: "As for me, I know that my Redeemer lives, and at the last He will take His stand on the earth. Even after my skin is flayed [lit., 'stripped off'], yet in (lit., from) my flesh I shall see God" (cf. 2 Sam. 12:23; Pss. 49:15; 73:24; 84:7; Isa. 25:8; 26:19; Hos. 13:14). Already in Daniel 12:2 we find a reference to the bodily nature of deceased persons as "sleeping" in the dust of the earth, from whence they shall be raised up.

In the New Testament this same resurrection of both the evil and the good is taken up by Christ Himself in John 5:28–29: "Do not marvel at this; for an hour is coming, in which all who are in the tombs shall hear His voice, and shall come forth; those who did the good deeds, to a resurrection of life, those who committed evil deeds to a resurrection of judgment" (NASB). The implication is that all humans after death remain in a state of sleep or suspended animation so far as their bodily nature is concerned. In the New Testament specific references to this state of sleep pertain to believers, at least so far as Paul's Epistles are concerned (1 Cor. 11:30; 15:51; 1 Thess. 4:14; 5:10). But their soul and spirit, which prior to the resurrection of Christ waited in that portion of hades referred to by Christ as "Abraham's bosom" (Luke 16:22), go to be with Christ immediately upon death (Phil. 1:23).

The second type of death taught in Scripture is *spiritual* death. It is this aspect of death that overtook our first parents immediately upon their act of sin. Alienation toward God was shown by their vain attempt to hide from Him when He came to have fellowship with them in the cool of the evening (Gen. 3:8). It was apparent from their attitude of guilty fear toward Him

(3:10), in the curse of expulsion from the Garden of Eden (where they had enjoyed intimate and cordial fellowship with Him), in the curse of toil and pain both in the eking out of a living from the soil and in the process of childbirth, and in the eventual death of the body and its reversion to the soil from which it was made (3:16–19,23–24). From that moment on, Adam and Eve fell into a state of spiritual death, separated from the living God through their violation of His covenant. As Ephesians 2:1–3 expresses it, they became "dead in trespasses and sins," walking according to the course of Satan and this present evil world, fulfilling the desires of the flesh and the mind, as children of disobedience and wrath.

Not only did Adam and Eve become guilty before God and thereby fall into a state of unrighteousness, but they also incurred that defilement and pollution that characterize the unholy life of the fallen *sarx* ("fleshly nature") that is basically alienated toward God and in a state of enmity toward Him (Rom. 8:5–8). Hence the mind-set (*phronēma*) of the *sarx* is death (v.6), and those who abide in this state are incapable of pleasing God (v.8). Hence they are alienated from the life of God, being completely helpless to save themselves or to earn any merit or favor in the eyes of God. They are utterly lost from the time they first begin their earthly life (Ps. 51:5), for they are born as "children of wrath" (Eph. 2:3).

Such was the condition of Adam and Eve as soon as they committed their first transgression. They were plunged immediately into a state of spiritual death, from which they had no prospect of recovery, despite the most strenuous efforts to lead a better life. Yet the biblical account goes on to tell of God's forgiveness and remedial grace. To that guilty pair He gave the promise (Gen. 3:15) that one of Eve's descendants would someday crush the head of the satanic serpent, at the cost of personal suffering (suggestive of His death on the Cross).

Instead of immediately inflicting the penalty of physical death on them, God gave Adam and Eve a set of guidelines for their life subsequent to their expulsion from Eden—which surely implied that their execution was to be delayed for some gracious purpose, even though they had forfeited the communion they had formerly enjoyed with God. God also provided them with animal pelts to cover up their nakedness and to protect them from the cold and the rigors of the outside world. But to furnish them with such pelts, it was necessary to take the lives of the animals whose fur they were to wear. It may have been in this connection that God taught Adam and Eve about blood sacrifice on the altar, as a means of their laying hold in advance of the atoning merit of the Cross—that vicarious, substitutionary death that the messianic "seed of the woman" was someday to offer up on the hill of Golgotha. As they responded in repentance and faith (bestowed on them by the Holy Spirit), they were rescued from their state of death and brought into a state of grace. This faith is deduced from the sacrificial practice of their son Abel, who presented the firstlings of his flock as a blood sacrifice on his altar in his worship of God. Blood sacrifice presupposes a concept of substitution, whereby the innocent dies in place of the guilty.

The third type of death referred to in Scripture is *eternal* death, that final, complete, and irremediable state of eternal separation from God, who is the only true source of life and joy. This death is referred to in Revelation 20:14 as the "second death." This is characterized by unending and unrelieved pangs of conscience and anguish of soul, corresponding to the ever-ascending smoke of the torment of the damned (Rev. 14:11). This is said to be the final state of Satan, the Beast (or the self-deifying world dictator of the last days), and his religious collaborator, the False Prophet (Rev. 20:10). All three are to be cast into the "lake of fire and brimstone," there to be tormented "day and night forever and ever." Revelation 21:8 reveals that every type of unrepentant, unforgiven sinner (the cowardly, the unbelieving or untrustworthy, the murderers, the sexually immoral, the sorcerers and idolaters, and all liars) will likewise be cast into the lake of fire and brimstone, which is the second death. This, then, is the ultimate destiny of those who willfully abide in a state of spiritual death until they experience their physical death. "He who believes in Him is not judged; he who does not believe has been judged already, because he has not believed in the name of the only begotten Son of God" (John 3:18, NASB). "He who believes in the Son has eternal life; but he who does not obey [or believe] the Son shall not see life, but the wrath of God abides on him" (John 3:36).

In the Garden of Eden, the serpent told Eve that if she and Adam ate of the forbidden fruit, they would be "as gods" (Gen. 3:5 KJV). Then in Genesis 3:22 God says, "Behold, the man has become like one of us" (NASB). Does "gods" and "us" imply the existence of more than one God?

Not at all. The usual Hebrew term for "God" is *ʾelōhîm*, which is the plural of *ʾelôah*. It is occasionally used as a true plural, referring to the imaginary gods of the heathen. But usually it refers to the one true God, and the plural ending is known to Hebrew grammarians as the "plural of majesty." Like *ʾadōnîm* ("lords" or "Lord") and *beʿālîm* (plural of *baʿal*, "lord," "master," "owner," "husband"), *ʾelōhîm* also may be used to give a heightened impressiveness of majesty to God. As such, this plural is modified by adjec-

tives in the singular and takes a singular verb.

In the case of the serpent, serving as Satan's mouthpiece, his previous uses of *ʾelōhîm* (3:1,5a) are unquestionably intended as a designation of the one true God; hence, it is altogether likely that it should be so used here. Therefore, the proper rendering of 3:5b should be (as ASV, NASB, NIV, and even the Luther Bible): "You will be like God, knowing good and evil." The last phrase acts as a qualifier; that is, "you will be like God in that you will have personal knowledge of the moral law, with the distinction that it draws between good and evil." No longer would they remain in a state of innocency, but they would have a (guilty) personal experience of evil and would be to that extent closer to God and His angels in the matter of full moral awareness.

Who, then, constitutes the "us" referred to in v.22? Conceivably the three persons of the Trinity might be involved here (as in Gen. 1:26), but more likely "us" refers to the angels surrounding God's throne in heaven (cf. 1 Kings 22:19; Isa. 6:1–3, etc.). There are a few passages in the Old Testament where the angels are referred to as *benê ʾelōhîm* ("sons of God," e.g., Job 1:6; 2:1; 38:6; cf. *benê ʾēlîm*—a shortened form of *ʾelōhîm*, Pss. 29:1; 89:6). In some cases, just as *benê Yiśrāʾēl* ("sons of Israel") is shortened to *Yiśrāʾēl* alone (referring to the nation of Israel rather than to Jacob), so also *benê ʾelōhîm* ("sons of God" in the sense of angels) is shortened to *ʾelōhîm*, as in Psalm 97:7.

It was certainly true of the angels of heaven that they too had acquired a knowledge of good and evil. Before the dawn of human history, there was apparently a revolt against God under the leadership of Satan or "Lucifer" (see Isa. 14:12–15, where Satan is addressed as the patron of the king of Babylon). This is probably alluded to in 2 Peter 2:4: "God did not spare angels when they sinned, but cast them into hell and committed them to pits of darkness, reserved for judgment." Therefore, those angels who remained true to the Lord were members of His heavenly court, having passed the tests of faithfulness and obedience in the face of temptation.

If it was not until after Adam and Eve had eaten of the fruit of the tree of knowledge and were hiding their nakedness in the garden that God knew they had disobeyed Him, how is this compatible with the belief that God is everywhere and knows what is in man's heart and what man will do?

The inference that God did not foreknow that Adam and Eve would yield to temptation and fall into sin is not supported by Scripture. If John the Baptist proclaimed Jesus as the "Lamb of God slain from the foundation of the world" (cf. Rev. 13:8), then God certainly foreknew that our first parents would sin and fall before they were even created. Even so, Jesus foreknew—and foretold—Peter's triple denial of Him in the courtyard of the high priest, even though Peter asserted his willingness to die for his Master if need be (Matt. 26:33–35). It was after Peter had denied knowing Jesus for the third time that Jesus turned His gaze in Peter's direction and their eyes met (Luke 22:60–61).

When the Lord called out to Adam in the garden (Gen. 3:9), He knew perfectly well where Adam was hiding (cf. Ps. 139:2–3), what he had been thinking, and what he had done (cf. Prov. 15:3). But there was no other way He could deal with Adam and Eve concerning their sin than to question them about it: "Have you eaten from the tree? . . . What is this that you have done?" (Gen. 3:11,13). Parents normally use this approach when they apprehend their children in wrongdoing, even though they are well aware of

their guilt. The use of a question leads to the necessary first step of confession: "Yes, Father, I broke it—by accident, of course."

Obviously, God was already aware of what Adam and Eve had done, and He had already decided how to deal with them in the light of their transgression (Gen. 3:14–19). This is simply an example of the general principle set forth in Acts 15:18: "Known to God are all His works from the beginning of the world." See also Isaiah 41:26; 42:9,23; 43:9,12; 44:7–8—all of which lay the strongest stress on God's foreknowledge of the future and His ability to predict exactly what is going to happen, even to revealing these matters to His prophets centuries in advance of their occurrence.

Were Adam and Eve saved? When God clothed them with animal skins after the Fall, did He also teach them about blood sacrifice and the atonement? Was Adam a high priest for his family?

The first people to be forgiven of their sin were undoubtedly Adam and Eve. Their repentance and forgiveness are presupposed in Genesis 3:9–21, even though it is not explicitly spelled out. To be sure, the recorded remarks of both Adam and Eve included some evasion of personal responsibility for eating the forbidden fruit—Adam blamed Eve, Eve blamed the serpent—but both admitted by implication that they had actually committed the very offense that they had promised never to do.

Even though no genuine, full admission of guilt and repentance for sin is recorded in this chapter, the disciplinary measures meted out by God—Eve is to have painful childbirth and be subordinate to her husband; Adam is to eke out a hard living from the soil, with the prospect of eventual death to his body—are governed by considerations of forgiveness and grace. God did not reject them and leave them to the punishment they deserved, but He put them under a chastening discipline out of motives of love. He showed His purpose to be a salutary reminder of their past unfaithfulness and of their need to put Him first in their lives.

Since Genesis 3:15 contains the first announcement of the coming of the Savior—"He [the Seed of the woman] shall bruise you on the head, and you [the satanic serpent] shall bruise him on the heel"—it seems logical to conclude that at the time God clothed the nakedness of Adam and Eve, He also instructed them in the significance of the atoning blood of the substitute sacrifice. Adam then doubtless passed on to his sons his understanding of the blood-sacrifice atonement; for it is clear that Abel, Adam's second son, was a true believer and was well instructed about substitutionary atonement, symbolized by his sacrifice of an innocent lamb on the altar (Gen. 4:4).

Cain and Abel seem to have approached their own altars directly, thus being personally responsible for their offerings, since there is no mention of Adam's serving them in a priestly capacity. Cain's vegetable offering would never have secured his father's approval, because Cain tried to approach God without atoning blood; and Adam would never have approved what God condemned (Gen. 4:5).

We conclude, therefore, that Adam and Eve were the first humans to conceive of saving faith in the grace of God, though Abel was the first person to die in a state of salvation, having predeceased his father by more than eight hundred years (Gen. 5:3–5).

One final comment about drawing conclusions from silence needs to be made. The Gospels never speak of Jesus ever kissing His mother. But would it be safe to conclude that He never did? Even so it is unjustified to infer from the absence of Adam's

words of self-condemnation and sorrow for sin that he never, in the 930 years of his earthly life, expressed his heartfelt repentance to the Lord.

What was there about Cain's offering that made it unacceptable to God? Was it the offering itself, or was it Cain's attitude? (D*)

It would appear that Cain was at fault, both in his attitude and in the offering he presented to the Lord. Cain's sacrifice consisted of crops he had raised in his garden (Gen. 4:3), rather than a blood sacrifice, as his younger brother Abel had set before the Lord.

That Abel presented a blood sacrifice and did so in faith (cf. Heb. 11:4) strongly suggests that he was claiming a divine promise of grace as he laid his lamb on the altar—a promise he had learned from his parents. God therefore was pleased with Abel's offering (Gen. 4:4) and responded to him with approval, in contradistinction to His rejection of Cain's offering. It would seem that Cain had followed his own judgment in choosing a bloodless sacrifice, disregarding the importance of blood as explained by God to Adam and Eve, and disregarding the principle of substitutionary atonement that later found its complete fulfillment in the crucifixion of Christ.

Cain's willful substitution of the work of his own hands in place of atoning grace was followed by a savage jealousy and burning resentment toward his younger brother (Gen. 4:5). This eventuated in his murder of Abel out in the field, where Cain supposed no one could see him. His proud self-will led him to commit homicide, and his descendants carried on something of his man-centered, God-denying attitude for many generations to come (see Gen. 4:18–24; cf. "the daughters of men" in Gen. 6:2).

Two of the sons of Adam and Eve had wives. Where did their wives come from? (D*)

Genesis 5:4 tells us that during Adam's long lifetime of 930 years (800 after the birth of Seth), he had other sons and daughters. Since he and Eve had been ordered to produce a large family in order to populate the earth (Gen. 1:28), it is reasonable to assume that they continued to have children for a long period of time, under the then ideal conditions for longevity.

Without question it was necessary for the generation following Adam to pair off brothers and sisters to serve as parents for the ensuing generation; otherwise the human race would have died off. It was not until the course of subsequent generations that it became possible for cousins and more distant relations to choose each other as marriage partners. There seems to be no definite word about the incestuous character of brother-sister marriage until the time of Abraham, who emphasized to the Egyptians that Sarah was his sister (cf. Gen. 20:12), thus implying to the Egyptians that if she was his sister, she could not be his wife (Gen. 12:13).

In Leviticus 20:17 the actual sanction against brother-sister marriage is spelled out. But as for Cain and Seth and all the other sons of Adam who married, they must have chosen their sisters as wives.

Why do people not live as long now as they did in early times (cf. Gen. 5:5; Ps. 90:10)? Was time calculated differently then? (D*)

At the time Adam and Eve were created, they were in an ideal environment for the preservation of human life. The Garden of Eden was ideally suited to maintaining their health and vigor unimpaired. Even after they were expelled from Eden, it would seem that conditions for longevity were still far more favorable than they later became after the Flood; and there may well have been a virtual absence of disease. When these conditions gradually changed for the worse, particularly after the terrible judgment of the Flood, the life expectancy of man became progressively shorter. By Moses' time a lifetime of seventy years was considered normal, and those who lived on to eighty or beyond were generally beset with discomforts and weaknesses of various sorts, until they finally passed off the scene (see Ps. 90:10, dating back to the time of Moses, around 1400 B.C.). It seems that there was a gradual working out of the cursed effects of sin on the physical well-being and stamina of the human race, even long after the Fall had taken place.

As for the suggestion that time may have been computed differently during the earlier history of mankind, this could only have been the case if the planet Earth revolved more rapidly around the sun then than it does now. By definition a year is reckoned as the time necessary for the earth to revolve around the sun. According to Genesis 1:14, this revolution, as well as the daily rotation of the earth, was pretty well set and standardized right from the beginning. It is rather unlikely (though not absolutely impossible) that these planetary movements would have greatly altered since the creation of man.

Why is so much emphasis put on the antediluvian genealogy in the Bible? If the whole world was destroyed with the Flood, wouldn't everybody be of the same bloodline through Noah and his family? In other words, aren't we all related? (D*)

Yes, we are indeed all descendants of Noah, for all other families in the

77

antediluvian human race were destroyed by the Flood (so Gen. 7:21: "And all flesh that moved on the earth perished, birds and cattle and beasts . . . and all mankind"). The reason for the genealogical listing in Genesis 5 was to give the family line of Noah himself, since his descent from Adam through the covenant line of true believers was a matter of prime importance. Likewise in the genealogy of our Lord Jesus Christ, as given in Luke's gospel, these same antediluvian ancestors are listed (see Luke 3:36–38) to show that the Second Adam was descended from the first Adam. Furthermore, the godly walk of leaders like Seth, the son of Adam (Gen. 4:26), and his son Enosh was a matter of great importance; so too was the close fellowship Enoch had with God before the Lord took him at the age of three hundred years to dwell with Him in heaven's glory.

Are there passages in the Old Testament indicating that the men and women of ancient Israel entertained a heavenly hope? (D*)

It is a mistake to suppose that God's people had no heavenly hope in Old Testament times. Genesis 5:24 records that, after a godly life, Enoch was taken away (*lāqaḥ*) by God—with the clear implication that from that time on he was in God's presence. (Hebrews 11:5 confirms this: "By faith Enoch was taken up so that he should not see death; and he was not found because God took him up" [NASB]. Enoch therefore never died but went directly to God's presence.)

Despite his moods of deep discouragement, the patriarch Job still showed confidence when he said, "After my skin has been destroyed, yet in [from the vantage point of] my flesh I will see God [just previously referred to as Job's Redeemer (*gō'ēl*) in Job 19:25]" (Job 19:26). (The rendering "without

my flesh I shall see" runs counter to the usage of the preposition *min* ["from"] wherever else in the OT it is used with the verb "see," whether *ḥāzāh*, the one used here, or with the more common *rā'āh*. Everywhere else *min* refers to the vantage point from which the looking is done.)

In the Psalms, David and his successors offer many intimations of future life with God. Even the assertion in Psalm 1:5 that ungodly men and sinners will "not stand in the congregation of the righteous" implies a final judgment either to condemnation or to acquittal and acceptance—terms that would be meaningless if moldering skeletons were all that remained after this earthly life is over. Psalm 16:10 mentions the hope of the bodily resurrection (clearly applied to the resurrection of Christ in Acts 2:27,31), and is followed by a strong affirmation: "In thy presence is fullness of joy; at thy right hand there are pleasures forever" (Ps. 16:11). "Forever" here is *neṣaḥ*, a term that can hardly be shown elsewhere to mean simply 'the rest of my earthly life' but that clearly suggests permanence beyond the grave. Again, Psalm 49:15 reads: "God will redeem me from the power of the grave, for He will receive me [*lāqaḥ*, or 'take me away']." This sounds like an assurance that God will not simply keep the psalmist from dying prematurely but rather that he will ever live on with God—in contrast to the spiritually foolish and wicked, whose ultimate home will be Sheol (vv.10–14). A similar confidence is expressed in Psalm 73:24: "Thou shalt guide me with thy counsel, and afterward ['*aḥar*] receive [*lāqaḥ*] me to [or "with"] glory."

Turning to the Prophets, we find that Isaiah has a remarkable passage on this theme in 25:8: "He will swallow up death in victory, and the LORD Yahweh will wipe tears away from all faces, and He will remove the reproach of His people from all the earth; for Yahweh has spoken." And again, Isaiah 26:19: "Your dead ones will live, My dead bodies will arise; those who dwell in the dust have awakened and they shout for joy . . . and the earth will give birth to the shades [of the deceased]." Compare this with Daniel 12:2: "Many of those who sleep in the dust of the ground will awake, these to everlasting life, but the others to disgrace and ever- lasting contempt" (NASB) (quoted by Jesus in Matt. 25:46, in a beyond-the- grave context). Daniel 12:13 contains this blessed promise to Daniel per- sonally: "You will enter into rest and rise again for your allotted portion at the end of the age."

There can be no question, in the light of the above, that the Old Testa- ment contained very definite teaching concerning the life of the believer be- yond the grave in the care of—even in the presence of—the Lord God Him- self.

Therefore the New Testament is abundantly justified in Christ's affir- mation that Abraham rejoiced to see the day of Christ's coming to earth (John 8:56), and that he looked for a heavenly city "whose builder and maker is God" (Heb. 11:10). But it should be added that apart from a few exceptions, like Enoch, Moses, and Elijah, it may well have been that the general congregation of redeemed be- lievers were not exalted to the full glory of God's presence until the price of their redemption had been actually paid at Calvary (see Matt. 27:52; Eph. 4:8; Heb. 11:39–40). It was therefore appropriate for the more detailed and glowing descriptions of the saved re- joicing in heaven's glory to be reserved for the pages of the New Testament.

Does "sons of God" in Genesis 6:2 refer to angels?

Genesis 6:1–2 reads: "When men began to increase in number on the earth and daughters were born to them, the sons of God saw that the daughters of men were beautiful, and they married any of them they chose" (NIV). The term "sons of God" ($b^e n\hat{e}$ $^{,e}l\bar{o}h\hat{i}m$) is used in the Old Testament of either angels or men who are true believers, committed to the service of God. Passages that refer to angels as $b^e n\hat{e}$ $^{,e}l\bar{o}h\hat{i}m$ include Job 1:6; 2:1; 38:7; Psalms 29:1; 89:6 (89:7 MT). The Masoretic text (MT) does not contain this phrase in Deuteronomy 32:43, but a fragment of a Hebrew text found in Qumran Cave Four reads: "Shout joy- ously, O heavens, with Him, and wor- ship Him, O sons of God [$b^e n\hat{e}$ $^{,e}l\bar{o}h\hat{i}m$], and ascribe to Him might, all you sons of the mighty [$b^e n\hat{e}$ $^{,}\bar{e}l\hat{i}m$]. Shout joy- ously, O nations, concerning His people, and accord strength to Him, all you angels of God [kol-$mal^{,a}k\hat{e}$ $^{,}\bar{e}l$]." This is considerably more expanded than the received Hebrew text (MT) of this verse, but it may possibly be the original wording. It was probably the passage quoted in Hebrews 1:6— though Psalm 97:7 may also be the source for that verse.

But the occurrences of $b^e n\hat{e}$ $^{,e}l\bar{o}h\hat{i}m$ referring to men standing in covenant relationship to God are fully as numer- ous in the Old Testament as those re- ferring to angels (cf. Deut. 14:1; 32:5; Ps. 73:15; Hos. 1:10 [MT=2:1]—and, we believe, Gen. 6:2 as well). The rea- sons for understanding Genesis 6:2 as referring to members of the covenant family, descendants of the line of Seth, are quite compelling. Scripture clearly teaches that angels are *spirits,* "minis- tering spirits sent to serve those who will inherit salvation" (Heb. 1:14, NIV). While they may on occasion appear in bodily form in the semblance of men, they have no physical bodies, and are therefore utterly incapable of carnal relations with women. The rabbinic speculation that angels are referred to in Genesis 6:2 is a curious intrusion of pagan superstition that has no basis at all in the rest of Scripture. The fact that some children of gigantic stature (*ne pilîm*, v.4) resulted from these marriages offers no evidence whatever of angelic paternity. No one claims that the sons of Anak, Goliath, and his brothers had any angelic forbears because of their great stature; nor is there any reason to suppose that the antediluvian giants had supernatural forbears.

What Genesis 6:1–2,4 records is the first occurrence of mixed marriage between believers and unbelievers, with the characteristic result of such unions: complete loss of testimony for the Lord and a total surrender of moral standards. In other words, the "sons of God" in this passage were descendants of the godly line of Seth. Instead of remaining true to God and loyal to their spiritual heritage, they allowed themselves to be enticed by the beauty of ungodly women who were "daughters of men"—that is, of the tradition and example of Cain. The natural result of such marriages was a debasement of nature on the part of the younger generations, until the entire antediluvian civilization sank to the lowest depths of depravity. "The LORD saw how great man's wickedness on the earth had become, and that every inclination of the thoughts of his heart was only evil all the time" (v.5, NIV). The inevitable result was judgment, the terrible destruction of the Great Flood.

Perhaps one last comment regarding angels would be in order here. If we were to concede that spirits could somehow enter into sexual relations with human beings—which they cannot—then they could not even so be fitted in with this passage here. If they were minions of Satan, that is, fallen angels, then they could not have been referred to as "sons of God." Demons of hell would never be so designated in Scripture. Nor could they have been angels of God, since God's angels always live in total obedience to Him and have no other yearning or desire but to do God's will and glorify His name. A sordid involvement with godless young women would therefore be completely out of character for angels as "sons of God." the only viable explanation, therefore, is the one offered in the previous paragraph.

Genesis 6:7 records God as saying, "I will destroy ... both man and beast, and the creeping things, and the fowls of the air; for it repenteth me that I have made them." This seems inconsistent with the generally accepted view of God, that He would repent about anything—or need to—since He could see in advance what the outcome of His creation would be. The word "them" seems to include the animals as well as men; what could the animals possibly have done to merit God's disgust? (D*)

While it is perfectly true that God in His sovereign omniscience knows all things in advance, and that nothing that happens can ever come to Him as a surprise, yet it is a mistake to infer from this that He is incapable of emotion or reaction to the willful depravity of His creatures. The Scriptures never present Him as an impassive Being, incapable of sorrow or wrath, but quite the contrary. This is because He is a God who cares, a God who loves and has a deep concern even for those ungrateful children of Adam who have mocked His gracious promises and have trifled with His mercy.

The depth of corruption to which the human race had plunged by Noah's time was utterly revolting to the God of holiness and justice, and He responded to these disgusting excesses as His righteousness and purity demanded. He was sorry He had created such an abominable generation of moral perverts as the antediluvian race had become. "And He repented" (Heb. *wayyinnāhem*, the niphal of *nāham*) is somewhat anthropomorphic (or anthropopathic) to be sure, for it serves to convey God's response to sin after a human analogy (just as the Bible speaks of God's having hands or eyes or a mouth, as if He had a body with physical parts and organs).

Of course the element of surprise by the unexpected or unlooked for is impossible for one who is omniscient, but His response to humanity was a necessary adjustment to the change in humanity's feeling about Him. Because they had stubbornly rejected and flouted Him, it was necessary for Him to reject them. The shift in their attitude required a corresponding shift in His attitude toward them, and it is this shift that is expressed by the Hebrew *niham* ("repent," "be sorry about," "change one's mind about").

Similarly, in the time of Jonah, God is said to have repented (*niham*) of the judgment He had threatened to bring down on the city of Nineveh, because He observed the Ninevites' sincere and earnest repentance after Jonah had preached to them. Their change in attitude toward God made appropriate a change in His attitude toward them. Therefore, much to Jonah's disgust, God allowed the forty days to elapse and withheld the blow of destruction He had threatened to bring on them. This shows that God may change His response from severity to leniency and mercy when people come to Him in repentance and with supplication.

Yet when it comes to His announced covenant purposes toward His covenant people. God is indeed incapable of repentance—as Balaam points out in Numbers 23:19: "God is not a man, that He should lie, nor a son of man, that He should repent; has He said, and will He not do it? Or has He spoken, and will He not make it good?" (NASB). The context here pertains to God's steadfast purpose to bless Israel, despite all the machinations of King Balak of Moab, who tried to bribe the prophet of Yahweh to bring down a curse on the Hebrew nation. In such a situation God is indeed incapable of repentance.

So far as the birds and the beasts were concerned, the context of Genesis 6:7 says nothing about their displeasing or angering God; so it is not really justified to interpret the purpose of judgment as directed at them equally with the depraved race of men. It was simply an inevitable consequence of the coming Flood, that it should destroy not only mankind but also all brute creation living in man's environment. The intended antecedent of "them" was really the preceding "man" (Heb. *hā'ādām*)—in the sense of the human race—rather than the various orders of bird and beast that are listed with man. Actually, God's solicitude for the survival of all these various species of animal and bird found expression in His command to Noah to preserve at least one pair of parents in order to propagate each species.

How can Genesis 6:19 be reconciled with Genesis 7:2?

Genesis 6:19 relates God's command to Noah: "You are to bring into the ark two of all living creatures, male and female, to keep them alive with you" (NIV). Genesis 7:2–3 records God's additional instruction: "Take with you seven of every kind of clean animal, a male and its mate, and two of every kind of unclean animal, a male and its mate, and also seven of every kind of bird, male and female, to keep their various kinds alive throughout the earth." Some have suggested that these diverse numbers, two and seven, involve some sort of contradiction and indicate conflicting traditions later combined by some redactor who didn't notice the difference between the two.

It seems strange that this point should ever have been raised, since the reason for having seven of the clean species is perfectly evident: they were to be used for sacrificial worship after the Flood had receded (as indeed they were, according to Gen. 8:20: "Then Noah built an altar to the LORD and, taking some of all the clean animals and clean birds, he sacrificed burnt offerings on it"). Obviously if there had not been more than two of each of these clean species, they would have been rendered extinct by their being sacrificed on the altar. But in the case of the unclean animals and birds, a single pair would suffice, since they would not be needed for blood sacrifice.

Is a universal Flood consistent with geologic evidence?

The biblical record in Genesis 7–8 describes no local inundation confined to the Mesopotamian Valley (as some scholars have suggested) but a water level that surpassed the summits of the highest mountains. Genesis 7:19 states: "And the water prevailed more and more upon the earth, so that *all* the high mountains *everywhere* under the heavens [lit., 'which were under all the heavens' or 'under the whole sky'] were covered" (NASB, italics mine). Verse 20 then indicates that the water level rose even fifteen cubits higher than that (fifteen cubits being about thirty feet).

Now the most elementary knowledge of physical law leads to the observation that water seeks its own level. A great tidal wave may temporarily reach a greater altitude than the general sea level, but the episode here described lasted for about a year; and there is therefore far more involved here than a temporary surge. If the water level rose thirty thousand feet so as to submerge the peak of Mount Everest, the world's tallest mountain, it must have reached that level everywhere else on earth. Even the overtopping of Mount Ararat, the resting place of Noah's ark, required a level well in excess of seventeen thousand feet. Water rising to such

an altitude would certainly engulf the entire surface of the planet, except for the highest peaks of the Andes and Himalayas, plus a few in North America and Africa. Therefore we must conclude that the Flood was indeed universal, or else that the biblical record was grievously in error. While it is doubtless true that mountain uplift is still going on, in North America, at any rate, even the reduction of a few thousand feet in the altitude of ranges so lofty as the Andes and Himalayas would not have substantially changed the necessity of worldwide distribution of the Flood waters.

The question of geological evidence is very much debated by geologists, according to the position they take toward the validity of the biblical record. Some Christian geologists feel that some of the major seismic disturbances indicated in various parts of the globe at the Cenozoic levels are best explained as triggered by the Flood (cf. Gen. 7:11: "On the same day all the fountains of the great deep burst open"). Some of the strata containing large boulders in the midst of coarse gravel are plausibly attributed to violent tidal movements and water agitation beyond anything known at the present time. But perhaps the most striking evidences of the violence of the Deluge throughout the earth are to be found in the amazing profusion of Pleistocene or Recent animals whose bones have been discovered in a violently separated state in several ossiferous fissures that have been excavated in various locations in Europe and North America.

Rehwinkel (*The Flood*) indicates that these fissures occur even in hills of considerable height, and they extend to a depth of anywhere from 140 feet to 300 feet. Since no skeleton is complete, it is safe to conclude that none of these animals (mammoths, bears, wolves, oxen, hyenas, rhinoceros, aurochs, deer, and many smaller mammals) fell into these fissures alive, nor were they rolled there by streams. Yet because of the calcite cementing of these heterogeneous bones together, they must necessarily have been deposited under water. Such fissures have been discovered in Odessa by the Black Sea, in the island of Kythera off the Peloponnesus, in the island of Malta, in the Rock of Gibraltar, and even at Agate Springs, Nebraska (which was excavated in 1876 over a ten-acre area).

Such geologic evidence is of decisive importance, even though it is seldom mentioned by scientists who reject the accuracy of Scripture. This is just exactly the kind of evidence that a brief but violent episode of this sort would be expected to show within the short span of one year. Of course there would be little sedimentary precipitation possible for such a short period of time. There are some negative evidences, to be sure, such as the cones of loose scoria and ashes from volcanoes in the region of Auvergne, France, which are alleged to be thousands of years older than the supposed date of the Flood. But until it is decisively proven that these volcanoes were antediluvian (the actual date of the Flood has not been precisely determined yet), and until it is demonstrated by a year's submergence under brackish water that such volcanic formations would show striking changes in appearance perceptible to the modern investigator, it seems premature to affirm that this type of evidence is even more compelling than that of the above-mentioned ossiferous fissures, which so definitely testify to the type of Deluge described in Genesis 7.

One notable feature of the biblical account sets it off from all other Flood narratives discoverable among other nations. Flood sagas have been preserved among the most diverse tribes and nations all over the world: the Babylonians (who called their Noah by

the name of Utnapishtim), the Sumerians with their Ziusidru, the Greeks with their Deucalion, the Hindus with their Manu, the Chinese with their Fah-he, the Hawaiians with their Nu-u, the Mexican Indians with their Tezpi, the Algonquins with their Manabozho. All these relate how this lone survivor (with perhaps his wife, children, and a friend or two) was saved from the destruction of a universal flood and was then faced with the task of repopulating a devastated earth after the flood waters had receded. But of all these accounts, only the Genesis record indicates with the exactitude of a diary or ship's log the date of the inception of the Deluge (when Noah was exactly 600 years old, on the seventeenth day of the seventh month of that same year), the length of the actual downpour (40 days), the length of time that the water-depth remained at its maximum (150 days), the date at which the tops of the mountains became visible once more (on the first day of the tenth month), the length of time until the first evidence of new plant growth was brought to Noah in the beak of his dove (47 days, according to Gen. 8:6–9), and the precise day of Noah's emerging from the ark on Mount Ararat (his 601st year, the first day of the first month). Here we have a personal record that apparently goes back to Noah himself.

The Babylonian account contains vivid details of how Utnapishtim built his ark, but there is no suggestion of a specific date. Like most legends handed down orally across the centuries or millennia, the Gilgamesh Epic (Tablet 11) fails to say anything at all about the year, even though the friendly sun-god, Shamash, had warned of the precise day when the prospective survivors would have to board their ark. It would seem that this Babylonian account is substantially closer to the Genesis record than any of the other Flood stories. Thus a friendly god warns the hero in advance and orders him to build an ark, to save not only his own family but also representative animals. That ark finally grounds on a mountain named Nisir (in the Zagros Range, northeast of Babylon); and Utnapishtim sends out a dove, a swallow, and a raven to bring back a report of conditions outside. Then finally he emerged with his family to offer sacrifice to the now-famished gods (who had been without altar-food for the weeks while the Flood was covering the earth).

Some comparative religionists have suggested that the Babylonian myth was earlier than the Hebrew, and that the compilers of Genesis 7 and 8 borrowed from it. But this is rendered most unlikely in view of the significant contrasts between the two. Thus, the ark built by Utnapishtim was completely cubic, equipped with six decks for all the animals to be quartered in. A more impractical and unseaworthy craft could hardly be imagined. But Noah's ark was three hundred cubits long, fifty cubits wide, and thirty cubits deep—an ideal set of measurements for an ocean liner. If the cubit measured twenty-four inches in that earlier period (as it may well have done in an age when men were bigger than they were after the Flood—cf. Gen. 6:4), then the ark of Noah would have been six hundred feet long, by one hundred feet wide, and sixty feet deep. If it was fairly boxlike in shape (as would be probable in view of its special purpose), it would have had a capacity of 3.6 million cubic feet. This is the capacity of about two thousand cattle cars, each of which can carry 18 to 20 cattle, 60 to 80 hogs, or 80 to 100 sheep.

At the present time, there are only 290 main species of land animals larger in size than sheep. There are 757 more species ranging in size from sheep to rats, and there are 1,358 species smaller than rats. Two individuals of each of these species would fit very comfortably into two thousand cattle cars, with plenty of room for fodder. But it is more than doubtful whether the same could be said of Utnapishtim's unwieldy craft, subject to frequent capsizing in heavy seas, in view of its cubic shape. Moreover, the stark contrast between the quarrelsome and greedy gods of the Babylonian pantheon and the majestic holiness of Yahweh, the absolute Sovereign over the universe, furnishes the strongest basis for classifying the Gilgamesh account as a garbled, polytheistic derivative from the same original episode as that contained in Genesis 7–8. The Hebrew account is couched in terms of sober history and accurate recording that reflect a source derived from the persons who were actually involved in this adventure. The Gilgamesh Epic is far more mythical and vague.

For readers who wish to do more extensive reading on the worldwide spread of the Flood saga, see James Frazer, *Folklore in the Old Testament,* vol. 1 (London: Macmillan & Co., 1918) or Richard Andree's more compendious work, *Die Flutsagen ethnographisch betrachtet* (Brunswick, 1891). For the Babylonian Flood epic, see Alexander Heidel, *The Gilgamesh Epic and Old Testament Parallels*, 2d ed. (Chicago: University of Chicago, 1949).

Are Christians still forbidden to eat blood?

After the Flood, the Lord renewed His covenant with Noah and gave him certain basic guidelines for the ordering of postdiluvian society (Gen. 9:1–16). Verse 4 has this important prohibition: "You shall not eat flesh with its life [*nepeš*], that is, its blood" (NASB). The special sanctity of the blood leads to a command for the capital punishment of any and all who commit murder. Later, in Leviticus 17:10–11, the reason for avoiding blood as food is spelled out more clearly: "Any man from the house of Israel, or from the aliens who sojourn among them, who eats any blood, I will set My face against that person who eats blood, and will cut him off from among his people. For the life [*nepeš*] of the flesh is in the blood, and I have given it to you on the altar to make atonement for your souls; for it is the blood by reason of the life that makes atonement" (NASB). The following verses go on to specify that even wild game must be completely bled before it may be eaten.

The question confronting believers in this New Testament era is whether this prohibition pertains to us today. The revelation granted to Peter in Acts 10:10-15 taught him that the ancient restrictions of the Mosaic Law concerning forbidden items of food were no longer to be observed. All the quadrapeds, crawling creatures, and birds were to be considered clean and fit for human consumption. The important factor here was the application of this principle by analogy to all the races of mankind, both Jew and Gentile—all of them were rendered suitable for salvation and grace through the shed blood of Jesus. The question remains, however, whether this removal of the categories of unclean food set forth in such detail in Leviticus 11:1-45 and Deuteronomy 14:3-21 actually lifts the restriction against the consumption of blood. Now that Christ has shed His sacred blood, does this remove all sanctity from blood as such? Or is it still to be honored as precious because of its symbolism of Calvary? In other words, does permission to eat all animals and birds without discrimination involve a license to eat the *blood* of these animals? Or should they first be properly bled by the butcher before being cooked and prepared for human consumption?

The answer to that last question seems to be yes. Some years after Peter had received God's special instruction

through his dream, the Jerusalem Council was held in order to consider whether the Gentile converts should be required to adopt the ceremonial requirements of Judaism in order to become Christians. As president of the council, James stated: "Therefore it is my judgment that we do not trouble those who are turning to God from among the Gentiles, but that we write to them that they abstain [1] from things contaminated by idols and [2] from fornication and [3] from what is strangled and from blood" (Acts 15:19-20, NASB). This found general approval by the rest of the assembly. So they decided on the following answer to the Gentile converts in Antioch, Syria, and Cilicia: "For it seemed good to the Holy Spirit and to us to lay upon you no greater burden that these essentials: that you abstain from things sacrificed to idols and from blood and from things strangled and from fornication; if you keep yourselves free from such things, you will do well" (Acts 15:28-29, NASB).

From the above passage we gather (1) that this admonition to avoid eating blood came subsequent to Peter's vision and therefore was not in any way modified or abrogated by the earlier revelation in Acts 10; (2) that this was coupled with a prohibition against fornication—which can never be regarded as an obsolete restriction but rather as an abiding principle binding on the conscience of all Christians; (3) that this insistence on the continuing sanctity of blood was decreed not only by men but by the authority of the Holy Spirit Himself. To be sure, some have inferred from Paul's later discussion in 1 Corinthians 8 concerning meat offered to idols that the prohibition contained in the letter of the Jerusalem Council was not really binding for all time to come. But actually Paul's objection centered not so much on the inherent sinfulness of eating such food but rather on the stumbling block such an example might furnish to newly converted pagans who had formerly sacrificed to idols.

In 1 Corinthians 10:27–28 Paul enlarges on this matter, saying: "If one of the unbelievers invites you, and you wish to go, eat anything that is set before you, without asking questions for conscience' sake. But if anyone should say to you, 'This is meat sacrificed to idols,' do not eat it, for the sake of the one who informed you, and for conscience' sake." This implies that whether or not a believer might partake in private of meat that had previously been offered on an idolatrous altar, his use of it before others would lead to his causing them to stumble. Therefore it was still forbidden to the New Testament believer on the ground of the spiritual harm that it might do to recent Gentile converts. The implication seems very clear that we are still to respect the sanctity of the blood, since God has appointed it to be a symbol of the atoning blood of Jesus Christ. Therefore it is not to be consumed by any believer who wishes to be obedient to Scripture.

Christ's solemn statement in John 6:53–58 concerning believers' partaking of His flesh and blood by faith quite obviously refers only to the *spiritual* response of true believers in regard to the atoning sacrifice of Christ on Golgotha. We appropriate His body and blood by faith, together with all His saving benefits, as we trust wholly in His sinless life and in His offering of His innocent body as a vicarious atonement for our sins. But this has no bearing whatever on the question of whether we may disregard God's earnest admonition not to partake of physical blood as an item of food.

In Genesis 9:24–28, why did Noah curse his youngest son and say that Canaan should be a slave? Was this the beginning of slavery? Was slavery all right in the sight of God? (D*)

The reason Noah cursed his son Ham was that he had derided and dishonored his father after he found him naked, sleeping off a drunken stupor. Ham should have treated him respectfully, even though his father (who had apparently never tasted liquor before) had made a fool of himself. But it should be carefully noted that only one of the sons of Ham, namely Canaan, was singled out for suffering the effects of Ham's curse. Genesis 9:25 quotes Noah as saying, "Cursed be Canaan; a servant of servants [or 'slave of slaves'—Heb. '*ebed* "*bādîm*] he shall be to his brothers" (NASB).

Ham had three sons besides Canaan, namely Cush, Mizraim, and Put (Gen. 10:6); but the penalty was announced only for Canaan, the ancestor of the Canaanites of Palestine, rather than for Cush and Put, who were probably the ancestors of the Ethiopians and the black peoples of Africa. The fulfillment of this curse came about in Joshua's conquest (ca. 1400 B.C.), and also in the conquest of Phoenicia and other Canaanites by the Persian Empire, since the Persians were descended, in all probability, from Japheth through Madai. This does seem to be the earliest occurrence of '*ebed* in the sense of "slave" that can be found in Scripture.

As to the moral status of slavery in ancient times, it must be recognized that it was practiced by every ancient people of which we have any historical record: Egyptians, Sumerians, Babylonians, Assyrians, Phoenicians, Syrians, Moabites, Ammonites, Edomites, Greeks, Romans, and all the rest. Slavery was as integral a part of ancient culture as commerce, taxation, or temple service. Not until the more exalted concept of man and his innate dignity as a person created in the image of God had permeated the world as a product of Bible teaching did a strong sentiment arise in Christendom in criticism of slavery and a questioning of its right to exist. No equivalent movement toward abolition is discernible in any non-Christian civilization of which we have any knowledge.

In Genesis 9:25, *'ebed* is used in the sense of being politically in subjection to a foreign power. Hebrew slaves were required under the Mosaic law to be set free after six years of service; they could not be made to serve out their entire lives as slaves unless they willingly chose to remain so, out of love for their masters (Exod. 21:2-7). In some cases slaves were held in great honor; that is to say, the nobles were generally called "servants" (*"bādîm*) of their king—a title of honor, something like Paul's reference to himself as a "bondslave of Jesus Christ."

In New Testament times slaves who became Christians were regarded as true brothers of the Christian free men and fellow heirs of the kingdom of God. They were bidden to serve their masters faithfully, respectfully, and with a right good will, as if they were serving the Lord Himself (Eph. 6:5-8)—even though they should seek to earn or purchase their freedom whenever possible (1 Cor. 7:21).

Yet there was inherent in the biblical concept of man as a person fashioned in the image of God and a candidate for heaven (on condition of repentance, faith, and commitment to the Lord) a dynamic principle that undermined slavery. This principle found expression first in the Christian world and then in other religions and cultures, which were shamed by the Christian example into abolishing slavery within their own domains. Thus God's ultimate purpose was brought to fruition.

What was meant by Noah's prophecy that Japheth would dwell in the tents of Shem (Gen. 9:27)?

The full statement by Noah was as follows: "May God enlarge Japheth,/ And let him dwell in the tents of Shem;/And let Canaan be his servant" (Gen. 9:27, NASB). This follows right on the heels of v.26, which indicates that the descendants of Canaan will serve as bondservants of both the Semites and the Indo-Europeans. This was fulfilled, in all probability, when in the 330s B.C. Alexander the Great subdued the entire territory of the Persian Empire and added it to his extensive European domains. As conqueror of the Phoenicians, Samaritans, Assyrians, and Babylonians, Alexander took over the reins of government through his special deputies and settled his veteran troops in various camps throughout the conquered territory. The empire he established endured for well over three centuries. In that sense, then, Japheth (ancestor of Javan or the Greeks) did "dwell in the tents of Shem."

Prior to Alexander's conquest, of course, Canaan had been invaded and taken over by the armies of Joshua around 1400 B.C. In that sense, then, Canaan became the servant of Shem as well as of Japheth (in the time of the Alexandrian conquest). But if the antecedent of the ambiguous pronoun "his" in "And let Canaan be *his* servant" is "Japheth"—as seems more likely—then this points forward particularly to the subjugation of the entire area of Canaan, or Palestine, by the Greeks and Macedonians of Alexander's army. Thus Canaan became the "servant" of Japheth.

Genesis 10:5,20,31 seem to indicate that mankind spoke many tongues. But Genesis 11:1 affirms that "the whole earth was of one language, and of one speech."

87

How are these two statements to be reconciled? (D*)

Genesis 10 describes the development of racial differentiation and dispersion that went on after the Flood and Noah's descendants began to repopulate the earth. This includes the entire process up to and including the third millennium B.C., just prior to the time of Abraham.

After this general survey, the author of Genesis reverts to a pivotal episode that occurred early in this postdiluvial era, the confusion of tongues that followed the vain attempt to build the Tower of Babel (Gen. 11:1-9). This must have been within a very few centuries after the Flood.

The various tribes that descended from Ham, Shem, and Japheth all spoke the same language (presumably that of Noah himself) but preserved their tribal distinction quite carefully. When God put an end to their arrogant humanism and their "one-world" policy (adopted in a rebellious attempt to get along without any need for God), He confused their speech so that one tribe could not understand another any longer; and it became impossible for them to continue with their collective project.

We have no way of knowing whether the pre-Babel worldwide language was preserved in any of the subsequent tongues that sprang up after that debacle. (Some have suggested that Hebrew may have been that original language and that we have the actual words of Adam, Eve, Cain, and so on, preserved in Gen. 3-4. But since Hebrew is demonstrably a later dialect of Northwest Semitic, or of the Canaanite language group within that division, it seems unlikely that biblical Hebrew could have been the most primitive or original of all human languages.)

We can only conjecture that within the various subtribes and clans the new language distribution or differentia-

tion was not so utterly complete as to keep even blood relatives from understanding one another. The fact that they continued to maintain their integrity according to their lineage strongly suggests that each of these smaller subdivisions was allowed a language mutually comprehensible to those within the clan, even after the confusion of tongues at Babel.

If Genesis 11:28 places the origin of Abraham's family in Ur of the Chaldees, why does Abraham in Genesis 24:4 locate his country and kinfolk in Haran?

Abraham's family originated in Ur but later migrated to Haran, which was located on the Belikh River, sixty miles from the Euphrates River, at the extreme north of the "Fertile Crescent." The entire clan joined in the migration, including Abram, Nahor, and Lot (the son of the deceased Nahor). Therefore they settled as a group in Padan Aram, of which Haran was the capital. There they all lived together for several decades, giving birth to children and rearing them in this Syrian setting. It is quite to be expected that Abraham would look back to the long sojourn in Haran as a second homeland from which he had migrated at the age of 75 (Gen. 12:4). It was also natural for him to refer to the children of his two older brothers as his "family" (*môledet*)—even though there may have been more distant relatives still living back in Ur (cf. 12:1).

Some have suggested that the Ur referred to as the ancestral home of Abraham's family may actually have been located much closer to Haran, up in the area of Padan Aram. There are references to "Uru" in the Eblaite tablets, according to G. Pettinato ("BAR Interviews Giovanni Pettinato," *Biblical Archaeology Review* 6, no. 5 [September-October 1980]: 51), located in northern Mesopotamia. But "Uru" was simply a Sumerian or Akkadian term for "the city," and as such it might be expected to occur in more than one region of Mesopotamia. Genesis 11:28 says very explicitly, however, that the Ur from which Abraham came was "Ur of the Chaldeans." This Ur was located very near the shoreline of the Persian Gulf back in ancient times, almost one hundred miles northwest of the present coast. As such it was very susceptible to raids by the Chaldean corsairs from the nearby region of what is now called Kuwait.

Just as the east coast of England finally became known as Danelaw, because of the increasing infiltration by Danish Vikings, so Ur became known as *Ur Kaŝdîm* (by Moses' time, at least, when Genesis was written), because of the establishment of a sphere of influence there on the part of the Chaldeans. But there is no way that any Uru up in the vicinity of Haran would have become subject to a Chaldean hegemony, for the Chaldeans never penetrated to that part of the Near East. (The suggestion that this might have reflected the Kassites of the Kassite dynasty in Babylon 1500–1200 B.C. has little to commend it. There was never any third radical *d* attached to the name *Kassî*.)

How could God allow Abraham to enrich himself through lying?

On two occasions (Gen. 12:10-20; 20:1-18), Abraham passed off his wife Sarah as his sister in order to save himself from getting killed. The first time he did so was when famine afflicted Canaan so severely that he felt he had to move to Egypt to survive (Gen. 12:10). But as he approached that corrupt pagan land, he realized he would be at the mercy of a society that would not stop at murder to seize his beautiful wife for the king's harem. Abraham felt sure they would kill him if they knew the truth about his marital status.

He therefore persuaded Sarah herself to join with him in the lie, feeling that this was the only way his life could be spared. It was understandable enough that she complied with his request under those circumstances. Yet it was a sin on the part of both of them, and it robbed them of all possibility of witnessing to the truth of God before the idolatrous society of Egypt.

Pharaoh's agents did as Abraham had foreseen; they took Sarah to Pharaoh as a lovely addition to his harem (she was still beautiful after sixty-five!). But to Abraham's embarrassment the king bestowed lavish gifts on him and greatly increased his wealth—in servants, livestock, silver, and gold (Gen. 12:16; 13:2). Even after Pharaoh was stricken with a sudden illness, as soon as Sarah entered his palace, and he was constrained to inquire of his soothsayers the reason for his affliction, he was restrained from exacting vengeance on Abraham for his deception. Perhaps Pharaoh understood the constraint that his visitor was under because of the likelihood of his being murdered for the sake of his wife. Pharaoh was also very uncomfortable about being involved in the sin of adultery—which was sternly forbidden even by the Egyptian religion (cf. *Book of the Dead,* chap. 125, sec. B19, in Pritchard, ANET, p. 35, where the deceased has to aver that he has never committed adultery). Pharaoh was awed by the power of Abraham's God, who could smite him so quickly that he could not take Sarah to his bed before he fell deathly sick. For these reasons he allowed Abraham to leave Egypt with all the handsome dowry he had bestowed on him as Sarah's guardian.

It seems quite clear that this account of Abraham's failure is an honest inclusion of his lack of faith as manifested by this entire episode. If he had not believed that Yahweh was able to protect him with honor and integrity if he went down to Egypt, then he should never have gone there at all. As it was, he brought dishonor on himself and the cause he stood for, discrediting himself before the moral standards of Egypt itself. As for his enrichment through Pharaoh's generosity, there was a very definite sense in which the king was under obligation to pay amends for the wicked constraint that his corrupt society put on strangers who visited his land. When he found out the truth, he had to admit that Abraham had acted logically when he lied himself out of peril. Therefore it hardly follows that God was responsible for Abraham's increase in wealth; it was Pharaoh's own doing, and he did not feel justified in demanding it back, even after he found out the truth. Abraham retained his added possessions as he returned to Canaan, the land God had promised to him. But it may well be that the subsequent years of agonizing delay (twenty or more until he was one hundred years old) were due in part to his failure and lack of faith in God's protecting power, both in Egypt and (later on) in Gerar.

Genesis 20 tells us how readily Abraham fell into the same subterfuge in Gerar, when he once again feared for his safety on account of his wife. As he later explained to Abimelech of Gerar, "I thought, surely there is no fear of God in this place; and they will kill me because of my wife" (v.11, NASB). He then went on to explain that in point of fact Sarah was his half sister (v.12), even though she lived with him as his wife. But here again Abraham showed a lack of confidence in God's power to preserve him from mortal danger and failed to uphold God's honor before the eyes of the unbelieving world. Even though he was given a thousand shekels by way of atonement for Abimelech's having taken Sarah into his palace, Abraham had to leave under a cloud of dishonor. Again we should observe that this account no more exonerates Abraham from his sin than

did the similar adventure in Egypt. He came away from both failures with dishonor and shame, and his influence on the Philistines was as nullified as it had been in the case of the Egyptians.

Can Abraham's defeat of the Mesopotamian kings in Genesis 14 be historically trustworthy?

While it is true that direct archaeological confirmation of this exciting episode in Abraham's career has not yet come to light, there are no valid scientific grounds for rejecting the account in Genesis 14 as unhistorical. Apart from the documents from twentieth-century B.C. Ur, there is no extensive source of information regarding this period apart from Genesis itself—at least so far as Mesopotamia is concerned. The name of Chedorlaomer, king of Elam, contains familiar Elamite components: *kudur* meant "servant," and *Lagamar* was a high goddess in the Elamite pantheon. Kitchen (*Ancient Orient*, p. 44) generally prefers the vocalization Kutir instead of Kudur and gives the references for at least three Elamite royal names of this type. He equates *Tid'al* with a Hittite name, Tudkhaliya, attested from the nineteenth century B.C. As for Arioch, one king of Larsa ("Ellasar") from this era was *Eri-aku* ("Servant of the Moon-god"), whose name in Akkadian was *Arad-Sin* (with the same meaning). The Mari Tablets refer to persons by the name of Ariyuk. The cuneiform original of Amraphel, formerly equated with Hammurabi of Babylon, is not demonstrable for the twentieth century (Hammurabi himself dates from the eighteenth century), but there may possibly be a connection with Amorite names like *Amud-pa-ila,* according to H.B. Huffmon (see Kitchen's footnote on p. 44 for documentation).

All the above information has come to light since the heyday of the Documentary Hypothesis, when learned scholars contemptuously dismissed this whole account as late and totally fictional. But even such notable experts as H. Gunkel and W.F. Albright in our own century have concluded that Genesis 14 rests on authentic backgrounds in the history of the early second millennium B.C. In H.C. Alleman and E.E. Flack's *Old Testament Commentary* (Philadelphia: Fortress, 1954), p. 14, W.F. Albright remarked: "In spite of our failure hitherto to fix the historical horizon of this chapter, we may be certain that its contents are very ancient. There are several words and expressions found nowhere else in the Bible and now known to belong to the second millennium. The names of the towns in Transjordania are also known to be very ancient." It should be added that according to G. Pettinato, the leading epigraphist of the Ebla documents dating from 2400–2250 B.C., mention is made in the Ebla tablets of Sodom (spelled *Si-da-mu*), Gomorrah (spelled in Sumerian cuneiform *I-ma-ar*), and Zoar (*Za-e-ar*). He feels that quite possibly these may be the same cities mentioned in the Abrahamic narrative (cf. "BAR Interviews Pettinato," p. 48).

The authenticity of the background is established with a high degree of probability by the evidence just cited, even from the standpoint of objective scholarship—even apart from the absolute trustworthiness of Scripture, to which all true believers are committed as a matter of faith. But as to the credibility of the episode itself, it must be acknowledged that it was a most exceptional feat of daring on the part of a peaceful nomad like Abraham, to attempt to rout a large invading force of professional soldiers like those of the Mesopotamian invaders. After their brilliant victory over the allied forces of the Sodomite confederacy (14:8–10), the booty-laden conquerors should have made short work of Abraham's

318 henchmen and his meager force of Amorite allies, who could hardly have exceeded 1000 men in all.

In normal daylight conditions, it would have been suicidal for Abraham's forces to attack the Mesopotamian soldiers on any battlefield. But Abraham caught up to them by forced marches and fell on them by night, when they were totally unprepared for combat. Dividing his forces up into several groups (Gen. 14:15), he apparently used a strategy somewhat similar to that of Gideon—who routed an even greater army of Midianites by the strategic use of only 300 men (Judg. 7:19–22). The secret of success, humanly speaking, was the inducement of panic among the heterogenous, polyglott forces of the invaders, who had no way of knowing how many attackers they had to face, and hardly knew which way to flee. But, of course, the real cause of victory was the miraculous power of God, who was pleased to give Abraham complete victory on this occasion—not only that he might rescue his nephew Lot, but also as a token of the ultimate triumph that Abraham's descendants would achieve under the leadership of Joshua 570 years later.

Was Melchizedek a historical person or a mythical figure?

The account in Genesis 14:18–20 sounds like a straightforward historical episode, just as truly as the rest of the chapter. It tells us that there was a priest-king of Salem (that is, Jerusalem, in all probability) named Melchizedek, who felt led to greet Abraham on his way back from the slaughter of the Mesopotamian invaders between Dan and Hobah (v.15) and to furnish him with provisions for his battle-weary fighting men. He also congratulated Abraham warmly for his heroic victory and bestowed a blessing on him in the name of "God Most

High" (*'Ēl 'Elyôn*)—a title never applied in Scripture to anyone else but Yahweh Himself. Obviously Melchizedek was a true believer, who had remained faithful to the worship of the one true God (just like Job and his four advisors in North Arabia; Jethro, Moses' Midianite father-in-law; and Balaam, the prophet of Yahweh from Pethor in the Euphrates Valley). The testimony of Noah and his sons had evidently been maintained in other parts of the Middle East besides Ur and Haran.

There was, however, one striking feature about the way Melchizedek was brought into this narrative: his parents are not mentioned, and there is no statement about his birth or death. The reason for this lack of information is made clear in Hebrews 7:3: "Without father, without mother, without genealogy, having neither beginning of days nor end of life, but made like the Son of God, he abides a priest perpetually" (NASB). The context makes it clear that Melchizedek was brought on to the scene as a type of the Messiah, the Lord Jesus. In order to bring out this typical character of Melchizedek, the biblical record purposely omits all mention of his birth, parentage, or ancestors. This is not to say that he *had* no father (for even the Antitype, Jesus of Nazareth, had the Holy Spirit as His Father—and certainly His mother, Mary, is mentioned in the Gospels) or that he had never been born (for even Jesus was in His human nature born on Christmas Eve). It was simply that his dramatic and sudden appearance was more clearly brought out by presenting him as God's spokesman to Abraham, serving as a type of the future Christ, bestowing the divine blessing on the people of God.

Melchizedek presented himself as a forerunner or type of the great High Priest, Jesus Christ, who would fulfill a priestly office far higher and more efficacious than that of Aaron and the Levites. This was taught back in David's time by Psalm 110:4, addressed to the future Deliverer of Israel: "The LORD has sworn and will not change His mind, 'Thou art a priest forever according to the order of Melchizedek'" (NASB). Hebrews 7:1–2 points out the significant features in Melchizedek as a type of Christ:

1. *Melchi-ṣedeq* actually means "King of Righteousness."
2. He was king of *šālēm*, which comes from the same root as *šālôm,* "peace."
3. He is presented without mention of birth, parentage, or genealogy, as befitted a type of the Son of God, the eternal God, without beginning and without end, who became incarnate in Jesus of Nazareth.
4. As a Priest forever after the "order of Melchizedek" (Ps. 110:4), Christ would carry on a priesthood that would completely supersede the priesthood of Aaron, established under the law of Moses, and which would endure forever because of the imperishable life of the High Priest Himself (Heb. 7:22–24).

Despite the fanciful traditions maintained by some of the rabbis (appearing even as early as the Qumran sect—cf. the Melchizedek Fragment from Cave 11) to the effect that Melchizedek was some kind of angel or supernatural being, the data of Scripture itself points clearly to the historicity of this man as a king of Jerusalem back in the days of Abraham. The description of Melchizedek in Hebrews 7:3 as *apatōr, amētōr, agenealogētos* ("without father, without mother, without genealogy") cannot be intended to mean that Melchizedek never had any parents or any ancestral line, for Melchizedek was a type of Jesus Christ, of whom none of the three adjectives was literally true. Rather, this verse simply means that none of those items of information was included in the Genesis 14 account and that they were purposely omitted in order to lay the stress on the divine nature and imperishability of the Messiah, the Antitype.

Why does the Bible use unscientific terms like "the going down of the sun" and "the four corners of the earth"?

Evidences of prescientific inaccuracy have been found by some critics of biblical authority in such expressions as Genesis 15:17: "When the sun went down," and Genesis 19:23: "The sun was risen upon the earth." If that charge is just, then it equally applies to our century, for we still—even the scientists among us—employ the words "sunrise" and "sunset" in our daily speech, even though we are well aware that it is really the earth that rotates rather than the sun that revolves. This is a perfectly acceptable type of phenomenal terminology, employed by all languages at all periods of their history. In fact the words for "east" and "west" in most of the Semitic languages are literally "place of rising" and "place of setting." This type of argument is really quite puerile and betrays an amazing naiveté on the part of the critic who raises it.

The same is true of the modern myth that the Bible teaches that the earth is a rectangle rather than a globe because it employs the expression "four corners of the earth" (e.g., Isa. 11:12). The word for "corners" is $k^e n\bar{a}p\hat{o}t$, which means "wings," i.e., wing-tips, such as one uses on compasses (even today!) to indicate the four directions: north, south, east, west. But as for the shape of the earth, Job 22:14, Proverbs 8:27, and Isaiah 40:22 all speak of the earth as a $\hbar\bar{u}g$ ("circle," "disk," or possibly even "sphere"). No one yet has come up with literal corners on a circle, not an ancient Hebrew—or a modern scientist!

Why did God command circumcision in Genesis 17?

Genesis 17 does not furnish any clear rationale for the establishment of this rite as mandatory for the family and descendants of Abraham. God simply says, "You shall be circumcised . . . and it shall be a sign of the covenant between Me and you" (v.11). Any of Abraham's people who refuse or willfully neglect circumcision are to be cut off from the covenant of grace altogether (v.14). Consequently circumcision mattered a great deal to Yahweh, so far as the Hebrew nation was concerned. Romans 4:9-10 explains that salvation was not dependent on circumcision but rather on the grace of God mediated to the guilty sinner through his acceptance and faith in the promises of God. God's righteousness was reckoned to Abraham *before* he was circumcised (cf. Gen. 15:6; 17:23-24). But then the apostle goes on to explain the purposes of circumcision in Romans 4:11: "He received the *sign* of circumcision, a *seal* of the righteousness of the faith which he had while uncircumcised, that he might be the father of all who believe without being circumcised, that righteousness might be reckoned to them" (NASB).

The rite of circumcision (i.e., the surgical removal of the prepuce) was intended as a sign and a seal of the covenant relationship between God and the believer. Even as a wedding ring is a sign and seal of the total and exclusive commitment of the bride and the groom to each other so long as they both shall live, so the sacramental removal of this portion of the male organ was a blood-sealed testimonial that the believer had turned his life over to the Lord, with the commitment to live for Him and in dependence on His grace for the rest of his earthly life. As a seal the act of circumcision amounted to a stamp of ownership on the Old Testament; it testified that he belonged not to the world, Satan, or self, but to the Lord Yahweh who had provided for his redemption.

Further explanation of the function of circumcision is found in Colossians 2:11–13: "And in Him you were also circumcised with a circumcision made without hands, in the removal of the body of the flesh by the circumcision of Christ; having been buried with Him in baptism, in which you were also raised up with Him through faith in the working of God, who raised Him from the dead. And when you were dead in your transgressions and the uncircumcision of your flesh, He made you alive together with Him, having forgiven us all our transgressions" (NASB). Three important insights concerning circumcision are included in these verses.

1. Circumcision involved the symbolic removal of "the body of the flesh" as an instrument of unholiness; apart from circumcision, the body of the sinner remained in a state of "uncircumcision of his flesh."
2. Circumcision entailed a commitment to holiness. Moses urged his congregation in Deuteronomy 10:16 (NIV): "Circumcise your hearts, therefore, and do not be stiff-necked any longer." This indicates that circumcision involved a commitment of heart to be holy unto the Lord and obedient to His word. (The opposite idea was stiffneckedness or stubborn willfulness on the part of the professing believer.) Leviticus 26:41 speaks of a future generation of Israelites taken off into captivity and promises them forgiveness and restoration to their land "if their uncircumcised heart becomes humbled so that they then make amends for their iniquity" (NASB). Shortly before the Babylonian captivity, the prophet Jeremiah (4:4) exhorted

his countrymen—all of whom had doubtless been circumcised physically as infants—"Circumcise yourselves to the LORD and remove the foreskins of your heart, men of Judah and inhabitants of Jerusalem, lest my wrath go out like fire . . . because of the evil of your deeds. (NASB). Circumcision, then, involved a commitment to a holy life, a life of faith in God and of obedience to His commands.

3. Circumcision represented to the Old Testament believer what baptism represents to the New Testament believer: an acceptance or adoption into the family of the redeemed. The benefits of Christ's future atonement on Calvary were by God's grace imparted to the circumcised believer prior to the Cross, even as the merit of Christ's atonement and the saving benefits of His resurrection victory are applied to the New Testament believer. In both dispensations the sacramental sign and seal was imposed on the believer (and also on the infant children of believers for whom the covenant promises were claimed by faith). The same God and Father of our Lord Jesus Christ commanded circumcision for the Old Testament believer and water baptism for the believer under the new covenant—which baptism constitutes spiritual circumcision, according to v.11.

Were there Philistines in Palestine by Abraham's time?

Genesis 20 relates Abraham's sojourn in Gerar, where he resorted to a lie about Sarah's true relationship to him to safeguard himself against assasination, should the truth about their marital status be known. Chapter 21 records the episode about Abraham's securing property rights to the well of Beersheba; and then it is said, "So they made a covenant at Beersheba; and Abimelech and Phicol ... returned to the land of the Philistines" (v.32). In Genesis 26:1 we are told that Isaac "went to Gerar, to Abimelech king of the Philistines." (We may safely assume that since there was an interval of over sixty years between chaps. 21 and 26 [cf. 25:26], the Abimelech mentioned in 26:1 was a son or grandson of the older Abimelech and was named after him, a frequent custom among the Egyptian and Phoenician dynasties.)

These references to Philistines before 2050 B.C. (in the case of Abraham) have been rejected as impossible by many authorities. The *Encyclopaedia Britannica* (14th ed., s.v. "Philistia") states categorically: "In Gen. 21:32,34 and Ex. 13:17; 15:14; 23:31 the references to Philistia and the Philistines are anachronistic." The ground for this assertion is found in the circumstance that up until now, at least, the earliest reference to Philistines in Egyptian records is found in the record of Ramses III concerning his victory over the "Sea Peoples" in a naval engagement fought in the Nile River in the 1190s B.C. It is supposed that after the *P-r-s-t* (as Egyptian spelled their name) and their allies were thus repulsed by the doughty Pharaoh, they retreated to the southern coastal region of Palestine and settled there as a military colony on a permanent basis. But to conclude from the mere fact that the earliest extant reference to the Philistines in Egyptian records dates from the 1190s constitutes any objective proof that there were no Philistine immigrants from Crete there at any time previously is an irresponsible violation of logic.

The Hebrew Scriptures constitute the most trustworthy of all archaeological documents (since they are invested with a divine trustworthiness from beginning to end); and they state very clearly that Philistines lived in Philistia as early as the twenty-first century B.C.

They also affirm that the Philistine fortresses that guarded the northern route from Egypt to Palestine were so formidable in the days of Moses (the 1440s B.C.) that a circuitous southern route remained the safest for the Israelites to use in their journey toward the Promised Land (Exod. 13:17). Obviously this record composed by Moses was centuries earlier than that of Ramses III, and there is no reason to assume that the earlier a record is the less trustworthy it must be. (Until recent times a similar argument from silence was used by some critics to dismiss the references in Gen. 18–19 to Sodom and Gomorrah as purely legendary and unhistorical. But now that the recently discovered Ebla tablets, dating from the twenty-fourth century B.C., contain references to both cities' maintaining commercial relations with Ebla, this critical contention is exposed as absurd. See G. Pettinato ["BAR Interviews Pettinato," p. 48], for Eblite references to *Si-da-mu* and *I-ma-ar*.) Once again the argument from silence is proven to be fallacious. The five main cities of the Philistines, or at least those that have been excavated, uniformly show occupation extending back to Hyksos times and before. The earliest level uncovered at Ashdod is certainly seventeenth century B.C. (cf. H.F. Vos, *Archaeology in Bible Lands* [Chicago: Moody, 1977], p. 146). Inscribed seals found at Gaza bear the names of Twelfth Dynasty Egyptian kings like Amenemhat III (ibid., p. 167). Hence there can be no doubt that this area was occupied by strong kingdoms back in the patriarchal age. To be sure, their population may have been pre-Philistine, but there is absolutely no proof that such was the case.

The southern coast of Palestine quite evidently became a favored region for trade and even for permanent settlement, so far as the Cretan population was concerned. The Philistines are referred to in Scripture as belonging to various groups, such as the Kaphtorim, the Cherethites, and the Pelethites. The commercial activity of Minoan Crete is known to have been most extensive; and its mariners must have discovered even before Abraham's time that the Philistine shore was blessed with an equable climate, rich soil, and a good rainfall for raising grain. They apparently migrated there in successive waves, more or less as the Danes kept migrating to the east coast of England over a period of several centuries until "Danelaw" was enlarged to cover all the region from the Scottish border to London itself. Migrations by the populations of a homeland across the sea are a frequent phenomenon throughout world history; so it surely should occasion no surprise that the Cretan emigrants continued their settlement activity over a period of several centuries, from before the time of Abraham until the unsuccessful naval expedition against Egypt in the early twelfth century. Therefore we conclude that there is no truly scientific evidence for classing the Philistine references in the Pentateuch as unhistorical or anachronistic.

How could God condemn human sacrifice in Leviticus 18 and 20 and yet command it in Genesis 22, or at least accept it in Judges 11?

It is a mistake to interpret Genesis 22:2 as a command by God for Abraham to sacrifice his son Isaac on the altar. On the contrary, God actually (through His angel, at least) restrained Abraham's hand just as he was about to plunge the knife into his son's body, saying, "Do not stretch out your hand against the lad, and do nothing to him; for now I know that you fear God, since you have not withheld your son, your only son, from Me" (v.12, NASB). While it is true that the Lord instructed Abraham previously to present Isaac as a burnt offering (*'ōlāh*), and Abra-

ham himself undoubtedly understood it as a command to kill his son on the altar, the point at issue was whether the doting father was willing to surrender even his only son (begotten by Sarah) to the Lord as a proof of his complete surrender. But v.12 is conclusive proof that Yahweh had no intention that Abraham should actually go through with this human sacrifice. It was simply a test of his faith.

As for the episode of Jephthah's daughter in Judges 11, see the article that deals with that passage. There is good reason to believe that in her case also, as in Isaac's (in both instances the term *'ōlāh* is used; cf. Judg. 11:31), the presentation did not eventuate in the death of the human "burnt offering." Rather, she was devoted to the service of the Lord as a virgin attendant in tabernacle worship for the rest of her life.

Leviticus 18:21 defines infant sacrifice as a profanation of the name of Yahweh, the God of Israel. Leviticus 20:2 prescribes the death penalty for any parent who does so—particularly in the worship of Molech, which especially featured infant sacrifice. It is logically indefensible to assume that God would expect or condone infant sacrifice on the part of Abraham or Jephthah, or any other of His servants, after such a stern prohibition of it in the Mosaic Law.

Is there archaeological evidence for Hittites living in southern Palestine in patriarchal times?

Genesis 23 states that "the sons of Heth" were in control of Hebron back in Abraham's time. Five or six centuries later the twelve spies reported back to Moses and the Hebrew host (Num. 13:29) that there were Hittite settlements in the hill country of Canaan. But since the main center of Hittite power was in eastern Asia Minor and their capital was Hattusas (Boghazkoy), and since their first rise to prominence in the Near East came in the reign of Mursilis I (1620–1590 B.C.), who sacked the great metropolis of Babylon around 1600, many modern scholars have questioned the historicity of Hittites in Palestine as early as 2050, when Sarah was buried in the cave of Machpelah. And yet archaeological evidence also indicates that the Hittites occupied or brought into vassalage many of the kingdoms of Syria; and in the days of Ramses II of Egypt there was a major showdown with Muwatallis (1306–1282) of the Hittite New Kingdom, and a remarkable nonaggression pact was made between the two superpowers, the text of which has been preserved both in Egyptian and in Hittite. The treaty line was drawn in such a way as to give northern Syria to the Hittites and southern Syria (plus all Palestine) to the Egyptian sphere of influence (cf. G. Steindorff and K.C. Seele, *When Egypt Ruled the East* [Chicago: University of Chicago, 1942], p. 251).

More recent archaeological discoveries have indicated further southward penetration than this line and an earlier stage of Hittite activity than that of the Old Kingdom and New Kingdom empires. Cuneiform mercantile tablets have been recovered from Kültepe (ancient Kanesh) in Cappadocia, left by early Assyrian merchants between 1950 and 1850 B.C. (Vos, *Archaeology*, p. 314). But even before the arrival of the Indo-European-Anatolian immigrants (the Nesili-speakers), there was an earlier race of Hattians of non-Indo European background. These were subdued by invaders of 2300–2000 B.C., who subsequently adopted the name Hatti for themselves, despite the linguistic and cultural differences between them and their predecessors.

O.R. Gurney, an eminent Hittite specialist, suggested that the original Hattians may have been much more widespread than in Asia Minor alone, and that they may even have set up colonies in regions as far south as Palestine (Tenney, *Zondervan Pictorial Encyclopedia*, 3:170). (Note that "Hatti" and "Hitti" would be written in the same consonants back in the B.C. era, and the vowels were supplied only by oral tradition.) In 1936 E. Forrer proposed on the basis of a Hittite text by King Mursilis II (ca. 1330 B.C.) that a Hittite group had migrated into Egyptian territory (i.e., regions of Syria-Palestine controlled by Egypt) earlier in the second millenium (cf. *Encyclopaedia Britannica*, 14th ed., s.v. "Hittites"; Tenney, *Zondervan Pictorial Encyclopedia*, 3:169–170).

Military penetration south of the Tarsus range began in the seventeenth century under Labarnas; Mursilis I succeeded in destroying Aleppo in Syria, and even ravaged Mari and plundered the Hurrians of the upper Euphrates. But the "Hittites" of Genesis may have had little in common with these Indo-European, Nesili-speaking conquerors, but rather may have come from the Hatti who historically preceded them in Asia Minor. Little can be concluded from the names referred to in Genesis 23, for Ephron and Zohar appear to be Semitic, Canaanite names—indicating an easy assimilation of the regional culture by these "Hittite" settlers in Hebron.

The Hittites are referred to later on in Israelite history. In Joshua's invasion they furnished resistance to his troops (Josh. 9:1–2; 11:3), but they were presumably crushed and annihilated by their Hebrew conquerors. Yet by the time of David there were some Hittites, at least, to furnish contingents for David's army. Such was Uriah, the husband of Bathsheba, who was clearly a committed believer and a devoted worshiper of Yahweh (2 Sam. 11:11). Solomon found the Neo-Hittites to be of sufficient political importance to have some of their princesses in his harem (1 Kings 11:1). Later on, in the 840s, Benhadad of Damascus led his troops in precipitous flight from their siege of Samaria because of their fear that "the king of Israel has hired against us the kings of the Hittites" (2 Kings 7:6).

During the earlier part of the first millennium B.C., various kings of northern Syria (whose territories had been part of the Hittite Empire in earlier centuries) bore names like Sapalulme (Suppiluliumas), Mutallu (Muwatallis), Lubarna (Labarnas), and Katuzili (Ḥattusilis). Hence they may have carried on something of the Hittite tradition, even though they had by now attained their independence. Among the "Neo-Hittite" principalities of Syria were Tuwana, Tunna, Hupisna, Shinukhtu, and Ishtunda (Tenney, *Zondervan Pictorial Encyclopedia*, 3:168). These names all appear in the cuneiform records (largely the Assyrian) of the time of the Hebrew divided monarchy.

Was Keturah Abraham's second wife (Gen. 25:1) or merely his concubine (1 Chron. 1:32)?

Genesis 25:1 states that after Sarah's death Abraham took to himself a wife (*'iššāh*) whose name was Keturah (*Qᵉṭûrāh*). Verse 2 gives the names of six sons she bore to him in his old age. Abraham lost Sarah when she was 127, and when he was 137 (Gen. 23:1; cf. 17:17). How soon after Sarah's death Abraham married Keturah, we have no way of knowing; but the six sons she bore him became ancestors of various Arabian tribes, and she is honored to this day by the Arab race as their ancestral mother.

There is really no discrepancy in 1 Chronicles 1:32, even though the term *pîlegeš* is used there rather than *'iššah*. Genesis 25:6 also refers to Keturah by implication as a *pîlegeš* to Abraham; for after v.5 has made it clear that God had confirmed Isaac, Sarah's son, as his principal heir, v.6 records: "But to

the sons of his concubines [the plural *pîlagᵉšîm* presumably includes Hagar as well as Keturah], Abraham gave gifts while he was still living, and sent them away from his son Isaac eastward, to the land of the East" (NASB). Obviously the term *pîlegeš* was used to indicate that although Keturah was the only lawfully wedded wife Abraham had (hence his *'iššāh*) during this twilight period of his life, she had a secondary status in relationship to Sarah, since only Sarah had been chosen by God to be the mother of Isaac, Abraham's only heir under the promise of the covenant. As for *pîlegeš* itself, it was a non-Semitic term of unknown origin, but which seems to have had the basic meaning of "secondary wife" (Ludwig Koehler and Walter Baumgartner, *Lexicon in Veteris Testament Libros* [Leiden: E. J. Brill, 1958], p. 761).

What concept of immortality is implied in "gathered to his people" (Gen. 25:8) and "slept with his fathers" (2 Kings 11:43)? Is there a connection with Jesus' depicting the deceased Lazarus in Abraham's bosom (Luke 16:22)? (D*)

The expression "gathered to his people" clearly implies something more than the mere proximity of corpses in some common tomb-vault or graveyard. Abraham was conceived of as joining his deceased loved ones in some sort of fellowship or personal association. Since Israel's neighbors all believed in the persistence of the soul after its departure from the body (so the Sumerians, Babylonians, Egyptians, and Homeric Greeks), it would be very surprising indeed if the Hebrews alone disbelieved in the conscious existence of the soul after death. Highly significant in this connection is King David's statement about the little son whose death had just been announced to him (2 Sam. 12:23): "I shall go to him, but he shall not return to me." In other words, David knew the infant's life would not return to his body so that he could resume his existence among the living. But David fully expected that he would go to join that little child after he himself passed away.

Again, "go to him" does not imply mere physical nearness to the deceased in their tombs. Asaph, David's contemporary, affirmed in Psalm 73:24 the following: "Thou shalt guide me [O God] with thy counsel, and afterward receive me to glory"—which seems to mean the glorious presence of God in heaven. There is a similar implication in Psalm 49:15: "But God will redeem my soul from the power of Sheol, for He shall receive me." One thinks of Enoch, who after three hundred years of fellowship with the Lord was taken (the same verb *lāqaḥ* is used in both passages) from this life, without leaving his body behind.

The expression "slept with his fathers" (1 Kings 11:43), which occurs quite frequently in connection with royal obituaries, seems to refer to the status of the believer's body as it awaits revivification in the grave—much like the term "fall asleep" is used occasionally in the New Testament of deceased believers. This expression contained within it a happy expectation that the dead body would someday be awakened once more. Isaiah 26:19 states: "Your dead will live; their corpses will rise. You who lie in the dust, awake and shout for joy, for your dew is as the dew of the dawn, and the earth will give birth to the departed spirits" (NASB).

In the light of the story of Lazarus and the rich man (Luke 16:19–31), there can be little doubt that Jesus believed that the souls of both the wicked and the just lived on in the life beyond and that the humble believer like Lazarus went to a place of blessed comfort and rest where Abraham was. Thus our Lord confirmed the trust of the Old Testament saints, who affirmed, "In thy presence is fulness of joy; at thy right hand there are pleasures forevermore" (Ps. 16:11), which follows that great resurrection verse: "For thou wilt not leave my soul in hell; neither wilt thou suffer thine Holy One to see corruption" (v.10).

How many wives did Esau have, and who were they?

Genesis 26:34 tells us that at the age of forty, Esau married two Hittite women—Judith, daughter of Beeri, and Basemath, daughter of Elon. Since Genesis 36 does not mention Judith at all, we can only conclude that she bore Esau no children; whether she was barren or died young is uncertain. Nevertheless, Judith was wife number one.

Wife number two was, as stated above, Basemath. But since Genesis 36 refers to her as Adah, it would seem that she bore that name as well. (Examples of men and women bearing more than one name are quite numerous in the Old Testament, both among Israelites and among Gentiles.) Since Esau later married a daughter of his uncle Ishmael, who was likewise named Basemath (apparently a common name in the Edomite region back in those days; Solomon also gave that name to one of his daughters [1 Kings 4:15]), it became expedient to call the former Basemath by her other name, Adah. She bore him one son, Eliphaz (36:4).

Wife number three was Oholibamah, daughter of Zibeon, a Hivite. We are given no information as to when he married her or under what circumstances. We only know that her father's name was Anah, the son of Zibeon. (Zibeon was therefore her grandfather rather than her father—as one might have gathered from Genesis 26:34. Hebrew has no technical term for grandparents or grandchildren; it simply uses the terms for "father" or "mother" for grandparent and "son" or "daughter" for grandchild.) Presumably Esau married Oholibamah before he married Ishmael's daughter Basemath. By Oholibamah Esau had three sons: Jesuh, Jalam, and Korah—in that order.

Wife number four was Basemath, daughter of Ishmael, who bore him just one son, Reuel (*Reʿûʾēl*, probably pronounced "Raguel"—the same name as that of Jethro, Moses' father-in-law [cf. Exod. 2:18; Num. 10:29]). It should be added that this Basemath also had a second name: Mahalath (cf. Gen. 28:9). But apparently she (or Esau) preferred Basemath (with its fragrant connotation, in the masculine form *bōśem*, of "balsam"), for so she is always referred to in Genesis 36.

This, then, constitutes the full list of Esau's wives and the sons they bore to him. Esau is also referred to in Genesis 36 as "the father of Edom" (vv.9,43), but in this case "father of" is equivalent to "founder of"—just as Jacob was the founder of the nation Israel.

Perhaps it is worth noting that the recurrence of favorite or fashionable names is reflected throughout Genesis 36 as characteristic of that Horite-Hivite culture into which Esau married down in the Edomite region. There are at least five examples of this, including the two wives named Basemath just mentioned.

First is Anah, the son of Zibeon, mentioned above as the father of Oholibamah. The Masoretic text actually reads *baṭ* ("daughter of") both in 36:2 and 36:14. But this appears to be a scribal error for *ben* ("son of"), because all the other parents referred to in these genealogical chains are always male rather than female (perhaps the scribal abbreviation for B-N [*ben*] was so close to B-T [*baṭ*] as to be confusing). It is highly significant that the Samaritan Hebrew text here does read B-N ("son of") rather than B-T

("daughter of"), and the Greek Septuagint (LXX) and Syriac Peshitta do the same. We note also that in v.24 a *son* of Zibeon son of Seir (v.20) was given the name Anah. While it is not uncommon for a nephew to be named after his uncle (which is what Anah son of Zibeon the Hivite would be to him), it is most unusual for a nephew to be named after his *aunt*. Therefore we conclude that the older Anah was indeed male rather than a female.

Second, the name Zibeon, as just noted above, was originally borne by the grandfather of Oholibamah, the wife of Esau. So far as we know, there was no blood relationship between Zibeon the son of Seir the Horite and Zibeon the Hivite, except by a distant in-law relationship, perhaps, through their common connection to Esau through marriage.

Third, the name Oholibamah was borne not only by the daughter of Anah who married Esau but also by a daughter of the younger (nephew) Anah (36:25). These were names that tended to recur in the same family line.

Fourth, the name of Timna was borne by the daughter of Seir who became a concubine to Eliphaz, the son of Esau by Basemath-Adah (36:12,22). It was also the name of a descendant of Esau whose paternity is not given but who is listed as a "chieftain" of Edom in a later generation (36:40). In this case, then, a male descendant was given the same name as a related female of an earlier century. Another remarkable example of this was a later chieftain of Edom named Oholibamah (v.41). This last example is all the more remarkable since it ends with the feminine -*ah*, which is not often to be found in a man's name. (The numerous masculine names ending in -*iah*—Isaiah, Jeremiah, Zechariah, etc.—are not feminine endings at all but a shortened form of Yahweh, the covenant name of God.)

One other pair of names is nearly

identical: Dishon and Dishan (36:21). Names that end in *-ān* in Aramaic, Arabic, or Akkadian generally appear as *-ôn* (by the so-called Canaanite shift, which tended to round off an original long ā as an ô in Hebrew and the other Canaanite dialects). Seir seems to have had a great fondness for this name pattern and hence used it on two different sons of his with a mere difference in the final vowel.

When was Rachel given to Jacob—after Leah's bridal week or after the fourteen-year contract with Laban had been completed? (D*)

From Genesis 29:27 it seems quite clear that Rachel was given to Jacob seven or eight days after his marriage to Leah: "Complete the bridal week of this one," Laban said to Jacob, "and we will give you the other also for the service which you shall serve with me for another seven years (NASB). It is true that the word rendered "bridal week" literally means only "week" (or even "heptad"); yet it is also true that apart from Daniel 9:24–27, it is not demonstrable that this word ever means anything other than a week of days in the Old Testament.

The subsequent narrative strongly suggests (in Gen. 30) that the two sisters were competing with each other simultaneously in the matter of childbearing, and that Leah was carrying off all the honors in this context, until finally, after years of trying, Rachel gave birth to Joseph. Not until after that event is mention made of the final period during which Jacob worked to earn livestock rather than wives (Gen. 30:25–32; 31:38).

How could God bless the conduct of Jacob and the lying of Rachel (Gen. 31)?

The evidence is very slight indeed that God "blessed the lying of Rachel." As a matter of fact, she did not live a very long time after the episode at Gilead but died at childbirth, while being delivered of her second child, Benjamin (Gen. 35:16–19). This could have allowed her only a few years of life after her useless and pointless theft of her father's household idols—which must have ended up with all the other idols carried about by Jacob's household, under the oak tree near Shechem (v.4).

As for the "conduct of Jacob," God continued to bless him, despite his devious and crafty ways, because He saw in him the makings of a true man of faith. It was only God's own providence that enabled Jacob to overcome the devious deceptions practiced on him by Laban, who foisted his eldest daughter on him (probably after making him so drunk that by the time he got to bed he could not tell one woman from another) instead of giving him the girl he really loved. After fourteen years Laban had left his son-in-law penniless, and had entered into an agreement about wages during Jacob's final six or seven years with him—with the hope and expectation of overreaching him and keeping him poor. As Jacob said to Laban, in their confrontation at Gilead: "I served you fourteen years for your two daughters, and six years for your flock, and you changed my wages ten times. If the God of my father . . . had not been for me, surely now you would have sent me away empty-handed" (Gen. 31:41–42, NASB).

Jacob was not simply expressing his own viewpoint. Genesis 31:12 records the statement of God's angel: "I have seen all that Laban has been doing to you" (NASB). It is clear from the following verses that Jacob's use of striped branches to induce controlled breeding among the sheep was prepared by God and made effectual for the purpose in the interests of fairness and justice. It is true that in this case the overreacher, Laban, was himself over-reached through the wise maneuvers of Jacob, who finally learned how to cope with him. Only in this way could Jacob have built up an estate and thus had wealth to transfer to his ancestral home when he and his family could finally get away from Padan Aram and settle at last in Palestine.

Laban's complaint that Jacob acted unfairly by not telling him he was planning to leave, thus denying him a chance to stage a farewell banquet, could hardly have expressed his true intention. He loudly protested that he was kindly disposed toward them all and would have given them a royal sendoff, but there is no evidence whatever that he would have done so. On the contrary, Jacob had good reason to fear him and to keep his intended departure a carefully guarded secret; thus Jacob said to him, "Because I was afraid, for I said, 'Lest you would take your daughters from me by force'" (Gen. 31:31, NASB). There is no reason to doubt that he would have done so, for vv. 1–2 make it clear that Laban had developed considerable suspicion and hostility toward Jacob because of the attrition of his livestock. It was sheer hypocrisy for him to claim that he would have granted them a gracious dismissal.

To sum the matter up, it is true that Jacob never notified his father-in-law about his intended departure; and in that sense Jacob deceived Laban the Syrian, by not telling him that he was fleeing. Nevertheless he told no overt lie, so far as the biblical record goes; and he withheld information concerning his imminent departure only because he was positive that Laban would never let him go voluntarily. He would have been sure to compel him to remain with him even after tensions and hostilities had arisen between Jacob and Laban's sons (Gen. 31:1) and the atmosphere had become too tense for Jacob to remain there in safety and harmony. The withholding of infor-

mation is not quite the same thing as lying. (Jesus certainly committed no sin by choosing to remain silent in front of Herod Antipas in Jerusalem [Luke 23:9]. In that sense He withheld information from Herod, information Herod would have appreciated.) The unusual circumstances dictated to Jacob the wisdom of departure without prior notification; otherwise they never could have gotten away, and God's promise to Jacob in Genesis 28:15 would have failed of fulfillment. Therefore the answer to the question "How could God bless the conduct of Jacob?" is "Because God is just and faithful to His children, even His less-than-perfect children."

Why is Genesis 31:49 referred to as the Mizpah "benediction"? Was it really intended as a blessing; or was it an expression of mistrust between Laban and Jacob, involving an appeal to God to ensure that both parties kept their agreement with each other? (D*)

A careful reading of Genesis 31:22–48 indicates the following background to this remarkable verse: "The LORD watch between me and thee, when we are absent one from another." Laban had caught up to Jacob after he had surreptitiously fled from Padan-aram, and he rebuked Jacob for leaving without giving him a chance even to say goodby to his daughters, Leah and Rachel. Laban then made a thorough but unsuccessful search for his missing teraphim (idols or family gods), which actually had been stolen by Rachel. Jacob, unaware of this theft, then proceeded to rebuke his father-in-law sternly, recalling how many times Laban had tried to cheat him in the years gone by, continually changing the employment contract in his own (Laban's) favor.

The result was a stand-off between the two; so they decided to erect a pile of rocks as a witness to a new compact of mutual nonaggression. Laban gave it the Aramaic name of "Jegar-sahadutha" (rockpile of witness); and Jacob gave it the Hebrew equivalent "Galeed" (Gilead). They also called it "Mizpah" (watchtower), saying, "The LORD watch [a form of the verb *ṣāpāh*, from which the term *miṣpāh* is derived] between me and thee, when we are absent from one another." This served as a testimony that neither Laban nor Jacob would pass beyond this boundary marker with intent to do the other any harm (Gen. 31:52).

Since the two sons of Jacob—Ephraim and Manasseh—were listed with the twelve tribes of Israel, the true number of tribes involved seems to have been thirteen. Why, then, does the Bible continue to speak of them as the Twelve Tribes rather than the Thirteen? Which tribe was left out in this reckoning? (D*)

There were actually only twelve sons of Jacob, not thirteen. But in Genesis 48:22 Jacob granted to Joseph a double portion of his inheritance rather than the single portion that each of Jacob's other eleven sons was to receive. This meant that, in effect, while there would be no tribe of Joseph as such, there would be two Joseph tribes: the tribe of Ephraim and the tribe of Manasseh. In other words, Ephraim was tribe A of Joseph and Manasseh was tribe B of Joseph.

On the other hand, the tribe of Levi was to serve as the priestly tribe and was to care for the spiritual welfare of all the rest of the tribes. Therefore, the tribe of Levi was to receive no tribal territory as such (Levites were distributed in designated cities and towns throughout Canaan after its conquest). This would have meant that there would be only eleven tribal territories rather than twelve, were it not for the fact that there were two Joseph tribes to make up for the subtraction of Levi from the number of landholding

tribes. Yet it was God's purpose that Israel should consist of twelve tribes rather than merely eleven. The double honor granted to Joseph by giving him—through his sons—a double inheritance came to him because of his outstanding services in preserving his whole family from death in time of famine and for supplying them with a haven of refuge in the land of the Nile.

How are the blessings and predictions in Genesis 49 and Deuteronomy 33 to be harmonized with each other?

Genesis 49 was a divine revelation to Jacob near the end of his life (ca. 1860 B.C.). Deuteronomy 33 was composed by Moses 455 years later (ca. 1405). Therefore Jacob's prophecy reflected a longer span of years than that of Moses, so far as the future career of Israel was concerned. Furthermore, Moses' song of blessing contained for the most part prayers for future blessing that expressed his hopeful desires but fell short of the status of actual predictions. These factors should be borne in mind as we compare the two passages in their bearing on each of the Twelve Tribes. For the sake of convenience, we shall follow the order of Genesis 49 in dealing with the various tribes, rather than the somewhat different order in Deuteronomy 33, which is the later oracle.

Reuben

Reuben's tribe is not to enjoy preeminence over the other tribes, despite his status of primogeniture (Gen. 49:4). Moses offers a prayer for his future survival as a tribe, and the hope that his descendants will be numerous enough to stand their ground (Deut. 33:6). As a matter of fact, the tribe of Reuben was one of the first to be overcome; for it was apparently subjugated by Moab in the ninth century, as the Mesha Stone inscription makes clear (ANET, Pritchard, p. 320). Medeba,

Baal-meon, Kiryathaim, and Dibon were all in the tribe of Reuben according to the original apportionment under Joshua.

Simeon

This tribe will, along with Levi, be dispersed or scattered among the other tribes (Gen. 49:5-7). There is no mention of Simeon at all in Deuteronomy 33. Although the population of Simeon was quite substantial (59,300 men at arms) at the time of the Exodus (Num. 1:23), it later proved unable to maintain its strength and numbers after settlement in the semiarid region assigned to it south and southwest of Judah. It therefore was, for all practical purposes, absorbed by Judah as its defender and ally even before the reign of King Saul. And yet its original identity was not completely forgotten, since even in David's time there was a Shephatiah placed by him in charge of the Simeonites (1 Chron. 27:16).

Levi

Jacob included Levi with Simeon in a common prediction of dispersion among the tribes of Israel (Gen. 49:5-7). As it turned out, however, the Levites were scattered throughout all Israel in forty-eight Levitical cities, in order to teach the twelve land-possessing tribes the statutes of the Lord. It was by no means the result of attrition and declining numbers that they were so scattered but rather part of the Lord's plan for the spiritual nourishment of the whole common-wealth. Deuteronomy 33 exalts the holy status of the tribe of Levi as the priestly tribe—an exaltation that Jacob apparently did not foresee—charged with the responsibility of teaching Israel the law of the Lord and of presenting incense and burnt offerings before Him. (There is no contradiction between these two prophecies but only a gracious transmutation of Levi's land-less condition into a matter of high privilege as the leading tribe in the spiritual life of the nation.)

Judah

Genesis 49:8-12 portrays Judah as a lionlike battle champion and as the tribe ordained to royal status as ruler over the whole nation, starting from the time of the first Judean king (namely David) until the coming of Shiloh, the Messiah. Deuteronomy 33 contains no predictions concerning Judah's future but only a prayer that the Lord will help him to overcome his adversaries.

Zebulun

Genesis 49:13 foretells the location of this tribe near the shore, affording a convenient passage for the cargoes of the ships unloading at the docks of the Mediterranean coast for transport to the Sea of Galilee and transshipment up to Damascus and beyond. (While Zebulun was located on neither coast, the Valley of Jezreel afforded an excellent highway for imported goods to be conveyed to the most important inland markets. Its northern border would point in the direction of the great commercial cities of Phoenicia, of which Sidon was then the leading emporium. As for Deuteronomy 33:18-19, nothing more definite is said of Zebulun than he will "rejoice" in his "going forth."

Issachar

Genesis 49:14-15 foresees the time when the hardworking, industrious people of this tribe will be subjected to foreign servitude—along with the rest of Israel and Samaria—which took place in 732 B.C., when Tiglath-pileser III annexed this territory to the Assyrian Empire and made it directly subservient to Assyrian rulers (cf. 2 Kings 15:29; Isa. 9:1). Deuteronomy 33:18-

19 looks forward to an earlier and more glorious stage of Issachar's future, when Deborah and Barak—who were natives of this tribe (Judg. 5:15)—would summon Israel's defenders to gather on the mountain (i.e., Mount Tabor [Judg. 4:12]), from which they would charge down against the armies of Jabin and Sisera and put them to flight. Like Zebulun, Issachar would also enjoy the benefits of being located along the major trade route of the Valley of Jezreel, thus dealing with the commerce of the Mediterranean as well as the good fishing of the Sea of Galilee ("the abundance of the seas"). But, of course, this prosperous condition of Issachar prior to the period of the Assyrian invasions had to give way to a new era of servitude, after the capitulation of Samaria to the Assyrians in 732. Ten years later Samaria was captured and consigned to destruction, and Israel was dragged away into permanent exile in the Middle East (2 Kings 17:6).

Dan

Genesis 49:16–18 foretells the career of Samson (although he is not mentioned by name, of course) as one of the best-known "judges" of Israel. (The name "Dan" comes from the root *dîn*, "to judge.") But then it mentions the vicious aggression that Dan—or at least a migrating portion of it—would display, snapping at its victims like a poisonous serpent. This refers to that rather sordid episode related in Judges 18, where a Danite expeditionary force of six hundred robbed Micah the Ephraimite of his silver idol and his hired priest and took them off with them northward. They then fell on the city of Laish, without provocation or warning of any sort, and butchered all its inhabitants before taking over the city for their own, renaming it Dan. As for Deuteronomy 33:22, it simply describes Dan as a leaping lion—which certainly has been illustrated above.

Gad

Genesis 49:19 indicates that Gad in its Transjordanian location will be subject to invasions and raids but will summon up the strength to put the aggressors to flight. Deuteronomy 33 enlarges on the theme of successful resistance and represents the Gadite warriors as bold like lions and as the instruments of God's justice inflicted on the guilty. The principal fulfillment in view here must have been that freebooter turned patriot named Jephthah. It was he who later turned back the Ammonite invaders and meted out severe punishment to those Ephraimite warriors that had sent no help during the Ammonite invasion. These Ephraimites felt so aggrieved that they had not been especially summoned to help out in routing the Ammonites that they made an issue of it before Jephthah, and they ended up being slaughtered by the fords of the Jordan (Judg. 12:4–6).

Asher

Genesis 49:20 speaks only of the future prosperity of this northern tribe; they will enjoy rich food, even "royal dainties." Deuteronomy 33:24–25 enlarges on this theme of prosperity, speaking of their abundance of oil and their fine gate-bars fashioned of bronze and iron (which were the most expensive kind). They will, in fact, surpass all the other tribes in their material plenty; and they will enjoy freedom from the devastation of war. (It was not until the debacle of 732 that Asher was invaded and taken over by the Assyrian Empire.)

Naphtali

Genesis 49:21 states that Naphtali will be like a doe let loose and will enjoy the eloquence of words. In other words, this tribe will enjoy a relatively free and easy life and cultivate the arts of literature and public speech.

Deuteronomy 33:23 lays more emphasis on the enrichment from fishing and commerce—largely that which came from the Sea of Galilee and the inland route from Phoenicia in the north. They will extend their influence to the regions south of them (i.e., Zebulun, Issachar, and Manasseh). Presumably this involved happy trade relationships with their kinsmen to the south.

Joseph

It is interesting that in both passages the tribes of Ephraim and Manasseh (which itself was subdivided into two half-tribes) should have been treated as a single tribe, both in the predictions of Jacob and in the Song of Moses. Since the division into three separate tribal holdings took place after the conquest under Joshua, it may reasonably be concluded that neither chapter was composed after the tribal division had taken place (as liberal scholars unthinkingly assume). It should be remembered, however, that this establishment of Joseph's two sons as tribal progenitors was occasioned by the blessing of Jacob himself, as recorded in Genesis 48. It was his decision to give Joseph the double portion of his inheritance, rather than to Reuben his firstborn (Gen. 48:13–22).

Genesis 49:22–26 predicts the future prosperity and fruitfulness of the Joseph tribes, as they successfully cope with their Canaanite enemies in securing their alloted portions in the forested uplands of the center of Palestine. The "archers" who shoot at Joseph may refer to the chariot troops of the coastal Canaanites as well as those who were headquartered in Beth-shean (Josh. 17:15–18). Judges 1:22–25 tells of the successful attack by the Ephraimites against Bethel (whose walls were doubtless manned by many an archer). Another possibility, favored by some writers, is that the "archers" were invading Egyptian troops who kept control of the most important trade routes and strategic fortress cities at various times during the period of the Judges, particularly during the reigns of Seti I (1320–1300) and Rameses the Great (1299–1234). In the earlier Tell el-Amarna correspondence (1400–1370), the Canaanite kings continually plead for the Pharaoh to send them "archers" (*pi-da-ti*) from his regular army in order to bolster their defenses against the invading Habiru (or SA.GAZ) (cf. Pritchard, ANET, p. 488). Whatever explanation we adopt for these archers, they were to be successfully dealt with by the men of Ephraim through the help of the Lord. The Ephraimites would also be blessed with a good rainfall and abundant crops ("blessings of the deep that lies beneath" [v.25]). Ephraim is to be a tribe notably distinguished above his brethren, a promise fulfilled by the splendid leadership of Joshua the son of Nun, an Ephraimite. (This verse by itself demonstrates the impossibility of dating Gen. 49 at any time later than the reign of Solomon, since no Judean author would have included such high praise of the arch rival of Judah in any such fashion as this.)

As for Deuteronomy 33:13–17, Moses predicts that Joseph's land will be blessed by the Lord with abundant rain and crops from a fertile soil. The surrounding hills will pour down their streams on the plowed fields to give them good harvests. By the special favor of the God who spoke to Moses from the burning bush, the warriors of Ephraim and Manasseh will be enabled to repel and subdue their foes. Thus we see an essential agreement between the two chapters in regard to the future of these two tribes.

Benjamin

Genesis 49:27 refers briefly to the fierceness and courage of this small tribe: it is like a ravenous wolf who devours the prey and divides the spoil. (Perhaps this foretells the prowess of Benjamin in holding off the troops of the other eleven tribes during the Benjamite War [Judg. 20], until finally they themselves were ambushed near Gibeah and almost completely annihilated, except for the six hundred who escaped.) But in Deuteronomy 33:12 Moses offers a prayer on Benjamin's behalf that God may show His love to him by protecting him night and day. Yet it should be understood that there is a substantial difference between a prediction and a prayer. Moses prayed for Benjamin's security and protection; but that prayer provided no guarantee that God's loving concern and care would extend into the indefinite future, if Benjamin should ever forsake its covenant obligations toward the Lord and fall into gross sin.

As long as they were obedient and faithful, the Benjamites certainly did enjoy God's deliverance—as in the example of Ehud, the patriot who managed to kill Eglon, king of Moab, by resorting to a ruse. Ehud was enabled to escape the Moabite guards and flee to safety in the hill country of Ephraim, where he gathered about him an army of courageous patriots and smashed the Moabite troops to regain Israel's independence (Judg. 3:15–30). But in later years, when the infamous atrocity was committed in Gibeah and the rest of the tribe of Benjamin rallied to protect the degenerate sodomites who had raped the Levite's concubine to death, the protecting favor of God was necessarily withdrawn. The rest of the tribes of Israel finally succeeded in avenging the dastardly crime, even though it meant wiping out almost the entire tribe of Benjamin (Judg. 20), as mentioned above.

Yet favor of the Lord was restored to the Benjamites after their wickedness had been thoroughly dealt with. Their six hundred survivors returned to fellowship with Israel and Israel's God;

and they so increased in numbers that by Saul's time (the eleventh century B.C.) they were once again a force to be reckoned with. It was from this smallest, severely battered tribe that God chose out the first king of the United Monarchy of Israel: Saul the son of Kish (1 Sam. 9–10). Thus it was that the Lord answered Moses' prayer to the extent that He was able to do so without compromising His own integrity and holiness.

We conclude this comparative study with the observation that no real discrepancies or contradictions can be found between the prophecy of Jacob in Genesis 49 and the prayer of Moses in Deuteronomy 33.

Is Genesis 49:10 really a prediction of Christ? What is the real meaning of Shiloh?

Genesis 49:10 appears in a stanza of Jacob's prophecies concerning his twelve sons; Judah is dealt with in vv. 8–12. That tribe is presented in a particularly warlike aspect, with such traits as "Your hand shall be on the neck of your enemies" (v.8, NASB) and "Judah is a lion's whelp.... as a lion, who dares rouse him up?" (v.9, NASB). Verse 10 emphasizes the coming role of Judah as the royal leader over all the tribes of Israel, and possibly over foreign nations as well. It reads as follows: "The scepter shall not depart from Judah, nor the ruler's staff from between his feet, until Shiloh comes, and to him shall be the obedience of the peoples ['ammím]" (NASB). The greatest stress is laid on the military prowess and kingly status of this royal tribe, and there is a clear affirmation that this kingly status is to continue until the appearance of a key figure referred to as "Shiloh." The scepter and lawgiver's ($m^e\hbox{-}\bar h\bar o q\bar e q$) staff will be wielded by this tribe until the arrival of Shiloh himself.

But the question arises, Who or what

is Shiloh? The Aramaic Targum renders v.10 as follows: "Until the Messiah comes, to whom the kingdom belongs." This seems to identify Shiloh as a title of the Messiah, but it also points to an interpretation of this name that involves the phrase "who to him" or "to whom." The Septuagint, dating from the third century B.C., renders the clause "until there come the things laid up [apokeimena] for him." This suggests that šîlōh was interpreted with a different vowel pointing, as šellô ("one to whom"). The second-century A.D. Greek translations of Aquila and Symmachus construe it more succinctly as "[the one] for whom it has been stored up," or: reserved, using the same Greek verb but in the form apokeitai. Jerome's Latin Vulgate derived it (incorrectly) from the verb šālaḥ ("to send") and translated it as "the one who is to be sent" (qui mittendus est).

It is fair to say, however, that the preponderance of modern authorities, both conservative and nonconservative, tend to prefer the explanation "the one to whom [it belongs]" and make the coming ruler the antecedent, understanding the "scepter" as the object that belongs to him. In other words, they render the clause thus: "The scepter shall not depart from Judah . . . until He comes to whom it belongs; and to Him shall be the obedience of the peoples." But whether the word is understood to be a mystical name for the Messiah (somewhat like the name Jeshurun for the nation Israel [Deut. 32:15]), or

whether it is a relative phrase "who to him" (šellô), it clearly refers to the Messiah, and possibly also to David, the ancestral type of Christ the King. (But to relate this promise to David raises the formidable difficulty that the scepter did not really depart from Judah when David came; on the contrary, it only began to be wielded by Judah when he assumed the throne and crown of the kingdom of Israel.)

We should not close this discussion without mentioning a most intriguing parallel passage in Ezekiel 21:27 (32 Heb.) that appears to be a reflection of Genesis 49:10: "A ruin, a ruin, a ruin, I shall make it [i.e., Jerusalem, about to be attacked by Nebuchadnessar in 588 B.C.]. This also will be no more [or else 'will not happen' (lō' hāyāh)], until He comes whose right it is [lit., "who to him the judgment" (ʾašer lō hammišpāṭ)]; and I shall give it to Him" (NASB). The similarity in wording can scarcely be an accident. ʾašer lō is the normal prose equivalent of šellô ("who to him"). In Ezekiel's statement we find hammišpāṭ ("the right of judgment"), replacing the kindred concept of "scepter" (šēbeṭ) in Genesis 49:10. If, therefore, Ezekiel 21:27 is intended to build on the foundation of Genesis 49:10 and reveal its ultimate application to the Messiah—as it certainly seems to do in Ezekiel—who will be descended from the royal house of Judah, then we are on firm ground in understanding Genesis 49:10 as intended by God to refer to His divine Son, the messianic descendant of David.

Exodus

How could God bless Shiphrah and Puah for lying to Pharaoh?

Exodus 1:16 contains the instructions of the Egyptian king to the Hebrew midwives concerning the murder of Hebrew male babies at the time of delivery: "When you are helping the Hebrew women to give birth ... if it is a son, then you shall put him to death; but if it is a daughter, then she shall live" (NASB). This, then, was a command for them to commit infanticide. The narrative goes on to say that in order to avoid perpetrating this heinous act, they resorted to a strategy of delay. That is to say, they managed to slow up their response to the call from a woman in labor to such an extent that the baby was already born and safely tucked away in its crib by the time they finally arrived at the house.

As the midwives explained to Pharaoh, "The Hebrew women ... are vigorous, and they give birth before the midwife can get to them" (Exod. 1:19, NASB). From the standpoint of the midwives' arriving too late, this was probably true. They simply did not divulge the fact that their tardy arrival was deliberately planned. They might easily have been caught by the Egyptian police if they had been put under twenty-four-hour surveillance; so they ran a real risk of detection, trial, and execution. But when faced with the choice between penetrating systematic infanticide against their own people

and misleading the king by a half-truth in order to avert this calamity, they rightly chose the lesser ill in order to avoid the greater. God did not honor and bless these two brave women for their withholding part of the truth; rather, he blessed them for their willingness to incur personal danger in order to save the lives of innocent babies.

In this connection the question is sometimes raised as to how just two midwives could have served a community of two million people during a period of high birthrate. Of course they could not have served so many Hebrew mothers without numerous assistants. But it was normal Egyptian practice to set up a bureaucratic chain of command in connection with almost every government agency or activity. Each department had its own overseer, directly responsible to the head of government, whether on the national level or on the provincial level. In this case the king appointed two seasoned professionals in this field to operate a regular obstetrical service under government supervision. We cannot tell how many assistants Shiphrah and Puah had at their disposal, but they apparently instructed them carefully about the technique of late arrival in order to preserve life. Thus Pharaoh had only the clever overseers to deal with and to interrogate, and they turned out to be more than a match for him. Hence God gave them both the blessing of raising many children of their own, as a reward for their courage in risking their lives to save the babies of others.

How could a good and loving God instruct the Hebrews to plunder the Egyptians (Exod. 3:22)? Was it not dishonorable for them to borrow jewels that they never intended to return?

First of all, there is one important matter of translation to clear up. The KJV translates the first clause as follows: "But every woman shall borrow of her neighbour, and of her that sojourneth in her house, jewels of silver, and jewels of gold, and raiment." The verb translated "borrow" is šā'al, which is the common word for "ask, ask for, request, inquire of." (F. Brown, S.R. Driver, and C.A. Briggs, *Hebrew and English Lexicon of the Old Testament* [Oxford: Clarendon, 1968], p. 981, cite three instances for the meaning "borrow": Exodus 22:14 [13 Heb.], 2 Kings 4:3, and 6:5. In these passages the context makes it clear that the items requested were intended for temporary use by the person who took them into custody, with the understanding that they were later to be returned to the owners.) In the case of Exodus 3:22; 11:2; 12:35 (where šā'al is also used), however, it is not at all clear that there was any pretext of mere temporary use. Therefore the normal meaning of "ask for" should be assigned to 3:22, as NASB renders it: "But every woman shall ask of her neighbor ... articles of silver and articles of gold, etc." They simply requested these items as gifts as they prepared to depart from Egypt, never to return. The Egyptian inhabitants were well aware of this intention and would have been under no illusions about getting their jewelry back again.

But why were the Egyptians so willing to donate such treasures to their erstwhile slaves? In the context it is quite apparent that they were desperately afraid that the disaster of the tenth plague might be repeated once more, and that they might lose still more of their children and their livestock. As Exodus 12:33 tells us, "The Egyptians urged the people [i.e., the Hebrew people], to send them out of the land in haste, for they said, 'We shall all be dead'" (NASB). The narrative then continues (vv.35–36): "Now the sons of Israel had done according to the word of Moses, for they had requested from the Egyptians articles of silver and articles of gold, and clothing; and the LORD had given the people favor in the sight of the Egyptians, so that they let them have their request. Thus they plundered the Egyptians" (NASB).

The verb for "plundered" in verse 36 is *wayyᵉnaṣṣᵉlû*, coming from *nāṣal*, which in the piel stem means "strip off, spoil, deliver someone from [danger]." It is not the usual term for plundering the enemy after he has been killed on the battlefield; that would be *šālal*. But *niṣṣēl* clearly is used here in a figurative sense, for the narrative plainly states that the Israelites simply made an oral request for a parting gift; and they received what they asked for. To be sure, there was a compelling factor of fear that moved the Egyptians to be so generous in parting with their treasures; so there was a certain sense in which they were despoiled by the departing Hebrews. They trembled with dread at the awesome power of Israel's God and the stroke of His destroying angel who had wrought such havoc on the night of the Passover.

As for the moral question whether such an act of spoliation (if we may describe a willing surrender of property by such a term) was ethically justifiable, or whether it was compatible with the goodness and love of God, we must bear in mind that for generations, even centuries, the Israelite population in Egypt had been subject to oppressive and brutal enslavement. Systematic infanticide was practiced toward their male offspring; they had been compelled to work for nothing in order to build Pharaoh's treasure cities and his other public works. There was a sense in which these jewels of silver, gold, and gems were only their just due; and they furnished only a partial compensation for all the anguish and toil to which they had been subjected. From this standpoint there can be no legitimate moral question raised concerning this whole transaction.

In Exodus 4:24 whom did the Lord meet? Why did He seek to kill him? What is the connection of the details of vv.25–26 to the subject of v.24? (D*)

In Exodus 4:24 the antecedent of "him" is "Moses." Why did God inflict him with such a near-fatal illness? In all probability it was because of Moses' neglect of the covenant sign of circumcision in the case of his own son, Gershom. We are driven to this conclusion by the fact that Moses could not recover and escape the death that threatened him until Zipporah had performed this rite on their son (v.25). Obviously she was strongly averse to this measure and did it only under compulsion, for she parted company with her husband after reproaching him as "a bridegroom of blood." It may have been that the Midianite practice was to reserve circumcision for lads who had just attained puberty rather than performing it on young and tender infants. But the Abrahamic tradition was to perform it when the child was eight days old (Gen. 17:12). Failure to receive circumcision meant that the boy would be "cut off from his people."

Now since Moses had been appointed for a responsible role of leadership, he was duty bound to serve as a good example to the people of Israel and to show faithfulness to the covenant obligations inherited from Abraham. The only way Moses could be forced into taking this step—against his wife's wishes—would be to afflict him with a potentially fatal illness. And so this is precisely what God did.

How could the Israelites have sojourned 430 years in Egypt if there were only three generations between Levi and Moses (Exod. 6:16-20)?

In common with almost all the genealogies of this type recorded in the Pentateuch (cf. Num. 26:28-34), the general practice is followed in Exodus 6 of listing a person's family tree by tribe, clan, and family group. As D.N. Freedman points out (in G.E. Wright, ed., *The Bible and the Ancient Near East* [London: Routledge and Kegan Paul, 1961], pp. 206–7), this type of classification was common in ancient Near Eastern practice. In Egyptian royal genealogies we find that several links are omitted between Rameses II in the Nineteenth Dynasty and the kings of the Twenty-first Dynasty in the Berlin genealogy published by Borchardt (in Kitchen, *Ancient Orient*, pp. 54–55).

It is quite obvious that if by Moses' time (according to Num. 3:27-28) the combined total of Amramites, Izharites, Hebronites, and Uzzielites came to 8,600—all of whom were descended from Kohath—the Amram who had perhaps one-fourth of 8,600 "children" (or 2,150) could not have been the immediate parent of Moses and Aaron. They could hardly have had over 2000 brothers in that one family! While Moses' father may in fact have been named Amram, he could not have been the same Amram as produced that many descendants.

Fortunately in 1 Chronicles we have many genealogies that are more complete, and these indicate that there were nine or ten generations between the sons of Jacob and the generation of Moses. For example, (1) 1 Chronicles

7:25 tells us there were ten links between Ephraim and Joshua: Beriah-Rephah-Resheph-Telah-Tahan-Ladan-Ammihud-Elishama-Nun-Joshua. (2) Bezalel, who designed the tabernacle (Exod. 31:2-11), was in the seventh generation from Jacob (cf. 1 Chron. 2:1,4-5,9,18-20). (3) Elishama, mentioned in Numbers 1:10, was in the ninth generation from Jacob (1 Chron. 7:22-27).

Nine or ten generations between Jacob and Moses harmonizes very well with a 430-year sojourn for the Israelites in Egypt (i.e., between 1875 and 1445 B.C.). This would average out to 43 years per generation. (The 215-year theory, espoused by those who follow the Septuagint reading for Exod. 12:40, would yield only 215 years for the sojourn, for an average of 21 years per generation. In the case of Bezalel and Joshua, this is well nigh incredible. So also is the increase of the original 70 or 75 in Jacob's immigrant group to over two million souls by Moses' time.)

Do not Exodus 6:26-27 and 16:33-36 indicate a biographer of Moses other than Moses himself?

Exodus 6:14-27 is a long paragraph giving the names of the first three of the twelve sons of Jacob and their first generations of descendants, who became the heads of the various subtribes through whom genealogical descent was reckoned by the time of the Exodus. But most of the attention is devoted to the priestly tribe of Levi and the line of Aaron and Moses. The survey concludes with the following words: "It was the same Aaron and Moses to whom the LORD said, 'Bring out the sons of Israel from the land of Egypt according to their hosts.' They were the ones who spoke to Pharaoh king of Egypt about bringing out the sons of Israel from Egypt; it was the same Moses and Aaron" (vv.26-27, NASB). These comments certainly

sound like those of a historian rather than the personal memoirs of Moses himself, at least so it is supposed by most Bible critics of a subevangelical or liberal persuasion.

To specialists in the field of comparative literature, however, an author's use of the third person singular when writing of his own deeds is entirely a matter of established literary convention, depending on the genre involved. In some genres, such as the personal autobiography, it was quite customary to refer to one's self in the first person singular. But in the case of a major historical account, it was more usual to refer to all actors on the scene in the third person rather than in the first, even though the author happened to be writing about an action in which he was personally involved.

The numerous historical records concerning the various kings of Egypt and their exploits were normally couched in the third person, except in instances where the words of the Pharaoh are directly quoted. The Greek historian Xenophon, in his *Anabasis,* characteristically refers to himself in the third person; likewise does Julius Caesar in his *Gallic Wars* and his *Civil Wars* as well. Yet no one questions that these were the genuine works of Xenophon and Caesar.

Furthermore, it would have appeared quite strange to the Hebrew reader (as well as to us modern readers) if in this genealogical account the author had suddenly brought himself into it with such wording as this: "These are the heads of the fathers' (households) of the Levites according to their families. It was actually *us*, Moses and Aaron, to whom the LORD said, 'Bring out the sons of Israel from the land of Egypt....' *We* were the ones who spoke to Pharaoh the king of Egypt about bringing out the sons of Israel from Egypt" (Exod. 6:25-26). Nothing could sound more bizarre than this sudden intrusion of first person forms in the midst of an objective account of this sort. Hence a conformity to the usual conventions governing this genre of the historical narrative furnishes no evidence whatever against Mosaic authorship of such verses as these.

As for Exodus 16:33–34, the same principle obtains. "And Moses said to Aaron, 'Take a jar and put an omerful of manna in it.... As the LORD commanded Moses, so Aaron placed it before the Testimony, to be kept" (NASB). Any normal historian, especially one who was not a boastful monarch of Egypt or Mesopotamia, would record actions in which he was personally involved in an objective style of speech just like this. Moses was writing an official record for the benefit of the entire nation; he had no intention of converting this record into a self-exalting personal memoir.

Why did the Egyptian magicians display the power (according to Exod. 8:7) of performing miracles as Moses and Aaron did (cf. also Exod. 7:11,22)? (D*)

Scripture indicates that Satan has power to perform "lying wonders" (2 Thess. 2:9) through his wicked agents for the express purpose of leading mankind astray. Christ warned that "false Christs and false prophets will arise and will show great signs and wonders, so as to mislead, if possible, even the elect" (Matt. 224:24). From Exodus 7 and 8 we learn that Satan displayed this power and employed this stratagem even in the time of Moses. Satan will continue to do so even in the final days of the Great Tribulation (Rev. 13:13), when his agent the False Prophet will perform "great signs, so that he even makes fire come down out of heaven to the earth in the presence of men" (NASB).

Counterfeit miracles, then, are Satan's stock in trade. Yet it should be carefully noted that Satan-empowered miracles are based largely on deception and illusion and generally involve some kind of clever trickery. Pharaoh's magicians showed a skill not much different from that of professional magicians today, who know how to produce rabbits or doves out of their hats. Their staffs that turned into serpents when cast on the ground may have been snakes that they had charmed into rigidity that made them look like staffs until their bodies hit the ground. Their frogs, apparently few in number compared to the overwhelming host that Moses' rod produced, may have been concealed at first like the rabbits in the magician's hat. But when they failed in their attempt to reproduce the stinging gnats that Aaron's rod had brought forth, they had to admit to Pharaoh that their art was merely human (or merely satanic, at least); for this new plague could only be explained as "the finger of God" (Exod. 8:19).

More importantly, the magicians' power was utterly inadequate to cope with the blood and the frogs produced by the Hebrew leaders. Neither were the magicians able to remove them from afflicting the land of Egypt. Hence their clever trickery was completely valueless and impotent before the true miracles performed by God in the ten plagues.

Why did God slay all the firstborn Egyptians when the Egyptian people had no control over Pharaoh's decision not to allow the Israelites to leave his country (Exod. 12:29–30)? (D*)

There is no way for nations to be dealt with other than on a collective basis. The fortunes of the citizens of any country are bound up with the government that guides their national policy, whether that government be a democracy, a party dictatorship, or monarchy. A wise and successful government passes on its benefit to all its

113

citizenry, as when its armed forces defeat an invading host on the battlefield.

A foolish or wicked government, like that of King Ahaz in the days of Isaiah the prophet, brings disaster and distress on all its subjects, regardless of personal merit. So it was with Egypt in Moses' day. The consequences of the decisions made by Pharaoh and his court were binding on all the people. Throughout history, ever since governments were first organized on the tribal level, it has been so.

Thus when Egypt's king decided to break his solemn oath by repeated acts of perjury and to set at defiance the almighty Lord of the universe, there could be no result other than the final, dreadful plague of which Moses had forewarned. By the terms of this judgment every firstborn male throughout Egypt, whether man or beast, was to lose his life, even as all previous nine plagues had affected the entire population of the Nile Valley.

Conceivably a coup d'état might have toppled Pharaoh from his throne in time to avert this approaching catastrophe, but his subjects were content to let him make the fateful decision as their lawful ruler. A loss of life in the family of the king alone—or even in the households of his aristocracy—would scarcely have sufficed to compel Egypt to grant a release of the entire Israelite nation and all its cattle. Nothing short of an all-inclusive calamity visited on the entire people would serve to bring about the deliverance of God's people from the bondage they had suffered in Egypt.

How could the various plagues fail to affect the Israelites as well as the Egyptians if they were imposed on the whole land of Egypt, as Exodus 8:16 and 9:22 say they were?

Neither in the Bible nor in any other literary document are we at liberty to take terms like "all" in an absolute sense if the context clearly indicates a qualifying restriction. In Exodus 9:6, for example, we read, "So the LORD did this thing on the morrow, and *all* the livestock of Egypt died; *but* of the livestock of the sons of Israel, not one died" (NASB). The exception is expressly made for the Hebrews living in Goshen, which was apparently populated only by the Israelite population along with their household servants (some of whom were apparently non-Israelite; cf. 12:38).

No explicit exception is made for the Hebrews in connection with the first three plagues, the plague of blood (7:17–25), the plague of frogs (8:1–14), and the plague of lice (8:16–19); yet there is no mention made of their afflicting the Israelites themselves. In the case of the first two, at least, it is stated that the Egyptians suffered their effect (7:21; 8:4), without reference to the Hebrews. But in connection with the fourth plague, that of flies, a clear distinction is drawn in 8:21: "I will send swarms of insects [or flies] on you and all your servants and on your people and into your houses; and the houses of the Egyptians shall be full of swarms of insects, and also the ground on which they dwell" (NASB). Likewise, in the case of the murrain, "the LORD will make a distinction between the livestock of Israel and the livestock of Egypt, so that nothing will die of all that belongs to the sons of Israel" (9:4, NASB).

As for the sixth plague, it is clearly stated that the boils came on the magicians and all the Egyptians, but there is no mention of Israelites (9:11). As for the seventh plague, that of the hail and lightning, it is expressly stated (v.25) that it struck "all that was in the field through all the land of Egypt, both man and beast. . . . Only in the land of Goshen, where the sons of Israel were there was no hail" (vv.25–26, NASB). Likewise with the ninth plague, that of darkness, "there was thick darkness in all the land of Egypt for three days.... But all the sons of Israel had light in their dwellings" (10:22–23, NASB). As for the tenth plague, it is undisputed and unquestioned that the death of the firstborn took place in every household except those in Goshen that had sprinkled the blood of the Passover lamb on the lintel and doorposts of the front door (12:29–30).

There is, then, no confusion or contradiction in the entire narrative. Those plagues that afflicted the rest of Egypt did not touch Goshen, where the Israelites lived. They struck *all* the land of Egypt and *all* the Egyptians *except* the believing children of Israel and their special enclave in Goshen.

Is there any evidence that any Pharaoh's son ever died in connection with the Israelite Exodus?

Exodus 12:29 states the episode in the following terms: "Now it came about at midnight that the LORD struck all the first-born in the land of Egypt, from the first-born of Pharaoh who sat on his throne to the first-born of the captive who was in the dungeon, and all the first-born of cattle" (NASB). The question arises as to whether there is any Egyptian evidence that might corroborate this tragic loss of the crown prince in a period corresponding to the Exodus itself. The answer to that question is affirmative, for it is implied in the Dream Stela of Thutmose IV.

To establish the time locus, we should take note of the fact that the Exodus, according to 1 Kings 6.1, took place about 480 years before the cornerstone was laid for Solomon's temple in Jerusalem. Since Solomon's reign began in 970 B.C., and since he commenced the building of the temple four years later (in 966), the Exodus must have occurred back in 1446 or 1445. According to the usual chronology agreed on for the Eighteenth Dynasty, Thutmose III (who was probably the "Pharaoh of the Oppression," from whom Moses fled after killing the Egyptian [Exod. 2:11–15]) died in 1447 B.C. His son Amenhotep II assumed the throne and became (if our chronology is correct) the Pharaoh of the Exodus. He reigned until 1421, when he was succeeded by his son Thutmose IV (1421–1410).

Now it so happens that a stela was found in a shrine connected with the great Sphinx at Gizeh, which recorded a dream appearance of the god Harmakhis, who solemnly promised the throne to Thutmose when he was only one of the princes in the royal family during the reign of his father: "I am thy father [i.e., his divine patron, not his biological father], Harmakhis-Khepri-Re-Atum. I shall give thee my kingdom upon earth [i.e., Egypt] at the head of the living" (Pritchard, ANET, p. 449). This elevation to kingship was, according to the god's instructions, to be followed by the pious undertaking of removing all the desert sand that had drifted against the recumbent figure of the Sphinx and rendered his chapel (located between his gigantic paws) inaccessible to the worshiping public.

The possibility exists that this oracle, which Thutmose later had recorded in this votive inscription, was simply an assurance that Thutmose himself would be preserved from death until his father had passed away, thus enabling him as crown prince to ascend the throne of Egypt. But since this would have been the normal sequence of events, hardly requiring any unusual favor from the gods, it is far more likely that Thutmose was *not* the crown prince at the time he had this dream. There must have been an older brother who was next in line for the throne. Therefore it would have to be a very special act of providence for Thutmose to become his father's successor. And that providence must have entailed the premature death of his older brother. How did it happen that this older brother met an untimely end? Exodus 12:29 seems to furnish the answer to this question.

How can the second commandment be reconciled with God's directions for pictorial ornamentation in the tabernacle (Exod. 25–27) and the temple (1 Kings 6:1–38; 7:13–51)?

The second commandment (Exod. 20:4–5) deals with the sin of idolatry and concerns itself, therefore, with the fashioning of carved images or other representations of "any likeness of what is in heaven above or on the earth beneath or in the water under the earth" (NASB) for the purposes of worshiping them as numinous powers or deities. The connection between the first commandment, "You shall have no other gods before Me" (v.3, NASB), and the second commandment is very close, and furnishes a setting in which to understand the true, full intent of this prohibition. Verse 5 continues this commandment by specifying, "You shall not worship them or serve them" (NASB). In other words, there are to be no material likenesses made of persons or things that are likely to be worshiped as supernatural or divine. That this is God's intention is clearly brought out by the passages cited in the question. Exodus 25:18,20 specifies: "You shall make two cherubim of gold, make them of hammered work at the two ends of the mercy seat.... And the cherubim shall have their wings spread upward, covering the mercy seat with their wings and facing one another" (NASB).

In the great temple of Solomon, the inner sanctum was to be guarded by two images of cherubim at least fifteen or eighteen feet tall ("ten cubits"), with a wing span of ten cubits as well (1 Kings 6:23–27). These cherubim would of course be invisible to the general public because of their location in the Holy of Holies, protected from view by worshipers outside by its drape or hanging. As such they could not become objects of worship. But there were also figures of cherubim that were carved into the wall of the "Holy Place," along with palm trees and open flowers (6:29,32). Apparently they were hardly susceptible of becoming cult objects when they were used as ornamentation along the walls in a recurring pattern of this sort. Therefore they were not considered objectionable or contrary to the mandate of the second commandment.

How can Sunday replace Saturday under the fourth commandment?

In Exodus 20:8 God's people are commanded: "Remember the sabbath day, to keep it holy." The seventh day of the week is to commemorate the completion of God's work of creation (v.11 concludes, "The LORD ... rested the seventh day; wherefore the LORD blessed the sabbath day, and hallowed it"). This commandment ranks with the nine others to form the Decalogue, and there is no suggestion even in the New Testament that the Ten Commandments are not binding on the conscience of Christian believers or that the number has been reduced to nine rather than ten. In the absence of any divine instruction to the contrary, we may assume that the fourth commandment is still binding on us. But the real question at issue is whether the sanction of the seventh day Sabbath has been by the New Testament transferred to the first day of the week, which the Christian church generally (apart from sabbatarian groups) honors as the Lord's Day, otherwise known as the Christian Sabbath.

New Testament Evidence for Sunday Worship

The heart of the apostolic manifesto to the Jewish and Gentile world from Pentecost onward was the bodily resurrection of Jesus Christ: "This Jesus God raised up again, to which we are all witnesses" (Acts 2:32, NASB). The bodily resurrection was God's certification to the world that the Savior of mankind had paid a valid and sufficient price for sinners and that He had for them overcome the curse of death. Christ's effectual atoning sacrifice and conquest over sin and death ushered in a new era, the age of the New Testament church. As the Lord's Supper replaced the Old Testament sacrament of the Passover, as the death of Christ replaced the sacrifice of animal offerings on the altar, as the high priesthood of Christ "after the order of Melchizedek" replaced the priesthood of Aaron and constituted every born-again believer as a priest of God, so also in the case of this one commandment out of the ten, which was in part at least ceremonial, there was to be a change in the symbol appropriate to the new dispensation, as the following facts seem to teach.

1. Jesus rose from the dead on the first day of the week, according to all four Evangelists (Matt. 28:1; Mark 16:2; Luke 24:1; John 20:1). Thus Sunday took on special importance as the weekly day of celebration for the triumph of the Resurrection.
2. Jesus personally appeared to His followers in visible, bodily form and conversed with them on Easter Sunday. (1) He first appeared to Mary Magdalene (John 20:11–18). (2) He next appeared to the other women who had brought spices for the embalming of His body (Matt. 28:7–10). (3) He appeared personally to Simon Peter (Luke 24:34). (4) He walked and talked with Cleopas and his companion on the road to Emmaus (Luke 24:15–32). (5) He appeared to the ten disciples and their friends on that same Sunday evening—His first appearance to a gathered assembly of Christian believers.
3. Exactly one week later, on a Sunday night, Jesus again appeared to His disciples; and this time the skeptical Thomas (who had been absent on the previous Sunday) was on hand. To him Jesus presented the physical evidence of His nail-pierced hands and feet and His spear-stabbed side in order to convince Thomas that He was alive again and was going about in the same body that had been crucified on Good Friday.
4. The outpouring of the Holy Spirit on the church took place on Pentecost. Since the Crucifixion took place on a Friday, the offering of the wave-sheaf (typical of the Resurrection) took place on the "morrow after the sabbath" (Lev. 23:10–11)—on a Sunday. This means that forty-nine days later, the Feast of Weeks (known in Greek as *Pentēkostē*, "Fiftieth [Day]") fell also on a Sunday. Obviously it was the Lord Himself who chose to honor Sunday by bringing about both the Easter victory and the "birthday" of the New Testament church on the first day of the week.

After Pentecost it seems that the Christian community continued to celebrate the seventh-day Sabbath as before, by gathering with other Jews (both converted and unconverted) for the reading of the Torah, for preaching, and for prayer. But there is no demonstrable reference to Christians ever gathering on the Saturday Sabbath to celebrate the Lord's Supper or to hold a distinctively Christian assembly. They joined in synagogue worship on Saturdays because they felt themselves to be Jews, even though they believed in Christ. In fact, they believed that they were better and more authentic Jews than those who had rejected the Hope of Israel. But they also met on Sunday mornings for worship and Holy Communion, and quite possibly on Sunday evening as well, when they had more preaching and the partaking of the *agapē* meal, or "love feast" (Acts 20:5–12).

5. In 1 Corinthians 16:2, Paul gave this instruction to the Corinthian church: "On the first day of every week let each of you put aside [lit., 'put by himself'] and save, as he may prosper, that no collections be made when I come" (NASB). The collection referred to was the relief fund for starving Hebrew Christians of Judea who were so hard hit by famine. Paul could hardly have been referring to a habit of saving carried on simply in private homes, for there would then have been no point to his referring to any one special day of the week. Anyone who is saving up for some special cause and setting the money aside in a "piggy bank" would be free to do so on any day of the week. He would hardly be expected to wait until Sunday to touch his private piggy bank. The only plausible basis for mentioning a particular day of the week was so that they might all contribute to the benevolence treasury (note the use of the word *thēsaurizōn*, "saving," which really means "putting into a treasury [*thēsauros*]," the very same term as was applied to the offering box set up in the court of the Jerusalem temple) according to what their income had been during the previous week ("as he may prosper"), presumably the 10 percent prescribed by the Old Testament. This pooling of their individual contributions into a common receptacle would enable them to amass a considerable sum for famine relief. With all these factors in view, it is safe for us to conclude that the Corinthian

church was in the habit of meeting on Sundays and that they took up offerings of some sort in connection with those Sunday worship services.

6. After Paul had spent an entire week at Troas, according to Acts 20:5–12, he concluded his stay with the Christian community there by presiding at their Sunday evening service. This could hardly have been a special meeting held for evangelistic or Bible-conference purposes, for otherwise there would have been no discernible motive for him to tarry there for seven days (v.6). Paul was quite pressed for time, since he had to make it to Jerusalem in time for the annual Feast of Pentecost (v.16). We must therefore conclude that he waited until the regular Sunday evening service at Troas so that he might have as large a congregation as possible. (There can be no legitimate question as to whether "first day of the week" could have referred to Saturday evening—as some have argued— since Troas was a city of major size and commercial importance, and it was beyond question predominantly Gentile. Therefore for them the "first day of the week" would have begun at midnight, as it did for the Roman world, and as it does for us today.) Paul then preached to a packed church at the upper story level; and they protracted the meeting all night until the dawn of Monday morning, when they held a simple love feast together before saying goodby (v.11). The institution of Sunday worship was firmly entrenched at Troas and obviously approved of by Paul.

7. The final New Testament reference to Sunday as a day of special meaning to Christians is to be found in Revelation 1:10: "I was in the Spirit on the Lord's day, and I heard behind me a loud voice like the sound of a trumpet" (NASB). The voice was

that of the glorified Christ Himself, who had come to commune with John on Sunday. "The Lord's Day" is expressed in the dative case: *tē kyriakē hēmerā*. There is no valid ground for questioning whether this really referred to Sunday. To this very day it is the regular word for "Sunday" in modern Greek, and it is plainly so intended in the earliest postbiblical witnesses (*Didache* 14:1, first quarter of the second century; *Epistle of Barnabas* 15:1, early second century). Justin Martyr (mid-second century) describes a typical order of service at a Christian service "on the day called Sunday" (*First Apology* 67). In his *Dialogue with Trypho* (a Jew), Justin argues that the command in Genesis 17 to circumcise an infant "on the eighth day" was intended by God as "a type of the true circumcision, by which we are circumcised from deceit and iniquity through Him who rose from the dead on the first day after the Sabbath, our Lord Jesus Christ" (Chap. 41). By the early third century, Tertullian went so far as to insist that "we [Christians] have nothing to do with sabbaths or other Jewish festivals, much less with those of the heathen. We have our own solemnities, the Lord's Day, for instance, and Pentecost" (*On Idolatry* 14). In *De Oratione* (23) Tertullian urged the cessation of labor on Sunday so that it might be preserved as a day of worship for God's people.

A very interesting testimony is found in the Syriac *The Teaching of the Apostles,* dating from the second half of the third century, to the effect that Christ's apostles were the first to designate the first day of the week as the day for Christian worship. "The Apostles further appointed: On the first day of the week let there be service, and the reading of the Holy Scriptures, and

the oblation: because on the first day of the week our Lord rose from the dead, and on the first day of the week He ascended up to heaven, and on the first day of the week He will appear at last with the angels of heaven" (*Ante-Nicene Fathers* 8.668). (For most of the quotations from the church fathers, I am indebted to Henry Waterman's fine article "The Lord's Day", [Tenney, *Zondervan Pictorial Encyclopedia,* 3:965–66].)

In the light of these early Christian testimonies, we can see the unsoundness of the contention made by some sabbatarian advocates that Sunday was not chosen to supersede Saturday as the day of Christian worship until the time of Constantine the Great (308–37). From apostolic times Sunday has been recognized by Christians as a day of worship and a day of rest. But what Constantine did was to issue a special edict prescribing Sunday as the official day of rest each week throughout the Roman Empire.

Sanctifying the Lord's Day

Now that we have covered the New Testament basis for the adoption of the first day of the week as the distinctive day of worship for Christians, we turn our attention to the question of how the Lord's Day was—and is—to be sanctified by God's people. If our initial premise is correct and the Lord's Day is basically intended to perpetuate the special sanctity of the Sabbath, then it would follow that our reverence for Sunday should be equal to that of the ancient Hebrew believer for the seventh-day Sabbath.

How is the Lord's Day to be sanctified? Well, if we consult the Decalogue, we find that it is to be marked by a cessation from self-serving, gainful employment that would be quite proper for the other six days of the week (Exod. 20:9–10). It is also, according to Leviticus 23:3, to be a day of public worship, a "holy convocation," and a day of special significance for the officiating priests. They were to replace the old showbread with fresh new loaves on the "table before the LORD" in the sanctuary (Lev. 24:8), and they were to double the normal offering on the altar of sacrifice (the "continual burnt offering") according to Numbers 28:9-10. But the most illuminating passage in the Old Testament concerning the true celebration of the Sabbath is found in Isaiah 58:13-14: "If because of the sabbath, you turn your foot from doing your own pleasure on My holy day, and call the sabbath a delight, the holy day of the LORD honorable, and shall honor it, desisting from your own ways, from seeking your own pleasure, and speaking your own word, then you will take delight in the LORD, and I will make you ride on the heights of the earth" (NASB).

Much of the concept conveyed by that passage found classic expression in the Westminster Shorter Catechism (60): "How is the [Christian] Sabbath to be sanctified? The Sabbath is to be sanctified by a holy resting all that day, even from such worldly employments and recreations as are lawful on other days; and spending the whole time in the public and private exercises of God's worship, except so much as is to be taken up in the works of necessity and mercy (Matt. 12:11-12)." This was the ideal standard of the Puritan movement, which represented the finest flower of the Protestant Reformation in the English-speaking world. While that standard is now more often honored by the breach than by observance, it would be difficult to prove that the modern permissive attitude toward hallowing the Lord's Day has any foundation in Scripture.

It is often urged by those who advocate pure voluntarism in the use of Sunday that Colossians 2:16 abolishes almost all the sanctions of the Old Testament fourth commandment. This verse says, "Therefore do not let anyone judge you by what you eat or drink, or with regard to a religious festival, a New Moon celebration or a Sabbath day" (NIV). A more accurate rendering of *sabbatōn* would be "Sabbaths"—plural rather than singular. This is important here, for the Hebrew religious calendar possessed not only seventh-day Sabbaths but also feast-day Sabbaths, which were to be celebrated in exactly the same way as the Saturday Sabbath, regardless of what day in the week the first and last days of the feast might fall (especially in regard to the Feast of Unleavened Bread and the Feast of Tabernacles, both of which ran for eight days).

The general purport of Colossians 2:16 is that the distinctive holy days of the Old Testament are no longer binding on New Testament believers because "these are a shadow of the things that were to come; the reality, however, is found in Christ" (v.17). Hence v.16 would seem to be referring primarily to obsolete Old Testament ordinances, of which the seventh-day Sabbath was one, and probably the feast-day Sabbath was another.

There is no good reason to believe that Paul intended to include the Christian form of the fourth commandment, that is, Sunday observance, as among the "shadows" that had already been fulfilled by Christ; the observance of the Lord's Day could hardly be classified as an Old Testament "shadow." In point of fact, it was a contemporary Christian ordinance zealously observed by those who trusted in Christ, the "Reality" (*sōma* literally means "body"), rather than in obsolete or obsolescent Old Testament types (or "shadows"). Therefore, it is altogether unwarranted to draw from this verse an unrestrained license to use the Lord's Day any way one pleases. Church attendance and group

120

Bible study are admittedly the most important elements in Sunday observance, but the principle of rest from self-seeking labor (except for those involved in works of real necessity or mercy) is surely at the heart of hallowing the Lord's Day—even in these days when the secularized culture around us holds that day in very low esteem.

For additional study of this topic see D.A. Carson, *From Sabbath to Lord's Day* (Grand Rapids: Zondervan, 1982).

Why is there so much killing of human beings mentioned in the Bible, along with the frequent references to animal sacrifice on the altar? How does this square with the divine command "Thou shalt not kill" (Exod. 20:13)? (D*)

Since the Bible is a book about man in his state of sin, and since there is so much violence and bloodshed in human society, it was inevitable that frequent mention of manslaughter should occur in Scripture. But much confusion has arisen from the misleading translation of Exodus 20:13 that occurs in most English versions. The Hebrew original uses a specific word for murder (*rāṣaḥ*) in this sixth commandment and should be rendered "You shall not murder" (NASB). This is no prohibition against capital punishment for capital crimes, since it is not a general term for the taking of life, such as our English word "kill" implies. Exodus 21:12, right in the very next chapter, reads: "He that smiteth a man, so that he die, shall be surely put to death." This amounts to a specific divine command to punish murder with capital punishment, in keeping with Genesis 9:6: "Whoever sheds man's blood, by man his blood shall be shed, for in the image of God He made man" (NASB).

Violence and bloodshed are occasionally mentioned in the record of man's history throughout Scripture, but never with approval. Yet there were specific situations when entire communities (such as Jericho) or entire tribes (such as the Amalekites) were to be exterminated by the Israelites in obedience to God's command. In each case these offenders had gone so far in degeneracy and moral depravity that their continued presence would result in spreading the dreadful cancer of sin among God's covenant people. Just as the wise surgeon removes dangerous cancer from his patient's body by use of the scalpel, so God employed the Israelites to remove such dangerous malignancies from human society. So far as sacrificial animals were concerned, this mode of worship, symbolizing the coming sacrifice of the Son of God on the cross, was taught to our forebears from the time of Adam and systematized for the believing community in the laws of Moses. "Without the shedding of blood, there is no remission of sins" (Heb. 9:22).

Why were there multiple marriages in Israel after the giving of the Ten Commandments?

The seventh commandment says, "Thou shalt not commit adultery" (Exod. 20:14). How did this affect the patriarchs like Abraham, who was given Hagar by his own wife, Sarah, to serve as her proxy in the marriage bed? Or Jacob, who not only married Leah and Rachel but also had children by their maids Bilhah and Zilpah? Perhaps the fact that the Decalogue was not given to Israel until five centuries later may have lessened the guilt of their multiple marriages. But how about King David, who lived four centuries later? Second Samuel 12:7–8 actually states that God "gave Saul's wives into David's arms" (cf. NIV), as if God Himself condoned this polygamy. How do we reconcile this with the monogamy that Jesus so clearly taught in Matthew 19:9 and which He asserted to have been God's intention from the very beginning of the human race?

Genesis 2:23–24, as Christ pointed out, teaches monogamy as God's will for man. After Adam was presented with his wife, Eve, the Bible records: "The man said, 'This is now bone of my bones, and flesh of my flesh.' ... For this cause a man shall leave his father and his mother, and shall cleave to his wife; and they shall become one flesh" (NASB). Now there is no possibility of a husband's constituting a unity with one wife if he also has another wife—or several others. This is made very clear by the analogy in Ephesians 5:23: "For the husband is the head of the wife, as Christ also is head of the church, He Himself being the Savior of the body" (NASB). The implication here is that there is but one true church and that it stands in a relationship to the heavenly Bridegroom like that of the wife toward her husband. Christ is not the Head of many different churches; He has but a single mystical body—not several different bodies—and therefore His one and only church is viewed as the antitype of monogamous marriage. Polygamy is absolutely excluded.

As we examine the scriptural record, we come to the realization that every case of polygamy or concubinage amounted to a failure to follow God's original model and plan. The very first reference to polygamy in Genesis is found in the life of Lamech son of Methushael, who, in addition to his bloodthirsty vindictiveness toward those with whom he had quarreled, is recorded in Genesis 4:23–24 as boasting of his prowess to his two wives. After that there is no mention of plural marriage until the time of Abraham.

In Abraham's case, Sarah is always represented as being Abraham's only legal wife as long as she lived. But when she became convinced that she could bear him no children of her own, she presented him with her maid Hagar, to be her proxy in the marriage bed. This meant that Hagar became a concubine to Abraham, not his lawfully wedded wife. But even this attempt to "help God" carry out His earlier promise, that Abraham would become the ancestor of a great nation, turned out to be a cause of great bitterness and strife within their home; and ultimately Hagar had to be sent away, along with Abraham's son by her, the lad Ishmael (Gen. 21:12–14).

Abraham's son Isaac was married to but one wife, Rebecca, and was faithful to her all his life. But their self-willed son Esau broke their heart by becoming involved in polygamy and by marrying out of the faith—both of Esau's wives were pagans (Gen. 26:34). Later on Esau even took a third wife, Mahalath the daughter of his uncle Ishmael (Gen. 28:9) and Oholibamah as well (cf. Gen. 26). In so doing, Esau is not presented as a model for believers to follow.

In the case of Jacob, his only desire was for one woman, Rachel, the daughter of Laban. It was only through Laban's crafty maneuvering that Jacob was tricked into marrying Rachel's older sister, Leah, as well. Later on, as unhappy rivalry broke out between the two sisters in the matter of childbearing, they resorted to Sarah's misguided expedient of presenting their husband with their handmaids, Bilhah and Zilpah, to serve as proxies in the marriage bed. But so far as Jacob was concerned, there never was any desire on his part to become a polygamist. All he had done was fall in love with Rachel; and after that one thing led to another, until he had four sets of children. These of course became ancestors of the twelve tribes of Israel, and God was gracious enough to accept them all within His plan for multiplying the race of Abraham. But even the home of Jacob was a rather unhappy one at first, rent with jealousy and strife, and marked by cruelty and falsehood.

This whole problem of polygamy in Old Testament times is not easy to handle. Yet it really should not be equated with adultery so as to make it a technical violation of the seventh commandment; for in Old Testament times when a man took a second wife, he bound himself to her as much as to his first wife. Thus all of David's wives were equally "Mrs. David," so to speak. The concubines were likewise an exclusive obligation for the man to cherish, support, and provide for in every way. This was a far different matter than entering into illicit relations with another man's wife. So far as Saul's wives were concerned—or the wives of any other deceased king, for that matter—they were normally entrusted to the protection and care of his successor. Otherwise a later marriage to a king's widow might give the second husband a legal claim to the throne. (This was the reason Solomon was so alarmed by Adonijah's proposal to marry King David's youngest wife, Abishag; Solomon took this maneuver as part of a plot to overthrow him [1 Kings 2:22].) Therefore the rule was that once a woman became a king's consort (whether as queen, secondary wife, or concubine), she had a right to retain that status even though her royal husband had died. His successor would take her over. Presumably, however, a son would treat all his father's wives as respected pensioners in the palace, rather than entering into incestuous relations with them.

The fact of the matter was that while polygamy was contrary to God's intention and ideal, nevertheless, because of what Christ called "the hardness of men's hearts" (Matt. 19:8), it was tolerated—especially in the case of a political leader whose dynasty would fail if he produced no son by his first wife. A state of civil war might well ensue from such a situation, with resulting bloodshed and disruption to the state. But then, of course, there were occasional references to plural marriages even in the case of private citizens, like Samuel's father, Elkanah. In the course of time, however, a better understanding of God's will in regard to marriage prevailed among God's people. From the time of the return from Babylonian exile (ca. 537 B.C.) onward, there is no reference to polygamy among God's people to be found in any of the post-Exilic books of the Old Testament. By Christ's time monogamy was the rule among the Greeks and the Romans as well as among the Jews, and Christ's affirmation of the "one flesh" principle of marriage (which makes sense only in a context of monogamy) found ready acceptance among His countrymen (Matt. 19:5–6).

Norman Geisler has a good summary of the biblical position on this question:

There is ample evidence, even within the Old Testament, that polygamy was not God's ideal for man. That monogamy was His ideal for man is obvious from several perspectives. (1) God made only one wife for Adam, thus setting the ideal precedent for the race. (2) Polygamy is first mentioned as part of the wicked Cainite civilization (Gen. 4:23). (3) God clearly forbade the kings of Israel (leaders were the persons who became polygamists) saying, "And he shall not multiply wives for himself, lest his heart turn away again" (Deut. 17:17). (4) The saints who became polygamists paid for their sins. 1 Kings 11:1,3 says, "Now King Solomon loved many foreign women . . . and his wives turned away his heart." . . . (6) Polygamy is usually situated in the context of sin in the O.T. Abraham's marriage of Hagar was clearly a carnal act of unbelief (Gen. 16:1f). David was not at a spiritual peak when he added Abigail and Ahinoam as his wives (1 Sam. 25:42-43), nor was Jacob when he married Leah and Rachel (Gen. 29:23,28). (7) The polygamous relation was less than ideal. It was one of jealousy among the wives. Jacob loved Rachel more than Leah (Gen. 29:31). Elkanah's one wife was considered a "rival" or adversary by the other, who "used to provoke her sorely, to irritate her..." (1 Sam. 1:6). (8) When polygamy is referred to, the conditional, not the imperative, is used. "*If* he takes another wife to himself, he shall not diminish her food, her clothing, or her marital rights" (Exod. 21:10). Polygamy is not the moral ideal, but the polygamist must be moral (*Ethics: Alternatives and Issues* [Grand Rapids: Zondervan, 1971], pp. 204-5).

What is the explanation of Exodus 24:9-11—the revelation of God enthroned to the elders of Israel who accompanied Moses to Mount Sinai? (D*)

According to Exodus 24:1, the Lord invited the seventy appointed elders of the Twelve Tribes to accompany Moses, Aaron, and his two sons, and to ascend the holy mountain for a certain distance up its slope, following at a suitable distance behind Moses. The purpose of this audience before the King of the Universe was to consecrate them for their holy task of assisting in the government of God's people.

It should be borne in mind that according to the earlier proclamation in Exodus 19:12-13, neither man nor beast was permitted even to touch or set foot on the holy mountain, under the penalty of death. Yet for this solemn occasion the seventy elders, along with Aaron and his sons, were permitted to gaze on the glory of God seated in blazing splendor on a sapphire throne. Normally they would have been struck dead for climbing even the lower reaches of Sinai, but in this case they were granted special permission to do so. Normally also it was impossible for mortal man to look on the glorious presence of God directly,

without being smitten with instant death: "For there shall no man see me, and live" (Exod. 33:20). And so it is stated in Exodus 24:11 that "upon the nobles of the children of Israel he laid not his hand: also they saw God, and did not eat and drink." That is to say, they all were permitted to partake of the sacred meal in view of God's throne on Mount Sinai; and they survived the exposure to His holy presence without any damage to themselves or loss of life.

It should perhaps be added that what was seen in this theophany was a glorious representation of God in His regal splendor, not the essence of God Himself; for that has never been vouchsafed to human eyes (John 1:18).

How can we reconcile Exodus 33:20, where the Lord tells Moses, "You cannot see My face, for no man can see Me and live!" and Exodus 33:11, which states, "Thus the Lord used to speak to Moses face to face, just as a man speaks to his friend"? (D*)

The Bible draws a clear distinction between gazing on God in His unveiled glory and beholding a representation or reflection of God in a personal interview or encounter with Him. John 1:18 declares, "No man has seen God at any time [that is, his full glory as Creator and Sovereign of all the universe]; the only begotten God [that is, Jesus Christ], who is in the bosom of the Father, He has explained Him" (NASB). The apostle Paul adds that God the Father "has shone in our hearts to give the light of the knowledge of the glory of God in the face of Christ" (2 Cor. 4:6, NASB).

We behold the face of God by faith as we look to Christ, "He who has seen Me has seen the Father" (John 14:9, NASB). God therefore showed His face and declared His glory through His Son, who was God Incarnate. But back in Old Testament times, God showed

His face through an angel (as at the interview with Moses at the burning bush [Exod. 3:2–6]), or else through His glory cloud, which led His people through the wilderness after the Exodus.

At the dedication of the tabernacle (Exod. 40:34–35), this glory cloud (*kābôd*) came to rest over the mercy seat of the ark of the covenant. Each week twelve loaves of sacred bread were offered to Yahweh on the table of "showbread," which was called in Hebrew *šulḥān weleḥem pānîm* ("the table with the bread of the Presence") because it was presented in front of the inner curtain (*pārō-ke-t*) that shielded the ark of the covenant from public view. The Presence (of God) remained over the mercy seat (*kappōret*), which surmounted the ark.

We are therefore to understand that Yahweh met with Moses and talked to him in some glorious representation that fell short of a full unveiling of His face. In that sense He talked with Moses face to face—somewhat as a speaker on television speaks face to face with his viewing public.

But what Moses was asking for in Exodus 33:18 went beyond this veiled appearance; to obtain full assurance of God's renewed grace to him and to the Israelite nation, Moses asked to see the very face of God. God warned that at such a vision Moses would instantly die (see 1 Tim. 6:16, which states that God dwells "in unapproachable light"). Yet, as a special confirmation of His personal favor and presence, Yahweh promised that He would reveal His back to Moses (Exod. 33:23), without showing His face. This Yahweh did when He passed by "in front of him" and set forth His gracious and glorious name (Exod. 34:6–7).

Leviticus

Does the rabbit really chew its cud?

Leviticus 11:5 refers to the *šāpān* (or *Hyrax syriacus*) as an unclean animal (e.g., unfit for sacrifice or human consumption) because "though it chews cud, it does not divide the hoof" (NASB). Clean animals had to do both to be eligible for food. The question at issue is the chewing of the cud. Did (or does) the *šāpān* (translated "coney" in KJV and "rock badger" in NASB) really "chew the cud" (Heb. *ma'ᵃ lēh gērāh*, lit., "raising up what has been swallowed")? Similarly in Leviticus 11:6 the same statement is made about the *'arnebet* ("rabbit," "hare"). Does the hare ruminate? The answer to both statements must be in the negative so far as the acutal digestive process is concerned. True ruminants normally have four stomachs, and that which has been worked over in these stomachs is regurgitated into the mouth when it is ready to be chewed again.

In this technical sense neither the hyrax nor the hare can be called ruminants, but they do give the appearance of chewing their cud in the same way ruminants do. So convincing is this appearance that even Linnaeus at first classed them as ruminants, even though the four-stomach apparatus was lacking. But we need to remember that this list of forbidden animals was intended to be a practical guide for the ordinary Israelite as he was out in the wilds looking for food. He might well conclude from the sideways movement of the jaws that these animals ruminated like the larger cattle; and since they fed on the same kind of grass and herbs, they might well be eligible for human consumption. Thus it was necessary to point out that they did not have hooves at all and therefore could not meet the requirements for clean food.

G.S. Cansdale gives this interesting information concerning the habits of the *'arnebet*:

Hares, like rabbits, are now known to practice "refection": at certain times of day, when the hare is resting, it passes droppings of different texture, which it at once eats. Thus the hare appears to be chewing without taking fresh greens into its mouth. On its first passage through the gut, indigestible vegetable matter is acted on by bacteria and can be better assimilated the second time through. Almost the same principle is involved as in chewing the cud ("Hare," in Tenney, *Zondervan Pictorial Encyclopedia*, 3:33).

How could leprosy affect clothing (Lev. 13:47–59) or house walls (Lev. 14:33–57)?

What is commonly known today as "leprosy" is usually equated with Hansen's disease. But the Hebrew term *ṣāra'at* is a far more general term for any kind of noticeable or disfiguring skin disease. Many of the types described in Leviticus 13:2–42 show symptoms unknown to Hansen's disease, such as

126

LEVITICUS

patches of white skin and areas of infection on the scalp. Verse 6 refers to a type of skin disease that is known, in some cases at least, to show spontaneous improvement within a week (which is never true of Hansen's disease). Verses 7-8 seem to refer to a phagedenic ulcer; v.24 to an infection in a burned area of the skin. Verse 30 refers to a scaly skin or scalp, strongly suggestive of psoriasis.

From the above data we may legitimately conclude that ṣāra'aṭ does not refer to any single type of skin disease (although Naaman's illness was quite certainly akin to Hansen's disease [2 Kings 5], likewise the affliction Uzziah was stricken with in the temple [2 Kings 15:5; 2 Chron. 26:19-20]); rather, it is a broadly descriptive term covering all kinds of disfiguring diseases of the skin or scalp.

As for Leviticus 13.47,59, these verses speak of ṣāra'aṭ on a garment or any piece of clothing. Obviously this cannot be the same as a skin disease afflicting the human skin. But a fungus or mold that attacks a fabric of cloth or leather or fur bears a surface resemblance to that which afflicts the skin. Because of its tendency to spread on contact and because of its highly disfiguring effect, this kind of ṣāra'aṭ had to be sequestered, to see whether it was something that could be washed away completely and permanently by a thorough scrubbing or laundering process. If these measures proved unavailing, the fabric in question was to be destroyed by fire.

As for Leviticus 14:33-57, the type of ṣāra'aṭ that afflicts the wall of a home seems to have been a kind of fungus, bacteria, or mold that occasionally appears on adobe walls, or even on wood, when the humidity is abnormally high and long sustained at temperatures that promote the spread of mold. Since the fungus could spread quite rapidly, mar the appearance of the entire room, and was possibly

promotive of other kinds of pollution and disease, it was necessary to deal with it as soon as it was detected. The afflicted areas of the wall were to be thoroughly scrubbed, scraped, and scoured, to see whether the mold could be eliminated and killed by these measures. Where mold had penetrated an individual brick or a particular patch in the wall, it was to be pried out and discarded completely, to keep the adjacent bricks from contamination. But if these drastic methods proved to be unavailing, then the entire house was to be destroyed.

There was always a suitable waiting period before a house was destroyed, generally of a week or two, at the end of which a confirmatory inspection was to be made by a priest. The same was true of "leprosy" on clothing or on the human skin. Inspections were to be made at the end of the first week or two in order to see whether the infection had been halted or whether it was continuing to spread. In all three cases or types of leprosy (ṣāra'aṭ), a ceremony or rite of purification was required, which is described in some detail in Leviticus 13-14.

Who is the scapegoat of Leviticus 16? Or what does it represent? (D*)

Leviticus 16 sets forth the procedure to be followed on the Day of Atonement (Yom Kippur), the tenth day of Tishri (usually late in September) each year. There were to be two goats set aside for this ceremony, one for a sin offering (ḥaṭṭāt-h) and the other for a burnt offering ('ōlāh). The former of the two was to be sacrificed on the altar, according to the usual requirement for sin offerings. But the latter was chosen by lot to be a live sacrifice, called 'ᵃzā'zēl, a term that perhaps should be vocalized as 'ēz 'āzēl ("a goat of departure"). (It should be understood that the Old Testament was originally written with consonants only;

vowel points were not added until about A.D. 800. In the case of proper names or obsolete technical terms, there was always a chance for a bit of confusion in the oral tradition concerning the vowels.) The Septuagint follows this latter reading, translating the Hebrew into the Greek as *chimaros apopompaios* ("the goat to be sent away").

The high priest was to lay his hands on the head of this goat, confess over him the sins of the nation Israel, and then send him away into the wilderness, symbolically carrying away all the guilt of Israel with him (Lev. 16:21). The tradition that the scapegoat was a name for a desert demon was of much later origin and quite out of keeping with the redemptive principles taught in the Torah. It is therefore altogether mistaken to suppose that the scapegoat represented Satan himself, for neither Satan nor his demons are ever suggested in Scripture as carrying out any atoning functions on behalf of mankind—as such an interpretation would imply.

On the contrary, each sacrificial animal referred to in the Mosaic Law symbolized some aspect of Christ's atoning work. The goat of the sin offering represented the substitution of Christ's blameless life for the guilty life of the condemned sinner. In the case of the scapegoat, the removal of sin from the presence of God is set forth. As the Father laid the sins of believers on the Son on the cross (Isa. 53:6) so that they might be removed far away, so the *'ēz 'āzēl*, on whom all the iniquities of Israel were symbolically laid by Aaron, carried them away into the wilderness to be remembered against them no more.

Numbers

How trustworthy are statistical numbers given in the Book of Numbers and in the Old Testament generally?

Some scholars have questioned the credibility of the numbers recorded in the two censuses of Numbers (chaps. 1–4 and 26). The arid conditions of the Sinai desert would hardly permit the survival of such a large host as 600,000 adult males, plus their wives and children, for a period of forty years. If, therefore, these statistics concerning the number of fighting men connected with each of the Twelve Tribes are to be accepted as having any historical basis whatever, we must then somehow reduce the total to a much smaller number than 2 million people or more and achieve an approximation within the limits of historical likelihood. Writers like G. Mendenhall (JBL 77 [1958]: 52–66), John Bright (*History of Israel* [Philadelphia: Westminster, 1959], p. 144), and R.E.D. Clark (*Journal of the Transactions of the Victoria Institute* 87 [1955]: 82ff.) suggest reading the word for "thousand" as merely clan." R.K. Harrison (*Old Testament Introduction,* p. 633), despite his generally conservative stance, surrenders the historical accuracy of these figures, suggesting that they have only a relative value as to the comparative size of the various tribes.

The word for "thousand" is the Hebrew *'elep,* which may have some original connection with the word for "bull." Although there is no clear occurrence of *'elep* with the meaning "family" or "clan" to be found in all the Hebrew Scriptures (so Brown-Driver-Briggs, *Lexicon,* pp. 48–49), yet the related noun *'allûp* means "chief," "commander of a thousand troops"; and there are some other passages that could be using the plural *'alāpîm* in the sense of a subdivision of a tribe (cf. Koehler-Baumgartner, *Lexicon,* p. 57). This is a most tenuous basis on which to erect a theory allowing for reduction; but if in these census chapters of Numbers one could render *'alāpîm* as "family complex" or "clan," then perhaps the total number of Israelite men-at-arms could be lowered to about 30,000. This would involve a much smaller number of mouths to feed and bodies to sustain during the many years of desert wandering. So goes the argument.

There are some fatal difficulties, however, that render this theory quite untenable. In the first place, it always happens that after the number of *'alāpîm* is cited, it is followed by the number of *mē'ōt* ("hundreds") as the next lower unit; and then it is followed by the decades and digits in descending order. Thus the first record given is that of the adult males of the tribe of Reuben (Num. 1:21): *šiššāh wᵉ'arbā'îm 'elep waḥᵃmēš mē'ōt* (lit., "six and forty thousand and five hundreds"). This being the case, there is no way that *'elap* in this total figure could have meant 46 clans (or families) and 500. Clearly the figure intended is 46,500. That such was the intention of the Hebrew author is rendered absolutely certain by the total of the "ransom money" raised from the male population of Israel according to Exodus 38:25: "100 talents and 1,775 shekels." Each man was to contribute half a shekel; there were 3000 shekels to the talent. Therefore, 100 talents and 1,775 shekels comes out to exactly 603,550 half-shekels (representing the same number of males, according to Num. 2:32). This total is confirmed by Exodus 12:37: "about 600,000 men on foot." Hence there has been no error in translation, nor any demonstrable garbling in transmission.

The objection that the natural resources of the Sinai desert could never have supported two million people or more for a period of forty years' wandering is absolutely valid. But it completely overlooks what the Pentateuch makes abundantly clear: Israel did not receive its food and drink from the ordinary natural resources of the Sinai terrain. This multitude was said to have been supplied in a miraculous way with manna from the sky and water from the cloven rock, all during the journey through the wilderness. The God who led the Israelites in the pillar of cloud was the one who supplied them with their nourishment by way of a supernatural intervention on their behalf. Apart from this, 30,000 would have perished of hunger and thirst in that wilderness just as quickly as 600,000; and it is quite futile to sidestep the factor of miracle by a mere reduction in numbers.

What we are dealing with here is the possibility of miracle. Miracles are recorded from the first chapter of the Bible to the last. Apart from the supreme miracle of God the Son becoming incarnate as Jesus of Nazareth, there is no gospel to preach or cross of Calvary to believe in. In fact, there is little point in bothering with the Bible at all, for its presuppositions are miraculous from start to finish. If all these miraculous events never really took place, then the Bible is too untrustworthy to be believed; it is only another sample of human speculation. No valid objection can be raised, therefore, on the ground that a biblical episode is miraculous in nature; and any line of argument or reinterpretation that presupposes the impossibility of miracle is a mere exercise in futility.

The credibility of a Hebrew host in excess of two million souls has been called in question by some authorities on the ground of the remarkably low number of firstborn sons as recorded in Numbers 3:42-43: "So Moses numbered all the first-born among the sons of Israel, just as the LORD had commanded him; and all the first-born males by the number of names from a month old and upward, for their numbered men were 22,273" (NASB). Quite obviously there must have been a far greater number of firstborn sons in Moses' congregation, numbering as it did over 600,000 men. But this apparent difficulty disappears when the setting of this incident is carefully examined.

It was apparently in the second year of the wilderness journey (cf. Num. 1:1), after the census of the Twelve Tribes and the tribe of Levi had been completed, that the Lord ordered Moses to number all the firsborn of the non-Levites and determine how many more of them there were than the number of the Levites themselves. The purpose of this was to compute how large a ransom offering should be contributed to the Lord's work, to compensate for the fact that the Levites totaled a little less than 10 percent of the total male population of Israel. Since there were 22,000 Levites (Num. 3:39) but 22,273 firstborn non-Levites (v.43), this meant that an offering of 22,273 times five shekels had to be raised for the excess number of non-Levites. (This is actually the origin of the so-called temple tax, which is still observed by worldwide Jewry today.)

Delitzsch (Keil and Delitzsch, *Pentateuch*, 3:9–13) points out that this requirement only applied to those babies born after the start of the Exodus; it was never intended to be retroactive. Well, then, out of a total of 603,550 males, there would within a year or so be a total of about 19,000 new marriages. If some of these allowed for two gestation periods, the probable number of births for male babies would be 22,000 or a few more. This agrees very well with the exact figure given of 22,273.

Another basis for postulating a small population among the Hebrews in Goshen is the record in Exodus 1:15, that two midwives were sufficient to handle all the obstetrical cases within the community. This observation is quite valid. Far more than two midwives would be necessary to care for a population of over two million. But surely this fact would have been just as obvious to an eighth-century B.C. author (like the putative "Elohist") as it is to us. Two midwives would have hardly been able to care for even 30,000 males plus wives and children. Quite obviously Shiphrah and Puah served as administrative superintendents over the obstetrical guild for the entire Hebrew community. It is hardly conceivable that the entire corps of midwives would have reported personally to the king himself; on the contrary, the king maintained control of their activities through approved overseers. This is quite in keeping with what we know of the highly bureaucratic structure of the ancient Egyptian government. Their documents refer to overseers (the Egyptian term was *imy-r*, "he who is in the mouth" of his employer or overlord) for nearly every craft, profession, or skill known to Egyptian society. They were all re-sponsible to report to and take orders from the government of the district in which they served. This makes the argument based on the small number of midwives completely invalid.

Another difficulty that has been proposed against the credibility of a congregation of over two million is derived from the amount of time necessary for so large a multitude to progress from point to point in their journey as they are said to have done according to the Pentateuchal narrative. How, for example, could such a large horde of people get across the Red Sea (or "Sea of Reeds," as the Hebrew puts it) so quickly as Exodus 14:21–24 seems to suggest? The parching east wind partially dried up the sea bed (after the waters had been miraculously removed to some distance above and below their point of crossing) for an entire night (v.21); and only after that, it would seem, did the Israelites make their way across.

It may have been by the fourth watch (i.e., 3:00 to 6:00 A.M.) of the following day that the Egyptian chariots began their crossing in pursuit of them. This means that the Hebrew host had barely twenty-four hours to make the passage. This would seem to be quite impossible if they had to keep to a paved highway of any sort as they made their advance. But in this situation there could have been no roads or highways at all (for what point would there be for a street leading into the waters of a sea?); and they had to proceed across directly over unpaved terrain from wherever they happened to be located in their overnight camp. Their maneuver would be just like that of an army advancing to do battle with an enemy host: their front line may have stretched out for two or three miles as they moved together simultaneously, livestock included. Hence there would have been very little time lost through waiting in line. The whole multitude simply moved ahead like

131

one enormous army advancing against an enemy battle line. If this was the way it was done, then there is no time problem to deal with.

The same observation applies to the day-by-day journeys of the Israelites during the forty years' wandering. If they had been packed up close together in one long column when they camped down for the night, then it would have taken several hours for their rearmost detachments to get moving after the journey had began for the vanguard. But we know from Numbers 2:3–31 that they camped down in the formation of a square, with three tribes to the east of the tabernacle, three to the south, three to the west, and three to the north. Thus they were distributed like a huge expeditionary force, with center, two wings, a vanguard, and a rearguard. When armies engaged each other in battle, they did not require much time before they engaged their front lines in hand-to-hand combat. They did not look around for paved roads but simply proceeded across the broken, rough terrain (if they had to) with their ranks carefully preserved in line. There were virtually no paved highways to be found in the Sinai (apart from the King's Highway, perhaps), and such as there were would only be used for wheeled vehicles—of which the Israelites had very few indeed, If, then, they began to move simultaneously after the signal trumpet was blown at the start of the day's march, they could very easily cover ten miles or more without overdriving the young of the livestock. They had no need to wait in line for their turn to move.

Considerable skepticism has been voiced by rationalist scholarship in regard to the historicity of such large armies as are referred to in subsequent periods of Israel's history. For example, at the Battle of Mareshah (2 Chron. 14:8–12), King Asa of Judah is said to have faced Zerah the Ethiopian with 580,000 troops against the invader's host of 1,000,000. Or again, back in David's time the Ten Tribes had 800,000 men at arms and Judah 500,000—which made up a total of 1,300,000 for the standing army and the militia in the early tenth century B.C. King Pekah of Israel slew 120,000 Judean troops in a single engagement and led off 200,000 more as captives, back in the reign of King Ahaz (2 Chron. 28:6–8). Modern scholars tend to cast doubt on these large numbers, feeling that the Chronicler especially was given to frequent exaggeration in his zeal to glorify Israel's past.

In answer to these charges of statistical unreliability, we make the following observations.

1. The ancient author, living within a few hundred years of the events he describes—or else even writing as a contemporary—is far more likely to be in secure possession of the facts than a modern skeptic who is separated from the event by three thousand years or more.

2. Modern criteria of likelihood or unlikelihood, if founded on the assumption that the unusual never happens, are virtually useless. If history teaches us anything, it teaches us that most of the major events of the past took place because the unlikely and unusual actually occurred.

3. Deductions based on recent observation and experience may lead to completely false results. It is unwarranted to assume from the climatic conditions that have prevailed in the Holy Land since A.D. 500 that the land was never more fertile nor could not have supported a large population in earlier times. The archaeological and geological evidence seems to indicate that the precipitation rates have fluctuated quite markedly since the third millennium B.C. The weather diary

kept by Claudius Ptolemaeus in Alexandria, Egypt, during the first century A.D. shows that in his time the summer drought was shorter than at present, with much greater thunderstorm activity and more of the north wind prevalent during the winter than at present (cf. Denis Baly, *Geography of the Bible*, rev. ed. [New York: Harper, 1974], pp. 66–67). The indications are that dry, hot conditions prevailed from 4500 to 3500 B.C.; cooler, damper weather prevailed from 3500 to 2300; followed by 300 years of drought (as witness Abraham's sojourn in Egypt). A better rainfall ensued from 2000 onward, though increased human activity has obscured the evidence for the real extent of the fluctuation from one century to another (ibid., p. 68). But such variables as these make it quite likely that the frequent description of fifteenth century Canaan as a "land flowing with milk and honey" points to an appreciably higher precipitation level in Moses' time than was true back in Abraham's time. The more fertile and productive the arable land became, the larger a population it could sustain.

4. Other ancient sources attest to the use of very large armies when military projects of special magnitude were under way. The Egyptian records are of little help in this connection, for apart from the Sixth-Dynasty inscription of Uni (Pritchard, ANET, p. 228), which states that King Pepi I sent into Asia an expeditionary force consisting of "many ten-thousands," the Pharaohs contended themselves with lists of prisoners taken from the enemy. Even Thutmose III in his account of the Battle of Megiddo (ca. 1468 B.C.) neglects to mention the size of the armies involved (ibid., p. 235). The same is true of Ramses II in his self-laudatory report of the stalemate Battle of Kadesh, in which he halted the southward advance of the Hittites; he simply refers to three separate army divisions that are involved in the conflict (ibid., pp. 255–56). As for the Assyrian records, the Assyrian kings never seem to refer to the size of their own armed forces but pretty largely confine themselves to the number of enemy slain or prisoners taken. In his account of the Battle of Karkar, however, which he fought with Benhadad and Ahab in 853, Shalmaneser III states that Adadizri (as he calls Benhadad) had 20,000 infantry, 1,200 cavalry, and 1,200 chariots; Ahab had 10,000 foot soldiers and 2000 chariots; the king of Hamath contributed 10,000 infantry, 700 cavalry, and 700 chariots (ibid., pp. 278–79). There were besides various smaller contingents from nine other kings arrayed against the Assyrians at Karkar; Shalmaneser claims to have killed 14,000 of them and to have chased the rest away. In another engagement he states that he slew 20,900 of "Hadaezer's" warriors (ibid., p. 280). Sennacherib in his 701 campaign against Hezekiah and his Philistine allies claims to have deported 200,150 prisoners taken from forty-six walled cities of Judah and taken them off as prisoners to Assyria (ibid., p. 288). His father, Sargon II, took 27,290 captives from Samaria back in 721 (ibid., p. 285). There are no figures at all given for the Persian troops in the Behistun Rock inscription of Darius I (ca. 495 B.C.).

As for the Greek historians, Herodotus (*Historia* 7) states that when Xerxes, king of Persia, reviewed his troops for the invasion of Greece, "the whole land army together was found to amount to

1,700,000 men." This total was arrived at by marshaling 10,000 soldiers at a time, until all the men had been counted. The naval forces included 1,207 triremes, with specified contingents from Egypt, Cyprus, Phoenicia, and many other maritime areas. As for the battle contingents involved in the campaigns of Alexander the Great, the largest conflict in which he was engaged was probably the Battle of Gaugamela in 331 B.C. Arrian estimated the infantry of Darius III at about 1,000,000, plus 40,000 cavalry. Alexander defeated him with only 40,000 infantry and 7000 cavaliers (Charles Anthon, *A Classical Dictionary, Containing an Account of the Principal Proper Names Mentioned in Ancient Authors* [New York: Harper & Bros., 1871], p. 107).

From these records we learn that even the army of Zerah the Ethiopian was by no means incredible in size for a major invasion force (cf. 2 Chron. 14:9). From the number of prisoners deported by the Assyrians, we gather that there was a rather high population level maintained in Palestine during the eighth and seventh centuries B.C. It is therefore a mistake to draw inferences from archaeological remains —as some scholars have done—that indicate a comparatively sparse population for the Near East during this period. One very interesting discovery from the recent excavations at Ebla includes a set of cuneiform tablets (published by G. Pettinato and P. Matthiae, in "Aspetti Amministrativi e Topografici di Ebla nel III Millennio Av. Cr.," *Rivista degli Studi Orientali* 50 [1976]: 1–30), one of which lists the superintendents and prefects of the four major divisions of the capital city itself back in 2400 B.C. From these data the estimated population of Ebla was about 260,000 (cf. Heinrich von Siebenthal, *Die könig-*

lichen Tontafelarchive von Tell Mardikh-Ebla n.38, trans. into French by Suzanne Ruckstuhl, and appears as app. 4 in G. Archer, *Introduction à l'Ancien Testament,* Edition Emmaus [Switzerland: St. -Legier, 1978], pp. 570–85; cf. also G. Pettinato, "The Royal Archives of Tell Mardikh-Ebla," *Biblical Archeologist* 39 [2, 1976]: 44–52). This renders quite credible the implied population of Nineveh in Jonah's day: "120,000 persons who do not know their right hand from their left" (Jonah 4:11)—i.e., infants and toddlers. This would indicate a total of nearly 1,000,000 inhabitants in Greater Nineveh alone.

All these ancient references to high population seem to remove any firm base for the skepticism of modern critics who question the accuracy of the figures given in the Old Testament. At the same time it is noteworthy that the Hebrew historical accounts seem to be almost unique among the extant literature of the ancient Near East in giving the numbers of soldiers involved in the various invasions and battles therein recorded. It goes without saying that it is rather difficult to make a well-documented comparison between Israelite and non-Israelite accounts of numbers involved in warfare or in national censuses when there are virtually no comparable accounts that have yet come to light from pagan sources from the same period.

Did the Levites enter their service in the sanctuary at the age of thirty (Num. 4:3), twenty-five (Num. 8:24), or twenty (Ezra 3:8)?

Numbers 4:3 states quite explicitly, "From thirty years and upward, even to fifty years old, [are] all [the Levites] who enter the service to do the work in the tent of meeting" (NASB). Eligibility for full service in assisting the priests in the transportation and upkeep of the furniture and holy vessels of the tabernacle was restricted to those who were at least thirty years of age.

In Numbers 8:24, however, it is stated in connection with their service at the sanctuary: "This is what applies to the Levites: from twenty-five years old and upward they shall enter to perform service in the work of the tent of meeting" (NASB). Jamieson (Jamieson-Fausett-Brown, *Commentary*, ad loc.) suggests: "They entered on their work in their twenty-fifth year as pupils and probationers, under the superintendence and direction of their senior brethren; and at thirty they were admitted to the full discharge of their official functions." This inference, drawn from a careful comparison of the two passages, seems to be altogether reasonable. It furnishes an analogy to the training period through which candidates for the gospel ministry are expected to pass before they receive full ordination, with the right to baptize or perform wedding ceremonies and the like.

For five years the younger Levites had an opportunity to observe the procedures and guiding principles followed by those engaged in full Levitical responsibility—the proper method of moving the lampstand, the table of showbread, the two altars, and so on—and the proper disposition of the bowls and jars, the spoons and snuffers, the holy oil and the water of purification, and all the rest. There were also chores related to the upkeep of the tabernacle grounds and the service to the worshipers who came to sacrifice at the altar. Apparently young Samuel, even as a lad much younger than twenty-five, was involved in such duties, with particular responsibilities as Eli's houseboy (1 Sam. 3:1). In other words, there were many different types and grades of service to be cared for by underage Levites, even before they were old enough to enter their apprenticeship at the age of twenty-five.

As for the Levites referred to in Ezra

3:8, two factors need to be carefully noted. The first is that in both Ezra 2:40 and Nehemiah 7:43 the number of Levites involved in the return from Babylon was only 74. There was a substantially larger number of gatekeepers and temple servants, and the priests who joined in the return to Jerusalem numbered 4,289 (Ezra 2:36-39). Therefore the Levites were in short supply, and it would have been appropriate to involve even the younger men (between twenty and twenty-five years of age) in order to provide an adequate number of Levitical overseers for the builders who were engaged in restoring the temple.

The second factor to note is that these Levites were not really engaged in the ministry of sacrifice and worship; they were only concerned with the building project as advisers or foremen. There was no sanctuary as yet in which they could officiate; so the question of being younger than twenty-five would hardly be raised at all. Thus there is no real discrepancy or contradiction in regard to the three age-limits given in the passage cited above, for each deals with a different level of authority.

How could God punish the Israelites for eating the quail He had miraculously provided as their food (Num. 11:31-34)?

If we read the whole account of Numbers 11 carefully, we can understand why God was so highly displeased with the Hebrew malcontents who were tired of His daily supply of manna and longed for meat and vegetables in their diet (vv.4-9). Moses himself was so disgusted at their complaining ingratitude that he was ready to resign from his responsibility of leadership. God thereupon encouraged him to delegate leadership to a supporting team of seventy godly elders, and then He told them how He would deal with their rebellious discontent. He would give them what they were asking for, thus bringing them to see how foolish they were to despise the good and sufficient food He had apportioned them in favor of that which they chose for themselves. As Psalm 106:15 recalls the episode: "He gave them their request, but sent a wasting disease among them [or, 'leanness into their soul']" (NASB). In other words, in order to teach them a much-needed lesson, God saw fit to give the discontented rabble exactly what they asked for—rather than that which would be best for them.

The result was that an enormous flight of quail were blown into the encampment at a height of two cubits (about three feet) above the surface of the ground (v.31). (The preposition 'al before "the surface of the ground" should be rendered "above," as NIV correctly renders it, rather than "on.") Flying at that low level, forced down by the strong wind, it was easy for the Israelites to bat them down with sticks and catch as many quail as they wanted—even to the amount of ten homers (about sixty bushels). But, of course, such a huge number of dead birds would speedily begin to rot in that hot desert, despite the people's best efforts to convert them into dried meat that could be preserved indefinitely by parching them under the sun (v.32). There is little wonder that they began to suffer from food poisoning and disease as soon as they began chewing this unaccustomed food. In the end a great many of them died of plague and had to be buried right there in the desolate wilderness, at *Qibrôt Hatt'avāh*, "The Graves of Greed."

How can Numbers 12:3, with its emphasis on Moses' humility, be an authentic comment from Moses' own pen?

Apart from Deuteronomy 34 (which must have been an obituary written after Moses' death), no passage in the Pentateuch has been more frequently cited as an evidence of non-Mosaic authorship than this verse. After the challenge to Moses' unique authority as God's spokesman (recorded in Num. 12:1-2), the humility statement occurs in v.3: "Now the man Moses was very humble, more than any man who was on the face of the earth." Unquestionably the first impression made by this judgment on the great leader's character is that it was contributed as a biographical note made by some admirer who knew him well, rather than by Moses concerning himself. M.G. Kyle ("Moses," *International Standard Bible Encyclopedia* [Grand Rapids: Eerdmans, 1939], p. 2090) tends to favor this explanation; even Jamieson (Jamieson-Fausset-Brown, ad loc.) allows for the possibility of its insertion here by some later prophet. But he also cites the parallel of Paul in 2 Corinthians 11:5; 12:11-12, where the apostle is compelled by the insolence and contempt of his detractors to emphasize the distinguishing excellence of his own character.

Likewise Elmer Smick (*Wycliffe Bible Commentary*, p. 129) allows for the possibility that this comment may have been contributed by a "divinely inspired *shōtēr* ([Num.] 11:16)." Yet he points out that this chapter "teaches that the prophet had so intimate a relationship with God that he could speak the truth objectively, as it was revealed to him, even when it regarded his own nature."

Haley (*Alleged Discrepancies*, p. 248) makes this observation:

Moses, under the impulse of the Holy Spirit, was writing history "objectively." Hence he speaks as freely of himself as he would of any other person. It is also to be observed that he records his own faults and sins with the same fidelity and impartiality. It is remarked by Calmet: "As he praises himself here without pride, so he will blame himself elsewhere with humility." The objectionable words were inserted to explain why it was that Moses took no steps to vindicate himself, and why, consequently, the Lord so promptly intervened.

It certainly must be conceded that in other ancient autobiographies where the author speaks of himself in the third person, self-evaluations occur that seem to be rather surprising; for they stand in contrast to the author's usual references to his own character. Thus in Julius Caesar's "Civil War" (*The Alexandrian War* 75), he speaks of his own discomfiture at the unexpected attack of the troops of Pharnaces in Pontus, saying: "Caesar was startled by this incredible rashness—or self-confidence. He was caught off guard and unprepared; he was simultaneously calling the troops away from the fortification work [which they had been engaged in], ordering them to arm, deploying the legions and forming the battle-line." In other words, Caesar had misjudged the enemy and therefore had been caught "flat-footed," as it were. Ordinarily Caesar presents himself as a paragon of foresightedness and a master strategist; so this derogatory comment about himself comes as a real surprise.

So far as Numbers 12:3 is concerned, it should be observed that Moses' failure to speak in his own defense, even when put under great pressure by Aaron and Miriam to lose his temper, calls for special explanation. That explanation is found in his complete deliverance from pride and his thoroughgoing commitment of himself to the Lord God as his vindicator and protector. Any other leader in his position would surely have faced them with a withering reply, but Moses turned the matter completely over to God. We really need the information contained in v.3 in order to make sense of his amazing meekness in this situation. Therefore it seems

rather unlikely that v.3 could have been a later interpolation, when it actually furnishes a key to the understanding of the whole episode that introduces it.

Did the mission of the twelve spies start from Paran (Num. 13:3) or from Kadesh Barnea (Num. 20:1)?

Both statements are true. The Wilderness of Paran extends from the port of Eloth (Eilat) on the Gulf of Aqabah in a north-northeast direction across the Nahal Paran and Har Ramon (cf. Baly, *Bible Geography*, p. 34) to include the site of Kadesh Barnea, which lies on the same latitude as Punon (ibid., p. 95). The spies therefore set out from Kadesh, which is located in the Wilderness of Paran (cf. Num. 13:26: "in the wilderness of Paran, at Kadesh").

How could Moses be said to have given Hoshea the name Joshua in Numbers 13:16 when he has already been referred to as "Joshua" in Exodus 17:9 and 24:13?

There is no difficulty here, for the final composition of Exodus by Moses undoubtedly occurred toward the end of the forty years' wandering. Even though Joshua may not have acquired the name from Moses until later in the journey from Egypt to Canaan, nevertheless in retrospect it would have been only natural to refer to Joshua by the name he bore at the time Exodus was composed by Moses. It should be added that $Y^e h \hat{o} \check{s} \hat{u}^a$ ("Jehovah is salvation") is virtually the same name as $H \hat{o} \check{s}^{e a \cdot}$ ("salvation"), both being derived from the root $y \bar{a} \check{s} a \cdot$.

How could the Israelite spies describe Canaan as a land that devours its inhabitants (Num. 13:32) if indeed it was a fertile land of milk and honey (Num. 13)?

It would be an obvious misinterpretation to take the expression in Numbers 13:32, which describes Canaan as "a land that devours its inhabitants," as implying that it was a poverty-stricken land that could not adequately support its population. In this context it can only mean that its lush fertility (enjoying a higher rate of precipitation than it has had in recent centuries) rendered it so desirable to aggressively competing nations and tribes as to make it a center of bloody strife. As rival claimants battled one another for possession of this desirable terrain, they suffered many casualties through warfare. There is no contradiction here whatsoever. The description of Canaan as a land flowing with milk and honey occurs at least thirteen times in the Pentateuch, as well as in Joshua, Jeremiah, and Ezekiel. There is absolutely no basis for interpreting the metaphor of Numbers 13:32 as relating to poverty or starvation.

If nearly the whole adult generation of Israel died during the forty years' wandering, why is not that whole region full of their graves (Num. 14:34–35)?

Under the nomadic conditions of the wilderness journey, with a constant shifting from one site to another, there is no way that sturdy or well-constructed graves could have been made as the adult generation passed away. Shallow burials beneath the surface of the sand or gravel would have failed to preserve any of the skeletons for a very long period, even though they might have escaped disturbance by carrion-eating wild animals (which is doubtful). No excavations conducted anywhere in the world have ever exhumed identifiable burials of this type, and in the nature of the case it would be very surprising if they did. The failure to uncover shallow, unprotected burials of this sort therefore constitutes no evidence whatever against the historical accuracy of the

account that all the adults involved in the rebellion at Kadesh Barnea passed away before the crossing of the Jordan under Joshua—except, of course, for Caleb and Joshua himself.

Did the Israelites under Moses pass "beyond" Edom (Num. 20:14–21; Deut. 2:8) or did they actually pass "through" it (Deut. 2:4–7)?

Apparently both statements are true, as one would expect in view of the fact that both of these prepositions are used in one and the same passage. Deuteronomy 2:4 says, "And command the people, saying, 'You will pass through [or, 'pass through in'; Heb. *ōḇerîm biḡeḇûl*] the territory of your brothers the sons of Esau who live in Seir; and they will be afraid of you" (NASB). The next two verses go on to explain that God will not permit the Hebrews to conquer any of Edom's territory since He originally bestowed it on Esau as a permanent possession. But they are to purchase food and water from the Edomites, along with the permission to march up through the international route known as the King's Highway, which passed through the midst of the Edomite domain.

The response of the king of Edom was in the negative, and he even drew up his troops to oppose their using the highway itself through his land. Numbers 20:21 then states, "Thus Edom refused to allow Israel to pass through his territory; so Israel turned away from him" (NASB). Moses later recalls this, saying, "So we passed beyond our brothers the sons of Esau, who live in Seir, away from the Arabah road [i.e., the King's Highway], away from Elath and from Ezion-geber" (Deut. 2:8, NASB). Therefore we are to understand that the northward line of march led along the eastern border of Edom to the border of Moab (a territory Israel was also forbidden by God to pass through forcibly, since it had been granted to the posterity of Lot, Moab's ancestor).

In what sense, then, did Israel pass through in the territory of Edom (as Deut. 2:4 said they would)? It was in the sense that they were inside the borders at the time they parleyed with the Edomite government. They may even have purchased some food and water from some of the local inhabitants before their government ruled against the Hebrews' using the King's Highway to go northward to Moab and the Plains of Shittim. They therefore did not force the issue—even though their army could have easily overwhelmed the Edomite armed forces. They refrained from passing up the highway and instead veered to the east and went up by the eastern border (in all probability), along the rugged, unpaved terrain of the Syrian desert.

If Israel's army was really so large, how could the Edomites have turned them back or the Canaanites have given them such difficulty in the conquest of the land (Num. 20:14–21; Josh. 7)?

According to Numbers 26 the Israelite armed forces totaled 601,730, which certainly would have exceeded the number of troops that Edom could have marshaled to oppose them. But Numbers 20:14–21 says absolutely nothing about an armed clash between these forces; so it is evident that Moses and his host turned away from Edom simply because the Edomites refused to give them permission to march through their land on their way northward to Moab and the east bank of the Jordan. Verse 21 says, "Thus Edom refused to allow Israel to pass through his territory; so Israel turned away from him" (NASB). The Hebrews evidently respected the right of the Edomites (who were distantly related to them through Abraham) to refuse them passage if they so insisted.

As for the conquest of Canaan, the only setback Israel experienced was when the defenders of Ai repulsed an Israelite expeditionary force of no more than 3000 (Josh. 7:4). They had 36 casualties—hardly a major military defeat! Every other armed conflict was attended by complete success. No country was ever more easily conquered than Canaan, so far as Joshua's troops were concerned. As for the ability of the land to support such large numbers of inhabitants as are indicated by the record in Joshua, it should be remembered that modern conditions are no reliable yardstick of population potential of ancient lands. In our own century large and beautiful Roman cities have been discovered under the sands of North Africa in areas that are now totally deserted, owing to a lowering of the precipitation rate. The soil of Israel today is remarkably fertile in most of its valleys, slopes, and plains, once it has adequate irrigation. Baly (*Bible Geography*, p. 67) reports Alan Crown's research as indicating that drought conditions recurred in Palestine between 2300 and 2000 B.C., but that there was "perhaps somewhat more assured rainfall than now just after 2000." Baly (p. 68) concludes his climatic study with these words:

Unfortunately, after 2000 B.C. the evidences for climatic fluctuation are increasingly obscured by human activity in the country, but we must certainly beware, and beware emphatically, of assuming that the climate figures given in this book [for the last century or so] can be used unchanged for the patriarchal period, the time of the monarchy, the New Testament, or any subsequent era. That would mean that the Palestinian climate had remained static for 4000 years, and this we can say with confidence is impossible.

The likelihood of a higher rainfall during the second millennium B.C. in the area of Syria-Palestine makes it quite feasible for that territory to have supported a large population, capable of fielding large armies and of supporting the Hebrew population there after the conquest. The present population of Israel is considerably in excess of the figures given for biblical times; so there should be little credence given to skepticism along these lines. Furthermore, the recent discoveries at the Syrian city of Ebla at the conclusion of the third millennium indicate quite conclusively that the population of that one city was at least 260,000 (cf. K.A. Kitchen, *the Bible in Its World* [Downers Grove, Ill.: Intervarsity, 1077], pp. 39–40).

We read in Numbers 22:17–23 that the prophet Balaam informed the messengers of King Balak of Moab that he could never do (or say) anything contrary to the command of Yahweh his God; but why then did the Lord send His angel to kill him (Num. 22:33)? (D*)

God sent His angel with a very stern warning to Balaam not to speak what Balak wanted him to say (namely, a curse against the host of Israel) but only the true message of God, a pronouncement of blessing on the covenant nation of Jacob. The encounter with the self-seeking prophet at the narrow mountain road was intended as a frightening reminder that Balaam was never to speak any other message than that which Yahweh was about to reveal to him in the presence of the Moabites and the Midianites. Because of his corrupt motive in going to Balak afterward, despite his earlier refusal to come to Balak at all (Num. 22:13), Balaam was guilty of yearning to comply with the king's request rather than God's desire, just for the sake of the earthly riches and honor the wicked monarch had promised him as a bribe to disobey God.

To be sure, the Lord had finally given Balaam grudging permission to go down to Moab, on the condition that he would faithfully repeat the true message of God in the presence of Balak and the Moabites (v.20). But because of the fierce struggle between duty and greed that went on in Balaam's soul as he responded to the king's invitation, Yahweh had to remind him very sternly that his failure to carry out his commission from God with complete faithfulness would result in his instant death. Hence the dramatic scene at the mountain pass occurred, where God used the donkey as His mouthpiece to rebuke the stubborn prophet and warn him of his mortal danger.

Is not the mention of Agag in Numbers 24:7 anachronistic, in view of his contemporaneity with King Saul in the eleventh century (1 Sam. 15:8)?

It is rather questionable whether "Agag" was a personal name at all; it may well have been a royal title among the Amalekites, somewhat similar to "Pharaoh" among the Egyptians or "Caesar" among the Romans (although, of course, the latter was originally the proper name of Gaius Julius Caesar). It has been found as a name (or title?) in Phoenician inscriptions (cf. *Corpus Inscriptionum Semiticarum* I. 3196) in a location and time far removed from the southern desert Midianites who were wiped out by Saul's army. But even if it was a royal name that appeared in the royal family of that branch of the Midianite nation, this is no more remarkable than the recurrence of Jeroboam as the name of a king of Israel who reigned from 793 to 753 rather than the original Jeroboam who began the northern kingdom back in 931. There is a similar recurrence of royal names in Phoenicia (with two or more kings named "Hiram" or "Ahiram"), in Syria (with at least two Benhadads), in Gerar of Philistia (with at least two Abimelechs), and in Egypt (where there were three Pharaohs named Senwosret and four named Amenemhet in the Twelfth Dynasty alone, and in the Eighteenth there were four named Thutmose and four named Amenhotep). Although no written records have survived from the Midianite culture, we may safely assume that they too followed the custom of using a favored name repeatedly in successive generations.

How many died in the plague of the apostasy of Baal-peor?

Numbers 25:9 indicates that as a divine judgment on the Baal worshipers of Baal-peor, no less than twenty-four thousand died of plague. Some have supposed that 1 Corinthians 10:8 refers to the same episode, which gives the number of the dead as only twenty-three thousand. But this is an unfounded objection, for 1 Corinthians 10:8 does not refer to the incident at Baal-peor (Num. 25:1-8) at all; rather, it refers to the plague that followed the apostasy of the golden calf. This is clear from the previous verse (v.7): "And do not be idolaters, as some of them were; as it is written: 'The people sat down to eat and drink, and stood up to play'" (NASB). Since this is a direct quotation from Exodus 32:6, the identification is beyond dispute.

Interestingly enough, Exodus 32:3 does not give the number of those that perished in that plague of the golden calf; it simply says, "Then the LORD smote the people, because of what they did with the calf which Aaron had made" (NASB). Not until this New Testament passage (1 Cor. 10:8) do we find out how many died in that plague, namely twenty-three thousand. There is no contradiction at all, just two different episodes!

Is there any record of the tribe of Dan to show where they eventually settled? (D*)

At the time of the second census, as recorded in Numbers 26:42, the military population of the tribe of Dan came to the very considerable figure of 64,400 (v.43). To these was allotted a rather restricted territory between the western border of Judah and the shore of the Mediterranean, including the northern part of Philistia (Josh. 19:40-46). This particular region, however, was very fertile and enjoyed good precipitation and might well have yielded enough crops to support this populous tribe. But for some reason the Danites failed to match the Philistines in determination and military prowess; and despite the heroism of Samson, their finest warrior, they became vassals to them in a few generations after Joshua's conquest.

Partly for this reason, the Danites became so restricted in their economic and political growth that some of the more enterprising of the younger men decided to form an expeditionary force and seek new land to settle outside the territory originally occupied by the Twelve Tribes. We cannot exactly date the time of this migration, which is detailed for us in Judges 18; but we know that only 600 men were involved in this operation.

After the Danite search committee had surveyed the entire land all the way up to southern Phoenicia (modern Lebanon), they chose the prosperous and peaceful city of Laish as the most attractive prospect for settlement. The armed troops thereupon proceeded through Kiriath-Jearim in Judah and went to the hill country of Ephraim, where they abducted a Levite who was serving as household priest to Micah, an Ephraimite. They also made off with Micah's silver ephod, to serve as their cult image in the worship of Yahweh (though this was contrary to the second commandment), and attacked the un-

141

suspecting Laishites in a surprise assault. Having taken possession of the city, they renamed it Dan. This Dan became the northernmost outpost of the Twelve Tribes, and as such was featured in the common phrase "from Dan to Beersheba."

After the secession of the Ten Tribes from the dynasty of David (931 B.C.), the founding king of the northern kingdom, Jeroboam I, took care to establish an official temple there, complete with the image of a golden calf (1 Kings 12:30). But this northern colony of the tribe of Dan probably remained much smaller in population than that of those living next to Philistia, in the territory originally allotted to them by Joshua. There was no question of a migration on the part of the whole tribe; it was a modest-sized colony that underjtook the conquest of Laish up near the territory of Sidon and Tyre.

How can the total destruction of Midian in Numbers 31 be morally justified?

Numbers 31 narrates the total destruction of the Midianites who had conspired to seduce the Israelites to fornication and idolatry at the incident of Baal-peor (Num. 25:1–9). The resultant plague against the Israelites on that occasion mounted to a total of twenty-four thousand and a serious alienation with God. The heinousness of their crime against the Lord's people and the threat of future allurement to apostasy made the Midianites ripe for judgment. Chapter 31 tells us very plainly that it was the Lord Yahweh Himself who commanded this punitive action; it did not originate with Moses or his men. They were commanded to "execute the LORD's vengeance on Midian" (v.3, NASB) by sending against them an army of twelve thousand warriors, one thousand from each tribe, under the leadership of Phinehas, the grandson of Aaron (v.6).

The attack was so successful that without a single casualty (v.49) the Israelites defeated and killed all five kings of the Midianites and all their men as well. Balaam, the unfaithful prophet of God from Beor, had been the instigator of the apostasy of Baal-peor; so he also was killed. The married women and all the younger women who had been sexually active were likewise put to death (vv.15–18), after Moses had given special orders to do so. Only the young girls and virgins had their lives spared, and they were taken as servants into the Israelite households. A stated percentage of the Midianite livestock was devoted to the Lord and the service of the tabernacle. Of the gold ornaments taken from the enemy, 16,750 shekels were also given to the Lord's service. Thus the entire affair was concluded and the baneful effects of fraternization with degenerate pagans became a thing of the past—all but the unhappy memory and the solemn warning against yielding to the seduction of Canaanite idolatry.

Was this action morally justified? Those who wish to argue that it was cruel and uncalled for will have to argue with God, for He commanded it. But it seems quite apparent in the light of all the circumstances and the background of this crisis that the integrity of the entire nation was at stake. Had the threat to Israel's existence as a covenant nation been dealt with any less severely, it is extremely doubtful that Israel would have been able to conquer Canaan at all, or claim the Land of Promise as a sacred trust from God. The massacre was as regrettable as a radical surgery performed on the ailing body of a cancer victim. If his life is to be preserved, the diseased portion must be completely cut away. (Further discussion concerning this whole problem of extermination will be found in connnection with Joshua 6:21—"Was Joshua justified in exterminating the population of Jericho?")

Does Numbers 35:30 make it wrong to condemn a murderer to death on mere circumstantial evidence?

Numbers 35:30 says, "If anyone kills a person, the murderer shall be put to death at the evidence of witnesses, but no person shall be put to death on the testimony of one witness" (NASB). Similarly we read in Deuteronomy 17:6: "On the evidence of two witnesses or three witnesses, he who is to die shall be put to death; he shall not be put to death on the evidence of one witness" (NASB).

If the term "witness" ('ēd) means only an eyewitness of the crime while it was actually being committed, this would seem to restrict the imposition of the death penalty to those comparatively rare instances where the murderer committed homicide in full view of the public. This might mean that less than 10 percent of the cases of the violations of the sixth commandment could lawfully be brought to trial and result in the achievement of justice. Yet the real thrust of the laws against first-degree murder was that the murderer should surely be brought to trial and executed. Nothing less than "life for life" was allowed under the Torah (cf. Exod. 21:23; Deut. 19:21).

Although some other legal systems (such as the Hittite Code) allowed for the payment of blood-money as an alternative to the death penalty, this was expressly forbidden by the law of God. Numbers 35:31 states: "Moreover, you shall not take ransom for the life of a murderer who is guilty of death, but he shall surely be put to death" (NASB). Verse 33 goes on to say, "So you shall not pollute the land in which you are; for blood pollutes the land and no expiation can be made for the land for the blood that is shed on it, except by the blood of him who shed it" (NASB).

The seriousness of an unsolved murder for the welfare of the district in which it occurred was such that Deuteronomy 21 required a solemn inquest to be held when it could not immediately be discovered who was guilty of the crime. Verses 3–8 specify:

> And it shall be that the city which is nearest to the slain man, that is, the elders of that city, shall take a heifer of the herd, ... and the elders of that city shall bring that heifer down to a valley with running water, ... and shall break the heifer's neck there in the valley. Then the priests, the sons of Levi, shall come near.... And all the elders of that city which is nearest to the slain man shall wash their hands over the heifer whose neck was broken in the valley; and they shall answer and say, "Our hands have not shed this blood, nor did our eyes see it. Forgive Thy people Israel whom Thou hast redeemed, O LORD, and do not place the guilt of innocent blood in the midst of Thy people Israel." And the bloodguiltiness shall be forgiven them.

This passage makes it clear that murder was a very heinous offense in the eyes of God, rather than a crime to be so lightly regarded as to be punishable perhaps one time out of ten (on the technicality that two men had not actually seen the killer strike the blow).

There is a far wider implication that results from this restrictive interpretation: the two-witnesses requirement applies not only to homicide cases but to any other crime for which a suspect could be brought to trial. Deuteronomy 19:15 says, "A single witness shall not rise up against a man on account of any iniquity or any sin which he has committed; on the evidence of two or three witnesses a matter shall be confirmed" (NASB). This two-witnesses rule therefore applies to theft, fraud, adultery (which is seldom performed in public view), embezzlement, or any other offense for which a man might be subject to criminal process. Every criminal guilty of any of these offenses would therefore get off scot-free if he had taken the prudent measure of committing his crime where two people did not happen to be watching him. It is safe to say that neither ancient Israel nor any other system of jurisprudence known to man could effectively function under such a restriction as that.

How then are we to understand this requirement for two or more witnesses in the prosecution of an accused suspect? The answer is found in a study of the actual usage of the term *'ēd* ("witness") as employed in the Hebrew Scriptures. In Leviticus 5:1 we read, "Now if a person sins, after he hears a public adjuration to testify, when he is a witness, whether he has seen or otherwise known, if he does not tell it, then he will bear his guilt" (NASB). This verse clearly establishes that there are two kinds of witnesses who may offer testimony in a criminal process: those who have seen the crime actually being committed, and those who, though not eyewitnesses, have seen some evidence relative to the identity of the offender. One who has found a written death-threat, for example, or who has heard the accused express a desire or intention to kill, rob, or rape the victim, would be acceptable as a witness within this definition of *'ēd* (one who has pertinent knowledge concerning the crime, even though he has not actually seen it being committed).

A slightly different use of *'ēd* is found in the law of responsibility for a missing animal that has been entrusted to the care of another, as in Exodus 22:13: "If it is all torn to pieces [i.e., by some predatory beast], let him bring it as evidence [*'ēd*]; he shall not make restitution for what has been torn to pieces" (NASB). Here then the lacerated corpse of the sheep or donkey, or whatever it may have been, will serve as a "witness" to the fact that the animal was killed without any fault on the part of the caretaker. Yet that corpse could hardly be described as an *eye*-witness! Similarly, also, documents or memorial stones may serve as a witness (*'ēd*)—such as the *gal-'ēd* that Jacob and Laban erected at the spot where Laban had overtaken his fleeing son-in-law, and they had finally come to a covenant agreement toward each other (Gen. 31:46–49). Both *gal-'ēd* (which gave rise to the name of "Gilead" for the whole region) and Laban's Aramaic equivalent, *yᵉgar śāhᵃdûṯā'*, signified "stone-pile of witness." Yet in these lifeless stones we can hardly find a visual observer.

Along the same line are references to written documents, which serve as a "witness" (*'ēd*, or its feminine form, *'ēdāh*) to the contract or covenant into which the contractual parties have entered. Thus Joshua 24:25–26 quotes Joshua himself as referring to the stone (or stela) that he had erected at Shechem, on which the words of their covenant commitment to Yahweh had been inscribed; he says of it in v.27: "Behold, this stone shall be for a witness against us, for it has heard all the words of the LORD which he spoke to us; thus it shall be for a witness against you, lest you deny your God" (NASB). The inscribed stela was certainly not an eyewitness (even though it is poetically represented as an auditor to the ceremony), but rather it served as a document in evidence.

We conclude, therefore, that concrete objects and written documents may be entered into evidence before a court hearing as valid testimony in any kind of a criminal process, whether or not a capital offense is involved. This falls more or less in line with the different types of evidence received in criminal cases even in our modern courts, and so there is no contravention of biblical principles in allowing such testimony, even though only one actual eyewitness may be found, or none at all. Each witness called to the stand is asked to testify only of matters within his personal observation and experience, and this satisfies the specifications of an *'ēd* in a perfectly adequate fashion according to actual biblical usage. (For further discussion, see article on John 8:11.)

Deuteronomy

How could the exact words of God in the Ten Commandments (Exod. 20:2-17) be altered in any way by Moses in Deuteronomy 5:6-21?

It should be understood that the purpose of Deuteronomy was to furnish a selective paraphrase of the law of God revealed to Moses in the earlier three books: Exodus, Leviticus, and Numbers. It was not intended to be a word-for-word repetition of the text of those books but rather a homiletical, hortatory application of their teaching to the new generation that had reached their majority during the forty years of the wilderness wandering. Those precepts and aspects of the law that would be most useful for the non-Levitical congregation were culled out and set before them in a hard-hitting yet encouraging fashion so that they would be ideologically prepared for the conquest and occupation of Canaan. Consequently it would be quite exceptional for the identical words to occur on a given subject, as between Exodus 20 and Deuteronomy 5. There are variations in phraseology, but never in sense or essential teaching, as between those two books (or between Deuteronomy and Leviticus or Numbers, for that matter).

In the case of the Decalogue, it was only to be expected that the wording of Exodus 20 should be very closely followed by Deuteronomy 5, since this was originally a text directly composed by God Himself. However, it should be remembered that Moses was free to follow the guidance of the Holy Spirit as he omitted or inserted a clause or two in the Deuteronomic restatement. While it is true that Moses quoted the Decalogue as being the very words of God ("He said" [Deut. 5:5]), this committed him only to insertions that quoted from God's own revealed word, whether in Exodus 20 or elsewhere in the book. Thus, in connection with the Sabbath commandment (v.14), he omits mention of the Creation in six days as a basis for the sanction (contained in Exod. 20:11), but adds at the end of this commandment (Deut. 5:15) the words of Exodus 13:3: "Remember this day in which you went out from Egypt, from the house of slavery; for by a powerful hand the LORD brought you out from this place." Those words also had been spoken by divine inspiration and authority, and they furnished Moses' people with an additional ground for showing kindness and consideration for the servile class in their society. The Lord had shown them great love and kindness when they had been a nation of slaves down in Egypt. It may not be quite clear as to the reason for omitting the Creation days basis for the Sabbath sanction; but the failure to include it constitutes no actual discrepancy—any more than pertains to quotations we may discuss, taken from the text appearing in some other book, but streamlined by the use of a succession of dots when we are leaving out a few of the words in the original passage.

As for the variation in word order occurring in the tenth commandment ("house" is mentioned before "wife" in Exod. 20:17, but "wife" before "house" in Deut. 5:21), the words and the meaning are both the same, despite the slight difference in sequence. There is also a different Hebrew word for "covet" used before "house" in Deuteronomy 5:21 (*tiṯ'awweh* instead of *taḥmōḏ*), but the meaning is virtually identical as between the two verbs; and the variation may simply have furnished a variant for the sake of a more agreeable style than that employed by Exodus 20:17 (*lōʾ taḥmōḏ*). That would certainly conform to the specifically homiletical purpose underlying the last book of the Pentateuch.

Just where did Aaron die? Deuteronomy 10:6 says that it was at Moserah, but Numbers 20:28; 33:38 say it was at the top of Mount Hor.

Deuteronomy 10:6 contains a parenthetical statement in the midst of Moses' reminiscences about events near Mount Sinai, which goes as follows: "Now the sons of Israel set out from Beeroth Bene-jaakan to Moserah. There Aaron died and there he was buried and Eleazar his son ministered as priest in his place" (NASB). But Numbers 20:28 relates how Moses and Eleazar accompanied Aaron to the summit of Mount Hor, where he passed away. This is confirmed by Numbers 33:38: "Then Aaron the priest went up to Mount Hor at the command of the LORD, and died there, in the fortieth year after the sons of Israel had come from the land of Egypt" (NASB).

In all probability Moserah was the name of the district in which Mount Hor was located (so P.A. Verhoef in Tenney, *Zondervan Pictorial Encyclopedia*, 4:279), just as Horeb was the name of the mountain complex in which the mountain known as Sinai was situated. There has been no archaeological investigation in the vincinity of Jebel Madurah that might give us additional information concerning the limits of the Moserah district; but it is fair to assume that the one ancient source that does mention it (namely, the Pentateuch) was well aware of its location, and that it placed it in the vicinity of Mount Hor.

Mount Nebo was alleged by Josephus (*Antiquities* 4.4.7) to be the same as Jebel Neby Harun, a mountain forty-eight hundred feet high, overlooking Petra. But since it was located in the middle of Edom rather than at its border, and since it is somewhat too rugged to ascend without special equipment, and too lofty for its summit to be easily observed from below, it is rather unlikely that this traditional identification is the correct one.

Stephen Barabas (in Tenney, *Zondervan Pictorial Encyclopedia*, 3:201) suggests Jebel Madurah as a more likely site for Aaron's death, for it lies northeast of Kadesh on the northwest border of Edom; and its summit can be observed by watchers standing at its base, as Numbers 20:27 specifies. But whether or not this is the correct identification, it is quite unwarrantable to assume that the Pentateuch erred in placing Hor in the district of Moserah.

What is the Old Testament teaching on the use of intoxicating liquor? Deuteronomy 14:26 seems to permit the purchase and use of wine and strong drink; libations of wine were even poured on the altar (Exod. 29:40). Yet Leviticus 10:8–9 contains a stern warning against wine so far as priests were concerned; and Proverbs seems to reject the use of wine

on the part of all believers (Prov. 20:1; 23:29–35), except perhaps for those who are sickly and near death (31:4–7). (D*)

The Old Testament abounds with warning examples of the misuse of wine and the very grave dangers it holds in store for those who drink it. When Noah first discovered the intoxicating effects of grape juice (Gen. 9:20–21), he made a fool of himself and met with derision on the part of his son Ham. The daughters of Lot plied him with wine until he became so befuddled that he committed incest with them unawares during nighttime. Immoderate use of wine became a national evil in the northern kingdom and led to its moral depravity and loss of spiritual understanding. Isaiah graphically described the revolting excesses and degrading addiction of those who drank to excess (Isa. 28:1–8). Proverbs 20 and 23 describe most vividly the depraving bestiality and folly of those who give themselves over to liquor for the purpose of intoxication. In a figurative sense also, Psalms 60:3; 75:8; Jeremiah 13:12–14; 25:15–18 speak of wine as a bitter and terrible potion for experiencing the wrath of God, visiting judgment on the wicked and ungodly. Quite in the spirit of these Old Testament passages, we read in Revelation 14:10, "He also [i.e., the worshiper of the beast] will drink of the wine of the wrath of God, which is unmixed in the cup of His anger; and he will be tormented with fire and brimstone" (NASB mg.).

As pointed out in the question, according to Leviticus 10:8–11, no priest was allowed to enter into the tabernacle or temple to perform divine service if he had partaken of wine. (It was probably because Aaron's two older sons, Nadab and Abihu, had been drinking that they brought unhallowed fire to light the incense of the golden altar and therefore lost their lives.) It is thus made clear that priests who drank were thereby prevented from carrying out their ministry of teaching the people the distinction between what was holy and what was profane.

This has implications for the New Testament priesthood of all believers (1 Peter 2:9) and suggests that they may be seriously handicapped in carrying on the work of soulwinning if they personally indulge in the use of alcohol. By doing so, they may cause millions of fellow citizens to stumble who have become enslaved to this degrading practice and are looking for some way out of their bondage. These are scarcely apt to take seriously the Christian witness of one who has not rid himself of "everything that hinders" (Heb. 12:1), especially when he starts speaking about the victorious life of faith.

It is clear that in the days of Christ and the apostles, wine was served as a table beverage at meals and used in communion services. At that time distilled liquor was as yet unknown, and there was no organized liquor industry dedicated to making every man, woman, and child addicted to their profit-making vice (as is true today), with attendant increase in crime and highway fatalities resulting from drunken driving. It is also very clear that the New Testament itself lays down a principle that makes it very difficult for a conscientious believer to carry on the use of liquor even on a temperate scale. That principle is found in Romans 14:21: "It is good neither to eat flesh, nor to drink wine, nor any thing where by thy brother stumbleth, or is offended, or is made weak." Verse 22 goes on to say, "Hast thou faith? have it to thyself before God. Happy is he that condemneth not himself in the thing which he alloweth."

In other words, the basic issue at stake is the law of love toward the weaker brother, and whether we as ambassadors of Christ are so concerned about souls that we are willing to forgo personal "rights" in order to win alcoholics and near-alcoholics to Christ. If we really care about the souls of men, and if we are really in business for Christ rather than for ourselves, then there seems (to this writer, at least) to be no alternative to total abstinence—not as a matter of legalism, but rather as a matter of love.

Are there not a number of contradictions between the laws of Deuteronomy and the earlier legal material found in Exodus? Compare Exodus 21:26 with Deuteronomy 15:12–18 and Exodus 23:10–11 with Deuteronomy 15:1–11.

The two sets of passages contain no contradiction whatever, so far as this writer can see (on the basis of his own legal training). In Exodus 21:26 it is laid down as a ruling that any slaveowner who strikes a male or female servant in such a way as to blind an eye must free that slave by way of compensation. In Deuteronomy 15:12–18 it is provided that after six years of service a Hebrew slave must be set free, and in addition he must be well provided with enough equipment to become self-supporting. These are two different grounds for manumission, but they do not in the slightest contradict each other.

Exodus 23:10–11 relates to the requirement that, after six continuous years of cultivation, plowed acreage is to be left fallow during the seventh or sabbatical year, and that which grows on it without cultivation is to be left to the poor or else to wild animals. Deuteronomy 15:1–11 has nothing to do with the cultivation of land but relates to the remission of debts (šᵉmiṭṭāh) at the end of seven years. It also contains a promise that there will be no poor in the land of Israel after the conquest and settlement by the Hebrews—provided only they will keep the Lord's commandments (both concerning the sabbatical year and concerning the other main guidelines for stewardship of the land as provided in the Mosaic Law). There is therefore no contradiction at all between these provisions.

For readers who may be interested in this general subject of allegedly conflicting laws in the Mosaic Code, we recommend the work of the British legal expert Harold M. Wiener, who in his "Essays on Pentateuchal Criticism" (1909) and "Pentateuchal Studies" (1912) (cited in R.K. Harrison *Old Testament Introduction,* p. 30) showed that there was no proven case of conflict between any of the pairs of laws that had been cited by Documentarian critics as proof of multiple authorship of the Torah. It is instructive to note that if a similar methodology were applied to the Code of Hammurabi (inscribed on a single diorite stela in Babylon ca. 1750 B.C.), a similar claim might be advanced. Kitchen (*Ancient Orient,* p. 134) remarks:

Thus, it is easy to group social laws and cult-regulations into small collections on the basis of their content or form and postulate their gradual accretion in the present books [i.e., of the Pentateuch], with the practical elimination of Moses. One may do this equally to the Hammurapi laws (on content), and postulate there a hypothetical process of accretion of laws into groups of themes prior to conflation in Hammurapi's so-called "code." But this does not eliminate Hammurapi from "authorship" of his "code." His laws are known from a monument of his own time in his own name; therefore, any accretions of laws in his collection occurred before his work.... Furthermore, there are apparent contradictions or discrepancies in the Hammurapi "code" that are "no less glaring than those which serve as the basis of analyzing strata in the Bible" (M. Greenberg, *Yehezkel Kaufmann Jubilee Volume,* 1960, p. 6). These obviously have no bearing on the historical fact of Hammurapi [sic] having incorporated them in his collection.

149

(See also Kitchen, *Ancient Orient*, p. 148.)

How can Deuteronomy 15:4—"There shall be no poor among you"—be reconciled with Deuteronomy 15:11—"For the poor will never cease to be in the land"?

Taken out of context, the promise "There shall be no poor among you" is indeed contradicted by vv.11–12 and by the subsequent experience of Israel. With Deuteronomy 15:11 in mind ("The poor will never cease to be in the land," NASB), our Lord Jesus Christ affirmed, in connection with the generosity of Mary in anointing His feet with costly perfume, "For the poor you have with you always; but you do not always have Me" (Matt. 26:11, NASB). But as we take the passage in context, it turns out to be a merely theoretical possibility conditioned on full and consistent obedience to God's law.

The KJV translates vv. 4–5 thus: "Save when there shall be no poor among you; for the LORD shall greatly bless thee in the land which the LORD thy God giveth thee.... only if thou carefully hearken unto the voice of the LORD thy God, to observe to do all these commandments." The ASV amends this slightly to read: "Howbeit there shall be no poor with thee; (for Jehovah will surely bless thee in the land).... if only thou diligently hearken unto the voice of Jehovah thy God, to observe to do all this commandment." The KJV's "Save when" and the ASV's "Howbeit" are different ways of handling the Hebrew *'epes kî*, with which v.4 begins. The lexicons tend to favor "howbeit" or "notwithstanding" (Koehler-Baumgartner, *Lexicon*, p. 78); Brown-Driver-Briggs (*Lexicon*, p. 87) defines this phrase as *save that howbeit* (qualifying a preceding statement)." Gesenius-Buhl (*Hebräisches und aramaisches Handwörterbuch*, p. 60) give "*nur, dass, aber, jedoch*" (i.e., "only

that," "but," "nevertheless"); Zorell (F. Zorell and L. Semkowski, edd., *Lexicon Hebräicum et Aramaicum Veteris Testamenti* [Rome, 1940], ad loc.) gives "*tantum* (est adnotandum) quod, = ceterum, utique, sed" (which means "yet [it is to be noted] that; = moreover, in any case, but"). Perhaps the best choice among these near-synonyms is "However," which is the equivalent appearing both in the NASB and the NIV, both of which begin v.5 with "if only you listen obediently."

The foregoing analysis makes it quite clear that the Lord is not predicting that there will be no poor among Israel, regardless of how the Israelites may break their promises of obedience to His laws and the obligations of brotherly kindness under their covenant with Yahweh. What v.4 is saying is that perfect and consistent obedience to the holy standards laid down by God will make possible a society free from poverty. Verse 5 is quite emphatic in the expression of the condition of total and sincere obedience that must be met. It begins with *raq 'im*, "only if." The particle *raq* means "only," "altogether," "surely." At the beginning of a sentence (observes Brown-Driver-Briggs, *Lexicon*, p. 956b), it adds a limitation on something previously expressed. In this particular passage it means "provided only."

In v.11 we find a true prediction: "For the poor will never cease to be in the land; therefore... you shall freely open your hand to your brother, to your needy and poor in your land" (NASB). In other words, there is no real expectation that the Israelites will long or consistently maintain biblical standards of holiness, fairness, consideration, and love among themselves; and the poverty-free state envisioned in v.4 is merely a theoretical possibility.

Is Deuteronomy 22:5—"The woman shall not wear that which pertaineth unto a

man, neither shall a man put on a woman's garment"—applicable today? (D*)

The word $k^e li$ (translated "what pertains to") is a rather imprecise word. Sometimes it means "vessel" or "container"; sometimes "implement," "equipment"; sometimes "weapon" or even "adornment." It is apparently only in this context that it refers to clothing ($k^e li$ is any kind of manufactured product); although conceivably it might refer to adornments or jewelry. The word for garment in the second part of the verse is *śimlāh*, which primarily means mantle or cloak, but then becomes more loosely applied to clothing of almost any kind that covers the body.

The basic principle here is that each of the two sexes is to appreciate and honor the dignity of its own sex rather than to adopt the appearance or role of the opposite sex. If a man is thankful to God that he was created a male and the woman that she was a female, then they should be happy to dress the part of a man or a woman, as the case may be, rather than imitating the costume of another.

Deuteronomy 22:5 completely excludes transvestism or any kind of impersonation of the opposite sex. Probably the practice of sex perversion and homosexuality, particularly in connection with pagan worship of fertility gods, accentuated the need of such a provision. Whether it implies God's disapproval of men's styles that resemble a woman's style of clothing (e.g., the Scottish kilt) or of women's clothing that resembles the costume of a man is another question. It is probably safe to say, for example, that most men would be quite reluctant to put on a pair of woman's slacks, even though they do superficially resemble men's trousers. Their style and cut are significantly different.

The specific range of styles worn by each sex tends to differ somewhat from one decade to another, and so it is impractical to lay down any hard and fast rule beyond the simple principle enunciated above. Yet it is a very important matter to God, since the verse ends with the solemn words "for all that do so are abomination unto the LORD thy God." It is therefore very questionable whether this particular provision of the Mosaic Law is to be relegated to the status of mere ritual matters, to be done away with by the emancipation of the New Testament believers from the yoke of the Old Testament legal code. Proper dress and modest clothing are certainly stressed in the New Testament as important for a convincing Christian testimony before the world (cf. 1 Tim. 2:9), and the dedicated believer is to dress to please the Lord rather than himself

Aren't the Mosaic instructions concerning divorce in Deuteronomy 24:1–4 at variance with the teaching of Jesus (Mark 10:2–12) and Paul (1 Cor. 7:10–16)?

Deuteronomy 24:1–4 does not actually bestow any divine approval or blessing on divorce as such. It simply recognizes that divorce was practiced in Israelite society and seeks to mitigate the hardship and injustice accruing to the wife when her husband, displeased with her for some reason, decides to put her away and send her back to her parents. The ASV renders v.1 thus: "When a man taketh a wife, and marrieth her, then it shall be, if she find no favor in his eyes, because he hath found some unseemly thing in her, that he shall write her a bill of divorcement, and give it in her hand, and send her out of his house." The NASB modifies the translation so as to eliminate the prescriptive thrust of the passage, rendering it: "When a man takes a wife . . . and it happens that she finds no favor in his eyes because he has found some indecency in her, and he writes her [$w^e k\bar{a}t\bar{a}b \, l\bar{a}h$ can be so rendered, instead of in a prescriptive way as it is in KJV and ASV] a certificate of divorce and puts it in her hand and sends her out from his house," leaving the sentence to continue on through vv.2–4, rather than stopping at the end of v.1.

Whichever way the verse is construed, it indicates that the husband must put the divorce certificate in his wife's hand as he sends her away. This had the effect of surrendering all his rights to the dowry that she had brought into the marriage. Otherwise he might wrongfully appropriate the dowry property as his own, falsely alleging that she had voluntarily left him for an indefinitely long visit at her parents' home and that no real divorce had taken place.

When this passage was mentioned to Jesus in Mark 10:2–12 (and in the parallel account in Matt. 19:1–9), He explained to the Pharisees who questioned Him, "Because of your hardness of heart he [Moses] wrote you this commandment" (NASB). He then discussed Genesis 2:24 with this closing comment: "AND THE TWO SHALL BECOME ONE FLESH; consequently they are no longer two, but one flesh. What therefore God has joined together, let no man separate" (vv.8–9, NASB). He then went on to specify (following Matthew's fuller report of the wording): "And I say to you, whoever divorces his wife, except for [sexual] immorality, and marries another commits adultery" (Matt. 19:9, NASB). In other words, it was never God's intention or desire for divorce to occur after a true and lawful marriage—unless the relationship was broken up by an adulterous union with a third party. The pre-Christian practice of divorce was therefore in that class of offenses that were permitted for a time because of the "hardness of men's hearts" but which would be done away

with (along with polygamy and slavery) by those who belonged to the kingdom of God. Under the new covenant these concessions to selfishness and unkindness would be abolished; and the true, original purpose of God would be exalted in the godly walk of believers who look to Christ Himself as their model.

In the sense that what Deuteronomy 24 permitted was no longer to be allowed in the New Testament age, there was a very definite change. But the Deuteronomy provision was to be recognized as a merely temporary measure, not really corresponding to God's ideal and purpose in marriage, and destined for abrogation in the new age ushered in by the Messiah, Jesus Christ.

As for 1 Corinthians 7:10–16, it is more than doubtful that this deals with true divorce. See the article discussing this passage, entitled: "Does 1 Corinthians 7:10–16 authorize divorce for desertion?"

Deuteronomy 24:16 says that children will not be killed for the sins of the fathers. Yet 2 Samuel 12:15–18 shows that the baby born to David and Bathsheba died because of their sin. Later, in 2 Samuel 21:5–9, Saul's seven grandchildren were put to death because of his sin, in order to bring the three-year famine to an end. How do we reconcile these?

Deuteronomy 24:16 lays down a general principle that human courts and human governments are not to impute to children or grandchildren the guilt of their parents or forebears when they themselves have not become implicated in the crime committed. It is clearly recognized in Scripture that each person stands on his own record before God. If one is personally guilty of unbelief or wickedness and fails to repent and trust in God's mercy through the blood shed on the altar, that person will die for his own sin—

not for that of his father. But if the child is upright and a true believer, he is justified before God; yet he cannot be justified on the basis of his father's righteousness if he himself rejects the grace of God (Jer. 31:29–30; Ezek. 18:1–20). On at least one occasion it is mentioned in the history of Judah that after the assassination of King Joash, his son Amaziah punished only his assassins themselves, sparing their children (2 Kings 14:6).

Although this legal principle of dealing with each person according to his deeds is firmly laid down in Scripture, it is also made clear that God retained for Himself the responsibility of ultimate judgment in the matter of capital crime. In the case of the child conceived by Bathsheba of David when she was married to Uriah, the loss of that baby (in that Old Testament setting) was a judgment visited on the guilty parents for their gross sin (which actually merited the death penalty under Lev. 20:10). It is by no means suggested that the child was suffering punishment for his parents' sin but that they were being punished by his death.

In the case of King Saul's grandchildren, no ordinary crime was involved. It was a matter of national guilt on a level that affected Israel as a whole. We are not given any information as to the time or the circumstances of Saul's massacre of the Gibeonites, but we are told that it was a grave breach of a covenant entered into back in the days of Joshua and enacted in the name of Yahweh (Josh. 9:3–15). All the nation was bound by this oath for all the days to come, even though it had been obtained under false pretenses. Therefore when Saul, as head of the Israelite government, committed this atrocity against the innocent Gibeonites, God saw to it that this covenant violation did not go unpunished. He sent a plague to decimate the population of all Israel, until the demands of justice could be met. God had delayed this visitation until it would do the least possible damage to the security of the nation, that is, until after the surrounding nations had been defeated and subdued to the rule of King David.

However, the high mortality resulting from the famine compelled David to inquire of the Lord what was the reason for this new calamity. God's answer came to him: "It is for Saul and his bloody house, because he put the Gibeonites to death" (2 Sam. 21:1, NASB). Saul himself and his sons had already fallen in battle, slain by the Philistines at the battle of Mount Gilboa; but the full measure of his guilt had yet to be paid for. This vengeance had to be visited on seven descendants of that king, for seven was a number symbolizing the complete work of God. Israel had to learn by this solemn object lesson that their covenants with foreign nations, sworn to in the name of Yahweh, had to be observed at all costs.

Under special circumstances, then, the general rule of safeguarding children against punishment for the sins of their parents was subject to exceptions, so far as God's administration of justice was concerned. In each of the above cases it is fair to conclude that if the children involved had been permitted to live out a normal lifespan, they would have chosen to follow in the evil example of their forebears and thus occasioned much suffering and woe to others. Only God could know that for a certainty, however, for only He can foreknow the potential of each new soul. For man to inflict such preventive penalty without express permission from God (as in the case of Joshua and the population of Jericho) would be the height of injustice and presumption.

How could Moses have written the first five books of the Bible when the fifth

153

book, Deuteronomy, reports his burial in an unknown grave?

Obviously Moses did not write in advance the account of his own death. Deuteronomy 34 is an obituary written by a friend and contemporary, possibly Joshua the son of Nun (v.9). Under the guidance and inspiration of the Holy Spirit, then, Joshua possibly appended an appropriate record of the death and burial of his revered master and framed the eloquent praise with which the book closes.

What inference may we draw from this? Does the insertion of an obituary in the final work of any author imply that he was not truly the author of the main text of that book? Before me lies a copy of Roland de Vaux's excellent volume *Archaeology and the Dead Sea Scrolls.* This is a revised English edition of the Schweich Lectures he delivered at Oxford in 1959, published by Oxford University in 1973. On page vi is a brief foreword signed by Kathleen Kenyon, which opens with the following words: "It is sad that Roland de Vaux did not live to see the translation of his Schweich Lectures appear." This, then, is a kind of obituary notice that is added to the main text of the book. In other terminal works produced by famous authors, the obituary appears as the last chapter in the book. Often that obituary is not signed.

So it is with Deuteronomy, the final work composed by Moses under the inspiration of God. Just as no responsible student of literature would think of impugning the authenticity of de Vaux's volume simply because of the obituary inserted by Kenyon, so doubts should not be raised as to the genuineness of the Mosaic authorship of Deuteronomy 1–33—or indeed of any of the books of the Pentateuch— simply on the ground of the obituary contained in chapter 34.

Joshua

Did God approve of Rahab's lie (Josh. 2:4-5)?

Scripture unequivocally condemns lying as a sin. In Leviticus 19:11 the Lord says, "You shall not steal, nor deal falsely, nor lie to one another" (NASB). In Proverbs 12:22 we read, "Lying lips are an abomination to the LORD, but those who deal faithfully are His delight" (NASB). In the New Testament Paul exhorts the Ephesians in 4:25: "Therefore, laying aside falsehood, SPEAK TRUTH, EACH ONE of you, WITH HIS NEIGHBOR, for we are members of one another" (NASB). These and many other passages make it clear that God is never pleased when people fail to tell the truth.

On the other hand, falsehood like every other sin can be fully atoned for by the blood of Christ on Calvary, when the liar becomes convicted in his conscience concerning his guilt and heartily repents of it. A contrite believer may claim the atoning merit of Christ and be completely forgiven. What this adds up to is the following principle that covers God's dealings with sinners: (1) the Lord has always condemned sin, so much so that He laid the guilt of every sin on His sinless Son when He died for sinners on the cross; (2) the Lord does not accept sinners as partakers of His redemption because of their *sins* but rather because of their *faith*. Even Abraham sinned in Egypt when he lied about Sarah's status

as his wife—though he felt compelled to do so in order to avoid being killed on her account (Gen. 12:12-19). David lied to the high priest Ahimelech when he told him that Saul had sent him to Nob on government business, even though he was actually fleeing from Saul to save his life (1 Sam. 21:2).

In Rahab's case there were special factors that operated in her favor, and they should not be overlooked, even if they do not altogether excuse her mendacity. In this particular case the lie meant for her a step of faith that put her very life in jeopardy. The safer thing for her to do was tell the truth and let the police officials of Jericho know that she had two Hebrew spies hidden under her piles of flax stalks drying under the sun on top of her roof. But she had given her solemn word, apparently, to the two fugitives that she would not betray them to the king's agents. At any rate, she professed a very firm conviction that the Israelite forces would capture and destroy Jericho, even though from the standpoint of military science it looked as if Jericho was virtually impregnable. "The LORD your God, He is God in heaven above and on earth beneath. Now therefore, please swear to me by the LORD" (Josh. 2:11-12, NASB). For a woman of ill fame and a completely pagan upbringing to attain such a conviction concerning the one true God was a far more striking display of faith than was the case of the patriarchs and ᴜe people of Moses who had been brought up in the truth of God. She had to turn her back on her own people and the cultural tradition in which she had been reared in order to take such a step as this and to throw in her lot with the covenant nation of Israel. She literally risked her life for the cause of the Lord, as she told that lie to the arresting officers. She might very easily have been discovered. A single sneeze or bodily movement on the part of the hidden spies would have sealed her doom—as well as theirs. Therefore we should recognize that there were very unusual extenuating factors involved in her deception.

The commitment Rahab made to Yahweh and His lordship led her to join the ranks of Israel after they captured Jericho and leveled it to the ground (Josh. 6:17-25); and she later married Salmon of the tribe of Judah and by him became the mother of Boaz and the ancestress of King David (Matt. 1:5-6). Despite her sinful past her faith was reckoned to her for righteousness, not only by the Lord, but also by His people; and she assumed a position of honor as an ancestress of the Lord Jesus Himself. In Hebrews 11:31 we read this tribute to her courage and faith: "By faith Rahab the harlot did not perish along with those who were disobedient, after she had welcomed the spies in peace" (NASB). In James 2:25 the apostle commends her faith as genuine and effectual because she expressed that faith by "works, when she received the messengers and sent them out by another way" (NASB).

Joshua 3:17 suggests that the Israelite host had already crossed the Jordan, but Joshua 4:4,10-11 imply that they had not done so. How can these verses be harmonized?

Joshua 3:17 tells us that the priests carrying the ark of the covenant re-

mained standing in the middle of the crossing until all the rest of the congregation had passed over to the west bank. Joshua 4:4 then relates how twelve men, one from each tribe, were directed to go back from the west bank to the midway point where the priests were still standing with the ark. There they were to dig up twelve sizable stones out of the bed of the river and carry them over to the location of the first encampment of the host on the Canaan side of the Jordan (v.8). This cairn of twelve mid-river stones was to serve as a memorial to this epoch-making event in Israel's history (vv. 6-7).

Joshua 4:10-11 concludes the episode by recording how the ark-carrying priests finally left their post at the midway point of the riverbed and finished their crossing with the ark all the way to the west bank. There they continued on their way until they had come to the forefront of the entire congregation and preceded them to their new camping ground at Gilgal (cf. v.19). Not until all Israel was safely across—including the priests and the ark—were the waters of the Jordan, which had been dammed up at Adam (3:16), allowed to flow downstream once more into the Dead Sea. There is therefore no discrepancy here at all, and the account is perfectly clear.

Has not the Joshua 6 account of the capture of Jericho by the Israelites been discredited by the modern archaeological investigations at Tell es-Sultan?

On the contrary, the testimony of the cemetery connected with City IV at Tell es-Sultan (which is generally agreed to be the site of Old Testament Jericho) is quite conclusive in favor of a date around 1400 B.C., which is in complete conformity with a 1446 date for the Exodus itself. After several years of thorough archaeological investigation, John Garstang discovered that of the many scarabs found in the graves of this cemetery, not a single one dates from a period later than Amenhotep III of Egypt (1412–1376 B.C.). It is impossible to explain why no scarabs bearing the cartouche of any later Pharaoh was ever found at that level if indeed the destruction of City IV took place in the mid-thirteenth century (as modern scholarship generally maintains today). How could there have been no scarabs from the reign of any of the numerous Pharaohs between Amenhotep III and Ramses II?

Furthermore, of the 150,000 fragments of pottery discovered in this cemetery, only a single sherd has been found that is of the Mycenean type. Since Mycenean ware began to be imported into Palestine from 1400 and onward, it is difficult to explain why virtually none of it was found in the City IV cemetery unless that cemetery was abandoned around 1400 B.C.

Kathleen Kenyon's later investigations at Tell es-Sultan led her to question Garstang's identification of the collapsed walls with City IV, because the potsherds found in the earth-fill of those walls were from a period centuries earlier than 1400 B.C. The soundness of this deduction is open to question, however, because the same phenomenon would be observable if the walls of Avila in Spain or Carcasonne in France were to be leveled by an earthquake in our own generation. Since those walls were erected several centuries ago, the Kenyon criterion would compel us to believe that they must have fallen centuries ago, because they would, of course, contain no internal evidence of twentieth-century construction. But no discovery of Kenyon or Vincent—or any other excavator at that site who came there with a prior commitment to a 1250 date for the Israelite conquest of Canaan—has ever been able to shake the objective findings of Garstang and his team in regard to the scarabs and

sherds found in the City IV cemetery. (See Garstang's remarks on this in the article on 1 Kings 6:1 and the date of the Exodus.)

Readers desirous of an extended discussion of the soundness of the biblical date for the Exodus itself (i.e., 1446 B.C.) are referred to my *A Survey of Old Testament Introduction*, pp. 223–34. A more recent work by an able young British scholar is that of John J. Bimson (*Redating the Exodus and the Conquest* [Sheffield: University of Sheffield, 1978]). Bimson shows how much of the archaeological evidence has been systematically manipulated by a process of circular reasoning on the part of the leading interpreters of archaeological data. He reviews the objective testimony of the stratigraphy and the artifacts and comes to a firm conclusion in favor of a fifteenth-century date of the Israelite Exodus and conquest of Canaan. This discussion is all the more impressive since Bimson himself does not hold to an Evangelical view of the inerrancy of Scripture but feels compelled to set the record straight so far as archaeology is concerned. (See also the article on 1 Kings 6:1 and the date of the Exodus.)

Was Joshua justified in exterminating the population of Jericho?

In Joshua 6:21 we read, "And they utterly destroyed everything in the city, both man and woman, young and old, and ox and sheep and donkey, with the edge of the sword (NASB). Verses 22–23 go on to say that Rahab the harlot, who had risked her life in order to save the two Israelite spies who had come earlier in order to reconnoiter the city, was spared from death, along with her entire family—as the two spies had promised that she would be. But everything combustible in the city was put to the torch; and all articles of gold, silver, iron and bronze were devoted to the treasury of the tabernacle.

Such complete destruction might appear to be needlessly harsh, since it included infants who were too young to have committed overt sin, even though the older children and the adults may all have fallen into utter depravity. Should we not understand this severity to be the result of a savage Bedouin mentality on the part of the wilderness warriors rather than a punitive measure ordained of God?

In answer to this humanitarian objection, we need to recognize first of all that the biblical record indicates that Joshua was simply carrying out God's orders in this matter. In other words, the same account that tells of the massacre itself is the account that tells of God's command to carry it out. Therefore we must recognize that our criticism cannot be leveled at Joshua or the Israelites but at the God whose bidding they obeyed. (Otherwise we must demonstrate our own special competence to correct the biblical record on the basis of our own notions of probability as to what God might or might not decide to do.) If criticism there be, we should not stop there, for the destruction of Jericho was far smaller an affair than the annihilation of the populations of Sodom and Gomorrah and their allies in Genesis 19:24-25. And then again this volcanic catastrophe was far less significant in the loss of life than Noah's Flood, which, except for Noah's family, wiped out the entire human race.

Back in Genesis 15:16 God had forewarned Abraham: "Then in the fourth generation [i.e., in four hundred years, after the migration to Egypt, since Abraham was one hundred before he became the father of Isaac] they [the Israelites] shall return here [to Canaan], for the iniquity of the Amorite is not yet complete" (NASB). The implication of this last statement was that when the wicked-

ness of the inhabitants of Canaan had reached a predetermined accumulation of guilt, then God would have them removed from the Land of Promise intended for Abraham and his seed.

The loss of innocent life in the demolition of Jericho was much to be regretted, but we must recognize that there are times when only radical surgery will save the life of a cancer-stricken body. The whole population of the antediluvian civilization had become hopelessly infected with the cancer of moral depravity (Gen. 6:5). Had any of them been permitted to live while still in rebellion against God, they might have infected Noah's family as well. The same was true of the detestable inhabitants of Sodom, wholly given over to the depravity of homosexuality and rape, in the days of Abraham and Lot. As with the Benjamites of Gibeah at a later period (Judg. 19:22-30; 20:43-48), the entire population had to be destroyed. So also it was with Jericho and Ai as well (Josh. 8:18-26); likewise with Makkedah (Josh. 10:28), Lachish (v.32), Eglon (v.35), Debir (v.39), and all the cities of the Negev and the Shephelah (v.40). In the northern campaign against Hazor, Madon, Shimron, and Achshaph, the same thorough destruction was meted out (Josh. 11:11-14).

In every case the baneful infection of degenerate idolatry and moral depravity had to be removed before Israel could safely settle down in these regions and set up a monotheistic, law-governed commonwealth as a testimony for the one true God. Much as we regret the terrible loss of life, we must remember that far greater mischief would have resulted if they had been permitted to live on in the midst of the Hebrew nation. These incorrigible degenerates of the Canaanite civilization were a sinister threat to the spiritual survival of Abraham's race. The failure to carry through completely the policy of the extermination of the heathen in the Land of Promise later led to the moral and religious downfall of the Twelve Tribes in the days of the Judges (Judg. 2:1-3, 10-15, 19-23). Not until the time of David, some centuries later, did the Israelites succeed in completing their conquest of all the land that had been promised to the descendants of Abraham (cf. Gen. 15:18-21). This triumph was only possible in a time of unprecedented religious vigor and purity of faith and practice such as prevailed under the leadership of King David, "a man after God's own heart" (1 Sam. 13:14; Acts 13:22).

In our Christian dispensation true believers possess resources for resisting the corrupting influence of unconverted worldlings such as were hardly available to the people of the old covenant. As warriors of Christ who have yielded our members to Him as "weapons of righteousness" (Rom. 6:13) and whose bodies are indwelt and empowered by God the Holy Spirit (1 Cor. 6:19), we are well able to lead our lives in the midst of a corrupt and degenerate non-Christian culture (whether in the Roman Empire or in modern secularized Europe or America) and still keep true to God. We have the example of the Cross and the victory of the Resurrection of Christ our Lord, and he goes with us everywhere and at all times as we carry out the Great Commission.

As New Testament believers, the weapons of our warfare are not carnal but spiritual, "mighty through God to the pulling down of strongholds; casting down imaginations, and every high thing that exalteth itself against the knowledge of God, and bringing into captivity every thought to the obedience of Christ" (2 Cor. 10:4-5). These weapons, far mightier than those of Joshua, are able to capture men's hearts for God; and we have no occasion as ambassadors for Christ to resort to physical weapons to protect our faith and land (as the Israelites were compelled to do, if they were to survive spiritually). But on the contrary we carry on a life-saving offensive as fishers of men, and we go after the unsaved and unconverted wherever they are to be found. But we must recognize that our situation is far more advantageous than theirs, and our prospects of victory over the world are far brighter than theirs. For this we can thank God. But we must refrain from condemnation of those who lived in the very different situation that prevailed before the Cross and recognize that they acted in obedience and faith toward God when they carried out his orders concerning the Canaanites.

How can Joshua's altar on Mount Ebal (Josh. 8:30) be reconciled with the later condemnation of the "high places"?

It should be quite obvious that a later denunciation of the idolatrous cult-centers known as "high places" (bāmôt) could have no retroactive effect on altars erected to the worship of Yahweh in a time prior to the establishment of Solomon's temple in Jerusalem (ca. 960 B.C.). Those strictures that were later directed at the rival shrines established by Jeroboam I (ca. 930 B.C.), to divert his subjects of the northern kingdom from worshiping at the Jerusalem temple at the various holy festivals during the year, were erected in clear violation of God's ordinance in Deuteronomy 12:2-14. This passage required the total destruction of every altar devoted to the worship of false gods, together with their sacred pillars (maṣṣēbôt) and wooden posts ('ašērîm)—which represented the abiding place of the male deity and his female consort, respectively, according to the Canaanite superstition—and confined worship to a single national sanctuary (vv.2-6). No particular location is designated for this central sanctuary—actually it shifted from Gilgal to Shiloh to Gibeon at various times between the conquest and the Solomonic temple—but it was set up wherever the tabernacle and its altar of burnt offering was located. After the Solomonic sanctuary was finally completed and solemnly dedicated at a great national assembly (1 Kings 8), it was understood that all sacrifice should be offered at that great temple and there alone.

Yet it was that same Solomon who later, under the influence of his idol-worshiping foreign wives, authorized the building of a *bāmāh* (or hilltop shrine) to Chemosh, the god of Moab, and to Milcom, the god of Ammon (1 Kings 11:5), and doubtless to other pagan deities as well, including those favored by his Egyptian wife, who was the daughter of the reigning Pharaoh. This evil example led to a more general disregard for the prohibition of Deuteronomy 12:2–14, and *bāmôṯ* began to be erected in many different cult centers, both in the northern kingdom (following the lead of King Jeroboam) and in the kingdom of Judah as well. The latter were periodically destroyed during times of religious revival under Asa (2 Chron. 14:3—although not in a thorough or permanent way; cf. 1 Kings 15:12–14), Jehoshaphat, Asa's son (2 Chron. 17:6), Hezekiah (2 Kings 18:4), and Josiah (2 Kings 23:4–8).

Apparently some of the Judean *bāmôtt* had been cult centers for Yahweh worship, and their purpose had been to serve the convenience of the local populace in the various provinces of the kingdom. Nevertheless they were maintained in violation of the law of the central sanctuary in Deuteronomy 12, and they were so denounced by the true prophets of God. Second Kings 23:8 suggests that some of these shrines were served by Levitical priests, but the fact that they were not put to death according to the law of Deut. 13, which required the execution of anyone guilty of idolatry, strongly suggests that they served at local altars dedicated to Yahweh. At the time of Josiah's reformation they were allowed to live and even to partake of food dedicated to the support of the Aaronic priesthood, but they were forbidden access to the true temple in Jerusalem.

Joshua's altar on Mount Ebal, which served the needs of the entire congregation of Israel at the solemn renewal of the national covenant (Josh. 8:30–35), was thoroughly in keeping with the earlier law of the altar promulgated in Exodus 20:24–25: "In every place where I cause My name to be remembered, I will come to you and bless you" (NASB). Even after the completion of the Solomonic temple, situations arose in the history of the northern kingdom where the erection of an altar was approved and blessed by God on the occasion of a great national crisis. Such was that of Elijah on the summit of Mount Carmel, where the miraculous fire from heaven on his burnt offering served to demonstrate to Ahab and his armies that Yahweh was the true and living God and that Baal was only a figment of the imagination of Jezebel's prophets (1 Kings 18:30–39).

Why did Israel have to keep its covenant with the Gibeonites after they obtained that covenant through fraud (Josh. 9)?

Joshua 9 recounts the crafty deception practiced by the Gibeonite envoys (vv.4–5) when they came to the camp of Israel to conclude a treaty of alliance and peace. They lied by saying that they had come "from a very far country" (v.9) because of their admiration for the God of Israel, who had so wonderfully prospered His people. They alleged that they had come from such a distance that their nice fresh bread had become old and brittle by the time they arrived at Gilgal. Actually Gibeon was less than a day's journey away. Unquestionably they had been guilty of misrepresentations and had lured Israel into an alliance by the use of deception. Under normal conditions, therefore, the Israelites would not have been obliged to keep their contract with them. Any court of law would have absolved them from adherence to their promises in view of the calculated deception practiced by the Gibeonites.

This however, was no ordinary contract engagement, for it was sealed by a solemn oath taken in the name of Yahweh their God. Since they did not first consult God about the matter, prior to entering into an agreement with these heathen Canaanites, they were bound to keep their covenant promises that had been sworn to in the name of Yahweh (v 15). Feeling that they could rely on their own good judgment and on the evidence of the dry, crumbling bread, the Israelites had neglected to go to God in prayer about the matter (v.14). Therefore they were bound by their oath, even into the indefinite future. Failure to keep this covenant obligation was one of the offenses for which God visited judgment on Israel, because Saul had put some of the Gibeonites to death (2 Sam. 21:1-14).

What is the explanation of the prolonged day in Joshua 10:12-14? (D*)

The Book of Joshua records several miracles, but none perhaps as noteworthy or as widely discussed as that pertaining to the twenty-four-hour prolongation of the day in which the battle of Gibeon was fought (10:12-14). It has been objected that if in fact the earth was stopped in its rotation for a period of twenty-four hours, inconceivable catastrophe would have befallen the entire planet and everything on its surface. While those who

believe in the omnipotence of God would hardly concede that Yahweh could not have prevented such catastrophe and held in abeyance those physical laws that might have brought it to pass, it does not seem to be absolutely necessary (on the basis of the Hebrew text itself) to hold that the planet was suddenly halted in its rotation. Verse 13 states that the sun "did not hasten to go down for about a whole day" (NASB). The words "did not hasten" seem to point to a retardation of the movement so that the rotation required forty-eight hours rather than the usual twenty-four.

In support of this interpretation, research has brought to light reports from Egyptian, Chinese, and Hindu sources of a long day. Harry Rimmer reports that some astronomers have come to the conclusion that one full day is missing in our astronomical calculation. Rimmer states that Pickering of the Harvard Observatory traced this missing day back to the time of Joshua; likewise has Totten of Yale (cf. Bernard Ramm, *The Christian View of Science and Scripture* [Grand Rapids: Eerdmans, 1954], p. 159). Ramm reports, however, that he was unable to document this report, possibly because those universities preferred not to keep records of this sort in their archives.

Another possibility has been deduced from a slightly different interpretation of the word *dôm* (translated in KJV as "stand thou still"). This verb usually signifies to be silent, cease, or leave off. F. W. Maunder of Greenwich and Robert Dick Wilson of Princeton therefore interpreted Joshua's prayer to be a petition that the sun cease pouring down its heat on his struggling troops so that they might be permitted to press the battle under more favorable conditions. The tremendously destructive hailstorm that accompanied the battle lends some credence to this view, and it has been advocated by men of unquestioned orthodoxy. Nevertheless it must be admitted that v.13 seems to favor a prolongation of the day: "And the sun stopped in the middle of the sky, and did not hasten to go down for about a whole day" (NASB).

Keil and Delitzsch (*Joshua, Judges, Ruth,* p. 110) suggest that a miraculous prolongation of the day would have taken place if it seemed to Joshua and all Israel to be supernaturally prolonged, because they were able to accomplish in it the work of two days. It would have been very difficult for them to tell whether the earth was rotating at a normal rate if the earth's rotation furnished their only criterion for measuring time. They add another possibility, that God may have produced an optical prolongation of the sunshine, continuing its visibility after the normal setting time by means of a special refraction of the rays.

Hugh J. Blair ("Joshua," in Guthrie, *New Bible Commentary,* p. 244) suggests that Joshua's prayer was made early in the morning, since the moon was in the west and the sun was in the east. The answer came in the form of a hailstorm that prolonged the darkness and thus facilitated the surprise attack of the Israelites. Hence in the darkness of the storm the defeat of the enemy was completed; and we should speak of Joshua's "long night" rather than Joshua's "long day." This of course is essentially the view of Maunders and Wilson. Such an interpretation necessitates no stopping of the earth on its axis, but it hardly fits in with the statement of Joshua 10:13 and is therefore of dubious validity.

Judges

Exactly how did Sisera die? Judges 5: 24–27 seems to disagree with Judges 4:21 at this point. And how could Jael be considered praiseworthy in this act of murder?

Judges 4:21 tells us that Jael, the wife of Heber, went up to her sleeping guest, placed a long, sharp tent-peg over his temple, and then drove it down into his skull with a single blow of her hammer. Presumably she had first made him comfortable on a cot, then placed a blanket over him to keep him warm. Judges 5:24–27 confirms the information that she had first given him a refreshing cup of yogurt before he settled down for his nap. Then, after he was fast asleep, she drove the tent peg into his skull in the same manner as 4:21 had described it, thus killing him instantly. Verse 27 adds the graphic detail that after the impact of that blow his body convulsively lurched on the floor of the tent, right between Jael's feet. There is no contradiction here at any level, and it is hard to see why this question should ever have been raised.

The more difficult question has to do with the moral evaluation of Jael's act. She certainly was guilty of violation of the sacred duty of protecting a guest who had been received peaceably into her home. Technically she was guilty of first-degree murder. And even though the text of Judges nowhere says that God Himself approved of her deed, there can be no doubt that Deb-orah, God's prophetess (4:4), regarded it as a praiseworthy act; and both she and her colleague Barak, who collaborated in the defeat of Sisera's army and the liberation of Israel from Jabin's oppression, gave dramatic expression in chapter 5 to their approval or admiration of her daring in thus dispatching this dreaded warrior.

In evaluating Jael's act, there are several factors to be brought into focus. For one thing, after the defeat of Sisera's army and the reestablishment of Israelite government, Jael would be liable to a charge of harboring a fugitive criminal if she did receive him as a guest into her tent. Furthermore, Jael, being apparently alone at the time, was in no position to refuse him entrance, armed and powerful warrior as he was, or to order him to go on and seek refuge somewhere else. Undoubtedly, had she attempted this, he would have forced his way into the tent anyway; and probably he would have killed her first, in order to keep her from betraying his whereabouts. Finally, Sisera represented a brutal and tyrannous oppression of God's people that might well be renewed at a later time, if he were permitted to escape. This meant that Jael herself would have been involved in the guilt of the slaughter of many innocent lives in Sisera's future career of aggression against the northern tribes of Israel. She was not ready to involve herself in complicity with this guilt. Nor was she willing to face the almost certain prospect that she and her husband would both be disgraced and put to death as traitors to Israel after the victorious troops of Deborah and Barak had traced Sisera's flight to her home. Nor would Jael's own sense of commitment to Yahweh and His people have permitted her to side with His enemy in this fashion. She therefore had little choice but to adopt the strategy that she did. Facing an anguishing alternative between two moral principles, she had to choose the lesser of two evils.

Why did God allow Jephthah's foolish vow to run its course? (D*)

The nature of Jephthah's vow has been much misunderstood. In Judges 11:30-31 Jephthah, on the eve of his decisive conflict with powerful Ammonite invaders, made a solemn promise to God that if He would grant victory over the foe, then whoever would come forth from the doors of his home to meet him would become the property of the Lord: "And I will offer him up for a burnt offering."

Obviously it was some human being who was to be involved, someone from Jephthah's household or some member of his family, and one who would care enough about Jephthah personally to become the first to greet him. The Hebrew text excludes the possibility of any animal serving as a candidate for this burnt offering since the phrase rendered "whatsoever cometh forth of the doors of my house" is never used of an animal (Keil and Delitzsch, *Josuha, Judges, Ruth*, p. 385).

Had it been a beast, there would of course have been no problem about sacrificing it on the altar as a blood offering (which the Hebrew word for burnt offering [*'ôlāh*] normally implied). But in this special case, since it was to be a human member of the household who would be the first to greet Jephthah, it was out of the question for a literal blood sacrifice to be performed. Why? Because human sacrifice was sternly and repeatedly forbidden by God in his law (see Lev. 18:21; 20:2-5; Deut. 12:31; 18:10).

It would have been altogether unthinkable for Jephthah or any other Israelite to imagine that he could please God by committing such a heinous and abhorrent abomination in His presence or at His altar. "You shall not behave thus toward [Yahweh] your God, for every abominable act which He [Yahweh] hates they [the Canaanites] have done for their gods; for they even burn their sons and daughters in fire to their gods. Whatever I command you, you shall be careful to do; you shall not add to nor take away from it" (Deut. 12:31-32). Again, we read in Deuteronomy 18:10-12: "There shall not be found among you anyone who makes his son or his daughter pass through the fire. . . . For whoever does these . . . detestable things Yahweh your God will drive them out before you."

In view of Yahweh's well-known prohibition and expressed loathing for this practice, it would have amounted to a complete renunciation of God's sovereignty for Jephthah to have undertaken such a thing. It would have been a repudiation of the very covenant that constituted Israel as God's holy people.

Equally incredible is the notion that God, foreknowing that Jephthah was intending thus to flout His law and trample on His covenant, would nevertheless have granted him victory over the foe. The understanding of the event involves an intolerable theological difficulty, for it hopelessly compromises the integrity of God Himself.

What, then, actually did happen if Jephthah did not offer up his daughter on the altar? As Delitzsch points out, the whole record of the manner in which this vow was carried out points to her dedication to the service of the Lord as a lifelong ministrant at the na-

164

tional sanctuary. Judges 11:37–38 states that she was allowed a mourning period of two months, not to bewail her approaching death, but rather to lament over her permanent virginity (*beṯûlîm*) and the resultant extinction of her father's line, since she was his only child. As one set apart for tabernacle service (cf. Exod. 38:8; 1 Sam. 2:22 for other references to these consecrated virgins who performed service at the tabernacle), she would never become a mother; hence it is emphasized that "she knew no man" (Judg. 11:39). This would have been a pointless and inane remark if in fact she were put to death.

Jephthah acted as a man of honor in carrying out his promise and presenting his daughter as a living sacrifice, as all true Christians are bidden to present themselves (Rom. 12:1). Had he committed a detested abomination like the slaughter of his own child, he never would have been listed with the heroes of faith in Hebrews 11. (An extended and skillful treatment of this whole issue is found in Keil and Delitzsch, *Joshua, Judges, Ruth*, pp. 384–95).

How could God have incited Samson to embark on a romance with a pagan girl as a means of stirring up strife between Israel and her neighbors (Judges 14:4)?

Samson seems to have enjoyed cordial relations with the Philistine overlords who held the tribe of Dan in vassalage. These aggressive and warlike foreigners from Crete had held much of Israel in humiliating bondage for many years; and they were destined to plague them all through the period of Samuel and Saul until the final successes of King David around 1000 B.C. Samson was the one figure who could break the power of the Philistines; yet he was too concerned with his personal interests and pleasures to assume that task in a responsible fashion. His enor-

mous physical strength and courage were hardly matched by his dedication to God's call. Consecrated from infancy to serve the Lord as a Nazirite, he had developed a willful spirit that was completely self-centered. Therefore the only way to rouse him against the oppressors of his people was to allow him to get into a quarrel with them on the ground of his personal interest. His godly parents had urged him to have nothing to do with Philistine girls, no matter how pretty they were; but Samson brushed their admonitions aside and insisted on having his own way.

It is in this context that v.4 informs us: "However, his father and mother did not know that it was of the LORD, for He was seeking an occasion against the Philistines. Now at that time the Philistines were ruling over Israel" (NASB). It was time for a new hero to appear and deliver the Israelites from heathen oppression, as had happened back in the days of Othniel, Ehud, and Gideon. But Samson was too wrapped up in himself to be attentive to God's call. Therefore he needed some strong incentive to turn against the Philistines in retaliation for a wrong he had received from them. God used even this carnal reaction on Samson's part to accomplish His gracious purpose in lightening the load of their oppressors. The result of Samson's resentment toward the Philistine wedding guests who had wormed out of his young bride the answer to his riddle was that he resorted to attacking the young men (possibly in the militia) at nearby Ashkelon in order to rob them of their garments in order to pay off his forfeited wager (14:19).

In the aftermath of this episode, Samson's unreasonable resentment at finding that the bride he had abandoned in disgust had later been given to another man led to his burning down all the standing crops of that town. The result of this was, of course, the organizing of an expeditionary force of Philistines to arrest and punish him for this deed (Judg. 15:6–8), a maneuver that led to their own destruction by the Rock of Etam and at Ramath-lehi (vv.14–17). This led to the weakening of the grip that Philistia had maintained for so long over the Israelites. Even Samson's folly in revealing the secret of his strength to his Philistine girlfriend, Delilah, led ultimately to the death of the flower of Philistine leadership in the collapse of the temple of Dagon. "So the dead whom he killed at his death were more than those whom he killed in his life" (Judg. 16:30, NASB).

How could Samson's marriage be "from the Lord," as Judges 14:4 says, if it was wrong to marry unbelievers?

Judges 14:3 makes it plain that Samson was doing the wrong thing by marrying the Philistine woman from Timnah, for his parents remonstrated with him about marrying out of the faith. Yet the headstrong young man insisted, "Get her for me, for she looks good to me." Then v.4, indicating how God was intending to use Samson as an aggressive champion against the Philistines in the years to come, says, "However, his father and mother did not know that it was of the LORD, for He was seeking an occasion against the Philistines."

It would be a mistake to conclude from this statement that God was pleased with Samson's violation of the Mosaic Law, which strictly forbade mixed marriages of this sort. But it does mean that God intended to use Samson as a champion in the deliverance of his people from the galling tyranny of the ungodly Philistines. Since up until that time Samson had enjoyed friendly relations with them, he was not likely to do anything to liberate Israel from the yoke of its heathen overlords. He needed to have a falling out with them before he would enter on his career as a champion for his country. The aftermath of this unhappy marriage, which was never really consummated, brought about the right conditions for Samson to raise a standard against Philistia.

How could Samson catch three hundred foxes for his prank at Timnah?

Judges 15 relates how Samson sought vengeance against the Philistine town of Timnah after his bride had been given to some other man. Verse 4 states that "Samson went and caught three hundred foxes, and took torches, and turned [the foxes] tail to tail, and put one torch in the middle between two tails." Then he lit the torches and let them run loose into the standing grain of the Timnite farmers so that they might lose their entire crop. As to the methods Samson may have used to capture so many foxes, when most people find it difficult enough to hunt down even one of them, we find no information at all in the text. Whether his superhuman strength was matched by a superhuman agility that enabled him to outrun them as they tried to escape, we cannot be sure. Or else he may have devised a set of unusually enticing traps and imprisoned them in cages until he had gathered a sufficient number for his purpose. Presumably he used a pair of thick leather gloves as protection against their sharp teeth. However he managed it, he was certainly in a class by himself. But any warrior who could slay a thousand armed soldiers with the jawbone of an ass as his only weapon (v.15) could surely take care of a mere three hundred foxes without too much difficulty.

Ruth

Is not the transaction between Boaz and the kinsman in Ruth 4:3–8 contrary to the stipulations in Deuteronomy 25:5–10? And is not levirate marriage at variance with the law against incest in Leviticus 18:16?

Deuteronomy 25:5–10 provides that a childless widow is to be taken over by a surviving brother of her deceased husband to be his wife and to bear a son (if biologically possible) who will be legally accounted as the son and heir of the deceased brother. This means that the dead man's name will be carried on by the son whom his brother has begotten so that the dead man's line does not become extinct. But vv.7–8 allow such a surviving brother to refuse the role of substitute husband if he so insists. If he should choose to do so, however, the widow may lodge a complaint against him before the authorities; and he may then be publicly disgraced. That is to say, the widow may publicly untie and remove his sandal and spit in his face, saying, "Thus it is done to the man who does not build up his brother's house" (v.9). Verse 10 goes on to say that he shall be known from then on as "The house of him whose sandal is removed" (NASB).

As we compare this provision, with its concern for the perpetuation of the memory and family line of the deceased, with the negotiations between Boaz and the unnamed nearer kins-

man in Ruth 4:3–8, we note the following additional features.

1. If there is no surviving brother in the immediate family (for Chilion had also died, as well as Ruth's husband, Mahlon), then the levirate obligation attached to the nearest surviving male cousin.

2. Along with the obligation to serve as a proxy for the deceased in the marriage bed, there was the related obligation to buy back any landed property of the deceased that was about to be sold or forfeited under foreclosure proceedings. (While this was not actually mentioned in connection with the ordinance of the levir in Deut. 25, it is specified in Lev. 25:25: "If a fellow countryman of yours becomes so poor he has to sell part of his property, then his nearest kinsman is to come and buy back what his relative has sold" [NASB]).

3. In the case of a non-Israelite widow like Ruth the Moabitess, it might be considered a little more justifiable to refuse to perform the duty of a surrogate husband (levir) than otherwise, since a taint attached to the descendants of a Moabite. Deuteronomy 23:3 provided: "No Ammonite or Moabite shall enter the assembly of the LORD: none of their descendants, even to the tenth generation, shall ever enter the as-

sembly of the LORD" (NASB). Whether this applied to a Moabite woman married to a Hebrew as much as it would to a Moabite male convert to faith in the Lord is an arguable question. But at least this possibility raised a doubt that was apparently perceived as being legitimate.

4. Whether for this reason, or whether Ruth herself had no desire to humiliate the kinsman (*gô'ēl*) when she had really set her heart on Boaz, the kinsman himself was permitted to remove his own sandal; and he was even spared the humiliation of having her spit in his face.

These four special features can hardly be regarded as contradictory to the general law of the levirate in Deuteronomy 25. The basic rules there for a formal rejection of the duty to the widow and also for a public acceptance of that responsibility were carried out by both men. Ruth's failure to carry out an active role in accusing and shaming the other *gô'ēl* amounted to the voluntary surrender of her right to perform this ceremony, in view of the fact that the essential purpose of the levirate ordinance was about to be achieved in a far more desirable and acceptable fashion through her kind benefactor, Boaz himself.

As for the law against incest with a brother's wife (Lev. 18:16), this obviously did not apply to a situation where the surviving brother took the childless widow into his home and undertook to act as his brother's proxy. If he had attempted to marry his sister-in-law under any other condition (as, for example, Herod the Tetrarch, who seduced his brother Philip's wife, Herodias, from him), that would have been a clear case of incest, which was a capital crime. Or if Ruth had borne a son to Mahlon, that would have made her ineligible to any surviving brother of his, or perhaps even to a first cousin (which Boaz apparently was not).

1 Samuel

How could Bethshemesh have contained over 50,000 men in Samuel's day (1 Sam. 6:19)? Why was such an extreme judgment visited on them?

It is quite true that 50,000 men would seem to have been far in excess of the normal population of a community like Bethshemesh in the eleventh century B.C. But there is very strong evidence to indicate that the original text of 1 Samuel 6:19 read a much lower number. That is to say, nowhere else is a figure like 50,070 written in this fashion according to the grammar of biblical Hebrew. Normally the wording would have been either *šib'îm 'îš waḥᵃmiššîm 'elep 'îš* (lit., "seventy man and fifty thousand man") or else in the descending order—which was far more usual—*ḥᵃmiššîm 'elep 'îš wᵃšib'îm 'îš* ("fifty thousand man and seventy man"). The fact that neither of these customary word orders was followed in the received Hebrew text of this passage gives rise to a very justified suspicion that the text was inadvertently garbled in the course of transmission. (Textual errors are demonstrable for 1 Samuel more frequently than for almost any other book in the Old Testament.)

While it is true that the Septuagint already found this same reading in its Hebrew *Vorlage* (*hebdomēkonta andras kai pentēkonta chiliadas andrōn*, "seventy men and fifty thousands of men"), it is highly significant that even in the late first century A.D., Josephus (*Antiquities* 6.1.4) refers to the loss of life at Bethshemesh as only seventy, with no mention whatever of the "fifty thousand." There are also a few Hebrew manuscripts that entirely omit "fifty thousand man." Hence it is not necessary to defend this huge number as part of the text of the original, inerrant manuscript of 1 Samuel. Nor is it likely that more than seventy men would have become involved in the sacrilege of removing the golden propitiatory (KJV, "mercy seat") from the ark of the covenant in order to see what was inside. It is hardly conceivable that fifty thousand persons would have filed by the opened ark in order to peer into its interior and satisfy themselves that it contained only the two tablets of the Decalogue (cf. 1 Kings 8:9). Therefore such an enormous loss of life is almost impossible to account for. Yet for the seventy who were involved in this sacrilege, they showed such an impious attitude toward the God who had invested this symbol of His presence with the most solemn of sanctions that it is hardly to be wondered at that they forfeited their lives in a sudden and catastrophic way—somewhat as Uzzah in the time of David, when he merely touched the exterior of the ark, to steady it in the lurching wagon (2 Sam. 6:6–8).

Why did God condemn the Israelites' request for a king (1 Sam. 8:7–9) after He had laid down rules for future kings of Israel to follow (Deut. 17:14–20)?

There can be no doubt that God's plan for Israel included a king, a specially chosen dynasty from the tribe of Judah (Gen. 49:10), and that in anticipation of that event He laid down certain basic guidelines for such a theocratic king to follow (especially the avoidance of multiplying riches, horses, or wives), as recorded in Deuteronomy 17. But this furnishes no problem at all in regard to the establishment of a monarchic form of government for Israel in the latter days of Samuel's career. After his own two sons, Joel and Abijah, had proved to be unworthy and incompetent for leadership, the Israelite people requested Samuel to choose out and anoint for office a ruler over them who should serve as a permanent king with full authority as a monarch (1 Sam. 8:5).

In view of the fluctuating fortunes of Israel under the long succession of "judges" who had followed after the death of Joshua, it was not altogether surprising for the people to look to such a solution for their ineffectiveness and disunity as a nation. But the reason why their request displeased the Lord was that it was based on the assumption that they should follow their pagan neighbors in their form of government. Their motive was to conform to the world about them rather than to abide by the holy and perfect constitution that God had given them under Moses in the form of the Pentateuchal code. There was a definite sense in which they were setting aside the laws of God as inadequate for their needs and falling in step with the idolatrous heathen. They expressed their desire to Samuel thus: "Now appoint a king for us to judge us like all the nations" (NASB). They had forgotten that God had called them out of the world, not to conform to the world, but to walk in covenant fellowship with Yahweh as a testimony of godliness before all the pagan world.

Nevertheless, it is also clear that the Lord had in mind from the very beginning a monarchic form of government for His people. Even to Abraham He had promised, "I will make nations of you, and kings shall come from you" (Gen. 17:6, NASB). He had also decreed that the chosen line of royalty should come from the tribe of Judah: "The scepter shall not depart from Judah, nor the ruler's staff from between his feet, until Shiloh comes" (Gen. 49:10, NASB) (i.e., until the coming of the Messiah, who would Himself be a descendant of the Judean royal line).

So it came about that when Samuel's contemporaries came clamoring for a king, God granted them their request, even though He rebuked them for their worldly motive in making it. He also warned them that the greater unity and efficiency of government they might achieve under a monarchy would be offset by the loss of their liberties under the oppressive and demanding rule of an autocratic king. Because of his supreme and concentrated power, he would not be as accountable to the personal and civic rights of his people in the same way the Judges had been; so the nation would have reason to regret their choice. Rather than being governed by the laws of God, they would fall under the autocratic rule of a single man and become subject to heavy taxation, corvèe labor, military draft, confiscation of property, and all the rest (1 Sam. 8:11–18).

In the sequel, God first chose out for them an able and gifted ruler in the person of King Saul, but one who was basically carnal, wilfully disobedient, insanely jealous, and bloodthirsty in the later years of his reign. The purpose of Saul's reign was to prepare Israel to appreciate all the more the reign of a true man of God, David son of Jesse, who came from the tribe of

Judah, and who was determined to serve as a faithful theocratic ruler and an obedient servant of Yahweh.

Do not the Scriptures give contradictory accounts of how Saul was anointed king over Israel (cf. 1 Sam. 9;10;12)?

There is actually only one account to be found in the scriptural record concerning the anointing of Saul to be king over Israel. That is found in 10:1, where we read that at the border of Samuel's city (presumably Ramah in the territory of Zuph [9:5]) Samuel privately anointed Saul, saying, "Has not the LORD anointed you a ruler over His inheritance?" (NASB). Therefore we must recognize that since there was only one account of the actual anointing ceremony itself, there could not possibly be any contradictory accounts of it.

What we are told in 1 Samuel 10:17–24 is that at a national assembly summoned by Samuel to Mizpah, there was a solemn casting of lots conducted with a view to finding out which man of Israel the Lord Himself had chosen to be king. The lot finally fell on Saul, who was modestly hiding himself from sight by lurking behind the baggage near the place of assembly. When searchers discovered him there and brought him out before the entire congregation, Samuel publicly acknowledged him, saying, "Do you see him whom the LORD has chosen? Surely there is no one like him among all the people" (v.24, NASB). Then all the multitude acclaimed him, saying, "Long live the king!" Yet there is not a word said here about a ceremonial anointing.

A still further confirmation by the military leadership of the nation came after Saul's successful lifting of the siege of Jabesh-gilead and his routing of the Ammonite besiegers themselves. First Samuel 11:15 tells us: "So all the people went to Gilgal, and there they made Saul king before the LORD in Gilgal. There they also offered sacrifices of peace offerings before the LORD; and there Saul and all the men of Israel rejoiced greatly" (NASB). But we are given no indication whatever that he was anointed at that time; there is no mention of a crowning ceremony either. It simply involved an enthusiastic reaffirmation of his royal authority and glory, in line with the previous appointment made at Mizpah. First Samuel 12 simply continues the narrative of the confirmation ceremony at Gilgal, with Samuel giving his farewell address before the people and solemnly warning all the nation as well as their new ruler that the favor and protection of the Lord Yahweh would be conditioned on their faithful adherence to His holy law and their maintenance of a consistent testimony of godliness before the idol-worshiping world (vv.14–15). He closed with a stern warning in v.25: "But if you still do wickedly, both you and your king shall be swept away"(NASB).

This record of the initial anointing of Saul by God's prophet, his subsequent acknowledgment by the nation, and his later vindication as leader by his first victory in war against the heathen all form a perfectly consistent and believable line of development as the very first king of Israel comes into office and the old system of intermittent "judges" (or charismatic rulers) comes to a close.

What is the correct number in 1 Samuel 13:1?

First Samuel 13:1 as preserved in the Masoretic or Received Text has lost the number that must have been included in the original manuscript. The Masoretic text literally says, "Saul was a son of . . . years when he became king, and he had ruled for two years in Israel, when [lit., 'and'] Saul chose out for himself three thousand from Israel." All we can say for certain is that he must have been more than twenty years old, since the number nineteen or less would have required the word for "years" to be put in the plural (*šāním*). Because the singular *šānāh* is used here, we can tell that a numeral of twenty or more must have preceded it (cf. E. Kautzsch, ed., *Gesenius' Hebrew Grammar* [Oxford: Clarendon, 1910], #134.2 and Rem. 1). (This peculiar rule in the syntax of numerals is followed in Arabic also.)

"Saul reigned one year" (KJV) is not justifiable, for the Hebrew text does not say "reigned" but "Saul was son of a year when he became king" (*bᵉmolkô*). The translation "Saul was [*forty*] years when he began to reign" (ASV) is sheer conjecture, as its marginal note acknowledges.

The NASB follows the conjectural "forty" but then adds a second conjecture: "And he reigned *thirty*-two years over Israel." This is quite unnecessary if the connection between the end of v.1 and the beginning of v.2 is handled in the way suggested above. RSV does no conjecturing at all but leaves the gaps where they are in the Masoretic text: "Saul was ... years old when he began to reign; and he reigned ... and two years over Israel." Jerusalem Bible leaves out v.1 altogether but gives a baldly literal rendering of the Masoretic text in a marginal note.

The NIV has "[thirty]" for the first number and "[forty-]two" for the second. In a footnote it refers the reader to Acts 13:21, which reads: "Then the people asked for a king, and he gave them Saul son of Kish, ... who ruled forty years." But if Saul ruled only forty years in all, as Acts 13:21 says, it is hard to see how he could be said in 1 Samuel 13:1 to have ruled forty-two years. Yet as indicated above, there is no need to amend the second number at all. Simply render it thus: "And he had ruled two years over Israel when he chose out for himself

three thousand from Israel." This serves as an appropriate introduction to the episode of Jonathan's remarkable exploit at Michmash.

How could the Philistines have used 30,000 chariots in a place like Michmash (1 Sam. 13:5)?

Michmash overlooks a fairly extensive valley, and it is not inconceivable that 30,000 chariots could have been deployed in its vicinity. But the problem lies in the magnitude of the chariot force itself. Delitzsch (Keil and Delitzsch, *Samuel*, pp. 126–27) points out in his commentary on this verse that the listing of a mere 6000 horsemen in this Philistine army makes it almost conclusive that the actual number of chariots was considerably smaller. That is to say, everywhere else in the Old Testament where an army inclusive of both cavalry and chariotry comes on the scene, the number of the cavalry exceeds that of the chariots (cf. 2 Sam. 10:18; 1 Kings 10:26; 2 Chron. 12:3, etc.). Furthermore, such a large number of chariots in a single army has never been recorded in the annals of any ancient power, not even of the Egyptians, the Assyrians, the Chaldeans, or the Persians. It is most unlikely, therefore, that a third-rate little pentarchy like Philistia could have fielded the largest chariot force in all human history. Delitzsch suggests: "The number is therefore certainly corrupt, and we must either read 3000 [*šᵉlōše-t ᵃlā-pím*] instead of [*šᵉlšším 'ele-p*] according to the Syriac [Peshitto] and the Arabic, or else simply 1000; and in the latter case the origin of the number thirty might be attributed to the fact, that through the oversight of a copyist the [*lamed*] of the word [*Yiśrā'ēl*] was written twice [dittography!], and consequently the second [*lamed*] was taken for the numeral thirty [since *lamed* with a dot over it was the cipher for 'thirty']."

In response to Delitzsch's suggestion, it is open to question which system of numerical notation was used by the Hebrew scribes prior to the third century B.C. The Septuagint already had the same reading as the Masoretic text (*triakonta chiliades harmatōn*), and it probably was translated in the latter part of that century. Much more likely, therefore, is the possibility that "3000" was the original number recorded in the earliest text of 1 Samuel 13:5 and that somehow in the course of later textual transmission the notation for "3000" was miscopied as "30,000." The accurate preservation of statistics and of the spelling of proper names is notoriously difficult in manuscript transmission, and 1 Samuel has more than its share of textual errors. But the doctrine of scriptural inerrancy guarantees only the original manuscripts of Scripture as preserved from all error; it does not guarantee absolute trustworthiness of all copies ever made from that original.

In 1 Samuel 13:13, how could God promise Saul an eternal kingdom if he did not belong to the tribe of Judah?

It was after Saul had violated God's law by offering sacrifice on the altar, instead of waiting for a priest, that Samuel said to him in 1 Samuel 13:13: "You have acted foolishly; you have not kept the commandment of the LORD your God, which He commanded you, for now the LORD would have established your kingdom over Israel forever." Does this last clause amount to a promise from God? Not really, for it simply sets forth what might have been if Saul had kept faith with God. He and his descendants would have occupied the throne of Israel on a permanent basis. But Saul failed God, both in the matter of the extermination of the Amalekites (1 Sam. 15) and in this episode at Gilgal, where Saul intruded on the prerogatives reserved

for the priesthood alone. The judgment on him was rejection and replacement by David, of the tribe of Judah.

It was to Judah that the throne of Israel had been promised, back in the closing days of Jacob's career, when he was inspired on his deathbed to prophesy of the future of all the Twelve Tribes. Genesis 49:10 contains the promise that "the scepter shall not depart from Judah, nor the ruler's staff from between his feet, until Shiloh comes" (NASB)—that is, until the coming of Jesus the Messiah. The throne was reserved for the house of David, of the tribe of Judah, and God knew very well beforehand that Saul would fall away into disobedience and apostasy. But 1 Samuel 13:13 simply sets forth what Saul had forfeited through his willful disobedience, namely, the enjoyment of the throne of Israel, both for himself and for his descendants.

In 1 Samuel 15:11 God is said to be sorry that He had ever set up Saul as king over Israel. Does this imply that God did not know in advance how poorly Saul would perform and that He had made a mistake in choosing him in the first place? Could this be a mere human interpretation of God's feelings in this matter? (D*)

Even though God, who knows all things, surely knew in advance that Saul the son of Kish would utterly fail in his duties of kingship during the later years of his reign, He nevertheless saw fit to use Saul in his earlier years to deliver Israel from its pagan foes. Saul proved to be an effective leader in coping with the Ammonites, the Amalekites, and the Philistines and inspiring the Twelve Tribes to new courage and pride in their nationhood. But God foreknew that Saul would fall into disobedience and rebellion and that He would have to discard Saul completely in favor of David the son of

Jesse. In fact, God made it clear through Jacob's deathbed prophecy (Gen. 49:8–10) that Judah was to supply the permanent royal line for the covenant nation of Israel. Saul was of the tribe of Benjamin, not Judah (as David was); so there could have been no doubt as to what God's choice would be.

Nevertheless, it was a matter of deep regret that Saul would disregard the instructions God had given him through Samuel and that he would substitute his own will for the revealed will of God. The Lord therefore said to Samuel, "I *regret* that I have made Saul king" (using the verb *niḥam,* a term that implies deep emotion and concern about a situation involving others). This does not imply that God was deceived in His expectations about Saul but only that He was deeply troubled about Saul and the suffering and failure that would come on Israel because her king had turned away from the path of obedience. Yet v.29 uses the same verb to state that God does not change His mind and adopt some plan other than that which He had originally conceived: "The Glory of Israel will not lie or change His mind; for He is not a man that He should *change His mind*" (NASB). This statement was unquestionably made by the prophet Samuel under divine inspiration and does not represent some fallible human interpretation, either in v.11 or v.29. Two somewhat different meanings occur for *niḥam* in the one and same chapter—a not uncommon occurrence in Hebrew words with two or more meanings.

Which name for David's brother is correct, Shammah or Shimea? (D*)

In 1 Samuel 16:9 the name of Jesse's third son (David's older brother) is given as Shammah (*šammāh*). But in 1 Chronicles 2:13 it is spelled *šimᵉ'ā'* (though the Syriac Peshitta reads *šamo'*

there as well as in 1 Sam. 16:9). There is still another passage (2 Sam. 21:21) where the name is given as Shimeah (*šimᵉ'āy*). From these data we must come to some conclusion as to which was the correct and original spelling of this man's name.

First of all, it is significant that even though the *'ayin* (') is missing from 1 Samuel 16:9, the *mêm* (m) does have a mark of doubling (dagesh forte) within it (*šammāh* rather than *šāmāh*), which makes it identical with the adverb for "thither" or "there"—and rather unlikely as a personal name. But it could represent an assimilation with a following consonant such as *'ayin.* It may be that in some regions of the Hebrew-speaking territory, such as Judah, there was a tendency to deemphasize or even omit the sound of *'ayin,* especially in proper names. Thus we find the name of the Moabitess spelled *rût* (Ruth), rather than *rᵉ'û-2t* ("Friendship"), which it probably should have been. (*Rû-t* is a meaningless word without an *'ayin.*) So also, Samuel is rendered *šᵉmú'ēl* (which could only mean "The name of God"), whereas according to Hannah's statements in 1 Samuel 1:20 and 1:27 it should have been *šᵉmú"ēl* ("Heard of God"). We must therefore conclude that the spelling in 1 Chronicles 2:13 (*šimᵉ'ā'*) is the correct one and that the reading in 1 Samuel 16:9 is a scribal error resulting from a regional pronunciation of the name.

How many sons did Jesse have? First Samuel 16:10–11 makes it eight, but 1 Chronicles 2:13–15 makes it seven.

First Samuel 16 names only the three oldest brothers of David: Eliab (v.6), Abinadab (v.8), and Shammah (v.9), who is called Shimea in 1 Chronicles 2:13. Yet it does specify that Jesse introduced seven of his sons to Samuel (v.10) before he had the youngest, David, called home from the field (v.11). First Chronicles 2:14 gives the names of the other three as Nethanel, Raddai, and Ozem, and specifies that David was the seventh. What became of the other son, unnamed in 1 Samuel 16 and totally ignored in 1 Chronicles 2? Delitzsch (Keil and Delitzsch, *Chronicles*, p.62) suggests that he might have died without posterity; therefore his name was not preserved as late as the period when Chronicles was composed. It may well have been that he died of illness or accident while still a young man, prior to marriage. Since he produced no descendants and contributed no exploits back in David's time, there was no special reason for retaining him in the later enumeration of Jesse's sons.

The writer of this article had an older brother who died quite young, which would bring up the count of the children to four. Yet after the death of that earlier son, the three surviving children always spoke of themselves as a family of three siblings. Perhaps a similar event happened in Jesse's family as well. The full number of his sons was eight, but only seven survived and played a role during David's career. (First Chron. 2:16 adds that there were two daughters as well, Zeruiah and Abigail. After they were married, their sons played an important role as well in the service of their uncle David.)

In 1 Samuel 16:19–21 Saul recognizes David as the son of Jesse, but in 17:58 Saul is said to have asked David, "Whose son art thou?" How can the two be reconciled? (D*)

It is true that Saul had already been introduced to David (1 Sam. 16:18) as "a son of Jesse the Bethlehemite who is a skillful musician, a mighty man of valor, a warrior, one prudent in speech, and a handsome man" (NASB). But it should be noted also that up until the contest with Goliath, David had shown to King Saul only his artistic side; and then David had been permitted to return home to Bethlehem. It is altogether true to life for Saul to see David in an entirely new light and to show a keen interest in his background. Apparently General Abner had no previous acquaintance with David except as a harp player and so was not even aware of Jesse's name (17:55). Abner had not been involved in David's earlier introduction to the palace as a soothing musician (16:18); rather, one of Saul's "young men" (that is, a retainer of the royal bodyguard) had mentioned Jesse's name to Saul.

Saul's rekindled interest, however, went far beyond the name of David's father—even though that was his lead-off question. It is quite apparent that Saul wanted to know whether there were any more at home like him; this was in line with his standard policy set forth in 1 Samuel 14:52: "When Saul saw any mighty man or any valiant man, he attached him to his staff" (NASB). That is to say, Saul was intent on building up a first-class bodyguard of champion fighters, and he saw in David a promising lead to obtaining more soldiers like him. From 18:1 we are informed that David then carried on a fairly extensive conversation with Saul, going far beyond the giving of his own father's name. Thus we find that when we view the two episodes in their own context and situation, they turn out to be very true to life; and there is no real contradiction between them.

First Samuel contains several instances of lying and deceit on the part of God's chosen servant David and of Samuel the prophet (1 Sam. 16; 20; 21; 27). Did the Lord really condone lying and deceit as means to a good end? (D*)

In dealing with this difficult question, we must keep the following factors in view.

1. Even though Scripture records the dishonesty of men, this does not necessarily mean that it approves or

condones such a sin. The same is true of other types of sin committed by religious leaders.

2. The duty to tell only what is true does not necessarily carry with it the obligation to tell the whole truth about the matter, especially if lives would be endangered or lost as a result of this information, or if divulging all the details would violate a trust of secrecy or amount to a betrayal of another's confidence.

3. The mere recording of an episode involving subterfuge or deception does not imply that the person resorting to it was acting responsibly on the highest level of faith or furnishing a valid example of conduct that believers might justifiably follow today.

With these factors in mind, we may profitably examine each of the episodes alluded to in the question.

First Samuel 16:2 relates Samuel's apprehension at carrying out the Lord's assignment to anoint a new king down in Bethlehem. "But Samuel said, 'How can I go? When Saul hears of it, he will kill me.' And the LORD said, 'Take a heifer with you and say, 'I have come to sacrifice to the LORD'" (NASB). Verse 5 relates that Samuel said to Jesse and his family, "I have come to sacrifice to the LORD" (NASB). Of course this was in fact true, for he had followed God's instructions in this matter. He had actually taken along a heifer to offer on the altar in Bethlehem, even though he really had a further purpose in mind. In this entire transaction he was carrying out the instructions of God Himself. It is quite clear that the Lord had approved a policy of withholding information from King Saul that would have moved him to violence or bloodshed had he known of it in advance. If Samuel had divulged his full intention (beyond the performing of a religious sacrifice in Bethlehem), Saul would have killed not only Samuel

himself but also David and his entire family. In this case then, it would have been altogether wrong and extremely harmful for Samuel to have told the entire truth or revealed his entire purpose. There is a clear distinction between resorting to actual deceit and to withholding information that would result in great harm and even failure to obey carrying out the will of God—in this case the anointing of young David to be king over Israel. In other words, Samuel was entirely within the will of God when he told only part of the truth rather than the whole truth.

First Samuel 20 relates how Jonathan handled the difficult matter of protecting the life of his dearest friend, David, in a situation where he knew (1) that God had chosen David to be the next king of Israel and (2) that his own father, Saul, was likely to attempt to prevent this purpose of God by having David killed, as a dangerous rival to the dynastic rights of the house of Saul. His loyalty to his father represented a definite conflict with his duty to the Lord Himself and to His chosen servant, David, whom he personally loved far more than himself or his insanely jealous and bloodthirsty father. Under these peculiar circumstances, Jonathan could pursue no other course than he did. That is to say, he agreed with David on a test of Saul's true intentions (which were difficult to determine, in view of his unbalanced mentality and his occasional change of mind; cf. 1 Sam. 19:6). The only way he could find out the king's real purpose was to present him with a situation to react to, namely David's failure to show up at the new moon feast at Saul's palace (which David had previously attended without fail, as a son-in-law belonging to the royal family). There had to be some plausible excuse arranged for his absence; so this was furnished by David's alleged summons to Bethlehem in order to join with the rest of his family in celebrating the new moon festival in the household of Jesse.

Unlike the previous example (1 Sam. 16:2), there seems to have been no such summons from David's oldest brother, Eliab, even though such an invitation would have been quite reasonable and justified on the part of the family in Bethlehem. Yet as the story unfolds, it is quite clear that David never went to Bethlehem after he found out that Saul was bent on having him killed. It is highly doubtful whether David would have gone home even if he had learned from Jonathan that Saul had relented in his hostility; David probably would have made his way back to the palace, instead. We can only conclude that this appointment to join the family in Bethlehem was a sheer concoction on David's part. And even though Jonathan accurately repeated what David had said to him by way of a request to be excused from attending the king's table, Jonathan, of course, knew that it was a mere subterfuge. And yet we can hardly fault Jonathan in this, for had he told his father all that he knew about the matter and the full content of his conversation with David, he would have been guilty of the basest betrayal of his trusting friend, who was also the chosen king of Israel according to Yahweh's own decision. David's blood would have been on Jonathan's head. As it was, he nearly lost his own life as he tried to defend David's rights before his father's fury; and Jonathan had to beat a hasty retreat when Saul attempted to pin him against the wall with his spear (1 Sam. 20:33).

First Samuel 21 records the sorry choice David made in fleeing to the town of Nob, where the high priest, Ahimelech, served at the tabernacle of the Lord. David should never had brought that community into such terrible danger from the wrath of the king, and his brief visit there brought on him the guilt of their subsequent massacre at the hands of Saul's agents, under the leadership of the despicable Doeg (22:18-19). In fairness to David, it may well be that he did not foresee the extreme to which Saul would go in slaughtering all those innocent priests. But after the atrocity was accomplished and Abiathar brought him the sorrowful tidings, David had to acknowledge how inexcusably guilty he was when he lied to Ahimelech about his mission at Nob and gave the priest no opportunity to choose whether he was willing to court death for David's sake.

In this entire episode David involved himself in the greatest guilt—as he himself recognized afterward. "Then David said to Abiathar, 'I knew on that day, when Doeg the Edomite was there, that he would surely tell Saul I have brought about the death of every person in your father's household'" (1 Sam. 22:22, NASB). But as for the Lord's involvement in this entire tragedy, there is really no indication whatever that He condoned David's deception toward Ahimelech. The only mitigation of David's guilt was that he really had not thought ahead about what harm he was going to cause to others when he sought refuge at Nob. But, in retrospect, David should have turned in some other direction when he fled from Saul. If David had really looked to the Lord for guidance, he might have found safety at Engedi or some other remote wilderness to which he later resorted. He certainly was out of the will of God when he lied his way into Nob and made off with the sword of Goliath.

It is interesting to notice that Jesus later used David's example at Nob, where he and his followers partook of the week-old showbread when they were starving, even though that bread was intended for the priests alone (Matt. 12:3-4). Our Lord seems to imply that under those unusual cir-

177

cumstances, David was justified in doing that, since the preservation of human life was even more important than strict observance of the ritual law. But even so, David certainly suffered the deepest humiliation when he allowed panic to lead him to King Achish at Gath, instead of waiting on the Lord for His guidance. David only succeeded in putting his life into even greater danger when he sought refuge with the ungodly Philistines. He only escaped from that peril by pretending to be hopelessly demented while he was in the palace of Achish, with the result that they utterly despised him and drove him from their borders like some wild animal (1 Sam. 21:13-15).

In 1 Samuel 27:8-12 we read of a long-continued deception David practiced toward King Achish. After he had been allowed to set up his headquarters in Ziklag (as a vassal or ally of Achish of Gath), David supported himself and his six hundred followers by raiding the tribesmen of the Negeb (the Geshurites, Girzites, and Amalekites) and slaughtering the entire population of every community that he invaded. The purpose of this bloody practice was to keep any survivors from informing the Philistines at Gath that David was not really attacking the Jerahmeelites and Judeans, as he claimed he was doing, but was actually raiding non-Israelite communities that were on good terms with the Philistines (vv. 11-12). He manged to keep Achish from ever finding out the truth about his activities and made him believe that he had become an enemy of his own countrymen by preying on their villages and carrying off their livestock.

After this review of those sorry episodes in the early career of David, we must recognize that God did not favor and protect the son of Jesse on account of his occasional deceptions or his occasional hardness toward pagan enemies (like the Ammonites in 2 Sam.

12:31). On the contrary, God put David through an arduous educative process of suffering, uncertainty, and danger, because He found in him an instrument well suited to deliver his nation from their heathen foes and to establish a strong and stable government in fulfillment of His ancient promise to Abraham (Gen. 15:18-21). It was not because of his virtue and his good deeds that God chose David for his role of leadership but because of his great faith. Despite the episodes where he failed to trust the Lord completely or to seek His guidance as carefully as he should have, David gave his heart to the Lord sincerely and made it his chief purpose and desire to do the will of God and glorify His name.

Who killed Goliath—David or Elhanan?

First Samuel 17:50 states that David cut off Goliath's head with the giant's own sword, after he had first felled him with a sling and a stone. Because of this amazing victory over the Philistine, David became the foremost battle-champion among the Israelite troops, even though he was still a mere teenager. But 2 Samuel 21:19 in the Hebrew Masoretic text states that "Elhanan the son of Yaare-oregim the Bethlehemite killed Goliath the Gittite, the shaft of whose spear was like a weaver's beam." As this verse stands in the Masoretic text, it certainly contradicts 1 Samuel 17. But fortunately we have a parallel passage in 1 Chronicles 20:5, which words the episode this way: "And Elhanan the son of Jair slew Lahmi the brother of Goliath the Gittite." It is quite apparent that this was the true reading, not only for the Chronicles passage but also for 2 Samuel 21:19.

The earlier manuscript from which the copyist was reading must have been blurred or damaged at this particular verse, and hence he made two or three mistakes. What apparently happened was the following:

1. The sign of the direct object, which in Chronicles comes just before "Lahmi," was '-*ṭ*; the copyist mistook it for *b-ṭ* or *b-y-ṭ* ("Beth") and thus got *Bêṭ hal-Laḥmî* ("the Bethlehemite") out of it.
2. He misread the word for "brother" ('-*ḥ*) as the sign of the direct object ('-*ṭ*) right before *g-l-y-ṭ* ("Goliath"). Thus he made "Goliath" the object of "killed" (*wayyak*), instead of the "brother" of Goliath (as the Chron. passage does).
3. The copyist misplaced the word for "weavers" ('-*r-g-ym*) so as to put it right after "Elhanan" as his patronymic (*ben Y-'-r-y'-r--g-ym*, or *ben ya"rêy 'ōrᵉ-gîm*—"the son of the forests of weavers"—a most unlikely name for anyone's father!). In Chronicles the *'ōrᵉgîm* ("weavers") comes right after *mᵉnôr* ("a beam of")—thus making perfectly good sense.

In other words, the 2 Samuel 21 passage is a perfectly traceable corruption of the original wording, which fortunately has been correctly preserved in 1 Chronicles 20:5.

First Samuel 18:10 says that an evil spirit from God came on King Saul. How can this be explained if only good comes from God? (D*)

It is not quite accurate to say that only good comes from God. While it is true that God's original creation was good (Gen. 1:31) and that God Himself is not tempted by evil, nor does He tempt (in the sense of attracting or enticing) any man to evil (James 1:13), nevertheless it remains true that genuine goodness in a moral God requires that a real difference be made between good and evil. As the ordainer and preserver of the moral order, it is absolutely necessary for God to punish sin, no matter how much love and compassion He may feel toward the sinner.

In Isaiah 45:7 we read, "[I am] the One forming light and creating darkness, causing well-being and creating calamity; I am the LORD who does all these" (NASB). The word rendered by NASB as "calamity" is the Hebrew *rā'*, which has the basic meaning of "evil" (either moral evil or misfortune evil). Here it points to the painful, harmful consequences that followed the commission of sin. Notice how James goes on to indicate how this process works: "But each one is tempted when he is carried away and enticed by his own lust. Then when lust has conceived, it gives birth to sin; and when sin is accomplished, it brings forth death" (James 1:14–15, NASB).

In Saul's case, he had knowingly flouted the law of God—first, by performing priestly sacrifice at the Lord's altar contrary to the divine command (1 Sam. 13:12–13), and, second, by sparing King Agag and some of the cattle of the Amalekites after he had been ordered to put them all to death (1 Sam. 15:20–23). Moreover in 1 Samuel 18:8 it is stated that Saul became insanely jealous of young David because of the public praise he had received for his prowess in slaying Goliath and the Philistines. By these successive acts of rebellion against the will and law of God, King Saul left himself wide open to satanic influence—just as Judas Iscariot did after he had determined to betray the Lord Jesus (cf. John 13:2).

Insofar as God has established the spiritual laws of cause and effect, it is accurate to say that Saul's disobedience cut him off from the guidance and communion of the Holy Spirit that he had formerly enjoyed and left him a prey to a malign spirit of depression and intense jealousy that drove him increasingly to irrational paranoia. Although he was doubtless acting as an agent of Satan, Saul's evil bent was by the permission and plan of God. We must realize that in the last analysis all penal consequences for sin come from God, as the Author of the moral law and the one who always does what is right (Gen. 18:25).

First Samuel 19:23-24 states of King Saul that "the spirit of God was upon him also, and he went on, and prophesied.... And he stripped off his clothes also, and prophesied before Samuel in like manner." Why did he prophesy naked? (D*)

The passage beginning with v.19 indicates that Saul was in pursuit of his son-in-law, young David, and that David had gotten to Naioth in Ramah. Saul was informed that David was there with the prophets who had been trained for the Lord's service under Samuel. So he sent his agents up to arrest David and to bring him down in chains.

When the king's agents got there, however, and saw the august figure of Samuel himself and his prophetic assistants all engaged in a joyous praise service before the Lord, they too came under the influence of the Holy Spirit. Unable to control themselves or carry out the business for which they had been sent, they could do nothing else but surrender to the same emotional excitement and join in the songs and shouts of adoration before the Lord. By that time they felt utterly unable to perform their mission, and they had to return to Saul empty-handed.

After the same thing had happened to two other teams of soldiers whom Saul sent up to Samuel's group, Saul finally resolved to carry out his mission himself. Until then he had hung back, hoping to avoid confrontation with Samuel, with whom he had had a complete falling out after the episode at Gilgal (1 Sam. 15:17-35), where Samuel had announced that Saul had been rejected by God from the kingship. Saul did not relish the prospect of facing that fearsome prophet again, but he felt there was no alternative.

Also, Saul was subject to manic depression and given to extreme changes of mood (cf. 1 Sam. 16:14-23; 18:10-11; 19:9). As he came near the praise service over which Samuel was presiding, Saul found himself coming under the spell of the excitement of the occasion; and he could not control himself. He too began to sing, shout, and dance along with the prophets themselves. (Somewhat similar cases have been reported at camp meetings during the Great Awakening in America in 1740 under George Whitefield and in 1800 at the revival meetings held in Kentucky.) Such an overpowering sense of the presence, power, and glory of God came over this wicked king that he recalled his earlier revival experience near Bethel (1 Sam. 10:5-6, 10), when he had first been called to the throne; and he succumbed to the same excitement again.

Unlike the other worshipers, Saul became so carried away with his enthusiasm that he stripped off his clothes as he shouted and danced, and he finally collapsed exhausted on the ground and lay there in a stupor or trance the rest of the day and all through the night (1 Sam. 19:24). Undoubtedly this humiliation came on him as a divine judgment because in his heart he was radically opposed to the will of God, insofar as it went counter to his own ambition.

What took place in 1 Samuel 28:8-16? Did Samuel really appear to Saul? Did Saul actually talk with him in the witch's cave? (D*)

There is little doubt that satanic powers are able to produce illusionary images and communicate with the living by this means. Such "lying wonders" (2 Thess. 2:9) are part of the Devil's stock in trade. On the other hand, it certainly lies within God's power as well to present an appearance for the purpose of conveying His message by a special revelation.

The oracle delivered by this shade or apparition sounded like an authentic message from God, with its announcement of doom on the guilty, unfaithful king. It even sounded like something Samuel himself would have said, had he remained alive after the massacre of Ahimelech and the priests of Nob (1 Sam. 22:11-19). Therefore it is entirely possible that this apparition was the actual shade of Samuel himself, when he asked, "Why has thou disquieted me, to bring me up?" Apparently Samuel had been directed by God to leave his abode in Sheol or Hades (where even the saved believers awaited the future resurrection of Christ, which would bring about their transferal to heaven itself) in order to deliver this final message to King Saul. Conceivably the deceased Samuel could have communicated long distance through an apparition in the cave of Endor, but the words "to bring me up" make this very doubtful.

On the other hand, it should be observed that the witch herself was quite startled by this ghostly visitor, as she said, "I see a god [Heb. '*e lōhîm*] coming up out of the earth" (v.13). This clearly implies that this authentic appearance of the dead (if such it was) was no result of her own witchcraft; rather, it was an act of God Himself that terrified her and that she had in no sense brought about in her own power. It would seem that God chose this particular occasion and setting to give His final word to the evil king who had once served His cause with courage and zeal. No scriptural basis for spiritism is furnished by this episode, nor for necromancy—both of which are sternly condemned as abomina-

tions before the Lord (Deut. 18:9-12; cf. Exod. 22:18; Lev. 19:26,31; 20: 6,27; Jer. 27:9-10).

First Samuel 31 gives an account of Saul's death that conflicts with another given in 2 Samuel 1. How can both be correct?

First Samuel 31:3-4 informs us that Saul was fatally wounded by a Philistine arrow at the disastrous battle of Mount Gilboa. Realizing that he was about to die, Saul himself appealed to his own armorbearer to thrust his sword through his heart and kill him immediately—"lest these uncircumcized [Philistines] come and pierce me through and make sport of me" (NASB). But since the armorbearer could not bring himself to take the life of his king, Saul took his own sword, fastened its hilt firmly in the ground, and then fell on it in such a way as to end his misery right then and there.

In 2 Samuel 1 we read that a certain Amalekite who had served in Saul's bodyguard fled from the battlefield and made his way to David's camp, in order to bring him news of Saul's death. According to the account he gave to David (vv.6-10), he was summoned by King Saul to his side while he was hopelessly surrounded by the triumphant Philistines; and he was ordered by the king to take his life immediately, in order to end his misery from his fatal wounds. The Amalekite then complied with his request (v.10): "So I stood beside him and killed him, because I knew that he could not live after he had fallen. And I took the crown which was on his head and the bracelet which was on his arm, and I have brought them here to my lord" (NASB).

This presents obvious discrepancies with the account in 1 Samuel 31, but it is not presented as being an actual record of what happened during Saul's dying moments; it is only a record of what the Amalekite mercenary said had taken place. Coming with Saul's crown and bracelet in hand and presenting them before the new king of Israel, the Amalekite obviously expected a handsome reward and high preferment in the service of Saul's successor. In the light of the straightforward account in the previous chapter, we must conclude that the Amalekite was lying in order to gain a cordial welcome from David. But what had actually happened was that after Saul had killed himself, and the armorbearer had followed his lord's example by taking his own life (1 Sam. 31:5), the Amalekite happened by at that moment, recognized the king's corpse, and quickly stripped off the bracelet and crown before the Philistine troops discovered it. Capitalizing on his good fortune, the Amalekite then escaped from the bloody field and made his way down to David's headquarters in Ziklag. But his hoped-for reward turned out to be a warrant for his death; David had him killed on the spot, saying: "Your blood is on your head, for your mouth has testified against you, saying, 'I have killed the LORD's anointed'" (2 Sam. 1:16; NASB). His glib falsehood had brought him the very opposite of what he had expected, for he failed to foresee that David's high code of honor would lead him to make just the response he did.

It should be added that this particular Amalekite came from a different Amalekite tribe from that which Saul had earlier destroyed at God's command—the tribe over which Agag had ruled (1 Sam. 15:7-8). Those Amalekites lived between Havilah and Shur. But there were other Amalekites not involved in this campaign, some of whom raided David's settlement at Ziklag (1 Sam. 30).

2 Samuel

How could David have reigned seven and a half years in Hebron if Ish-bosheth, his rival, reigned only two years before he died?

In 2 Samuel 5:5 we are told that the length of David's reign in Hebron as king of Judah (before he became acknowledged by the northern tribes as king over all Israel) was seven and a half years. This is confirmed by 1 Chronicles 3:4. Yet 2 Samuel 2:10 reports that David's rival, Ish-bosheth son of Saul, ruled over Israel (under Abner's sponsorship) for only two years. But this did not prevent the very next verse from affirming that David's rule in Hebron was indeed seven and a half years. How could both statements be true? On the assumption that the two years for Ish-bosheth represented the true interval, the Jerusalem Bible even amended 1 Chron. 3:4 to read, "Hebron, where he reigned for *three* years and six months" [italics mine]—even though no similar alteration has been made in the other two passages [2 Sam. 2:11; 5:5], interestingly enough!

A careful survey of the circumstances surrounding the career of Ish-bosheth furnishes a clue for the brevity of his reign. After the total collapse of Israel's army at the disaster of Mount Gilboa, it became necessary for Abner and the other fugitives from the victorious Philistines to take refuge east of the Jordan, leaving the entire area of Ephraim and Manasseh to the control of the conquerors. Abner must have set up his headquarters at Mahanaim, where he placed Ish-bosheth for safekeeping in the hinterland of the tribe of Gad. It apparently took Abner five long years of hard fighting to force the Philistines back from Beth-shan (where they had displayed the impaled bodies of Saul and his sons) all the way up the Valley of the Esdraelon, and thus link up the northern tribes of Issachar, Naphtali, and Asher with Benjamin to the south. But until that was accomplished, it was premature to celebrate any formal coronation of Ish-bosheth as king of Israel.

However, at the end of five years Abner had been sufficiently successful to call representatives from all Ten Tribes to a public coronation ceremony in Mahanaim—which remained the provisional capital for the time being, safely out of the reach of retaliatory expeditions launched by the Philistines. Thus it came about that Ish-bosheth actually reigned for only two years, at the end of which he was assassinated in bed by two of his army commanders, Baanah and Rechab (2 Sam. 4:5–6), sometime after they had heard of Abner's murder at the hand of the treacherous Joab (2 Sam. 3:27).

David, however, had been crowned by the men of Judah at Hebron quite soon after the battle of Mount Gilboa; and thus he wore the crown for a full seven and a half years, even though

Ish-bosheth had formally begun his reign only two years before his death.

What is the correct number of horsemen that David took in his battle over Hadadezer, seventeen hundred (2 Sam. 8:4) or seven thousand (1 Chron. 18:4)?

In the war against Hadadezer of Zobah, David won a significant victory near Hamath, capturing many prisoners, listed in 2 Samuel 8:4 as "a thousand and seven hundred horsemen, and twenty thousand footmen." But in 1 Chronicles 18:4 the number taken in this engagement is given as "a thousand chariots, and seven thousand horsemen, and twenty thousand footmen [i.e., infantry]." There is no question but that these two accounts refer to the same episode, and therefore the prisoner count should be the same in both instances. There has been a scribal error or two either in Samuel or in Chronicles.

Keil and Delitzsch (*Samuel*, p. 360) have a most convincing solution, that the word for chariotry (*rekeb*) was inadvertently omitted by the scribe in copying 2 Samuel 8:4, and that the second figure, seven thousand (for the *pārāsîm* "cavalrymen"), was necessarily reduced to seven hundred from the seven thousand he saw in his *Vorlage* for the simple reason that no one would write seven thousand after he had written one thousand in the recording of the one and the same figure. The omission of *rekeb* might have occurred with an earlier scribe, and the reduction of seven thousand to seven hundred would have followed by chain reaction when the defective copy was next copied by a later scribe. But in all probability the Chronicles figure is right and the Samuel numbers should be corrected to agree with it.

Second Samuel 14:27 says Absalom had three sons; 2 Samuel 18:18 says he had none. Which is right? (D*)

Second Samuel 14:27 says, "And to Absalom there were born three sons, and one daughter whose name was Tamar" (NASB). But 2 Samuel 18:18 states, "Now Absalom in his lifetime had taken and set up for himself a pillar which is in the King's Valley, for he said, 'I have no son to preserve my name.' So he named the pillar after his own name, and it is called Absalom's monument to this day" (NASB)—that is, to the time of the final composition of 2 Samuel, which may have been in the middle of the eighth century B.C. (The so-called Absalom's Tomb that now stands in the Kidron Valley probably dates from Hellenistic times, ca. second century B.C., judging from the style of its façade [cf. K.N. Schoville, *Biblical Archaeology in Focus* (Grand Rapids: Baker, 1978), p. 414].) This establishes the fact that by the time he set up his monument (which may have been a year or two before his rebellion against his father, David), Absalom had no male heirs surviving to him. But it does not prove that none had been born to him previously.

Keil and Delitzsch (*Samuel*, p. 412) point out, in regard to 2 Samuel 14:27, that "contrary to general usage, the names of the sons are not given, in all probability for no other reason than because they died in infancy. Consequently, as Absalom had no sons, he afterwards erected a pillar to preserve his name (ch. xviii. 18)." Apparently he endured the heartbreak of losing all three little boys in their infancy, and it had become apparent that his wife would not bear him any more. It would seem that Tamar was the only one to survive out of all his children; and that meant he had no male heir to carry on his name, hence the poignancy of his remark in 18:18, and the rather pathetic attempt to compensate by the erection of a monument in stone. Within a few years Absalom himself died in disgrace, as the would-be slayer of his own father, David, and as a defiler of his father's wives. Thus any son of his would have had a sorry heritage had he survived to adulthood.

As for the daughter, Tamar (named after Absalom's beautiful sister, whom her half-brother Amnon had raped, but whom Absalom later avenged by having Amnon assassinated), she apparently lived on and married well. Her husband was Uriel of Gibeah (cf. 2 Chron. 11:20–22; 13:1). Their daughter was the infamous Maacah (=Micaiah), who married King Rehoboam (1 Kings 15:2) and became the mother of his successor, Abijam. Her grandson King Asa finally removed her from the position of Queen Mother because of her involvement in idolatry (1 Kings 15:10–13; 2 Chron. 15:16).

How could a kind and loving God take the life of Bathsheba's first child just because of the sin of its parents (2 Sam. 12:15–23)?

One of the profoundest insights granted to us through Holy Scripture is the true meaning of death. Apart from divine revelation we may think of death as a fearsome menace, a terrible curse, a final stroke of judgment. Insofar as death—that is to say, physical death with its separation of the soul from the body—means the end of all opportunity to find God and to glorify Him with a godly life, there is something very solemn and awesome about death. But God's Word tells us very plainly that physical death, regardless of how it looks to the human observer, is not the end for any man. He goes right on into the eternal phase of his career, whether in heaven or in hell—whichever he has chosen during his earthly life. But since the Son of God has come and given His trustworthy assurance to all believers, that everyone who lives and believes in Me shall never die" (John 11:26), death has taken on an entirely new meaning. Because it was through death—death

as the sinner's substitute on the cross—that our Savior "conquered death and brought life and immortality to light through the gospel" (2 Tim. 1:10) death has been robbed of its sting and the grave has been deprived of its victory (1 Cor. 15:54–56). "Blessed are the dead who die in the Lord. . . . that they may rest from their labors" (Rev. 14:13, NASB).

In the case of children who die in infancy, it may well be that they are spared a life of tragedy, heartbreak, and pain by their immediate departure from this world. It is perhaps too simplistic to maintain that all children dying in infancy are thereby guaranteed a place in heaven, as if the saving benefits of Calvary were somehow imputed to them without any response of faith on their own part. Such a doctrine would be a powerful encouragement to parents to kill their babies before they reached the age of accountability, as the only sure way of their getting into heaven. But since infanticide is sternly condemned in Scripture as an abomination before God (Lev. 18:21; Deut. 12:31; 2 Chron. 28:3; Isa. 57:5; Jer. 19:4–7), even when perpetrated in the name of religion, we must conclude that there is some other principle involved in the salvation of infants besides their managing to die in infancy. That is to say, the omniscience of God extends not only to the actual but also to the potential. He foreknows not only whatever *will* happen but also whatever *would* happen. In the case of babies who die at birth or before they reach the age of accountability, God knows what their response would be to the proffers of His grace, whether acceptance or rejection, whether faith or unbelief.

It was probably for this reason that David took comfort after he learned that his prayers had been fruitless, and that God had taken his little one "home." He resigned his baby to the grace of God and said only, "I shall go to him, but he will not return to me" (2 Sam. 12:23, NASB). David had a quiet confidence in the perfection of God's will, even in a heart-rending situation like this. And, furthermore, he understood why God had seen fit to chasten the guilty couple by taking from them the fruit of their sinful passion. He saw that they needed this rebuke as a reminder that God's children, even though forgiven, must bear the temporal consequences of their sin and patiently endure them as an important part of their repentance.

Was Absalom actually buried in Absalom's Tomb in the Kidron Valley?

Second Samuel 18:17 relates what happened to Absalom after Joab caught him hanging by the hair from the bough of an oak and dispatched him with a spear: "And they took Absalom and cast him into a deep pit in the forest and erected over him a very great heap of stones" (NASB). The "forest" in question was the so-called Forest of Ephraim, which was apparently located in the land of Gilead (on the East Bank—whereas the tribal territory of Ephraim was on the West Bank). As soon as Absalom's body was cut down from the tree branch it was given an inglorious burial in a deep pit, even before Absalom's father, King David, had heard of his death.

The background for the so-called Tomb of Absalom in the Kidron Valley is to be found in 2 Samuel 18:18, which refers to a pillar (*maṣṣebeṭ*) that Absalom had erected in that valley as a compensation for his childlessness so far as sons were concerned. "So he named the pillar after his own name, and it is called Absalom's monument to this day" (NASB, i.e.; the day when 2 Samuel was finished, ca. 750 B.C.). But this pillar was at most a cenotaph; it never represented the actual place of interment for Absalom's body, which

rotted away in the forest pit on the East Bank, on the other side of Jordan.

Who moved David to number his people, God or Satan?

In 2 Samuel 24:1 we read, "And again the anger of the LORD was kindled against Israel, and He moved David against them to say, Go, number Israel and Judah." In the parallel account in 1 Chronicles 21:1-2 it is stated: "And Satan stood up against Israel, and provoked David to number Israel. And David said to Joab and to the rulers of the people, Go, number Israel from Beer-sheba even to Dan; and bring the number of them to me, that I may know it." The wording of 1 Chronicles 21:2 is very similar to that of 2 Samuel 24:2; there is no significant difference. But so far as the first verse of each chapter is concerned, it appears in 2 Samuel 24 that God Himself incited David to conduct the census, whereas in 1 Chronicles 21 it was Satan, the adversary of God. This would seem to be a serious discrepancy— unless both statements are true.

In neither book are we given a definite context for this census taking, and we have no way of knowing whether it took place before or after Absalom's revolt. But since it led indirectly to the acquisition of the hill (Mt. Moriah) that became the location of the temple and of the royal palaces, it must have occurred several years before the end of David's career. Only thus could he have had opportunity to amass the large amount of costly ornamentation and material that Solomon was later to use in fashioning that temple (1 Chron. 29:3-5).

Without being fully aware of what was going on in his heart, David had apparently been building up an attitude of pride and self-admiration for what he had achieved in the way of military success and economic expansion of his people. He began to think more in terms of armaments and troops than in terms of the faithful mercies of God. In his youth he had put his entire trust in God alone, whether he was facing Goliath with a slingshot or an army of Amalekites with a band of four hundred men. But in later years he had come to rely more and more on material resources, like any hardheaded realist, and he learned to measure his strength by the yardstick of numbers and wealth.

The Lord therefore decided that it was time for David to be brought to his knees once more and to be cast on the grace of God through a time of soul-searching trial. He therefore encouraged David to carry out the plan he had long cherished, that of counting up his manpower resources in order to plan his future military strategy with a view to the most effective deployment of his armies. Quite possibly this would also afford him a better base for assessment of taxes. And so God in effect said to him: "All right, go ahead and do it. Then you will find out how much good it will do you."

Though he was a hard-bitten and ambitious commander, General Joab felt a definite uneasiness about this whole project. He sensed that David and his advisors were becoming increasingly puffed up over their brilliant conquests, which had brought the Palestinian, Syrian, and Phoenician kingdoms into a state of vassalage and dependency on Israel. Joab was fearful that the Lord was displeased with this new attitude of self-confidence and self-esteem, and he tried to dissuade David from his purpose. First Chronicles 21:3 records Joab as saying, "The LORD make his people an hundred times so many more as they be: but, my lord the king, are they not all my lord's servants? Why then doth my lord require this thing? Why will he be a cause of trespass to Israel?" There is a defi-

nite sense in which Yahweh gave David a final warning through the lips of Joab, before David finally committed himself to the census.

It was not that census taking was inherently evil. The Lord was not displeased with the two censuses taken in the time of Moses; in fact, He gave Moses positive directions to number all his military effectives (Num. 1:2–3; 26:2), both at the beginning of the forty years' wandering in the desert and at the end of that period, as they were on the threshold of the conquest. The second census was designed to show that the total of Israel's armed forces was actually a bit less than it had been forty years earlier. And yet with that smaller force they would sweep all their enemies before them, rather than cowering in fear at the prospect of war as their fathers had done at Kadesh-Barnea. The second census would also serve a useful purpose as a basis for the distribution of the conquered territory among the Twelve Tribes. The more numerous tribes should be awarded the larger tracts in the apportionment of land. But this census on which David had set his heart could serve no other purpose than to inflate the national ego. As soon as the numbering was complete, God meant to chasten the nation by a disastrous plague that would cause a considerable loss of life and a decrease in the numbers of their citizens.

But as we turn back to the opening verse in 1 Chronicles 21, we are faced with the statement that it was Satan who moved David to conduct the census even over Joab's warning and protest. The verb for "incited" is identical in both accounts (*wayyāset*). Why would Satan get himself involved in this affair if God had already prompted David to commit the folly he had in mind? It was because Satan found it in his own interest to do so. The situation here somewhat resembles the first and second chapters of Job, in which it was really a challenge to Satan from God that led to Job's calamities. God's purpose was to purify Job's faith and ennoble his character through the discipline of adversity. Satan's purpose was purely malicious; he wished to do Job as much harm as he possibly could, and if possible drive him to curse God for his misfortunes. Thus it came about that both God and Satan were involved in Job's downfall and disaster.

Similarly we find both God and Satan involved in the sufferings of persecuted Christians according to 1 Peter 4:19 and 5:8. God's purpose is to strengthen their faith and to enable them to share in the sufferings of Christ in this life, that they may rejoice with Him in the glories of heaven to come (4:13–14). But Satan's purpose is to "devour" them (5:8), that is, to draw them into bitterness or self-pity, and thus drag them down to his level and his baneful destiny. Even in the case of Christ Himself, it was Satan's purpose to deflect the Savior from His messianic mission by the three temptations he offered Him; but it was the Father's purpose for the Second Adam to triumph completely over the very tempter who had lured the first Adam to his fall.

Also, at the Crucifixion it was Satan's purpose to have Jesus betrayed by Judas (whose heart he filled with treachery and hate [John 13:27]); but it was the Father's purpose that the Lamb slain from the foundation of the world should give His life as a ransom for many—and this was symbolized by the cup that Christ was forced to accept at Gethsemane. And in the case of Peter, Jesus informed him before his triple denial in the court of the high priest: "Simon, Simon, Satan has asked to sift you as wheat. But I have prayed for you, Simon, that your faith may not fail. And when you have turned back, strengthen your brothers" (Luke 22: 31–32, NIV).

Here, then, we have five other examples of incidents or situations in which both Satan and God were involved in soul-searching testings and trials—God with a basically benevolent motive and a view to eventual victory and increasing usefulness for the person so tested, but Satan with an altogether malicious motive, hoping to do as much damage as he possibly can. Therefore we can say without hesitation that both accounts of David's incitement were correct. God incited him in order to teach him and his people a lesson they needed to learn and to humble them in a way that would promote their spiritual growth. Satan incited him in order to deal a severe blow to Israel and to mar David's prestige before his subjects. As it turned out (and this is true of virtually all the other examples as well), Satan's success was limited and transient; but in the end God's purpose was well served and His cause was substantially furthered.

In the aftermath of the plague, which cost the lives of seventy thousand Israelites (2 Sam. 24:15), the angel of the Lord designated the exact spot on Mount Moriah where the plague was stopped as the chosen spot for the future temple of the Lord (v.18). This structure was destined to bring much blessing into the lives of God's people for many generations to come. Once again Satan's malice was surpassed by the overruling grace of God.

Second Samuel 24:9 gives the total population for Israel as 800,000, which is 300,000 less than the corresponding figure in 1 Chronicles 21:5. On the other hand, 2 Samuel 24 gives 500,000 for Judah, as over against a mere 470,000 in 1 Chronicles 21. How can these apparent discrepancies be reconciled? (D*)

A possible solution may be found along these lines. So far as Israel (i.e., the tribes north of Judah) is concerned, the 1 Chronicles figure includes all the available men of fighting age, whether battle seasoned or not. But from 2 Samuel 24 we learn that Joab's report gave a subtotal of "mighty men" ('iš ḥayil), i.e., battle-seasoned troops, consisting of 800,000 veterans. But in addition there may have been 300,000 more men of military age who served in the reserves but had not yet been involved in field combat. These two contingents would make up a total of 1,100,000—as 1 Chronicles 21 reports them, without employing the term 'iš ḥayil.

So far as Judah was concerned, 2 Samuel 24 gives the round figure of 500,000, which was 30,000 more than the corresponding item in 1 Chronicles 21. Now it should be observed that 1 Chronicles 21:6 makes it clear that Joab did not complete the numbering, for he did not get around to a census of the tribe of Benjamin (nor that of Levi, either) before David came under conviction about completing the census at all. Joab was glad to desist when he saw the king's change of heart. The procedure for conducting the census had been to start with the Transjordanian tribes (2 Sam. 24:5) and then shift to the northernmost tribe of Dan and work southward back toward Jerusalem (v.7). This meant that the numbering of Benjamin would have come last. Hence Benjamin was not included with the total for Israel or that for Judah, either. But in the case of 2 Samuel 24, the figure for Judah included the already known figure of 30,000 troops mustered by Benjamin (which lay immediately adjacent to Jerusalem itself). Hence the total of 500,000 included the Benjamite contingent.

Observe that after the division of the united kingdom into North and South following the death of Solomon in 930 B.C., most of the Benjamites remained loyal to the dynasty of David and constituted (along with Simeon to the south) the kingdom of Judah. Hence it was reasonable to include Benjamin with Judah and Simeon in the subtotal figure of 500,000—even though Joab may not have itemized it in the first report he gave to David (1 Chron. 21:5). It would seem then that the completed grand total of the fighting forces available to David for military service was 1,600,000 (1,100,000 of Israel, 470,000 of Judah-Simeon, and 30,000 of Benjamin).

Why is there a discrepancy in the number of years of famine mentioned in 2 Samuel 24:13 and in 1 Chronicles 21:11–12? (D*)

Second Samuel 24:13 relates the visit of the prophet Gad to King David after he had finished the census of his kingdom in a spirit of pride. Gad relays God's message to him in the following terms: "Shall seven years of famine come to you in your land? Or will you flee three months before your foes while they pursue you? Or shall there be three days' pestilence in your land?" (NASB). To this David replies in a spirit of humble repentance, "Let us now fall into the hand of the LORD, for His mercies are great, but do not let me fall into the hand of man" (v.14, NASB).

In 1 Chronicles 21:11–12, Gad comes to David and says to him, "Thus says the LORD, 'Take for yourself either three years of famine, or three months to be swept away before your foes, ... or else three days of the sword of the LORD, even pestilence in the land.'" (NASB). Note that the wording here is significantly different from that of 2 Samuel 24:13 (i.e., "Shall seven years of famine come to you?"). Rather than that simple question in 2 Samuel, we have it given here in 1 Chronicles as an alternative imperative ("Take for yourself either three years of famine...").

From this we may reasonably conclude that 2 Samuel records the first approach of Gad to David, in which the alternative prospect was seven years; the Chronicles account gives us the second and final approach of Nathan to the king, in which the Lord (doubtless in response to David's earnest entreaty in private prayer) reduced the severity of that grim alternative to three years rather than an entire span of seven. As it turned out, however, David finally opted for God's own preference (whether famine or pestilence); and God sent three days of severe pestilence, which carried off the lives of seventy thousand men of Israel.

In 2 Samuel 24:24 it says that David "bought the threshing floor and the oxen for fifty shekels of silver." But in 1 Chronicles 21:25 it says David gave to Ornan for the place "600 shekels of gold by weight." How are these two statements to be reconciled? (D*)

The record in 2 Samuel 24:24 refers to the immediate purchase price paid by King David to Araunah (or "Ornan," as his name was alternatively spelled) for the two oxen and the wooden threshing cart being used by the Jebusite owner at the time David came up to see him. David's exact words in v.21 are as follows: "To buy the threshing floor from you, in order to build an altar to the LORD" (NASB). A threshing floor is generally an area of modest dimensions, not usually broader than thirty or forty feet. The market price for the two oxen and the cart would scarcely exceed the sum of fifty shekels of silver under the market values then prevailing.

In 1 Chronicles 21:25, however, we are told that David paid the much larger price of six hundred shekels of gold, which was possibly 180 times as much as fifty shekels of silver. But the Chronicles figure seems to include not merely the oxen and the threshing sledge but also the entire site. The Hebrew *wayyittên . . . bammāqôm* ("And he gave for the place") seems to be far more inclusive than the mere threshing floor. Neither in the fifth century B.C., nor in any other period in ancient history, would a threshing floor have cost anything like six hundred gold shekels. Consequently we may safely conclude that Ornan possessed the entire area of Mount Moriah.

About sixteen hundred feet long and on a commanding elevation, Mount Moriah was an extremely valuable piece of real estate, easily worth six hundred shekels of gold. The advisability of acquiring enough square footage for a temple site must have commended itself to King David, as he viewed the area of the threshing floor and realized how advantageous it would be to have the entire hilltop set apart for religious and governmental purposes. It was probably a somewhat later transaction with Ornan when David paid him the much larger price for the whole tract, and the Chronicler saw fit to record this entire transaction from the standpoint of its end result.

1 Kings

How can 1 Kings 6:1 be accepted as accurate if Rameses the Great was Pharaoh of the Exodus?

First Kings 6:1 states, "Now it came about in the four hundred and eightieth year after the sons of Israel came out of the land of Egypt, in the fourth year of Solomon's reign over Israel, ... he began to build the house of the LORD" (NASB). Since Solomon's reign began in 970 B.C., his fourth year would have been 966. Four hundred and eighty years before 966 comes out to 1446 or 1445. (There may have been a rounding off of numbers here, but essentially the time locus of the Exodus would have been between 1447 and 1442, if 1 Kings 6:1 is correct.) This would have been early in the reign of Amenhotep II, who according to the usual estimates reigned between 1447 and 1421. (Some more recent discussions of Egyptian chronology tend to lower these dates by a few years, but they have not yet been generally accepted as valid.)

The most-favored date for the Exodus in scholarly circles is about 1290, or quite early in the reign of Ramses II (1300–1234). In most of the popularizations of the Exodus drama, such as Cecil B. DeMille's "The Ten Commandments," the late date theory is assumed to be correct. The principal arguments in its favor are as follows:

1. The Israelites are stated in Exodus 1:11 to have labored as slaves in the building of the city of "*Raamses*"—which presupposes that there was already a King Rameses for this city to have been named after.

2. Since the Hyksos Dynasty was in charge of Egypt at the time Jacob migrated into Egypt—at least according to the Jewish historian Josephus—and since the Hyksos may not have seized power much before 1750 B.C., the 1445 date is precluded. Exodus 12:40 testifies that the Israelites sojourned in Egypt for 430 years, a subtraction of 430 from 1750 would come out to 1320—which is much closer to the time of Rameses II in the Nineteenth Dynasty than to the period of Amenhotep II of the Eighteenth Dynasty.

3. The early chapters of Exodus presuppose the proximity of the royal residence to the land of Goshen up in the Delta, whereas the capital of Egypt in the Eighteenth Dynasty was five hundred miles further south, in the city of Thebes. But Rameses built up Tanis in the Delta as his northern capital and as the base of his military expeditions against Palestine and Syria.

4. The archaeological evidence of the destruction levels in key Palestinian cities like Lachish, Debir, and Hazor points rather to the thirteenth century than to the early fourteenth century, as the early date theory would require. Furthermore, the extensive explor-

ations of surface sites in the various tells throughout Transjordan carried on by Nelson Glueck indicate that there was no strongly entrenched, sedentary population to be found in Moab, Heshbon, or Bashan, such as is indicated in the Mosaic campaigns of conquest against Sihon and Og according to the record of Numbers 21 and Deuteronomy 1.

5. The failure of the Book of Judges to mention any Egyptian invasions of Palestine during the late fourteenth and thirteenth centuries is a strong indication that those invasions were already past history by the time of Joshua and the Israelite conquest of Canaan.

These five arguments present an impressive case for the inaccuracy of 1 Kings 6:1. If the Exodus actually took place around 1290 B.C., then the figure should have been 324 years rather than 480. Some Evangelical scholars who adhere to the late date theory point out that 480 may be an "artificial" number, intending to convey no more than that there were about twelve generations intervening between the Exodus and the temple (thought of as 40 years each, because of the prominence of the number 40 in the lives of leaders like Moses and Joshua). But the true average length of generations is 30 years rather than 40, and so we may perhaps correct the total number to 360 rather than 480 (so R. K. Harrison, *Old Testament Introduction*, pp. 178–79).

However, careful examination of the case for the late date theory shows that it is incapable of successful defense in the light of all the evidence. Not only does 1 Kings 6:1 unequivocally affirm the 1445 date for the departure of the Israelites from Egypt (the whole theory of symbolical or artificial numbers in matters of dating in the Old Testament has no objective support

whatever), but so does Judges 11:26. This contains a question put by Jephthah to the Ammonite invaders who laid claim to the Israelite territory east of the Jordan: "For three hundred years Israel occupied Heshbon. Aroer, the surrounding settlements, and all the towns along the Arnon. Why didn't you retake them in that time?" Since the probable date of Jephthah was about half a century before King Saul, Jephthah's parley with the Ammonites must be dated around 1100 B.C. His remarks therefore imply a conquest dating back to about 1400, which fits in perfectly with a 1445 Exodus. Since this is a casual reference to chronology and adduces a time interval apparently well known to Israel's enemies and acknowledged by them, it carries special credibility as evidence for the early date.

Nor is this the only corroboration of 1 Kings 6:1. In his speech at Antioch Pisidia, the apostle Paul affirms in Acts 13:19–20: "And when He had destroyed seven nations in the land of Canaan, He distributed their land as an inheritance—all of which took about four hundred and fifty years. And after these things [i.e., after the division of the land to the Twelve Tribes] He gave them judges until Samuel the prophet" (NASB). Quite clearly the interval included the first departure from Egypt to take possession of the Holy Land, all the way to the end of Samuel's career, as the prophet who anointed David as king. In other words, about 450 years elapsed between the Exodus and the establishment of David in the Holy City of Jerusalem: 1445 to 995 B.C.

Thus it turns out that if the 1290 date is correct, then we must condemn as inaccurate at least two other passages in Scripture besides 1 Kings 6:1 itself; and the Bible then loses all claim to complete trustworthiness in matters of historical fact—even the major events of the history of Redemption. It

192

is therefore of particular importance to examine the case for the accuracy of the 1445 date indicated by these two passages from the Old Testament and the one from Acts 13.

First, as to the reference to the slave labor of the Israelites in the city of Rameses in Exodus 1:11, it should be noted that even by the late date theory this would have to be regarded as an anachronism (i.e., a later name applied to the city than the name it bore at the time of their taskwork in it). The reference to this work project occurs before any mention of the birth of Moses, and Moses was eighty years of age by the time of the Exodus event. It would have been impossible for Moses to have been born after the commencement of Rameses's reign in 1300 B.C. and then be eighty years old ten years later! Consequently the city in question could not have borne the name "Raamses" back in the period referred to by Exodus 1:11. Therefore its evidential value for the late date theory is fatally undermined. It should also be observed, however, that even though a later name was inserted in place of the original name of the city that was current in Moses' time, this furnishes no more difficulty than to refer to Kiriath Arba as Hebron, even though narrating an event that took place there prior to its change of name. Nor would a history of England be justly accused of inaccuracy if it spoke of Constantius I of Rome making a triumphant march into "York" back in a day when it was called "Eboracum."

Second, as to the argument that there could not have been a 430-year interval between a Jacob migration in the Hyksos period and a 1445 Exodus, we freely admit the force of this objection. If the Hyksos rule began around 1750 B.C., a 1445 Exodus would be out of the question. But we hasten to add that the textual evidence of both Genesis and Exodus make it quite certain that it was a native Egyptian

dynasty that was in power back in Joseph's day; it could not have been Hyksos—Josephus to the contrary notwithstanding. Consider the following facts:

1. The reigning dynasty looks down with contempt on Semitic foreigners from Palestine and forbids such to eat at the same table with Egyptians (Gen. 43:32: "The Egyptians might not eat bread with the Hebrews; for that is an abomination unto the Egyptians"). But the Hyksos themselves had originally come down from Palestine into Egypt, speaking a Semitic language like theirs. (Thus their first king was named Salitis, representing the Semitic term šallîṭ; they named their cities in Egypt Succoth, Baal-zephon, and Migdol, all good Canaanite names.) It is therefore inconceivable that they would have regarded other visitors from Palestine as an inferior breed of humanity. But the ethnic Egyptians certainly did so, as their literature abundantly testifies.

2. Joseph is obviously uneasy about his family admitting to the Egyptian authorities that they were shepherds as well as cattle raisers. (Gen. 46:34 states quite plainly: "For every shepherd is an abomination unto the Egyptians.") But this could scarcely have been true of the Hyksos, who were so closely associated with sheep-herding in the recollection of the later Egyptians that they (like Manetho) construed the name "Hyksos" to mean "Shepherd Kings." During their era certainly there could have been no reproach attachable to the raising of sheep.

3. The Pharaoh "who knew not Joseph" came to power a considerable interval after Joseph's death and after his family had already settled in Goshen. Therefore we are

warranted in assuming that this new Pharaoh was a Hyksos rather than a native Egyptian. This emerges from his concern expressed in Exodus 1:8-10 as to the alarming population growth of the Hebrews, whom he states to be "more and mightier than we" (NASB). The population of Egypt was unquestionably much larger than the two million or so Israelites (who only became that numerous by the time of the Exodus, many years later). But for the leader of the warrior caste of the Hyksos, who dominated the native population only through their superior military organization (something like the Spartans as they kept the more numerous Helots and Messenians subject to their rule), this would not have been an exaggerated apprehension. Because of the steadfast loyalty of Joseph and his family to the Egyptian government, a Hyksos monarch might well have feared that they might make common cause with a native Egyptian uprising ("Let us deal wisely with them, lest they multiply and in the event of war, they also join themselves to those who hate us, and fight against us" [v.10]). It was at a later time, then, after the Hyksos themselves had finally been expelled from Egypt by Ahmose—who however left the Hebrews undisturbed in Goshen because of their consistent loyalty to the native Egyptians—that Amenhotep I of the Eighteenth Dynasty adopted the oppressive policy of the Hyksos rulers. Amenhotep I also was uneasy at the phenomenal growth of the Hebrew population in Goshen and tried to discourage this growth by hard labor and, finally, by the time of Moses' birth, by infanticide. If it is at v.13 that this Eighteenth-Dynasty oppression begins, then we must understand the Hyksos as hav-

ing compelled the Israelites to work on the storage cities of Pithom and Raamses. In this connection it might be pointed out that the name "Raamses" itself may have been of Hyksos origin. The father of Rameses II was "Seti," which means "Follower of Seth" or "Sutekh," the Egyptian equivalent of "Baal," who was the patron god of the Hyksos dynasties. A great many of the Hyksos royal names ended likewise in "Ra," the name of the sun god of Egypt (names such as Aa-woser-Ra, Neb-khepesh-ra, Aa-qenen-ra, etc.), and Ra-mose (a name already current in the Eighteenth Dynasty, by the way) means "Born of Ra." (Ra-mes-su, the Egyptian spelling of Rameses, actually means "Ra has begotten him.") But it is most significant that Rameses II went to great effort and expense to restore and build up the old Hyksos capital of Avaris, even though he named it after himself. At all events, nothing could be more unlikely than that Joseph and his family moved into Egypt during the Hyksos period. Hence this objection to the 1445 Exodus is without weight.

Third, the argument that an Eighteenth Dynasty Pharaoh would have kept his royal residence far down (or up) the Nile, five hundred miles away from Goshen, also proves to be untenable in the light of the inscriptional evidence. We offer the following data:

1. Thutmose III, the probable "Pharaoh of the Oppression," erected two red granite obelisks in front of the temple of Ra (or $R\bar{e}'$, as it is more usually vocalized today) in Heliopolis, describing himself as "Lord of Heliopolis." This city was at the base of the Delta, and therefore hardly remote from Goshen. It is fair to assume that up in the Delta he had frequent need of slave labor

194

for his building projects, especially in view of the barracks and military installations that had to be erected in the Delta as a base of operations against Palestine and Syria (which he invaded no less than fourteen times).

2. An Eighteenth-Dynasty scarab has been found that refers to the birth of Amenhotep II as having occurred in Memphis, likewise at the base of the Delta. From this we must assume that at least part of the time Thutmose III must have maintained a palace in Memphis.

3. In an inscription set up by Amenhotep himself (translated in Pritchard, ANET, p. 244), he recalls how he used to ride out from the royal stable in Memphis to practice archery near the pyramids of Gizeh. W. C. Hayes (*The Scepter of Egypt*, 2 vols. [Cambridge: Harvard University, 1959], 2:141) concludes that Amenhotep must have maintained large estates at Perwennefer, a large naval dockyard near Memphis, and that he resided there for extended periods of time. So much for the theory that Eighteenth-Dynasty kings resided only at Thebes.

Fourth, the archaeological evidence of thirteenth-century destruction levels at cities like Lachish, Debir, and Hazor, mentioned in the narrative of Joshua's conquests, fails to furnish any decisive evidence that Joshua's invasion in fact took place in the thirteenth century. In the turbulent, unsettled conditions that characterized the period of the Judges, such as the total destruction meted out to Shechem by Abimelech the son of Gideon, episodes of this sort must have been frequent, even though our scanty records do not permit any specific identification of the victorious aggressor in most instances. As for the date of the destruction of City IV in Old Testament Jericho, even though the collapsed walls may have been erected considerably earlier than 1400 B.C. (as Katherine Kenyon deduced from the sherds discovered in the earth-fill), these walls may still have been the same as those that fell before Joshua at the time of the Israelite conquest. After all, the walls that now surround Carcassonne in France and Avila in Spain were erected many centuries before our present era—yet they still stand today. But their earth-fill must contain artifacts and sherds coming from several centuries ago, rather than from the late 1900s.

But more significant for dating the Fall of Jericho to the end of the fifteenth century is the fact that the associated cemetery (contemporaneous with City IV) yielded numerous Egyptian scarabs bearing the name of Eighteenth-Dynasty Egyptian kings, but none of them later than Amenhotep III, in whose reign (1412–1376) the capture of Jericho would have occurred, according to the early date theory. Over 150,000 sherds were discovered in City IV, according to John Garstang's published reports, but only one piece was found of the Mycenean type. Since Mycenean ware was introduced into Canaan soon after 1400, we are forced to conclude that City IV was destroyed before the early fourteenth century. Concerning this, John Garstang wrote:

We are aware that varying opinions have appeared in print which conflict with our interpretation of the date of the fall of Jericho about 1400 B.C. Few such opinions are based on first-hand knowledge of the scientific results of our excavations; while many of them are devoid of logical reasoning, or are based upon preconceptions as to the date of the Exodus. No commentator has yet produced from the results of our excavations, which have been fully published in the Liverpool Annals of Archaeology, any evidence that City IV remained in being after the reign of Amenhotep III .... We see no need therefore to discuss the date as though it were a matter for debate (*The Story of Jericho* [London: Marshall, Morgan and Scott, 1948], p. xiv).

Perhaps it should be added that the reference to iron implements as part of the booty taken from Jericho, according to Joshua 6:24, is no decisive evidence that the city fell during the Iron Age (twelfth century and thereafter). In fact the contrary is the case, for during the Iron Age iron objects would hardly have been mentioned with gold and silver as valuable booty, for by the Iron Age this metal had come into common use. Yet iron itself was known and used long before 1200 B.C. in the Near East, for iron objects have been found at Tell Asmar dating from about 2500 B.C. (*Oriental Institute Communications*, ASOR, 17:59–61). The Hebrew word for "iron" is *barzel*, corresponding to the Babylonian *parzillu*, and it was probably derived from the ancient Sumerian language, which spells the word for "iron" as [na]AN.-BAR (Deimel, *Šumerisches Lexikon*, Heft 2).

As for the often-cited negative findings of Nelson Glueck concerning the nonexistence of sedentary occupation in the Transjordan during the fifteenth century B.C., the most recent (though unofficial) reports indicate that sherds that Glueck could not identify he did not mention in his survey—and some of them may well have been from that period (cf. H. J. Franken and W. J. A. Power, "Glueck's Exploration in Eastern Palestine in the Light of Recent Evidence," VT 9 [1971]: 119–23). In the last thirty years an increasing number of excavated sites have testified to urban centers that flourished during the supposedly unoccupied era. Thus G. Lankaster Harding reported in the *Biblical Archaeologist* for February 1953 the discovery of an ancient tomb in Amman containing numerous artifacts (black-pricked ware, buttonbase vases, oil flasks, scarabs, and toggle pins) dating from about 1600. In his *Antiquities of Jordan* (1959, p. 32), Harding described characteristically Middle Bronze pottery and other artifacts found at Naur and Mount Nebo. In 1967 a sixteenth-century tomb was discovered in Pella (ASOR Newsletter, December 1967). Under a runway at the Amman airport a Late Bronze temple was uncovered in 1955. The excavations at Deir Alla by Franken and those of Siegfried Horn at Heshbon have shown that the pottery of Transjordan was quite dissimilar to contemporary pottery produced on the West Bank; since Glueck was unaware of this fact, an important margin of error entered into his calculations (cf. E. Yamauchi's article in *Christianity Today*, 22 December 1971, p. 26).

The site of Ai is usually identified with Et-Tell, which according to the archaeological evidence was unoccupied between 2200 B.C. and 1200 B.C. or a little afterward. There are many reasons for rejecting the identification of Ai with Et-Tell, but since its period of nonoccupation agrees neither with the early date nor the late date theory, it hardly seems worth discussion. W. F. Albright's suggestion was that the account in Joshua 7 was garbled and that it was Bethel itself that the Israelites captured and destroyed rather than Ai. But Albright failed to explain how the observers from Bethel were able to descry the pretended flight of the Israelites from the charge of the Aites (Josh. 8:17), or how the inhabitants of *both* cities could have taken part in the pursuit. The true location of Ai has yet to be discovered, but until further excavation reveals a Late Bronze level of occupation (which is entirely possible) Et-Tell has no bearing whatever on the dating of the Conquest.

On the other hand, the archaeological data from the Wadi Tumilat (ancient Goshen) is quite decisive *against* a Nineteenth-Dynasty date for the events of the Exodus. In the Nineteenth Dynasty, Rameses II carried on extensive building in that area occupied formerly by the Hebrews. This cannot be reconciled with the situation of exclusive Israelite occupation during the Ten Plagues. The details of the plague of flies, the plague of hail, and the plague of darkness make it clear (in Exod. 8:22; 9:25-26; 10:23) that the Hebrews were exempted from these afflictions in the region that they inhabited. This strongly suggests that no Egyptians were living at all in Goshen during this period, in view of the fact that all the Egyptians had to bear the brunt of these three plagues. But back in the days of Thutmose III and Amenhotep II of the Eighteenth Dynasty, there was no Egyptian building activity in the Wadi Tumilat at all—so far as the present state of our knowledge goes.

As far as the fifth argument for a 1290 date is concerned, that the Book of Judges contains no references to the Egyptian invasions of Seti I and Rameses the Great in the land of Canaan, this turns out to be of little weight. The Book of Judges is equally silent concerning Egyptian invasions of Palestine that took place after the death of Rameses II and prior to the establishment of the Hebrew monarchy. His son Merneptah records in the so-called Israel Stela (on display at the Museum of Egyptian Antiquities in Cairo) an allegedly devastating invasion in 1229 throughout the land of the Hittites, Yanoam near Laish-Dan, Gezer near the Valley of Aijalon, Ashkelon in Philistia, and also against the Horites and the Israelites themselves. This would have to have occurred in the time of the Judges, even according to the late date theory.

Nor is there any mention of the campaigns of Rameses III (1204-1172) of the Twentieth Dynasty. Inscriptions of his (published in Pritchard, ANET, p. 262) record that he subdued the Tjeker (Palestinians) and burnt the cities of the Philistines to ashes. Some of the bas-reliefs on his monuments depict his triumphant progress up to Djahi (Phoenicia) to the north. In Beth-shan at the eastern end of the Plain of the Esdraelon, stelae have been discovered attesting his authority in that region. These examples show that the Hebrew account did not see fit to refer to the Egyptian invasions at any period during the time of the Judges. The reason for this silence is not quite clear, but at any rate its supposed evidence for a 1290 date for the Exodus turns out to be valueless.

John Garstang and J.B. Payne both offered the suggestion that the periods of "rest" referred to in Judges may have coincided with periods of time when the Egyptians were in firm control of the main strongholds and important highways of Palestine, thus insuring no major movements of aggression on the part of Mesopotamian invaders or Moabites or Ammonites or Philistines. Thus the eighty years of peace following the death of King Eglon of Moab would have coincided with the pacification of Canaan by Seti I and Rameses II. The quiet period after the overthrow of Jabin and Sisera by Deborah and Barak may have been the result of the firm control by Rameses III. Perhaps the references to the "hornet" sent by the Lord to drive out the Canaanites before the Israelite attack is a covert reference to the Egyptian invasions (cf. Exod. 23:28; Deut. 7:20; Josh. 24:12). The hieroglyphic symbol for the king of Lower Egypt was a wasp-shaped bee. Whether or not this was the case, the fact remains that there is no specific reference to any Egyptian invasion of the Holy Land until the time of Solomon, so far as the Hebrew records go.

After this rather extensive survey of the biblical, historical, and archaeological evidence, we are forced to conclude that only the 1445 date can be sustained. It is quite obvious that the Pharaoh from whom Moses had to flee after his slaying of the Egyptian taskmaster remained on the throne until near the close of Moses' forty-year sojourn in Midian; for Exodus 4:19 reports Yahweh as saying to Moses, "Go, return into Egypt; for all the men are dead which sought your life." The whole tenor of the narrative in Exodus 2 leads us to believe that it was the Pharaoh of 1:22 who "after many days" passed away, as mentioned in 2:23. No other Pharaoh meets all these qualifications besides Thutmose III. He alone was on the throne long enough (1501–1447) to have been reigning at the time of Moses' flight from Egypt until near the time of his return.

Thutmose's son Amenhotep II, who doubtless hoped to equal his father's prowess, proved unable to launch any invasion of Palestine apart from his modest campaigns in his fifth year and his seventh year—or was it the ninth year? The Memphis stela dates his first campaign in the seventh year and the second in his ninth year, but the Amada stela puts his first campaign in the third year (cf. J. A. Wilson's footnote in Pritchard, ANET, p. 245). This suggests that some major disaster, such as the loss of his main chariot force in the Red Sea crossing (Exod. 14), was a factor in his diminished scale of foreign aggression.

As for Amenhotep II's son and successor, Thutmose IV, the evidence of his "Dream Stela" strongly suggests that he was not the firstborn son but a younger son who would not ordinarily have been eligible to succeed him. In this text (which had apparently been somewhat damaged and then later restored) the god of the Sphinx, Harem-akht, appeared to the young prince

and promised him the throne of Egypt if he would have his sand-engulfed shrine dug out and restored for worship. Obviously if Thutmose had already been his father's oldest son, he would have needed no such promise from the god but would have automatically succeeded his father upon the latter's decease. It is reasonable to infer from this that the oldest son of Amenhotep II was carried off by some accident or illness prematurely—such as the tenth plague.

Many other evidences could be advanced in support of the 1445 B.C. date for the Exodus and in refutation of the 1290 theory, but what has already been adduced is more than sufficient to prove the point. (See further my *Survey of Old Testament Introduction*, pp. 215–19; Bimson, *Redating the Exodus*, pp. 35–146; Leon Wood, *A Survey of Israel's History* [Grand Rapids: Zondervan, 1970], pp. 88–109.)

Doesn't 1 Kings 7:23 give an inaccurate value for pi?

First Kings 7:23 says, "He [Hiram] made the sea of cast metal ten cubits from brim to brim, circular in form, and its height was five cubits, and thirty cubits in circumference" (NASB). Some critics have urged this approximate value of three to one as the relationship between the diameter and the circumference of the circle amounts to a geometrical inaccuracy, inconsistent with a truly errorless Scripture. The true value of pi is calculated to be 3.14159 rather than 3.0.

This criticism is, however, devoid of merit. While it is true that the more exact calculation of pi is essential for scientific purposes, or for the manufacture of precision parts in a factory, the use of approximate proportions or totals is a familiar practice in normal speech, even today. If the statistical statements concerning the population of cities or nations were subjected to the same stringent standard as that leveled at 1 Kings 7:23, then we would have to say that all population statistics are in error. A certain number of people are dying each minute, and babies are being born at a standard rate every sixty seconds; therefore any exact sum that might be true at 1:00 P.M. on a given day through computer calculation would be "inaccurate" by 1:01 P.M. that same day. It is perfectly proper to speak of the circumference of any circle as being three times its diameter if we are speaking approximately, just as one may legitimately state that the population of China is from 800 million to one billion. The Hebrew author here is obviously speaking in the approximate way that is normal practice even today.

There is one interesting feature about this that might well be added. If the rod used to mark out a length of five cubits (approximately ninety inches) for the radius were used to measure the inside circumference of the same bowl-shaped vessel here described, then it would take exactly six of those five-cubit measures to complete the circumference. Let the skeptic try it and see!

Despite 1 Kings 9:22, didn't Solomon impose forced labor on Israelite citizens?

First Kings 9:22 says that in contrast to the descendants of the conquered Canaanite nations, "Solomon did not make slaves [lō' nā-tan ... 'ā-bed] of the sons of Israel; for they were men of war, his servants [ʿăbādîm], his princes, his captains, his chariot commanders, and his horsemen" (NASB). In other words, he treated them as free men, as citizens of honorable standing. Yet earlier, in 1 Kings 5:13 (5:27 Heb.), it is stated that "King Solomon levied forced laborers [lit., 'raised a levy of forced labor'] from all Israel; and the forced laborers [hammas] numbered 30,000 men" (NASB). Each of three con-

tingents of ten thousand worked for four months of the year, by shifts or in rotation. Besides these there were seventy thousand burden bearers and eighty thousand stonecutters to assist in procuring and preparing the materials for the temple and palace that were to be erected on the temple mount in Jerusalem.

It is not stated whether the burden bearers and stonecutters were non-Israelite Canaanites, but it is a fair assumption that they were. Nothing is said about the division into shifts that characterized the Israelite workers, as just described. It is a fair assumption also that the thirty thousand Israelites who participated in the felling and processing of building materials for the temple were specially selected for their experience and skill along these lines, and that they considered it a privilege to have a part in this work for God. Hence there is no real contradiction between the two statements (5:13 and 9:22).

It should be noted, however, that Solomon did not restrict the drafting of an Israelite labor force to the temple mount structures. He apparently used this kind of work crew to strengthen the defenses of Jerusalem as well: the filling up of the depression between Mount Zion and Mount Moriah as a heightened and fortified Millo ("Filling"), along with a general improvement of the entire city wall (1 Kings 9:15). Some of the provincial capitals required this type of additional fortification, such as Hazor and Megiddo—and even Gezer, after Pharaoh had turned the city over to Solomon (as a dowry for his daughter, who became Solomon's wife). Indeed the maintenance of corvée labor on the part of Israelite citizens may have continued intermittently until the close of Solomon's reign, for while it uses the word sēbel rather than mas, 11:28 mentions that Jeroboam was originally a supervisor or foreman of such a "burden-bearing" force for the "house of Joseph" (which presumably included Manasseh as well as Ephraim). Perhaps Solomon resorted to this system of corvée for Israelite citizens as the building operations progressed and as his own original high principles suffered eclipse under the pressure of his ambitious goals.

In the light of his dealings with Bathsheba and her husband, Uriah, how could David be regarded by the Lord as a servant whose heart was "perfect" before Him (cf. 1 Kings 11:4; 15:3; Acts 13:22)? (D*)

Even before David became king of Israel, he had committed several sins and offenses to his discredit. His deception of the high priest Ahimelech resulted in the massacre of nearly every priest in the city of Nob by the agents of King Saul, even though they were completely unaware of David's status as a wanted fugitive (1 Sam. 21–22). Later on, as a vassal of King Achish of Gath, David systematically deceived him as to the various tribes and communities his warriors had raided in their forays from Ziklag; and he was willing to put every one of his victims to death in order to keep the truth about his activities from getting back to Achish (1 Sam. 27:8–12). His affair with Uriah's wife, Bathsheba, and the subsequent cover-up that he engineered by having Uriah killed in battle before the walls of Rabbath Ammon (2 Sam. 11) were by no means the only shameful blots on his record, even though they are doubtless the best known.

From these considerations it is quite apparent that David did not gain God's favor or approval because of a sinless life. Although his conduct was for the most part exemplary and his courage and ability as a leader beyond comparison, it was not because of these things that he especially pleased God. It was rather because of his tremendous faith in the power and grace of God that his heart was adjudged to be *šālēm* (KJV, "perfect"; NASB, "wholly devoted"; NIV, "fully devoted") with Yahweh his God (1 Kings 11:4; 15:3). The adjective *šālēm* basically means "complete, whole, sound, finished" or even "at peace with [*'im*] someone." (The word is cognate with *šālôm*, "peace, welfare.") That is, David's heart was all there for God, and God was his very reason for living. Many of his psalms eloquently express his deep attachment to the Lord, his joy in fellowship with God, and his complete trust in His redeeming power.

Furthermore, David could never remain out of fellowship with God for very long. Psalm 32 reveals what unbearable agony he went through after the affair with Bathsheba, until finally the prophet Nathan came to him and condemned his crimes in the name of Yahweh (2 Sam. 12:7–10). A lesser man would have flared up against this daring prophet and had him put to death. But one of the greatest assets in David's character was his ability to receive rebuke, to acknowledge his utter sinfulness (cf. Ps. 51:3–5), and to cast himself on the mercy of God to forgive him, cleanse him, and restore him to holy fellowship once more.

The believer who can face guilt and failure in the way David did is in a profound sense a man after God's own heart—the kind that God told Samuel He was going to look for after Saul had forfeited favor by his disobedience (1 Sam. 13:14). David was that kind of a son and servant to the Lord; he was an *'iš kileḇāḇô* ("a man according to His heart"). As such he became a model for all believers to follow, in regard to wholehearted commitment to pleasing the Lord, obeying His word, and furthering the cause of His kingdom on earth. God could trust him with great responsibility and consistent victory on the battlefield because David's central purpose was to glorify God, not to glorify or please himself. Recalling these dominant traits in David's life, the apostle Paul commended him to the congregation in Antioch Pisidiae, saying: "And after He had removed him [Saul], He raised up David to be their king, concerning whom He also testified and said, 'I have found David the son of Jesse, a man after My heart [*kata tēn kardian mou*], who will do all My will" (Acts 13:22, NASB).

The glory of God, the will of God, and the loving fellowship of God were what mattered most to King David, even though there were temporary lapses in that relationship. But even after he had fallen into sin and failure, David knew how to trust God's grace and forgiving love enough to confess and forsake his iniquity in an attitude of true repentance so as to get back in step with the Lord on the highway of holiness. Such a believer is certain to be a man or woman after God's own heart!

Was Elijah's prediction of the dogs' licking up Ahab's blood at Jezreel really fulfilled by the Pool of Samaria?

First Kings 21:19 reads: "Thus says the LORD, 'Have you murdered, and also taken possession?'... Thus says the LORD, 'In the place where the dogs licked up the blood of Naboth the dogs shall lick up your blood, even yours'" (NASB). But in the record of the fulfillment of this sentence of doom, which occurs in 1 Kings 22:37–38, we read: "So the king died and was brought to Samaria, and they buried the king in Samaria. And they washed the chariot by the pool of Samaria [*berē-ka-t šōmerôn*], and the dogs licked up his blood... according to the word of the LORD which He spoke" (NASB). The licking up of Ahab's blood by dogs is certainly confirmed by this narration. But what about the detail "in this place where the dogs licked up the blood of Naboth"? The Hebrew text lays stress on

the very spot: "where the dogs licked up" (*bimeqôm "šer lāqequ hakkelābîm*) Naboth's blood (21:19). This calls for further investigation.

Where was Naboth stoned to death by the two false witnesses and the mob that accompanied them? Could it have been by a pool located just outside the city of Samaria? This is barely conceivable; but it hardly seems likely, in view of the circumstances surrounding the whole transaction of Ahab's offer to Naboth outside of Jezreel (21:2–3), which met with Naboth's refusal. Jezebel sent orders "to the elders and to the nobles who were living with Naboth in his city." In all probability Naboth was tried and convicted on a trumped-up charge of blasphemy in the city square of Jezreel itself, and he was then led to a place just outside the city wall of Jezreel; so it must have been there (rather than in Samaria, which was many miles distant) that his innocent blood was spilled. Yet this is not actually stated in so many words.

If Naboth's accusers had taken Naboth "outside of the city" of Jezreel, they may have carried him all the way to Samaria in order to hold his execution by stoning right outside the capital of the kingdom of Israel, at the pool just outside the city wall. Nevertheless this would have been an exceptional procedure according to Old Testament law. Normally a punishment or execution was inflicted on an offender in the same jurisdiction as his crime was committed. (Yet this was not invariably the case. Joshua 7:24 records that Achan, whose theft of spoil from the accursed city of Jericho took place at Jericho itself, was not stoned to death outside Jericho but rather in the valley of Achor [which seems to have been part of the Wadi Qilt, at some distance from Tell el-Sultan, Old Testament Jericho], a site fairly removed from the scene of the crime.)

There remains one other intriguing possibility, as we study the probable route traveled by Ahab's henchmen during their retreat from the disaster at Ramoth-gilead. They would almost certainly have crossed the Jordan just below Beth-shan and then made their way in a west-northwesterly direction until coming to the summer capital of Jezreel, just beyond which they would have to take the highway leading through the pass through the Esdraelon range. By the time they reached Jezreel, with their melancholy task of interring Ahab's corpse in the cemetery of Samaria after their arrival there, they may well have decided to wash off his chariot before it entered Samaria itself. By that time his dried gore must have been quite malodorous and disfiguring to the appearance of the royal chariot—which presumably would have been part of the later funeral procession. A pool outside Jezreel would have been most convenient for their purpose. But how could a pool at Jezreel have been called "the Pool of Samaria"? Perhaps in the planning of this new summer palace and its adjacent landscaping, Ahab and Jezebel decided that a pool would enhance the beauty of the grounds. They might well have called it "Samaria Pool" in honor of the regular capital city (founded by Ahab's father, Omri), which would serve as the seat of government during the cooler seasons of the year.

Not all pools connected with ancient Near Eastern cities bore the name of the city itself, particularly if there was an older pool already in existence. In Jerusalem, for example, there were the Pool of Siloam, the Pool of Bethesda (Beth-zatha), the King's Pool, and the Pool of Shelah. Since the "Pool of Samaria" here mentioned was one at which the city's prostitutes normally bathed (1 Kings 22:38), it was probably not the only pool in use, but only a later pool, constructed by the landscapers connected with the summer palace. It is therefore reasonable to infer that there was another pool known as the Pool of Jezreel, intended for the general public of Jezreel itself. Hence Ahab's palace pool, if such there was, would have to have borne some other name. What, then, would have been more appropriate than the name of the national capital, where Ahab resided in his ivory-inlaid palace for the greater part of the year?

Is there not a contradiction between 1 Kings 22 and 2 Chronicles 20, as to Jehoshaphat's ill-fated fleet at Ezion-geber?

First Kings 22:48 agrees with 2 Chronicles 20:35-36 that a fleet of ocean-going merchantmen ("ships of Tarshish") was constructed at the Red Sea port of Ezion-geber, for the purpose of engaging in trade with Ophir—a trade that Solomon had found very profitable back in the previous century (1 Kings 9:28). They also agree that Ahaziah the son of Ahab, king of Israel, was somehow involved in this venture. Apparently the plan originally agreed on by both rulers (2 Chron. 20:35-36) was that this would be a joint commercial venture, with both the costs and the profits to be shared by both governments. First Kings 22:49 says: "Then Ahaziah the son of Ahab said to Jehoshaphat, 'Let my servants go with your servants in the ships.' But Jehoshaphat was not willing" (NASB). But 2 Chronicles 20:35-36 contributes the interesting information that Jehoshaphat actually was at first quite willing for Ahaziah to join with him in this undertaking, even though it was wrong for him to act in partnership with a degenerate Baal-worshiper like the son of Ahab and Jezebel. It was only under the pressure of the prophet Eliezer son of Do-davahu, who denounced the alliance as highly displeasing to God, that Jehoshaphat finally backed away from the agreement. Second Chronicles 20:37 tells us that Eliezer predicted that Yahweh would destroy all the ships that Jehoshaphat had built, and then the Lord apparently proceeded to do so by sending a violent storm on the harbor of Ezion-geber.

There is really no basic contradiction between the two accounts, even though there is perhaps a difference in emphasis. But we still cannot be quite certain whether Jehoshaphat notified Ahaziah that the deal was off at some time before the storm struck or whether it was after it had smashed up the ships. In the latter case, the only thing that Jehoshaphat could have vetoed, so far as Ahaziah was concerned, was a project to attempt a rebuilding of the ruined fleet as a joint venture for a second time.

2 Kings

When did Jehoram son of Ahab begin his reign?

Second Kings 1:17 states that Jehoram, Ahab's younger son, began his reign as king of Israel in the *second* year of *Jehoram* son of Jehoshaphat, king of Judah. (Quite confusing is this appearance of identical names among the children of both Ahab of Israel and Jehoshaphat of Judah, but apparently their treaty of alliance and friendship extended even to the naming of their children!) This appears to be in conflict with the notation in 2 Kings 3:1, that Jehoram ben Ahab became king in the "eighteenth year of Jehoshaphat." But the discrepancy arises from the fact that just prior to joining Ahab in the unsuccessful attempt to recapture Ramoth-gilead from the Syrians, Jehoshaphat took the precaution to have his son Jehoram installed as coregent on the throne of Judah.

In the battle of Ramoth-gilead, in which Ahab was fatally wounded by an arrow (1 Kings 22:34–35), Jehoshaphat himself nearly lost his life; so his foresight was well grounded. But Jehoram began his reign as *coregent* in that year, 853 B.C. Yet Jehoshaphat lived on until 848, five years later. Thus it came about that the second year of Jehoram ben Jehoshaphat was 851-850. It was also the eighteenth year of Jehoshaphat (who began to reign in 869-868 as sole

king, that being the year when his father Asa died). Since Jehoram ben Ahab ascended the throne of Israel in 850, *both* synchronisms were correct: the second year of Jehoram ben Jehoshaphat was the same as the eighteenth of Jehoshaphat.

It should be pointed out in this connection that this precedent for installing the crown prince as coregent in his father's lifetime was followed at least six times in the course of the Judean monarchy: (1) Asa died in 869, but his son Jehoshaphat became coregent in 872 (making three or four years of coregency); (2) Jehoshaphat died in 848, but his son Jehoram became coregent in 853; (3) Amaziah died in 767, but his son Azariah (or Uzziah, as he is variously known) became coregent in 790 (possibly when Amaziah was taken captive to Israel by Jehoash ben Jehoahaz, king of Israel); (4) Uzziah died in 739, but his son Jotham became coregent in 751 (when his father was stricken with leprosy); (5) Jotham died in 736 or 735, but his son Ahaz became coregent in 743; (6) Ahaz died in 725, but his son Hezekiah became coregent in 728. From the technical legal standpoint, Jehoiachin was the senior king of Judah from 597 (Ezekiel always dates his prophecies by Jehoiachin's regnal years); and so during the entire reign of his brother Zedekiah (597–587), the latter ruled only as coregent. If we bear these guidelines in mind, many apparent confusions in the dates of the period of the divided monarchy can be readily cleared up.

The young men who mocked Elisha because he was bald were cursed, and forty-two of them were killed by two she-bears (2 Kings 2:23-24). How could a man of God curse people for such a mild personal offense? (D*)

A careful study of this incident in context shows that it was far more serious than a "mild personal offense." It was a situation of serious public danger, quite as grave as the large youth gangs that roam the ghetto sections of our modern American cities. If these young hoodlums were ranging about in packs of fifty or more, derisive toward respectable adults and ready to mock even a well-known man of God, there is no telling what violence they might have inflicted on the citizenry of the religious center of the kingdom of Israel (as Bethel was), had they been allowed to continue their riotous course. Perhaps it was for this reason that God saw fit to put forty-two of them to death in this spectacular fashion (there is no evidence that Elisha himself, in imposing a curse, prayed for this specific mode of punishment), in order to strike terror into other youth gangs that were infesting the city and to make them realize that neither Yahweh Himself nor any of His anointed prophets were to be threatened or treated with contempt.

Certainly from that time on, the whole Israelite community became convinced that Elisha was a true prophet and that he bore an authoritative word from God. Even the ungodly king Jehoram son of Ahab treated him with great deference and respect (see 2 Kings 3:11-13) after this had taken place.

Was not Elisha the prophet guilty of lying to the Syrian troops in 2 Kings 6:19?

Technically Elisha's statement to the foreign invaders was true in the light of the situation in which he made it. He said to the expeditionary force of Benhadad, sent to capture him by surprise, "This is not the way, nor is this the city; follow me and I will bring you to the man whom you seek" (NASB). While it is true that Dothan had been Elisha's location the night before and that they had taken the right way to get up to Dothan, nevertheless neither of those facts was now true. Why? Because Elisha was no longer in Dothan; he had come out of the city to meet them. Therefore the way up to Dothan was no longer the right path for them to use if they wished to capture the troublesome prophet. Thus he was only speaking the truth when he said, "This is not the way, nor is this the city." It was now Elisha's purpose to go in front of them down the highway to Samaria, the city where he would remove the "blindness" (i.e., their inability to recognize him) from their eyes. Consequently the rest of his statement was likewise true: if they would follow him all the way down to Samaria, then he would indeed bring them to Elisha inside the city of Samaria. The following verse (v.20) shows how he fulfilled his promise to the letter. Samaria was the right city for them to see the prophet they had come to capture. But unfortunately for them, when they did get into Samaria, they saw their hoped-for quarry surrounded by the regimental troops of the king of Israel; and it was the Syrians who were taken prisoner.

This delightful episode certainly does record the complete discomfiture of the foreign invaders by a supernatural blindness cast on them by the Lord (somewhat like the blindness sent on the Sodomites who riotously attempted to break down the door to Lot's house [Gen. 19:11]). But it is not really justified to call Elisha's statement a lie, for every part of it was technically correct. Nowhere does he actually say, "I am not the man you are looking for." He only said that he would lead them to that man in the city where they would find him (as soon as he got there).

When did Ahaziah ben Jehoram become king?

Second Kings 8:25 says that Ahaziah son of Jehoram of Judah became king in the twelfth year of Jehoram son of Ahab of Israel. Yet in 2 Kings 9:29 it is stated that it was in his eleventh year. Which is right? Is there not a discrepancy of one year?

The answer is that Ahaziah ben Jehoram became king in 841 B.C., which according to the nonaccession-year system came out to Jehoram ben Ahab's twelfth year, but according to the accession-year system was his eleventh year. In 2 Kings 8:25 the nonaccession-year system was used, but in 2 Kings 9:29 it was the accession-year system that was followed. Confusing?

The fact of the matter is, however, that the Northern Kingdom followed the nonaccession-year system from 930 B.C. until 798 B.C., but from 798 (the beginning of the reign of Jehoash ben Jehoahaz) till the Fall of Samaria in 722 B.C., it switched to the accession-year system. The southern kingdom, on the other hand, used the accession-year system from 930 until the beginning of the reign of Jehoram ben Jehoshaphat (848–841), or possibly a couple of years earlier, in 850 B.C., before Jehoshaphat died. Around 850 the southern kingdom of Judah switched to the nonaccession-year system and stayed on it until the end of the reign of Joash ben Ahaziah (835–796)—when it finally reverted to the

accession-year system (i.e., the first official regnal year did not begin until New Year's Day of the year following the year when the new king came to the throne). Therefore, by the accession-year system, what was the eleventh year of Jehoram was the twelfth year by the nonaccession-year system, i.e., 841 B.C. No discrepancy!

How old was Ahaziah when he began to reign (cf. 2 Kings 8:26 with 2 Chron. 22:2) and Jehoiachin when he began to reign (cf. 2 Kings 24:8 with 2 Chron. 36:9–10)?

Copyists were prone to making two types of scribal errors. One concerned the spelling of proper names (especially unfamiliar proper names), and the other had to do with numbers. Ideally, we might have wished that the Holy Spirit had restrained all copyists of Scripture over the centuries from making mistakes of any kind; but an errorless copy would have required a miracle, and this was not the way it worked out.

It is beyond the capability of anyone to avoid any and every slip of the pen in copying page after page from any book—sacred or secular. Yet we may be sure that the original manuscript of each book of the Bible, being directly inspired by God, was free from all error. It is also true that no well-attested variation in the manuscript copies that have come down to us alter any doctrine of the Bible. To this extent, at least, the Holy Spirit has exercised a restraining influence in superintending the transmission of the text.

These two examples of numerical discrepancy have to do with the decade in the number given. In 2 Chronicles 22:2 Ahaziah is said to have been forty-two; in 2 Kings 8:26 he is said to have been twenty-two. Fortunately there is enough additional information in the biblical text to show that the correct number is twenty-two. Second Kings 8:17 tells us that Ahaziah's father Joram ben Ahab was thirty-two when he became king, and he died eight years later, at the age of forty. Therefore Ahaziah could not have been forty-two at the time of his father's death at age forty!

Similar is the case of Jehoiachin, whose age at accession is given by 2 Chronicles 36:9–10 as eight but by 2 Kings 24:8 as eighteen. There is enough information in the context to show that eight is wrong and eighteen is right. That is to say, Jehoiachin reigned only three months; yet he was obviously a responsible adult at the time, for he "did what was evil in the sight of the Lord" and was judged for it.

Observe that in each case it is the decade number that varies. In Ahaziah's case it is forty-two as against twenty-two. In Jehoiachin's case it was eight as against eighteen. It is instructive to observe that the number notation used by the Jewish settlers in the Elephantine in the time of Ezra and Nehemiah (fortunately we have a large file of documents in papyrus from this source) consisted of horizontal hooks to represent decades. Thus eight would be /III IIII, but eighteen would be /III IIIII. Similarly twenty-two would be I ⹀, but forty-two would be /I ⹀⹀. If, then, the manuscript being copied out was blurred or smudged, one or more of the decade notations could be missed by the copyist.

The same was probably the case with the date of Sennacherib's invasion of Judah in 701 B.C. This is stated in 2 Kings 18:13 to have occurred in the "fourteenth" year of Hezekiah, which implies that Hezekiah must have begun his reign in 715. Yet the other six references to Hezekiah's chronology in 2 Kings make it clear that he was crowned as assistant king in 728 and became sole king in 725. Since Sennacherib did not become king in Assyria until 705 and the invasion occurred in the fourth year of his reign,

the 701 date for the invasion is absolutely certain. Therefore we are to understand the "fourteen" in 2 Kings 18:13 as a miscopying of an original "twenty-four." The difference in the Hebrew notation would have been as follows: fourteen was /IIII, and twenty-four was ⹀. A blurred manuscript probably confused the scribe of Isaiah 36:1, who originated the error; and it may have been that the later scribe of 2 Kings 18 was so impressed by the number fourteen with which he was familiar in the Isaiah text that he decided to "correct" v.13 to conform with it. At least that is the likeliest explanation I know of. (See also the discussion of Sennacherib's invasion in Hezekiah's fourteenth year at 2 Kings 18:13.)

How could God commission Jehu to destroy the house of Ahab (2 Kings 9:6–10; 10:30) and then later condemn him for the bloodshed (Hos. 1:4)?

There can be no question that Jehu fully carried out the commission he received from the Lord: "You shall strike the house of Ahab your master, that I may avenge the blood of My servants the prophets, and the blood of all the servants of the LORD, at the hand of Jezebel. For the whole house of Ahab shall perish" (2 Kings 9:7–8, NASB). After Jehu, racing back from Ramoth Gilead to Jezreel, shot King Jehoram dead, and Ahaziah of Judah as well (for he was the grandson of Jezebel), he then proceeded to the city of Samaria and intimidated the elders of that city into decapitating all seventy of Ahab's sons who were living in the palace (2 Kings 10:1–10). Not long after that he managed to lure all the Baal-worshiping leaders of Israel into the temple of Baal on the pretext of leading them in a great celebration of worship there. Once they were locked up inside the temple itself, he had them all massacred by his troops and destroyed the entire building, desecrating it in such a way that it could never be used for worship again (vv.18–27).

It was after Jehu had carried out all these stern measures for the suppression of idolatry in Israel that the commendation came to him from the Lord: "Because you have done well in executing what is right in My eyes, and have done to the house of Ahab according to all that was in My heart, your sons of the fourth generation shall sit on the throne of Israel" (2 Kings 10:30, NASB). Jehu had served as God's executioner on behalf of the many hundreds of prophets of the Lord whom Jezebel and Ahab put to death (1 Kings 18:4,13), and he had taken the most thorough means of suppressing the soul-destroying curse of idolatry. Therefore he would be granted security on his throne, and his descendants after him unto "the fourth generation" (i.e., Jehoahaz 814–798, Jehoash 798–782, Jeroboam II 793–753, and Zechariah, who was assassinated within a few months of his accession in 752).

In the course of his own career, however, Jehu did not enjoy a great deal of success as a ruler or defender of his country. The Black Obelisk of Shalmaneser III of Assyria depicts Jehu "the son of Omri [sic!]" prostrate before the invader and paying him tribute as his vassal (cf. Pritchard, ANET, p. 281), in connection with an expedition against Benhadad of Damascus and the Phoenician cities of Byblos, Sidon, and Tyre. But 2 Kings 10:33 indicates that even before that invasion by Assyria (in the twenty-first year of Shalmaneser, which would have been about 832 B.C.), Jehu had lost all Transjordanian Manasseh, Gad, and Reuben (which later had for the most part been conquered by Moab under King Mesha) to King Hazael of Damascus. His son Jehoahaz (814–798) was reduced to complete vassalage by Hazael and his son Benhadad II (2

Kings 13:1–3). But Jehoash (798–782) was allowed by the Lord to expel the Syrians in three decisive engagements (v.19) and also to crush the pretensions of King Amaziah of Judah in the Battle of Bethshemesh (14:13), with a resultant spoliation of Jerusalem itself. But it was Jehu's great-grandson Jeroboam II who achieved very great success on the battlefield, for he regained possession of the Transjordanian tribal territory and all the area formerly ruled over by Jeroboam I—just as the prophet Jonah had predicted (vv.25–27).

On what basis, then, did the prophet Hosea proclaim the judgment of the Lord on the dynasty of Jehu (Hos. 1:4–5)? It was because of the impure motive with which Jehu himself had carried out his commission from Yahweh to blot out the race of Ahab. Although Jehu had only done what God had commanded, he did so out of a carnal zeal that was tainted with protective self-interest. Second Kings 10:29 says of him: "However, as for the sins of Jeroboam the son of Nebat, [by] which he made Israel sin, from these Jehu did not depart, even the golden calves that were at Bethel and ... Dan" (NASB). But v.31 goes on to say: "But Jehu was not careful to walk in the law of the LORD, the God of Israel, with all his heart; he did not depart from the sins of Jeroboam, [by] which he made Israel sin" (NASB). This same mixture of motives showed up in Jehu's descendants as well, for Jehoahaz "did evil in the sight of the LORD, and followed the sins of Jeroboam. . . . So the anger of the LORD was kindled against Israel, and He gave them continually into the hand of Hazael king of Syria, and into the hand of Benhadad the son of Hazael. Then Jehoahaz entreated the favor of the LORD, and the LORD listened to him" (2 Kings 13:1–4; NASB).

Jehoash, Jehoahaz's son, did not do much better; for he too followed his father's evil example (2 Kings 13:11), even though he did retain a respectful relationship with the prophet Elisha (vv.14-19). And even though Jeroboam II enjoyed such remarkable success in war (14:25) and had a long reign of forty-one years (v.23)—i.e., from 793-782 as viceroy under his father, and 782-753 as sole king—yet his relationship toward the Lord was no better than his father's. "He did evil in the sight of the LORD; he did not depart from all the sins of Jeroboam the son of Nebat, [with] which he made Israel sin" (v.24; NASB). The whole prophecy of Amos, especially Amos 2:6-16; 4:1; 5:5-13; 6:1-8, is a commentary on the corruption of government, society, and personal morality that prevailed in the Northern Kingdom during Jeroboam's reign. (Amos's ministry came "two years before the earthquake" [1:1], in the reign of Uzziah of Judah. This must have been some time between 760 and 755.)

The important principle set forth in Hosea 1:4 was that when blood is shed, even in the service of God and in obedience to His command, blood-guiltiness attaches to God's agent himself if his motive was tainted with carnal self-interest rather than by a sincere concern for the purity of the faith and the preservation of God's truth (such as, for example, animated Elijah when he had the 450 prophets of Baal put to death after the contest with them on Mount Carmel). The "bloodshed of Jezreel" was finally visited on the house of Jehu when his great-great-grandson Zechariah was murdered at his own birthday party by his trusted chariot captain Shallum (2 Kings 15:10).

Did Pekah really rule over Samaria for twenty years?

Second Kings 15:27 states that "Pekah son of Remaliah became king over Israel in Samaria—twenty years."

(NASB inserts "and reigned" in italics before "twenty years.") This raises an apparent difficulty because he did not establish his headquarters in Samaria itself until 739 B.C., when he assassinated King Pekahiah son of Menahem (15:25). Since he in turn was assassinated by Hoshea in 732, Pekah would appear to have reigned only eight years in Samaria rather than twenty.

To understand the basis for the "twenty years," we must go back to the coup d'état of 752, when Zechariah son of Jeroboam II was murdered by an army commander named Shallum. Shallum, however, lasted for only one month on the throne; for he was defeated by Menahem, who launched an invasion of Samaria from the city of Tirzah (2 Kings 15:8-16). Menahem succeeded in buying off the Assyrian invader Tiglath-pileser III, who came against Israel sometime after 745. After a large tribute was given to Assyria, Tiglath-pileser "confirmed" Menahem in office as his vassal-king (v.19). Possibly he felt he needed Assyrian support because he was facing opposition within his own kingdom. And indeed he was, for Pekah son of Remaliah had apparently laid claim to the throne of Israel back in 752, the year of Zechariah's assassination; and he established his headquarters in Gilead, ruling over most of the East Bank territory of the Israelite kingdom. Apparently Pekah held out against Menahem until Menahem died in 742. Then he must have entered into a treaty of reconciliation with Menahem's son and successor, Pekahiah, according to the terms of which Pekah received a command in the army headquarters in Samaria. He then conspired with fifty of his trusted supporters from Gilead and murdered Pekahiah in his palace. Then, of course, Pekah had himself proclaimed king.

How then is the interval of "twenty years" to be justified? It was simply the official position of Pekah's government that after Zechariah (or Shallum) was murdered, Pekah became the only lawful king over Israel. To be sure, he was unable to dislodge Menahem from the West Bank; but still, as the only legitimate king of Israel (in his own opinion, at least), his right to Samaria as capital of the kingdom was ipso facto established. He finally took up official residence in Samaria (after the coup d'état against Pekahiah) from 740 or 739, but his reign in Samaria was theoretically computed from 752, when he first asserted his right to the throne.

Are there not historical inaccuracies in Kings and Chronicles, such as "So, king of Egypt" and "Zerah the Ethiopian," of whom there is no record in secular sources (cf. 2 Kings 17; 2 Chron. 14)?

The plainest and shortest answer to this question is that there are no *proven* inaccuracies in any of the historical records in Scripture. The second observation to make is that if a historical statement in the Bible is factually true, it does not require any corroboration from secular sources to become true. This is a basic canon of logic. Undoubtedly there are multitudes of events that have taken place in earlier times that have never been recorded either in sacred or secular written sources. They nevertheless actually took place, even though they were not recorded. And if an event was recorded only in a nonscriptural document, it needs no attestation from Scripture to preserve it from being a non-event. And, of course, the reverse is true. An episode that actually took place became a fact of history whether or not it was recorded in an extrabiblical source.

The only way to justify skepticism of scriptural veracity when it records names or events not found in extant secular accounts is to establish that the Bible is demonstrably inferior to all other ancient sources in the matter of its trustworthiness. To assume that the failure up until now to find a mention of Zerah or So in any pagan document proves that they never existed is to fall into a blatant non sequitur quite unworthy of true scholarship. Those who follow such a criterion in their handling of scriptural testimony should be reminded that the number of such unverified names and events has been sharply reduced by the archaeological discoveries of the last 150 years. Back in 1850, for example, many learned scholars were confidently denying the historicity of the Hittites and the Horites of Sargon II of Assyria and Belshazzar of Chaldean Babylon, or even of Sodom and Gomorrah. Yet all of these have more recently become accepted by the scholarly world because of their appearance in ancient documents discovered within the last fifteen decades of archaeological investigation.

The skeptical approach toward the historical statements of Scripture has thus been proven to be completely unjustified. This furnishes strong evidence that the cynical suspicion toward the Bible's accuracy is basically unfounded and that a far sounder approach—considering the excellent record of Bible history in the light of archaeological discovery—would be to assume that any biblical notice is accurate and dependable until proven false. Up until now, so far as this writer is aware, there is no biblical record that has ever been proven false by any evidence exhumed by the excavator's spade.

It is not altogether certain that So (*Sô'*), the king mentioned in 2 Kings 17:4 as a potential ally of Hoshea of Samaria, during the final years of its existence in the 720s B.C., is the name of a king at all. The Hebrew text could be translated as follows: "He [i.e., 'Hoshea'] sent to Sais [the name of the Egyptian capital city at that time], the king of Egypt." During that time the king of Egypt was named Tefnakht (ca. 730–720) and he made his headquarters in Sais. (This is suggested by K.A. Kitchen in his article on "So" in J.D. Douglas, ed., *New Bible Dictionary* [Grand Rapids: Eerdmans, 1962], p. 1201.)

It is true that no mention of Zerah the Ethiopian (Heb., *kûšî*) has yet turned up in any ancient text outside the Bible itself (2 Chron. 14:9–15). Apparently he was not a reigning monarch of Egypt during the time of King Asa of Judah (910–869), since none of the Egyptian rulers bore such a name during that period. K.A. Kitchen (*The Third Intermediate Period in Egypt* [Warminster: Aris & Phillips, 1973]) estimates the date of the Battle of Mareshah to be about 897 B.C., which would have been the twenty-eighth year of Pharaoh Osorkon I (who was of a Libyan dynasty rather than a Cushite). But Kitchen (ibid., p. 309) says: "By 897 B.C. Osorkon I was already an old man, and so he may well have sent a general of Nubian [or Cushite] extraction to lead a force into Palestine. . . . However, Zerah proved no match for the Judean king, and so we have no trace of a triumphal relief of Osorkon to adorn anew the temple walls of Egypt"—as Osorkon's father, Sheshonq (Shishak) had done back in the days of Rehoboam.

How could Sennacherib's invasion have occurred in the fourteenth year of Hezekiah?

Second Kings 18:13 in the Masoretic text states: "Now in the fourteenth year of King Hezekiah, Sennacherib king of Assyria came up against all the fortified cities of Judah and seized them." Since Sennacherib's own record in the Taylor Prism establishes 701 B.C. as the date of that invasion, the fourteenth year of Hezekiah would mean that he did not ascend the throne until

715 B.C. Yet 2 Kings 18:1 (the very same chapter, be it noted) states that Hezekiah became king in the third year of Hoshea king of Israel—which comes out to 729 or 728. This would have been the year in which he was crowned as subordinate king, under his father Ahaz (who did not die until 725). The Masoretic text of 2 Kings 18:13 therefore stands in clear contradiction to 18:1,9, and 10, which confirm that Hezekiah's fourth year was Hoshea's seventh and that Hezekiah's sixth was Hoshea's ninth (i.e., 722 B.C.). We must therefore conclude that the Masoretic text has preserved an early textual error (which also appears in Isa. 36:1—where the error probably originated), in which a mistake was made in the decade column. The word "fourteen" was originally "twenty-four." (For further details, see the articles on 2 Kings 8:24 and on Ezra 2 and Nehemiah 7. Compare also my *Survey of Old Testament Introduction*, pp. 291–92, and E.J. Young, *Book of Isaiah: New International Commentary*, 2 vols. [Grand Rapids: Eerdmans, 1969], 2:540–42.)

In 2 Kings 29:8–11 and Isaiah 38:8, how was it possible for the shadow on the stairway of Ahaz to retreat by ten steps?

Obviously this phenomenon, asked for by Hezekiah (2 Kings 20:10), prayed for by the prophet Isaiah (v.11), and graciously granted by the Lord (Isa. 38:7–8) in answer to his prayer, was intended as a miraculous confirmation of God's promise to heal Hezekiah of his potentially fatal carbuncle or cancer after he had previously been warned that he had not long to live. Had it been some unusual occurrence that could be explained by the laws of astronomy or meteorology, it could hardly have served as a God-given sign of the imminent fulfillment of a difficult promise. Conceivably there might have been some extraordinary intervention of a cool, moisture-laden stratum in the sky that caused an unusual refraction of the sun's rays; but the precise timing of such a condition to coincide with Hezekiah's request and Isaiah's prayer would have itself constituted a miraculous event. Would it really have been difficult, however, for a God who had already created the entire universe of matter out of nonmatter to do a thing like this simply by the word of His power? Obviously not!

How could the embassy from Merodach-baladan have come to Hezekiah after 701 B.C., if by that time Merodach-baladan had been expelled from Babylon (2 Kings 20:12–15)?

Merodach-baladan (or *Marduk-apa-iddin*, as it is spelled in cuneiform) was in secure control of Babylon from 721–710. If Hezekiah's illness occurred fifteen years before his death in 698 or 696 (as it is variously reckoned), then it must have occurred in 712 or 711 B.C. This coincides very well with a diplomatic approach on the part of the king of Babylon (who was technically a vassal of the king of Assyria) Sargon II (722–705), to organize an east-west *entente cordiale* against the Assyrian overlord. If we place Hezekiah's illness back in that period rather than after the Sennacherib invasion of 701, then the embassy from Babylon fits in very well with the chronology of Hezekiah.

But how can we date Hezekiah's illness before the Assyrian invasion of Judah in 701? Is it not narrated in Isaiah after the invasion is over? Does not the introductory phrase "In those days" (Isa. 38:1) refer to the episode just narrated in chapter 37, which tells how the angel of the Lord took the lives of 185,000 Assyrian troops in a single night, thus compelling the God-defying, blaspheming Sennacherib to retreat to Nineveh without capturing Jerusalem? Normally we would be justified in making this con-

nection, but in this particular case we encounter the difficulty that the last episode referred to in 37:38 did not take place until 681. Therefore a strict construction of "In those days" in 38:1 would mean that Hezekiah did not become ill until 681, and that he must have had fifteen more years of life (v.5) after that. But all authorities, even Edwin Thiele (who mistakenly defers the accession of Hezekiah until 715 B.C. [cf. his *A Chronology of the Hebrew Kings* (Grand Rapids: Zondervan, 1977), p. 65]), accept the statement of 2 Kings 18:2 that Hezekiah reigned only twenty-nine years. No authority has ever suggested that he reigned any later than 686; yet fifteen years after 681 would come out to 666 or 665. Therefore "In those days" cannot be construed as referring to the event immediately preceding, namely, the murder of Sennacherib by his sons in 681.

We must understand "In those days" as an introductory formula for a new episode—e.g., "Now it came about in those days when Hezekiah was king that he became mortally ill." Similar uses of this formula may be found in Esther 1:2 (where it introduces the account of the king's feast without any tie-in with a preceding event), in Judges 17:6 ("In those days there was no king in Israel"), likewise Judges 18:1; 19:1. Compare also in the New Testament Matthew 3:1: "Now in those days John the Baptist came, preaching in the wilderness of Judea." There is no clear connection with Matthew 2:22 (the verse immediately preceding), which probably refers to the return of the holy family from Egypt to Nazareth after the close of the reign of Herod Archelaus in A.D. 6—at which time John the Baptist would have been only eleven years old!

If, then, the formula "In those days" does not refer to the days following Sennacherib's departure from Palestine in 701, what are the indications as to the time of his illness? As we have already suggested, the promise of fifteen more years points to a date of around 713 for his medical crisis. Since Hezekiah must have died sometime between 698 and 696 (his successor, Manasseh, was only twelve at the time of his accession, and he ruled until 642, as all authorities agree—after a reign of fifty-five years, according to 2 Kings 21:1), the choice must lie with 713 or 711 at the latest. Now Isaiah 39:1 informs us that Merodach-baladan sent his embassage to Hezekiah in order to congratulate him on his recovery from his nearly fatal illness. Since Merodach-baladan was expelled from Babylon by 710 and did not get back there, except very briefly in 704 or 703, the evidence points very strongly to a date of no later than 711 for the arrival of his envoys at Jerusalem subsequent to Hezekiah's illness. This shows that the placement of Isaiah 38 after the narrative of Sennacherib's invasion in chapter 37 was due, not to chronological sequence, but to a shift of topic, which served some other purpose in Isaiah's mind than a sequential order of events. What could that purpose have been?

In order to clear up this question, we must observe the implications of the prediction uttered by Isaiah after he transmitted God's message to the king concerning his foolish pride in showing off his treasures to the Babylonian envoys. Isaiah 39:6 contains this ominous warning: "Behold, the days are coming when all that is in your house, and all that your fathers have laid up in store to this day shall be carried [off] to Babylon; nothing shall be left, says the LORD" (NASB). In view of the contemporary situation, with Babylon a subject province under the Assyrian yoke, this was a very surprising prophecy indeed. Yet this was the judgment God had ordained for His backslidden nation, and He had revealed His plan to His prophet Isaiah.

It would be the Babylonians, specifically the Chaldeans in charge of Babylon, who would finally carry out the sentence of total depopulation and exile for the disobedient people of Judah. From this standpoint Isaiah 39 forms an appropriate introduction to chapter 40 and the subsequent chapters of Isaiah's prophecy, all of which were probably composed in the reign of Hezekiah's ungodly son, Manasseh. Chapter 40 presupposes the Babylonian captivity as a sure and settled prospect in store for Judah. The focus of attention is largely diverted from Assyria to the future crisis of Nebuchadnezzar's destruction of Jerusalem and deportation of the Jews, along with the promise of their ultimate restoration to their homeland after the Exile is over. Thus we see that the contents of chapter 39 make a most fitting introduction to chapter 40, since it explains the reason for the coming deportation to Babylon, the headquarters of Merodach-baladan.

How, when, and where did Jehoiakim die?

Second Kings 24:6 states, "So Jehoiakim slept with his fathers, and Jehoiachin his son became king in his place" (NASB). (This suggests that this wicked king enjoyed a normal burial and was buried in a royal tomb— although "slept with his fathers" might mean simply that he joined his forefathers in the realm of the dead—Sheol.)

Second Chronicles 36:5–8 reads: "Jehoiakim was twenty-five years old when he became king, and he reigned eleven years in Jerusalem.... Nebuchadnezzar king of Babylon came up against him and bound him with bronze chains to take him to Babylon. Nebuchadnezzar also brought some of the articles of the house of the LORD to Babylon and put them in his temple in Babylon.... And Jehoiachin his son became king in his place"

(NASB). This could be construed to mean that Jehoiakim was taken off to Babylon as a prisoner and remained there the rest of his life—an event that would have to have occurred in 598 B.C. (since he ruled eleven years from 608 B.C.) Yet the text here does not actually say that he never returned from Babylon, as a chastened vassal of Nebuchadnezzar, having given him solemn promises of loyalty and assurances that he would never again team up with Pharaoh Necho and the Egyptians against the Chaldean overlordship. If it was the latter, then this event probably took place in 604 B.C., after Nebuchadnezzar had extended his rule over Syria, Phoenicia, Samaria, and Judah, taking with him an assortment of hostages, such as Daniel, Hananiah, Mishael, and Azariah.

Just as Ashurbanipal of Assyria took King Manasseh from his kingdom and imprisoned him for a considerable length of time in Babylon (2 Chron. 33:11–12), until he became repentant for his previous unfaithfulness to God and was finally restored to his throne by the Assyrian king, so also Jehoiakim was probably restored to his throne in Jerusalem as a chastened vassal king under the Chaldean overlordship. The Chronicles passage does not describe his deportation to Babylon in terms clearly suggestive of the downfall of Jerusalem in 597, when the young son and successor Jehoiachin was thus deported, along with "all the captains and all the mighty men of valor, ten thousand captives, and all the craftsmen and the smiths. None remained except the poorest people of the land" (2 Kings 24:14, NASB). Moreover, on the occasion of that second deportation, Nebuchadnezzar did not remove just "some of the articles of the house of the LORD" (2 Chron. 36:7) but, rather, "*all* the treasures of the house of the Lord, and the treasures of the king's house" (2 Kings 24:13, italics mine).

It therefore appears that the episode of 2 Chronicles 36:5–8 was not the same as that of 2 Kings 24:14. The former took place in 604, along with the captivity of Daniel and his friends; the latter took place in 597 and involved a different king (Jehoiachin), with a far larger amount of treasure and a huge number of captives. Thus the case for establishing a discrepancy completely fails; the data of the biblical text precludes identifying the two events as the one and same transaction.

But the manner and place of Jehoiakim's death were a bit more pathetic than the brief statement in 2 Kings 24:6 would indicate, for we read in Jeremiah 22:18–19: "Therefore thus says the LORD in regard to Jehoiakim the son of Josiah . . . 'They will not lament for him:' . . . He will be buried with a donkey's burial, dragged off and thrown out beyond the gates of Jerusalem" (NASB). This predicts the shameful treatment meted out to Jehoiakim's corpse after he died (apparently around 7 December 598 B.C.). Instead of a normal interment in a royal tomb—whether at the time of the funeral or sometime thereafter—that body was tossed into some open pit like that intended for a dead animal; and he was permanently interred outside the city walls by a citizenry that deeply resented his wicked and disastrous reign. His unhappy son, Jehoiachin, remained to face the full consequences of his father's oath breaking toward Nebuchadnezzar—as noted above.

What was the correct age for Jehoiachin when he came to the throne, eight or eighteen?

Second Kings 24:8 tells us that Jehoiachin "was eighteen years old when he became king." But the parallel passage in 2 Chronicles 36:9 states that he was "eight" years old when he began to reign. Obviously there has been a textual error committed by the copyist either in 2 Kings or in 2 Chronicles. This type of error occurs now and then because of blurring or surface damage in the earlier manuscript from which the copy is made. A numerical system generally in use during the fifth century (when Chronicles was probably composed—very likely under Ezra's supervision) features a horizontal stroke ending in a hook at its right end as the sign for "ten"; two of them would make the number "twenty." (See article on 2 Kings 8:26.) The digits under ten would be indicated by rows of little vertical strokes, generally in groups of three. Thus what was originally written as a horizontal hooked stroke over one or more of these groups of short vertical strokes (in this case, eight strokes) would appear as a mere "eight" instead of "eighteen."

The probabilities are that 2 Chronicles 36:9 is incorrect, both because the age of eight is unusually young to assume governmental leadership—though Joash ben Ahaziah was only seven when he began to reign (2 Kings 11:21) and Josiah was only eight (2 Kings 22:1)—and because the Chaldeans treated him as a responsible adult and condemned him to permanent imprisonment in Babylon after he surrendered to them in 597 B.C. Moreover, it is far less likely that the copyist would have mistakenly seen an extra ten stroke that was not present in his original than that he would have failed to observe one that had been smudged out.

While it is true that Jehoiachin's father, Jehoiakim, must have been unusually young to have begotten him (sixteen or seventeen), nevertheless some of the Judean royalty seem to have married at an early age (in other words, if Jehoiakim was twenty-five at his accession in 608 [2 Kings 23:36], and if Jehoiachin was eighteen in 598 when his father died [2 Kings 24:8], then there must have been only a difference of seventeen or eighteen years between them). Note that Ahaz appears to have fathered Hezekiah at the age of thirteen or fourteen, judging from the fact that Ahaz was twenty on his vice-regency in 743 and that Hezekiah was twenty-five at his father's death in 725 (hardly at his first appointment as vice-regent in 728!) (cf. 2 Kings 16:2 [2 Chron. 28:1] and 2 Kings 18:2 [2 Chron. 29:1]).

1 Chronicles

Special note: For a general discussion of the distinctive purposes of the author of 1 and 2 Chronicles consult the first discussion under Jonah, p. 300 concerning the alleged midrashic elements in Jonah.

Why are there so many genealogies in 1 and 2 Chronicles?

The Chronicles were apparently compiled by Ezra in the middle of the fifth century B.C., or at least by a contemporary of his. After the long ordeal of the Babylonian captivity, which lasted from 586 to 539, a group of Jewish colonists was led back by Zerubbabel and Jeshua to establish a new commonwealth of Israel in their ruined homeland. The Israelites had lost every material possession—every building, every home—as a result of the Chaldean devastation. All that was left were the people, their memories, their traditions, and their Bible—and, of course, the God who had given it to them and who had kept His promise by restoring them to their land after the Exile was over. It was therefore of utmost importance to establish their lines of descent, from Abraham and the twelve sons of Jacob, and from the later ancestors to whom specific territories, cities, and towns had been assigned back in the days of Joshua. There are many people today who will spare no effort to trace their ancestry back as far as they can. But in Israel's case there was the added factor that Yahweh Elohim had made a personal covenant with Abraham and his "seed," a series of gracious promises and special requirements for them to lead a godly life. Probably the great majority of the deported Israelites elected not to undertake the hardships involved in making the trek back to Jerusalem; the 42,000 freemen who made up the group of returnees could hardly have been more than 10 percent of those eligible to go back from Babylon. (cf. Isa. 6:13) It was very important to establish definitely which families were represented in the second commonwealth, for God's plan of redemption was bound up with them rather than with the 90 percent who preferred to stay in Exile.

This emphasis on genealogies continues even until New Testament times, for early in Matthew and Luke we find the lines of descent recorded for our Lord and Savior, Jesus Christ—the son of David, the son of Abraham, the son of Adam. Jesus' human ancestry was very important for His status as the Son of Man, the Messiah, the Savior of all true believers, both from Israel and from the Gentiles.

What was the genealogical relationship between Sheshbazzar, Shealtiel, and Zerubbabel?

First Chronicles 3:16–19 states: "And the sons of Jehoiakim were

Jeconiah his son, Zedekiah his son [i.e., Jehoiakim's younger son—not to be confused with his uncle Zedekiah son of Josiah, who became the last king of Judah]. And the sons of Jeconiah [or Jehoiachin, cf. 2 Kings 24:8] the prisoner [reading *'āsîr* rather than *'Assîr*, as the Masoretes have wrongly pointed it] were Shealtiel his son, and Malchiram, Pedaiah, Shenazzar [and three others]. And the sons of Pedaiah were Zerubbabel and Shimei. And the sons of Zerubbabel were Meshullam and Hananiah" (plus one daughter and five more sons, according to v.20).

This passage establishes that Zerubbabel, the governor of the province of Judah in Zechariah's time (Zech. 4:6–9), was the son of Pedaiah and, therefore, a nephew of Shealtiel (Pedaiah's older brother). But Ezra 3:2 refers to Zerubbabel as the "son" of Shealtiel; so Shealtiel apparently had adopted Zerubbabel after the premature death of his natural father, Pedaiah. (There is no reference to Pedaiah's early demise elsewhere, but this is the only reasonable explanation for Zerubbabel's being taken over by Shealtiel. Other references to Zerubbabel as "the son of Shealtiel" are Ezra 3:8; 5:2; Neh. 12:1; Haggai 1:1.)

As for Sheshbazzar, Ezra 1:8 states that Cyrus, king of Persia, had his treasurer, Mithredath, turn over the fifty-four hundred gold and silver vessels of the destroyed Jerusalem temple (seized by Nebuchadnezzar as booty back in 587) into the hands of "Sheshbazzar, the prince [*nāśî'*] of Judah." Verse 11 states that these vessels were safely conveyed by Sheshbazzar to Jerusalem (in 537) as the returned Israelites began building their new colony there. Later on, Ezra 5:14 corroborates the fact that these temple vessels were given over by Cyrus (doubtless through his treasurer, Mithredath) "to one whose name was Sheshbazzar, whom he had appointed governor [*peḥâh*]."

There are two possible deductions to draw from the foregoing evidence: "Sheshbazzar" is another name for Zerubbabel, or "Sheshbazzar" is another name for Shealtiel, the "father" of Zerubbabel. The former has some strong advocates, such as C.F. Keil (Keil and Delitzsch, *Ezra, Nehemiah, Esther,* p. 27), who suggests that "Sheshbazzar" was Zerubbabel's official court name (analogous to "Belteshazzar," the court name of Daniel [Dan. 1:7]). The difficulty with this theory is that "Sheshbazzar" (derived possibly from *Shamash-mar-*(u)*ṣur,* "Sun-god, protect the son!" which is what one would expect for an official court name) is no more clearly of Babylonian origin than "Zerubbabel" (*zērû-Babili,* "Seed of Babylon"). This weakens the supposition that one is the given name and the other a Gentile name later imposed.

The latter view, that Sheshbazzar was the court name of Shealtiel, the (adoptive) father of Zerubbabel, has more to commend it; for Shealtiel is a genuine Hebrew name (meaning, "I asked God," or possibly, "My request is God"). It is not inconceivable, perhaps, that Zerubbabel or Sheshbazzar was the name originally given to the baby by the parents at circumcision, since they had become accustomed to such non-Hebraic names during the long captivity in Babylonia. But it seems far more likely that Shealtiel was a name bestowed originally by his Hebrew parents and that Sheshbazzar was the court name later assigned to him by the Babylonian government. This would mean, then, that the temple vessels were entrusted to Shealtiel-Sheshbazzar, the aged adoptive father (actually the uncle) of Zerubbabel, by the Persian authorities. It would have to follow that Shealtiel was originally given the status of *peḥâh,* or governor, of the new Jewish colony to be established in Judea, and that both he and his "son" Zerubbabel participated in the laying of the foundations of the second temple in 536.

It should, however, be carefully noted that Sheshbazzar is never mentioned again after the foundation ceremony itself (Ezra 5:16). This might indicate that soon after that event he passed away and left the mantle of authority with his "son," Zerubbabel, who from then on probably served as the *pehâh* (though this is nowhere expressly affirmed of him). Admittedly, this explanation is cumbered with attendant suppositions that are otherwise unsubstantiated; and it lacks the simplicity of the first view, that Sheshbazzar is another name for Zerubbabel (an interpretation strongly argued by Unger, *Bible Dictionary,* p. 1014). From the standpoint of sheer likelihood, the objection based on the Babylonian etymology of both names (Sheshbazzar and Zerubbabel) may not seem to loom as large as the necessity of imagining that Zerubbabel's father held the honor of senior governor and shared with him in the laying of the cornerstone of the temple, when there is no actual mention of *two* such leaders in connection with the foundation ceremony. If so, the fairest thing to say is that either explanation would solve the problem of the apparent discrepancy, but the available evidence does not point strongly to either of them in preference to the other.

Before leaving this topic, it ought to be added that if Sheshbazzar was the same person as Shealtiel, then we may suppose that there might have been a levirate marriage involved. That is to say, according to Deuteronomy 25:5, if a man died without having had a son by his wife, his surviving brother (or nearest male relative, if he had no brother) had the responsibility of taking the widow into his home and marrying her, so as "to raise up seed unto his brother." The first son born to them after this levirate marriage was to be accounted, not the son of the sec-

ond man, but the son of the deceased man. If, then, Pedaiah died young without leaving issue, Shealtiel may have taken his widow over and thus became the biological father of her first-born child, Zerubbabel. But legally he would be accounted the son of Pedaiah, just as 1 Chronicles 3:19 attests. And yet, since he was actually begotten by Shealtiel and raised up by him in his home, he would also (unofficially) be known as the son of Shealtiel.

There remains just one more difficulty to deal with in this connection. Luke's genealogy of Jesus (3:27–28) lists the following links in the series: *Addi–Melchi–Neri–Salathiel–Zarobabel–Rēsa–Iōanan,* et al. Since Salathiel is the Greek form of Shealtiel, and Zorobabel is obviously Zerubbabel, the question arises as to whether there is any relationship here between Shealtiel and Zerubbabel (descendants of King Josiah of the Davidic dynasty) and those two who are descended from Melchi and Neri in the Lucan genealogy. The answer must be in the negative; for not only are the names of Neri and his forbears impossible to be fitted into the Davidic line, but their time locus is definitely wrong. In Matthew's genealogy of Christ, Salathiel and Zorobabel are generations fifteen and sixteen after David, whereas in the Lucan series Salathiel and Zorobabel are twenty-one and twenty-two after David. Even though some links are occasionally omitted in the Matthew list (such as Ahaziah-Joash-Amaziah between Joram and Uzziah), the discrepancy of five generations is hardly overcome.

How then are we to account for the sequence Shealtiel and Zerubbabel in the line descended from Jeconiah (Matt. 1:12) and the sequence Shealtiel and Zerubbabel in the branch of David's family that descended through Nathan (Luke 3:27–31) to Neri? It is, to be sure, quite unusual for the same father-to-son pair to occur in two different family lines; yet there is an interesting analogy to be found back in the time of Ahab and Jehoshaphat. Both kings, during a time of cordial relations between the governments of Judah and Israel, named their two sons Jehoram and Ahaziah (2 Kings 1:17 and 8:16; 1 Kings 2:51; 2 Kings 1:1; 8:25). Thus it is quite conceivable that a descendant of King David named Shealtiel living in the post-Exilic period (i.e., Shealtiel son of Neri) might have decided to name his own son Zerubbabel, in honor of the well-known pair who led the remnant back to Jerusalem at the close of the Exile. In the previous millennium, the Twelfth Dynasty and the Eighteenth Dynasty of Egypt had a series of Amenemhat-Senwosret kings and Amenhotep-Thutmose kings, respectively. And so there are both precedents and analogies for the recurrence of father-son pairs, so far as names are concerned.

How could a good God, a God of peace, condone warfare (1 Chron. 5:22), give instructions as to how war should be fought (Deut. 20), and be acclaimed by His people as "the Lord is a warrior" (Exod. 15:3)? (D*)

The key element in 1 Chronicles 5:22 (which tells of the tribal conquests of Reuben, Gad, and Manasseh over the pagan races of Transjordan) is: "For many fell slain, because the war was of God."

Underlying this question are certain assumptions that require careful examination as to their soundness. Is it really a manifestation of goodness to furnish no opposition to evil? Can we say that a truly good surgeon should do nothing to cut away cancerous tissue from his patient and simply allow him to go on suffering until finally he dies? Can we praise a police force that stands idly by and offers no slightest resistance to the armed robber, the rapist, the arsonist,

or any other criminal who preys on society? How could God be called "good" if He forbade His people to protect their wives from ravishment and strangulation by drunken marauders, or to resist invaders who have come to pick up their children and dash out their brains against the wall?

No policy would give freer rein to wickedness and crime than a complete surrender of the right of self-defense on the part of the law-abiding members of society. No more effective way of promoting the cause of Satan and the powers of hell could be devised than depriving law-abiding citizens of all right of self-defense. It is hard to imagine how any deity could be thought "good" who would ordain such a policy of supine surrender to evil as that advocated by pacifism. All possibility of an ordered society would be removed on the abolition of any sort of police force. No nation could retain its liberty or preserve the lives of its citizens if it were prevented from maintaining any sort of army for its defense. It is therefore incumbent on a "good God" to include the right of self-defense as the prerogative of His people. He would not be good at all if He were to turn the world over to the horrors of unbridled cruelty perpetrated by violent and bloody criminals or the unchecked aggression of invading armies.

Not only is a proper and responsible policy of self-defense taught by Scripture from Genesis to Revelation, but there were occasions when God even commissioned His people to carry out judgment on corrupt and degenerate heathen nations and the complete extermination of cities like Jericho (cf. the article on "Was Joshua justified in exterminating the population of Jericho?" in connection with Joshua 6:21). The rules of war laid down in Deuteronomy 20 represented a control of justice, fairness, and kindness in the use of the sword, and as such they truly did reflect the goodness of God. Special hardship conditions were defined as a ground for excusing individual soldiers from military duty until those conditions were cleared up (Deut. 20:5–7). Even those who had no such excuse but were simply afraid and reluctant to fight were likewise allowed to go home (v.8). Unlike the heathen armies, who might attack a city without giving it an opportunity to surrender on terms (cf. 1 Sam 11:2–3; 30:1–2), the armies of Israel were required to grant a city an opportunity to surrender without bloodshed and enter into vassalage to the Hebrews before proceeding to a full-scale siege and destruction. Even then, the women and children were to be spared from death and were to be cared for by their captors (Deut. 20:14). Only in the case of the degenerate and depraved inhabitants of the Promised Land of Canaan itself was there to be total destruction; a failure to carry this out would certainly result in the undermining of the moral and spiritual standards of Israelite society, according to vv.16–18. (This corrupting influence was later apparent in the period of the Judges [Judg. 2:2–3,11–15].)

In the New Testament itself, the calling of a soldier is considered an honorable one, if carried on in a responsible and lawful fashion (Matt. 8:5; Luke 3:14; Acts 10:1–6,34–35). Paul even uses the analogy of faithful service in the army as a model for Christian commitment (2 Tim. 2:4), without the slightest suggestion of reproach for military service. In a similar vein is the description in Ephesians 6:11–17 of the spiritual armor to be put on by the Christian warrior in the service of his Lord. There does not appear to be any basis in Scripture, either in the Old Testament or the New, for the concept of a "good" God who enjoins pacifism on His followers. (For a more extensive discussion of the Bible evidence on this point, see G. L. Archer, "Does Pacifism Have a Scriptural Basis?" *The Evangelical Beacon* [December 28, 1971]: 4–6.)

First Chronicles 6:16ff says that Samuel's father was a Levite, but 1 Samuel 1:1 says that he was an Ephraimite. Which is correct?

First Chronicles 6:16,22–28 says that Elkanah the father of Samuel (to be distinguished from Elkanah the son of Assir, who was five generations before him) was descended from Kohath the son of Levi, just as Moses and Aaron were. For this reason Samuel was accepted as a lad by the high priest Eli (1 Sam. 1:24,28; 2:11) to be an apprentice under him. When Samuel reached adulthood, he functioned as a priest and held sacrifices in the leading centers of Israel—which he could not have done had he not been of the priestly tribe.

So far as 1 Samuel 1:1 is concerned, this simply states that Elkanah was "from" (*min*) Ramathaim-zophim on Mount Ephraim. All Levites were assigned to certain "Levitical cities" or towns throughout the Twelve Tribes, according to the regulation laid down in Numbers 35:6. We do not have a list of these forty-eight towns, but quite possibly Ramathaim-zophim was one of them. By ancestry, then, Elkanah was a Levite; by location he was an Ephraimite. Hence there is no contradiction whatever between these two passages.

In 1 Chronicles 21 David is said to have yielded to Satan's temptation to number Israel. As a result of this God destroyed seventy thousand people through pestilence. Was it just of God to punish the people for David's sin? (D*)

From the human standpoint, it would certainly seem far more ideal for the evil consequences of sin to be limited to the wrongdoer alone. But because of the interrelated involvements of family and society, no such limitation is possible. There is a sense in which the millions who perished during the Nazi era suffered death because of one man, Adolf Hitler. In David's case, of course, there was no malicious or cruel intent behind his stubborn purpose to have a census taken of all the citizens in his kingdom. His motive was more likely to have been a self-congratulatory pride in his achievements as a military genius and in the prosperity that the entire kingdom had attained under his leadership.

It is a mistake, however, to assume that David's countrymen were not also involved in this same attitude of pride. Second Samuel 24:1 tells us, "Now again the anger of the LORD burned against Israel, and it incited David against them to say, 'Go, number Israel and Judah.'" (NASB). It may very well have been that the advisability of conducting a census had been suggested by David's advisers, both on the grounds of military expediency and for the sake of a more accurate basis for taxation. There must have been a high level of nationalistic pride that tended to minimize God's sovereign grace and power rather than to acknowledge Him as the author of all their astonishing victories on the battlefield and the extension of their hegemony from the borders of Egypt to the banks of the Euphrates and the northernmost reaches of Syria. As a nation they must have been ripe for a judgment of warning, or else it would never have been said that the "anger of the LORD burned against Israel."

From 1 Chronicles 21:1 we are apprised of how Satan capitalized on this situation: "Then Satan stood up against Israel and moved David to number Israel." As is his custom, when Satan found the situation ripe for exploitation, he moved in to encourage the desire on David's part and in the hearts of his leaders to carry through this egotistical undertaking, even though General Joab strongly advised against it (cf. v.3). It should not be a matter of surprise, therefore, that the totalling up of all the manpower of the Twelve Tribes at the height of their power constrained God to remind them that it was not by their great numbers they would prevail but only by His great grace.

Why does Chronicles consistently give a higher numerical figure than Samuel or Kings, wherever there is a discrepancy?

Some eighteen or twenty examples may be found of discrepancy in numbers between Chronicles and Samuel-Kings in reporting the same transaction. This has been interpreted by some critics as evidence of a consistent policy to glorify the past as the Chronicler resorts to deliberate exaggerations. It should be pointed out, however, that in the vast number of instances Chronicles does agree perfectly with Samuel and Kings in the matter of numbers and statistics; and so the alleged desire to embellish the record and exaggerate the glory of the past must have been a very modest one on the Chronicler's part.

A careful examination of the eighteen or twenty examples of true discrepancy (for most of the apparent discrepancies turn out to be referring to a different group of people or things not occurring at precisely the same time or belonging to exactly the same category) yields the interesting result that fully a third of them display a *smaller* number in Chronicles than in Samuel-Kings. For example, see 1 Chronicles 11:11 as compared with 2 Samuel 23:8; 1 Chronicles 21:5b as compared with 2 Samuel 24:9b; 2 Chronicles 3:16b as compared with 1 Kings 7:20b (cf. v.42); 2 Chronicles 8:10 as compared with 1 Kings 9:23; 2 Chronicles 36:9 as compared with 2 Kings 24:8. A good example of a more modest (and credible) figure is

2 Chronicles 9:25, which gives four thousand as the number of stalls Solomon built for his cavalry, whereas 1 Kings 4:26 puts the figure at forty thousand. Or again, 1 Chronicles 11:11 gives the number of enemies slain by Jashobeam in a single battle as reaching three hundred; 2 Samuel 23:8 gives it as eight hundred—according to the Masoretic text.

One interesting example of a suspiciously high figure appears in 1 Samuel 6:19 (unfortunately there is no parallel in Chronicles). The number of persons slain by a divine plague at Bethshemesh, where the inhabitants had opened up the sacred ark of the covenant and looked inside it, is reported as 50,070—a figure probably exceeding the total population of Bethshemesh (though we cannot be sure of that).

In explanation of these transmissional errors (as we believe them to be), let it be understood that numerals and proper names are always more liable to copyist errors than almost any other type of subject matter (especially when we are dealing with non-Hebraic foreign names). Almost all suspiciously high numbers are round numbers expressed in thousands. In the later stage of transmission particularly (but prior to the imposing of a system of spelling out in full, as prescribed by the guild of sō-p̄erîm, or professional scribes), alphabetic letters were often used. Thousands were indicated by supralinear dots appearing over the digit letter. (Thus an aleph with two dots over it indicated one thousand.) As a manuscript became worn, brittle, or moth-eaten, it would be difficult to tell whether the multiplying dots were over the letter or not. But even the earlier types of notation, such as that employed in the fifth-century B.C. Elephantine Papyri, were also subject to garbling in the attempt to copy from a faded or smudged document. In line with the Egyptian hieratic style, the Jewish authors would use superimposed horizontal fish hooks in order to indicate decades. A serious consequence of this may be instanced in the case of 2 Kings 18:13, where an original "twenty-four" was copied out as "fourteen," apparently because the upper fishhook was smudged in the manuscript copied from. (This case is discussed in a separate article. Compare also the discussion of Ezra 2 and Nehemiah 7 in regard to the numbers who returned from Babylon.)

To revert to the original question about the Chronicler who has been unjustly accused of propagandist tendencies, the elimination of seven instances described above (which actually show smaller statistics than Samuel-Kings) leaves us only a dozen well-accredited numerical discrepancies in which Chronicles shows a higher number. Considering the large amount of text involved, it is almost incredible that so few numerical discrepancies do occur, out of hundreds of instances where numbers are cited by both sources. In other cases the unit of measurement reflects a later, lighter standard of weight than that specified in the earlier source. See, for example, the discussion of 1 Chronicles 22:14 and the halving of the weight of the shekel by the fifth century B.C.

(For a more thorough discussion of the numbers included in the text of Chronicles, see J. B. Payne, "The Validity of Numbers in Chronicles," *Bulletin of the Near East Archeological Society*, n.s. 11 [1978]: 5–58.)

How could David say in 1 Chronicles 22:14 that he had provided for 100,000 talents of gold for the future temple and then say in 1 Chronicles 29:4 that he had donated only 3000 talents? (D*)

The answer to this is very simple. In 1 Chronicles 22 David makes his principal donation to the work of building and equipping the future temple of

Yahweh so that Solomon will have everything needful when he sets about its construction. But in 1 Chronicles 29 David holds another building fund rally in which he appeals to his well-to-do supporters to make a supplemental donation beyond that which they have already given in chapter 22. The language of 29:3–4 is quite explicit on this: "And moreover, in my delight in the house of my God, the treasure I have of gold and silver, I give to the house of my God, over and above all that I have already provided [i.e., the 100,000 talents of 22:14—concerning which consult the article following] for the holy temple, namely, 3000 talents of gold, ... and 7000 talents of refined silver, to overlay the walls of the buildings" (NASB). In other words, he sees a need for a supplemental contribution even beyond the large sum he had already devoted to the project. The nobles and wealthy businessmen followed their king's example and gave an additional 5000 talents, plus 10,000 darics, of gold—along with 10,000 talents of silver, 18,000 talents of brass, and 100,000 talents of iron. There is no contradiction whatsoever between these two chapters; 29 records a later donation supplemental to that of 22.

First Chronicles 22:14 lists "100,000 talents of gold" as donated by David to the future temple in Jerusalem. Is this a credible figure, or is it a transmissional error?

Both in the Masoretic text and in the Septuagint this remarkably large figure of "100,000 talents of gold and 1,000,000 talents of silver" is given. Such a sum as this might have been beyond the resources of the Caesars themselves. It would be quite possible to commit an error in textual transmission in the act of copying out large numbers of this sort. We have a probable example of this as we compare 2 Chronicles 9:25 (which gives four thousand as the number of stalls built for Solomon's chariot horses) and 1 Kings 4:26 (which gives the figure as forty thousand). The latter citation has undoubtedly undergone multiplication by ten because of an obscurity in or misunderstanding of the *Vorlage*. It may be that here also, in 1 Chronicles 22:14, there has been the error of one decimal point. Perhaps the original figure was "10,000 talents of gold"; perhaps the silver total of 1,000,000 was miscopied from an original 100,000. Another possibility would be the misinterpreting of an abbreviation for "manehs" as "kikkars" (there were sixty manehs or minas to the kikkar or talent).

At the same time it should be observed that the Masoretic text figure cannot be excluded from the realm of possibility. Keil (Keil and Delitzsch, *Chronicles*, pp. 246ff.) makes the following points:

1. The ordinary civil or "royal" shekel seems to have been only one-half the Mosaic "shekel of the sanctuary." This appears from a comparison of 1 Kings 10:17 ("300 shields of beaten gold, using three minas [150 shekels] of gold on each large shield") and 2 Chronicles 9:16 ("300 shields of beaten gold, using three hundred shekels of gold on each shield"). (Three hundred shekels would equal six minas; hence the figure in 1 Kings involves a shekel twice as heavy as that of 2 Chronicles.) This means that the 100,000 talents referred to in Chronicles would be equal to only 50,000 talents back in the earlier period. The Chronicles talent would weigh about thirty-seven and a half pounds rather than the seventy-five pounds of the Solomonic age.

2. Keil also points out that Alexander the Great is reported to have plundered the Persian royal treas-

ury of 40,000 to 50,000 talents of gold and silver bullion, plus 9000 talents in coined gold (i.e., darics). In Persepolis alone he captured 120,000 talents, in Parsagada 6000 more, and in Ecbatana 180,000 talents. There may be some overlap in these figures, but if they are added end to end, they total about 355,000 talents of gold and silver.

3. David is recorded as conquering the Edomites, Philistines, Moabites, Ammonites, and the Sykrian kingdoms of Damascus, Hamath, and Zobah—and the Amalekites as well. These defeated nations are listed in 2 Samuel 8:7 13, and there it is stated that all their treasures taken as spoil were dedicated by David to the Lord.

Over the forty years of David's reign, these must have accumulated to a very large total—especially since David did rather little in the way of expensive public works. Moreover his friendly political relations with the prosperous merchant cities of Tyre and Sidon must have resulted in considerable revenue from commerce. Thus a total accumulation of "100,000 talents of gold" (i.e., 50,000 talents by the earlier standard) and "1,000,000 talents of silver" (equaling 500,000) can hardly be shown to be so far beyond his capacity to donate to the erection of the future temple, on which he had set his heart.

2 Chronicles

How can 2 Chronicles 16:1 (thirty-sixth year of Asa) be reconciled with 1 Kings 16:8 (Elah began to reign in the twenty-sixth year of Asa)?

If Asa began his reign in 911 B.C., the thirty-sixth year of his reign would have been 876 or 875. He reigned for forty-one years (1 Kings 15:10); so this would have been a possible date—except for the fact that Baasha himself reigned from 909 to 886. Therefore he could not have built a fortress at Ramah in 875, eleven years after his death. Here we have a clear discrepancy in the Received Text. There are two possible solutions.

One solution is that the phrase *maleˉ-kûˆ-t 'Asā* in 2 Chronicles 16:1 does not refer to Asa's own reign but rather should be understood as "the kingdom of Asa," i.e., the southern kingdom of Judah as distinguished from the northern kingdom of the Ten Tribes. Since the southern kingdom began under Rehoboam in 931 or 930 B.C., the thirty-sixth year would come out to 895 for the expedition of Baasha—which is the correct year, in all probability. (Leon Wood, *Israel's History*, p. 346, dates it as occurring in the sixteenth year of Asa, or 895.) This would mean that the Chronicler copied out his information from an older official record in Judah that at first used 931 as the "era" date rather than a regnal date. Later on, however, the Chronicler's sources seem to have shifted to a regular regnal system of dating; for there are no other examples of such an era date except 2 Chronicles 15:19, which puts the war between Asa and Baasha in the thirty-fifth year of his reign. Jamieson (Jamieson-Fausset-Brown, *Commentary*, 1:274) favors this solution, saying, "The best Biblical critics are agreed in considering this date to be calculated from the separation of the kingdoms, and coincident with the sixteenth year of Asa's reign. This mode of reckoning was, in all likelihood, generally followed in the book of the kings of Judah and Israel, the public annals of the time (v.11), the source from which the inspired historian drew his account."

In defense of this theory it should be said that *maleˉ kûˆt* is often used even in the post-Exilic books to mean "kingdom" or "realm" rather than "reign" (e.g., 2 Chron. 1:1; 11:17; 20:30; Neh. 9:35; Esth. 1:14, etc.) In 1 Chronicles 17:14 it is used of "royalty" as belonging to Yahweh; in Esther 1:2 and 5:1 as the "kingdom" of Persia. But it is without parallel to refer to the kingdom of a nation as a whole and identify it thus with one particular king who comes later on in the ruling dynasty. And the fact that in its account of the later history of Judah no such usage can be instanced in Chronicles raises a formidable difficulty to this solution, even though it does avoid the necessity of textual emendation.

The other solution, presented by

Keil (Keil and Delitzsch, *Chronicles*, pp. 366–67), prefers to regard the number "thirty-six" in 2 Chronicles 16:1 and the number "thirty-five" in 15:19 as a copyist's error for "sixteen" and "fifteen," respectively. There is no way in which such an error could have arisen if the *Vorlage* recorded the number of words fully spelled out (for "sixteen"— *šiššāh 'āśār*—cannot possibly be misunderstood as "thirty-six"—*šᵉlōšim wāšēš*). But if the number was written in numerical notation of the Hebrew alphabetic type (rather than the Egyptian multiple-stroke type used in the Elephantine Papyri), then "sixteen" could quite easily be confused with "thirty-six." The reason for this is that up through the seventh century B.C. the letter *yod* (= 10) greatly resembled the letter *lamed* (= 30), except for two tiny strokes attached to the left of the main vertical stroke. That is to say, *yod* was ⟨ and *lamed* was ⟨. It required only a smudge from excessive wear on the scroll-column to result in making the *yod* look like a *lamed*—with a resultant error of twenty. It is possible that this error occurred first in the earlier passage, in 2 Chronicles 15:19 (with its "thirty-five" wrongly copied from an original "fifteen"); then to make it consistent in 16:1, the same scribe (or perhaps a later one) concluded that "sixteen" must be an error for "thirty-six" and changed it accordingly on his copy.

If this is the true explanation for the discrepancy, then it would bear a similarity to the problem arising in 2 Kings 18:13, in which the relevant data compel an emendation of the "fourteenth year of King Hezekiah" to the "twenty-fourth year of King Hezekiah." Another example of this involves 2 Chronicles 36:9, which gives the age of Jehoiachin as eight at the time of his accession, whereas the parallel in 2 Kings 24:8 indicates the true number as "eighteen." Still another instance is 2 Chronicles 22:2, which gives the age of Ahaziah

son of Jehoram as "forty-two" when he began to reign, whereas 2 Kings 8:26 gives it as "twenty-two" (which is more probably the correct number).

How could Jehoram of Judah receive a letter from Elijah long after his departure from this life (2 Chron. 21:12–15)?

Obviously he could not have done so. But the question presupposes something that never happened, namely the demise of Elijah at some time prior to the reign of Jehoram son of Jehoshaphat. The reader is invited to consult W. Crockett, *A Harmony of Samuel, Kings, and Chronicles*, p. 247. There he will see that "The Translation of Elijah" is placed in the reign of Jehoram the son of Ahab. Therefore it was perfectly possible for Elijah to compose a letter of warning and rebuke as late as 847 B.C., for the reign of Jehoram of Judah (848–841) largely overlapped the reign of Jehoram of Israel (852–841).

Elijah was certainly still active in the reign of Jehoram's immediate predecessor, Ahaziah of Israel (853–852), who also was a son of Ahab. We know this because of the exciting encounter Elijah had with Ahaziah's platoons of soldiers sent to arrest him but who were destroyed by fire from heaven in answer to Elijah's prayer (2 Kings 1:3–16). In all probability the aged prophet would have lived on for another four or five years until the character and policies of Jehoshaphat's unworthy son had become apparent. (Second Chron. 21:4 relates how Jehoram had all his own brothers put to death as soon as he became king. Probably his bloodthirsty wife, Athaliah daughter of Jezebel, encouraged him to this fratricide. She herself later tried to kill off all the survivors of Ahab's house after her son Ahaziah was slain by Jehu in 841.)

It is true that the account of Elijah's translation to heaven is given in 2

Kings 2:1–11, whereas the reign of Jehoram of Judah is not spoken of until 2 Kings 8:16. But it should be remembered that the narrator of First and Second Kings continually shifts from the careers of reigning kings to the adventures of the principal prophets, Elijah and Elisha. On occasion he carries a theme through in a proleptic way when he is describing the exploits of Elijah, not desiring to leave off that theme until he is through with it. So it was with the story of Elijah's departure to heaven. This was closely related to the enduement of Elisha with the charismatic power of his revered teacher. Elijah had first called him to discipleship back in the reign of Ahab, after he had symbolically cast his mantle on him (1 Kings 19:19–21), not long after the memorable contest on Mount Carmel.

As Elijah later came near the end of his earthly career during the reign of Jehoram son of Ahab (852–841), the most important theme from the author's standpoint was the prophetic succession. Therefore he very logically related that first (i.e., the bestowal of Elijah's cloak and a double portion of his spirit on Elisha at the time of their parting). Not until then was it appropriate for the author of Kings to backtrack and pick up the narration of the national affairs of Israel and Judah in chapter 3. (A similar proleptic procedure is followed in 2 Kings 19:37, which relates the assassination of Sennacherib, which took place in 681 B.C., before the illness of Hezekiah, which occurred in 714.)

So far as the narrative in 2 Chronicles is concerned, there is no notice at all of Elijah's demise, whether before or after the accession of Jehoram son of Jehoshaphat; so there is no problem of apparent anachronism to deal with. In all probability the letter of Elijah to Jehoram was composed in 847 and delivered to him that same year, shortly before Elijah was taken up into heaven by the celestial chariot of fire (2 Kings 2:11).

Why is there no mention of Manasseh's repentance in 2 Kings?

Second Chronicles 33:13–16 tells of King Manasseh's repentance and dedication to God after his release from captivity in Babylon (cf. v.11). In despair Manasseh cast himself on the mercy of the God he had hated and mocked during the decades of his wicked reign. Amazingly, the Lord responded to his cry and released him. According to vv.15–16, Manasseh then removed all the idols he had installed in the Jerusalem temple and all the pagan altars throughout the city and cast them into the trash heap outside the city walls. He then restored the worship of Yahweh in the temple according to the law of Moses and ended his days in restored fellowship with God.

But why was this final conversion of that wicked king not mentioned at all in the account in 2 Kings 21? The first nine verses of this chapter detail his sinful violation of God's covenant and the baneful influence he exerted for the spiritual downfall of his people. The next six verses record God's stern sentence of total destruction for Jerusalem and the southern kingdom because of Manasseh's unparalleled wickedness. The account closes (vv.16–18) with a summary of the unchecked bloodshed and crime that afflicted Jerusalem under his rule and makes no mention whatever of a change of heart before his death and burial.

It seems a bit strange that such an important development as the latter-day repentance of this long-reigning king receives no mention whatever in 2 Kings 21. But the reason seems to lie in the different focus of interest that guided the author of Kings. He was not quite so concerned with the personal

227

relationship of individual leaders to the Lord as he was with the response of the nation as a whole to its responsibilities under the covenant. From the standpoint of lasting results, Manasseh's reign added up to a severe spiritual setback for Judah; and even his personal reform and restoration to fellowship with God came as too little and too late, so far as influencing the nation was concerned. Under his son and successor, Amon, the people reverted to their immoral, idolatrous lifestyle, just about as they had done before Manasseh's return from captivity. The curse of God was not lifted from the city, and the disaster of 587 B.C. came upon them just the same.

The author of Chronicles, however, takes more of a personal interest in the relationship each leader or king maintained toward God. Thus in 1 Kings 15:9–24 there is a relatively short account of Asa's reign, which centers attention on Asa's grave blunder in bribing Benhadad of Damascus to invade Israel from the north, thus compelling Baasha of Israel to give up his fortification of Ramah on his southern border. The maneuver seemed successful, and Baasha's fortress was later completely dismantled by Asa's troops; but there were sinister consequences for the future. In 2 Chronicles 16:7–9 God's prophet Hanani had to rebuke Asa for relying on the king of Syria for deliverance rather than on God. Hanani reminded Asa of the wonderful way Yahweh had come through for him in his combat with the huge army of the Ethiopians and Egyptians, when he had cast himself wholly on God's faithful mercy (an episode described at length in 2 Chron. 14:9–15 but entirely omitted in 1 Kings).

Going still further back, we find in 2 Chronicles 13:2–20 a long, detailed account of a victory won by Abijah son of Rehoboam over Jeroboam I. This was completely omitted by 1 Kings because it had no lasting results for the political struggle between the divided kingdoms. But for the Chronicler it was important because it showed how wonderfully God delivers those like Abijah who trust in Him in the presence of great difficulties and discouraging odds. Thus we can discern a pattern of selection as between the two historians. First Kings focused on the overall result of each king's reign, in the light of his faithfulness to the covenant. But the Chronicler was interested in recording great moments of faith, even when no lasting consequences ensued for the nation as a whole. Omission of an event in Kings is therefore not to be regarded as casting doubt on its historicity in Chronicles—anymore than the omission of an event in one synoptic Gospel justifies doubt as to its historicity when it appears in another gospel.

Ezra

How do we resolve the statistical discrepancies between Ezra 2 and Nehemiah 7?

In Ezra 2:3–35 and Nehemiah 7:8–38 there are about thirty-three family units that appear in both lists, starting with the sons of Parosh (2,172 in both cases). Of these thirty-three there are fourteen that differ; two of them differ by 1 (sons of Adonikam, sons of Bezai), one differs by 4 (sons of Lod, Hadid, and Ono, 725 as against 721), two by 6 (Pahath-moab of the sons of Joshua and Joab, i.e., 2,812 as against 2,818; and the sons of Bani or Binnui—note the variant vocalization for the same consonants—642 as against 648). For the men of Bethlehem and Netophah, the total is 9 less for Ezra 2:21–22 (179) than in Nehemiah 7:26 (188). The sons of Bigvai are 11 less in Ezra 2:14 (2,056) than in Nehemiah 7:19 (2,067). In the case of the sons of Zattu, Ezra reports 945, which is exactly 100 more than the 845 given by Nehemiah 7:13; similarly, the men of Bethel and Ai (223 in Ezra 2:28 vs. 123 in Neh. 7:32). For the sons of Adin, Ezra 2:15 has 201 less (454) than in Nehemiah 7:20 (655); 105 less in Ezra for the sons of Hashum (223 in Ezra 2:19 vs. 328 in Neh. 7:22). Ezra 2:35 gives 300 less for the sons of Senaah than Nehemiah 7:38 (3,630 vs. 3,930). The largest difference of all is found between Ezra's figure for the sons of Azgad (1,222 in

2:12) and Nehemiah's (2,322 in 7:17). The other nineteen are identical in the two lists.

How, then, are we to account for the fourteen discrepancies? There are two important factors to bear in mind as we deal with these various discrepancies in the Received Text. The first is that consideration adduced by Jamieson, Fausset, and Brown (*Commentary*, 1:289):

> It is probable that all mentioned as belonging to this family repaired to the general place of rendezvous, or had enrolled their names at first as intending to go; but in the interval of preparation, some died, others were prevented by sickness or insurmountable obstacles, so that ultimately no more than 652 [sc. of the family of Arah] came to Jerusalem.

Later, the same writer observes:

> The discrepancy is sufficiently accounted for from the different circumstances in which the two registers were taken: that of Ezra having been made up at Babylon, while that of Nehemiah was drawn out in Judea, after the walls of Jerusalem had been rebuilt. The lapse of so many years might well be expected to make a difference appear in the catalogue, through death or other causes (ibid., 1:297).

To be sure, regardless of the date when Nehemiah recorded this list (ca. 445 B.C.), his expressed purpose was to give the exact number of those who actually arrived at Jerusalem under the leadership of Zerubbabel and Jeshua back in 537 or 536 (Neh. 7:7). So also Ezra (in the 450s, apparently) recorded their numbers (2:1–2). But it may well be that Ezra used the earlier list of those who originally announced their intention to join the caravan of returning colonists back in Babylonia, whereas Nehemiah's list reproduces the tally of those who actually arrived in Judea at the end of the long trek from Mesopotamia.

In some cases there may well have been some individual families who at first determined to go with the rest and actually left their marshaling field (at Tel Abib, or wherever it may have been in Babylonia) under Zerubbabel and proceeded to the outskirts of that province before new factors arose to change their mind. They may have fallen into disagreement as to the advisability of all of them going at once with the initial group; others may have discovered business reasons to delay their departure until later. In some cases there may have been illness or death, as Jamieson suggested in the quotation cited above. In other cases there may have been some last-minute recruits from those who at first decided to remain in Babylonia. Perhaps they were caught up in the excitement of the return movement and joined the company of emigrants after the official tally had been taken at the marshaling grounds. Nevertheless, they made it safely back to Jerusalem, or wherever their ancestral town in Judea was, and were counted in the final list made up at the completion of the journey.

Only four clans or city-groups came in with shrunken numbers (Arah, Zattu, the men of Bethel and Ai, and the men of Lod, Hadid, and Ono). All the rest picked up last-minute recruits, varying from 1 (in the case of Adonikam and Bezai) to 1,100 (in the case of Azgad). It would be fascinating to know what special, emotional, or economic factors led to these last-minute decisions. At any rate, the differences in totals that do appear in these two tallies should occasion no surprise whatever. The same sort of augmentation and attrition has featured every large migration in human history.

A second consideration should also be kept in mind, and that is the difficulty of preserving complete accuracy in the copying out of numerals as between the *Vorlage* and its would-be duplicate. Numbers are very difficult to verify; and if the *Vorlage* was by any chance worn, smudged, or even worm-eaten (as most of the Qumran manuscripts were, for example), it is very easy to see how uncertainty as to the digit might join with absentmindedness on the part of the copyist to produce an inaccuracy in reproducing the figures. (A similar difficulty arises in the copying of rare or unfamiliar names, especially if they are non-Israelite names.)

Strong confirmation of this type of copyist error is found in various pagan records that have been preserved to us for the purposes of comparison. For example, in the Behistun Rock inscription set up by Darius I, we find that #38 gives the figure for the slain of the army of Frada as 55,243, with 6,572 prisoners—according to the Babylonian column. In a duplicate copy of this inscription found at Babylon itself, the number of prisoners was 6,973. But in the Aramaic translation of this inscription discovered at the Elephantine in Egypt, the number of prisoners was only 6,972—precisely the same discrepancy as we have noted in the comparison of Ezra 2 and Nehemiah 7 (cf. F.W. König, *Relief und Inschrift des Königs Dareios I am Felsen von Bagistan* [Leiden: Brill, 1938], p. 48.) Similarly in #31 of the same inscription, the Babylonian column gives 2,045 as the number of slain in the rebellious army of Frawartish, along with 1,558 prisoners, whereas the Aramaic copy has over 1,575 as the prisoner count (ibid., p. 45).

How can we reconcile Ezra 3:8–13; 5:13–17, which say that the second temple was begun in the reign of Cyrus the Great; Ezra 4:24, which says it was begun in the second year of Darius I; and Haggai 2:15, which implies that the work had not yet begun in 520 B.C.?

Ezra 3:10–11 speaks only of the laying of the foundation of the temple in the seventh month of the year, when the fifty thousand returnees from the Babylonian captivity recommenced sacrificial worship on the site of Solomon's temple. Presumably this occurred in 537 or 536. But as Ezra 4:4 makes clear, the Samaritans and other neighboring nations brought such influence to bear on Cyrus's court at the imperial capital that the government suspended their building permit.

Ezra 4:24 informs us that because of this opposition, all further work on the building of the temple was suspended until the second year of Darius the Great, about 520 or 519 B.C. While the wealthier members of the Judean colony were busily building nice homes for themselves, they made no effort at all to pursue the task of rebuilding the temple of the Lord (Hag. 1:3–4).

In the year 520 or 519, Haggai was directed by the Lord to stir up the people of Judah and Jerusalem to start building on the foundation that had been laid sixteen years before. In response to this challenge, the Jewish governor Zerubbabel and the high priest Joshua rallied to this undertaking with their whole heart, along with the rank and file of the people (1:14). This new beginning was made on the "twenty-fourth day of the sixth month" that same year (1:15).

On the twenty-first day of the seventh month, almost a month later (according to 2:1), Haggai gave them

an encouraging prediction about the glory of the second temple as surpassing that of the first (v.9). Two months later still (v.10), the prophet called attention to the fact that their farming activities had been beset with blight, mildew, and hail, ever since they discontinued building the temple sixteen years before ("the day when the foundation of the Lord's temple was laid" [v.18]).

Despite the interference of Tattenai, the governor of Trans-Euphrates, Shethar-bozenai, and their colleagues, King Darius himself had a search made for King Cyrus's original decree back in 537; and after it had been located at Ecbatana, he issued a rescript ordering the Jerusalem temple to be completed without any interference on the part of the neighboring nations (Ezra 6:3–12). The happy result was that the second temple was finished in 516, "on the third day of Adar, in the sixth year of the reign of King Darius" (v.15).

Thus we see that when all the scriptural data are properly sorted out and compared, there is no discrepancy whatever among them, nor any difficulty at their reconciliation.

What was the real reason why the rebuilding of the temple was delayed?

Ezra 4:7–23 states that it was foreign interference (Rehum and Shimshai) that caused the delay in rebuilding the temple, after a hopeful beginning had been made by Zerubbabel and Jeshua in 536 B.C. But Haggai 1:2 accuses the Jerusalem leaders themselves of indifference towards the project and lays the blame on them for making no attempt to renew the building campaign. Haggai's message came in 520, or a good fourteen years later than the suspension of the work late in the reign of Cyrus.

Actually, both statements are true. Back in the time of Cyrus, the surrounding nations became alarmed at the establishment of a new settlement of Jews in Jerusalem; and they hired counselors at the Persian court to persuade the king to suspend the building license. But later on, after the death of Cambyses in 524 and the assassination of Gaumata (Pseudo-Smerdis) in 522, followed by the rise of Darius I to a position of power, the situation was somewhat more favorable to the Jews' renewing their efforts to get their temple built. Yet by that time the leading classes in Jerusalem had become so preoccupied with their own interests and concerns that they felt no zeal to renew the building project—especially if there was any danger of their getting in trouble for rebuilding the temple without a permit.

There has been much misunderstanding, however, concerning the sequence of events in Ezra 4; Rehum and Shimshai were not even around when Haggai's building campaign began in 520. Note that the date of their letter was later than 464, since it was addressed to Artaxerxes (464–424 B.C.) Nor does either their letter to the king or his reply to them make any mention of the building of the temple as such, but only of the rebuilding of the city walls and outer defenses. The temple itself had been completed back in 516 (Ezra 6:15). In the course of the campaign to rebuild the templle, there was a remonstrance raised by Tattenai, governor of Trans-Euphrates, and Shethar-bozenai and their associates; and they actually wrote to King Darius to see whether the claim of the Jews that Cyrus had originally given them official permission was actually true (Ezra 5:3–17). His researches finally located the decree, and he cordially validated their right to go ahead with the completion of the temple without interference from anyone—and with royal subsidies to help them meet expenses (Ezra 6:1–12).

The opposition of Rehum and Shimshai was several decades later (even though it is mentioned earlier in Ezra), and it had only to do with rebuilding the walls of the city. It was apparently the concern of Ezra himself to aid in the repair of the city walls (cf. Ezra 9:9) as well as the religious reformation of the city. But for reasons not given in the Bible record, Ezra's efforts were frustrated; and it remained for Nehemiah to complete that important task (cf. article on Daniel's prophecy of the Seventy Weeks).

Nehemiah

What was the real name of Nehemiah's Arab opponent, "Geshem" (Neh. 2:19) or "Gashmu" (Neh. 6:6)?

Arabic names preserved (and still do, in modern literary Arabic) the original Semitic three-case inflectional endings (u for the nominative, i for the genitive, and a for the accusative). The Arabic pronunciation of the man's name is given with the u ending in 6:6. But the usual practice of the Hebrew-speaking and Aramaic-speaking populations of Palestine was to omit the short-vowel ending for all nouns, including proper names. Hence Gashmu would more normally be referred to as Geshem, as was the case in Nehemiah 2:19.

Esther

Was it right for Esther to take part in a pagan beauty contest and become part of Xerxes' harem?

Even though God's name is not explicitly mentioned in the Book of Esther, the providential guidance of the Lord is marvelously attested throughout all ten chapters, from beginning to end. No time was more fraught with peril for the Jewish nation; for it was then that Haman, the prime minister of Persia, undertook to have the entire population of the Hebrew captivity wiped out in a genocidal massacre. To thwart this evil purpose, God raised up a woman—a very beautiful, intelligent, and courageous woman—who made herself totally available for the deliverance of her people. The only way she could achieve this goal was by presenting herself before the king as a candidate in the beauty contest held in the royal palace.

Whether Esther actually volunteered to participate, or whether she was compelled by the king's agents to join with the other contestants, we have no way of knowing. Esther 2:8 simply says, "Esther *was taken* to the king's palace" (NASB). This could well imply that she had no freedom to refuse. At any rate, there can be no doubt that she was to serve as God's instrument to frustrate the purpose of the vengeful premier, Haman, and to entangle him in a web of guilt as one who plotted the death of Xerxes' new queen. Because of all the special factors, we may say with assurance that in this particular case Esther acted completely within the will of God. She was willing to risk her life for the sake of her people, saying, "If I perish, I perish" (4:16).

Yet on the other hand, this remarkable adventure of Queen Esther can hardly be said to offer a precedent for young Christian women to follow at the level of a modern beauty contest. It is true that God used Esther's beauty to deliver His chosen people from total destruction. No such issues, however, are at stake in beauty contests as we know them in our modern civilization; and young believers are well advised to avoid them.

Job

Was Job a historical person or just a fictional hero?

Because of the poetic form in which 39 of the 42 chapters of Job are composed, and because of the supernatural forces involved in the hero's disasters and afflictions (as well as in his restoration to good fortune), some scholars have questioned the historicity of the whole episode. Was there ever such a person as Job; and, if so, where did he live and when? Many have speculated that he was a mere fictional character, somehow representative of the Hebrew people during their period of deep affliction in the Babylonian captivity. They allege that the high frequency of loan words from Aramaic and the high level of pure monotheism reflected in the viewpoint of all five persons—or six, if we include Yahweh Himself—involved in the dialogues indicate a post-Exilic date of composition.

In answer to this skeptical theory of a late, fictional origin of Job, we should observe that ample grounds may be found to support the complete historicity of both Job himself and the details given concerning his life experiences. First, it should be observed that Job 1:1 states very positively that "there was a man in the land of Uz, whose name was Job." This is expressed in just as truly a matter-of-fact way as 1 Samuel 1:1: "Now there was

a certain man from Ramathaim-zophim, . . . and his name was Elkanah the son of Jeroham, etc." (NASB). Or again, in Luke 1:5 we read, "In the days of Herod, King of Judea, there was a certain priest named Zacharias" (NASB). If Job is part of the sacred canon of Scripture, it logically follows that the same credibility must be granted to its opening historical statement as is accorded to 1 Samuel or to Luke—or to any other book in Scripture that affirms the historical existence of a character whose career it records.

Second, the historicity of Job is definitely confirmed by the references to him found elsewhere in Scripture. In Ezekiel 14:14 he is grouped with Noah and Daniel as a paragon of godliness and an effective intercessor before God: "Even though these three men, Noah, Daniel, and Job were in its [i.e., Israel's] midst, by their own righteousness they could only deliver themselves, declares the Lord GOD" (NASB). Here we find God Himself affirming the factual existence of Job on the same level with the existence of Noah and Daniel. If, therefore, no such person as Job ever lived, the historicity of both Noah and Daniel is likewise called in question. And actually it would follow that God Himself must be understood as deceived about the whole matter and in need of correction by the present-day scholars of skeptical persuasion! In this connection it is significant that even W.F. Albright, who inclined to a late date of the composition of Job, entertained no serious doubt as to the actual existence of Job himself. In his chapter on "The Old Testament and Archeology" (H.C. Alleman and E.E. Flack, eds., *Old Testament Commentary* [Philadelphia: Fortress, 1954]), Albright suggested that Job may have been a contemporary of the patriarchs in the pre-Mosaic age. He supports the credibility of Job by the authentic second-millennium employment of the name *'Iyyōḇ*. (It should be noted that in the Berlin Execration texts, *'Iyyōḇ* appears as the name of a Syrian prince living near Damascus; in the Mari documents of the eighteenth century B.C., *Ayyabum* is mentioned; and in the Tell el-Amarna correspondence from about 1400 B.C., *Ayab* is referred to as a prince of Pella.) Albright also certifies the credibility of the name of Bildad (one of Job's three "comforters") as a shortened form of *Yabil-Dadum,* a name found in the cuneiform sources of the early second millennium.

Third, objections based on the confrontation between Yahweh and Satan recorded in the first two chapters of Job are no more soundly based than those regarding Christ's temptation by Satan in the wilderness, as recorded in Matthew 4 and Luke 4. If the Bible cannot be regarded as trustworthy in such matters as these, it is difficult to say in what respect it retains any authority or credibility as a document of divine revelation.

Fourth, the linguistic argument based on the presence of terms more characteristic of Aramaic than Hebrew is tenuous indeed. The Aramaic language was evidently known and used in North Arabia for a long period of time. The numerous first-millennium inscriptions of the North Arabian Nabateans are almost invariably written in Aramaic, and commercial relations with Aramaic-speaking peoples probably began before 2000 B.C. Jacob's father-in-law, Laban, was certainly Aramaic speaking (cf. Gen. 31:47). Commercial contacts with the great Syrian center of Ebla were very extensive as early as 2400 B.C. (though the Eblaites themselves seem to have spoken an Amorite dialect, rather than Aramaic).

Furthermore, it should be pointed out that the extent of Aramaic influence has been somewhat overrated. A. Guillaume ("The Unity of the Book of Job," *Annual of Leeds University,* Oriental Sec. 14 [1962–63]: 26–27) has convincingly argued that there are no demonstrable Aramaisms in the speeches of Elihu (Job 32–37), which reputedly have the highest incidence of them. He contends that nearly all of them are terms existing in Arabic that happen to have cognates in Aramaic as well. He deals with no less than twenty-five examples of this, citing the Arabic originals in every case. Since the setting of the narrative is in Uz, located somewhere in North Arabia, this admixture of Arabic and Aramaic vocabulary is exactly what should be expected in the text of Job, whether it was originally composed in Hebrew (which is rather unlikely), or whether it was translated out of an earlier text written in the language prevalent in North Arabia during the pre-Mosaic period.

In view of the above-mentioned considerations, we must conclude that there are no tenable grounds for the theory of a fictional Job. The apostle James was therefore quite justified in appealing to the example of the patriarch Job in his exhortation to Christian believers to remain patient under tribulation. James 5:11 states: "You have heard of the endurance of Job and have seen the outcome of the Lord's dealings, that the Lord is full of compassion and is merciful" (NASB, an allusion to Job's ultimate restoration to health, wealth, and happiness as the father of a large and God-fearing family). It is needless to point out that the Lord could hardly have been merciful and compassionate to a fictional character who never existed!

In Strong's Concordance we are told that the word translated "curse" in Job 1:11 and 2:5 is *bērak*, a word that elsewhere is translated "bless." How can the same Hebrew word mean two such opposite things?

It is true that *bārak* in the *piel* stem (*bērak*) normally means "bless," "greet with a blessing." It occurs very frequently throughout the Old Testament with this meaning. But in Job 1:5,11; 2:5,9, and possibly also in Psalm 10:3 (where it is coupled with *ni'ēṣ*, "despise," "reject"), it seems to have the very opposite meaning to "bless." This is explained by Brown-Driver-Briggs (*Lexicon*, p. 139) as follows: "Bless with the antithetical meaning *curse* ... from the greeting in departing, saying adieu to, taking leave of; but rather a blessing overdone and so really a curse as in vulgar English." In this connection, 1 Kings 21:10,13 may also be cited.

The verb *bērak* means "say goodby to" in Genesis 24:60; 32:1; 47:10; Joshua 22:6, 2 Samuel 13:25; and 1 Kings 8:66, generally with the connotation of invoking a parting blessing on the person taking his leave. From this usage we may surmise that an insolent sinner might say goodby to God Himself, with the intention of dismissing Him from his mind and conscience, of totally abandoning Him (so Zorell, *Lexicon*, p. 130, and this seems as satisfactory an explanation as any). Delitzsch (Keil and Delitzsch, *Job*, 2:51) calls this use of *bērak* an antiphrastic euphemism. He feels that in Job 2:9 it clearly means *valedicere* ("say goodby to") as a benedictory salutation at parting. But in his general handling of these negative usages, he prefers to render it "dismiss God from one's heart" (ibid., 2:49).

The statement of Eliphaz in Job 5:13 is quoted in 1 Corinthians 3:19 as valid and true; does this mean that the words of Job's three comforters were also inspired?

In Job 5:13 Eliphaz says of God, "He captures the wise by their own shrewdness and the advice of the cunning is quickly thwarted" (NASB). The first portion of this is quoted in 1 Corinthians 3:19: "He is the one who catches the wise in their craftiness" (NASB). But if Eliphaz was right in this affirmation about God, how are we to understand the Lord's reproof to Eliphaz, Zophar, and Bildad as expressed in Job 42:7: "The LORD said to Eliphaz the Temanite, 'My wrath is kindled against you and against your two friends, because you have not spoken of Me what is right as My servant Job has'" (NASB)? This adverse judgment calls into question the reliability of any statement made by any of the three.

While it is true that the basic position of the three "comforters" was seriously in error (that all misfortune and misery that befalls an apparently righteous believer must be the consequence of unconfessed, secret sin), nevertheless 42:7 does not go so far as to say that nothing else they ever said about God was true. On the contrary, even Job himself conceded the correctness of some of their teachings about God, for he rephrased many of the statements they themselves had made and wove them into his own eloquent eulogies of God.

On the other hand, it hardly seems doubtful that some of Job's own sentiments were incorrect and subject to the rebuke of both Elihu and Yahweh Himself. In fact, Job is led by God's direct teaching to see the presumptuous folly he had shown in criticizing God for unfairness and unkindness toward him. Job even says of himself in 42:3: "Who is this that hides counsel without knowledge? Therefore I have declared that which I did not understand, things too wonderful for me, which I did not know" (NASB). Later on, in v.6, Job adds, "Therefore I retract, and I repent in dust and ashes" (NASB). Obviously, if Job had to retract things that he had said amiss in criticism of God's treatment of him, then not everything Job himself said about God is to be received as true.

Therefore we must rely on the context in each case in order to discover which of Job's sentiments were divinely inspired and approved of, and which expressed the distortions of insight to which grief and provocation had driven him. After all, the inerrancy of Scripture assures the truthfulness and accuracy of the record of what was said and done, according to the intention of the author within the context of his message. If by careful, objective exegesis it can be ascertained that the scriptural author meant to give a faithful record of what men said mistakenly or untruthfully, the inerrancy inheres in the accuracy of the report; it does not necessarily vouch for the truthfulness of what was said. No reader would imagine, for example, that what Satan said to God in Job 1 and 2 is to be received as truthful.

There is, however, one other significant observation to be made. Concerning Job's comforters, in all the New Testament this one statement from Eliphaz in 1 Corinthians 3:19 is the only quotation to be found from them. Nothing said by Bildad or Zophar is ever quoted, nor is any other comment from Eliphaz. Similar sentiments may be found elsewhere in the New Testament, but never any quotations—only vague allusions. (For a fuller discussion of this point, see 1 Cor. 3:19.)

In Job 2:1–2, Satan presents himself before the Lord. Does this mean that Satan has access to heaven and is able to go freely between heaven and earth? Also, who are the "sons of God" referred to in v.1? (D*)

In Ephesians 2:2, Satan is spoken of as the "prince [*archōn*] of the power [or 'authority'—*exousia*] of the air" (*aēr*, the atmosphere surrounding the earth, not the outer atmosphere or "space" indicated by *aithēr*). His sphere of action, even in his fallen and confined state (cf. 2 Peter 2:4), seems to be extensive enough so that he comes in contact with the archangel Michael (Jude 9) and even has communication with God over his administration of judicial authority.

Thus in Zechariah 3:1, the prophet sees a vision (admittedly symbolic) of the contemporary high priest of Israel standing before the judgment throne of God: "He showed me Joshua the high priest standing before the angel of Yahweh, with Satan standing on his right to accuse him. The angel of Yahweh said to Satan, 'May Yahweh rebuke you, Satan!'"

This establishes quite clearly the fact that Satan, prior to the Cross at least, had occasional access to the court of God in situations where man's sinfulness gave him the right to interpose the claims of strict, retributive justice, or where the sincerity of believers' motives toward the Lord might be called in question. For this cause Satan is called "the Accuser" (Greek *ho diabolos*), who accuses Christians before the Lord night and day (Rev. 12:10). There is ample support from Scripture that Satan does have at least occasional and limited access before God in the presence of the angels of heaven— referred to as "the sons of God" (both in Job 1:6 and 2:1; cf. also Job 38:7— "when the morning stars sang together, and all the sons of God shouted for joy," i.e., back in the primeval beginning, long before the creation of the human race).

Present in this scene are some unexpected features that are not easily explained. If this celestial court session is held in heaven, in what part of heaven might this have taken place? There are at least three levels according to 2 Corinthians 12:2, where Paul mentions being caught up to the *third* heaven to behold the glories above. Presumably the scene of Job 2 would not be the highest and holiest level, as nothing abominable or profane is granted admittance to the City of God (Rev. 21:27). But perhaps in some lower level, on occasion at least, the Lord holds sessions of His celestial council; and to such gatherings Satan may come as an uninvited guest.

The other puzzling feature about this confrontation is that God seems to treat the Prince of Evil in such a casual and relaxed manner, asking him what he has been doing recently, and whether he has observed the consistent godliness of Job. We have no way of knowing whether Satan still puts in such appearances before the judicial throne of God; but it is certainly true that he later challenged and tried to tempt the Son of God in the wilderness at the commencement of His active ministry (cf. Matt. 4; Luke 4).

Satan's doom is sure; he is destined to be bound for a thousand years during the Millennium (Rev. 20:2-3). And after the final revolt against Christ at the close of that period (vv.7-10), Satan will be cast into the lake of fire and brimstone, there to undergo the endless torment of all the cursed and condemned (21:8).

Does Scripture use mythology from pagan sources (e.g., Leviathan [Job 41:1; Isa. 27:1], Rahab [Isa. 30:7], Behemoth [Job 40:15], Tartarus [2 Peter 2:4])?

The poetic books, such as Job and Psalms, and occasionally the poetic passages of the Prophets contain references to mythological figures. There is a far more sparing use of them than appears in the hymns and religious poetry of the non-Hebrew literature of the ancient Near East, and there is furthermore a basic difference in their use. The pagans for the most part believed in the real existence of these mythological characters, whereas the biblical authors employed them in a purely figurative and metaphorical way.

The same practice can be observed in English literature as well, especially in the seventeenth century and earlier, when frequent allusions occur in the works of the great masters who were trained in the Greek and Latin classics. Thus in the opening lines of John Milton's "Comus" (11.18-21) we read:

Neptune, besides the sway
Of every salt flood, and each ebbing stream,
Took in by lot 'twixt high and nether Jove,
Imperial rule of all the sea-girt Isles.

Or, again, we read in lines 46-53:

Bacchus, that first from out the purple grape
Crushed the sweet poison of misused wine,
After the Tuscan mariners transformed
Coasting the Tyrrhene shore, as the winds listed,
On Circe's island fell (who knows not Circe
The daughter of the Sun? Whose charmed cup whoever tasted, lost his upright shape,
And downward fell into a groveling swine).

It would be a very naive and ill-informed critic of English literature who would imagine that John Milton, that notable Christian apologete who composed the most outstanding of all English epics pertaining to the Fall of Adam and the redemption of man by Christ ("Paradise Lost" and "Paradise Regained"), betrayed a taint of pagan belief in his references to the Roman and Greek deities and demigods of Vergil and Homer. And yet many a

239

nineteenth-century higher critic of biblical literature has fallen into this obvious fallacy in his attempt to link up the religion of ancient Israel with the superstitions of their idolatrous neighbors. A careful study of the religious documents of the Egyptians, Sumerians, Babylonians, and Canaanites (as set forth in Pritchard's *Ancient Near Eastern Texts*, for example) will show the distinction clearly and underline the fact that the attitude of the biblical authors towards Behemoth, Leviathan, and Rahab was very similar to the Miltonian references to Jove, Bacchus, Neptune, and Circe cited above.

To be more specific, "Leviathan" refers to an aquatic monster of great size and fearsome power. In Psalm 104:26 it is described in such a way as to suggest a whale. In Job 41 it probably refers to a monster-sized crocodile, as a prime example of an untamable beast too fierce and powerful for man to deal with—and yet perfectly cared for by Yahweh its Creator. In Isaiah 27 it symbolizes the empires of Assyria (the "fleeing" or "piercing" serpent—possibly suggestive of the winding Tigris River) and of Babylonia (the "crooked" or "twisted" serpent of the River Euphrates). In Psalm 74:14, on the other hand, Leviathan is used in parallelism with the *ṭannîn* ("sea monster," "whale," or even perhaps "river monster"), referring to the Nile River or the Red Sea. In Ezekiel 29:3–5 it clearly refers to the crocodile of Egypt, with its scales and gaping jaws.

"Behemoth" (a plural of intensity derived from *bᵉhēmāh*, a large quadruped, whether domestic or wild) appears in Job 40:15 as a fierce, huge beast that also frequents the water. On the whole it seems best to identify it with a giant hippopotamus, native to the upper reaches of the Nile. (An Egyptian etymology has been suggested: *pᵉ iḥ mw*, "the water-ox," but this presents serious phonetic problems and was never so used by the Egyptians themselves, so far as we know. The three commonest terms for hippopotamus in Egyptian were *ḥ·b*, *db*, or *nḥs* [cf. R.O. Faulkner, "A Concise Dictionary of Middle Egyptian," handwritten lithographed (Oxford, 1962), pp. 184,311,136 respectively].)

"Rahab" (Hebrew *rāhāb*—not the same as Rahab the harlot, which is *Rāḥāb*, a different root) is a term meaning "pride," "arrogance"; but it appears in Job 26:12 and 38:8–11 as a personification of the turbulent forces of the raging deep. It serves as a symbol of Egypt at the time of the Exodus, as employed in Psalm 87:4, or as the loud, blustering do-nothing Egypt of Isaiah's day in Isaiah 30:7.

Tartaros, the Greek term for hell as a place of torment, appears only in the verb form *tartaroō* ("consign to Tartaros") and refers to no deity, only a place.

Does Job 19:26 envision a resurrection body or not?

Job 19:25–27 was uttered by Job in an exalted moment of faith, as he turned away from his wretched circumstances and fastened his gaze on God: "But as for me, I know my Redeemer lives, and at the last He will stand on the earth [lit., 'dust']; and after they [i.e., the worms] have consumed away my skin, yet from my flesh I shall behold God—whom I shall behold and my eyes shall see—I and not another, [when] my inward parts have been consumed within me." The passage is highly poetic and capable of minor variations in rendering here and there. But the most discussed matter of interpretation concerns the word-cluster *ûmibbᵉśārî* (composed of the waw-connective—"and" or "yet," the preposition *min*—"from" or "away from," and *bāśār*—"body" or "flesh," plus -*î*, meaning "my."

The question at issue is the real significance of *min*: does it mean "in [my flesh]" as KJV and NIV render it? Or does it mean "from [my flesh]" as RSV and JB have it? Or does it mean "without [my flesh]" as ASV and NASB have rendered it? If Job intends here to say that his soul or spirit will behold God in the Last Day, then the *min* should perhaps be rendered "without." But no other passage uses *min* to mean "without" in connection with a verb of seeing; rather it is only used in combinations such as Job 11:15—"Then you will lift up your face without spot [*mimmûm*]"; Proverbs 1:33—"when they are at peace without fear [*mippaḥad*]"; Jeremiah 45:48—"They stand without strength [*mikkōaḥ*]" (cf. Brown-Driver-Briggs, *Lexicon*, p. 578b).

It is poor exegetical procedure to prefer a rare or unusual meaning for a word when a common and frequent meaning will agree perfectly well with the context. Therefore, it is far better to take *min* here in its usual sense of the point of reference from which an observation is taken, a vantage point from which the spectator may view the object of his interest. (Thus *min* is often used in specifying a compass direction or a relative location of one person in reference to another.)

In this case, then, it is hard to believe that the Hebrew listener would gain any other impression from *mibbeśārî 'eḥezeh 'elôah* than "from [the vantage point of] my flesh [or 'body'] I shall behold God." Taken in this sense, the passage indicates Job's conviction that even after his body has moldered away in the grave, there will come a time in the Last Day—when his divine Redeemer stands on the soil (*'āpār*) of this earth—that from the vantage point of a postresurrection body he will behold God. It is for this reason that the rendering of RSV and JB ("from") and of KJV and NIV ("in," which expresses the same idea with the preposition more agreeable to our idiom) is much to be preferred over the "without" of ASV and NASB. Construed as "from" or "in," this passage strongly suggests an awareness of the bodily resurrection that awaits all redeemed believers in the Resurrection.

Psalms

Do not Psalms 5:5 and 11:5 contradict the teaching that God loves the sinner but hates the sin?

Psalm 5:4–6 reads: "For Thou art not a God who takes pleasure in wickedness; no evil dwells with Thee. The boastful shall not stand before Thine eyes; Thou dost hate all who do iniquity. Thou dost destroy those who speak falsehood; the LORD abhors the man of bloodshed and deceit" (NASB). Psalm 11:5 reinforces this as follows: "The LORD tests the righteous and the wicked, and the one who loves violence His soul hates" (NASB). To this may be added the often-cited passage in Malachi 1:2–3: "'Was not Esau Jacob's brother?' declares the LORD. 'Yet I have loved Jacob; but I have hated Esau, and I have made his mountains a desolation, and appointed his inheritance for the jackals of the wilderness.'" (NASB).

From such passages as these we learn that God makes a difference between good and evil and between good men and evil men. Evil does not really exist in the abstract (except as a theoretical idea) but only in the evil nature and wicked deeds of ungodly men and the demons of hell. Scripture describes the wicked and immoral as those who love sinners in their defiance of God and in their contempt for His moral law. Thus the prophet Hanani rebuked even good King Jehoshaphat for his alliance with Ahab, saying, "Should you help the wicked and love those who hate the LORD and so bring wrath on yourself from the LORD?" (2 Chron. 19:2, NASB). The apostle John warns in his first Epistle (2:15): "Do not love the world, nor the things in the world. If any one loves the world, the love of the Father is not in him" (NASB). We are not to love the wicked as sinners in rebellion against God, lest we become involved in their guilty ways and attitudes of mind. Therefore, we are to recognize that only Satan loves sinners in their transgression and opposition to the moral law. God does not love them in that way; rather, He condemns and punishes them in His capacity as righteous Judge over all the universe.

There is yet another aspect of God's attitude toward sinners that reflects His unfathomable mercy and matchless grace. He so loved the wicked, sinful world that He gave His only Son, Jesus, to die as an atonement for sin. "All we like sheep have gone astray, ... but the LORD has caused the iniquity of us all to fall on Him" (Isa. 53:6). This means that even though God opposes and hates the sinner as a co-worker with Satan and a tool of his malice, God's love reaches out in compassion and grace to all sinners everywhere, seeking to deliver them from sin by the Atonement and the

New Birth, and to adopt them as His children in the family of the redeemed. Here, then, we find to our amazement that while God hates and condemns the unrepentant, unconverted sinner, yet His heart reaches out to him in mercy and love—a holy love operating through the Cross, "that He might be just and the justifier of the one who has faith in Jesus" (Rom. 3:26, NASB). In other words, God is able to love the one whom He hates; but His hatred is of the sinner in his sin, and His love is for the sinner who repents of his sin and puts his trust in Jesus. Why is this so? Because from the moment he sincerely turns from his wicked way and puts his trust in Jesus, he becomes united with Christ by faith—and the Father cannot hate His Son, or anyone who is a member of His body and a temple of His Spirit.

How can the superscription to Psalm 30 be accurate, when it seems so inappropriate for the contents of the psalm?

The title for Psalm 30, according to the Masoretic text, is "A Psalm; a Song at the Dedication of the House. A Psalm of David" (NASB). The substance of Psalm 30 deals largely with a very personal experience on the part of the poet himself—an experience of rescue from the hand of his enemies—together with an earnest plea that the Lord will not allow him to be killed by his enemies, but will rather preserve him for further years of fellowship and service for God on earth. There seems to be nothing in the twelve verses of this psalm that would lend itself to use in tabernacle or temple by way of public worship. It should be added that the titles of the psalms, informative and illuminating though they often are, do not enjoy the status of inspired and authoritative Scripture. Only the words of the psalm itself as originally composed are included in the inerrant text.

The titles are at best to be considered as highly reliable notations added sometime subsequent to the composition of the poem itself.

However, we observe one significant fact about Psalm 29, which immediately precedes the title of Psalm 30. Psalm 29 is eminently suited for use in public worship and shows some of the grandeur and exalting sublimity that we associate with the Hallelujah Chorus. This brings to mind a treatise by J.W. Thirtle (*The Titles of the Psalms, their Meaning and Nature Explained*, 2d ed. [London: H. Froude, 1905], ad loc.). In this discussion Thirtle suggests that many of the Psalms had not only a prescript but also a postscript. Some of the ancient Egyptian and Akkadian hymns have been preserved to us with a final notation. This makes it quite possible that in the later compilation of the canonical Psalms the scribes became confused by the presence of postscripts and assumed that they should be taken as part of the prescript for the psalm following. This establishes a certain likelihood that the first part, at least of the title of Psalm 30 ("A Psalm; a Song at the Dedication of the House") was originally a closing notation attached at the end of Psalm 29. This would leave only "A Psalm of David" as the true heading for Psalm 30. If this was the case, then the problem of inappropriateness disappears completely.

Should not the name in the title to Psalm 34 be Achish rather than Abimelech?

The title to Psalm 34 reads: "A Psalm of David; when he feigned madness before Abimelech, who drove him away and he departed" (NASB). This is probably a reference to the episode related in 1 Samuel 21:13, when in order to escape arrest as an enemy of the Philistines, David pretended before King Achish of Gath that he had become insane. Reluctant to treat him like a responsible wrongdoer, King Achish ordered him to be expelled from the city and sent away. The appearance of the name "Abimelech" instead of "Achish" may be an error on the part of the editors of the Psalter, who added the titles to the Psalms for which titles are supplied. On the other hand, the biography of King David was known to the Hebrew people better than that of any other king of Israel; and it is most unlikely that this kind of a blunder could have been made by a knowledgeable editor of a later generation.

It is far more likely that the reference to Abimelech was no blunder at all, but actually refers to a second name of King Achish. Just as Gideon also bore the name of Jerubbaal (Judg. 6:32; 7:1, etc.), Solomon was also named Jedidiah (2 Sam. 12:25), and Zedekiah was also called Mattaniah (2 Kings 24:17), so also the kings of the Philistines may have borne more than one name. Actually the earliest Philistine king ever mentioned in Genesis was King Abimelech of Gerar (20:2), followed later in the time of Isaac by Abimelech II (26:1). It would seem that Abimelech became a kind of recurrent dynastic name, a little like "Darius" in Persia (the first Darius actually bore the name Spantadāta before his coronation in 522, and the personal name of Darius the Mede [Dan. 5:31; 6:1; 9:1] was probably Gubaru [Dārᵉyāwēš was probably a throne-name meaning "Royal One"]). All the kings of Egypt bore at least two names (the nesu-bity name, which was a personal name; and a sa-Ra' name, which was a dynastic title, often recurring in the titulary of members of the same dynastic chain); so it should occasion no surprise if some of the Philistine kings, profoundly influenced by the culture of their neighboring super-power, followed a similar practice.

No other names of Philistine kings are given in the Old Testament except the two already mentioned, Abimelech and Achish. Assyrian sources, however, mention an Aziri or Azuri, king of Ashdod (Pritchard, ANET, p. 286), whom Sargon II replaced by his younger brother, Ahimiti, and Sidqia, king of Ashkelon, preceded by Rukibtu and succeeded by Sharruludari (ibid., p. 287), along with Padi, king of Ekron, whom Sennacherib restored to his throne as a loyal vassal. At the same period Ṣillibēl was king of Gaza (ibid., p. 288). Essarhaddon mentioned Mitinti as king of Ashkelon (ibid., p. 291) and Ikausu as king of Ekron—and very significantly, also, an A-himilki (the same name as Ahimelech, and very close to Abimelech in formation) as king of Ashdod. This furnishes a strong degree of likelihood that names like Abimelech persisted among Philistine royalty from the eleventh to the eighth century B.C.

What is the significance of "O Lord, when thou awakest" in Psalm 73:20? According to Psalm 121:3-4, God does not sleep. (D*)

The verb translated "awakest" is bā'ir, meaning "to awake," "to act in aroused manner." It is used here figuratively for bestirring oneself into action appropriate to a situation. In this context no Hebrew would draw the inference that God had to be literally asleep before He could rouse Himself into action. This is anthropomorphic language when applied to God; that is, God is represented as behaving or reacting in terms appropriate to humans with bodily parts and limbs. In His essential being, God is spirit and therefore does not have a "body, parts or passions," as traditional theology defines it. (Yet the Bible definitely teaches that He does feel the emotions of love, sorrow, or anger, when the occasion calls for it.)

So in this case, while it is true that God "neither slumbers nor sleeps" in the sense of losing consciousness or contact with the reality about Him, He may remain unresponsive or inactive in situations where we might expect Him to act decisively. When He finally bestirs Himself to display His power and enforce His will, it is *as if* He had aroused Himself into action, like a man awakening out of slumber and confronting a situation demanding his immediate response. (Compare the similar language in Ps.35:23: "Stir up yourself [using the same verb as above] and awake [*hāqîṣāh* from the verb *qîṣ*, meaning 'awake' in the hiphil stem] to the justice due me.")

How could a true man of God, as the psalmist in Psalm 137:8-9, rejoice at the prospect of dashing infants against the rocks?

Psalm 137 was composed by a member of the captivity of Judah, who had witnessed the sadistic brutality of the Chaldean soldiers in the time of the capture of Jerusalem in 587 B.C. He had seen how those heartless monsters had wrenched away helpless babies from their mothers' arms and then had smashed out their brains against the corner of the nearest wall, laughing uproariously in their malicious glee, and uttering the grossest blasphemy against the God of Israel as they carried on their wanton butchery. The challenge to the sovereignty and honor of the one true God, which they hurled at Him as they massacred His people, could not forever go unanswered. As the guardian and enforcer of His own moral law, God could manifest His glory only by visiting a terrible vengeance on those who had so dealt with their unresisting captives and poured contempt on their God.

The captive exile who composed these words, therefore, felt altogether justified in calling on God to enforce the sanctions of His law and mete out appropriate retribution to those malevolent brutes who had committed these atrocities. Only thus could the pagan world be taught that there is a God in heaven who requires all men to regard the basic standards of right and wrong as truly binding on their consciences. They needed to learn that bloody violence practiced on others was sure to come back on themselves. The only way the heathen world could learn this lesson was to experience the fearsome consequences of trampling on the sanctions of humanity and have done to them what they had done to others.

The time was to come when the victorious Medes and Persians would deal with the Babylonian babies just as the Babylonians had dealt with the Hebrew babies at the time the Jews went into captivity. The Babylonian babies would meet up with the same brutality the Babylonians had inflicted on others. Only thus could they be convinced of the sovereignty and power of the God of the Hebrews. So the chief motive for this prayer is not a vindictive desire for revenge; but, rather, it is an earnest wish that Yahweh would manifest Himself before the jeering world by catastrophically overthrowing the Chaldean power that had wrought such misery and needless woe back in the days of Jerusalem's demise.

It should, of course, be added that in our present age subsequent to Calvary, God has another way in which to show His terrible judgment on sin. He sacrificed His only beloved Son in order to atone for the guilt of all sinners everywhere. The overthrow of wicked, bloodstained political leaders and their degenerate followers still goes on even down to our present generation; but it is not quite so necessary now as it was before the coming of the Lord Jesus that God vindicate His righteousness and justice by spectacular strokes of retributive justice. Moreover, since the sinless Son of God has supremely manifested God's wrath against sin by offering up His own life on the cross as an atonement for the sins of mankind, it is not so imperative as it was in the Old Testament age for God to manifest His righteousness through penal judgments of a catastrophic kind.

It is less appropriate for New Testament believers to offer up the same call for vengeance as this psalm expresses. Nevertheless we must not ignore the passages found even in the latest New Testament book of all, Revelation, which in 6:10 articulates the appeal of the martyred saints from the time of the Tribulation: "How long, O Lord, holy and true, wilt Thou refrain from judging and avenging our blood on those who dwell on the earth?" As the arrogant godlessness of the End Time mounts to a Satan-inspired climax of brutality and bloodshed, it is appropriate to pray with great earnestness that God will intervene to crush the wicked and visit on a rebellious world the destruction that it so richly deserves.

Does the Bible class abortion with murder?

Surgical abortion was hardly possible until the development of modern techniques in the operating room; in ancient times the babies were killed in the womb only when their mother was also slain. An example is Amos 1:13: "Thus says the LORD, 'For three transgressions of the sons of Ammon and for four I will not revoke its punishment, because they ripped open the pregnant women of Gilead in order to enlarge their borders'" (NASB). But now that the United States Supreme Court has questioned the human status of a fetus in the womb until it reaches an advanced stage of gestation, it becomes essential to establish from Scripture what God's view is on this matter.

At what stage does God consider the fetus to be a human being, so that the taking of its life may be considered manslaughter?

Psalm 139:13 indicates very definitely that God's personal regard for the embryo begins from the time of its inception. The psalmist says, "For Thou didst form my inward parts; Thou didst weave me in my mother's womb" (NASB). Verse 16 continues, "Thine eyes have seen my unformed substance; and in Thy book they were all written, the days that were ordained for me, when as yet there was not one of them" (NASB). It is reassuring to know that even though many thousands of embryos and fetuses are deliberately aborted every year throughout the world, God cares about the unborn and takes personal knowledge of them just as truly before they are born as after their delivery. He has their genetic code all worked out and has a definite plan for their lives (according to v.16).

In Jeremiah 1:5 the Lord says to the young prophet on the threshold of his career, "Before I formed you in the womb I knew you, and before you were born I consecrated you; I have appointed you a prophet to the nations" (NASB). This certainly implies that God foreknew this lad even before he was conceived in his mother's womb. Apparently we human beings have an identity in God's mind that is established "from everlasting"—long before conception as an embryo. Second, the verse teaches that it is God Himself who forms that fetus and governs and controls all those "natural" processes that bring about the miracle of human life. Third, God has a definite plan and purpose for our lives, and each of us really matters to Him. Therefore anyone who takes the life of any human being at any stage in his life's career will have to reckon with God. "Whoever sheds man's blood, by man his blood shall be shed, for in the image of

God He made man" (Gen. 9:6, NASB). When does an embryo begin to be a creature made in the image of God? From the moment of conception in the womb, Scripture says. Therefore God will require his blood at the hands of his murderer, whether the abortionist be a medical doctor or a nonprofessional.

In Isaiah 49:1, the messianic Servant of the Lord is quoted as saying, "Yahweh has called Me from the womb; from the body of My mother He named Me." This raises the interesting question for the Supreme Court to answer: At what point in the gestation period of Christ in Mary's womb did the Lord Jesus begin to be the Son of God? At what time between conception and birth would an abortion of that Baby have amounted to heinous sacrilege? After three months? After three days? After three minutes? The angel said to Mary at the Annunciation: "The Holy Spirit will come upon you, and the power of the Most High will overshadow you; so the holy one to be born will be called the Son of God" (Luke 1:35). When did the miracle of the Incarnation take place? Was it not at the very moment of conception?

Luke 1:15 brings out a similar point concerning John the Baptist: "For he will be great in the sight of the Lord . . . and he will be filled with the Holy Spirit even from birth." We are not told at what stage in his mother's pregnancy that greatest of all human prophets (Matt 11:11) began to be filled with the Third Person of the Trinity; but it may well have been earlier than the stage set by the Supreme Court as being "viable." What we do know for certain is that at about six months of gestation John's mother, Elizabeth, felt him leap in her womb when Mary entered the room (Luke 1:41,44); for Elizabeth cried out with joy after Mary greeted her: "When the sound of your greeting reached my ears, the baby in my womb leaped for joy." The Third Person of the Trinity responded with joy when the future mother of Jesus Christ, the Second Person, came into the same room. How fortunate for the human race that no abortionist's knife came near either of those two embryos!

In earlier years of the current abortion controversy, it used to be said even by some Evangelical scholars that Exodus 21:22-25 implied that the killing of an unborn fetus involved a lesser degree of culpability than the slaughter of a child already born. This was based on an unfortunate mistranslation of the Hebrew original. Even the text rendering of the NASB perpetuates this misunderstanding, quite as much as the KJV: "And if men struggle with each other and strike a woman with child so that she has a miscarriage, yet there is no further injury, he shall surely be fined as the woman's husband may demand of him; and he shall pay as the judges decide. But if there is any further injury, then you shall appoint as a penalty life for life, eye for eye, tooth for tooth, hand for hand, foot for foot, etc."

In the margin the NASB acknowledges that $w^e y\bar{a}s^{e'}\hat{u}$ $y^e l\bar{a}dey\bar{a}h$ (which it renders "so that she has a miscarriage") literally means "her children come out." The same term used for a child from infancy to the age of twelve is used here: yeled in the singular, $y^e l\bar{a}d\hat{\imath}m$ in the plural. (The plural is used here because the woman might be pregnant with twins when this injury befalls her.) The result of this blow to her womb is that her child (children) will be aborted from her womb and (if she is fortunate) will come forth alive.

The second important observation is that the "further" inserted by NASB (in italics) does not appear in the Hebrew, nor—in the opinion of this writer—is it even implied in the Hebrew. The Hebrew as it stands (for the third clause) is perfectly clear: "and there is no injury" ($w^e l\bar{o}'$ $yihyeh$ $'\bar{a}s\hat{o}n$). Thus the whole sentence really should be translated "And when men struggle together and strike a pregnant woman [or 'wife'] and her children come forth, but there is no injury, he shall be certainly fined, as the husband of the woman shall impose on him, and he shall give [or 'pay'] in [the presence of] the judges; but if there shall be an injury, then you shall pay life for life [*nepeš taḥaṭ nāpeš*]."

There is no ambiguity here whatever. What is required is that if there should be an injury either to the mother or to her children, the injury shall be avenged by a like injury to the assailant. If it involves the life (*ne-peš*) of the premature baby, then the assailant shall pay for it with his life. There is no second-class status attached to the fetus under this rule; he is avenged just as if he were a normally delivered child or an older person: life for life. Or if the injury is less, but not serious enough to involve inflicting a like injury on the offender, then he may offer compensation in monetary damages, according to the amount prescribed by the husband of the injured woman. Monetary damages usually are required when a baby is born prematurely, for there are apt to be extra expenses both for medical attention and for extra care.

If, then, the taking of the life of a human fetus is to be classed as homicide—as the Bible clearly implies—the question arises as to whether such homicide is ever justifiable. Naturally we are not talking about the imposition of public justice against offenders who have been officially tried and convicted of such crimes as the worship of false gods, infant sacrifice, witchcraft, blasphemy against Yahweh, first-degree murder, adultery, incest (execution for these crimes was to be by stoning, the sword, or burning at the stake [cf. Lev. 20:2–5,14,20,27; 24:15–17; Deut. 13:1–5, 15; 17:2–7; 22:22–24]). Such punitive

measures are to be classed as execution rather than homicide. But in a case of self-defense or of defending the home against a burglar during the night (Exod. 22:2), the taking of human life was considered justified in order to prevent an even greater injustice by allowing the criminal to victimize or slaughter the innocent.

There is no specific treatment in the Bible of the problem posed when the continuance of the fetus in the womb means a serious threat to the life of the mother. It may be reasonably concluded that an actual life is of more intrinsic value than a potential life—especially if the well-being of other children is at stake.

In most cases it turns out that babies who would have turned out to be so defective as to be incapable of a meaningful life die at childbirth or soon afterward. Nevertheless, there are some who never achieve human rationality and survive for a period of years. Unlike the ancients, we now have diagnostic techniques that can warn the obstetrician or the expectant mother that the uterus contains such a freak and that only a harrowing heartbreak is in store for the family and parents if the fetus is allowed to come to full term. Conceivably a case can be made out for the termination of its life by abortion. But this is a very dubious procedure to follow unless the malformation of the embryo is established beyond all doubt. It is usually better to let "nature" (i.e., the good providence of God) take its course.

In the case of involuntary conceptions such as rape or incest, while the injustice to the pregnant woman is beyond question, it is more than doubtful whether the injustice done to the unborn child is not even greater, should its life be terminated by surgery before it is born. The psychological trauma to the mother may be severe, and yet it is capable of being successfully handled by one who is innocent of wrongdoing and has no consciousness of personal guilt in the whole affair. It can be coped with by a submissive faith and trust in God for ability to handle the new situation created by the arrival of the baby. If the mother should feel unwilling to raise the child herself, there are many other childless couples who would be glad to adopt the little one and raise it as their own.

In the case of incest, adoption is almost obligatory, since it would be almost impossible for a child fathered by its grandfather or uncle to maintain any kind of self-respect if it should later find out the truth. Nevertheless this tragic consequence can be avoided through adoption, and it is very questionable whether abortion would be justified even under such an extreme circumstance as incest. The child's right to live should remain the paramount consideration in almost every instance. (Perhaps it should be pointed out in this connection that according to Gen. 19:36-38, the ancestor of the Moabite nation and that of the Ammonite nation were both born from an incestuous relationship—though in that special case the father, Lot, was hardly responsible for this offense.)

Proverbs

In view of Solomon's personal life, how could his writings be part of Holy Scripture? How could the Bible call him the wisest of men? (D*)

Solomon began his career on the basis of high ideals and lofty principles. First Kings 3:3 states: "Now Solomon loved the Lord, walking in the statutes of his father David, except he sacrificed and burned incense on the high places" (NASB)—as well as at the Jerusalem sanctuary of Yahweh, where he should have carried on all his altar worship (Deut. 12:10–14). In his solemn dedication of himself to the Lord for service, he modestly asked nothing for himself but the gift of "an understanding heart" (lit., "a hearing heart") so as to "judge Thy people to discern between good and evil" (1 Kings 3:9). God said He would give him "a wise and discerning heart, so that there has been no one like you before you, nor shall one like you arise after you" (v.12, NASB). In 1 Kings 4:29 [MT: 1 Kings 5:9] we read, "Now God gave Solomon wisdom [ḥo-kmāh] and very great discernment [tᵉ-bûnāh] and breadth of mind [rōḥa-b lē-b], like the sand that is on the seashore" (NASB). Verse 30 then states, "And Solomon's wisdom surpassed the wisdom of all the sons of the east and all the wisdom of Egypt" (NASB). Verse 31 affirms that he was "wiser than all men"—even wiser than the most famous sages before his time (Ethan, Heman, Calcol, and Darda), and his reputation spread throughout all the Near East.

The gift of wisdom bestowed on Solomon pertained particularly to matters of government—as a judge between quarreling litigants (1 Kings 3:16–28), as the builder of architectural and artistic masterpieces, as an inspired leader in public worship (at the dedication of the temple), as fortifier of city defenses and the formation of large armies with advanced military equipment, and as the promoter of worldwide commerce and a thriving domestic economy. The Lord also gave him wisdom in matters of science (all branches of botany and zoology), according to 1 Kings 4:33, and in the mastery of poetry and proverbial literature (v.32 speaks of 3000 proverbs and 1,005 songs).

The Book of Proverbs contains some of the finest teaching ever written concerning a godly and fruit-bearing life, and it contains repeated and eloquent warnings against sexual license and toleration of crime and collaboration with ruthless criminals. It teaches the fine art of getting along harmoniously with others, yet without compromising moral principle. There can be no doubt of the high caliber of Solomon's surpassing wisdom and skill as a teacher and as a leader in government. There is no good reason to doubt the inspiration of his three great works: Proverbs, Ecclesiastes, and the Song of Solomon.

On the other hand, we read in 1 Kings 11 how he engaged in plural marriage to utter excess, partly on the basis of diplomacy with foreign nations. Verse 1 says, "Now King Solomon loved many foreign women along with the daughter of Pharaoh: Moabite, Ammonite, Edomite, Sidonian, and Hittite women" (NASB). Verse 2 goes on to point out Solomon's sin in contracting all these marriages with pagan women, referring to Exodus 34:12–16 and its prohibition of marrying or covenanting with unbelieving heathen. Verse 3 records his enlargement of his harem to seven hundred wives and three hundred concubines and his consequent toleration of—or even cooperation with—the worship of the false gods that his foreign wives brought with them. His particular attention went to Ashtoreth of Sidon and Milcom of the Ammonites (v.5). Verse 6 concludes with this depressing report: "And Solomon did what was evil in the sight of the LORD, and did not follow the LORD fully, as David his father had done" (NASB). He even built a shrine for Chemosh, god of Moab, and one for Molech "the detestable idol of the sons of Ammon" (v.7).

Quite clearly, then, the gift of wisdom did not include the gift of faithfulness to moral principle, so far as his personal relations were concerned. He knew perfectly well that Deuteronomy 17:16–17 had sternly warned against the very vices he had indulged in: multiplying of horses, wives, silver, and gold. He was well able to instruct others in the wisdom of moderation and self-control, and he had a fine mental grasp of the insight that the "fear of Yahweh is the beginning of wisdom" (Prov. 1:7). But as he found himself invested with absolute power, boundless wisdom, honor, and limitless wealth to acquire or pay for whatever he wanted, he began to indulge his carnal desires without restraint.

In Ecclesiastes 2:10 Solomon confesses "And all that my eyes desired I did not refuse them. I did not withhold my heart from any pleasure, for my heart was pleased because of all my labor and this was my reward for all my labor" (NASB). He condemned himself to a life of experimentation with every pleasure or advantage that spells happiness to the child of this world. And yet, as he testifies in Ecclesiastes, he found that all this "satisfaction" brought neither contentment, happiness, nor a feeling of meaningful accomplishment after it was all over. Hence he was driven to see on the basis of his own personal experience, as well as on the basis of theory and revelation from God, that no activity or accomplishment "under the sun" (i.e., relating to this present sin-ridden, transient world, without reference to God above or the world beyond) amounts to anything but frustration, futility, and despair. "Vanity of vanities! all is vanity," says the Preacher.

The life of Solomon is a solemn reminder that wisdom is an attainment quite distinct from a sincere heart animated by a real love for God's will. Wisdom is not equivalent to godliness—"the fear of the Lord." And yet without godliness no wise man will use his wisdom to a consistently good purpose, so far as his own life is concerned. There is a radical evil in the human heart (Jer. 17:9), and it can coexist with a perfect knowledge of God's truth. There is no logical reason for Solomon to have defiled his personal life the way he did. It was simply that he allowed himself to be corrupted by his wealth and power, and he gradually sank into a state of alienation toward God without fully realizing it.

Nevertheless, at the end of his life, Solomon came to see that no attainment or enjoyment brought any real or lasting satisfaction if it was done for self and for this world—"under the sun." He found it all meaningless and empty, and he ended up with one big zero. From the tone of Ecclesiastes and its clear warning that it is profitless to gain the whole world and lose one's own soul, we are led to believe that Solomon tried to get right with God and repented of his unfaithfulness and folly in sinning against the light that had been given him. His legacy to all believers with a wandering, willful, self-centered heart was that any life not lived for God turns to dust and ashes, heartbreak and despair. Solomon concluded by saying, "Now all has been heard; here is the conclusion of the matter: Fear God and keep His commandments, for this is the whole duty of man" (Eccl. 12:13).

Our conclusion is this: The three books Solomon wrote are true and profitable because he was inspired by God as he wrote them. He was a man of surpassing wisdom but also of surpassing folly so far as his private life was concerned. And he himself came to recognize and bitterly regret this before he died.

Does Proverbs 22:6 always work for the children of believers?

Proverbs 22:6 says, "Train up a child in the way he should go, even when he is old he will not depart from it" (NASB). NIV renders the second line thus: "And when he is old he will not turn from it." Before discussing the practical application of this verse, we should examine quite carefully what it actually says. The literal rendering of the Hebrew $h^a n\bar{o}\underline{k}$ $lanna'ar$ is "Initiate, train the boy" ($na'ar$ refers to a young male from childhood until he reaches majority); the verb $h\bar{a}na\underline{k}$ does not occur elsewhere in the Old Testament with the meaning "train up." Normally the verb means "dedicate" (a house or a temple [Deut. 20:5; 1 Kings 8:63; 2 Chron. 7:5], or else a dedication offering [Num. 7:10]). This seems to be cognate with the Egyptian h-n-k

("give to the gods," "set up something for divine service"). This gives us the following range of possible meanings: "Dedicate the child to God," "Prepare the child for his future responsibilities," "Exercise or train the child for adulthood."

Next we come to what is translated "in the way he should go." Literally, it is "according to his way" ('al-pî darkô); 'al-pî (lit., "according to the mouth of") generally means "after the measure of," "conformably to," or "according to." As for darkô, it comes from dere$\underline{k}$ ("way"); and this may refer to "the general custom of, the nature of, the way of acting, the behavior pattern of" a person. This seems to imply that the manner of instruction is to be governed by the child's own stage of life, according to his personal bent, or else, as the standard translations render it, according to the way that is proper for him—in the light of God's revealed will, according to the standards of his community or his cultural heritage. In this highly theological, God-centered context ("Yahweh is the maker" of both the rich and the poor [v.2]; "The reward of humility and the fear of Yahweh is riches, honor, and life" [v.4]), there can be little doubt that "his way" here implies "his proper way" in the light of the goals and standards set forth in v.4 and tragically neglected by the "perverse" in v.5. Yet there may also be a connotation that each child is to be reared and trained for God's service according to the child's own personal and peculiar needs and traits.

The second line reads gam kî ("even when") yazqîn ("he gets old"—zāqēn is the word for "old" or "an elder"), lō' yāsûr ("he will not turn away") mimmennāh ("from it," i.e., from his dere$\underline{k}$), which seems to strengthen the interpretation "his proper way," "behavior pattern," or "lifestyle" as a well-trained man of God or good citizen in his community.

What this all adds up to, then, is the

general principle (and all the general maxims in Proverbs concerning human conduct are of this character, rather than laying down absolute guarantees to which there may never be an exception) that when a godly parent gives proper attention to the training of his child for adult responsibility and for a well-ordered life lived for God, then he may confidently expect that that child—even though he may stray during his young adulthood—will never be able to get away completely from his parental training and from the example of a God-fearing home. Even when he becomes old, he will not depart from it. Or else, this *gam kî* may imply that he will remain true to this training *throughout* his life, even when he gets old.

Does this verse furnish us with an iron-clad guarantee that all the children of conscientious, God-fearing, nobly living parents will turn out to be true servants of God? Will there never be any rebellious children, who will turn their backs on their upbringing and fall into the guilt and shame of a Satan-dominated life? One might construe the verse that way, perhaps; but it is more than doubtful that the inspired Hebrew author meant it as an absolute promise that would apply in every case. These maxims are meant to be good, sound, helpful advice; they are not presented as surefire promises of infallible success.

The same sort of generality is found in Proverbs 22:15. "Foolishness is bound up in the heart of a child; the rod of discipline will remove it far

from him" (NASB). This surely does not mean that all children are equally willful and rebellious and that all of them stand in need of the same amount and type of discipline. Nor does it guarantee that a person brought up in a well-disciplined home will never stray off into the folly of sin. There may be exceptions who turn out to be worldly minded egotists or even lawbreakers who end up in prison. But the rate of success in childrearing is extremely high when the parents follow the guidelines of Proverbs.

What are those guidelines? Children are to be accepted as sacred trusts from God; they are to be trained, cherished, and disciplined with love; and they are to be guided by a consistent pattern of godliness followed by the parents themselves. This is what is meant by bringing them up "in the discipline and instruction of the Lord (Eph. 6:4)." This type of training implies a policy of treating children as even more important than one's own personal convenience or social life away from home. It means impressing on them that they are very important persons in their own right because they are loved by God, and because He has a wonderful and perfect plan for their lives. Parents who have faithfully followed these principles and practices in rearing their children may safely entrust them as adults to the keeping and guidance of God and feel no sense of personal guilt if a child later veers off course. They have done their best before God. The rest is up to each child himself.

Ecclesiastes

How could such a skeptical book as Ecclesiastes be canonical?

It is often alleged that *Qōheleṭ* ("the Preacher," the Hebrew term rendered by the Septuagint as *Ekklēsiastēs*) represents a cynical departure from normative Hebrew faith. Solomon, the Preacher, expresses an agnostic attitude about what happens to a man after he dies: "For who knows what is good for a man during his lifetime, during the few days of his futile life? He will spend them like a shadow. For who can tell a man what will be after him under the sun?" (6:12, NASB). Or again, "I have seen everything during my lifetime of futility; there is a righteous man who perishes in his righteousness, and there is a wicked man who prolongs his life in his wickedness. Do not be excessively righteous, and do not be overly wise. Why should you ruin yourself?" (7:15–16, NASB). Extreme pessimism in the face of death seems to be conveyed by 9:4–5: "For whoever is joined with the living, there is hope; surely a live dog is better than a dead lion. For the living know they will die; but the dead do not know anything, nor have they any longer a reward, for their memory is forgotten" (NASB).

Taken in isolation, these above passages do indeed sound skeptical about the spiritual dimension of human life and the worthwhileness of earnest endeavor. There are some statements that sound almost hedonistic, such as "For what does a man get in all his labor? . . . Because all his days his task is painful and grievous. . . . There is nothing better for a man than to eat and drink and tell himself that his labor is good" (2:22–24, NASB). But this work is a masterpiece of philosophical insight that must be taken together as an organic whole, rather than its being taken out of context. Only then can its real contribution to the whole counsel of God set forth in Scripture be properly and intelligently evaluated.

A careful synthetic study of Ecclesiastes brings out the true purpose and theme of its author. After he has tried every other avenue to the highest value in human life, Solomon gives his personal testimony as to the emptiness and disgust that resulted from his tasting to the full all that the world could offer him in the way of satisfaction and pleasure. It all turned out to be futile and unworthy, completely lacking in ultimate satisfaction. "Vanity of vanities, all is vanity" (1:2). The announced purpose of his search for the *summum bonum* was to try out every type of pleasure or practical achievement possible (2:2–8), even including the achievement of top distinction in philosophy and knowledge (v.9). "All that my eyes desired I did not refuse them. I did not withhold my heart from any pleasure, for my heart was pleased because of all my labor and this was my [temporary and evanescent] reward for all my labor. Thus I considered all my activities which my hands had done and the labor which I had exerted, and behold all was vanity and striving after wind and there was no profit under the sun" (vv.10-11, NASB). In other words, it is as if this wise, wealthy, and powerful king had undertaken a trial of Jesus' later challenge: "What shall it profit a man if he gain the whole world and lose his own soul?" (Matt. 16:26). And so he set about gaining the whole world and the full enjoyment of all the pleasures and satisfactions that this life could give him, and he found that in the long run they added up to zero.

The key term throughout this book is *taḥaṯ haššemeš* ("under the sun"). The whole perspective is of this world. The natural man who has never taken God seriously falls into the delusion that "this world is all there is." Well then, replies the Preacher, if this world is all there is, let us find out by experience whether there is anything ultimately worthwhile in this world— anything that yields real satisfaction. The result of his extensive experiment, carried on under the most favorable conditions possible, was that nothing but meaninglessness and profound disappointment await the secularistic materialist. All his ambitions, though fully achieved, all his lusts, though fully indulged, lead only to revulsion and nausea. For him life is "a tale told by an idiot, full of sound and fury, signifying nothing."

The message that comes through loud and clear in Ecclesiastes is that true meaning in life is found only in a relationship with God. Unless there is in man's heart a sincere regard for the will of God and an earnest desire to carry out His purposes, man's life will end up a meaningless tragedy. "Although a sinner does evil a hundred times and may lengthen his life, still I know that it will be well for those who fear God, who fear Him openly" (8:12,

NASB). This life takes on real meaning only as an arena of opportunity for man to serve God before he steps out into eternity.

It is true that death overtakes the wise man and the fool alike, and all living creatures end up in the grave. After we are dead and confined in Sheol (or Hades), we have no more knowledge of what goes on in the world; there is no longer any opportunity for earning rewards (9:5), and our memory may be forgotten by future generations on earth. But the only conclusion to draw before we pass off this earthly scene is the need of coming to terms with God and His will for our lives. "Let us hear the conclusion of the whole matter: Fear God and keep His commandments, for this is the whole duty of man" (12:13). "Remember your Creator in the days of your youth, before the evil days come" (12:1). "Remember Him before the silver cord is broken and ... the pitcher by the well is shattered ... then the dust [of your body] will return to the earth as it was, and the spirit [or 'breath'] will return to the God that gave it" (vv.6-7). Otherwise, "all is vanity" (v.8), for "God will bring every act to judgment, everything that is hidden, whether it is good or evil" (v.14; cf. Matt. 10:26; Rom. 2:16).

If Solomon was not really the author of Ecclesiastes, how can 1:1 be correct?

Ecclesiastes 1:1 affirms that the book was composed by "the Preacher, the son of David, king in Jerusalem" (NASB). Yet many modern biblical scholars (Delitzsch, Hengstenberg, Leupold, Young, Zoeckler, etc.) believe otherwise. For example, G.S. Hendry states, "The author does not really claim to be Solomon but places his words in Solomon's mouth" (in Guthrie, *New Bible Commentary*, p. 571).

While it is true that the author does not call himself "Solomon" but only refers to himself as *Qōhelet* (related to the word *qāhāl*, "assembly," "congregation"), it does violence to the rights of language to assert that the author of this philosophical discourse does not claim to be the son of David, king in Jerusalem. While "son" (*ben*) occasionally is used of later generations (such as a grandson, great-grandson, or even remoter descendants than that), the other details the author gives concerning himself leave no doubt that he presents himself to his readers as being King Solomon himself. He refers to his unrivaled wisdom (1:16), his unsurpassed wealth (2:8), his tremendous retinue of servants (2:7), his unlimited opportunities for carnal pleasure (2:3), and his very extensive building projects. No other descendant of David measures up to these specifications except Solomon, David's immediate successor.

Most modern scholars admit that the *purported* author of Ecclesiastes is Solomon; but they maintain that this was simply a literary device employed by a later author, now unknown to us, who wished to teach the ultimate futility of a materialistic worldview. If this could be accepted as valid, it would certainly put in question almost every other affirmation of authorship to be found in any other book of the Bible. Some later, unknown author might equally well have pretended to be Isaiah, Jeremiah, Hosea, or the apostle Paul, simply as "a literary device to express his own views." If it were any other book than the Bible, this would have to be classified as forgery, a mere product of deception, which would render the actual author of such a spurious work liable to damages in a court of law. It is more than doubtful that a Bible that holds to such high standards of integrity and honesty and that was certified by the Lord Jesus and His apostles as being the infallible Word of God could be composed of spurious work by authors who paraded under assumed names.

The chief argument against the authenticity of Ecclesiastes as a work of the historic Solomon is drawn from the data of linguistics. It is urged that the language and vocabulary of this book differ markedly from other tenth-century B.C. works composed in Hebrew and contains many terms found in Aramaic documents (such as Daniel and the Talmud) or in late biblical or postbiblical Hebrew (such as Esther, Nehemiah and the Mishnah). Delitzsch drew up a list of ninety-six words, forms, and expressions found nowhere else in the Bible except in Exilic and post-Exilic books like Ezra, Esther, Nehemiah, Chronicles, Malachi, or the Mishnah. Zoeckler claimed that there are Aramaisms in almost every verse, but Hengstenberg found only ten demonstrable Aramaisms in the entire twelve chapters. From the standpoint of possible political and social allusions, the fifth century B.C. is suggested as a possible time of composition. But these scholars fail to discuss the problem that Ecclesiastes no more resembles fifth-century Hebrew works than it does those of the tenth century (apart from the Song of Solomon and Proverbs).

James Muilenberg ("A Qohelet Scroll from Qumran," *Bulletin of the American Schools of Oriental Research* 135 [October 1954]: 20) comments on the discovery of mid-second-century fragments of Ecclesiastes discovered in Qumran Cave Four:

> Linguistically the book is unique. There is no question that its language has many striking peculiarities; these have been explained by some to be late Hebrew (discussed by Margoliouth and Gordis) for which the language of the Mishnah is said to offer more than adequate support (a contention effectively answered ... in the *Jewish Encyclopedia* V, 33, where he points out the lin-

guistic affinities of Qohelet with the Phoenician inscriptions, e.g., Eshmunazar, Tabnith). The Aramaic cast of the language has long been recognized, but only within recent years has its Aramaic provenance been claimed and supported in any detail (F. Zimmerman, C.C. Torrey, H.L. Ginsburg) ... Dahood was written on Canaanite-Phoenician influences in Qohelet, defending the thesis that the book of Ecclesiastes was originally composed by an author who wrote in Hebrew but was influenced by Phoenician spelling, grammar and vocabulary, and who shows heavy Canaanite-Phoenician literary influence (*Biblica* 33, 1952, pp. 35-52, 191-221).

In weighing the force of the linguistic argument, it should be noted that a comprehensive survey of all the data—including vocabulary, morphology, syntax, and style—indicates that the text of Ecclesiastes does not resemble the literary style or vocabulary of any book of the Hebrew Bible, or indeed of any later Hebrew work preserved to us up into the second century B.C., when the earliest fragments of Ecclesiastes from Qumran are to be dated paleographically. The sole exception would be the apocryphal Book of Ecclesiasticus, which is admittedly composed by an author (Jesus ben Sirach) who was profoundly influenced by *Qōhelet* and tried to imitate its style and approach in many passages.

In the judgment of this writer, the only convincing case of affinity is that advanced by Mitchell Dahood, referred to by Muilenberg as quoted above. The reason for the peculiar vocabulary, syntax, and style seems to be found in the literary genre to which Ecclesiastes belonged—the genre of the philosophical discourse. If this particular genre was first developed in Phoenicia, and if Solomon was well read in this whole area of wisdom literature (cf. 1 Kings 4:30-34), there is every reason to believe that he deliberately chose to write in the idiom and style that had already been established for that genre. Dahood's evidence is quite conclusive. *Qōhelet* shows a marked tendency toward Phoenician spelling (which omitted vowel letters even for inflectional sufformatives), distinctively Phoenician inflections, pronouns, particular, syntactical constructions, lexical borrowings, and analogies of various sorts. The alleged Aramaisms turn out to be employed also in the Phoenician inscriptions as well; so they prove little in the way of a late date of composition.

As for Dahood himself, he tries to account for this close affinity to Phoenician by supposing that some sizable colony of Jewish refugees settled up in Phoenicia after the Fall of Jerusalem in 587 B.C., and then he suggests that it was this 'emigre' group that composed *Qōhelet*. But this theory is well-nigh untenable in view of Nebuchadnezzar's relentless pursuit of all Jewish refugee groups, even to the point of invading Egypt in order to massacre the Jews who had fled there.

Only one reasonable alternative remains. That period when Israel enjoyed the closest relations with Tyre and Sidon, on both the commercial and the political levels—and cultural as well (it was a Phoenician Jew named Hiram who designed and produced all the art work connected with the temple in Jerusalem, and large numbers of Phoenician artisans and craftsmen worked under his supervision)—was unquestionably the age of Solomon, that period when wisdom literature was most zealously cultivated. This was the era when Solomon composed his Proverbs, and he may have had a hand in popularizing the venerable Book of Job. From the standpoint of linguistics, then, and from the standpoint of comparative literature and the known proclivities of the age, Solomon's period in the tenth century B.C. must be regarded as the most likely time for the composition of Ecclesiastes. (For the various arguments from internal evidence and "telltale expressions" advanced by advocates of the late date theory, see my *A Survey of Old Testament Introduction*, pp. 484–88.)

Does Ecclesiastes 3:21 teach that animals have a spirit just as man does?

Ecclesiastes 3:21 reads, "Who knoweth the spirit of man that goeth upward, and the spirit of the beast that goeth downward to the earth?" (KJV). Since it is usually understood that the spirit of man is the focal point of the divine image in man that enables him to reason and respond to God religiously, it sounds a bit startling to hear that the "spirit" of an animal goes downward, as its body (like man's body) turns to dust in the grave (v.20). NASB alleviates the problem by translating it as "breath": "Who knows that the breath of man ascends upward and the breath of the beast descends downward to the earth?" But the basic problem still remains, for the term *rûaḥ* ("breath," "spirit") is used for both man and beast. This is true whether we understand v.21 as a question implying that there is real doubt as to where the "spirit" of man or beast really goes after death; or whether we are to take it as a regretful question, implying, "How many people really know this fact, that the breath of man goes upward and the breath of the beast goes downward, when they die?" (I personally incline to the latter interpretation, but it is possible that the author meant the question skeptically.)

In this use of *rûaḥ*, we face a familiar phenomenon in the history of the development of transcendental terms in almost every language. From the observation that a living man or animal breathes in and out as long as it is alive, it is natural to derive a term such as

"breath" and make it a symbol of life. Thus we have quite frequently in the Flood narrative the phrase *rûaḥ ḥayyîm* ("the breath of life") as attributed to animals, both those that drowned in the Flood (Gen. 6:17; 7:22) and those that were preserved in the ark (Gen. 7:15). In Genesis 7:22 it is even combined with *nišmaṭ rûaḥ ḥayyîm* ("the breath of the spirit of life"—*nešāmāh* being a word used almost exclusively for literal breathing and nothing beyond). The Egyptian phrase *ṯ̣w 'nḫ* ("breath of life," conventionally pronounced *tchau 'anekh*) occurs very frequently in Egyptian literature, and it is possible that Moses had this expression in mind and translated it into the Hebrew equivalent.

Here, then, we have a general, nontechnical use of *rûaḥ* as applied to animals possessed of life. I am not aware of any other passages where *rûaḥ* is used with respect to animals. Apart from the 100 times where *rûaḥ* is applied to "wind" or "winds," the rest of its 275 occurrences pertain to human beings, angels (who are essentially *rûaḥ* without any real, physical body), demonic spirits (who were formerly angels of God, before Satan was cast out of heaven), or God Himself: the Third Person of the Trinity is spoken of as *rûaḥ 'elōhîm* ("the Spirit of God") or *rûaḥ Yahweh* ("the Spirit of Yahweh [or, as mispronounced, 'Jehovah']").

As is so often the case with terms that began with a primitive and general meaning, it later became specialized so as to acquire a technical, figurative meaning on a metaphysical level. The observation that living creatures breathe leads to the use of "breath" as a term for "life-principle." From that point on it becomes a matter of usage whether to employ *rûaḥ*, *nešāmāh*, or some other word referring to air in motion as a symbol for the spiritual element in man's being—that which makes him distinctively human, as opposed to subhuman creatures that also have lungs and breathe. It is not because of some inherent root meaning, then, but because of established usage that *rûaḥ* became the technical term for the image of God in man, that capacity for thinking of God and responding to Him, that ability to comprehend the difference between right and wrong and make moral decisions, that ability to reason in a generalizing, philosophical manner, which distinguishes man from beasts. The corresponding term for this in the Septuagint and in the New Testament is *pneuma*. In biblical usage, then, *pneuma* became equivalent to *rûaḥ*. Appropriately enough, *pneuma* also was derived from the verb *pneō* ("to blow").

A closely related term for the non-physical element in man was *nepeš* ("soul"). This too was derived from a root idea of breathing (*napāšu* in Akkadian meant "breathe freely," then, "become broad or extended"; the noun *napištu* meant "breath" or "life"). But it became specialized to mean the individual identity of any living, breathing creature, whether man or animal (for both *nepeš* and *psychē*, its Greek equivalent, are used freely for beasts as well as men). The *nepeš* is the conscious center of emotions, desire or appetite, or inclination or mood. It is the locus of each man's personality and the point of reference for his self-consciousness. Gustav Oehler defines *nepeš* as springing from the *rûaḥ* and as existing continually through it (a statement that could not be applied to animals, however); individuality resides in it, that is, in the man's ego or self. It is interesting to note that *nepeš* with the appropriate possessive pronoun is the most frequent way of expressing the reflexive pronoun in a specific way. Thus "he saved himself" would be expressed by "he saved his *nepeš* [or 'soul']" (cited by J.I. Marais,

"Soul," in *The International Standard Bible Encyclopedia*, 5 vols., ed. by J. Orr [Grand Rapids: Eerdmans, 1939], p. 2838).

It is to be noted, therefore, that there is a distinction between "spirit" (*rûaḥ*) and "soul" (*nepeš*) in the Old Testament, just as there is between *pneuma* and *psychē* in the New Testament. These, in turn, are differentiated from the term for "body" (*bāśār*), which also (when used figuratively) has a psychological meaning as well as the basic physical idea of a literal, flesh-and-blood body. The *bāśār* is the seat of all sensations and the data supplied by the five senses: but it is also used in Psalm 84 in parallelism with *nepeš* as the vehicle of a spiritual longing for the living God. The same is true in Psalm 63:1: "My soul [*nepeš*] thirsts for Thee, my flesh [*bāśār*] yearns [lit., 'faints'] for Thee, in a dry and weary land where there is no water" (NASB). Again, in Psalm 16:9 it is used in parallelism with "heart" (*lēb*) and "glory" (*kābod*—a surrogate for *rûaḥ*, which is the divine element in man): "Therefore my heart is glad, and my glory rejoices; my *flesh* also will dwell securely" (NASB). Thus the "flesh" is capable of feeling satisfaction in a state of security in the loving presence of God.

The triune makeup of man is brought out even more clearly in the New Testament. In 1 Thessalonians 5:23 Paul expresses this prayer for his readers: "Now may the God of peace Himself sanctify you entirely; and may your spirit [*pneuma* = *rûaḥ*] and soul [*psychē* = *nepeš*] and body [*sōma* = *bāśār*] be preserved complete, without blame at the coming of our Lord Jesus Christ..." (NASB). Quite clearly the spirit and the soul are differentiated here as distinct elements of the human psyche, and man is represented as triune in nature. This is exactly what we should expect, if man was really created in the image of the Triune God (Gen. 1:26–27).

A clear distinction between *pneuma* and *psychē* is unquestionably implied by 1 Corinthians 2:14–15, which defines the difference between a believer who is dominated by the *pneuma* (the *pneumatikos,* "spiritual man") and the once-born "natural" man (the one dominated by his egoistic *psychē*): "But a natural [*psychikos*] man does not accept the things of the Spirit of God; for they are foolishness to him, and he cannot understand them, because they are spiritually [*pneumatikōs*] appraised" (NASB).

Similarly, in 1 Corinthians 15:44,46, the same distinction is maintained in reference to the transformation from a merely physical body (prior to death and resurrection) and a spiritual body (i.e., a body especially adapted to the needs and desires of the glorified spirit of the redeemed believer): "It is sown a natural [*psychikon*] body, it is raised a spiritual [*pneumatikon*] body" (NASB). In v.46 we read, "However, the spiritual is not first, but the natural; then the spiritual . . ." (NASB). Quite clearly then, the spirit is distinct from the soul, or else these verses add up to tautological nonsense. We therefore conclude that man is not dichotomic (to use the technical theological term) but trichotomic. (The fullest discussion of this question may be found in Franz Delitzsch, *A System of Biblical Psychology,* reprint ed. [Grand Rapids: Baker, 1966].)

Song of Solomon

How did such a book as Song of Solomon get to be part of the Bible?

There is no denying that the Song of Solomon (or Song of Songs, or Canticles, as it is variously called) is a very different book from the rest of the Bible. Its theme is not doctrine but inner feeling—that most exciting and uplifting of all emotions, the emotion of love. Love is that which knits two souls together into a larger unity, an organic partnership that responds to and reflects the love of God for His children and the love of Christ for His chosen bride, the church. The importance of Canticles is that it is a book about love, especially love between husband and wife as a paradigm of the love between the Savior and His redeemed people.

Many times this sacred, typical character of marriage is referred to in Scripture. In Isaiah 54:4-6 the Lord addresses His sinful, straying, chastened people Israel in terms of an aggrieved but graciously forgiving husband: "Fear not for you will not be put to shame... and the reproach of your widowhood [i.e., the period of alienation from Yahweh during the Babylonian exile] you will remember no more. For your husband is your Maker, whose name is Yahweh of hosts; and your Redeemer is the Holy One of Israel.... For Yahweh has called you, like a wife forsaken and grieved in spirit, even like a wife of one's youth when she is rejected."

In other words, the deep, emotional commitment of a good husband toward the wife he adores bears a typical relationship (albeit a faint and finite one) to the inexhaustible and eternal love that God has toward His redeemed (cf. Eph. 3:18-19). This is spelled out most fully in the classic passage from Ephesians 5:21-27 (NIV): "Submit to one another out of reverence for Christ. Wives, submit to your husbands as to the Lord. For the husband is the head of the wife as Christ is head of the church, his body, of which he is the Savior....Husbands, love your wives, just as Christ loved the church and gave himself up for her to make her holy, cleansing her by the washing with water through the word, and to present her to himself as a radiant church without stain or wrinkle or any other blemish, but holy and blameless" (NIV).

From this perspective, then, we turn to the Song of Solomon and its lyric, emotional imagery, which is constructed like some mood-creating symphony, written by a musical genius and performed by a magnificent orchestra. It is a heart-stirring account of Solomon's romance with a humble but surpassingly beautiful girl from the country, perhaps from Shunem up in the territory of Issachar (the Septuagint renders "Shulamite" in 6:13 as *Sounamitis*, "Shunemite"). It may be that Solomon originally wooed her in the garb of a shepherd and thus came to know her as she was tending her sheep in an adjacent field.

It is quite possible that in the earlier part of his reign, at least, Solomon took time off from his official duties to enjoy a vacation in the country (apparently in an estate at Baal-hamon—8:11). His preference was for the tending of sheep, vines, and flowers, rather than golfing, fishing, boating, or tennis (such as our modern executives enjoy). So he spent a few weeks away from Jerusalem incognito. (Some scholars prefer to introduce some local swain who was a shepherd by profession and who became a successful rival to the king for the girl's affections; but this is very hard to sustain from the wording of the text itself, and it is most unlikely that Solomon, the apparent author of this production, would have written up this episode as a monument to his own defeat in love.)

As he picked up an acquaintance with this charming young shepherdess, Solomon found himself unexpectedly falling in love; and she apparently became deeply enamored of him before she discovered his true identity. As he secured her hand in marriage, he took her off with him to Jerusalem and the splendors of his court. There she was faced with the sixty wives and eighty concubines who already made up his harem, and in these palace surroundings she felt abashed at the unfashionable deep tan she had picked up from her outdoor life, to which she had been compelled by her own brothers (1:6).

The memoir Solomon wrote of this deeply meaningful episode in his life, in which he experienced the most authentic relationship of love he was ever to know, has been recorded for us in an amazingly beautiful way by this consummately gifted poet. Although through his foolish self-indulgence this misguided polygamist failed to live up to the exalted insights to which this lovely girl had brought him, he gave us an unsurpassable expression to the glory of a love that reflects the incomparable love of God. "Many waters cannot quench love; rivers cannot wash it away. If one were to give all the wealth of his house for love, it would be utterly scorned" (8:7, NIV).

The poet has not followed a strict logical or chronological order in the way he has brought his material together; rather, there is an emotional stream-of-consciousness technique throughout these eight chapters. This greatly resembles the recurrent flashback technique followed by certain television shows of our own day. But if the basic guidelines and presuppositions we have suggested above are borne in mind, the various components come together in a coherent and convincing way. Try it again, dear reader, maybe you will like it! And please bear in mind, as you go through passages like 4:1-5 and 7:1-9, that a beautiful woman who loves the Lord is God's supreme masterpiece of artistry; and external though that beauty may be, it serves as a fitting symbol of the spiritual loveliness of the temple of the Lord to which the body of every true believer has been transformed as a habitation of the Holy Spirit of God. The woman's viewpoint finds expression equally eloquent in 2:3-6 and 5:10-16—although a male reader may not find himself emotionally attuned to respond to those passages as well as a woman can.

The Song of Solomon serves as a reminder to all believers that God rejoices in His handiwork and knows how to invest it with thrilling beauty that deserves a full and proper appreciation. Yet along with this warm response to all that God has made beautiful—whether landscape, sky, sea, the magnificent trees, gorgeous flowers, or the transient charms of human loveliness, we must never forget to give all the glory and worship to the One who fashioned them so. We must always remember to exalt the Creator above all His creation and above all His creatures.

Isaiah

What solid evidence is there for the unity of *Isaiah*?

Isaiah 6:11–13 records a revelation made by God to Isaiah at the beginning of his prophetic ministry (ca. 739 B.C.). After he heard God's call and had been commissioned to preach to a people who would only harden their hearts against the truth, he asked the Lord with troubled heart, "Lord, how long?" Then Yahweh answered him, "Until cities are devastated and without inhabitant, houses are without people, and the land is utterly desolate, the LORD has removed men far away, and the forsaken places are many in the midst of the land" (NASB). Here we have a clear prediction of the total devastation and depopulation of Judah meted out by Nebuchadnezzar in 587 B.C., over 150 years later! This is of extreme importance as evidence, since all scholars of every viewpoint admit that Isaiah 6 is an authentic work of the eighth-century Isaiah.

Continuing on in v.13, we read of the return of a remnant of the exiles back to the land of Israel, to found a new commonwealth from which "a holy seed" (*zera' qōḏeš*) will arise. Literally translated, v.13 says, "But [there will] still be a tenth-part in it [i.e., the exiled people], and it will return [*wᵉšāḇāh*] and it will be for burning [i.e., subjected to fiery trials], like a terebinth or like an oak, which in [their] felling [still have] a root-stump in them, a holy seed [shall be] its root-stump." In other words, although the parent tree was hewn down by the Chaldean conquest and deportation in 587, yet from around the base of the stump a new sucker would spring up that would some day grow into a strong and vigorous tree. That is to say, the Fall of Jerusalem and the destruction of Solomon's temple would not really mean the end for God's people. After their exile, they would return and establish a new state for God and prepare the way for the Holy Seed.

Crucial to this interpretation is the translation of *wᵉšāḇāh*, which is often construed to have mere adverbial force, tantamount to "again" (i.e., "and it will again be subject to burning"). But in this case we have proof positive that Isaiah himself did not so interpret it. On the contrary, he must have understood it as meaning "It shall return" (from the verb *šûḇ*, "to return"). We know this because of the name he gave to his firstborn son, Shear-jashub, mentioned just three verses later. That name means "a remnant will return," as all scholars admit. Where did Isaiah learn about an exile from which the future people of Israel would return? From 6:13! The same verb *šûḇ* is used both in 6:13 and in 7:3. This leaves no ground for doubt, then, that back in 739 B.C. Isaiah the prophet knew by revelation what was going to happen in 587 B.C., when Jerusalem fell, and also what would happen in 537 B.C., when the exiles would return from Babylon to the Holy Land by permission of

King Cyrus of Persia—an event that was not to occur until more than two hundred years later.

Isaiah 6:13 therefore destroys the basic premise of the entire Deutero-Isaiah theory, which assumes that it would be impossible for an eighth-century Hebrew prophet to foretell or even foreknow the events of 587 and and 539-537 B.C. (the Fall of Babylon and the return of the first settlers to Jerusalem). It was on this premise that J.C. Doederlein (1745-92) built his entire argument and based his case for some unknown author living quite near to 539 B.C., who began his prophetic composition with chapter 40 (with its awareness that the Babylonian exile has taken place and that there is now a prospect of their return to Palestine) and ending with chapter 66.

In other words, Doederlein assumed that no genuine predictive prophecy was possible, and that no eighth-century prophet could have seen that far into the future. His theory was built on antisupernatural presuppositions, and so also were the elaborations of this theory by J.G. Eichhorn (ca. 1790), H.F.W. Gesenius (ca. 1825), E.F.K. Rosenmueller (ca. 1830), and Bernhard Duhm (ca. 1890)—who opted for three Isaiahs instead of just two. Every one of them assumed the impossibility of genuine prophecy by a personal God; therefore every apparent evidence of it had to be explained away as "prophecy after the fulfillment" (*vaticinium ex eventu*). But Isaiah 6:13 cannot be explained away as prediction concocted after the event since its time of composition was unquestionably in the 730s B.C.

Second, the internal evidence of Isaiah 40-66 speaks decisively against the possibility of post-exilic composition. Many of the same evils deplored and denounced by Isaiah 1 and 5 are still prevalent in "Deutero-Isaiah." Compare Isaiah 1:15: "Yea, when you make many prayers, I will not hear [you]; your hands are full of blood" and 59:3,7: "For your hands are defiled with blood, and your fingers with iniquity; your lips have spoken lies, your tongue has muttered perverseness....Their feet run to evil, and they make haste to shed innocent blood." Compare also Isaiah 10:1-2 with Isaiah 59:4-9.

Moreover, there is a revolting hypocrisy that corrupts the religious life of the nation. Compare 29:13: "Forasmuch as this people draw near me with their mouth, and with their lips do honour me, but have removed their heart far from me, and their fear toward me is taught by the precept of men" and Isaiah 58:2,4: "Yet they seek me daily, and delight to know my ways, as a nation that did righteousness, and forsook not the ordinance of their God; they ask of me the ordinances of justice; they take delight in approaching to God.... Behold, ye fast for strife and debate, and to smite with the fist of wickedness."

Third, idolatry is set forth in Isaiah 40-66 as a current vice in Israel. The prophet addresses his countrymen as flagrant idol worshipers in 57:4-5: "Against whom do ye sport yourselves? ... Enflaming yourselves with idols under every green tree, slaying the children in the valleys under the clifts of the rocks?" Compare with this Isaiah 1:29: "They shall be ashamed of the oaks which ye have desired" (oak groves being the setting for ritual prostitution and excesses connected with Baal worship). The reference to infant sacrifice suggests the conditions prevailing during the reign of Manasseh (697-642 B.C.), who made a practice of sacrificing babies to Moloch and Adrammelech in the Valley of Hinnom (2 Kings 21:6; 2 Chron. 33:6). Isaiah 57:7 makes a clear allusion to sacrifice on the "high places," which was practiced in Judah during the time of Ahaz (743-728 B.C.) and Manasseh. Again, in Isaiah 65:2-4 we read: "'I have spread out my hands all the day to a rebellious people.... a people that provoke me to my face continually, sacrificing in gardens and burning incense upon bricks; that sit among the graves and lodge in the secret places; that eat swine's flesh; the abomination, and the mouse. They shall come to an end, all of them,' says Yahweh."

These references to the practice of idolatry by the Israelites demonstrate conclusively that the author is writing in a historical setting prior to the Babylonian exile. This is so for two reasons.

First, the mountainous terrain, the high and lofty hills, are not to be found in Babylonia at all; for there is nothing but a broad, flat, alluvial plain. Moreover, the trees that are mentioned as possibilities for making wooden images out of and then using the scrap for the stove or fireplace—the cedar, the cypress, and the oak (41:19; 44:14)—are all unknown to Babylonia. Therefore, if we have any respect at all to the internal evidence of the text itself, we have to conclude (Doederlein to the contrary notwithstanding) that Isaiah 40–66 could never have been composed in Babylonia.

Second, the references to idol worship exclude the possibility (advocated by Duhm and many of the later scholars) that Isaiah 40–66 was really composed *after* the Fall of Jerusalem, up in Lebanon, and partly back in Judah, after the Fall of Babylon. The reason that this possibility is excluded is that only the earnest, pious men of religious conviction were involved in the resettlement of Jerusalem and Judah after Cyrus gave permission for the Jewish exiles to return to their homeland. Only a mere 10 percent of them responded to the invitation (about fifty thousand in all), and their expressed purpose was to reestablish a commonwealth dedicated to the worship and service of Yahweh as the one true God.

We have positive control evidence that no idolatry was practiced in post-Exilic Judah within the sixth and fifth centuries BC. That evidence comes from the writings of Haggai, Zechariah, Ezra, Nehemiah, and Malachi. In the prophecies and historical records of these five post-Exilic authors, we meet with a good deal of denunciation of sins that were prevalent among their countrymen at that time; but there is never a mention of idolatry in Israel. There was intermarriage with foreign women of idolatrous background, there was oppression of the poor by the rich, there was desecration of the Sabbath, there was a withholding of tithes, and there was the presentation of diseased or defective animals on the altar to God. But there was never a mention of idolatry—which had been emphasized by the pre-Exilic prophets as the cardinal sin of the nation, the very particular sin for which God would bring down on them the weight of His wrath and the total destruction of their country. There is no other logical deduction to draw from the evidence of the text of Isaiah 40–66 but that it demands a pre-Exilic setting, which absolutely destroys the Deutero-Isaiah and the Trito-Isaiah theories. Such antisupernatural hypotheses can be maintained only in the teeth of the objective evidence of the Hebrew text, on which they were allegedly founded.

The final consideration we adduce at this point is the attitude of Christ and the New Testament authors toward the authorship of the Book of Isaiah. Consider the following: (1) Matthew 12:17–18 quotes Isaiah 42:1 as "that which was spoken by Isaiah the prophet." (2) Matthew 3:3 quotes Isaiah 40:3 as "spoken by the prophet Isaiah." (3) Luke 3:4 quotes Isaiah 40:3–5 as "in the book of the words of Isaiah the prophet." (4) Acts 8:28 reports that the Ethiopian eunuch was "reading Isaiah the prophet," specifically Isaiah 53:7–8. He then inquired of Philip, "Of whom is the prophet speaking, of himself or of some other man?" (5) Romans 10:20 quotes Isaiah 65:1, stating, "Isaiah is very bold and says. . . ." (6) In John 12:38–41 we find two quotations from Isaiah: Isaiah 53:1 (in v.38) and Isaiah 6:9–10 (in v.40). Then in v.41 John affirms concerning these two verses, one from Isaiah "I" and the other from Isaiah "II": "These things Isaiah said when he saw His glory and spoke of Him." This surely implies that the inspired apostle believed that both Isaiah 6 and Isaiah 53 were written by the same Isaiah.

In view of this decisive New Testament testimony, it is hard to see how those who claim to be Evangelical can espouse the Deutero-Isaiah theory, or even regard it as a legitimate option for Evangelicals to hold. Or are there really Evangelicals who can embrace antisupernatural theories that completely deny the possibility of predictive prophecy and still call themselves Evangelical? It is questionable whether they can do so with integrity!

How can Isaiah 7:14 be considered a prophecy of the virgin birth of Christ? Isaiah 7:16 seems to preclude this entirely, and Isaiah 8:3 seems to fulfill the prophecy. (D*)

In a time of great national crisis, the kingdom of Judah was threatened with conquest by the northern alliance of apostate Samaria and pagan Damascus (Isa. 7:4–6). Had they succeeded, Judah would have become a mere satellite to Samaria and later would have been destroyed as a nation by the Assyrian invaders (who destroyed Samaria itself within fifteen years of this time).

Since Judah was governed by a wicked and ungodly king named Ahaz, its position as the one Bible-believing nation on the face of the earth was gravely imperiled. Therefore its great-

est need was for a deliverer who would rescue it from sin and exalt it to a position of great spiritual force, witnessing to the rest of mankind about the way of salvation. In these prophecies concerning Immanuel, the Lord met Judah's needs.

Isaiah 7:14 promises that "the Lord himself shall give you a sign; Behold, a virgin shall conceive, and bear a son, and shall call his name Immanuel [i.e., 'God with us']." Who is this sign to be? In what sense will he be "God with us"? From the references that follow, it is quite apparent that there is to be a *type* of Immanuel who will be born in the near future as proof that God is with His people to deliver them.

Yet also an *antitype* will be born in the more remote future who will be both God and man, and He will deliver His people not only from human oppressors but also from sin and guilt. Furthermore, He will reign as David's descendant and successor forever and ever. Thus the twofold need will be met both by the typical Immanuel and by the antitypical divine Redeemer.

Isaiah 7:16 clearly refers to a child who is to be born within a very few years: "For before the boy will know enough to refuse evil and choose good [i.e., before he reaches the age of full moral responsibility], the land whose two kings you dread [i.e., Pekah of Samaria and Rezin of Damascus] will be forsaken" (NASB). Normally at the age of twelve or thirteen, the Jewish lad was considered old enough to assume full responsibility for his own sins; then he would learn to read and expound the Pentateuch as a barmitsvah (a "son of the commandment").

Now if this promise was given in 735 B.C., and if the time-indicator child was born within a year or so thereafter, then he would have been twelve by 722 B.C., when Samaria fell to the Assyrian besiegers and was permanently destroyed as a nation. Damascus had already been stormed and pillaged by the troops of Tiglath-pileser III in 732. This earlier date was also predicted, for in Isaiah 8:4 we read of the son who is to be born to Isaiah by the prophetess: "Before the boy knows how to cry out 'my father' or 'my mother,' the wealth of Damascus and the spoils of Samaria will be carried away before the king of Assyria" (NASB).

By 732 the boy who served as the type of Immanuel would be two years of age, and therefore old enough to say "Daddy" and "Mommy." Quite clearly this little son of the prophet who bore the God-given name of Maher-shalal-hash-baz (see Isa. 8:3) was to be the time-indicator for the fulfillment of this prediction of Judah's deliverance from the current crisis.

At the time Isaiah 7:14 was given, the "prophetess" mentioned in 8:3 would have been a virgin and would have been known to King Ahaz and his court as the woman to whom Isaiah (presumably a widower by this time, having lost through death the mother of Shear-jashub mentioned in 7:3) was engaged. Before they married, the Lord revealed to Isaiah that the first child he would have by this godly young woman would be a boy: and the Lord told him what name to call him: "Hasten to the booty, the spoil is running away!" (which is the meaning of Maher-shalal-hash-baz, intended as an encouragement to the Assyrian invaders against the Damascus-Samaria coalition).

By the time this boy reached the age of twelve the invaded regions of Israel would be so utterly laid waste by the Assyrians that much of it would revert to pastureland; and the erstwhile cultivator of orchards and wheatfields would find his property reduced to a mere "heifer and a pair of sheep" (Isa. 7:21), and he would be living on a diet of curds and wild honey (vv. 15,22). Clearly, then, Isaiah's second son was

to serve as the type of the coming Immanuel.

Yet it is also apparent from what follows that there is a far greater person in view, who will come as the divine-human antitype and will in His own person be Immanuel, God Incarnate. It is significant that Palestine is from that time on to be known as the land of Immanuel (see Isa. 8:8: "your land, O Immanuel"). This is something far more meaningful than the land of Maher-shalal-hash-baz. It is because of Immanuel that the people and land of Israel are guaranteed a key role in God's program of redemption. There will come that mighty Redeemer of whom it is promised in 9:6; "For a child will be born to us, a son will be given to us; and the government will rest on his shoulders; and his name will be called Wonderful Counselor, Mighty God, Father of Eternity [as the Hebrew *'ăbi-'ad* should properly be rendered], Prince of Peace." Verse 7 continues to speak of His messianic rule. Plainly, this refers to God Incarnate, the divine-human King, Jesus Christ, whose sovereign rule will eternally endure, because He Himself will never pass away.

In confirmation of this Christ reference of Isaiah 7:14, the New Testament says in Matthew 1:22–23: "Now all this took place that what was spoken by the Lord through the prophet might be fulfilled, saying, 'Behold, the virgin shall be with child, and shall bear a Son, and they shall call His name Immanuel,' which translated means, 'God with us'" (NASB).

Perhaps a brief comment should be made concerning the word for "virgin" used in Isaiah 7:14. The root meaning of *'almāh* is "maiden" or "young woman." It is therefore not as precise a word for virgin as the Hebrew *bᵉṯûlāh*, which is defined in Genesis 24:16 (in reference to Rebekah) as a young woman who has never had sexual relations.

Yet it is also true that in the seven occurrences of 'almāh in the singular throughout the Hebrew Scriptures, the word never refers to a maiden who has lost her virginity but only to one who is in fact unmarried and chaste—as in Genesis 24:43, where Rebekah the virgin (beṭûlāh) is also referred to as an 'almāh. By Hebrew usage, then, this word is about equivalent to the idea of "virgin," even though it is less precise than beṭûlah.

It should be observed that 'almāh was an ideal term for the twofold aspect of the Immanuel prophecy in Isaiah 7:14. The future mother of the antitype, Isaiah's wife-to-be, was a virgin up until the night of her wedding. But the Virgin Mary was a *virgo intacta* at the time the angel announced to her that she would become the mother of Jesus. Joseph had no carnal knowledge of her until after her firstborn Son was delivered, according to Matthew 1:24–25.

If Christ is God the Son, how is it that he is called "the everlasting Father" in Isaiah 9:6?

Isaiah 9:6 says of the coming Savior, the God-man Jesus Christ, "His name shall be called Wonderful Counselor, Might God, *Everlasting Father,* Prince of Peace." At least, this is the way it is usually translated. But the basis for so doing is very dubious, since the Hebrew reads 'abî 'ad, which literally means "Father of Eternity." It is true that both 'ad and 'olām are often used as constructs in an adjectival sense and might be so construed here, were it not for the context. The preceding portion of the verse stresses His sonship in terms suggestive of His incarnation, in such a way as to make an assertion of His paternity or paternal status within the Godhead seem quite incongruous. For this reason we should understand this phrase in the most literal way, that He is father of

(that is, the author of) 'ad, a term meaning "perpetuity," used at least nineteen times in connection with 'ôlām ("age," "eternity"). It usually points to the indefinitely continuing future and is often used to imply "eternal" or "everlasting," in much the same way as 'ôlām is. In other words, 'ad and 'ôlām seem to be nearly synonymous and may even be substituted for each other without any change in meaning.

In view of the above, it seems reasonable to understand the phrase 'abî 'ad as "Father of Eternity" in the sense of "Author of Eternity"—not in the sense of beginningless and endless eternity (such as would be predicated of God), but in the sense of all the stretch of time between the beginning of creation and its ultimate termination. In other words, this title points to Christ as the Creator of the world—the world viewed as a time continuum—the fullest statement of which is found in John 1:3 ("All things came into being through Him . . .").

Who is Lucifer in Isaiah 14:12? Satan or the king of Babylon?

The passage involved is rendered as follows: "How you have fallen from heaven, O star of the morning [mg.: 'Lit., Hêlēl; i.e., shining one'], son of the dawn! You have been cut down to earth, you who have weakened the nations!" (NASB). The title Hêlēl, which KJV (following the Latin Vulgate) translates as "Lucifer," is rendered Heōsphoros in the Septuagint (meaning "Dawn-bringer" and referring to the morning star); the Syriac Peshitta simply gives it as a proper name closely resembling Hêlēl, i.e., 'Aylel. A possible cognate in Arabic is hilālun, "a new moon." If this is derived from the root hālal in Hebrew (halla in Arabic), which means "shine brightly" (the Akkadian cognate ellu is an adjective meaning "bright"), then we may understand Hêlēl as meaning the "Shining One." Obviously this is a poetic name for the person or entity who is addressed in this passage (somewhat like *Jeshurun,* "the Upright," which is applied to Israel in Deut. 32:15; 33:5, 26; also in Isa. 44:2). (somewhat like *Jeshurun,* "the Upright," which is applied to Israel in Deut. 32:15; 33:5,26; also in Isa. 44:2). A similar designation for Assyria (or a specific king of Assyria) in Hosea 5:13 and 10:6 is *Yārē* ("Let him contend," or "[one who] contends"—from the verb *rî,* "strive, contend, dispute"). These appellations probably do not refer to any one historic personage.

Some speculation has been devoted to the various possibilities of identification of this king of Babylon with Nabonidus (as Duhm and Marti suggested) or Belshazzar, the last kings of Babylon; but the arrogant self-confidence and overweening ambition expressed in v.13 of this chapter can hardly be reconciled with the declining power and beleaguered status of Babylonia during the last two decades of its existence as an empire. Only Nebuchadnezzar himself could have entertained such extravagant ideas of achieving complete supremacy over earth and heaven. (O. Proksch argued for this identification in his *Jesaja I, Kommentar zum Alten Testament* [Leipzig, 1930].) But as W.H. Cobb pointed out ("The Ode in Isaiah XIV," *Journal of Biblical Literature* 15 [1896]: ad loc.), Nebuchadnezzar "was very far from being a cruel oppressor." J. Muilenburg ("The Book of Isaiah chaps. 40–66," in G. Buttrick, ed., *Interpreters Bible* [Nashville: Abingdon, 1956] ad loc.) contended that "in many ways it appears that the Babylonian rule was neither tyrannical nor oppressive, certainly not in comparison with the role of Assyria." (Seth Erlandsson, in *The Burden of Babylon* [Lund: Gleerup, 1970, pp. 109–27], has a fine survey of modern scholarly discussion concerning the interpretation of this chapter.)

This elimination of possible candi-

dates for identification with the "king of Babylon" in Isaiah 14:4–23 leads to the conclusion that this figure was really intended to be a comprehensive personification for Babylon as a whole, as one of the series of God-defying world powers that met its doom when its day of judgment came. It is highly significant that this oracle concluded (in vv.24–27) with a decree of destruction to be visited on "Assyria" in the land of Israel, and, indeed, on all the Gentile nations as well (v.26). This prophecy was therefore given to Isaiah sometime prior to the Assyrian invasion of 701 B.C., which resulted in shattering losses for the apparently invincible army of Sennacherib. Yet it also has in view the future rise and temporary supremacy of the city of Babylon, even though in Isaiah's day it was a mere subject province of the Assyrian Empire.

All this has a bearing on the identification of Lucifer, the Shining One, who is tauntingly addressed as the "son of the dawn" (*šāḥar*). His proud boast (vv.13–14) that he will ascend to heaven and raise his throne above the stars of God and sit on the mount of assembly in the recesses of the north (*ṣāpôn,* a possible allusion to the fabled Mount Ṣapûnu of Canaanite mythology, the Mount Olympus of the Ugaritic epics) points to a level of expectation far beyond that conceivable by any human ruler concerning himself. It is for this reason that *Hêlēl* must be identified with Satan himself, as the archrebel of heaven, who was cast out of God's presence and glorious abode and consigned to earth and hell as his proper sphere. The Lord Jesus seems to have had this passage in mind when, after receiving the report of His disciples' success in casting out demons, He declared, "I was watching Satan fall from heaven like lightning" (Luke 10:18, NASB). In the Greek this statement uses about the same words as the Septuagint of Isaiah 14:12, except that "lightning" (*astrapē*) has replaced "Lucifer" (*Heōsphoros*). We may reasonably conclude that Jesus identified Satan with *Hêlēl*.

How are we then to relate Satan with the "king of Babylon"? Plainly the king himself is viewed as human, for he is the father of descendants. Verse 21 proclaims the command: "Prepare for his sons a place of slaughter because of the iniquity of their fathers" (NASB). In other words, the Empire of Babylon will go down in defeat and ruin, and the survivors of the coming catastrophe (marked by the Fall of Babylon to the Medes and Persians in 539 B.C.) are to be decimated and forever bereft of political power. On the other hand, the fallen state of Chaldean Babylon (picturesquely described as a maggot-ridden corpse moldering in a grave, now brought down to inhabit Sheol [v.11]) is greeted by the spirits of the dead rulers of earlier civilizations with taunts and jeers. It is they who address fallen Babylon as the *Hêlēl* cast down ignominiously from heaven, after he has uttered his foolish and extravagant boasts. What we have here, then, is the defeat of Satan's henchmen mirroring the defeat of Satan himself. This clearly implies that the Wicked One was the animating and inspiring force that manipulated Babylon—and, in all probability, Assyria as well.

It is noteworthy that the four-empire statue of Nebuchadnezzar's dream, as set forth in Daniel 2:35, possesses a certain identity throughout all four periods involved, right down until the time of the End, when the fifth kingdom (the millennial rule of Christ) shatters the whole structure to pieces. In all likelihood it is Satan who is to be the integrative principle behind each of the four. It is for this reason that Babylon emerges in the End Time as the symbol of the corrupt world culture and world church, which is to be overthrown in a sudden disaster of unparalleled severity. Revelation 14:8 says, "And another angel, a second one, followed, saying, 'Fallen, fallen is Babylon the great.'" The fall of earthly Babylon is followed by the fall of the satanic dragon himself (Rev. 20:2). This seems to confirm the involvement of two personalities in Isaiah 14 as well, with both of them brought under the fearful judgment of almighty God—both the satanic principal and his human agents as well. It is very dramatic how this final moment of arrogant contempt and defiance toward the God of the Hebrews as expressed by King Belshazzar at his birthday banquet is brought to an end by the sinister handwriting on the palace wall, announcing irreversible and sudden doom, "That same night Belshazzar the king of the Chaldeans was slain" (Dan. 5:30).

Does not the explicit mention of Cyrus the Great by name in Isaiah 44:28 and 45:1 compel us to adopt a sixth-century date for this portion of Isaiah?

This question presupposes the inability of God to predict any future leaders in human history—by name at least. No logical reason can be found for this assumption, unless it can be proven that none of the other instances of specific naming in the Old Testament prophets can have been authentic either but are all the result of pious fraud. Yet such a contention can be easily refuted by the data of Scripture itself. In 1 Kings 13:2 it is recorded that a certain prophet from Judah, who visited Jeroboam's new sanctuary in Bethel (ca. 930 B.C.), invoked God's curse on this new altar at which Jeroboam was officiating and specifically predicted the name of the future king who would someday destroy this altar. The prophet specified that it would be a king named "Josiah." In 2 Kings 23:15 we read the account of how Josiah actually fulfilled this prediction around 620 B.C., over three hundred years later.

In Micah 5:2 the prophet names the birthplace of the future Messiah as being "Bethlehem." Now there is no possibility that Micah was composed after the birth of Jesus (ca. 6 B.C.). (Actual fragments of the Hebrew text of Micah in a third-century B.C. manuscript of the Minor Prophets were found in Qumran cave 4 [cf. F. M. Cross and S. Talmon, *Qumran and the History of the Biblical Text* (Cambridge: Harvard University, 1975), p. 406].) Since Jesus was unquestionably born in Bethlehem, the above-mentioned presupposition against specific naming is untenable.

Furthermore, it is important to observe that such a specific naming of captive Judah's future liberator was especially appropriate for Isaiah's own generation. During the reign of Manasseh, the moral breakdown and disregard of God's Word as manifested by all classes of Judean society made the doom of Judan and Jerusalem absolutely certain. The warnings of Leviticus 26 and Deuteronomy 28 would surely be fulfilled. But what reasonable hope could remain of the Israelites ever returning to their ancestral home once it had been completely depopulated and the survivors all driven off into exile? There was none whatever, except for a rather vague indication in Leviticus 26:40–45, and perhaps a few hints elsewhere in pre-Isaianic Scripture.

If the future generation living at the time of the Fall of Babylon in 539 B.C. was to have any clear confirmation that the God of Abraham and Moses was still watching over their national destiny, and was ready to do for them a work of restoration that had never been the experience of any other exiled nation, then they needed a very striking and decisive token of His continuing favor and care. This could hardly be communicated in any other way so decisively as if God back in Isaiah's time would actually specify the name of their liberator. As the discouraged and disheartened exiles could hear of the rise of Cyrus and his successive victories over the Medes and the Lydians, they would remember Isaiah's prophecy concerning this man and would have faith to believe that God would really do a new thing on their behalf and would restore them to their land.

The revelation of the very name of the future liberator is presented as the climax of the entire prophecy in chapter 44 of Isaiah and then continues on with this theme through the first portion of chapter 45. It cannot be regarded as a later insertion, for it serves as the capstone of the arch in the structure of the passage in which it occurs. Therefore, we may rest assured that it is an authentic prediction of a pivotal event in holy history, destined to take place over 150 years later than the date of the prophecy itself.

Jeremiah

How can Jeremiah 7:22-23 be reconciled with Exodus 20:24 and the rest of the sacrificial ordinances attributed to Moses in the Pentateuch?

Jeremiah 7:22-23 quotes God as saying to Israel: "For I did not speak to your fathers, or command them in the day that I brought them out of the land of Egypt, concerning burnt offerings and sacrifices. But this is what I commanded them, saying, 'Obey My voice, and I will be your God, and you will be My people; and you will walk in all the way which I command you, that it may be well with you'" (NASB). This sounds like a denial of any sacrificial requirements whatever back in the days of Moses, at least insofar as divine sanction is concerned. Yet many chapters containing these various provisions concerning offerings and sacrifices are introduced by the rubric "And Yahweh spoke to Moses and Aaron, saying, . . ."

Liberal scholars invariably point to the Jeremiah passage as proving that the sacrificial regulations of the Mosaic Code were unknown in the seventh century B.C. as having any sanction from God or from Moses himself. This deduction is totally without foundation, however. Jeremiah 7:22-23 refers quite clearly to what God said to Moses and the Israelites in Exodus 19:5: "Now then, if you will indeed obey My voice and keep My covenant, then you shall be My own possession among all the peoples. . . and you shall be to Me a kingdom of priests and a holy nation" [NASB]). Apart from the Passover ordinance in Exodus 12, which had nothing to do with offerings on an altar, no sacrificial requirements were made by God to the Israelites until chapter 20, when the Ten Commandments were promulgated and the first reference to a sacrificial altar appeared in v.24.

It should be carefully observed that the whole thrust of Jeremiah 7 is to the effect that for sacrificial worship to be acceptable to God, worshipers must come to the altar with yielded and believing hearts, with a sincere purpose to do God's will. Verses 22-23 then point out that in the very book that records God's deliverance of the enslaved Hebrew people from Egyptian bondage, the first essential was a heartfelt commitment to a covenant relationship to God. They were to understand themselves as a holy people, called out to a new life of total obedience to the known will of God. Apart from that surrender of heart, that pledge of their soul to live to the glory of God, no acts of ritual or formalized worship could avail to please God.

In point of fact, then, God never said anything to them at the beginning—"*in the day that* I brought them out of the land of Egypt"—about offerings or sacrifices. What He did emphasize to them was the commitment of their hearts to Him with a full purpose to obey His will. Without that purpose, acts of religion mean nothing but abominable hypocrisy. Isaiah 1:11–17 and Amos 5:21–26 teach exactly that same principle.

Which king is involved in Jeremiah 27:1–11, Jehoiakim or Zedekiah?

The Masoretic text reads: "In the beginning of the reign of Jehoiakim, the son of Josiah king of Judah, this word came to Jeremiah from Yahweh." The KJV adheres to this; so does the ASV, with the marginal note: "Properly, *Zedekiah*." The NASB has "In the beginning of the reign of Zedekiah the son of Josiah," with the marginal note: "Many mss. read, *Jehoiakim*." The NIV has "Early in the reign of Zedekiah," with the following footnote: "A few Hebrew manuscripts and Syriac . . . ; most Hebrew manuscripts *Jehoiakim*." The Greek Septuagint omits this first verse altogether and commences the chapter with v.2. Even v.3 of this chapter militates against the correctness of the Masoretic reading, for it reads, "Send word to the king of Edom . . . Moab . . . Tyre . . . Sidon by the messengers who come to Jerusalem to Zedekiah king of Judah."

How likely is it that an oracle of God would be transmitted to Jehoiakim in 608 or 607 B.C., at a time when Pharaoh Necho of Egypt was the overlord of Palestine (subsequent to his victory at Megiddo in 609), and Nebuchadnezzar had not even made an appearance in western Asia (his victory at Carchemish came about three years later than the beginning of Jehoiakim's reign)? Moreover, the actual contents of this oracle point to a collective embassage to Zedekiah, rather than Jehoiakim, sent to the Judean court by the surrounding nations (not including Egypt). It would seem, then, that the Masoretic text contains its own refutation of the reading "Jehoiakim" in v.1.

Textual authorities suspect that at some point in the transmission of the Sopherim-Masoretic text a scribe inadvertently copied in the words of Jeremiah 26:1 as the heading for chapter 27. This seems to be a plausible explanation for this textual error. The original copy undoubtedly read "Zedekiah" instead of "Jehoiakim" in 27:1.

Please explain Jeremiah 31:31, with its prophecy of the "new covenant." Does this prophecy refer only to the New Testament church, or does it await fulfillment in the days when Israel will be converted to faith in Christ on a national level?

This remarkable prediction very clearly found its first fulfillment in the raising up of the New Testament church in the days of the apostles, beginning with the outpouring of the Holy Spirit on the 120 believers at the Feast of Pentecost, after the bodily resurrection of our Lord Jesus Christ. Jeremiah 31:31–33 reads as follows: "'Behold, days are coming,' declares the LORD, 'when I will make a new covenant with the house of Israel and with the house of Judah, not like the covenant which I made with their fathers in the day I took them by the hand to bring them out of the land of Egypt. My covenant which they broke, although I was a husband to them [or, according to another interpretation, w^e'*ānōkî bā'altî bām* should rather be rendered 'so that I rejected them,' as Heb. 8:9 suggests],' declares the LORD. But this is the covenant which I will make with the house of Israel after those days,' declares the LORD, 'I will put My law within them, and on their heart I will write it; and I will be their God, and they shall be My people.'" (NASB).

The context of this passage in Jeremiah clearly refers to a restoration of national Israel after the close of the Babylonian captivity; the specific predictions of the rebuilding of the Tower of Hananel, the Corner Gate, the hill of Gareb, the wadi of the Kidron, and the Horse Gate that follow in vv.38–40 found a preliminary fulfillment, at least in the days of Nehemiah (446–445 B.C.), as attested in Nehemiah 3:1,24,28. But the inauguration of the new covenant itself awaited the bestowal of the Holy Spirit as a permanent indwelling Paraclete, according to the promise of Christ Himself in John 14:17: "You know Him because He abides with you, and will be in you" (NASB).

Jesus made it clear that the Spirit could not be bestowed on believers until after his death on the cross and His subsequent victory over sin and death at the Resurrection. "For if I do not go away, the Paraclete shall not come to you; but if I go, I will send Him to you" (John 16:7). The Holy Spirit was poured out on the church (which then consisted only of Jewish believers) at Pentecost (fulfilling the promise of Joel 2:28–32 [3:1–5 according to the Masoretic text]), and thus inaugurated in a miraculous, dynamic way the age of the new covenant. From then on believers are said to be dwelling places or temples of God the Holy Spirit (1 Cor. 6:19; 1 Peter 2:5), who is Himself the essence of God's law (tôrāh) referred to in Jeremiah 31:33. Because the Holy Spirit dwells within the souls or hearts of the born-again believers, that law is truly written on their hearts.

As we have pointed out, the church at Pentecost consisted almost entirely of Jewish Christians and so continued for some years, until the conversion of the centurion Cornelius and his household, when the Gentiles were welcomed into the fellowship of the redeemed. The Jewish apostle Paul made it clear in Romans 2:28–29 that in the age of the new covenant (even more clearly than under the old covenant, when Gentile converts were only occcasionally added to the ranks of redeemed Israel), God accepted those who were spiritually circumcised—whether Hebrews or Gentiles—as true Jews (that is, saved believers, children of God under the covenant of grace). He accounted them as true children of Abraham, by faith (Gal. 3:7,29). In the course of the apostolic age, the membership of the Christian church was recruited largely from the ranks of the Gentiles, both because there were more of them to recruit and because the gospel message was obviously superior to their degenerate pagan beliefs (the Jews already had the Old Testament). Note that Hebrews 8:6–13 applies this Jeremiah passage to the first-century Christian church, contemporary with the author.

On the other hand, it is quite clear that the raising up of the New Testament Jewish-Gentile church did not furnish complete fulfillment for Jeremiah 31:31–33. As we have already noted, the context shows that in the latter days national Israel is going to experience a life-transforming faith resulting in its becoming spiritually born again. This same promise is clearly repeated in Ezekiel 36:24–28:

> For I will take you from the nations, gather you from all lands, and bring you into your own land. Then I will sprinkle clean water on you, and you will be clean; I will cleanse you from all your filthiness and from all your idols. Moreover, I will give you a new heart and put a new spirit within you; and I will remove the heart of stone from your flesh and give you a heart of flesh. And I will put My Spirit within you and cause you to walk in My statutes, and you will be careful to observe My ordinances (NASB).

This gracious promise is in this context addressed to the captivity of Israel during the time of the Babylonian exile. Here again, then, there is a clear prophecy pertaining to Israel as a nation—the same nation that had prior to the Babylonian exile fallen into idolatry and unfaithfulness (under the old covenant). As we turn to the New Testament, which so strongly affirms a preliminary fulfillment in the raising up of the New Testament Jewish-Gentile church, we find that Paul likewise makes it clear that a national awakening and conversion movement is in store for national Israel in the last days. He reveals in Romans 11:25-27:

> For I do not want you, brethren, to be uninformed of this mystery [the restoration of Israel], . . . that a partial hardening has happened to Israel until the fulness of the Gentiles has come in; and thus all Israel [i.e., true, spiritual Israel—all the true children of Abraham by faith] will be saved. . . . And this is My covenant with them, when I take away their sins (NASB).

Here, then, we have a clear case of two-stage fulfillment of Old Testament prophecy. Jeremiah 31:31-33 has been fulfilled in the New Testament church; and it will be consummated in the last days when there shall be a major national awakening among the Jewish people, and they turn to the Lord Jesus as their true Messiah and Savior (Zech. 12:10).

It is stated in Jeremiah 36:30 that Jehoiakim "shall have none to sit upon the throne of David." Yet in 2 Kings 24:6 and 2 Chronicles 36:9 we read that his son Jehoiachin reigned in his stead. Isn't this a contradiction? (D*)

The point of this sentence of doom on Jehoiakim (who had just sliced up Jeremiah's written prophecies and cast them into the fire) was that he would have no dynasty to succeed him. In fulfillment of this condemnation, it turned out that in 597 B.C., when Jehoiakim died, his son Jehoiachin took over Jerusalem for a mere three months, before it fell to the besieging armies of Nebuchadnezzar. Probably there was no official coronation ceremony during that period of unrest as the siege continued. At any rate, that son was not permitted to remain on the throne of Judah from that time on; rather, it was Zedekiah, his uncle, who was installed as a vassal king under the Chaldean Empire, and Jehoiachin was dragged off to captivity in Babylon, from which he never returned.

It should be noted that when the Hebrew verb *yāšab* ("sit enthroned") is used of a king, it implies a certain degree of permanence rather than so short a time as ninety days. As Jehoiakim's son, Jehoiachin was not permitted to sit on the throne and carry on the career of the Davidic dynasty. On the contrary, he was removed; and no son or descendant of his was ever permitted to reign as king thereafter on the throne of David. Zerubbabel may have been descended from Jehoiachin through Shealtiel (see Matt. 1:12), and he may have exercised a leadership role after the restoration of captive Judah from Babylon; but he never achieved the status of king. (The later Jewish kings of the second and first centuries B.C., the Hasmoneans, were of the tribe of Levi and had no connection whatever with Jehoiakim.)

Was not Jeremiah mistaken in his prediction of a Babylonian invasion of Egypt (Jer. 43:7-13; 44:30)?

If Jeremiah had been guilty of false prophecy in regard to this important event, and if Nebuchadnezzar never really made an invasion of Egypt, then surely Jeremiah would have been exposed as a false prophet (cf. Deut. 18:22) and hence eliminated from all canonical status in the Hebrew Bible. The very fact that his writings were received and preserved as authoritative by the believing community is proof positive that the invasion actually did take place. The archaeological confirmation for this will be found in the article on Ezekiel 26, which also predicts the same coming event, Nebuchadnezzar's full-scale invasion of Egypt in the thirty-seventh year of his reign (ca. 569 B.C.).

Ezekiel

Was not Ezekiel mistaken in some of his prophecies? How then can his writings be accepted as canonical?

Ezekiel 26:3–14 contains a striking series of prophecies that foretell the complete downfall of the proud merchant city of Tyre, to be brought about by the armies of Nebuchadnezzar. Yet from 29:18 it is clear that Nebuchadnezzar had not succeeded in capturing the island city offshore from the mainland port of Tyre. Undoubtedly the inhabitants had removed their most valuable possessions from the old city when they saw that its defenses could not hold out against the Chaldean siege engines. They had conveyed these possessions by ship to their island fortress, which was securely protected by Tyre's formidable navy against the landings attempted by Nebuchadnezzar's sea forces. Thus he had experienced years of frustration in the vain attempt to capture that prize. By way of compensation the Lord promised the king a successful venture against Egypt.

A careful examination of 26:3–14 indicates a two-stage level of punishment for Tyre. Verses 3–4 predicted that "many nations would come up against" it and would break down its towers and walls. This fits in well with the Chaldean campaign and its thorough destruction of the mainland city. Verses 5–6 go on to speak of the removal of all the bricks and rocks and

everything movable from the site of that ruined city—a most unusual procedure in dealing with a city taken by storm. Generally such locations would be left a chaos of rubble rather than being swept clean.

Verses 7–11 specify that Nebuchadnezzar will capture, plunder, and thoroughly destroy the parent city on the shore. But v.12 seems to usher in the later phase, using an unspecific "they" as the subject of "shall make a spoil of thy riches." Continuing through vv.13–14, the specifics point very strikingly toward the later attack on the island city of Tyre that was successfully carried through by Alexander the Great (ca. 332 B.C.). History tells us that after Alexander's naval forces proved incapable of storming the island (due to the determined resistance of the superior Tyrian fleet), he resorted to an ambitious engineering effort, consisting of a mile-long mole built out from shore to the east wall of the island. In order to get material for this causeway, the Greek invaders used every movable piece of rock or stone to cast into the sea, until after several months of strenuous endeavor the wall was reached, broken through, and the city sacked. Exasperated by the long delay in his invasion schedule, Alexander resolved to make a fearsome example of Tyre; so he had the island city totally destroyed so that it should never be rebuilt (v.14).

In point of fact, the mainland city of

276

Tyre later was rebuilt and assumed some of its former importance during the Hellenistic period. But as for the island city, it apparently sank below the surface of the Mediterranean, in the same subsidence that submerged the port of Caesarea that Herod had built up with such expense and care. All that remains of it is a series of black reefs offshore from Tyre, which surely could not have been there in the first and second millennia B.C., since they pose such a threat to navigation. The promontory that now juts out from the coastline probably was washed up along the barrier of Alexander's causeway, but the island itself broke off and sank away when the subsidence took place; and we have no evidence at all that it ever was built up again after Alexander's terrible act of vengeance. In the light of these data, then, the predictions of chapter 26, improbable though they must have seemed in Ezekiel's time, were duly fulfilled to the letter—first by Nebuchadnezzar in the sixth century, and then by Alexander in the fourth.

But was the promise of Ezekiel 29:17–20 fulfilled? In vv.8–16 a general prediction of crushing defeat of Egypt at the hand of foreign invaders is foretold, with devastation inflicted on the whole stretch of territory from Migdol in the Delta to Assuan in the far south. This unhappy condition was to endure for forty years, with considerable numbers of the Egyptians fleeing to other countries for refuge.

Then in vv.17–20 a specific promise is made to Nebuchadnezzar personally. He will be compensated for his disappointment at Tyre by dazzling success in Egypt. He will penetrate to the refugee groups of Jews who fled from Palestine after the murder of Gedaliah in 582 B.C., abducting Jeremiah with them. Jeremiah himself predicted in Jeremiah 43:8–13 that Nebuchadnezzar would track them down there, both in Tahpanhes and wherever else they had settled in Egypt. There he would slaughter them or take them captive and would burn down the temples of Egypt.

The oracle of Ezekiel 29:17ff. was given to the prophet "in the twenty-seventh year"—which was probably intended to be the regnal year of Nebuchadnezzar himself, rather than that of the captive Jewish king Jehoiachin, even though in discussing specifically Jewish affairs Ezekiel normally does refer to Jehoiachin's reign. Since Nebuchadnezzar was crowned in 605 B.C., this would come out to about 578. Very likely this was the year of the first invasion of Egypt by Nebuchadnezzar, since this would allow for the forty years of affliction predicted back in v.11. Thus the Chaldean domination and maltreatment of Egypt came to an end in 539, when Babylon fell to the forces of Cyrus the Great. While it is true that Egypt kept up national resistance through it all during the reigns of their native kings, such as Hophra (Uah-ib-Ra) 588–569 and Amasis (Ahmose II) 569–526, they were not able to repair the severe damage inflicted on their land by the Chaldean kings; nor were they able to repel them at their borders.

The Greek historians received no information from Egyptian or Persian sources concerning this period of successful Chaldean aggression. But Josephus (Antiquities 10.9.5–7) refers to Nebuchadnezzar's conquest of Egypt around 582 B.C. While this date seems a bit early, there is little reason to condemn his whole account as fictitious. More recent discoveries of documentation in both Babylonian cuneiform and Egyptian hieroglyphics confirm Josephus in a remarkable way. A cuneiform tablet discovered by Pinches and translated by Pritchard (ANET, p. 308) dates one of Nebuchadnezzar's invasions in his thirty-seventh year (569 or 568 B.C.). There is also the biographical funerary stela of *Nes-Hor* in the Louvre, in which this commander in the reign of *Uah-ib-Ra,* though not furnishing us with an exact date, speaks of an invasion of the Nile Valley by an "army of northerners" and Asiatics who penetrated so far up the Nile Valley as to threaten the Ethiopian border.

These contemporary records from Babylon and Egypt serve to belie the skepticism of Ezekiel's detractors. But even they will have to concede that Ezekiel's long-range prediction concerning Egypt came true as stated in 29:15. After the forty years of Chaldean oppression were over and Babylon itself had succumbed to the Medo-Persian Empire in 539, there was but little respite for Egypt before Cambyses, the son of Cyrus, launched his invasion and proceeded to annex Egypt to his empire in 525. Despite a few brief intervals of independence, the Egyptians remained subjects of the Persian Empire right up until 332 B.C., when they were taken over by Alexander the Great and the Ptolemaic Dynasty that came into power after his death in 323. The Ptolemies ruled Egypt until Cleopatra's navy was defeated by Augustus at the Battle of Actium in 31 B.C. From that point on the Romans retained control right down to the Byzantine era, until finally the Arabs overwhelmed the Nile Valley in the A.D. 630s. In other words, there was no strong or enduring native Egyptian dynasty on the throne of Egypt from the time of Nebuchadnezzar until our present millennium; and in that sense it could be regarded as the "basest of kingdoms," according to Ezekiel 29:15.

As for the predictions concerning a future temple on the devastated Mount Moriah in Jerusalem, the main subject matter of Ezekiel 40–48, it is perfectly true that there has never been a real fulfillment of these chapters up until the present time. Nevertheless, as we shall show in a separate article, they will find their fulfillment on the threshold of Christ's millennial kingdom. If that is so, they can hardly be condemned as false prophecy.

Who was the "prince of Tyre" in Ezekiel 28? Did he have any relationship to Satan?

Very specific prophecies concerning the future of the Phoenician seaport of Tyre have been given in Ezekiel 26 and 27, predicting the destruction of the mainland city by Nebuchadnezzar (26:6–11) and of the offshore island city of Tyre by Alexander the Great in 332 B.C. (26:3–5, 12–14). The devastating effect on the commerce and economic prosperity of the various cities and nations that have traded with Tyre is set forth in 26:15–21 and all through chapter 27. The passages concerning the lamentation over the downfall of Tyre and the resultant ruination of world trade furnish a motif that is taken up on an even more impressive scale in Revelation 18, which pictures all the great merchant cities of earth mourning and sorrowing over the sudden destruction of latter-day Babylon.

These ancient trading centers, then, whether Tyre or Babylon, typify the collapse of the materialistic culture of the godless world in the End Time. All the luxuries and mercantile wealth for which that depraved civilization will have sold their souls will be stripped from them and leave them with nothing but disillusionment and despair. There is a sense, then, in which Tyre serves as an apocalyptic symbol of world overthrow in the final agony of the Tribulation.

From this perspective we move on to a consideration of chapter 28. The "prince" or "leader" (*nāgîd*) of Tyre is quoted in 28:2 as saying, "I am a god, I sit in the seat of gods, in the heart of the seas" (NASB). God replies to him, "Yet you are a man and not God, although you make your heart like the heart of God" (NASB). That is to say, in his folly and pride, this ruler of Tyre put himself and his material interests above the will and glory of God. In his imbecility he imagines himself to be more important than the Creator and Sovereign of the universe—as indeed every unsaved human being does who has not come to terms with the demands of God's lordship.

Tyre had become proverbial for its business acumen and brilliant success in pursuing its material goals. God says ironically, "Behold, you are wiser than Daniel [who had already risen to prominence by this juncture in Ezekiel's life]; there is no secret that is a match for you" (v.3, NASB). No other business capital could exceed Tyre in the acquisition of the luxuries and treasures that money could buy, and it was this financial supremacy that the witless world equated with real wisdom. This heady success had led the Tyrian people to the folly of self-deification. They imagined that their riches could buy them security and power without the need of divine protection or favor. "Because you have made your heart like the heart of God [that is, you imagine yourselves to be divine, and suppose that you are the captains of your own destiny], therefore, behold, I will bring strangers upon you, the most ruthless of the nations [i.e., the Chaldeans under Nebuchadnezzar]" (v.7, NASB).

Ezekiel 28:12–15 describes the self-flattering illusion into which the Tyrian state had fallen. To the king of Tyre, God says: "You had the seal of perfection, full of wisdom and perfect in beauty. You were in Eden, the garden of God; every precious stone was your covering: the ruby, the topaz, and the diamond; etc." (vv. 12–13, NASB). In other words, all the paradise that Tyre wanted was unlimited enjoyment of the costliest material treasures that money could buy. Having that, they supposed themselves to be enjoying heaven on earth. Verse 14 continues:

"You were the anointed cherub who covers [a comparison to the cherubim whose wings overshadowed the lid of the ark of the covenant in the Most Holy Place in the Jerusalem temple]; and I placed you there [i.e., God favored Tyre with this unparalleled prosperity on which its megalomania was based]" (NASB).

The Tyrians imagined themselves to be beyond reproach in their moral status because they considered wealth to be the reward and certification of ethical perfection—insofar as ethics really mattered in the world of the hard-headed businessman. "You were blameless in your ways from the day you were created [that is to say, that is how they viewed themselves], until unrighteousness was found in you" (v.15, NASB)! As their proud city finally succumbed to the Chaldean battering ram and the pillaging warriors from Babylon, they discovered how deluded they had been about themselves. They had thought they were safely settled at the summit of the mountain of God (or of their own god, Baal); but they were cast down from that mountain by the righteous judgment of Yahweh and plunged into the depths of humiliating defeat.

There is no possibility of identifying the leader or king of Tyre with any specific monarch in the Tyrian dynasty. Like the "king of Babylon" in Isaiah 14, this "king" serves as a symbol or personification of the government and people of the entire city-state of Tyre. As for a relationship with Satan, there does not seem to be any decisive evidence in the text that the Prince of Hell is being indirectly addressed through the prince of Tyre. There is hardly a verse to be found that could be applied to the Devil alone rather than to the human rulers of the city itself. Certainly the theory advanced by some writers that this chapter contains a flashback to Satan's personal career prior to his rebellion and expulsion from heaven is at best an unsupported conjecture. All the hyperbolic language employed in the verses discussed above can best be understood as the flattering self-delusion of the Tyrian millionaires and their money-loving leaders, whose concept of heaven rose no higher than their treasures of rubies and gold, and whose yardstick for virtue consisted of material wealth. Yet it should be clearly understood that in a very real sense every culture that has sold out to materialistic values is under the domination of Satan and is influential in promoting his cause. It will also share in his ultimate judgment and eternal destruction (Rev. 20:10).

What is the significance of the temple in Ezekiel's prophecy (Ezek. 40–44)? Since Jesus died to atone for the sins of the world, it is puzzling to read of the renewal of animal sacrifices once again at some future age. (D*)

This question rightly assumes that the temple prophecy in Ezekiel does refer to a future age, since it has never been fulfilled up until the present time. While it is true that there was a Jewish temple completed in 516 B.C., subsequent to Ezekiel's prediction (made about 580 B.C.), nevertheless there were many differences between the layout of the second temple and the specifications of this temple with its precincts. Herod's renovation, grandiose as it was, likewise failed to fulfill the requirements of Ezekiel's blueprint. No temple has stood on this site (apart from Islamic mosques) since the total destruction of the second temple in A.D. 70. Nor is it possible to construe these five chapters (containing even more detailed specifics than the description of the first temple in 1 Kings 6–7) as merely symbolic of the New Testament church, as Christ's spiritual temple.

How then are we to understand the sacrifices referred to in Ezekiel 43:18–27? This passage specifies burnt offerings ('ōlôt), sin offerings (ḥaṭṭā'ôt), and peace offerings (šᵉlāmîm), all of which during the Old Testament era before the Cross typified Christ's atoning sacrifice. Hebrews 10:11–14 explains to us that these Old Testament sacrifices were not inherently effective in and of themselves to remove the guilt of the believer's sins. They all pointed forward to our Savior's atonement on Calvary, and every offering presented by the Israelite believer was in the nature of a bank check drawn on the unlimited credit of Christ's future payment on his behalf. When His blood was finally shed on our behalf, then the guilt of all the sins of all redeemed mankind was effectually atoned for once and for all; and there was no longer any need (or even possibility) of propitiatory blood-sacrifice on any altar to God.

We may therefore be confident that the sacrifices mentioned in Ezekiel 43 have nothing to do with atonement for sin. Their function will be parallel to that of the Lord's Supper, which Christ established as a communion ordinance during our present church age. The Eucharist of bread and wine is only intended for this present dispensation, however. Jesus said, "This do in remembrance of Me. . . . For as often as you eat this bread and drink the cup, you proclaim the Lord's death *until He comes*" (1 Cor. 11:24–26). But during the age of the millennial kingdom, when our Lord Jesus Christ will come again to set up the rule of God over all the earth, what type of Communion ordinance will replace our present Lord's Supper with its bread and wine? Apparently it will be in the form of blood sacrifices once again, yet without any of the atoning function of the Old Testament period.

It is true that the same Hebrew terms are used in Ezekiel 43 as were employed in the law of Moses, but they will have a new meaning. They were used by the Old Testament prophet because they furnished the closest analogy to the millennial offerings that the Hebrew believer had any acquaintance with. But like so many other terms employed in connection with the end times, so these designations of sacrifice were sublimated and altered to fit the new conditions of the new age yet to come. Even so the millennial temple itself will have a triumphal or doxological meaning rather than a typical significance pointing forward to the atoning and sanctifying work of a future Redeemer. It will serve as a headquarters of worship and praise for all the citizens of the glorious, messianic kingdom, over which Jesus Christ will reign for a thousand years after He comes again to claim the earth for God.

Daniel

Must Daniel be dated in the sixth century?

With the possible exception of Isaiah, no prophet of the Old Testament presents such a serious challenge to the rationalist as Daniel. His book contains not only short-range predictions, like the seven years of Nebuchadnezzar's insanity (chap. 4) and the imminent Fall of Babylon to the Medo-Persian attackers (chap. 5), but also such long-range predictions as the four-kingdom sequence (chap. 2), the elaboration of that sequence and—with its emphasis on the last days (chap. 7, as well as in chap. 8, with its special attention to the third kingdom)—the prediction of the date of Christ's first advent and the framework of the Seventy Weeks (chap. 9), and then the detailed account of the confrontation between the Seleucid and Ptolemaic empires and the career of the two Little Horns (chap. 11).

In order to avoid the impact of the decisive evidence of supernatural inspiration with which Daniel so notably abounds, it was necessary for rationalistic scholarship to find some later period in Jewish history when all the "predictions" had already been fulfilled, such as the reign of Antiochus Epiphanes (175–164 B.C.), when such a pious fraud could most easily be prepared. In order to do this, however, it was necessary for J. D. Michaelis and J. G. Eichhorn (who in the eighteenth century revived the old Maccabean date

hypothesis of the third-century neoplatonic philosopher Porphyry) to make a few adjustments in the evidence of the text. For the actual text of Daniel indicates that the empire sequence was as follows: first kingdom: Chaldean; second kingdom: Medo-Persian; third kingdom: Greek; fourth kingdom: Roman. But since the Roman Empire did not take over the Holy Land until 63 B.C., it was necessary to eliminate that identification altogether in order to preserve the rational defensibility of a Maccabean date hypothesis. The Maccabean period would have been around 167 to 165 B.C., or over a hundred years before Pompey seized Palestine for the Romans; so that would have allowed a successful prediction to remain in the Book of Daniel, a hundred years in advance of the fulfillment. Consequently the effort was made to prove that the fourth kingdom was Greek rather than Roman and that the true sequence was Chaldean, Median, Persian, and Greek. Otherwise the late date theory could not survive, for it was not late enough to account for Pompey.

In the article on "Darius the Mede," we will furnish the evidence for the rejection of that revised identification and demonstrate that the fourth kingdom has to be Rome after all. But in this preliminary discussion we shall be centering our attention on the linguistic evidence in Daniel that tends to eliminate all possibility of dating the composition of Daniel any later than the Persian period. With the wealth of new data from the manuscripts of the Dead Sea caves (the Qumran literature), it is possible to settle this question once and for all. Now that we have at least one fairly extensive midrash originally composed in third-century B.C. Aramaic and several sectarian documents in second-century Hebrew, it has become possible to perform a careful linguistic comparison of the Aramaic and Hebrew chapters of Daniel and these unquestionably·third- or second-century B.C. documents, which were close to the era of the Maccabean struggle.

If Daniel had in fact been composed in the 160s, these Qumran manuscripts should have exhibited just about the same general characteristics as Daniel in the matter of vocabulary, morphology, and syntax. Yet the actual test results show that Daniel 2–7 is linguistically older than the Genesis Apocryphon by several centuries. Hence these chapters could not have been composed as late as the second century or the third century, but rather—based on purely philological grounds—they have to be dated in the fifth or late sixth century; and they must have been composed in the eastern sector of the Aramaic-speaking world (such as Babylon), rather than in Palestine (as the late date theory requires). The evidence for this is quite technical, and hence it would hardly be suitable for this type of encyclopedia (which does not presuppose a thorough knowledge of Hebrew, Aramaic, and Greek on the part of most of our reading public). But those who have had training in Hebrew and Aramaic are encouraged to consult the summaries of this evidence as contained in this author's *A Survey of Old Testament Introduction* (pp. 391–93). But my more thorough and definitive work, "The Aramaic of the Genesis Apocryphon Compared with the Aramaic of Daniel," appears as chapter 11 in Payne, *New Perspectives*. See also my article "The Hebrew of Daniel Compared with the Qumran Sectarian Documents," in Skilton, *The Law and the Prophets* (chap. 41).

The following conclusion concerning the Apocryphon comes from my *A Survey of Old Testament Introduction* (p.169):

> The fact that Targumic and Talmudic words abound in this document indicates a considerable interval in time between its composition and that of *Ezra* and *Daniel*. Its use of normal Semitic word order in the clause as over against Daniel's policy of placing the verb late in the clause points to a definite difference either in geographic origin (which would eliminate the possibility of *Daniel's* Maccabean composition in Palestine) or in time of composition. Either inference is fatal to the pseudepigraph theory. It is fair to say, therefore, that the overall testimony of this scroll [the Genesis Apocryphon] leads to an abandonment of a long-cherished position of higher criticism, and makes the genuineness of Danielic authorship an even more attractive option than it was before.

In *New Perspectives* (pp. 480–81), we find the following concluding remarks:

> In the light of all the data adduced under the four categories just reviewed, it seems abundantly clear that a second-century date for the Hebrew chapters of *Daniel* is no longer tenable on linguistic grounds. In view of the markedly later development in the areas of syntax, word-order, morphology, vocabulary, spelling and word-usage, there is absolutely no possibility of regarding *Daniel* as contemporary [with the sectarian documents]. On the contrary the indications are that centuries must have intervened between them.... But any fair-minded investigator when faced with such an overwhelming body of objective data pointing to the temporal interval of centuries between the two

bodies of literature must conclude that a second-century date for the book of Daniel is completely out of the question.... The complete absence of Greek loan-words, apart from musical instruments of international currency [mentioned in Dan. 3:5], points unmistakably to a time of composition prior to the Alexandrian conquest. It is utterly inconceivable that after 160 years of Greek overlordship (as the Maccabean theory insists) there would be a complete absence of Greek terms pertaining to government and administration, whether in the Aramaic chapters or in the Hebrew, in a literary product of the 160's B.C. But now that the considerable body of new documentation exhumed from the First Qumran Cave has been published and subjected to thorough analysis, it becomes patently evident that the Maccabean-date theory, despite all of its persuasive appeal to the rationalist, is altogether wrong. Only a dogma-ridden obscurantist can adhere to it any longer, and he must henceforth surrender all claim to intellectual respectability.

Are we then driven back to the late sixth century B.C. for the composition of the Book of Daniel? Since Daniel himself must have been born between 620 and 615 B.C., we can hardly assume that he lived beyond 530, to the age of 85 or 90. This means that the final form of his memoirs was completed by 530 and that we should look for a linguistic locus of about that period if his work is genuine. Unquestionably he lived to see the Fall of Babylon to the Medo-Persian armies of Cyrus the Great in 539. He served under Cyrus's viceroy, Darius the Mede, for a year or so, and thus became deeply involved with the new Persian terminology that had begun to infiltrate the Aramaic of Babylon in matters of administration and government. The fifteen loan-words from Persian that appear in Daniel's Aramaic are adequately accounted for by the close contact Daniel enjoyed with Persian officialdom during the 530s. Once we establish that the Book of Daniel must have been com-

posed before the Greek conquest—and therefore back in the Persian period—there is no good reason for refusing the adequacy of a 530 date. Certainly the phenomenon of successful prediction of events extending even into the first century A.D. becomes a characteristic that can only point to divine inspiration behind it, and all the presuppositional incentive for late dating the book has been removed. We may as well accept it for what it purports to be, the personal composition of Daniel himself (as is affirmed by 7:1-2,15,28; 8:1, 15,27; 9:2,21-22; 10:1-2; 12:5).

For the consistent Evangelical, however, the matter is definitely settled by the reference to Daniel that occurs in Christ's Olivet Discourse (Matt. 24:15). There Jesus mentions "the abomination of desolation which was spoken of through [dia with genitive] Daniel the prophet." The phrase "the abomination of desolation" (or "which makes desolate") occurs in Daniel 9:27; 11:31; 12:11. The important thing to observe is that Christ was not simply referring to some book in the Old Testament named "Daniel" but rather to the agency of Daniel personally, since dia with the genitive always implies personal human agency. If these words of Christ are reliably reported—as of course they are—we can only conclude that Christ personally believed that the historic personage Daniel was the author of the book that contained this eschatological phrase. Moreover Christ made it plain that the fulfillment of the prediction concerning this "abomination of desolation" yet lay in the future. It was not fulfilled by what happened back in 168 B.C., even though a type of this abomination may have been erected by Antiochus in the Jerusalem temple.

Is Daniel 1:1 wrong about the date of Nebuchadnezzar's invasion?

Daniel 1:1 says that Nebuchadnezzar first invaded Palestine in the "third" year of Jehoiakim of Judah. But Jeremiah 46:2 says that the first year of Nebuchadnezzar was the "fourth" year of Jehoiakim. Which is right? Actually, both are right. Nebuchadnezzar was crowned king of Babylon in 605 B.C., which according to the Babylonian system would have been the "accession year" of Nebuchadnezzar. His first regnal year did not begin, therefore, until New Year's Day in 604. But according to the Judean system, the accession year counted as the first year of a king's reign. Since Jehoiakim was appointed king of Judah in 608 by Pharaoh Necho, 605 would be reckoned his fourth year (which Jeremiah, as a resident of Jerusalem, would naturally have followed). But according to the Babylonian reckoning (which Daniel, as a resident of Babylon naturally followed), 605 would have been Jehoiakim's "third" year (reckoning his first regnal year from New Year's Day 607). Hence both statements are correct, and both come out to the same year: 605—the year of Nebuchadnezzar's great victory at the Battle of Carchemish.

Why does Daniel refer to soothsayer-priests as *Chaldeans*?

Daniel 2:2 first introduces the "Chaldeans" (Heb. *Kaśdîm*) as a class of astrologer-priests, along with the "magicians, the conjurers, and "the sorcerers." Obviously there is nothing ethnic about this use of the term. From the ethnical standpoint, Nebuchadnezzar himself and most of his political and military leaders were "Chaldeans." Some have argued that this nonethnic use of the term in Daniel 2:2 and elsewhere reflects a confusion in the understanding of the late author of the Book of Daniel, who probably wrote around 165 B.C. This theory is completely shattered, however, by the fact that the real author of "Daniel" (namely, Daniel himself, writing around 530 B.C.) also uses *Kaśdîm* in an

ethnic way. In 5:30 he refers to Belshazzar as "the king of the Chaldeans" (Aramaic *malkā' Kaśdā'ē*). (Probably the certain "Chaldean men" [*gubrîn Kaśda'în*] in 3:8, who were the accusers of Daniel's three friends, were high government officials rather than soothsayer-priests [so Brown-Driver-Briggs, *Lexicon*, p. 1098].) Such a varying use of the term cannot be explained by a theory of late authorship. The fact of the matter is that the author of Daniel used this name in two different senses: (1) as astrological, (2) as ethnical. How could this have come about? Is there any explanation for these homonyms? Yes, there is, but it is to be found in the handing down of an ancient term through three languages.

As Robert Dick Wilson of Princeton pointed out (*Studies in the Book of Daniel*, Series 1 [New York: G.P. Putnam's Sons, 1917]), the Sumerian combination *Gal-du* would have meant "Master Builder," a title given to those astrologer-priests who drew star charts by dividing the visible stars up into little rooms on a chart resembling the floor-plan of a house. The term *Gal-du* so appears in a tablet dated in the fourteenth year of Shamash-shumukin of Babylon (668–648 B.C.).

Confusion of *Kal-du* (the Akkadian spelling of Sumerian *Gal-du*) with the name of the Chaldean nation came about as follows: That name, originally *Kasdu* or *Kašdu* later came to be pronounced *Kaldu* in the Babylonian dialect of Akkadian. This resulted from a modification of a sibilant to an *l* before a dental; thus, the preposition *ištu* ("out of") was pronounced *ultu* in later Babylonian; *aštur* ("I wrote") was changed to *altur*. The final stage came in the rise of the Neo-Babylonian Empire under Nabopolassar and his son Nebuchadnezzar; for in this time of national resurgence (having thrown off the Assyrian yoke at last), they tried to restore their literary language to its earlier classical form. This meant that all the sibilants that had become *l* before dental consonants had to be changed back to their original sibilants. It was only natural, therefore, for the *Kaldu*, which originally came from *Kal-du* (*Gal-du*), to be unhistorically changed to *Kaśdu* (the plural of which was *Kaśdī*, Hebrew *Kaśdîm*, Aramaic *Kasdîn*, or *Ḳaśdā'ē* in the emphatic state). This term thus fell together with the ethnic *Kaldu* (plural *Kaldî*), which had come originally from *Kaśdu*. (Note that the Greeks picked up the name before the Neo-Babylonian reform, for they called the nation *Chaldaioi*, whence comes our English translation "Chaldeans."

Is not Daniel 5 in error regarding the identity of the last king of Babylon? Wasn't it Nabonidus rather than Belshazzar?

On the contrary, the biblical notice has been strikingly confirmed by archaeological evidence. During the previous centuries many scholars mistakenly assumed that "Belshazzar" was a mere legendary figure because none of the Greek historians, from Herodotus on, knew anything about Belshazzar or referred to his name. While it is true that Nabonidus (the cuneiform spelling is *Nabu-na'id*) was indeed the head king of Babylon at the demise of the Chaldean Empire, it has now been well established that he was quartered at Tema in North Arabia at the time of Cyrus's invasion of Babylonia. It was therefore his son, Belshazzar, who was in charge of Babylon itself (which at that time was considered impregnable to any besieging army), and who had been crowned as viceroy several years earlier during his father's reign.

Excavations at Ur turned up an inscription of Nabunaid containing a prayer, first for himself, then for his firstborn son, *Bel-shar-uṣur*. Such prayers were offered only for the reigning monarch (in a manner quite similar to the celebration of Holy Communion in the Anglican Church). Still other cuneiform documents record how Belshazzar presented sheep and oxen at the temples of Sippar as "an offering of the king." Since the name of Belshazzar had been forgotten by the time of Herodotus (ca. 450 B.C.), it is clear that the author of Daniel 5 must have written this work a good deal *earlier* than 450 B.C. That author was also well aware that Belshazzar was only number two king of Babylon in 539 B.C., for all he could offer Daniel as a reward for deciphering the inscription on the wall of the banquet hall was "the *third* place in the kingdom." (For further details on this matter, the reader is encouraged to consult Raymond P. Dougherty, *Nabonidus and Belshazzar* [New Haven: Yale, 1929].)

Is there any confirmation for the existence of "Darius the Mede"?

"Darius the Mede" is first mentioned in Daniel 5:31: "So Darius the Mede received the kingdom [over the erstwhile Chaldean Empire] at about the age of sixty-two" (NASB). Some scholars, advocating a late date theory for the composition of Daniel, argue (1) that there never was a Median Darius, since he is never mentioned in any other ancient document preserved to us; (2) that the name Darius was picked up by the Maccabean author, who was confused about the real sequence in Persian history and mixed up a legendary Median king with Darius I (522–484), who was a Persian rather than a Mede; (3) that the author mistakenly supposed that it was the Medes who conquered Babylon (rather than Cyrus the Persian), and that under this legendary "Darius" they were supposed to have maintained a world empire for some years before they fell to the Persians.

In this way the Maccabean date

advocates are able to account for the four "kingdoms" in Nebuchadnezzar's dream (Dan. 2) as (1) Chaldean, (2) Median, (3) Persian, (4) Greek—which would have the advantage of extending the prophetic horizon of "Daniel" no farther than 165 B.C. (The problem with the traditional identification of the fourth kingdom with Rome is that it would presuppose genuine predictive prophecy—which cannot be permitted by rationalist higher criticism.) The tenability of the Maccabean date hypothesis rests on this explanation for "Darius the Mede." Therefore Darius is a pretty important fellow and deserves our special attention.

No identification can be made out between Darius the son of Hystaspes and Darius the Mede for the following reasons:

1. Darius I was a Persian by birth, a cousin of King Cyrus; he was not a Median.
2. Darius was a young man when he assassinated the imposter Gaumata (who claimed to be Smerdis, the son of Cyrus) in 522. Darius could not have been 62; he was more likely in his twenties.
3. Darius did not precede Cyrus as king of Babylon; rather, he began his reign seven years after the death of Cyrus the Great; yet the liberal theory alleges that the author supposed that he came before Cyrus.
4. Such confusion as to the true nationality and time sequence of Darius the Great would have been unthinkable in the second-century B.C. Hellenistic world; for even in the Near East every schoolboy was required to read Xenophon, if not Herodotus, and other Greek historians from the fifth and fourth centuries B.C. Even in Hellenistic Palestine, these authors were widely read and admired. It is from Xenophon and Herodotus that we gain our information concerning Cyrus and Darius. Any Greek-writing author,

or author within the Hellenistic orbit, who attempted to put Darius before Cyrus would have been laughed off the stage by the general public; and no credence would have been given to anything he wrote.

We must therefore conclude that Darius the Mede and Darius the Persian have nothing to do with each other, and that the confusion is in the minds of the late date theorists rather than in the mind of the author of Daniel. And yet it is true that no reference to "Darius the Mede" has been discovered as yet in the findings of archaeology. (Until the late nineteenth century, the same would have been true of Belshazzar, viceroy under his father Nabonidus. Maccabean date critics used to allege that he was another fictional character in Daniel, before the discovery of Babylonian tablets from that period, which confirm that Belshazzar was serving as junior king in the final years of Nabonidus's reign.) Yet there is a very obvious and attractive identification to be found as we shall see.

There are several indications in the text of Daniel that Darius was not king in his own right but had been temporarily appointed to the throne by some higher authority. In 9:1 it is stated that Darius "was made king." The passive stem (*hophal*) is used in the verb *homlak*, rather than the usual *mālak* ("became king"), which would have been used had he obtained the throne by conquest or by inheritance. In 5:31 we are told that Darius "received" (*qabbēl*) the kingship, as if it had been entrusted to him by a higher authority. It is also appropriate to point out that subordinate or vassal kings were similarly appointed by Cyrus according to the Behistun Rock inscription set up by Darius I in the late sixth century. (Thus Darius's own forebear, Hystaspes, is said to have been "made king" during the time of

Cyrus the Great.) As the incumbent of the time-honored throne of Babylon, it was only a matter of proper protocol for Cyrus's appointee to assume in his official decrees the same titles as had always attached to that title. Thus the decree of 6:25 is addressed to the inhabitants of "all the earth" ('ar'ā' could also be translated "land," rather than being as comprehensive as "the earth"). Traditional titulary, going back to the time of Hammurabi (eighteenth century B.C.), was šár kiš-šati ("king of the universe"). Therefore this phrase need not be construed as implying that Darius was claiming to be king over all the inhabited world, including Persia itself, as some critics have assumed.

Who, then, was Darius the Mede? In his careful study of the relevant archaeological documents, J.C. Whitcomb (Darius the Mede [Grand Rapids: Eerdmans, 1959]) has assembled all the texts referring to (1) Ugbaru, the general who engineered the capture of Babylon in 539 B.C.; (2) Gubaru, who is often referred to in tablets dating from 535 to 525 as the governor of Babylon; and (3) Gaubaruva, a leader mentioned in the inscriptions of Darius the Great. Ugbaru was not the same person as Gubaru (Xenophon spells his name as Gobryas but confuses him with Ugbaru) but an elderly general who died within a few weeks after the Fall of Babylon. Gaubaruva is plainly a later personage who came into prominence after Ushtani was appointed governor of Babylon in the late 520s. Concerning Gubaru, we have little evidence of his ethnic background, but he could very well have been a Mede. Certainly it was consistent with Cyrus's policy to put talented and loyal Medes like General Harpagus into key positions in his government. As for the name "Darius" (Persian Dārayawush), it seems to be related to dara, which appears in Avestan as a term for "king." Like augustus among the Romans,

dārayawush ("the royal one") may have been a special honorific title, which could also be used as a proper name (just as "King" may be a name in English).

It would appear, then, that right after the Fall of Babylon to the Medo-Persian troops, Cyrus's presence was urgently needed on another front of his expanding empire. He therefore found it expedient to put Gubaru-Darius in charge, with the title King of Babylon, to rule for a year or so until Cyrus could return in person and celebrate a formal coronation as king in the temple of Marduk. After his year of rule as viceroy, then, Darius was retained as the governor of Babylon, but with the crown transferred to his overlord, Cyrus (who subsequently had his older son, Cambyses, crowned king of Babylon). It is clear from Daniel's failure to mention any date later than Darius's "first year" (9:1) that his reign must have been of very brief duration. It should be observed that an empire that lasted for only a single year introduces an element of utter implausibility into the Maccabean date hypothesis; for a one-year empire could hardly have been set up as number two in a series that included the Chaldean Empire, which lasted for 73 years, the Persian Empire, which lasted for 208 years, and the Greek Empire, which would have lasted for 167 years by 165 B.C.

We close this discussion with the episode that first ushers Darius onto the stage in Daniel's narrative. Daniel 5 relates the dramatic episode of the divine handwriting on the wall of Belshazzar's banquet hall. The third term in that fateful inscription is PERES, which Daniel himself (in v.28) interprets as "PERES—your kingdom has been divided [pᵉrîsat, from the same p-r-s root as PERES] and given over to the Medes and Persians [Pārās]" (NASB). This double word-play on the root p-r-s makes it absolutely certain that the author of this book believed that kingdom number one (the Chaldean Empire) passed directly and immediately into the control of the Persians, allied with the Medes, as kingdom number two. This leaves no room for the critics' theory of an earlier and separate Median Empire as being intended by the author of Daniel. That author must therefore have believed that kingdom number two was Persian (i.e., Medo-Persian), that kingdom number three (of Dan. 2) was the Macedonian-Greek-Syrian Empire, and that kingdom number four would overthrow and replace the Greek Empire. The only power that ever did that was the Roman Empire. Therefore, successful predictive prophecy cannot be eliminated from Daniel even by a Maccabean date hypothesis!

How can we make any sense out of Daniel's prophecy of Seventy Weeks?

The prophecy of the Seventy Weeks in Daniel 9:24–27 is one of the most remarkable long-range predictions in the entire Bible. It is by all odds one of the most widely discussed by students and scholars of every persuasion within the spectrum of the Christian church. And yet when it is carefully examined in the light of all the relevant data of history and the information available from other parts of Scripture, it is quite clearly an accurate prediction of the time of Christ's coming advent and a preview of the thrilling final act of the drama of human history before that advent.

Daniel 9:24 reads: "Seventy weeks have been determined for your people and your holy city [i.e., for the nation Israel and for Jerusalem]." The word for "week" is šābūʿac, which is derived from šebaʿ, the word for "seven." Its normal plural is feminine in form: še bûʿôt. Only in this chapter of Daniel does it appear in the masculine plural šābūʿîm. (The only other occurrence is in the combination še bu'ê še bu'ôt ["heptads of weeks"] in Ezek. 21:28 [21:23 English text]). Therefore, it is strongly suggestive of the idea "heptad" (a series or combination of seven), rather than a "week" in the sense of a series of seven days. There is no doubt that in this case we are presented with seventy sevens of years rather than of days. This leads to a total of 490 years.

At the completion of these 490 years, according to v.24b, there will be six results: (1) "to finish or bring transgression [or 'the sin of rebellion'] to an end"; (2) "to finish [or 'seal up'] sins"; (3) "to make atonement for iniquity"; (4) "to bring in everlasting righteousness"; (5) "to seal up vision and prophecy"; and (6) "to anoint the holy of holies." By the end of the full 490 years, then, the present sin-cursed world order will come to an end (1 and 2), the price of redemption for sinners will have been paid (3); the kingdom of God will be established on earth, and all the earth will be permanently filled with righteousness, as the waters cover the sea (4); and the Most Holy One (Christ?), or the Most Holy Sanctuary (which seems more probable, since Christ was already anointed by the Holy Spirit at His first advent), will be solemnly anointed and inaugurated for worship in Jerusalem, the religious and political capital of the world during the Millennium (5 and 6).

Daniel 9:25 reads: "And you are to know and understand, from the going forth of the command [or 'decree'; lit., 'word'—dābār] to restore and [re]build Jerusalem until Messiah the Prince [nāgîd] will be [or 'there are; the Hebrew omits the verb 'to be' in this case] seven heptads and sixty-two heptads." This gives us two installments, 49 years and 434 years, for a total of 483 years. Significantly, the seventieth heptad is held in abeyance until v.27. Therefore we are left with a total of 483 between the issuance of the decree to rebuild Jerusalem and the coming of the Messiah.

As we examine each of the three decrees issued in regard to Jerusalem by kings subsequent to the time Daniel had this vision (538 B.C., judging from Dan. 9:1), we find that the first was that of Cyrus in 2 Chronicles 36:23: "The LORD, the God of heaven, ... has appointed me to build Him a house in Jerusalem, which is in Judah" (NASB). This decree, issued in 538 or 537, pertained only to the rebuilding of the temple, not of the city of Jerusalem. The third decree is to be inferred from the granting of Nehemiah's request by Artaxerxes I in 446 B.C., as recorded in Nehemiah 2:5-8. His request was "Send me to Judah, to the city of my fathers' tombs, that I may rebuild it." Then we read, "So it pleased the king to send me, and I gave him a definite time [for my return to his palace]" (NASB). The king also granted him a requisition of timber for the gates and walls of the city.

It should be noted that when Nehemiah first heard from his brother Hanani that the walls of Jerusalem had not already been rebuilt, he was bitterly disappointed and depressed—as if he had previously supposed that they had been rebuilt (Neh. 1:1-4). This strongly suggests that there had already been a previous decree authorizing the rebuilding of those city walls. Such an earlier decree is found in connection with Ezra's group that returned to Jerusalem in 457, the seventh year of Artaxerxes I. Ezra 7:6 tells us: "This Ezra went up from Babylon, ... and the king granted him all he requested because the hand of the LORD his God was upon him" (NASB; notice the resemblance to Neh. 2:8, the last sentence). According to the following verse, Ezra was accompanied by a good-sized group of followers, including temple singers, gatekeepers, temple servants, and a company of laymen ("some of the sons of Israel"). After arriving at Jerusalem, he busied himself first with the moral and spiritual rebuilding of his people (Ezra 7:10). But he had permission from the king to employ any unused balance of the offering funds for whatever purpose he saw fit (v.18); and he was given authority to appoint magistrates and judges and to enforce the established laws of Israel with confiscation, banishment, or death (v.26). Thus he would appear to have had the authority to set about rebuilding the city walls, for the protection of the temple mount and the religious rights of the Jewish community.

In 9:9 Ezra makes reference to this authority in his public, penitential prayer: "For we are slaves; yet in our bondage, our God has not forsaken us, but has extended lovingkindness to us in the sight of the kings of Persia, to give us reviving to raise up the house of our God, to restore its ruins, and to give us a *wall* in Judah and *Jerusalem*" (NASB; italics mine). While this "wall" may have been partly a metaphor for "protection," it seems to have included the possibility of restoring the mural defenses of Jerusalem itself. Unfortunately, we are given no details as to the years that intervened before 446; but it may be that an abortive attempt was made under Ezra's leadership to replace the outer wall of the city, only to meet with frustration—perhaps from a lack of self-sacrificing zeal on the part of the Jewish returnees themselves or because of violent opposition from Judah's heathen neighbors. This would account for Nehemiah's keen disappointment (as mentioned above) when he heard that "the wall of Jerusalem is broken down and its gates are burned with fire" (Neh. 1:3, NASB).

If, then, the decree of 457 granted to Ezra himself is taken as the *terminus a quo* for the commencement of the 69 heptads, or 483 years, we come out to the precise year of the appearance of Jesus of Nazareth as Messiah (or Christ): 483 minus 457 comes out to A.D. 26. But since a year is gained in passing from 1 B.C. to A.D.1 (there being no such year as *zero*), it actually comes out to A.D. 27. It is generally agreed that Christ was crucified in A.D. 30, after a ministry of a little more than three years. This means His baptism and initial ministry must have taken place in A.D. 27—a most remarkable exactitude in the fulfillment of such an ancient prophecy. Only God could have predicted the coming of His Son with such amazing precision; it defies all rationalistic explanation.

Daniel 9:25 goes on to say, "It will again be built with street and moat, even when times are difficult." It is fair to deduce from this that the actual completion of the reconstruction of the city, both walls and interior appointments of the city, would take up about seven heptads, or forty-nine years. Soon after 400 B.C., then, the walls, the defensive moat, and all the streets and buildings behind those walls had been completely restored.

Daniel 9:26 goes on to foretell the tragic death of the Messiah: "And subsequent to the sixty-two heptads [ensuing upon the earlier installment of forty-nine], the Messiah will be cut off and shall have no one [or 'nothing']." This suggests that the Messiah would be violently put to death, without any faithful followers to protect Him. He would die alone! This refers to the great event that took place on Golgotha in A.D. 30. There are some able scholars who prefer the date 33 but the calendrical data seem to favor the earlier date. At all events, the earlier statement "until Messiah the Prince" in v.25 refers to His first appearance to Israel as the baptized and anointed Redeemer of Israel; it does not refer to the year of His death, since His "cutting off" is not mentioned until v.26.

Daniel 9:26b then foretells what will happen by way of retribution to the "holy city" that has rejected Jesus and voted to have Him "cut off": "And the people of the prince who shall come [i.e., Titus, the victorious commander of the Roman troops in A.D. 70] will destroy the holy city, and its end will come with a flood [of disaster], and war is determined down to the [very] end, with devastation." These vivid terms point to the total destruction that overtook Jerusalem in that fateful year.

Daniel 9:27 reads: "And he will confirm a covenant with the many for one heptad [i.e., seven years], but in the middle of the heptad he will terminate sacrifice and offering." The subject of "confirm" is indefinite in the Hebrew, for no subject is expressed; but it is easily inferred from the last personal subject mentioned in the previous verse: "the prince who shall come," that ruler who will establish a covenant or concordat with the Jewish community ("the many"—a term originating in Isa. 53:11–12) is an antitype of the Roman general who destroyed Jerusalem after the termination of the sixty-ninth heptad (i.e., Titus in A.D. 70). That antitype has already appeared back in Daniel 7:25 as the Little Horn of the last days who will persecute "the saints of the Most High" for "a time [Aramaic *'iddān*], times, and half a time," i.e., for three and a half years. This same period recurs in Daniel 12:7, where the mighty angel swears to Daniel that "it will be for a time [Heb. *mô'ēḏ*), times, and a half; and as soon as they finish shattering the power [lit., 'hand'] of the holy people, all these things will come to an end"—i.e., that final heptad of years will be over. The data of v.26 indicate that a long but indeterminable interval is intended between A.D. 27 (the end of the sixty-ninth heptad)—after Messiah appears; then the Crucifixion occurs; Jerusalem is destroyed by the Romans; and finally there is a period of overwhelming disaster, war, and desolation—and the inception of the final seven years of the last days (v.27), in the midst of which the antitypical prince or supreme dictator covenants with the Jewish people for seven years of religious tolerance, only to revoke his promise after three and a half years.

By the use of proper grammatical exegesis, then, it is possible to make perfect sense of the Seventy Weeks prophecy of Daniel 9 and see a remarkable correspondence with subsequent history up through the sixty-ninth heptad and the events that have ensued between then and now. But the reference to "sacrifice and offering" in 9:26 does seem to presuppose the prior erection of a valid temple and altar on the Temple Mount as a feature at the inception of the final seven years before the Battle of Armageddon and the establishment of the kingdom of God on earth in the millennial rule of Christ on the throne of David.

Do not the detailed predictions of Daniel 11 regarding events taking place during the third century and early second century B.C. strongly indicate a date of composition during the 160s B.C.?

Daniel 11 presents a panorama of future history subsequent to the reign of Cyrus the Great all the way to the appearance of the Antichrist or Beast of the last days, prior to the return of Christ and the Battle of Armageddon. Verse 2 refers to three more Persian kings (i.e., Cambyses, Darius, and Xerxes) prior to the Persian invasion of Greece in 480 B.C. Verse 3 predicts the conquests of Alexander the Great in the 330s, and v.4, the quadripartite division of his empire after his death. Verses 5–9 cover the period of conflict between the Ptolemaic and the Seleucid empires from the 320s to the death of Seleucus III in 223. Verses 10–19 foretell the career of Antiochus III (the Great), and v.20 that of his successor, Seleucus IV. Verses 21–35 give a vivid and detailed description of

Antiochus IV (Epiphanes), who was destined to make a supreme effort to stamp out the faith of Israel and to convert the Jews to Hellenic paganism.

Up until this point, the rationalist scholar, who seeks to avoid the supernatural factors involved in foretelling the events of 365 years to the future, will necessarily be driven to the explanation that the author of Daniel actually lived and wrote in the 160s B.C., rather than in 530 B.C. But unfortunately for this explanation, vv.36–45 do not conform to what is known of the life and career of Antiochus Epiphanes. A fine discussion of these verses and their bearing on the career of the future Antichrist may be found in Leon Wood's *A Commentary on Daniel* (Grand Rapids: Zondervan, 1973), pp. 304–14.

The significant phrase "At the end time" in Daniel 11:40 points unmistakably to the last days rather than to the events of the 160s B.C. Many of the distinguishing traits and policies attributed to this "king of the North" do not at all conform to what we know of Epiphanes; and the manner and location of his death stand in striking contrast to the manner of the death of Antiochus, which took place in Tabae, Persia, after an unsuccessful attempt to raid a wealthy temple in Elymais. Tabae was nearly two thousand miles away from Palestine. But Daniel 11:45 reads: "And he [the king of the North] will pitch the tents of his royal pavilion between the seas and the beautiful Holy Mountain; yet he will come to his end, and no one will help him" (NASB). This means that this eschatological tyrant will meet his end somewhere between the Mediterranean and the Dead Sea, in the proximity of Mount Zion. No theory of Maccabean composition can account for so serious a blunder as this—if indeed v.45 was intended to prophesy the end of Antiochus Epiphanes.

Lastly, it should be pointed out that

from Daniel 2 through Daniel 7 the perspective of the author of Daniel includes the Roman Empire as the fourth kingdom in the four-kingdom scheme of chapter 2. All attempts to insert a separate, earlier Median Empire as preceding the Persian Empire are rendered nugatory by the handwriting on the wall of Belshazzar's palace. That is to say, the third term of that inscription is PERES, which is interpreted by Daniel himself to mean "Your kingdom has been divided [*perisat*—a verb derived from the root *P-R-S*] and has been given over to the Medes and Persians [*Pārās*]." Nothing could be plainer from this verse (5:28) than that the author of Daniel believed that imperial power passed directly from the Babylonian to the Medo-Persian as a federated empire—*not* to the Median Empire first, then a few years later to the Persian Empire (as the Maccabean date hypothesis demands). On the contrary, the author himself must have believed that the second kingdom was the Medo-Persian one. This means that the Greek Empire, founded by Alexander the Great, must have been kingdom number three and that the Roman Empire, which did not take over the Near East in a decisive and final way until 63 B.C., was kingdom number four. This factor renders the Maccabean date hypothesis logically indefensible.

There is only one alternative left. The author of Daniel knew of the whole future course of history from Cyrus the Great to the Roman Empire through direct revelation from God. No other theory fits the objective data of the text or the known facts of history.

Hosea

How could a holy God command Hosea to marry a harlot?

From the standpoint of Hosea himself, looking back on his domestic tragedy, it was quite clear that when God had encouraged him to marry Gomer, the daughter of Diblaim, who He foreknew would be unfaithful to Hosea after he had married her, this amounted to a divine directive to marry a harlot. This does not necessarily mean that she had already shown a tendency to sexual promiscuity when he was courting her or that she was already a woman of ill fame when he married her. It is clearly implied in Hosea 1:3-4 that the prophet himself was the father of their firstborn child, Jezreel. We cannot be sure about the paternity of the next two children, Lo-ruhamah and Lo-ammi, though there is no clear indication that Hosea had not also begotten them as well. All that we can be sure of is that after their birth Hosea was given a message from God (2:2-13) in which the names are related to the religious harlotry of the northern kingdom of Israel. Since Hosea's marriage relationship is intended to serve as a type of Yahweh's relationship to Israel, it could legitimately be inferred that Gomer had become pregnant by some paramour rather than by her lawful husband. Chapter 3 strongly suggests that Gomer had deserted Hosea's home and had run off with some lover, ultimately ending up as a slave (perhaps as a prostitute in a house of ill fame) who had to be purchased from the person to whom she had sold herself.

To sum up, then, Hosea's unhappy marriage was intended by God to serve as a heartrending illustration of the apostasy of the northern kingdom, whose citizens had turned from the worship of Yahweh to the worship of the various Baals of the degenerate religions of Canaan and Phoenicia. God, of course, foreknew that Israel would prove false to Him in later centuries, even when He first took her as His covenant wife in the solemn marriage that took place in the days of Moses at Mount Sinai. Yet in His marvelous grace He bore with her infidelities, welcomed her back in her times of repentance and revival, and kept faithful to her even though she repeatedly betrayed His love. Even so was it to be with Hosea. Gomer would be unblemished in the beginning of their marriage, but would stray from him later on.

In retrospect, therefore, Hosea interpreted God's encouragement to him to enter into this unhappy match as a directive at the very start: "Go, take to yourself a wife of harlotry" (1:2, NASB), even though the Lord may not have used such shocking terms in His original response to Hosea's prayer concerning this attractive girl with whom he had fallen in love. God knew very well what was in her heart; yet He said nothing to warn or dissuade Hosea before he married her. This amounted to the language of 1:2 in the light of God's foreknowledge and His overriding purpose in allowing this unhappy marriage to take place. The tragedy of Hosea was to serve as a parable of the tragedy of God's marriage to Israel. No more eloquent illustration of this could be found than that of the infidelity of Gomer to her godly husband.

Is there a contradiction between Hosea 8:13 ("Ephraim will return to Egypt") and Hosea 11:5 ("They will not return to Egypt")?

Hosea 11:5 states in full: "They [i.e., Israel or Ephraim; cf. 11:1–2] will not return to the land of Egypt; but Assyria—he will be their king, because they refused to return to Me" (NASB). This passage reaffirms that the tribes of Israel generally, and the Northern Kingdom headed up by the tribe of Ephraim in particular, will not be driven back to Egypt as a nation of enslaved exiles. This reiterates the promise of Deuteronomy 17:16: "Moreover, he [the future king of Israel] shall not multiply horses for himself, nor shall he cause the people to return to Egypt to multiply horses, since Yahweh has said to you, 'You shall never again return that way.'" Deuteronomy 17:16 suggests, however, that developing a large force of chariotry and relying on this type of armament rather than on the Lord's deliverance would lead to an Egyptian attitude of materialism and pride. In that sense such a king, as Solomon turned out to be (cf. 1 Kings 4:26), would in effect be turning the people back to Egypt on that spiritual level of materialistic arrogance.

It is surely in this figurative sense that Hosea intends 8:11–13: "Since Ephraim has multiplied altars for sin.... As for My sacrificial gifts, they sacrifice the flesh and eat it, but Yahweh has taken no delight in them. Now He will remember their iniquity, and punish them for their sins; they will return to Egypt." While it is true that taken by itself this last clause might amount to a threat of actual deportation to Egypt, it seems more harmonious with the context to understand this as figurative and translate the verb *yāšûbû* as "they are returning" —which is legitimate for the Hebrew imperfect tense (i.e., an imperfect indicates noncomplete action, and this may have either a future reference or a present reference—as here—depending on the context). In other words, they are becoming spiritually Egyptian-pagan in their attitude toward God as they engage in sacrifice. Rather than coming to Him with full repentance for sin, with full trust in God's grace, and with a sincere purpose to do His will, they come to God's altar to buy Him off or earn His favor—as any heathen would do to his god. (Another striking example of using the name of a country or city as a symbol of wickedness, rather than an actual geographical location, is found in Isa. 1:9–10: "Hear the word of the LORD, you rulers of Sodom"—long after the historical Sodom had ceased to exist.)

Joel

Does not Joel's mention of the "Greeks" (3:6) indicate the late fourth century as the earliest possible date for the composition of the book?

Joel 3:6 reads: "You [Phoenicians and Philistines] sold the sons of Judah and Jerusalem to the Greeks [$Y^ewānîm$] in order to remove them far from their territory" (NASB). The very wording of this verse precludes dating the composition of Joel at any time subsequent to the conquest of Asia by Alexander the Great. The Greeks are referred to here as a people living "far from the territory" of Judah, and probably also far from the territory of the Phoenician and Philistine slave-raiders themselves, who swooped down on defenseless Judean towns in order to sell the captives on slave markets very far from Canaanite territory. But after Alexander's conquest the Greeks were very close at hand. In fact, they were in full control of the government of Phoenicia, Israel, and Philistia, and began to carry on all the administration in the Greek language. Therefore Joel must have been composed while the Greeks were still remote from the Near East.

The Greeks already came to public notice, of course, after the collapse of Xerxes' attempted conquest of Greece in 480–479 B.C. But Greek coins are found in Palestinian hoards from as early as the late sixth-century issues of Peisistratus. Greek mercenaries or adventurers served in the court and army of the Babylonians as early as the Lesbian poet Alcaeus, who refers to his brother Antimenidas as engaged in such service. Alcaeus's date was the seventh century B.C. Neo-Babylonian ration tablets published by F. F. Weidner mention Ionian carpenters and shipbuilders as recipients of these rations. (Edwin Yamauchi's *Greece and Babylon* [Grand Rapids: Baker, 1967], p. 33, discusses the Cretan Linear B tablets dating from 1500 B.C., and gives full documentation for all these references, and also includes references to Egypt, Beirut, Tyre, and Phoenica, in general.) In the light of such data as these, it is nothing short of naive to suppose that a late ninth-century Joel could not have known anything about the Greeks, or to imagine that no slave-traders ever went to Greek ports with captives from Near Eastern slave raids.

Amos

Does the prophecy in Amos 8:11–12 refer only to Israel? If so, has it been fulfilled? Are "the words of the Lord" (v.11) those that we have in the Bible today? (D*)

The ministry of Amos was to the apostate northern kingdom of Israel, near the close of the reign of King Jeroboam II (793–753 B.C.). The earlier portion of Amos 8 deals quite specifically with the approaching downfall of Samaria which took place about thirty-three years later, in 722 B.C., when the Assyrians destroyed both the city and the northern kingdom as an independent state.

Amos 8:11–12 reads: " 'Behold, days are coming, declares the Lord Yahweh, when I will send a famine on the land, not a famine for bread or a thirst for water, but rather for hearing the words of Yahweh. And people will stagger from sea to sea, and from the north even to the east; they will go to and fro to seek the word of Yahweh, but they will not find it.' " This warning refers to the final decade of Israel's history (i.e., of the northern kingdom), during which the government, the clergy, and the people all sought in vain for some words of comfort and guidance from the Lord Yahweh but found none. (This parallels the final frantic efforts of King Saul just before the battle of Mount Gilboa, to receive some word from the Lord [cf. 1 Sam. 28:6]. Because of his stubborn rebellion and disobedience, Saul had forfeited all right to receive direction from God.)

In this context "the words of the Lord" were not the Hebrew Scriptures that had thus far been revealed; rather, they were the words of special guidance the people were seeking from God in this coming crisis. The prophecy was, of course, fulfilled during the last tragic years when the kingdom of the Ten Tribes, founded by Jeroboam I back in 931 B.C., finally came to a close, never to rise again. The kingdom of Judah, however, continued for another 135 years under the Davidic dynasty and later experienced a rebirth after the Babylonian captivity.

It should be added, however, that the basic warning to northern Israel applies with continuing application to national apostasy wherever a nation or people puts aside the authority of Holy Scripture and lives in rebellion against God. Those who do not heed the teaching of the Bible find that they have no more access to God's mercy or favor and receive no comfort or deliverance from Him when disaster closes in on them. "Whatsoever things were written aforetime were written for our learning," wrote Paul in Romans 15:4.

Obadiah

Which is the correct rendering of Obadiah 13?

The KJV renders this verse thus: "Thou [Edom] shouldest not have entered into the gate of my people in the day of their calamity; yea, thou shouldest not have looked on their affliction in the day of their calamity, nor have laid hands on their substance in the day of their calamity." Translated in this past subjunctive way, it seems to indicate that Edom participated in the storming and pillage of Jerusalem when it was finally and permanently destroyed (such is the implication of "shouldest not have entered . . . looked . . . laid hands on"). But when we turn to the Hebrew original, we find to our surprise that in each case the verb is in a normal negative-imperative construction (i.e., in the jussive mood with the negative *'al*). Therefore it should be translated "Do not enter. . . Do not look upon . . . Do not stretch forth [hands] against." Similarly in v.14 the Hebrew says, "Do not stand. . . Do not deliver over. . ., etc." So far as I am aware, KJV never translates *'al* with the jussive as a past subjunctive anywhere else in the entire Hebrew Scripture; and if it were not for incorrect rabbinical tradition, it would never have done so here.

The NASB has a good and faithful rendering of vv.13–14: "Do not enter the gate of My people in the day of their disaster. Yes you, do not gloat over their calamity in the day of their disaster. And do not loot their wealth in the day of their disaster. And do not stand at the fork of the road to cut down their fugitives; and do not imprison their survivors in the day of their distress." This straightforward rendition of the Hebrew text points to a situation that might arise in the future, similar to an attack on Jerusalem in the days gone by. It was probably in connection with the time of Jehoram son of Jehoshaphat (848–841 B.C.) that the Edomites joined with the Philistines and the Arabians who came up against Jerusalem and took it by storm (2 Chron. 21:16–17). Earlier in the reign of this ungodly king, Edom had revolted against Judean overlordship (2 Kings 8:20); and Jehoram had launched a punitive invasion in a determined effort to bring them back under his control. Since he did not succeed in his purpose, despite the great damage he had inflicted on them, it was only to be expected that anti-Jewish feeling would have run high in Edom.

While the record in 2 Chronicles 21 does not include the name of Edom as a prime mover in the invasion against Jerusalem, it is quite conceivable that after the Philistines and South Arabians had captured Jerusalem, the Edomites joined with them for the dividing up of the spoil. It was this unduly cruel and vengeful attitude that called for God's stern rebuke, conveyed through

Obadiah. The warning against ever doing that again in the future (a warning that of course implied that Jerusalem was still standing and capable of being thus victimized again by a combination of invaders) was no mere idle threat. As a matter of fact, in their later career the Edomites apparently did join with the Ammonites and Moabites in attacking Jerusalem as allies of Nebuchadnezzar in 588–587 (even though that episode is *not* the one referred to in Obadiah), and thus incurred the judicial wrath of the Lord. As a result He brought up the Nabatean Arabs against them in the sixth and fifth centuries, and the Edomites were completely driven out of the ancestral holdings in the region of Mount Seir. As the Nabateans established their kingdom in the former Edomite territory, the Edomites themselves found refuge in the depopulated areas of southern Judea and converted them into "Idumea."

Jonah

Are there any good grounds for classifying Jonah and portions of Chronicles as midrashic in nature?

A midrash is a special study and vividly imaginative expansion of some portion of Scripture. The term is derived from *dāraš*, which means "search," investigate," particularly with a view to adding vividness and color to the narrative contained in the scriptural account itself. For example, the *Genesis Apocryphon* (composed in Aramaic ca. 200 B.C.) expands on Genesis 12:11–19, the account of Abraham and Sarah during their visit to Egypt, and supplies lengthy conversations and colorful detail concerning the striking physical attractiveness and charm of Sarah herself, the deadly danger to which Abraham was exposed because of her beauty, and the utter necessity of resorting to falsehood in order to save Abraham from assassination on the part of the agents of Pharaoh. The technique resembles that employed by a Sunday school teacher who wishes to make a Bible story come to life before a children's group. There is often a tendency to justify the motives and magnify the wisdom or prowess of the biblical hero whose exploits are described.

So far as Jonah is concerned, it should be pointed out that apart from the four chapters that compose the book so named, there is only one certain reference to the prophet Jonah in the rest of the Hebrew Bible, namely 2 Kings 14:25: "He [Jeroboam II] restored the border of Israel from the entrance of Hamath as far as the Sea of Arabah, according to the word of the LORD, the God of Israel, which He spoke through His servant Jonah the son of Amittai, the prophet, who was of Gath-hepher" (NASB). There is virtually no connection between this verse and the subject matter of Jonah itself, except that it suggests a strong patriotic zeal on the part of the man of Gath-hepher. Insofar as a midrash furnishes an imaginative expansion and vivid elaboration of a passage in Scripture, Jonah cannot possibly be classified as midrashic; for it has nothing whatever to say about the wars of Jeroboam II. Only in the sense of vivid and exciting narration can the book be so classified—though in point of fact its style is far more pithy and succinct than is any genuine midrash. Yet if such thrilling adventure is to be regarded as midrash, this would apply equally well to Abraham's rescue of Lot from the Mesopotamian invaders as described in Genesis 14, or to the encounter between Christ and Satan in Matthew 4. Since elaborate visions are also part of the repertoire of midrash, the Book of Revelation in the New Testament might also have this label attached to it; although it is more usual to classify it as apocalyptic.

If Jonah fails to qualify as midrash, what about those dramatic passages in

First and Second Chronicles that are characterized by lengthy speeches (such as David's to Solomon in 1 Chron. 28, or Asa's prayer before the battle with Zerah in 2 Chron. 14:11)? Do these indicate a late storyteller's dramatic embellishments, as over against the more succinct and concise narrative in Kings? The basis for this judgment is meager; however, when a harmony such as Crockett's *Harmony of Samuel, Kings, and Chronicles* is consulted, it appears that long and dramatic episodes occur in Kings that do not appear at all in Chronicles. For example, the account of the ministry and tragic death of the prophet of Judah who came to Bethel in order to denounce Jeroboam I (1 Kings 13) is there related in as fully circumstantial and dramatic a manner as any episode recorded in Chronicles but missing in Kings.

The occasional differences in the choice of material that set Kings and Chronicles in contrast stem from the differing purpose that animated the author of each of these works. The chief concern of the historian who wrote Kings was the response of each ruler of the divided kingdom to the covenant requirements imposed on Israel back in the days of Moses. But the main purpose of the Chronicler was to emphasize the religious institutions that were meant to safeguard Israel's relationship to the Lord (hence the attention devoted to cultic ordinances and celebrations, to the regulations relating to the duties of priest and Levite). Likewise he tended to dwell on the great moments of testing and triumph that featured the career of each of the great leaders of the southern kingdom. These elements have nothing in common with the midrashic literature as we know it, and the allegation of late embellishment on the part of professional storytellers cannot be sustained against Chronicles in the light of all the objective data when fairly considered. (For further information as to midrash as a genre, the reader is directed to the article on "Midrash" in *Encyclopaedia Brittanica*, 14th ed., 15:415–16.)

Must Jonah be taken as literal history?

The Book of Jonah has often been challenged as to its credibility and historical value because of the amazing adventures it narrates concerning the prophet from Gath-hepher. How could a man be saved from drowning by the friendly offices of a whale (or "large fish"), who kept him safely in his stomach for three days and then ejected him safely onto the shore? And how could a pagan capital like Nineveh be so moved by an unknown foreigner addressing them in a strange language, threatening them with destruction from a God they knew nothing about, that they all went into mourning, fasting, and prayer so that they might be spared the threatened doom? Should we not therefore take Jonah as a historical short story with an allegorical purpose, intended to deflect the fifth-century Jews in Palestine from their nationalistic narrow-mindedness and to stir them up to evangelize the pagan nations about them?

There are several serious weaknesses to this fashionable modern theory, the most significant of which is that, according to Matthew 12:40, Jesus the Son of God believed that Jonah was completely historical. He showed this by stating, "For as Jonah was three days and three nights in the belly of a huge fish, so the Son of Man will be three days and three nights in the heart of the earth" (NIV). This puts the issue on a very clear footing. Jesus here affirms that Jonah's experience in the belly of the whale was a type of the death, burial, and resurrection that awaited Him between Good Friday and Easter morning. The coming experience of Christ, which certainly was historical, would serve as an antitype to the experience of the prophet Jonah. If the antitype was historical, then the type must also have been historical. No fictional past episode can serve as a prophetic type of a future literal fulfillment. Only fiction can correspond to fiction; only fact can correspond to fact. All other types of Christ in the Old Testament were historical (Isaac's near sacrifice on Mount Moriah, the priest-king Melchizedek, Moses, David, Solomon as types of Christ), as were the Exodus events referred to in 1 Corinthians 10 in a series of types and examples for believers in Paul's day.

The amazing response of Nineveh to the preaching of Jonah, unlikely though it may seem, was confirmed historically by Jesus when He said, "The men of Nineveh will stand up at the judgment with this generation and condemn it; for they repented at the preaching of Jonah, and now one greater than Jonah is here" (v.41). If in point of fact the Ninevites never did repent (as rationalist higher critics would have us believe), then any eschatological judgment on Jesus' unbelieving contemporaries would be quite unfair. Jesus claimed that the men of Nineveh really did repent and set an example for the Israelites of His time to follow. But if the Ninevites did not repent and Jonah was only a folk tale, their example could not shame Jesus' contemporaries because of their unbelief. Jesus, however, was sure that everything actually did happen as the Book of Jonah relates. Therefore His true followers must believe it, too.

Zechariah

What solid evidence is there that Zechariah 9-14 was written by the same author who composed Zechariah 1-8?

This is an extensive subject and requires a long, involved, and technical discussion in order to be dealt with properly. This writer has set forth the case for the unity and authenticity of Zechariah in his *Survey of Old Testament Introduction* (pp. 425-30). All the usual arguments in favor of a third-century or early second-century date for Zechariah 9-14 have been described and refuted in those six pages. The period of Zechariah's service extended from 520, when he assisted Haggai in the building campaign for the second temple in Jerusalem, to some period subsequent to 480 B.C., after the defeat of Xerxes' army in their attempt to conquer and subdue the Greeks (cf. 9:13). It is quite possible that a few decades intervened between the composition of chapters 1-8 and chapters 9-14, for there is a difference in focus and style that point to a later situation in the career of the second commonwealth of Judah than that of the earlier chapters, which are more closely related to the rebuilding of the temple (completed in 516 B.C.) and the ideological issues involved in that whole enterprise. But there is no good literary evidence for denying the composition of the two parts by the one and same author.

Special Note on Difficulties in Zechariah

It would be helpful to many readers if some attention could be devoted to the symbolism of the visions in chapters 1-6 and some of the predictive passages in chapters 7-14. These passages require very careful study and a painstaking comparison of all of the historical sources and ancient documents bearing on this period if one is to come to a clear understanding of this fascinating prophet. In this encyclopedia, however, I could do no more than suggest the correspondences and fulfillments that I have worked out in my personal study and classroom teaching of Zechariah over a period of three decades. But to present the conclusions without all of the supporting evidences on which they are based would be less than helpful to the reader. And because the only satisfactory procedure—the presentation of a brief commentary on the particularly troublesome portions that occur throughout these fourteen chapters—would far exceed the purview of this encyclopedia and would necessitate a similar treatment of the book of Revelation, I have decided to forgo delving into the involved symbolism of Zechariah. Instead, I refer the interested reader to some of the best recent treatments that are now on the market, including David Baron, *Vision and Prophecies of Zechariah* (London, 1918); George L. Robinson, *The Twelve Minor Prophets* (New York:

303

Doran, 1926); Charles L. Feinberg, *God Remembers: Studies in Zechariah* (Wheaton: Van Kampen, 1950). The forthcoming volume 7 in Zondervan's *Expositor's Bible Commentary* will include Kenneth L. Barker's commentary on Zechariah. In view of the proven ability of this scholar, this will be an outstanding piece of work.

Malachi

What is the best translation of Malachi 2:15? Why do our various English versions come up with such different renderings?

Malachi uses an especially conversational style in discussing the various grievances that God charges against His spiritually backward people in Jerusalem. In ordinary conversation we are apt to omit words that can be implied from the context. Because Hebrew does not have case endings like Greek, it is sometimes hard to tell the relationship of nouns to the verb in the clause in which they stand. So it is with this difficult verse. The KJV reads: "And did not he make one? Yet had he the residue of the spirit. And wherefore one? That he might seek a godly seed. Therefore take heed to your spirit, and let none deal treacherously against the wife of his youth." (The ASV differs from this only in substituting "although" for "Yet" and in capitalizing "Spirit," so as to indicate the Spirit of God.)

There are several problems with this rendition, the first of which is that it construes the first clause as a question, even though a negative question in biblical Hebrew usually is introduced by the interrogative particle h^a-; $h^a l\bar{o}$, occurs very frequently in negative questions. The second problem is that this wording does not yield a very clear sense in line with the stream of the

thought preceding. Thirdly, the reference to "one" is rather mystifying; who is this "one" who is spoken of in the first two sentences of this verse? The best way to determine the answer to these questions is to study the preceding context with some care and thus arrive at the contribution that this particular verse makes to the completion of the thought.

Verse 10 presents God's indictment against those men of Jerusalem who have divorced their first wives, who were Jewish believers, in order to marry younger women of pagan background and conviction. This involvement in mixed marriages amounts to a grave violation of God's law as revealed through Moses (cf. Exod. 34:16; Deut. 7:3-4) and leads to surrendering to idol worship. This danger is spelled out very clearly in v.11: "Judah has profaned the holiness of the LORD ... and married the daughter of a strange god." Verses 12-13 reveal this treachery as the reason for God's refusal to answer the prayers of Jewish worshipers who come to His altar for His blessing. Malachi says that the Lord does not accept their offerings because of the "treachery" that they have shown toward their older, legitimate wives. To each offender He declares: "Yet is she thy companion, and the wife of thy covenant"—a covenant made with her before God at the time of their marriage (v.14). From this

305

background we come to v.15, which goes as follows (in the Hebrew word order):

"And/ But/ Yet/ not one has done/ made [*wᵉlō' 'eḥād 'āśāh*] and/ but/ while/ a remnant of the Spirit/ spirit to him/ Him [*ûšᵉ'ār rûaḥ lô*]; and what/ why/ the one seeking for a posterity God/ of God? [*ûmāh hā'eḥād mᵉḇaqqēš zera' 'ᵉlōhîm*]. Therefore take heed to your spirit, and against the wife of thy youth let no one deal treacherously [*ûḇe'ēšeṯ nᵉ'ûreykā 'al-yiḇgōḏ*]."

The KJV takes Yahweh as the subject of "made" (*'āśāh*) and assumes that it is the original wedding pair that is intended (following the clue of Gen. 2:24: "And they two shall be one flesh [*ḇāśār 'eḥā-ḏ*]"). This is certainly a possible rendering, though it does require making the clause interrogative ("Did He not make one?"), even though the interrogative *hᵃ*- is almost mandatory before the negative *lō'*, according to normal biblical usage. A much more straightforward interpretation would be "But no one has done [so]" (i.e., has dealt treacherously with the wife of his youth, his first, Yahweh-worshiping wife, as implied from the previous verse). RSV makes *'eḥāḏ* the subject but understands it to refer to the one true God; but then it resorts to free paraphrase in the remainder of the sentence and blurs out the second *hā'eḥāḏ* altogether, saying, "and sustained for us the spirit of life."

If, then, the first clause refers to the individual Jewish believer who has kept faith with his first wife, the second clause probably refers to him as well: "But no one has done so who [taking the waw connective *û* before *šᵉ'ār* as a circumstantial or virtual-relative clause] has a residue of the Spirit ['has' is regularly expressed by *lô* ('to him') in Hebrew]." This means that *rûaḥ* refers not to the human spirit of the individual believer but to the Spirit of God

who wrought faith within the heart of all true believers who stood in covenant relationship with God right from the beginning of mankind. The following clause then asks, "And what does the one—the covenant-keeping husband just referred to—seek for? An offspring of God!" That is, the God-fearing father, faithful to his covenant with his Jewish wife and with the God whom they both love and serve, seeks to bring his children up as true believers, who will likewise be faithful to the covenant of grace. For these reasons, therefore, the men of Jerusalem are strongly urged to take heed to themselves and to the Holy Spirit who has made them children of God under the covenant and resist any temptation to deal treacherously with their first wife by marrying some other woman—who, while prettier and younger, does not love the Lord, and who will very likely produce children who will themselves reject the one true God in favor of the false gods of their mother.

The best rendition of this verse, then, would seem to be as follows: "But no one has done so who has a residue of the Spirit. And what does that one seek for? A godly offspring! Therefore take heed to your spirit [as a true believer under the covenant] and let none of you deal faithlessly with the wife of his youth [i.e., the wife he married when he was young]." This interpretation fits so smoothly into the flow of the thought in this paragraph that is seems almost certain to be the intention of the prophet himself. If so, the NASB is to be preferred over the NIV in the treatment of this verse. (NASB: "But not one has done so who has a remnant of the Spirit. And what did that one do while he was seeking a godly offspring?" NIV: "Has not the LORD made them one? In flesh and spirit they are his. And why one? Because he was seeking godly offspring.")

The New Testament
and the Old Testament

Why is it that many of the Old Testament quotations in the New Testament are not literal?

Many careful Bible students have noticed this phenomenon. Often this is accounted for by the fact that a completely literal translation from the Hebrew does not make clear sense in Greek; therefore some minor adjustments must be made for the sake of good communication. But in a few instances the rewording amounts to a sort of loose paraphrase. This is particularly true of quotations from the Septuagint (the translation into Greek of the entire Old Testament by Jewish scholars in Alexandria, Egypt, during the third and second centuries B.C.). Generally, the Septuagint is faithful to the Hebrew wording in the Old Testament, but in some instances there are noticeable deviations in the mode of expressing the thought, even though there may be no essential difference in the thought itself.

Some scholars have concluded from such deviations that the New Testament authors did not hold to the theory of verbal inspiration; otherwise they would have gone back to the Hebrew text and done a meticulously exact translation of their own as they rendered that text into Greek. It has even been argued that the occasional use of an inexact Septuagint rendering

in a New Testament quotation demonstrates a rejection of inerrancy on the part of the apostolic authors themselves. Their inclusion of Septuagint quotations containing elements of inexactitude seems to indicate a cavalier attitude toward the whole matter of inerrancy. On the basis of inference from the phenomena of Scripture itself, it is therefore argued that the Bible makes no claim to inerrancy.

To this line of reasoning we make the following reply. The very reason for using the Septuagint was rooted in the missionary outreach of the evangelists and apostles of the early church. The Septuagint had already found its way into every city of the Roman Empire to which the Jews of the Dispersion had gone. This was virtually the only form of the Old Testament the Jewish believers outside Palestine had, and it was certainly the only form available to Gentile converts to the Jewish faith or to Christianity. The apostles were propagating a gospel that presented Jesus Christ as the fulfillment of the messianic promises of the Old Testament. Their audiences throughout the Near East and the Mediterranean world were told to consult the Old Testament to verify the truth of the apostolic claims, that Jesus in His person and work had fulfilled the promises of God. Had the New Testament authors quoted these prom-

307

ises in any form other than the wording of the Septuagint, they would have engendered uncertainty and doubt in the minds of their hearers. For as they checked their Old Testament, the readers would have noticed the discrepancies at once—minor though they may have been—and would with one voice have objected, "But that isn't the way I read it in my Bible!" The apostles and their Jewish coworkers from Palestine may have been well-equipped to do their own original translation from the Hebrew original. But they would have been ill-advised to substitute their own more literal rendering for that form of the Old Testament that was already in the hands of their public. They really had little choice but to keep largely to the Septuagint in all their quotations of the Old Testament.

On the other hand, the special Hebrew-Christian audience to which the evangelist Matthew addressed himself—and even more notably the recipients of the Epistle to the Hebrews—did not require such a constant adherence to the Septuagint as was necessary for a Gentile readership. Hence Matthew and Hebrews often quote from the Old Testament in a non-Septuagintal form, normally in a form somewhat closer to the wording of the Hebrew original.

It should also be observed that in a few cases, at least, the Greek renderings (whether Septuagintal or not) of the Old Testament point to a variant reading in the original form of the text that is better than the one that has come down to us in the standard Hebrew Bible. It should be carefully noted that none of this yields any evidence whatever of carelessness or disregard on the part of the apostles in respect to the exact wording of the original Hebrew. Far from it! In some instances Christ Himself based His teaching on a careful exegesis of the exact reading in the Torah. For exam-

ple, He pointed out in Matthew 22:32 the implications of Exodus 3:6 ("I *am* the God of Abraham, and the God of Isaac, and the God of Jacob") on the basis of the present tense implied by the verbless clause in Hebrew. He declared that God would not have spoken of Himself as the God of mere corpses moldering in the grave ("God is not the God of the dead but of the living"). Therefore Abraham, Isaac, and Jacob must have been alive and well in the life beyond when God addressed Moses at the burning bush, four or five centuries later. Similarly Christ's discussion with the Pharisees concerning the identity of the one referred to as "my Lord" in Psalm 110:1 really turned on the exact terms used in that clause or sentence. He therefore asked them, "If David then calls Him 'Lord,' how is He his son?" (Matt. 22:45, NASB). In other words, the Messiah must not only be David's lineal descendant, but He must also be his divine Lord (*kyrios*)!

Returning, then, to the apostolic use of the Septuagint, we find that this line of reasoning (that inexact quotations imply a low view of the Bible) is really without foundation. All of us employ translations of the Bible in our teaching and preaching, even those of us who are thoroughly conversant with the Greek and Hebrew originals. But our use of any translation in English, French, or any other modern language by no means implies that we have abandoned a belief in scriptural inerrancy, even though some errors of translation appear in every modern version. We use these standard translations to teach our readers in terms they can verify from the Bibles they have. But most of us are careful to point out to them that the only final authority as to the meaning of Scripture is the wording of the original languages themselves. There is no infallible translation. But this involves no surrender of the conviction that the original manuscripts of Scripture were free from all error. We must therefore conclude that the New Testament use of the Septuagint implies nothing against verbal inspiration or scriptural inrancy.

Doesn't the Old Testament present a different kind of God than the New Testament?

It is commonly thought by those who have not studied the Bible very carefully that the Old Testament presents a God who is full of vengeance and wrath as He enforces the standards of righteousness, whereas the New Testament reveals Him to be full of compassion and love, always seeking to forgive and restore guilty sinners. In point of fact, however, the Hebrew Scriptures (partly because they make up three-fourths of the Bible) contain far more verses on the mercy and lovingkindness of God than the New Testament does. Deuteronomy lays the greatest emphasis on the faithful, unquenchable love of God for His people. Deuteronomy 7:8 says, "But because the LORD loved you and kept the oath which He swore to your forefathers, the LORD brought you out by a mighty hand, and redeemed you from the house of slavery, from the hand of Pharaoh king of Egypt" (NASB). Psalm 103:13 reads, "As a father has compassion on his children, so the LORD has compassion on those who fear him" (NASB). Verse 17 says, "But the lovingkindness of the LORD is from everlasting to everlasting on those who fear Him, and His righteousness to children's children" (NASB). Jeremiah 31:3 has the same message: "The LORD appeared to us in the past, saying: 'I have loved you with an everlasting love; I have drawn you with loving-kindness'" (NIV). Psalm 136 affirms no less than twenty-six times that "His [Yahweh's] love endures forever."

In the New Testament there is a tremendous display of the love of God. In fact, the supreme display is in the sacrifice of His only Son on the cross of Calvary; and no one ever spoke more movingly about the love of God the Father than did His Son in the Sermon on the Mount, in John in 3:16, and throughout the Gospels. Perhaps no sublimer words can be found than Romans 8:31-38, which describes the unfailing and unquenchable love of God for His children.

But at the same time it should also be observed that the New Testament teaches the wrath of God just as forcefully as the Old Testament does. John 3:36 says, "But he who does not obey the Son shall not see life, but the wrath of God abides on him" (NASB). Romans 1:18 states, "For the wrath of God is revealed from heaven against all ungodliness and unrighteousness of men, who suppress the truth in unrighteousness" (NASB). Again, in Romans 2:5-6 we read, "But because of your stubbornness and unrepentant heart you are storing up wrath for yourself in the day of wrath and revelation of the righteous judgment of God; who will render to every man according to his deeds" (NASB). And consider 2 Thessalonians 1:6-9:

> For after all it is only just for God to repay with affliction those who afflict you, and to give relief to you who are afflicted and to us as well when the Lord Jesus shall be revealed from heaven with His mighty angels in flaming fire, dealing out retribution to those who do not know God and to those who do not obey the gospel of our Lord Jesus. And these will pay the penalty of eternal destruction, away from the presence of the Lord and from the glory of His power (NASB).

This theme recurs right through to the end of the New Testament, as in Revelation 6:15-17: "And the kings of the earth and the great men ... hid themselves in the caves and among the rocks of the mountains; and they said to the mountains and to the rocks, 'Fall on us and hide us from the presence of Him who sits on the throne, and from the wrath of the Lamb; for the great day of their wrath has come; and who is able to stand?'" (NASB). No passage in the Old Testament can compare with the fearsome description of God's judicial wrath found in Revelation 14:9–11. Truly our just and holy God is "a consuming fire"—in both Testaments, the Old and the New (Deut. 4:24; Heb. 12:29).

The portrait of God is altogether consistent throughout the sixty-six books of the Bible. God's wrath is the reverse side of His love. As the up-holder of the moral law—and He would be an unholy, Satan-like God if He failed to uphold it— God must pass judgment and execute sentence on every unrepentant sinner, whether demon or man. The sacrifice of His Son on the cross was the supreme exhibition of God's indignation against sin, for in the hour of final agony even Jesus had to cry out with anguish of soul, "My God, My God, why hast Thou forsaken Me?" And yet the Cross was also the supreme revelation of His unfathomable love, for it was the God-man who suffered there for us, the Just for the unjust, that He might bring us to God.

The Synoptic Gospels

Why are there differences among the synoptic Gospels?

Of the three Synoptists, only Matthew was one of the twelve disciples. Mark seems to have been an assistant to Peter, at least according to church tradition; but he probably accompanied the Twelve much of the time during Jesus' later ministry. At least the special mention (found only in Mark) of a certain young man who fled away naked from the scene of the arrest at Gethsemane quite possibly refers to him, even though he does not give his name. Luke became associated with Paul on his first journey to Macedonia (Acts 16:10), and later became intimate with the Jerusalem apostles and Jesus' mother, as he devoted himself to a careful biography of Jesus' life. Apparently Luke was not a Jew (unlike the other NT authors), if we may judge from Colossians 4:11 and 14. Evidently he had enjoyed a fine education in literary Greek, even though much of his narration was couched in simple Hebrew style (contrast Luke 1:1–4 and the remainder of that chapter). John, of course, was one of the inner circle of the original Twelve; and he composed his gospel after the Synoptics had been published. Much of his material consisted of private discourses spoken to believers who were more mature in their understanding and faith.

As we compare the accounts given by each of the three Synoptists, we find a special set of emphases or circle of interests that characterizes each of them and exerts a controlling influence on their selection of material—both as to what they include and as to what they leave out. Even in the manner of arranging their material, there are differences appropriate to their own special perspective. They have about fifty-three units in common among themselves. Matthew has forty-two units unique to him, Mark has only seven, and Luke has fifty-nine (there are ninety-two in John) according to Westcott's tabulation. About one-half of Mark is found in Matthew, but only one-fourth of Luke. As we investigate cases of divergence between the three Synoptics, it may be helpful to recognize their special emphases and concerns as they relate to us the life of our Lord.

Matthew lays special emphasis on Christ as the Messiah and King who fulfills the promises and predictions of the Hebrew Scriptures. He seems to have a Jewish constituency in view as he brings in numerous quotations from the Old Testament, many of which are not from the Septuagint (as the other Evangelists' quotations tend to be), but which show a greater faithfulness to the Masoretic text (the standard form of the Hebrew that has come down to us today). This indicates that his audience is not dependent on a Greek translation; and this serves as a

311

confirmation that the original form of his gospel was "in Hebrew" (this statement is found not only in Papias [A.D. 130] in his "Exposition of the Oracles of the Lord" [cited by Eusebius] but also in Irenaeus, Origen, and Jerome). By "Hebrew" Papias probably meant the Jewish dialect of Aramaic. Apparently only afterwards was Matthew's gospel translated into Greek, the form in which it has come down to us. Matthew makes more frequent reference to the law of Moses than the others do, and he uses the pious Jewish locution "kingdom of heaven" as a substitute for "the kingdom of God" in the oral teaching of Jesus. (This tendency to refer to God by the locution "Heaven" is also apparent in the Mishnaic Jewish tradition of the rabbis, but not in the Aramaic Targums, which use the phrase "kingdom of God" almost as consistently as Mark, Luke, and John. Matthew himself uses "kingdom of heaven" thirty-two times and "kingdom of God" only four times [12:28; 19:24; 21:31,43]. The probabilities are that Jesus used both expressions, but Matthew used "of heaven" as more congenial to his special audience, the Palestinian Jews.)

The Palestinian focus is also found in Matthew's attention to details about contemporary Jewish life and religious customs. The teaching of Jesus was designed to correct unsound interpretations of the Torah that were sophistic evasions of the true intent of God's law; these receive special emphasis in Matthew's gospel. Matthew devotes particular attention to Jesus' teaching ministry and tends to group logically cohesive themes of instruction into major blocks, of which there are four outstanding examples. Especially prominent are (1) the Sermon on the Mount (which may have been delivered all at one time, though it must have been partially repeated elsewhere, judging from the Sermon on the Plain in Luke 6:17–49); (2) the parables of the king-

dom, which are similarly collected in Matthew 13:1–52 but tend to occur separately in Mark and Luke; (3) the Olivet Discourse in Matthew 24 which does not substantially differ from Mark 13 and Luke 21; but insofar as it is tied right in with Matthew 25 (the foolish virgins, the parable of the talents, and the judgment of the nations), it does represent a cluster grouping not found in the others; and (4) the long denunciation of Pharisaical hypocrisy and casuistry in Matthew 23, which is not found in the others.

There is also an interesting tension between the theme of salvation through Christ as being primarily intended for the Jews (in fulfillment of the Old Testament promises and the widening of its scope to the Gentile nations in accordance with the Great Commission [Matt. 28:16–19]). On the one hand, Jesus emphasizes that His primary mission was to "the lost sheep of the house of Israel" (15:24), and that was the ground of His tendency to avoid any of the Gentile areas around Palestine (10:5). (Only Mark 7 mentions Jesus' short visit to the region of Tyre.) Jesus even encourages His disciples to follow the teaching of the law of Moses as explained by the scribes and Pharisees (23:2). On the other hand, Matthew alone records the visit of the Gentile Magi soon after Christ's birth (2:1–12), as if to emphasize the potential outreach of Christ's rule to all the nations of the earth. In the record he gives of the parable of the wicked husbandmen, Matthew records the full text of Jesus' judgment on His unbelieving countrymen: "Therefore I tell you that the kingdom of God will be taken away from you and given to a nation that produces the fruits of it" (21:43). The parallels in Mark and Luke summarize His statement by saying simply "shall be given to others."

Mark is not so much concerned with Jesus as the messianic Prophet as he is with Jesus as the Conqueror over Satan, sin, sickness, and death—the Man of action who triumphs as the Suffering Servant (Isa. 53). Mark focuses on Jesus' dynamism and redemptive deeds rather than on His philosophy and theological teaching. In this biography the action moves rapidly, and the characteristic word is "straightway" (*euthys*). The church tradition that Mark, having served at first with Barnabas and Paul, became an assistant to Peter at Rome (if Peter in fact did go to Rome) may be correct. If so, much of his narrative concerning Christ would have tended to summarize Peter's own characteristic presentation of Christ's life and deeds, with its heavy emphasis on the suffering of Christ and the events of Passion Week (chaps. 11–16), nearly two-fifths of the entire text of the Gospel). The detailed reference to Simon of Cyrene, who bore Christ's cross, as the "father of Alexander and Rufus" may tie in with the Rufus mentioned in Romans 16:13 as a member of the Christian community in Rome.

Mark has several interesting quotations from Jesus' *ipsissima verba* in His native Aramaic, such as *Boanērges* (rendered "Sons of thunder") in Mark 3:17; *ephphatha* (for *'etpāttah*, meaning "open up!") in 7:34; *talitha koum(i)* (rendered "Maiden, arise!") in 5:41; and *Elōi* (or better *Ēlī*) *lema sabachthani* (rendered "My God, My God, why hast Thou forsaken Me?") in 15:34. These sound like explanations intended for Dispersion Jews unfamiliar with Aramaic or for Gentiles, who might especially appreciate these interpretations. Mark also took particular pains to explain Jewish religious customs (cf. 7:3ff.). Clark Pinnock summarizes Mark's emphasis by saying that Mark is especially concerned to present Jesus as the "Son of God, the glorious Son of man, and the Redeemer" (in Tenney, *Zondervan Pictorial Encyclopedia*, 2:786).

Luke came to his task from the perspective of an educated Greek, a physician who took a special interest in the details of Christ's miracles of healing. He was concerned to present a comprehensive, historically accurate biography of Jesus as the perfect Son of Man, bringing out His excellencies and surpassing tenderness in dealing with people.

It was his announced purpose to set forth a carefully researched account, "having investigated everything carefully from the beginning," so that Theophilus and his other readers "might know the exact truth" about the words and deeds of the Lord Jesus. The terms *akribōs kathexēs* ("accurately in correct order") indicate his policy of following fairly strict chronological order in the arrangement of his material and also of including biographical material omitted by the other Synoptists that he felt would help complete the portrait of Jesus in all its beauty and grandeur. (One notable departure from chronological order may be found in his account of Christ's wilderness temptation, and even that exception is disputed by many scholars.) Luke includes more details of our Lord's life than do the other Evangelists. He gives all the background for the birth of John the Baptist and includes all the prophetic utterances that accompanied John's birth as well as that of Jesus. Luke alone records the angelic annunciation to Mary, the visit of the shepherds to Bethlehem, and the birth of our Lord in a stable. He alone narrates Jesus' presentation in the temple, the prophecy of Simeon, and Jesus' adventure in Jerusalem as a lad of twelve. In chapter 4 Luke tells of Jesus' rejection by the angry mob at Nazareth and alone relates the story of the raising of the dead son of the widow of Nain (7:11–17).

Much interest is devoted to Jesus' dealings with women and children and His tender regard and consideration for them. Luke mentions not only well-known women like Mary and

Martha (who figure so prominently in John's gospel) but also a good many others (perhaps as many as thirteen) not mentioned elsewhere. Of particular moment is the emphasis on Jesus' concern for those who were considered social outcasts, such as Samaritans and publicans (like Matthew-Levi and Zacchaeus), the band of ten lepers (17:11–19), the weeping women of Jerusalem (23:27–31), and the repentant thief who hung on the cross beside Him (23:39–43). Valuable details omitted by others pertain to important developments on Easter Sunday, such as His meeting with the two disciples on the road to Emmaus and His first visit to the assembled disciples after the Crucifixion (24:36–39). Luke alone gives us details of Christ's ascension from the Mount of Olives (24:50–53; Acts 1:9–11).

In his zeal for accuracy and precision, Luke used about 180 terms in his gospel that occur nowhere else in the New Testament, and many of them are rare and technical. He devotes special attention to various types of disease and physical sufferings, such as the "great fever" that afflicted Peter's mother-in-law (4:38). Especially noteworthy is his description of Christ's agony in the Garden of Gethsemane, with His sweat dropping from His face and frame like great drops of blood (22:44). Similar attention to detail characterizes Luke's other book, Acts, where in chapter 28, for example, he describes the shipwreck at Melita (Malta)—using at least 17 nautical terms with technical accuracy—the deadly adder that failed to do Paul any harm by its venomous fangs, and the fever and dysentery that afflicted Publius.

Luke, then, is preeminently the gospel of Christ's humanity and of His surpassing love and tenderness as the Son of Man. Also, Luke is certainly the most comprehensive of the four biographers in covering the details of Christ's earthly life.

The purpose of this brief characterization of each of the three Synoptists has been to furnish some sort of guideline or rationale in accounting for what each Evangelist includes in his record and what he omitted, and for the particular manner of his presentation. But it should be understood that all three of them accurately related the events of Christ's career and the words of His mouth, even though they included only what was pertinent to their particular approach. When any room is photographed in a person's home, the camera may well capture different views of the contents, depending on the angle from which the picture is shot. All of them are accurate, even though they are by no means identical. The same is true with a classroom of students who are engaged in taking notes on their teacher's lecture. Each student will note at least a few details that are not reported by the others, and yet none of them will be making a false report of what the instructor said.

In the same way we are to fit together the testimony of each of the three Synoptists. Each one is on the alert for details that fit in with his own special view of Jesus, and so there are naturally going to be inclusions and omissions that correspond with the particular aim of each Evangelist. (Students of classical Greek literature notice a similar phenomenon in regard to Plato's portrait of Socrates, his revered teacher in Athens, and the quite different emphasis of Xenophon, who was another of Socrates' pupils. Plato dwells on his teacher's skill in dialogue and his masterful treatment of philosophical themes: Xenophon in the *Symposium* concentrates on the character and personality of Socrates, as indicated by various anecdotes from personal experience. The two witnesses bring out different aspects of their master, but neither is in error!)

As we deal with episodes in our Lord's life that are of such importance that all three (or even John as well) furnish an account, our task is to line them up beside one another and see how each fits in with or supplements the others. In almost every case, a careful consideration will yield a synthetic account that bears a resemblance to a stereophonic player as contrasted with a monaural player, or a trio of monaural recorders. Some writers deprecate Tatian's *Diatessaron* (which interweaves material from all four Gospels to form a composite, sequential account of Jesus' works and words), but with dubious justification. Essentially the same method is followed in every inquest or court hearing where a multiplicity of witnesses are to be heard. Each of them may contribute differing details that bear on the case, but the judge and jury that hear the various testimonies are expected to fit together the contribution of each witness into a self-consistent, coherent picture of the entire episode or transaction.

Bible critics who have never had any training in the law of evidences may decry the "harmonistic method" all they wish; but like it or not, it is essentially the harmonistic method that is followed every day that court is in session throughout the civilized world. This method has a very definite bearing on valid procedures in biblical criticism, as well as in the practical conduct of a tort or criminal action, or even a contract case in a court of law, today. Then the critics would find that most of their artificial, logically fallacious and basically biased approaches to the text of Holy Scripture would be successfully challenged by even the most inexperienced attorney and thrown out by the presiding judge. From a truly scientific and objective approach such as is followed in a responsibly conducted action at law, the three Synoptists have nothing to fear so far as credibility and verification are concerned. The same is true with the rest of Scripture.

Matthew

From which of David's sons was Jesus descended? In Matthew 1:6 Jesus' ancestry is traced through Solomon, while in Luke 3:31 it is traced through Nathan. (D*)

Matthew 1:1–16 gives the genealogy of Jesus through Joseph, who was himself a descendant of King David. As Joseph's adopted Son, Jesus became his legal heir, so far as his inheritance was concerned. Notice carefully the wording of v.16: "And Jacob begat Joseph the husband of Mary, of whom was born Jesus, who is called Christ" (NASB). This stands in contrast to the format followed in the preceding verses of the succession of Joseph's ancestors: "Abraham begat [*egennēsen*] Isaac, and Isaac begat Jacob, etc." Joseph is not said to have begotten Jesus; rather he is referred to as "the husband of Mary, of whom [feminine genitive] Jesus was born."

Luke 3:23–38, on the other hand, seems to record the genealogical line of Mary herself, carried all the way back beyond the time of Abraham to Adam and the commencement of the human race. This seems to be implied by the wording of v.23: "Jesus. . .being (as was supposed) the son of Joseph." This "as was supposed" indicates that Jesus was not really the biological son of Joseph, even though this was commonly assumed by the public. It further calls attention to the mother, Mary, who must of necessity have been the sole human parent through whom Jesus could have descended from a line of ancestors. Her genealogy is thereupon listed, starting with Heli, who was actually Joseph's father-in-law, in contradistinction to Joseph's own father, Jacob (Matt. 1:16). Mary's line of descent came through Nathan, a son of Bathsheba (or "Bathshua," according to 1 Chron. 3:5), the wife of David. Therefore, Jesus was descended from David naturally through Nathan and legally through Solomon.

Does not Matthew 1:9 err in listing Uzziah as the father of Jotham?

Matthew 1:9, which gives the genealogy of Jesus through His legal father, Joseph, states, "Ozias begat Joatham." These are the Greek forms of Uzziah and Jotham. Some are confused by this mention of Uzziah, because Jotham's father is called Azariah in 2 Kings 15:1–7 and in 1 Chronicles 3:12. On the other hand, 2 Kings 15:32,34 calls him Uzziah rather than Azariah and refers to him as the father of Jotham. The same is true of 2 Chronicles 26:1–23; 27:2; Isaiah 1:1; 6:1; 7:1. The names are different, but they refer to the same king. *ʿazaryāh* ("Azariah") means "Yahweh has helped," whereas *ʿuzzî-yāhû* ("Uzziah") means "Yahweh is my strength." The reason for the two names is not given in the biblical record, but the fact that he bore them both (perhaps Azariah was later replaced by Uzziah) is beyond dispute.

There are various reasons for the acquisition of second names in the case of Israel's leaders. Gideon acquired the name Jerubbaal because of his destruction of the altar of Baal at Ophrah (Judg. 6:32; 7:1; 8:29, etc.). Rehoboam's son Abijam was also called Abijah (cf. 1 Kings 14:31; 15:1, 7–8 for Abijam and 1 Chron. 3:10; 2 Chron. 12:16 for Abijah). Jehoahaz son of Josiah also bore the name of Shallum (2 Kings 23:21 and 1 Chron. 3:15; Jer. 22:11). Jehoiakim, Josiah's oldest son, was originally named Eliakim; but Pharaoh Necho changed his name to Jehoiakim (i.e., "Yahweh will establish" rather than "God will establish"), according to 2 Kings 23:34. Likewise Jehoiachin son of Jehoiakim was also known as Jeconiah, and Zedekiah's original name was Mattaniah.

Astrology is condemned in the Bible as a form of idolatry. Yet in Matthew 2:2 the birth of Christ was told to the Magi by the appearance of His star in the heavens. How can this be? (D*)

First of all, we need to define astrology as a superstitious belief in the movement or the position of the planets and stars as forewarnings of the will of the gods (or the forces of fate), which the devotees of astrology may somehow cope with by taking some sort of evasive or preventive action. Or else, as with the horoscopes and study of the signs of the zodiac so much in vogue today, astrology may indicate special potentialities in those born under a certain constellation, or signify good or bad luck for activities that might be engaged in during that particular day. In ancient pre-Christian times, this concern for astrology was accompanied by actual worship of the heavenly bodies in a ritualistic way. All who carried on such practices in ancient Israel were subject to execution by stoning (Deut. 17:2–7).

In the case of the natal star of Christ, however, none of the above elements was involved. The star the Magi saw in the East constituted an announcement that the Christ child had been born. We know this because of the scope of Herod's command to his corps of butchers sent to Bethlehem: "When Herod realized that he had been outwitted by the Magi, he was furious, and he gave orders to kill all the boys in Bethlehem and its vicinity who were two years old and under, in accordance with the time he had learned from the Magi" (Matt. 2:16, NIV). Therefore the star must have appeared when Jesus was born, and it must have required the Magi more than a year to get to Jerusalem and have their interview with Herod. The star was not a fore warning but the announcement of an already accomplished fact.

Second, no worship of false gods or of deterministic powers of fate was involved in this pilgrimage of the Magi. They simply received God's announcement through the star as requiring them to seek the newborn King, because they understood that He was destined to be Ruler over the entire world—including their own country (which might have been Persia, since the Magi were most active there in ancient times). They therefore decided to make up a caravan for the group (whether there were three of them or more, we cannot be sure, except perhaps for the three types of gifts mentioned: gold, frankincense, and myrrh) and conduct a pilgrimage to the kingdom of the Jews. They wished to do homage to the God-sent Baby destined to become King of the Jews and of the whole earth as well.

Third, it should be understood that the Scripture speaks in several other passages of divine announcements in the heavens set forth by the sun, moon, and stars. For example, Jesus speaks of "the sign of the Son of Man" that will "appear in the sky, . . . with power and great glory" (Matt. 24:30, NIV). It is fair to assume that this sign will include the sun, moon, or stars—though it could be some sort of blazing apparition. But certainly at Pentecost the apostle Peter, quoting from Joel 2:28–32, was referring to these signs of the Second Coming when he said, "I will show wonders in the heaven above. . . . The sun will be turned to darkness and the moon to blood before the coming of the great and glorious day of the Lord" (Acts 2:19–20, NIV). These celestial manifestations have nothing to do with astrology as a pagan superstition.

One last word about the star of Bethlehem. Much speculation and astronomical calculation have been devoted to the question of how such a bright and outstanding star could have been visible to the Magi. Some have suggested that there was an unusual lining up of planets or stars so that their combined light could have produced such a noteworthy brilliance. While such a cause might be assigned to the appearance of the original star, it is highly unlikely that any normal star was capable of directing its glow so specifically over Bethlehem that the wise men could identify the place where the Christ child was then residing. And yet according to Matthew 2:9, "The star they had seen in the east went ahead of them until it stopped over the place where the child was." This was plainly a supernatural star sent by God for their special guidance.

Is not Matthew 2:6 a distortion of Micah 5:2 that significantly alters its meaning?

There are several minor variants in wording as between the Hebrew text of Micah 5:2 and the quotation of it in Matthew 2:6. There is also one major deviation of an unusual sort: a nega-

tive has apparently been substituted for a positive. As seems often to be the case, Matthew did not quote from the Septuagint version (LXX) but from some other Greek translation, possibly Proto-Theodotion. Actually the LXX is very close to the Masoretic text (MT) in this verse, and its only deviations are minimal concessions to Greek idiom. But Matthew used a more paraphrastic version, or perhaps injected a bit of interpretation as he dealt directly with the Hebrew original, endeavoring to bring out implications rather than giving a merely literal rendering.

In the first clause, addressed to Bethlehem, the house of Ephrathah, Matthew substitutes for "Ephrathah" the phrase "land of Judah." The LXX uses "house of Judah," as if repeating after *leḥem* the *bêt* that appears before it. Matthew may have derived from the etymology of Ephrathah a poetic name for Judah as "Fruitful One" (from the root *p-r-y*, "fruit" or "be fruitful") the rendering above given.

The MT and the LXX agree in rendering the second clause "Thou art small to be among the thousands of Judah." Surprisingly enough, Matthew injects a strong negative in this main clause. Where the other two say positively, "Thou art small [*ṣā'îr*; LXX says 'very small' (*oligostos*)] to be among the thousands of Judah [*bᵉ 'alᵉ pê Yᵉ hûdāh*; LXX has *en chiliasin Iouda*], "Matthew resorts to a paraphrase in order to bring out the implication behind the positive statement used by Micah himself. In other words, if Micah is saying to Bethlehem that it is small in size to be reckoned among the thousand-family towns of Judah, yet the messianic ruler is destined to come from there, this adds up to the insight that Bethlehem is really a very important town indeed, one of commanding leadership. Consequently Matthew feels justified in commencing the clause with a strong negative; that is, if the promised Messiah is destined to come out of Bethlehem, then it is by no means the least in Judah, despite the modest size of its normal population. So Matthew ends up with "Thou art by no means [*oudamōs*] least among the rulers of Judah."

The second variation in the second clause has to do with the treatment of the word *ªlāpîm*, "thousands"—which even the LXX renders as *chiliasin* (dative plural of *chilias*, "a thousand"). Matthew 2:6 refers to it as *hēgemosin* ("rulers"). How can this change be justified? Well, in this context it is clear that it is a town that is being addressed, rather than a literal army unit. Possibly towns were so referred to (cf. 1 Sam. 23:23) because they contained a thousand families, or else because they were capable of mustering at least a thousand men-at-arms for the national militia. The standard term for a subdivision of a tribe was either *mišpāḥāh* ("family," "clan," "sub-tribe") or else *'elep* (1 Sam. 10:19,21). From that specific submeaning it was but a step to refer to its military commander or civil ruler by the same term, just as the Latin *centurio* ("centurion") was derived from *centuria* ("a company of one hundred soldiers").

There is also a possibility, however, that Matthew (or the non-Septuagintal Greek version from which he was quoting) read *'allûpîm* (actually in the construct plural, *'allûpê*) instead of MT's *ªlepê* ("thousands of"). This would involve no change of spelling in the consonants themselves, and vowel points were not added to the consonantal text of the Hebrew Bible until about A.D. 700. *'Allû-pîm* is the plural of *'allûp* ("chieftain," "colonel in command of a thousand troops"). This is adequately rendered by *hēgemōn* ("ruler") and would therefore justify Matthew's interpretation of this term. For all we know, this was the word Micah actually intended to write back in the late eighth century B.C., when the *waw*, which is characteristic of post-Exilic or-

thography, had not yet been introduced into the spelling of this word. In view of the clear suggestion of a messianic deliverer, destined by God to rule the world, the context tends to support this interpretation of *'-l-p-y* almost as strongly as the vocalization put on it by the Masoretes. The only problem is to relate the concept of "ruler" with the town of Bethlehem as a municipality. Yet even this may be understood as implying that a great messianic ruler (*môšēl*) might logically be expected to come from a leading city in the territory of Judah, such as Hebron, Lachish, or Bethshemesh, rather than from a small community like Bethlehem in Micah's day.

It is quite significant that the final portion of Matthew 2:6 is really not taken from Micah 5:2 at all, even though it somewhat resembles it. Micah 5:2b says, "From you One will go forth for Me to be a ruler in Israel" (NASB). Matthew 2:6b concurs in part: "For out of you shall come forth a Ruler," but then it concludes with the words "who will shepherd My people Israel" (NASB). Notice that "will shepherd My people" is not found at all in Micah. Rather, it is inserted from 2 Samuel 5:2, which contains a promise from the Lord to King David, quoted to him by the leaders of the Ten Tribes at Hebron: "And the LORD said to you, 'You will shepherd My people Israel, and you will be a ruler over Israel.'" (NASB). Therefore the words "will shepherd My people" are taken from 2 Samuel 5 rather than from Micah 5 (both contain "Israel" as the concluding word); and we find ourselves dealing with a conflate quotation, combining portions of Micah 5:2 and 2 Samuel 5:2.

From this commingling of passages, we are to gather that Matthew did not intend to furnish a literal rendering of a single Old Testament verse, but meant rather to bring together two passages bearing on the fulfillment of divine prophecy in regard to the place of Messiah's birth, and apparently in regard to His royal lineage as well. The phrase from 2 Samuel 5 suggests by implication that the Ruler who is to be born in Bethlehem will fulfill perfectly the model of the theocratic King first exemplified by His ancestor David. (For other examples of conflate quotations in the New Testament, cf. Matt. 27:9-10, which combines elements from Zech. 11:12-13 with an important element taken from Jer. 19:2,11, and 32:6-9. Another case is Mark 1:2-3, which combines Isa. 40:3 with Mal. 3:1.)

In light of the author's intention, therefore, it is clear that Matthew did not contradict or pervert the meaning of Micah 5:2 (or of 2 Sam. 5:2) in the way he interpreted their implication according to the divine purpose that underlay them both. Furthermore, it is entirely possible that Herod's Bible experts quoted from more than one Old Testament passage. In a sense, therefore, they were the ones responsible for the wording, rather than Matthew himself.

Why do Matthew and Luke differ in the order of Christ's temptations?

Matthew 4:5-10 puts the proposal to jump from the pinnacle of the temple as the second of Christ's three temptations and the offer of the world empire as the third. Luke 4:5-12 makes the offer of the empire temptation number two and the jump from the pinnacle number three. Here we have a clear-cut discrepancy. How are we to account for it without sacrificing the doctrine of scriptural inerrancy?

This is understandably one of the often-debated questions raised in any discussion of the Synoptic accounts of Christ's life. But is is not really unique, for similar problems arise in connection with the cursing of the fig tree in Matthew 21:18-19 and Mark 11:12-

21. Likewise, compare the "staff" passage in Mark 6:8 ("only a staff") with Matthew 10:10 and Luke 9:30 ("no staff"). In each case the technical differences arise from the special aim of the various Synoptists as they draw their portrait of Jesus.

In the case of the conflicting order of the second and third temptations as recorded by Matthew and Luke, we must take note of the adverbs and conjunctions employed by each in relating the episode. In the case of Matthew, there is a more definite emphasis on the sequence of the two temptations than in Luke. Matthew 4:5 says, "Then [tote] the Devil takes Him along to the holy city, and he set Him on the pinnacle of the temple." After Jesus has refused to cast Himself down from it, as Satan proposed, we read, "Again [palin] the Devil takes Him along to a very high mountain and shows Him all the kingdoms." These two adverbs, tote and palin, seem to be quite specific indeed—so specific that if the second and third temptations did not take place in that order, then Matthew would definitely have been in error.

In Luke's case, however, a simple kai ("and") is all that introduces the second temptation mentioned (the offer of a world empire). Likewise the third temptation (the jump from the pinnacle) is led into with a mere de ("and" or " but"). This account is by no means so emphatic in regard to sequence as are Matthew's tote and palin. It is much like the report of the little girl who said, "Do you know what we had for Thanksgiving yesterday? We had apple pie and turkey and everything!" The chances are that a more careful interrogation would reveal that she had been served the turkey before she had her apple pie. But she mentioned the pie first because she thought of it first, no doubt preferring the dessert to the main course. Could her report be faulted as erroneous under these circumstances? Hardly!

No more should Luke be reproached for reversing the order from the chronological standpoint so as to keep to an ideational order—if indeed it was he who reversed the order rather than Matthew.

From the evidence of the two adverbs mentioned above, we may reasonably deduce that Matthew adhered to the historical sequence in putting the pinnacle before the mountain top. But for Luke, there may have been a more logical order in putting the temptation of taking an immediate shortcut to world power as an appropriate middle stage in the ascending order of testings, rather than the climactic display of supernatural powers before the great throng worshiping at the Jerusalem temple.

That Luke should be less exact than Matthew in matters of chronological order may seem surprising, since Luke normally is the most careful of all the Synoptists in regard to correct sequence. But in this particular chapter he seems to have preferred a proleptic order in the interests of dramatic effect. This is very clearly brought out by the ensuing episode: Jesus' visit to His hometown of Nazareth. It was a very striking development that right after He had passed through the gauntlet of spiritual battle with Satan (vv.1–13), and thus proved His mettle as Messiah, Jesus should have made His way first of all back to His own people in Nazareth. But there He met with incredulity and rejection and even had His life threatened before He finally departed for Capernaum.

Very significantly in the course of His sermon at the Nazareth synagogue, Jesus quoted the people as murmuring against Him, "Physician, heal yourself! Those great things that we heard took place in Capernaum, perform them here as well, in your own hometown!" (v.23). But the interesting thing about this remark is that up until this point Luke had made no mention of Capernaum at all, and yet Jesus' audience had already heard about the miracles He had performed there. Not until after He escaped from the riot His sermon evoked does our Lord make His way back to Capernaum, which He had begun to use as His headquarters. His reception there was far more cordial and appreciative than at Nazareth (4:31–32), and it was there that He performed the notable miracles of healing the demoniac in their synagogue (vv.33–37) and instantaneously curing Peter's mother-in-law as she lay at death's door with a high fever (vv.38–39). It may have been that these particular cures were performed after His visit to Nazareth; but there can be no doubt (on the basis of v.23) that Jesus had already been to Capernaum and had done some notable miracles there *before* He went over to Nazareth (cf. vv.14–15). Yet Luke does not mention Capernaum by name until *after* Nazareth. The advantage he gained from the heightened contrast between the two cities may have prompted him in this case also to depart from strict chronological sequence.

When the centurion's servant was ill, who actually came to Jesus, the centurion (Matt. 8:5–13) or the servant himself (Luke 7:2–11)?

Matthew 8:5 states: "Now when he had entered Capernaum, a centurion came to Him, beseeching Him." This states very explicitly that it was the centurion who came to Jesus; the servant himself was paralyzed and confined to his bed, suffering great pain. It would obviously have been impossible for him to come to Jesus in person.

Luke 7:2 says, "A servant of a certain centurion was very sick and about to die, and he was highly esteemed by him." From the context, it was the servant who was highly esteemed by the centurion; therefore, the "by him" must refer to the centurion rather than the servant. This establishes the fact that the subject of the next sentence is necessarily the centurion also. In other words, when v.3 begins "And hearing of Jesus he sent to Him elders of the Jews, asking Him that He would come and heal his servant," it is perfectly evident that Luke also reports that it was not the servant who came to Jesus in person; rather, it was the centurion. The nearest eligible antecedent for the participle *akousas* ("hearing") and for *apesteilen* ("he sent") is *autō* ("by him"), which was the last to be mentioned. Hence these two accounts are in perfect agreement.

Perhaps it should be added that Luke contributes the detail that the centurion sent on a committee of Jewish elders to intercede with Jesus on his behalf. Only after the elders had explained to Christ how deserving the centurion was of His favorable consideration did He enter into direct conversation with the Roman officer. He had come part way to the centurion's house before He met him in person, and there in the street He spoke with him.

Why did Jesus always speak of Himself as Son of Man?

Matthew 8:20 is the first occurrence of the title "Son of Man" applied by the Lord Jesus to Himself: "The foxes have holes, and the birds of the air have nests; but the Son of Man has nowhere to lay His head" (NASB). (This title is used of Christ thirty-two times in Matthew, fourteen in Mark, twenty-six in Luke, and twelve in John.) Jesus never refused to accept the title "Son of God" when He was so addressed by God the Father at His baptism (Mark 1:11: "Thou art my beloved Son, in whom I am well pleased") or on the Mount of Transfiguration (Mark 9:7). Nor did He refuse it when the demons so hailed Him as He cast them out

of their victims (Mark 3:11: "You are the Son of God!"), or even when Satan challenged Him in the wilderness temptations (Luke 4:3: "If you are the Son of God, tell this stone to become bread").

The disciples hailed Him as "truly the Son of God" after He had miraculously stilled the storm; and Peter came up with his identification of "the Son of Man" (Matt. 16:13) with the Spirit-taught recognition: "Thou art the Christ, the Son of the living God" (v.16, NASB). Jesus commended him for this confession of faith and conferred on him the "keys of the kingdom." At His trial before Caiaphas (Matt. 26:64), Jesus affirmed the divine title when the high priest challenged Him: "Tell us whether you are the Christ, the Son of God!" Jesus responded, "You have said it [yourself]; nevertheless I tell you, hereafter you shall see the Son of Man sitting at the right hand of power and coming on the clouds of heaven." At this solemn moment, when He was on trial for the crime of blasphemy, Jesus of Nazareth appropriated the title of the divine-human Messiah, the universal King, who was revealed to the prophet Daniel (Dan. 7:13).

Daniel 7:13-14 reads: "I kept looking in the night visions, and behold, with the clouds of heaven One like a Son of Man was coming, and He came up to the Ancient of Days [who was God Almighty on His throne] and was presented before Him. And to Him was given dominion, glory and a kingdom, that all the peoples, nations, and men of every language might serve Him" (NASB). It was this celestial figure with whom Jesus identified Himself at that dramatic moment of crisis, thereby announcing that there would be a future trial some day in which Caiaphas and all his cohorts would stand condemned before the bar of divine and eternal justice. Then sentence would be pronounced on them, and they would be led away into everlasting doom.

This raises the question of what the title "Son of Man" (*Bar ᵉnāš* in the Aramaic of Dan. 7) signified. Why was the Messiah represented as a glorified human being rather than as the divine King of Glory? The answer is to be found in the necessity of the Incarnation as indispensable to man's redemption. The fallen, guilty race of Adam could not have their sins atoned for except by a Sin-Bearer who represented them as a true human being as He laid down His life for their sake. The Old Testament term for Redeemer is *gô'ēl*, which implies "kinsman-redeemer." He therefore had to be related by blood to the person whose cause he took over and whose need he supplied, whatever it was, whether to buy him back from slavery (Lev. 25:48), to redeem his forfeited property foreclosed on a mortgage (Lev. 25:25), to care for his childless widow (Ruth 3:13), or to avenge his blood on the murderer (Num. 35:19).

God revealed Himself to Israel as *gô'ēl* of His covenant people (Exod. 6:6; 15:13; Isa. 43:1, Ps. 19:14 [15 Heb.], et al.); but before God became Man by the miracle of the Incarnation and the Virgin Birth, it was a mystery to God's ancient people how He could ever qualify as their *gô'ēl*. God was their Father by creation, to be sure, but *gô'ēl* implies a blood relationship on a physical level. And so God had to become one of us in order to redeem us from the guilt and penalty of our sin. "And the Word became flesh and dwelt among us, and we beheld his glory, the glory as of the only begotten from the Father, full of grace and truth" (John 1:14, NASB).

God as God could not forgive us for our sins unless our sins were fully paid for; otherwise He would have been a condoner and protector of the violation of His own holy law. It was only as man that God in Christ could furnish a satisfaction sufficient to atone for the sins of mankind; for only a man, a true human being, could properly represent the human race. But our Redeemer also had to be God, for only God could furnish a sacrifice of infinite value, to compensate for the penalty of eternal hell that our sin demands, according to the righteous claims of divine justice. Only God could have devised a way of salvation that made it possible for Him to remain just and at the same time become the Justifier of the ungodly (Rom. 4:5), instead of sending them to the everlasting perdition they deserved. But through the Cross the broken law was more fully satisfied than if all mankind had gone to hell forever; for it was the perfect Man who was also infinite God that furnished an effectual sacrifice for all believers of every age.

The miracle of the Incarnation, which alone made possible the rescue of Adam's race, was perhaps the greatest miracle of all time. How could God remain God and yet also become man by assuming a human nature and by birth into the world from a human mother? And how could He become a single person in two distinct natures, one human and one divine? Other religions might speak of a godlike man or a manlike god, but only God the Son, the Second Person of the Trinity, could find a way to become a true human being—eligible to represent man at the Cross.

Lest Christians become confused about the divine-human elements in their Savior and fall into the Docetic error of supposing that He was really God in His essential being and that His human form and body were only a temporary disguise that He discarded at the Ascension, Jesus may have felt it best to emphasize that He was really and truly man, even though He was also God. For only as man could He serve as Messiah and redeem His people through His sacrificial death. And, of course, it was only as man—the Man who had lived a completely sinless life—that He could be qualified to sit in judgment on the sins of men at His second coming. As the man who perfectly obeyed the law of God and never yielded to temptation, Christ is in a position to condemn those who have transgressed the moral law and who have in addition rejected His atonement and lordship for their lives.

The need to stress the genuineness of His humanity was therefore a contributing factor in leading Jesus to speak of Himself consistently as the Son of Man. Yet the principal reason was unquestionably the identification with the sublime figure of Daniel 7:13, who is destined to come in clouds of glory, sitting on the right hand of Power, and assuming absolute dominion over all the earth, after He has meted out justice to all who in this lifetime refused God's mercy.

What did Jesus mean by "Let the dead bury their dead" (Matt. 8:22; Luke 9:60)?

The situation Jesus was dealing with at the time He gave this injunction involved an important decision a young follower of His had to face. The young man had to choose between remaining at home until his father died or leaving his home and family in order to follow the Master and enter into His service. Quite possibly the man's father was in poor health, and it was uncertain how long he would live. The basic issue at stake was which has the higher priority: God or family?

Jesus saw that the young man was ready for discipleship; therefore He said to him, "Follow Me; and allow the dead to bury their own dead" (NASB). By this He meant that the rest of the young man's family would be on hand

to care adequately for the ailing father and to take care of the funeral services. They apparently were not believers in the Lord Jesus and therefore had not yet emerged from spiritual death into eternal life. That is to say, they were still "dead in trespasses and sins" (Eph. 2:1). As we read in John 3:36, "He who believes in the Son has eternal life; but he who does not obey the Son shall not see life, but the wrath of God abides on him" (NASB). From the standpoint of their spiritual relationship to God, therefore, the other members of the family were dead; and they were perfectly suited to the responsibility of attending to the father's needs and his ultimate interment. Rather than waiting around for him to die and thus losing all opportunity for training under Christ's instruction, the young disciple was bidden to put first the call of God to Christian service. "He who loves father or mother more than Me," said Jesus, "is not worthy of Me" (Matt. 10:37).

How can Matthew 8:28-34 (the maniacs of Gadara) be reconciled with Mark 5:1-20 and Luke 8:26-39 (the maniac of Gerasa)?

There are two principal variations between these two accounts (the Marcan and Lucan accounts are in essential agreement). The first is the location of the episode itself; was it Gadara, Gerasa, or Gergesa (as the Sinaiticus, the Coridethian, the Bohairic Coptic, and Family 1 of the minuscules read for this name)? An examination of the map for this region to the east of the Sea of Galilee reveals that Gerasa (now called Jerash) was far removed from the Sea of Galilee to the southeast, more than twenty miles east of the Jordan Valley. It is virtually impossible to relate Gerasa with an episode that seems to have taken place on the eastern shore of Gennesaret (the Sea of Galilee).

As for Gadara (which is the reading

in most manuscripts of Matt. 8:28— although Washingtonensis, Family 1, Family 13 of the minuscules, and the Bohairic Coptic attest "of the Gergesenes"), it was located about eight miles southeast of the southern tip of Gennesaret; so it is entirely possible that the political control of this region was centered in Gadara as the capital city. Hence it would be called "the land of the Gadarenes," even though Gadara itself lay south of the Yarmuk River. Although Mark and Luke both point to Gerasa (Alexandrinus, Washingtonensis, Family 13, and the Syriac Peshitta attest "of the Gadarenes" for Luke 8:26), the distinct preference should be given to Gadara because of its greater proximity to Genessaret.

None of the synoptic Gospels strongly supports Gergesa (despite the manuscripts cited above), though Gergesa enjoys the distinct advantage of being located right on the eastern shore of Gennesaret, about one-third of the way down from the northern end of the lake. From the standpoint of location merely, it should receive the preference; but in view of the much stronger manuscript evidence, Gadara is more likely to have been the original reading in all three Synoptics, with scribal error substituting the name of Gerasa, possibly because at a later period the name of Gerasa had become more widely known than that of Gadara. Perhaps it is worth noting that the shape of D (daleth) and the shape of R (resh) are very similar in the Hebrew alphabet; therefore if the name was being transcribed into Greek characters from the Hebrew/Aramaic alphabetical form, GaDaRa' might have been misread as GaRaRa[Da]. Gergesa also begins G-R—, which might have been misread from G-D—. But Gadara has the strongest claim to being the authentic, original spelling of the name in all three Gospels.

The second distinction between the Matthew account and that of Mark and Luke is that there were really two maniacs who came out to meet Jesus as He disembarked on the eastern shore of the lake, rather than just the one demoniac of Mark and Luke. How serious a problem is this? If there were two of them, there was at least one, wasn't there? Mark and Luke center attention on the more prominent and outspoken of the two, the one whose demonic occupants called themselves "Legion."

As a seminary professor I have occasionally had small elective courses containing only two students. In some cases I remember only one of them with any distinctness, simply because he was the more brilliant and articulate of the two. If I were to compose a set of memoirs and speak of only one of my two-student class, I could hardly be charged with contradicting the historical fact that there were actually two of them in the elective course. A similar case in the synoptic Gospels is found in the episode of the healing of Bartimaeus outside Jericho. Matthew 20:30 records that Bartimaeus actually had a companion with him who also was blind. Luke (18:35) does not give any names at all but refers to only one blind beggar. It is Mark (10:46) who spells out his name both in Aramaic (*Bar-Tim'ay*) and Greek (*huios Timaiou*) form. The reason for this emphasis on him, as over against his companion, was that he was the more articulate of the two.

Whatever the differing inclusions or omissions as between the various Synoptics, they all agree as to what became of the demonic occupants of the maniacs of Gadara: they were all sent into the nearby herd of swine, and thus permitted to carry out on these ceremonially unclean animals the full destruction of life that had at first been intended for their two human victims. The hapless pigs dashed down the cliff into the waters of Gennesaret and were drowned (cf. Matt. 8:30-34; Mark 5:11-14; Luke 8:32-37.)

In Jesus's commissioning of the twelve disciples, were they or were they not to take a "staff" (cf. Matt. 10:10; Mark 6:8)?

In Matthew 10:5-6 Jesus commissioned His twelve disciples to go out on an Evangelistic tour of the cities of Israel, preaching the arrival of the kingdom of heaven, and healing the sick and the demon possessed. Then He cautioned them in regard to their equipment for this journey: "Do not acquire [*ktēsēsthe*] gold or silver or bronze for your money belts; or a bag [*pēran*, "knapsack"] for your journey, or even two tunics, or sandals, or a staff; for the worker is worthy of his support" (Matt. 10:9-10). The parallel in Luke 10 mentions other articles for the journey in Christ's commission to the seventy, but this must have been a later episode. At any rate the word "staff" is not used at all. But in Mark 6:7-9, where His commission to the Twelve is likewise recorded, we read in vv. 8-9: "And He instructed them that they should take nothing [*mēden airōsin*] for their journey, *except a mere staff* [*ei mē rabdon monon*]; no bread, no bag, no money in their belt; but to wear sandals; and He added, 'Do not put on two tunics'" (NASB).

Both Matthew 10 and Mark 6 agree that Christ directed the disciples to take along no extra equipment of any kind for this journey but simply to go on their mission with what they already had. Luke 9:3 agrees in part with the wording of Mark 6:8, using the same verb *airō* ("take"); but then, like Matthew, adds: "neither a staff, nor a bag, nor bread, nor money; do not even have two tunics apiece." But Matthew 10:10 includes what was apparently a further clarification: they were not to *acquire* a staff as part of their special equipment for the tour. Mark 6:8 seems to indicate that this did not involve their necessarily discarding or leaving behind even the walking stick that they normally took with them wherever they went, while they were following Jesus during His teaching ministry. As Lange (*Commentary on Mark*, p. 56) says, "They were to go forth with their staff, as they had it at the time; but they were not to seek one carefully, or make it a condition of their travelling." Lange then sums up the paragraph as follows: "The fundamental idea is this, that they were to go forth with the slightest provision, and in dependence upon being provided for by the way.... We find in them [i.e., Mark's expressions] no other than a more express view of their pilgrim state, burdened with the least possible encumbrance, and as free as might be from all care." So understood, there is no real discrepancy between the two passages.

In Matthew 16:28, did Jesus mean that He would come again in the lifetime of His disciples?

After speaking of His second advent in great power and glory to judge the world in righteousness (Matt. 16:27), Jesus added, "Truly I say to you, there are some of those who are standing here who shall not taste death until they see the Son of Man coming in His kingdom" (v.28, NASB). By this He apparently referred to a preliminary phase of His coming, rather than to the final and climactic phase, when He will be accompanied by His glorious angels. This preliminary manifestation would take place before the death of some of those who were then listening to His voice. There are three possible fulfillments of v.28.

The first possible fulfillment would have been the glorious Transfiguration up on the high mountain referred to in Matthew 17:1-8, where Moses and Elijah appeared to Jesus and discussed with Him His approaching death and resurrection (cf. Luke 9:31).

In a certain sense Christ appeared to Peter, James, and John in His heavenly glory as the Founder of the messianic kingdom of God. But since the principal emphasis was laid on His "departure" (*exodos*, v.31) rather than on His return, this could hardly have been the fulfillment our Lord had in mind.

The second possible fulfillment would have been the powerful descent of the Holy Spirit on the church at Pentecost (Acts 2:2–4). Jesus had promised His disciples, during His discourse in the Upper Room, "I will not leave you orphans; I will come to you" (John 14:18, NASB). This He said right after He had spoken to them of the imminent bestowal of the Holy Spirit ("another paraclete... the Spirit of truth"). Evidently, then, Jesus meant that He would come again to them in and by the Third Person of the Trinity, the Holy Spirit. In v.23 Jesus added this further confirmation: "If anyone loves Me, he will keep My word; and My Father will love him, and We will *come* to him, and make Our abode with him" (NASB). Since it was at Pentecost that the Holy Spirit came with miraculous power on the 120 disciples who had been praying together, and manifested Himself by tongues of fire on their heads and the ability to proclaim the gospel in foreign languages, it is quite evident that Christ returned to His followers at Pentecost through the Holy Spirit. Thus He did not leave His disciples "orphans" but actually came to them. This understanding is reinforced by Revelation 3:20: "Behold, I stand at the door and knock; if any one hears My voice and opens the door, I will *come* in to him, and will dine with him, and he with Me" (NASB). This could not refer to a bodily appearance of Christ but rather to the invasion and capture of the heart of a truly converted believer by the transforming power of the Holy Spirit. So it can only mean

that when the Holy Spirit enters the heart of a regenerate sinner, it is Christ Himself who comes to him as indwelling Savior and Lord. Numbers of the people who heard Christ's promise of Matthew 16:28 were privileged to enter into that experience, and in that preliminary sense Jesus came again to them within their lifetime.

A third possibility of fulfillment might be the events of A.D. 70, when the no-longer-needed temple in Jerusalem was destroyed by the Romans under Titus, and the no-longer-holy city itself—the city that had rejected Christ in A.D. 30 and had called for His death by crucifixion—was totally demolished. In the sense that Christ's prophecy of Jerusalem's destruction was fulfilled (Matt. 24:2; Mark 13:2; Luke 19:43–44), Jesus may be said to have come in judgment on the city that had witnessed His judicial murder. But this could hardly be said to display Christ's regal splendor or the glory of His mighty angels (which was indirectly manifested by the marvelous outpouring of the Spirit at Pentecost); so it is a less likely fulfillment than the preceding.

On which day of the week was Christ crucified?

Matthew 12:40 states: "For as Jonah was three days and three nights in the belly of a huge fish, so the Son of Man will be three days and three nights in the heart of the earth." If the general tradition—that Christ was crucified on Friday of Holy Week, died at 3:00 P.M. (the "ninth hour" of the day), and then rose again from the dead on Sunday at dawn—is correct, how can it be said that Jesus was three days and three nights in the grave? He was interred about 6:00 P.M., according to Luke 23:54. ("And it was the day of preparation [*hēmera paraskeuēs*] and the Sabbath was coming on [*epephōsken*].")

This would mean that the period of interment was only from Friday night to Saturday night before the Resurrection on the dawn of Sunday; and it would also mean only one dawn-to-sunset day, namely Saturday, had passed. How do we get "three days and three nights" out of two nights and one day? Must not the actual day of crucifixion have been Thursday or even Wednesday?

It is perfectly true that a Friday Crucifixion will not yield three full twenty-four-hour days. But neither will a Thursday afternoon Crucifixion, nor a Wednesday afternoon Crucifixion either. This results from the fact that Jesus died at 3:00 P.M. and rose at or about 6:00 A.M. The only way you can come out with three twenty-four-hour days is if He rose at the same hour (three days later, of course) that He was crucified, namely, 3:00 P.M. Actually, however, He rose "on the third day" (1 Cor. 15:4). Obviously, if He rose on the third day, He could not already have been buried for three whole nights and three whole days. That would have required His resurrection to be at the beginning of the fourth day.

What, then, is the meaning of the expression in Matthew 12:40: "three days and three nights in the heart of the earth"? (NASB). This can only refer to three twenty-four-hour days in part or in whole. That is to say, Jesus expired at 3:00 P.M. near the close of Friday (according to the Hebrew method of reckoning each day as beginning at sundown), which would be one day. Then Friday 6:00 P.M. to Saturday 6:00 P.M. would be the second day, and Saturday 6:00 P.M. to Sunday 6:00 P.M. would constitute the third day—during which (i.e., Sunday 6:00 A.M. or a little before) Christ arose. Christ rested in hades (where paradise, or "Abraham's Bosom," still was, according to the indications of

Luke 16:22–26; cf. Luke 23:43) for a portion of the three days: Friday, Saturday, and Sunday. The same would be true, of course, if the Evangelists had been reckoning according to the Roman method, from midnight to midnight.

Why then are three portions of day referred to in Matthew 12:40 as "three days and three nights"? The simple answer is that the only way "day" in the sense of dawn-to-dusk sunlight could be distinguished from the full twenty-four-hour cycle sense of "day" was to speak of the latter as "a night and a day" (i.e., an interval between 6:00 P.M. and 6:00 P.M. of the day following). In other words, Friday as a twenty-four-hour unit began on Thursday at 6:00 P.M. and lasted until Friday 6:00 P.M. Correspondingly, Sunday began at 6:00 P.M. Saturday, according to Hebrew reckoning (but 12:00 P.M. Saturday according to Roman reckoning). According to ancient parlance, then, when you wished to refer to three separate twenty-four-hour days, you said, "Three days and three nights"—even though only a portion of the first and third days might be involved.

A similar usage is apparent from the narrative in 1 Samuel 30:12, where "he had not eaten bread or drunk water for three days and three nights" is equated in v.13 with hayyôm šᵉlōšāh ("three days ago")—which could only mean "day before yesterday." But if the Egyptian slave fell ill on the day before yesterday (with relationship to the day on which David found him), then he could not have remained without food or water for three entire twenty-four-hour days. We simply have to get used to slightly different ways of expressing time intervals. (Similarly the Feast of Pentecost was originally called the "Feast of Weeks" because it fell on the forty-ninth day after the offering of the wave sheaf on the first day of the Feast of Unleavened Bread. Yet it was known actually as the *Fiftieth* Day—*Pentēcostē* in Greek.)

Is the mustard seed really the smallest of all seeds?

In Matthew 13:31-32 Jesus describes the mustard seed (*kokkos sinapeōs*) as being "smaller than all the seeds." The question arises as to whether this statement could be supported by a knowledgeable botanist, or did Christ make a mistake in His rating of the comparative size of the mustard seed? In all probability, He was referring to the black mustard (*Brassica nigra*; cf. W.E. Shewell-Cooper, "Mustard," in Tenney, *Zondervan Pictorial Encyclopedia*, 4:324-25). J.C. Trever (Buttrick, *Interpreter's Dictionary*, 3:477) suggests that the orchid seed is even smaller than the seed of the black mustard. But it is highly questionable whether Jesus was discussing all plant life on planet Earth when He made this statement. No one yet has proved that ancient Palestinians planted anything that bore a smaller seed than that of the black mustard, and that was the framework within which Jesus was speaking. There is no record of the orchid ever being cultivated in Palestine.

As for Jesus's description of the growth of the black mustard, there seems to be some divergence of opinion. Trever states that the *Brassica nigra* does not grow to tree size, nor are its branches large enough to make nests in. But Shewell-Cooper quotes L.H. Bailey as stating that some mustard plants grow to a height of ten feet; if so, its branches would certainly be suited for smaller birds to nest in.

How can we resolve the discrepancies in the Synoptic accounts of the rich-young-ruler episode?

The three reports of the encounter between Christ and the rich young ruler are found in Matthew 19:16-30, Mark 10:17-31, and Luke 18:18-30. These contain special details, some of which are found only in one of the three accounts, others in only two out of the three. But when we synthesize the information contributed by all three of the Synoptics, we obtain a fuller picture of all that transpired than would be the case with any single account. Therefore we may be grateful for their occasional diversity.

Stonehouse (*Synoptic Gospels*, pp. 95-96) furnished the following statistics. The Marcan account is considerably longer than the others, employing 279 Greek words, as against Matthew with 270 (of which 38 occupy the unique 19:28) and Luke with only 202. This ratio is of unusual interest inasmuch as most New Testament scholars regard Mark as the earliest of the four Evangelists. If so, his longer and fuller account cannot be regarded as a "later" embellishment of a more primitive "tradition"—as liberal critics usually assume when one synoptic account is longer than the others.

Stonehouse devotes much discussion to the interesting question of the principles followed by each of the Synoptists in selecting his material. Quite obviously Matthew's special interests included demonstrating to Jews (1) that Jesus was the fulfillment of Old Testament prophecy, i.e., the authentic Jewish Messiah; (2) that Jesus was the divine Prophet and finally authoritative Teacher of the holy life (brought together in five major blocks of connected instruction); and (3) that Jesus fulfilled the promises to Israel and yet was also the Light of the Gentiles—to whom the kingdom of God would be transferred.

As for Mark, his focus is on Christ's redemptive deeds even more than on His oral teaching; the emphasis is on action more than discussion. Hence the characteristic word is "straightway." His concern is to interpret Palestinian customs (with occasional quotations in Aramaic) to a Gentile public—probably Roman, in view of his many Latinisms.

Luke, on the other hand, stresses the personal dynamic of the Lord Jesus and His tender concern for individual people, including women and children. But his guiding principle is to follow a consistently historical methodology and to cover the whole sweep of Jesus' biography from the very beginning (even to the birth of the forerunner, John the Baptist; the annunciation to Mary and the shepherds; and the visit to the temple at age twelve) to the very end (the Ascension from the Mount of Olives). He includes an extraordinary number of episodes and heart-searching parables not included by the other two. The Perfect Man, incarnating the love and grace of God, opens up the way to a new life for all true believers, whether Jew or Gentile.

It is a profitable exercise to correlate the insertions as well as the omissions that mark each synoptist in his treatment of the episodes in Christ's career from the vantage point of these three areas of interest. All three are to be regarded as trustworthy, helpful witnesses, even though they emphasize slightly different facets of Christ's life and personality. But it is when we have the benefit of all three reports that we can assemble the fullest understanding of each of Jesus' encounters with people and His responses to their needs.

As we compare the testimonies of Matthew, Mark, and Luke, we will bring out the particular contributions from each as we combine them all into a full composite.

The Query of the Rich Young Ruler

As he makes his first approach to Jesus on the matter of his own standing before God as a justified believer, the ruler asks, "Good [Mark, Luke] Master, what good [Matt.] thing shall I do, that I may obtain [Matt.] or: inherit [Mark, Luke] eternal life?" Jesus answers him with a question, to probe his understanding of the divine nature of Christ's goodness and of the nature of goodness itself. "Why do you call Me good [Mark, Luke], or: ask Me about what is good [Matt.]? There is just One who is good [Matt.]; in fact, there is no one good but God alone [Mark, Luke]. But if you wish to enter into life [Matt.], you know the commandments [Mark, Luke]; keep them [Matt.]!"

Christ's Challenge to the Ruler's Sincerity

The young man countered with a request for specifics: "Which of them [Matt.]?" he enquired. Jesus pointed him to the most basic of all—the Decalogue. "Do not murder, do not commit adultery, do not steal, do not bear false witness, honor your father and mother. And also [Matt.] you shall love your neighbor as yourself."

The young man [Matt.] said to Him, "All these I have kept, from [Mark, Luke] my youth up. What [Matt.] do I still lack? And Jesus looked [Luke] on him and loved him, and said, "You do lack one thing [Mark, Luke]; if you wish to be perfect [Matt.], go [Matt., Mark] and sell all the possessions [Matt.] you have, and give them out to the poor, and you will have treasure in heaven. And come and follow Me."

The Young Man's Refusal and Departure

When he heard this statement, the young ruler became downcast [Luke] and very grieved [Matt., Luke] as he went away—for he had many possessions [Matt., Mark] and was very rich [Luke]. On observing this, Jesus looked around [Mark] on His disciples and said to them, "I tell you truly [Matt.] that it is with difficulty that a rich man will enter the kingdom of heaven [Matt.]. In fact, those who possess wealth will enter God's kingdom only with difficulty [Mark, Luke]." But the disciples were amazed [Mark] at His words. Again He said, "Children, how hard it is to enter into the kingdom of God [Mark]! It is easier for a camel to go into [Matt., Luke] and pass through [Mark] the eye of a needle than to enter the kingdom of God [so, even Matt.!]."

The Rewards of Dedicated Discipleship

The disciples were astonished [Matt., Mark] at hearing this; and they said [Mark] to one another, "Who then can be saved?" And looking on them [Matt., Mark] Jesus said, "With men this is impossible, but all things [Matt., Mark] are possible with God."

Then answering [Matt.] Peter began [Mark] to say to Him, "Behold, we have left all [Matt., Mark] that is ours [Luke] and have followed You [Matt.]. What then shall there be for us?" Jesus said to them [Matt., Luke], "Truly I say to you, that you who have followed [Matt.] Me in the regeneration, when the Son of Man sits on His glorious throne, you yourselves also will sit on twelve thrones, judging the twelve tribes of Israel [Matt. only]." (Note that on another occasion, in Luke 22:30b, Christ repeats that same promise about sitting on the twelve thrones.)

Then Jesus continued with a promise for this present world: "There is no one who has left [Mark, Luke—but Matt. phrases it: 'And everyone who has left'] home [Matt.: 'homes'] or wife [Luke] or brothers or sisters, or father or mother [Matt., Mark] [Luke: 'or parents'], or children or lands, for the sake of My name [Matt.] and the gospel [Mark] and the kingdom of God [Luke], who will not receive many times as much [Matt., Luke; Mark: 'a hundred times as much'] at this present time [Mark, Luke], homes and brothers and sisters and children and lands [Mark only], along with persecutions; and in the age to come [Mark, Luke] he will inherit [Matt.] eternal life. But many who are first [Matt.,

Mark; Luke: 'And behold, there are last who shall be first'] shall be last, and those who are last shall be first [Matt., Mark; Luke: 'and there are first who shall be last'].

As we conclude this synthesis of the three synoptic accounts, we note that there are three verbal variations that convey exactly the same thought but that are technically different in wording: (1) Matthew 19:29: "And everyone who has left," as opposed to Mark 10:29 and Luke 18:29, which read "There is no one who has left"; (2) Mark 10:30 reads "a hundred times," as opposed to Matthew 19:29 and Luke 18:30, which read "many times as much"; (3) Luke 18:29 reads "parents," as opposed to Matthew 19:29 and Mark 10:29, which read "father or mother." Perhaps it should be mentioned also that Matthew 19:29 reads "homes" (*oikias*) while the other two read "home" (*oikian*).

This pericope, then, gives us an instructive example of the range of verbal variation present in the Synoptics, displaying a genuine overlap or alternative rather than related items that may be fitted together as a composite. Apart from possible scribal error (the Peshitta Syriac version of Luke 18:29 does not read a special word for "parents" but employs *'abohē*, "fathers"; so it looks as if Luke had this word in mind when he chose the Greek word *goneis* ["parents"] and preferred not to break it up into "father and mother," as Matt. and Mark decided to do), items 1 and 2 leave us uncertain as to which exact Aramaic term our Lord used in His actual discourse as originally given. But we may be content with the observation that each case can be explained on the basis of the same original statement in Aramaic, which is susceptible of being handled in more than one way when it is cast into Greek (as in the case of "parents" vs. "father and mother" in item 3). In the latter case, perhaps, it should be added that to this day it is still customary in literary Arabic to use the dual number (*'abawāni*) of the word for "father" (*'abun*) in order to express the idea of "parents." Thus "his parents" would in Arabic be *'abawāhu* (lit., "his two fathers").

How can Matthew 20:20 be reconciled with Mark 10:35?

Matthew 20:20–21 states that it was the mother of James and John who came to Jesus with the request that they might be appointed as Jesus' foremost officials after He should come into His kingdom. But Mark 10:35 records James and John themselves as presenting this request to our Lord. Which account is correct? In all probability both versions are correct. It would be altogether natural for the mother and her two sons to agree on the petition and then for the mother to pave the way by approaching Christ first concerning this matter. Soon afterwards the two sons came up to second her request on their own behalf.

This is just as understandable as the somewhat similar strategy followed by the prophet Nathan, when he first put Solomon's mother, Bathsheba, up to making the first approach to aged and sickly King David (1 Kings 1:11–21). Then came Nathan himself and verified her tidings that Adonijah was seizing power as David's successor, rather than Solomon himself, whom David had earlier designated as heir of his throne (vv.22–27). This is a very true-to-life account and furnishes no improbabilities to reconcile.

How many did Christ heal of blindness, and was it when He was entering Jericho or leaving it?

In Matthew 20:29 we are told that Jesus and His disciples were coming out of Jericho when they were appealed to by two blind men. Mark 10:46 agrees that it was when Jesus was leaving Jericho that the healing occurred; but at the same time he mentions only one blind man and gives his name quite precisely (Bartimaeus, the son of Timaeus). Luke 18:35 states that "a certain blind man" (no companion is mentioned, nor is this man's name actually given) first heard of Jesus when He and His followers were entering into Jericho. Verse 36 adds that it was while the crowd was passing by (*ochlou diaporeuomenou*) that he started making inquiry as to what was going on. Then he cried out, saying, "Jesus, Son of David, have mercy on me!" (v.38, NASB). Then the leaders of the procession began to rebuke him, in order that he might be quiet. Yet he only cried out all the more, repeating the same petition. In v.40, Jesus hears him calling out and stops in order to help him. Then (as in Matt. and Mark) he is brought to Jesus and makes his personal appeal to Christ for the gift of sight.

It is only after we compare the testimony of all three witnesses that we obtain a fuller understanding of the whole episode. From Luke 18:35 we learn that Bartimaeus first learned of Jesus' visit to Jericho as He and his followers were entering the town. Then, as the crowd was passing by, he tried to gain Christ's attention by calling out directly to Him from where he was sitting. Yet it would seem that he was not at first successful; for it was not until Jesus had entered the town, had His contact with Zacchaeus, taught the people the parable of the pounds (or: minas), and was on the point of leaving the city that Bartimaeus finally managed to engage Christ's attention. Possibly this was because the crowd was quieter on Jesus' departure than it had been at His arrival. At any rate, it was not until that point that Jesus stopped walking and gave orders for Bartimaeus to be brought to Him.

Mark 10:46–47 makes this clear:

"And they come to Jericho. And as He was going out from Jericho ... Bartimaeus ... was sitting by the road. And hearing that it was Jesus the Nazarene, he began to cry out and say, 'Jesus, Son of David, have mercy on me!'" We cannot be certain whether vv.47–48 refer to his first (and unsuccessful) appeal, or whether it was his subsequent outcry on Jesus' departure. From Matthew 20:30 we get the clear information that it was the latter. For Matthew 20:29 states quite explicitly that this dialogue with Jesus took place as the Lord was emerging from the city. Matthew also informs us that Bartimaeus had picked up a blind colleague in the meantime. It seems that Bartimaeus spoke to him of his high hopes of getting through to Jesus when He would depart from the city, by the same gate He had entered. It may not have been a close friend of his, since Bartimaeus seems to have called out on his own behalf, in the first instance at least (Mark 10:48; Luke 18:39).

Bartimaeus and his unnamed companion moved forward at more or less the same time to where Jesus was standing. As they made their way to the Savior, they jointly petitioned Him (Matt. 20:33). Yet for some reason it was Bartimaeus who showed the greater energy in his importunity to Christ, and it was therefore to him that Jesus addressed His remarks and questions. He next healed the other man as well, and apparently touched their sightless eyes with His hand, thus restoring their sight to them (Matt. 20:34). The result was that both men joined Jesus' following and rejoiced as they witnessed to everyone they saw concerning what the Lord had done for them.

The three accounts supplement one another very helpfully in such a way as to bring out the facts that (1) Bartimaeus was the prime mover and the undiscourageable man of faith in this approach to Jesus for healing, while his companion was a less aggressive personality who was content to chime in with whatever Bartimaeus said; (2) Bartimaeus' persistence was such that he would not take no for an answer, no matter how sternly the public ordered him to be silent. He even kept waiting for a second opportunity to contact Jesus, no matter how long it took for our Lord to accomplish His purposes in Jericho. Therefore he was most intently waiting for Jesus as He finally emerged once more through that same city gate.

Matthew was concerned to mention all who were involved in this episode (just as he alone of the Synoptists recorded the fact that it was really two maniacs that met Jesus on the territory of Gadara [Matt. 8:28], whereas both Mark and Luke speak only of one demoniac possessed by the Legion demons). Matthew is content to record that actual scene of healing, whereas Luke gives particular attention to the entire proceedings, from the moment that Bartimaeus first heard about Jesus' arrival—a feature only cursorily suggested by Mark 10:46—because he is interested in the beggar's persistence in request before the cure was actually performed on him. As for the second blind beggar, neither Mark nor Luke find him significant enough to mention; presumably he was the more colorless personality of the two.

How many donkeys were involved in the Palm Sunday entrance into Jerusalem? One or two?

Matthew 21:2 mentions two animals involved in Christ's entrance into Jerusalem: the mother donkey and her foal. In the parallel accounts in Mark 11:2 and Luke 19:30 only the male foal is referred to; nothing is said about the mother. But this does not constitute a contradiction, because all three gospels agree that Jesus rode on a young donkey foal (*pōlos*) that had not been ridden before. Only the mother donkey is at issue. Rather than being guilty of embellishing the narrative, however, Matthew was simply pointing out (21:5) that the prediction in Zechariah 9:9 was fulfilled to the letter by this symbolic action of Christ. Zechariah 9:9 closes with the words "humble, and mounted on a donkey [*ḥᵃmôr*], even on a foal ['*ayir*], the son of a she-ass ["ᵃ-*tōnô-t*]." Matthew goes on to record that the mother donkey went on ahead of Jesus as He rode on her young foal (v.7).

What was the point of involving the she-ass in this transaction? A moment's reflection will bring out the fact that if the foal had never yet been ridden (and that was an important factor for the sake of the symbolism), then he probably was still dependent on his mother psychologically or sentimentally, even though he may have been completely weaned by this time. It simply made it an easier operation if the mother donkey were led along down the road toward the city gate; then the foal would naturally follow her, even though he had never before carried a rider and had not yet been trained to follow a roadway.

The Zechariah passage does not actually specify that the parent donkey would figure in the triumphal entrance; it simply describes the foal as "the son of a she-ass" by way of poetic parallelism. But Matthew contributes the eyewitness observation (and quite possibly neither Mark nor Luke were eyewitnesses as Matthew was) that the mother actually preceded Jesus in that procession that took Jesus into the Holy City. Here again, then, there is no real contradiction between the synoptic accounts but only added detail on the part of Matthew as one who viewed the event while it was happening.

Did Christ curse the barren fig tree before or after He expelled the moneychangers from the temple?

In Matthew 21:12-17 we are told that after Christ entered Jerusalem on Palm Sunday, He went straight to the temple and proceeded to cast out those selling animals for sacrifice within the court and those converting the monetary gifts of worshipers into currency acceptable for the temple treasury. Luke 19:45-46 contains a much-shortened version of the same account and states that the cleansing took place after Jesus had entered the temple. But in Mark 11:11-19 it is clearly stated that Jesus did not expel the tradesmen from the temple until Monday, after He had cursed the barren fig tree (vv.12-14). Matthew does not speak of the fig tree until after he has described the cleansing of the temple (21:18-19). Luke does not refer to the fig tree incident at all; so we have to deal only with Matthew and Mark in regard to this problem of sequence. How are we to reconcile these two accounts? Quite obviously Jesus would not have cleansed the temple court on two successive afternoons, using precisely the same terms: "My house shall be called a house of prayer."

As we study the narrative technique of Matthew in general, we find that he sometimes arranges his material in topical order rather than in the strictly chronological order that is more often characteristic of Mark and Luke. Matthew's collection of teachings contained in the three chapters (5-7) of the Sermon on the Mount may perhaps have been delivered all at one time, as the multitude sat on the hillside below Him on the traditional site of the Mount of the Beatitudes, by the north shore of the Sea of Galilee. The fact that portions of the Sermon-on-the-Mount teachings are found sometimes in other settings, such as in the Sermon on the Plain in Luke (6:20-49) and elsehwere, may mean no more than that Jesus often spoke on these same themes wherever He went during His three-year ministry in Palestine and its adjacent regions. But Matthew's tendency to group his material in themes according to a logical sequence is quite clearly exhibited in the series of eight parables of the kingdom of heaven that make up chapter 13. Once a theme has been broached, Matthew prefers to carry it through to its completion, as a general rule.

Matthew and Mark agree that as soon as Christ entered Jerusalem on Palm Sunday, He made His way straight to the temple (Matt. 21:12; Mark 11:11). They also agree that He actually entered the temple on that Sunday. Mark contributes that it was in the late afternoon that this took place, and that after He entered He took a careful look around at what was going on. Doubtless He was deeply disturbed by the loud, irreverent commercialism, just as He had been three years before, when He had chased the merchants out at the end of His lashing whip (John 2:13–17). On that occasion He had denounced them for making God's house a place of merchandise (rather than quoting Isa. 56:7, as He did in this Holy Week episode).

Mark then tells us that Jesus did nothing publicly to express His indignation on that late Sunday afternoon. On the contrary, Jesus returned to Bethany—presumably to the home of Lazarus, Mary, and Martha—and spent the night there. We may be sure that He spent part of that night in prayer, seeking from the Father guidance as to what He should do on the next day. It may well be that Jesus saw in the barren fig tree He encountered on His way back to Jerusalem that Monday morning of Holy Week a vivid reminder of the unfruitfulness of Israel as a nation; and for that reason He made it a special object lesson for His disciples.

The fig tree had produced its foliage without having put forth its fruit—which in that climate normally precedes the full leafage itself. (Mark 11:13 observes that it was not the regular season for the production of figs, but apparently this particular tree had gone into full foliage without developing any figs at all.) Jesus also used the rapid withering of the fig tree (apparently before Monday was over) to teach the disciples that the prayer of faith (and His curse had been in the nature of a prayer for judgment on that tree) could accomplish such marvels as these, and even greater (such as the moving of mountains into the sea; cf. Matt. 21:20–22; Mark 11:20–25).

Mark then goes on to relate, following his principle of chronological sequence, that Christ went back to Jerusalem and into the temple; there He expelled the noisy, venal tradesmen and moneychangers from the hallowed court, employing the language referred to above: "'My house shall be called a house of prayer for all nations,' says the Lord, 'but you have made it into a house of thieves'" (Matt. 21:13; Mark 11:17; Luke 19:46). Matthew, however, felt it suited his topical approach more effectively to include the Monday afternoon action with the Sunday afternoon initial observation, whereas Mark preferred to follow strict chronological sequence. (Luke says nothing about this matter either way, since he does not include the fig tree episode at all.)

Does Matthew 22:39 teach a godly love of self?

Matthew 22:39 contains Christ's quotation of Leviticus 19:18: "You shall love your neighbor as yourself" (NASB). Some have inferred from this that Jesus taught a godly love of self, for one cannot very well love his neighbor unless he also loves himself. There may be a measure of truth in this, but it involves a somewhat different understanding of the word "love" than what is normally used. Certainly the second great commandment involves a proper regard, acceptance, and respect for oneself; but it seems to be quite misleading—if not altogether dangerous—to speak of the Bible as teaching self-love.

Interestingly enough, there is only one passage in Scripture that speaks of self-love explicitly, and that is 2 Timothy 3:1–3: "But realize this, that in the last days difficult times will come. For men will be *lovers of self* [*philautoi*], lovers of money, boastful, arrogant, revilers, disobedient to parents, ungrateful, unholy, unloving" (NASB). It is interesting to see the categories of character weakness and sinful perversion in which this *philautoi* appears. And it should be carefully noted that "lovers of self" are grouped with the "unloving" (*astorgoi* —lacking the natural affection toward one's own flesh and blood), "haters of good," and "lovers of pleasure rather than lovers of God." There can be no question but what the term "self-lovers" is presented here as a serious character weakness, a trait of sin. For this reason there is little justification for a Christian minister or a Christian counselor to speak with approval of "self-love." Are we ever justified in praising what Scripture condemns? Hardly. Rather, because of the self-deceptiveness of the human heart (Jer. 17:9), we would do well to allow ourselves to be taught by Scripture in this matter, rather than falling into a fallacy that comes from a sophistic juggling of terms.

The first appeal to self-love to be found in the Bible occurs in Genesis 3:4–5, where the satanic serpent poses as the friend and helpful counselor of man: "You surely shall not die [despite what God may have said to you]! For God knows that in the day you eat from it your eyes will be opened, and you will be like God [or 'gods'], knowing good and evil" (NASB). So saying, he stirred up a strong realization of self love on Eve's part, and she felt moved to partake of the forbidden fruit. Satan has been appealing to self-love in fallen man ever since. The influence of self-love and self-will has been to lead away from the will of God into a life of shameful bondage to evil. "Self-love" is the name of the disease of our soul; it cannot possibly be the correct label for its cure!

How, then, are we to understand Matthew 22:39: "Love your neighbor as yourself"? We should observe that it commands the very opposite of self-love, for self-love dictates the love of self *in preference* to others. This second commandment bids us to do the very contrary of this: we are to put the rights and needs of others in the very same level as our own. Hence this is a negation and a rejection of self-love (in the sense of self-preference). The same idea is brought out very clearly by Christ's "Golden Rule" in Matthew 7:12: "Therefore all things that you wish men to do to you, do even so to them." We are to treat them with as much consideration and love as we should like to have them do to us. This again is the very antithesis of self-love.

When the early Christians of the Jerusalem church sold their property and gave the proceeds to be distributed among all the church members as each might have need, this was a distribution of love to all alike; it was anything but a manifestation of self-love. Self-love would have dictated a retaining of one's wealth for personal advantage and enjoyment. Fallen mankind already knows this kind of self-love and needs no exhortation or encouragement by professional counselors —Christian or otherwise—to further self-love.

What really concerns the Christian counselor is that tendency towards low self-esteem or outright self-rejection that he often encounters in people who are emotionally disturbed. Often they have disappointed themselves in a vain attempt to achieve their own personal goals; and they condemn themselves for their failure, out of a feeling of wounded pride. Or else they have been so rejected and put down by others that they end up despising themselves. The psychologist seeks to counteract this self-contempt or self-rejection by a totally different concept of self—and so he should. But the remedy is not found in resurrecting the same vice that may have contributed to their downfall in the first place. Self-love is not the answer; rather, it is Christ-love. "For the love of Christ controls us, having concluded this, that one died for all, therefore all died [i.e., all believers united to Him by faith died with Him as He suffered for them on the cross]; and He died for all, that they who live should no longer live for themselves [as all self-lovers do], but for Him who died and rose again on their behalf" (2 Cor. 5:14–15, NASB).

The fact that the Son of God loved me enough to die for me confers on me a standing of privilege and glory far higher than anything a self-lover might seek to gain for himself. 'Blessed be the God and Father of our Lord Jesus Christ, who has blessed us with every spiritual blessing in the heavenly places in Christ, just as He chose us in Him before the foundation of the world" (Eph. 1:3-4, NASB). If God has loved us, delivered us, showered such blessing on us, and guaranteed a place for us up in the glory of heaven above—all because of His free grace and not because of any merit or goodness in us—how can we condemn, reject, or despise ourselves? "Who shall lay any thing to the charge of God's elect?" asks Romans 8:33. If no one else in heaven, earth, or hell can bring any charge against those justified by the blood of Jesus, no more can we despise or abhor ourselves. That amounts

to a rejection of God's own judgment of love toward us (who by faith are *in* His beloved Son, Jesus).

Self-contempt and self-hate are completely excluded by the mighty love of God, which He has showered on us. He has entrusted us with a high and holy calling; He has summoned us to be ambassadors of the court of heaven, commissioned to preach Christ and reconciliation to God through His atoning death (2 Cor. 5:19–20). He has consecrated our bodies to be temples of His Holy Spirit (1 Cor. 6:19). What higher dignity, what greater glory is possible for any man? I must daily, hourly, present my body as a living sacrifice to Him on the altar of devotion; I must constantly draw on Him for His enablement to fulfill my stewardship in a worthy and appropriate manner. But I will never, never despise myself or reject myself if I truly believe what God has said about me in His word. This kind of self-assurance and self-esteem is derived completely from Jesus by faith and lifts me immeasurably above the level of "self-love." I am lost in the love of Christ, and in Him I find myself again!

How could Zechariah son of Berechiah be the last of the martyrs? And wasn't he really the son of Jehoiada?

In Matthew 23:34-35, Jesus says to the scribes and Pharisees who are plotting His death, "Therefore behold, I am sending you prophets and wise men and scribes; some of them you will kill and crucify, ... that upon you may fall all the righteous blood shed on earth, from the blood of righteous Abel to the blood of Zechariah the son of Berechiah, whom you murdered between the temple and the altar." It is generally supposed that Jesus was actually referring to Zechariah the son of Jehoiada, who was stoned to death in the court of the temple at the order of King Joash, because Zechariah had the temerity to rebuke the government and the citizenry for their cultivation of idolatry. This is recorded in 2 Chronicles 24:20–22. But once this apparent error concerning the name of the martyr's father has been explained away as a textual error, then it is observed that Zechariah ben Jehoiada, who died 800 B.C., was by no means the last of the Old Testament martyrs; hence he makes a poor balance to Abel, who certainly was the first.

The obvious solution is to start all over again and assume that Matthew 23:25 correctly reports the words of Jesus, and that He knew what He was talking about. If so, then we discover that the Zechariah He was referring to was indeed the son of Berachiah (not Jehoiada), and that he was indeed the last of the Old Testament martyrs mentioned in the Hebrew Scriptures. In other words, Christ is recalling to His audience the circumstances of the death of the *prophet* Zechariah, son of Berechiah (Zech. 1:1), whose ministry began around 520 and ended a bit later than 480 B.C. The Old Testament contains no record of events during the first few decades of the fifth century B.C. until about 457, the date of Ezra's return to Jerusalem. But it may very well have been that sometime between 580 and 570 Zechariah the prophet was martyred by a mob in much the same way Zechariah the son of Jehoiada was some three centuries earlier. Since Jesus referred to Zechariah as the *last* of the Old Testament martyrs, there can be no legitimate doubt that it was the eleventh of the twelve minor prophets He had in mind. Therefore we can only conclude that the later Zechariah died in much the same way the earlier one did, as a victim of popular resentment against his rebuke of their sins.

Since there are about twenty-seven different individuals mentioned in the Old Testament bearing the name Zechariah, it is not surprising if two of them happened to suffer a similar fate. In other words, if we take Matthew 23:35 just as it stands, it makes perfect sense in its context; and it offers no contradiction to any known and established facts of history. In the absence of any other information as to how the prophet Zechariah died, we may as well conclude that Jesus has given us a true account of it and add him to the roster of the noble martyrs of biblical times.

Did Jesus mean in Matthew 24:34 that all the signs of His second coming were really fulfilled before His generation passed away?

Matthew 24:34 reports our Lord as saying, "Truly I say to you, this generation [*genea*] will not pass away until all these things take place" (NASB). What things? The rise of false teachers and prophets, the persecution and martyrdom of believers, and all the horrors of the Great Tribulation will occur (vv.9–22). Also, there will be false Christs, deceitful miracles, and strange phenomena in the heavens (vv.23–29). Then at last the "sign of the Son of Man" (v.30) will appear in the heavens; and all the world will witness His return to earth with power and great glory, when he sends forth His angels to gather together all the "elect" from every part of the earth.

Obviously these apocalyptic scenes and earth-shaking events did not take place within the generation of those who heard Christ's Olivet discourse. Therefore Jesus could not have been referring to His immediate audience when He made His prediction concerning "this *genea*." What did He mean by this prophecy?

There are two possible explanations. One is that g*enea* ("generation") was used as a synonymn of *genos* ("race," "stock," "nation," "people"). This would then amount to a prediction that the Jewish race would not pass out of existence before the Second Advent. Whatever other races would die out before that event—and most of the races contemporaneous with Jesus of Nazareth have in fact died out already—the Jewish race, however persecuted and driven from one country to another, would survive until our Lord's return. No other nation has ever managed to live through all the dispersions and persecutions and up-rooted conditions to which the Jews have been subjected. Yet they live on until this day and have reestablished their independence in the State of Israel. Although this meaning for *genea* is not common, it is found as early as Homer and Herodotus and as late as Plutarch (cf. H.G. Liddell and R. Scott, *A Greek-English Lexicon,* 9th ed., [Oxford: Clarendon, 1940], p. 342).

The other possibility is that *genea* does indeed mean "generation" in the usual sense of the word, but refers to the generation of observers who witness the beginning of the signs and persecutions with which the Tribulation will begin. Many of these will live to see the Lord Jesus come back to earth, as Conqueror and Judge, with great power and glory. This interpretation has the merit of preserving the more common and usual meaning of the word. But it suffers from the disadvantage of predicting what would normally be expected to happen anyway. Whether the Tribulation will last for seven years or for a mere three and a half years, it would not be so unusual for most people to survive that long. Seven years is not a very long time to live through, even in the face of bloody persecution.

Perhaps it should be added that if the Olivet Discourse was originally delivered in Aramaic (as it probably was), then we cannot be certain that the meaning of this prediction hinged entirely on the Greek word used to translate it. *Genea* and *genos* are, after all,

closely related words from the same root. The Aramaic term that Jesus Himself probably used (the Syriac Peshitta uses *sharbᵉtā'* here, which can mean either "generation" or "race") is susceptible to either interpretation, and thus could mean the Jewish "race" rather than the circle of Christ's own contemporaries.

How can the various accounts of Peter's denial of Christ be reconciled?

Concerning Peter's denial, Christ is quoted in Matthew 26:34 as stating, "Truly I tell you that this night, before the rooster crows, you will three times deny Me." Mark 14:30 quotes Jesus a little more fully: "And Jesus says to him, 'Truly I tell you that today, this very night, before the rooster crows twice, you will three times deny Me.'" (Luke 22:34 substantially follows Matthew's wording, though in a somewhat briefer version.) Is this a real discrepancy, as some critics allege? Hardly, since we may be very sure that if the rooster crows twice, he has at least crowed once.

Apparently Jesus did specify that the cock would crow a second time by the time the third denial had been expressed by Peter. The important part of the prediction, however, lay not in the number of times the rooster would sound out but in the number of times Peter would basely deny to his interrogators that he belonged to Jesus—or even that he was acquainted with Him. To add or include additional information does not amount to a contradiction of the testimony of a witness who has given a somewhat briefer account. Such variation is observed in the lecture notes taken by students in a classroom: some include more details than others. But that does not mean they are not all equally valid witnesses to what their instructor said.

The same observation applies to the account of the triple denial itself. Each synoptist includes some items of information not included by the others, and John furnishes many details not found in the Synoptics at all. But it is perfectly clear that none of the statements are actually contradictory. When they are lined up in parallel columns, their rich wealth of information gives us a fuller account than could be gathered from any single one of them. Such a comparison yields the following composite narrative of Peter's miserable experience during Christ's trial before Caiaphas.

Peter was admitted to the outer court of the high priest after John had spoken to the doorkeeper (*thyrōros* is probably masculine here) who guarded the approach from the street (John 18:15–16). After Peter entered, he sat down by a fire to warm himself on that chilly night (Luke 22:56). But a girl who served as a doorkeeper on the inner side of the gate began looking intently at him and finally blurted out, "You too were with Jesus, the Galilean from Nazareth!" (Mark 14:67) (Luke 22:56 reads "You too were with him!"). Then she asked him point blank, "Aren't you one of His disciples?" (John 18:17). To this Peter uttered his first denial, "I am not!" He added, "I don't know or understand what you are talking about" (Matt. 26:70; Mark 14:68). Then he stoutly affirmed, "I don't know Him, woman!" (Luke 22:57).

After this brush with danger, Peter wandered off to the portico of the building itself; but even there he attracted some unwelcome attention. Another servant girl, who may well have been tipped off by the female gatekeeper, remarked to one of the bystanders, "This man was with Jesus the Nazarene" (Matt. 26:71). "He certainly was one of them," she insisted (Mark 14:69).

At this point, one of the men in the group leveled an accusing finger at Peter and declared, "You are one of

them!" (Luke 22:58). Peter had by this time joined some men standing around a charcoal fire (apparently not the same fire he had stopped by in the outer court); they also picked up the accusation: "You too were with Jesus the Galilean!" (Matt. 26:73; Mark 14:70). They followed this charge with a forthright question: "Are you one of His disciples?" (John 18:25). With mounting intensity Peter replied, "Man, I am not!" (Luke 22:58). "I neither know nor understand what you are talking about!" (Matt. 26:72).

Somewhat later, perhaps as long as an hour after the second denial (Luke 22:59), a relative of the servant Peter had wounded at Gethsemane spotted him and shouted out, "Didn't I see you in the garden with Him? You certainly must have been with Him, for you are a Galilean" (Luke 22:59). At this the bystanders chimed in: "You are certainly one of them, for you are a Galilean" (Mark 14:70). "You must be, for you talk with a Galilean accent" (Matt. 26:73). At this, Peter began to panic; so he broke out into cursing and swearing: "By God, I don't even know the man you're talking about!" (Mark 14:71).

As soon as he had uttered this lie, Peter heard a rooster crowing. Suddenly he remembered how he had boasted the night before that he was ready to go to his death rather than deny his Lord. It was at that moment that Jesus Himself, who was still standing before Caiaphas under trial, looked over in Peter's direction—and their eyes met (Luke 22:61). Covered with shame and full of self-loathing, Peter hurried out of the high priestly palace into the darkness of the night, now graying into dawn; and he sat down to weep and sob out his contrition before God.

In conclusion, then, the four testimonies of the Evangelists contain no contradictions, even though the information they yield may be somewhat diverse. As in any properly conducted court hearing, it is the task of the judge and jury to piece together the full account of the occurrence under investigation on the basis of the report of each individual witness. Much of their testimony will, of course, be identical; but in each case there will be some details recalled or thought worth mentioning that are not forthcoming from the other witnesses. There is under the laws of legal evidence no good ground for concluding, as some biased scholars mistakenly do, that the differences between the Gospels involve genuine discrepancies and unresolvable contradictions. Critics such as these would be utterly incompetent to sit in judgment in any court of law.

Does the New Testament teach pacifism or the abolition of capital punishment?

Matthew 26:52 records our Lord Jesus as saying to Peter, after he had drawn his sword in defense of his Master, "Put your sword back in its place, for all who draw the sword will die by the sword" (NIV). This could be interpreted as a condemnation of all resistance against crime or aggression by means of force, especially force leading to the death of the aggressor. Those who so interpret it often cite 2 Corinthians 10:4–5, where Paul describes the battle procedure of the Christian minister: "The weapons we fight with are not the weapons of the world. On the contrary, they have divine power to demolish strongholds. We demolish arguments and every pretension that sets itself up against the knowledge of God, and we take captive every thought to make it obedient to Christ" (NIV). Unquestionably this passage describes the weaponry of Christian evangelism as being far more effective than any instrument of physical violence when it comes to capturing and subduing the souls of men for God. But the real question is whether

either of these citations have a bearing on the question of war or capital punishment as exercised by the state government in the defense of society and in the maintenance of justice.

The Sermon on the Mount sets forth the wholly different standard of life that characterizes a true child of God in his role as a private citizen. His conduct is governed by the holy love and kindness of God. The Christian is to come to an agreement with his adversary before they actually present their case in court (Matt. 5:25). When he is smitten on one cheek, he is to turn to him the other (v.39), rather than retaliating in kind. In general, he is not to resist evil; that is, he is not to fight back in the defense of his own personal rights. He is never to return evil for evil (Rom. 12:17). By faithfully following this policy he will be "walking in the light," and that bright testimony of holy love will draw others to the light of Christ Himself (Matt. 5:16).

All these directives pertain to the personal conduct of the Christian as a citizen of the kingdom of God in the midst of a depraved and sin-cursed world. But they have very little bearing on the duty of the state to preserve law and order and to protect the rights of all its citizens. Romans 13 spells this out very clearly: "The authorities that exist have been established by God. ... Do you want to be free from fear of the one in authority? Then do what is right and he will commend you. For he is God's servant to do you good. But if you do wrong, be afraid, for he does not bear the sword for nothing. He is God's servant, an agent of wrath to bring punishment on the wrongdoer" (vv.1,3–4).

It hardly needs to be pointed out that "the sword" is not a symbol of imprisonment but of capital punishment. When he appeared before the Sanhedrin under the protection of Festus, Paul said, "If then I am a wrongdoer, and have committed anything worthy of death, I do not refuse to die" (Acts 25:11, NASB). Very clearly this constitutes an acknowledgment on the part of the inspired apostle that the state continued to have the power of life and death in the administration of justice, just as it did from the days of Noah, when God solemnly committed that responsibility to human government (Gen. 9:6: "Whoever sheds man's blood, by man his blood shall be shed, for in the image of God He made man" [NASB]).

If Matthew 5:39 applied to the state and to human government, then the principle of "Resist not evil" would mean the abolition of all law enforcement. There would neither be police officers nor judges nor prisons of any kind. All society would immediately fall prey to the lawless and criminal elements in society, and the result would be total anarchy. Nothing could have been further from Christ's mind than such Satan-glorifying savagery and brutality. In connection with the parable of the pounds (or minas), Christ pronounced this judgment on those who had rebelled against their king (Luke 19:27): "But these enemies of mine, who did not want me to reign over them, bring them here, and slay them in my presence" (NASB). This sounds very much like an endorsement of capital punishment. Again, in Luke 20:14–16, as He concluded the parable of the wicked husbandmen (or tenants), our Lord said: "But when the tenants saw him [the son of the landlord], they talked the matter over. 'This is the heir,' they said, 'Let's kill him, and the inheritance will be ours.' So they threw him out of the vineyard and killed him. What then will the owner of the vineyard do to them? He will come and kill those tenants and give the vineyard to others." Thus it is very clear that neither Christ nor His apostles intended to abrogate the God-given responsibility of the government (under Old Testament law) to protect its citizens and enforce justice by capital punishment.

There is nothing in the New Testament that sets aside the solemn sanction against unavenged murder contained in Numbers 35:31,33: "You shall not take ransom [i.e., allow mere monetary damages] for the life of a murderer who is guilty of death, but he shall surely be put to death.... So you shall not pollute the land in which you are; for blood pollutes the land and no expiation can be made for the land for the blood that is shed on it, except by the blood of him who shed it" (NASB). So far as God's Word is concerned, then, neither life imprisonment, nor that brief term of years (with time off for "good behavior") that is usually meted out to murderers in modern society, nor any kind of monetary damages to the survivors of the victim can discharge the solemn obligation of the state to impose capital punishment on those guilty of first-degree murder. After the long reign of unavenged murder in Jerusalem during the days of King Manasseh, when the city was "filled with bloodshed from one end to the other" (2 Kings 21:16)—as a natural consequence of abandoning the standards of Scripture and substituting false idols (or modern concepts of penology based on humanism)—God pronounced His judgment on the Jewish state and allowed it to be totally destroyed by Nebuchadnezzar of Babylon.

On the related issue of national defense against foreign aggression, does a "Christian" government—and whether there are any such today is a matter of definition—have a right to summon its citizens to arms in order to repel an invader? Or may it send an expeditionary force abroad in order to crush an invader before he has an opportunity to land his troops on our soil? No one questions whether this right was accorded to Israel under the Old Testament; the God-blessed careers of Joshua and David are a sufficient demonstration of that right. But what about the New Testament and the teaching of Jesus?

We have already seen that Christ's dictum to Peter in Matthew 26:52 ("All they that take the sword shall perish with the sword") has to do with the personal witness of the Christian soulwinner; it has nothing to do with the Christian's obligations as a citizen, concerned with the protection of society or the defense of his country. Jesus also upheld the right of kings to resort to warfare if the circumstances warrant it, for this is certainly implied in Luke 14:31: "What king, going to make war against another king, does not first sit down and take counsel as to whether he is able with ten thousand troops to meet in battle with one who comes against him with twenty thousand?" No pacifist could use such an illustration as this without appearing to condone warfare as a legitimate measure for a head of state. But even more clearly is this implied by what Jesus said to Pilate in John 18:36: "My kingdom is not of this world. If it were, My servants would fight to prevent My arrest by the Jews." It was only because Christ's kingdom (prior to the kingdom age of the end time) was not of this world that Peter's resort to the sword was restrained and Christ allowed Himself to be arrested by the Jewish authorities. But the implication is unavoidable that a kingdom that *is* of the world has a perfect right to resort to warfare and the killing of enemy aggressors.

In the parable of the wedding feast, Jesus seems to speak approvingly of the action of the king (who clearly represented God Himself) when he "sent forth his armies and destroyed those murderers and burned up their city." The prediction of Jesus in the Olivet Discourse, that wars will continue to be fought on earth until He returns in sovereign power and imposes peace by overwhelming force (Matt. 24:5–7, 25:31; Mark 13:7–8), leaves little room for the dream entertained by pacifistic socialism of the establishment of a warless society that abolishes murder and violence by doing away with capital punishment and the use of arms in national defense.

Nor is there any hint of disapproval of military service as a legitimate calling for a true believer in Christ. In fact, our Lord reserved His highest praise for the faith of the centurion whose servant He healed at Capernaum (Matt. 8:10). There was no suggestion that he would have to give up his martial calling in order to be saved. The same was true of the centurion Cornelius of Caesarea, who was honored by Peter as the first of the converts from the Gentiles and was welcomed into the family of God as a true believer (Acts 10:47–48). Nothing was said about his promising to change to a more peaceful profession as a condition for his being baptized. Paul frequently draws analogies from the obligation, commitment, and selfgiving devotion of a good soldier in his description of a dedicated Christian life: "Suffer hardship with me, as a good soldier of Christ Jesus. No soldier in active service entangles himself in the affairs of everyday life, so that he may please the one who enlisted him as a soldier" (2 Tim. 2:3–4), NASB).

The military profession is linked up with the professions of vinedressing and the raising of livestock in 1 Corinthians 9:7: "Who at any time serves as a soldier at his own expense? Who plants a vineyard and does not eat the fruit of it? Or who tends a flock and does not use the milk of the flock?" (NASB). It is hard to see how on the basis of this verse a pacifist would not also have to condemn a farmer, for they are here both put on the same level of legitimacy.

A pacifist position is impossible to reconcile with the praise heaped by

Hebrews 11:32–34 on warriors like Gideon, Barak, Samson, Jephthah, Samuel, and David, who along with the Old Testament prophets "by faith conquered kingdoms, performed acts of righteousness, obtained promises, shut the mouths of lions, quenched the power of fire, escaped the edge of the sword, from weakness were made strong, became mighty in war, put foreign armies to flight" (NASB). It would be quite difficult to imagine the author of this passage as adding, in agreement with the pacifist advocate, "Oh yes, all those who did engage in warfare in Old Testament times would have to be condemned as wicked sinners today, according to the law of Christ." Of such a "law of Christ" neither Christ Himself nor any of His apostles betray the slightest awareness, according to the text of the New Testament itself. We must therefore conclude that pacifism is completely lacking in support from the Word of God.

How did Judas Iscariot die?

Matthew 27:3–10 records Judas's remorse at having betrayed Jesus to the Jewish authorities. Judas first attempted to return the thirty shekels that they had paid him for leading the temple posse to Gethsemane, where Jesus was arrested. But the priests and temple officials refused to take the money back, since it was the price of blood and therefore unsuitable as an offering to God. Judas therefore cast the money pouch onto the floor of the temple treasury, departed from the city, and "hanged himself" (*apēnxato*— the aorist middle third person singular from *apanchō*, a verb used with that specific meaning ever since the fifth century B.C). This establishes the fact that Judas fastened a noose around his neck and jumped from the branch to which the other end of the rope was attached.

In Acts 1:18 the apostle Peter reminds the other disciples of Judas's shameful end and the gap he left in the ranks of the Twelve, which called for another disciple to take his place. Peter relates the following: "He therefore acquired a plot of land [*chōrion*] from the reward of wrongdoing." (This could mean either that Judas had already contracted with the owner of the field that he originally had wanted to buy with the betrayal money; or—as is far more likely in this context—Peter was speaking ironically, stating that Judas acquired a piece of real estate all right, but it was only a burial plot [*chōrion* could cover either concept], namely, the one on which his lifeless body fell.)

Acts 1:18 goes on to state: "And he, falling headlong, burst asunder, and all of his inwards gushed out." This indicates that the tree from which Judas suspended himself overhung a precipice. If the branch from which he had hung himself was dead and dry— and there are many trees that match this description even to this day on the brink of the canyon that tradition identifies as the place where Judas died—it would take only one strong gust of wind to yank the heavy corpse and split the branch to which it was attached and plunge both with great force into the bottom of the chasm below. There is indication that a strong wind arose at the hour Christ died and ripped the great curtain inside the temple from top to bottom (Matt. 27:51). This was accompanied by a rock-splitting earthquake and undoubtedly also by a thunderstorm, which normally follows a prolonged period of cloud gathering and darkness (Matt. 27:45). Conditions were right for what had started out as a mere suicide by hanging to turn into a grisly mutilation of the corpse as the branch gave way to the force of the wind and was hurtled down to the bottom.

Why does Matthew 27:9 attribute to Jeremiah a prophecy from Zechariah?

Matthew 27:9-10 describes the purchase of Potter's Field with Judas Iscariot's money as a fulfillment of Old Testament prophecy: "Then that which was spoken through Jeremiah the prophet was fulfilled, saying, 'And they took the thirty pieces of silver, the price of one whose price had been set by the sons of Israel; and they gave them for the Potter's Field, as the Lord directed me" (NASB). The remarkable thing about this quotation is that the greater portion of it is actually from Zechariah 11:12-13, which reads as follows: "And I said to them, 'If it is good in your sight, give me my wages; but if not, never mind!' So they weighed out thirty shekels of silver as my wages. Then Yahweh said to me, 'Throw it to the potter, that magnificent price at which I was valued by them.' So I took the thirty shekels of silver and threw them to the potter in the house of Yahweh." There are significant differences between the Zechariah passage and the quotation in Matthew, which has the prophet paying out—or at least giving—the purchase money, and has him turning over the money for a field rather than giving it to the potter personally. Yet the whole point of the quotation in Matthew is directed toward the purchase of the field. The Zechariah passage says nothing at all about purchasing a field; indeed, it does not even mention a field at all.

But as we turn to Jeremiah 32:6-9, we find the prophet purchasing a field in Anathoth for a certain number of shekels. Jeremiah 18:2 describes the prophet as watching a potter fashioning earthenware vessels in his house. Jeremiah 19:2 indicates that there was a potter near the temple, having his workshop in the Valley of Hinnom. Jeremiah 19:11 reads: "Thus says Yahweh of hosts: 'Even so I will break this people and this city as one breaks a potter's vessel, that cannot be made whole again; and they shall bury them in Tophet.'" It would seem, therefore, that Zechariah's casting of his purchase money to the potter dated back to the symbolic actions of Jeremiah. Yet it is only Jeremiah that mentions the "field" of the potter—which is the principal point of Matthew's quotation. Matthew is therefore combining and summarizing elements of prophetic symbolism both from Zechariah and from Jeremiah. But since Jeremiah is the more prominent of the two prophets, he mentions Jeremiah's name by preference to that of the minor prophet.

A similar procedure is followed by Mark 1:2-3, which attributes only to Isaiah a combined quotation from Malachi 3:1 and Isaiah 40:3. In that case also, only the more famous of the two prophets is mentioned by name. Since that was the normal literary practice of the first century A.D., when the Gospels were written, the authors can scarcely be faulted for not following the modern practice of precise identification and footnoting (which could never have become feasible until after the transition had been made from the scroll to the codex and the invention of the printing press).

What was the exact wording of the inscription on the cross?

The slight differences between the four Evangelists in the exact wording of the *aitia*, or criminal charge, against Jesus that was composed by Pilate and affixed as a *titulus* over Christ's head on His cross have puzzled Bible students for years, especially since biblical inerrancy has become prominent in recent discussion. The version of each Evangelist is given below, as rendered in the NIV:

Matthew 27:37: "This is Jesus, the King of the Jews."

Mark 15:26: "The written notice of the charge against him read: The King of the Jews."

Luke 23:38: "This is the King of the Jews."

John 19:19: "Pilate had a notice prepared and fastened to the cross. It read: Jesus of Nazareth, the King of the Jews."

The only element common to all four citations is "King of the Jews." How are these to be reconciled? John contributes a valuable clue: "Many of the Jews read this sign, for the place where Jesus was crucified was near the city, and the sign was written in Aramaic, Latin and Greek" (19:20). If the sign was written in three languages, it is quite certain that Pilate himself, however well versed in Latin (his native language) and Greek (the language he used in conversing with all non-Italians in Palestine), would scarcely have been able to write in either Hebrew or Aramaic. (John 19:20 uses for this the adverbial form *Hebraisti*, which in gospel usage did not mean "in Hebrew" but in the Jewish dialect of Aramaic. We know this because wherever *Hebraisti* is used elsewhere, as in John 5:2; 19:13, 17; 20:16, the word is given in its Aramaic form, transcribed into Greek letters.) It is quite conceivable that Pilate first wrote in Latin in brief form. Then, as he wrote beneath in Greek, he may have felt like adding the name of Jesus and the city that He belonged to, since the Greek form would be legible to all bystanders of whatever race. The Aramaic version may have copied the Greek with the omission of "Naza-

rene." This could account for the variations reported in the four versions.

I venture to suggest a possible format for the title on the cross as follows:

Matthew 27:37 probably contained the Aramaic wording, since Matthew's gospel, according to Papias, was originally composed in Aramaic.

Mark 15:26 seems to be an abridged form of the Latin wording—a reasonable supposition if indeed Mark assisted Peter in Rome and wrote down Peter's oral teaching after Peter was martyred. We cannot be sure how reliable this church tradition may be (especially if José O'Callaghan is right in dating 7Q5 as Mark 6:52–53 as *Zierstil*, copied down in the 50s), but at least there is some basis for supposing that Matthew would have inclined to Pilate's original Latin form (dropping the demonstrative pronoun *HIC*; "This").

As for John, his ministry seems to have been confined to a Greek-speaking population, wherever he served. The last decades of his life were almost certainly spent in or around Ephesus. We might therefore expect him to have inclined to the Greek form of the title.

This indicates the following as the exact wording on the cross, following the order in John 19:20: Aramaic, Latin and Greek:

(Aramaic) דנא ישויט מלכא דיהודיא
(Latin) *REX IVDAEORVM HIC*
(Greek) ΙΗΣΟΥΣ Ο ΝΑΖΩΡΑΙΟΣ Ο ΒΑΣΙΛΕΥΕΣ ΤΩΝ ΙΟΥΔΑΙΩΝ.

What did the centurion really say as he watched Jesus die (Matt. 27:54; Mark 15:39; Luke 23:47)?

Matthew 27:54 quotes the centurion and the soldiers who were standing guard at the cross of Christ, in the midst of the terrifying darkness, wind, earthquake, and storm that took place at the moment He expired, as remarking, "Truly [*alēthōs*] this man was a son [or possibly 'the Son'] of God!" The wording in Mark 15:39 is virtually the same (with only the word for "man" [*anthrōpos*] included in the Greek, though it was already inferred by the masculine singular demonstrative *houtos* ["this"]). In Luke 23:47, however, the centurion is quoted as saying, "Truly [*ontōs*] this man was righteous."

Are we presented with an irreconcilable contradiction here? Certainly not! Those who express admiration of the performance of some actor, musician, or orator on the stage usually employ more than one laudatory epithet in order to describe their feelings about him—even if they do not resort to the standard promotional hyperbole: "That was terrific! Stupendous! Colossal! Magnificent!" There is no reason whatever to suppose that the military bystander limited his expressed sentiments to one terse sentence. He must at least have said, "This was truly a righteous man. This was surely a son of God!" Luke found "righteous man" particularly striking because the words were voiced by the chief executioner of one who had been condemned to death by Hebrew and Roman justice as a blasphemer and a rebel against the authority of Caesar. Matthew and Mark were more impressed by his later expression regarding the divine dimension he had perceived in the expiring Sufferer.

Do not the many discrepancies in the four Resurrection narratives cast doubt on the historicity of the Resurrection itself?

Each of the four Evangelists contributes valuable details concerning the events of the resurrection of our Lord Jesus Christ. Not all these distinctive items of information are contained in all four Gospels; some are contained only in one or two. But nothing could be clearer than that all four were testifying to the same epoch-making event, that the same Jesus who was crucified on Good Friday rose again in His crucified body on Easter Sunday morning. The very fact that each of the four writers contributed individual details from his own perspective and emphasis furnishes the most compelling type of evidence possible for the historicity of Christ's conquest over death and the grave. A careful examination of these four records in comparison with one another demonstrates that they are not in any way contradictory, despite the charges leveled by some critics. It is helpful to synthesize all four accounts in order to arrive at a full picture of what took place on Easter itself and during the weeks that intervened until the ascension of Christ.

The Women's First Visit to the Tomb

On Saturday evening three of the women decided to go back to the tomb belonging to Joseph of Arimathea, where they had seen Christ's body laid away on Friday at sundown. They wanted to rewrap His corpse with additional spices, beyond those which Nicodemus and Joseph had already used on Friday. There were three women involved (Mark 16:1): Mary Magdalene, Mary the wife (or mother) of James, and Salome (Luke does not give their names; Matthew refers only to the two Marys); and they had bought the additional spices with their own means (Mark 16:1). They apparently started their journey from the house in Jerusalem while it was still dark (*skotias eti ousēs*), even though it was already early morning (*prōi*) (John 20:1). But by the time they arrived, dawn was glimmering in the east (*tē epiphōskousē*) that Sunday morning (*eis mian sabbatōn*) (Matt. 28:1). (Mark 16:2, Luke 24:1, John 20:1 all use the dative: *tē miā tōn sabbatōn*.) Mark 16:2 adds that the tip of the sun had actually appeared above the horizon (*anateilantos tou hēliou*—aorist participle; the Beza

347

codex uses the present participle, *anatellontos,* implying "while the sun was rising").

It may have been while they were on their way to the tomb outside the city wall that the earthquake took place, by means of which the angel of the Lord rolled away the great circular stone that had sealed the entrance of the tomb. So blinding was his glorious appearance that the guards specially assigned to the tomb were completely terrified and swooned away, losing all consciousness (Matt. 28:2-4). The earthquake could hardly have been very extensive; the women seemed to be unaware of its occurrence, whether it happened before they left Jerusalem or while they were walking toward their destination. There is no evidence that it damaged anything in the city itself. But it was sufficient to break the seal placed over the circular stone at the time of interment and roll the stone itself away from its settled position in the downward slanting groove along which it rolled.

The three women were delightfully surprised to find their problem of access to the tomb solved; the stone had already been rolled away (Mark 16:3-4)! They then entered the tomb, side-stepping the unconscious soldiers. In the tomb they made out the form of the leading angel, appearing as a young man with blazing white garments (Mark 16:5), who, however, may not have shown himself to them until they first discovered that the corpse was gone (Luke 24:2-3). But then it became apparent that this angel had a companion, for there were two of them in the tomb. The leading angel spoke to them with words of encouragement, "Don't be afraid, for I know that you are looking for Jesus who was crucified" (Matt. 28:5). Nevertheless they were quite terrified at the splendor of these heavenly visitors and by the amazing disappearance of the body they had expected to find in the tomb.

The angel went on: "Why do you seek the living among [lit., 'with'—*meta* with the genitive] those who are dead? He is not here, but He has risen [Luke 24:5-6], just as He said [Matt. 28:6]. Look at the place where they laid Him [Mark 16:6], the place where He was lying [Matt. 28:6]. Remember how He told you when He was still in Galilee, saying that the Son of Man had to be betrayed into the hands of sinful men, crucified, and rise again on the third day" (Luke 24:6-7).

After the angel had said this, the women in fact did remember Christ's prediction (especially at Caesarea Philippi); and they were greatly encouraged. Then the angel concluded with this command: "Go quickly and tell His disciples that He has risen from the dead!" Then he added: "Behold, He goes before you into Galilee; there you will see Him. Lo, I have told you" (Matt. 28:7). Upon receiving these wonderful tidings, the three delighted messengers set out in haste to rejoin the group of sorrowing believers back in the city (possibly in the home of John Mark) and pass on to them the electrifying news. They did not pause to inform anyone else as they hurried back (Mark 16:8), partly because they were fearful and shaken by their encounter at the empty tomb. But in their eagerness to deliver their tidings, they actually ran back to the house (Matt. 28:8) and made their happy announcement to the disciples who were gathered there.

Mary Magdalene took pains to seek out Peter and John first of all; and she breathlessly blurted out to them, "They have taken the Lord away from the tomb, and we don't know where they have laid Him!" (John 20:2). She apparently had not yet taken in the full import of what the angel meant when he told her that the Lord had risen again and that He was alive. In her confusion and amazement, all she could think of was that the body was not there; and she did not know what had become of it. Where could that body now be? It was for this reason that she wanted Peter and John to go back there and see what they could find out.

Peter and John at the Tomb

The synoptic Gospels do not mention this episode, but it was extremely important to John, who therefore took pains to record it in detail. As the two men got closer to Joseph's tomb, they began to run in their eagerness to get there and see what had happened (John 20:3-4). John arrived there first, being no doubt younger and faster than Peter. Yet it turned out that he was not as perceptive as Peter, for all John did when he got to the entrance was stoop down and look into the tomb, where he saw the shroud, or winding sheet, of Jesus lying on the floor (v.5). But Peter was a bit bolder and more curious; he went inside the chamber and found it indeed empty. Then he looked intently at the winding sheet, because it was lying in a very unusual position. Instead of being spread out in a long, jumbled strip, it was still all wrapped together in one spot (*entetyligmenon eis hena topon*). Moreover, the *soudarion* ("long kerchief") that had been wound around the head of Jesus was not unwound and tossed on the shroud but was still wrapped together and lying right above it (vv.6-7).

In other words, no one had removed the graveclothes from the corpse in the usual way, it was as if the body had simply passed right out of the headcloth and shroud and left them empty! This was such a remarkable feature that Peter called John back and pointed it out to him. All of a sudden it dawned on the younger man that no one had removed the body from that tomb. The body had simply left the tomb and left the graveclothes on its own power, passing through all those layers of cloth without unwrapping

them at all! Then John was utterly convinced: Jesus had not been removed by other hands; He had raised Himself from the dead. That could only mean He was alive again. John and Peter decided to hurry back and report to the others this astounding evidence that Jesus had indeed conquered death and was alive once more.

The Private Interviews With the Women and With Peter

For some reason, Peter and John did not tell Mary Magdalene about what they had deduced before they left. Perhaps they did not even realize that she had followed along behind them at her slower pace. In fact, she may not have gotten back to the tomb until they had already left. She arrived all alone, but she did not immediately reenter until she had paused to weep for a little while. Then she stooped down once more to look through her tear-stained eyes into the tomb (John 20:11). To her astonishment it was ablaze with light; and there she beheld two angels in splendid white robes, sitting at each end of the place where Jesus had lain (v.12). Immediately they—the very same pair that had spoken to the three women at their earlier visit—asked her wonderingly, "Why are you crying?" Had she not understood the glorious news they had told her the first time? But all Mary could think about was the disappearance of Christ's body. "They have taken my Lord away, and I don't know where they have laid Him," she lamented. To this the angels did not need to give any answer, for they could see the figure of Jesus standing behind her; and they knew His response would be better than anything they could say.

Mary could sense that someone else had joined her, and so she quickly turned around and tried to make out through her tear-blurred eyes who this stranger might be. It wasn't one of her own group, she decided; so it had to be the gardener who cared for this burial ground of Joseph of Arimathea. Even when He spoke to her, Mary did not at first recognize Jesus' voice, as He kindly asked her, "Woman, why are you crying? Whom are you looking for?" (v.15). All she could do was wail at Him accusingly, "Sir, if it is you who have taken Him away, tell me where you have laid Him; and I will carry Him off"—as if somehow her womanly strength would be equal to such a task.

It was at this point that the kindly stranger revealed Himself to Mary by reverting to His familiar voice as He addressed her by name, "Mariam!" Immediately she realized that the body she was looking for stood right before her, no longer a corpse but now a living, breathing human being—and yet more than that, the incarnate God. "Rabbouni!" she exclaimed (that is to say, "Master!") and cast herself at His feet. It was only for a brief moment that she touched Him; for He gently withdrew Himself from her, saying, "Don't keep touching Me [the negative imperative *mē mou haptou* implies discontinuance of an action already begun], for I have not yet ascended to My Father." Whether He did so later that afternoon and then returned afterward to speak to the two disciples on the road to Emmaus and the rest of the group back in Jerusalem that evening is not altogether clear. But if Mary was asked not to touch Him at this point in the day and the disciples were freely permitted to touch Him that evening, it must be inferred that He did report briefly back to God the Father in heaven before returning to earth once more for His postresurrection forty-day ministry.

This private interview with the risen Lord did not continue much longer, so far as Mary was concerned; for He commissioned her to hurry back to the group in the city and prepare them for His coming to join them in His resurrection body. "Go to My brethren," He said, "and tell them I am going up to My Father and your Father, My God and your God" (John 20:17). This definitely confirms the deduction that Christ did in fact make a brief visit to heaven during the middle of Easter Sunday before reappearing to Cleopas and his companion on the Emmaus road.

Nevertheless Jesus did not make His ascent to heaven at this precise moment, for He waited around long enough to meet with the other two women who had earlier accompanied Magdalene to the tomb at daybreak. Apparently Mary the mother (or wife) of James, and Salome with her, had decided to go back once more to visit the empty tomb. Presumably they noticed that Mary Magdalene had slipped away again after conferring with Peter and John, and they must have guessed where she had gone. Very soon after Magdalene had left Jesus and headed back toward the city (but not so soon that they actually met one another on the way), the two women drew near to the same spot where they had encountered the two angels on their first visit (Luke 24:4).

We are not told whether the women actually entered the tomb once again, or whether they met Jesus just outside; but at any rate He apparently accosted them after they had arrived, and He greeted them (Matt. 28:9). (The Greek *chairete* here probably represents either the Hebrew *šālôm* or the Aramaic *šᵉlāmā'*. Literally the Greek means "Rejoice!" whereas the Hebrew means "Peace!") Their reaction at seeing their risen Lord was similar to Magdalene's; they cast themselves at His feet and kissed them as they clung to Him. Jesus reassured them as they were adjusting to the shock of seeing Him alive again, "Don't be afraid." Then He continued with a mandate similar to the one He had given to Magdalene: "Go and pass on the word [*apangeilate*] to My brethren that they are to depart for Galilee, and there they will see Me."

It is highly significant that our Lord first revealed Himself in His resurrection body, not to the men, the eleven disciples themselves, but rather to three of the women among the group of believers. Apparently He found that they were even readier in their spiritual perception than the eleven men of His inner circle, on whom He had spent so much of His time during the three years of His teaching ministry. Be that as it may, it seems quite clear that Jesus chose to honor the women with His very first postresurrection appearances before He revealed Himself to any of the men— even to Peter himself.

Yet we must gather that Peter was the first of the male disciples to see his Lord alive after the Resurrection; for at some time after Mary Magdalene came back from her second visit to the tomb and her confrontation with Jesus there, Simon Peter must have had a personal reunion with Jesus. This we learn from Luke 24:34, where we are told that the disciples in the house of John Mark in Jerusalem had learned from Peter that he had already seen Jesus and had talked with Him, even before the two travelers returned from their journey toward Emmaus and reported back that they had broken bread with Jesus at the inn. They found as they came back with their exciting news and expected everyone there to be surprised at their account of talking with the risen Lord that the rest of the group were already aware of the stupendous event. The two travelers were delighted to meet with ready acceptance by all who heard them, for they were assured by all their friends, "Yes, yes, we know that Jesus is alive and has returned to us; for He has appeared to Simon Peter as well" (Luke 24:34). Presumably they were already aware (cf. v.22) of the earlier interviews reported to them by Mary Magdalene (who told them, "I have seen the Lord," and then relayed His announcement about ascending to the Father in heaven; cf. John 20:18) and by the other Mary and her companion, Salome, who had passed on His instructions about the important rendezvous to be held up in Galilee.

As for this personal interview between Christ and Peter, we have no further information; so we cannot be certain as to whether it was before or after His ascension to the Father and His subsequent return in the afternoon of Easter Sunday. All we can be sure of (and even this is perhaps arguable) is that He talked with Peter before He met with Cleopas and the other disciple on the road to Emmaus. It is interesting to note that Paul confirms that Christ did in fact appear to Peter before He revealed Himself to the rest of the Eleven (1 Cor. 15:5).

The Interview With the Disciples on the Way to Emmaus

The next major development on that first Easter Sunday involved two disciples who were not of the Eleven (the number to which they were reduced after the defection of Judas Iscariot). Cleopas was relatively undistinguished among the outer circle of Jesus' following; at least he is hardly mentioned elsewhere in the New Testament record. As for his companion, we are never even told what his name was, even though he shared in the distinction of being the first to walk with Christ after His resurrection. Jesus apparently chose these two disciples outside the circle of the Eleven in order to make it clear to all of His church that He was equally available or accessible to all believers who would put their trust in Him as Lord and Savior, whether or not they belonged to any special circle or had come to know Him at an earlier or a later date. Perhaps He also felt that for their future testimony to the world—that they had become convinced of His bodily resurrection even in the face of their initial assumption that He was already dead and gone—such a manifestation would be of special helpfulness to future generations.

One thing is certain: a true believer does not have to belong to the original band of chosen apostles in order to experience a complete transformation of life and the embracing of a new understanding that life with Jesus endures forever, in spite of all the adversities of this life and the malignity of Satan and the terrors of the grave. The Emmaus travelers replied, "Did not our hearts glow within us on the way and as He opened the Scriptures to us?" (Luke 24:32). They thus became the first example of what it means to walk with Jesus in living fellowship and hear Him speak from every part of the Hebrew Scriptures.

This account is contained only in the Gospel of Luke, that Evangelist who took such special interest in the warm and tender personal relationships that Jesus cultivated with individual believers, both male and female. We may be very grateful to him (and the Holy Spirit who guided him) that this heart-stirring record was included in the testimonies of Jesus' resurrection; for this encounter more fully than the others shows how life may be transformed from discouragement and disappointed hope into a richly satisfying and fruitful walk of faith with a wonderful Savior who has conquered sin and death for all who put their trust in Him.

One interesting feature about this interview deserves comment. As in the case of Mary Magdalene, Jesus did not appear to the Emmaus travelers at the first with His customary form, features, or voice; and they failed to recognize His identity. They took Him for a stranger who was new to Jerusalem (Luke 24:18). It was not until after He had taught them how the Old Testament had clearly foretold how Messiah would first have to suffer before entering into His glory—and indeed not until after they had sat down for a bite to eat at some roadside café and heard Him give thanks to God for the food—that they realized who He was. And then, at the moment of recognition, He suddenly left them, vanishing from their sight. This sudden disappearance showed them that this new friend of theirs, who had flesh and bones and could use His hands to break bread with them, was a supernatural Being. He was the God-man who had triumphed over death and had risen from the grave to resume His bodily form, a marvelous new body with power to appear and disappear according to His will and purpose, as He saw fit.

As soon as Jesus had left them, the two wayfarers sped back to Jerusalem as fast as their legs could carry them. They lost no time in making their way to the assembled believers and sharing with them the electrifying news of their lengthy encounter with the risen Lord. "And they began to relate their experiences on the road, and how He was recognized by them in the breaking of the bread."

The Interviews With the Assembled Disciples

Luke tells us that while the Emmaus travelers were finishing their report to the assembled believers, the Lord Himself entered through the locked doors and appeared in their midst (Luke 24:36), much to the amazement of all those who had not previously seen Him risen from the dead. Graciously He greeted them with His customary "Peace be with you" (the Greek *eirēnē hymin* doubtless represents the Aramaic *šᵉlāmā' 'ammᵉkôn* [John 20:19]). Then He hastened to allay their fears by showing them physical evidence of His bodily resurrection and restoration to life. "Why are you troubled and why do doubts arise in your heart?" He asked (Luke 24:38), as He held out His pierced hands for them to see and removed His sandals to show the nail holes through His feet (vv.39–40). He even uncovered the scar of the gash that the Roman spear had made in His side as He hung lifeless on the cross (John 20:20). "Look at My hands and feet," He said to them, "for it is really I. Feel Me and see, for a mere spirit does not have flesh and bones such as you behold Me to have" (Luke 24:39).

How many took advantage of Christ's offer to touch Him, we cannot be sure. But numbers of those in the room found even this evidence too amazing to be believed; so He offered a yet more dramatic proof. "Do you have anything to eat?" He asked them. They gave Him a piece of broiled fish, and He proceeded to eat it as they looked on with wonder and delight (Luke 24:42–43).

Having thus demonstrated that He was none other than their beloved Master risen from the dead, Jesus proceeded to explain to them, as He had explained to the two on the road to Emmaus, that all the amazing occurrences of Passion Week were fully predicted in the Hebrew Scriptures—all the way from Genesis to Malachi. The portions referred to were threefold: Moses (i.e., the Pentateuch), the Prophets, and the Psalms. (Notice that by this period all the Old Testament books other than the Pentateuch and the Psalms were included under the classification of "Prophets"—including all the books of history, Daniel, and probably the wisdom books of Proverbs and Ecclesiastes as well, unless "Psalms" is intended to represent all five books of poetry.) The entire Hebrew Bible is about the Son of God. But His particular focus was on those predictions of His ministry, sufferings, and death found in the Pentateuch (Gen. 3:15; 49:10; Deut. 18:15–18, and all the types of priesthood and sacrifice contained in the Torah), the Prophets (e.g., Isa. 7:14–9:6; 52:13–53:12), and the Psalms (esp. Ps. 16:10 and Ps. 22), which foretold all the events that found their culmination on this Easter Day (Luke 24:44–46). Thus He assured them that all the apparently tragic events of the last few days were in exact fulfillment of the great plan of human redemption that God had decreed from before the beginning of all time. Instead of feeling intimidated and disappointed by the shame of the Cross, they were to see in it the greatest victory of all time; and they were to trumpet abroad the good news of salvation, which by His atonement He had purchased for repentant sinners everywhere.

This led Jesus quite naturally to the earliest pronouncement of the Great Commission. He told the disciples that repentance was to be preached in His name to all nations for the forgiveness of sins, beginning from Jerusalem, and that they as eyewitnesses were under special obligation to carry out the proclamation of this message. But He recognized that in order to accomplish this mission effectively, they would need divine empowerment, the special dynamic that God had promised in His Word (cf. Joel 2:28–29). Then He concluded His exhortation with this formula of evangelistic commission: "As the Father has sent Me, so do I send you." Having said this, He breathed on them and said to them, "Receive the Holy Spirit" (John 20:22). Even in advance of the general bestowal of the Holy Spirit on the entire church at Pentecost, these apostles received Him as their permanently indwelling, sanctifying power. As temples for His residence, the apostles were entrusted with the awesome responsibility of conveying to the human race the knowledge of the Lord Jesus as the Way, the Truth, and the Life, without whom no one can come to God for salvation (John 14:6).

As prophets of God, therefore, preachers and missionaries of the gospel, empowered and used by the Holy Spirit, were to make available to lost sinners everywhere the benefits of Calvary. But since man cannot believe the gospel until it has been presented to him, the availability of God's forgiveness through Christ is practically limited to those evangelized by the faithful witness of His servants. In this sense, then, "if you forgive the sins [*aphēte tās hamartiās*] of any"—that is, by presenting them with Christ—"they have been forgiven them" (John 20:23, NASB). That is to say, they have been numbered among God's elect according to His foreknowledge and elective grace (the Greek perfect passive *apheōntai* so implies); and through the agency of God's messengers of the gospel, they enter the ranks of the forgiven and redeemed. By the same token, however, those who remain unevangelized have no access to this forgiveness and salvation; and failure to get out the message to them seals their eternal doom. "If you retain the sins of any, they have been retained" (by God Himself, in His predestinative will), NASB. Christ had spoken of this solemn responsibility earlier, at the time of Peter's confession of His messiahship; and there Jesus had symbolized it as the "power of the keys" (Matt. 16:19). It was at Pentecost, by his heart-stirring and conscience-piercing message, that Peter first used the power of the keys. With them he opened up the gateway to heaven to all the three thousand who believed.

John records that of the Eleven, there was just one who was not present. Thomas (whose Greek name was Didymus—"Twin"). Perhaps it was providential that he had been absent during the initial meeting of the church with the resurrected Christ, for he might later have wondered whether he had not been unduly swayed in his critical judgment by the contagion of the enthusiasm of the others. Thomas was one who insisted on concrete, objective proof before he could be intellectually convinced. He had to be convinced almost against his will, for he firmly believed that once a man was dead, that was the end. How could a buried corpse ever come to life again? An impossible, absurd notion if he had ever heard one! Therefore he would not lend credence to the most solemn protestations of his trusted fellow disciples, that they had actually seen and talked with their resurrected Lord (John 20:25). Surely they must have fallen victim to mere hallucination!

No one could ever expect Thomas to believe in anything so contrary to nature. Yet it was exactly one week later, on the Sunday following Easter, that Jesus appeared to the group for the second time (cf. John 21:14). This time Thomas was present, that stubborn skeptic who had declared, "Unless I see the print of the nails in His hands and put my finger into the place of the nails and put my hand into His side [i.e., where the spear had entered His chest], I will not believe" (John 20:25). As Jesus entered the room, again passing through the closed doors, He gave them the same general greeting as before: "Peace be unto you." Then He went up to Thomas and stood before him, saying, "Reach here your finger and look at My hands, and reach your hand here and put it into My side; and be not faithless but believing."

The very type of proof Thomas had demanded was now presented to him in a way that could admit of no other explanation: the same body that had been crucified on the cross now stood alive before him. All of a sudden, as Thomas touched the scar and nail prints with his hands, all of his hardheaded skepticism seemed foolish and unworthy. All he could do was fall to his knees in repentance and adoration as he exlaimed, "My Lord and my God" (John 20:28).

We now pass to the third interview between Christ and His apostles subsequent to the Resurrection. By this time the disciples had left Jerusalem and had gone up to Galilee to keep their rendezvous with Him as He had bidden them (Matt. 28:10; Mark 16:7). This was a much less formal occasion, and only five of them were present— on the fishing expedition at least (Peter, Thomas, Nathanael, James, and John). It was Peter's idea to go fishing, for it might help to relieve some of the tension of waiting for the Lord to appear to them. There is no good reason to infer, as some have done, that Peter was intending to leave his apostolic calling and go back to his old job as a fisherman. Even in our own day many a full-time pastor occasionally relaxes by following Peter's example. From Peter's scanty attire (John 21:7), we gather that it was a hot summer night; and it may have been hard to sleep. At any rate, they all went out with Peter and caught absolutely nothing.

Finally, as the dawn mist came on them, they made out the form of a bystander greeting them from the shore. "Children," He called out to them, "you don't have anything to eat, have you?" "No," they answered Him. "Well then," the stranger shouted, "throw your net on the right-hand side of the boat, and you will have a catch!" This seemed very unlikely, but they complied nevertheless. Immediately the net ropes began to jerk and pull about this way and that, and it seemed as if they had run into a whole school of unwary fish. John immediately recognized that this was a special work of God; only Jesus could turn such dismal failure into thrilling success. "It is the Lord," he exclaimed.

The rest of the story is so well known, it is unnecessary to repeat it all here. But the important feature about the incident so far as John was concerned—and he makes it the final item in his gospel—was the correlation between love and service. "Simon, if you love Me, feed My sheep." Love for Jesus was absolutely foundational. Jesus compelled Peter to reaffirm his love for Him three times—corresponding to the number of times he had denied Him in the palace of the high priest. Nothing Peter might do for the Lord would satisfy or please Him unless it was based on an all-consuming personal affection and commitment to Him, in sincere fulfillment of the first and great commandment. But if that love was real, it had to express itself in loving outreach to all of God's people: Christ's lambs and sheep (both children and adults). In Peter's case, at least, Peter's faithfulness to Jesus would some day mean his death on the scaffold or cross (John 21:18–19). As a lover of Christ, Peter also would have to be willing to lay down his life for his "friends."

There may have been numerous other times of fellowship between Christ and His apostles during the remainder of the forty-day period between the Easter resurrection and the acension of our Lord to heaven recorded in Acts 1:9. Luke simply indicates that Jesus was repeatedly seen (optanomenos) by His disciples over a period of forty days, and He taught them "concerning the kingdom of God" (Acts 1:3). But the record of the Galilean retreat closes with a large assembly of Christ's followers—quite possibly the gathering included more than five hundred at that time (cf. 1 Cor. 15:6)—on some mountain in Galilee (Matt. 28:16), which though unnamed may have been Tabor, the highest and most impressive hill in Galilee. There Jesus issued a stirring appeal for lives devoted to evangelism. He assured His disciples that the Father had committed to Him as the risen Messiah all authority (*pāsa exousia*) in heaven and on earth; and even after His ascension to Glory, He would be with them always, to the very consummation of the age (Matt. 28:20). Their responsibility would be to go and make disciples of all the nations, baptizing them in the name of the Triune God, and teaching them to observe all of His commandments. Matthew 28:19-20 gives us the fullest form of the Great Commission.

The final day of Christ's postresurrection ministry did not take place in Galilee. That may have been the site of the largest assembly of His followers, as we have just seen; but His actual departure was from the crest of the Mount of Olives, not far from Bethany. There was something especially fitting that this should be the point of His departure, since from the prophecy in Zechariah 14:4 we know that the Mount of Olives will be the place of His return in the day of Armageddon. As He sets His foot down there, a mighty earthquake will split the hill of Olivet into a broad valley running from west to east.

We have no way of knowing how many of Jesus' disciples gathered on the summit of Olivet for that last memorable interview with their Lord, on His final day of earthly ministry. Perhaps there were about 120 there, judging from the statement in Acts 1:15. It is conceivable that the "over five hundred brethren at once" (1 Cor. 15:6) were there rather than up in Galilee. Matthew 28:16 only mentions the Eleven as being certainly of that number; yet the Eleven may have simply been a core group, and a great many more may have gathered around them. On the other hand, if there were over 500 assembled at Olivet on Ascension Day, it is unlikely that 380 of them would have disregarded Christ's solemn instructions and would have failed to tarry for the specified ten days until Pentecost (Luke 24:49; Acts 1:4), when the Spirit would descend from heaven on them.

As the disciples gathered about Jesus to take their leave of Him before His departure to heaven, they asked Him one question of pressing importance: Will the kingdom of God very soon be established on earth? They were anxious to know what their Lord's plan was for the triumph of His cause and the establishment of His sovereignty over all the earth. In response to this question, Jesus does not correct their underlying premise—that He some day will establish the kingdom of God on earth—but indicates that there will be intervening times and seasons in phraseology reminiscent of the Olivet Discourse (Matt. 24:5-14), with its clear indication that much would have to happen before the present age would draw to its close. It was unnecessary and inappropriate for them to know about the exact date of the Second Advent; their task was simply to carry out the Great Commission and spread the gospel to the very ends of the earth (Acts 1:7-8).

As His final gesture there on the hilltop near Bethany, our Lord lifted His hands to bless His disciples (Luke 24:50); and in that attitude He was suddenly lifted up from the ground, to disappear from their sight beyond the clouds. As they stood there looking up, transfixed with wonder, two angels suddenly appeared beside them (perhaps the same angels who had greeted the visitors to the empty tomb) and assured them that Jesus would some day return to earth in bodily form—in the same form as they had seen Him ascend to heaven. With this glad assurance ringing in their ears, they made their way down from Olivet in order to spend the next ten days in communion and prayer, until the outpouring of Christ's Holy Spirit came on them all at Pentecost.

Does the Bible really teach that God is a Trinity?

Christian baptism commanded by Christ in the Great Commission (Matt. 28:19) is to be "in the name of the Father and the Son and the Holy Spirit" (NASB). Notice that it says "name," not "names." This suggests that the name of God is Father-Son-Holy Spirit. It is true that the term "Trinty" was not employed by the actual Hebrew or Greek text of the Bible; but neither is "soteriology"—yet there is a systematic doctrine of salvation found in Scripture—neither is "hamartiology" nor "transcendence" nor "immanence" nor "preexistence" nor "Christology." Few people who discuss biblical teaching raise a red flag and object to the use of these terms when they discuss the nature of the gracious working of God. Such designations serve as convenient labels for concepts or complex teachings concerning subjects that belong together. It is impossible to discuss theology as a systematic, philosophical discipline without using these technical terms. None of them is found in the Bible text, to be sure; but all of them sum up in a coherent, organized way the major concepts that are taught in Scripture. Therefore we must dismiss as irrelevant the objection that the precise word "Trinity" is not used in the Bible text.

On the other hand, we venture to insist that some of the most basic and fundamental teaching about God remains nearly incomprehensible without a grasp of the doctrine of the Trinity.

First, let us be very clear as to what is meant by "Trinity." This implies that God is a Unity subsisting in three Persons: the Father, the Son, and the Holy Spirit—all three of whom are one God. That God is One is asserted in both the Old and New Testaments: Deuteronomy 6:4: "Hear, O Israel! Yahweh our God is one Yahweh"; Mark 12:29: "Jesus answered, 'The first [great commandment] is, "Hear, Israel, the Lord our God is one Lord'"; Ephesians 4:6: "[There is] one God and Father of all, who is over all and through all and in all." These are all clear, unequivocal affirmations of monotheism. God is One. There are no other gods besides Him. Isaiah 45:22 quotes God as saying, "Turn to Me, and be saved, all the ends of the earth; for I am God, and there is no other" (NASB). Or again, Psalm 96:4-5 reads: "For great is Yahweh, and greatly to be praised; He is to be feared above all gods. For all the gods of the peoples are idols [the Hebrew 'ᵉlilîm connotes 'weak, worthless ones']." This is made very explicit in 1 Corinthians 8:5-6: "For even if there are so-called gods whether in heaven or on earth, as indeed there are many gods and many lords, yet for us there is but one God, the Father, from whom are all things, . . . and one Lord, Jesus Christ, through whom are all things" (NASB).

On the other hand, the Bible teaches that God is not a sterile monad but eternally exists in three Persons. This is suggested by the Creation account in Genesis 1:1-3: "In the beginning God ['ᵉlohîm, plural in form, with the îm ending] created [bārā', a singular verb, not the plural bārᵉ'û] the heavens and the earth [this plural for 'God' is probably a 'plural of majesty'; yet compare Gen. 1:26-27, discussed below]. And the earth was formless and void . . . and the Spirit of God was moving over the surface of the waters [showing the involvement of the Third Person in the work of creation]. Then God [ᵉlohîm] said, 'Let there be light!'" (NASB). Here we have God speaking as the Creative Word, the same as the Logos (John 1:3), who is the Second Person of the Trinity.

The Bible teaches that each Person of the Trinity has a special function, both in the work of creation and in the work of redemption.

The Father is the *Source* of all things (1 Cor. 8:6: "from whom are all things"). He is the one who *planned* and *ordained* redemption. "For God so loved the world, that He *gave* His only begotten Son" (John 3:16). This incarnation was a fulfillment of His previously announced *decree* in Psalm 2:7; "I will surely tell of the decree of Yahweh: He said to Me, 'Thou art My Son, today I have *begotten* Thee.'" He also has given His messianic Servant as an atonement for our sins (Isa. 53:6,10). He has likewise given the Holy Spirit to His people (Acts 2:18; Eph. 1:17). He bestowed salvation on the redeemed (Eph. 2:8–9) through the faith that is also His gift. And to His Son He has given the church (John 6:37).

As for God the Son, it was *through Him* that all the work of creation was accomplished (John 1:3; 1 Cor. 8:6), which means that He was also the Lord God addressed in Psalm 90 as the Creator who fashioned the mountains, hills, and all the earth. He is also the Sustainer and Preserver of the material universe that He created (Heb. 1:2–3). Yet He is also the God who *became "flesh"* (John 1:18), that is, a true human being—without ceasing to be God—in order to explain ("exegete") God to mankind. He was the *Light* that came into the world to save men from the power of darkness (John 1:9;8:12) by means of His *perfect obedience* to the law and by His *atoning death* on the cross (Heb. 1:3). He was also the one who overcame the power of death; and as the risen Savior, He established and commissioned His church as His living temple, His body and His bride.

The Holy Spirit is that Person of the Godhead who *inspired* the writing of *Scripture* (1 Cor. 2:13; 2 Peter 1:21), who manifests the gospel to God's redeemed (John 16:14). He *communicates* the *benefits of Calvary* to all who truly believe and receive Christ as Lord and Savior (John 1:12–13); and He enters their souls to *sanctify* their bodies as living temples of God (1 Cor. 3:16; 6:19), after they have been born again by His transforming grace (John 3:5–6). Then He teaches believers to understand and believe the words of Christ (John 14:26; 1 Cor. 2:10), as He bears witness of Christ both by external signs and by inward conviction (John 15:26; Acts 2:33,38,43). He sanctifies and brings together the members of Christ into a living organism that is the true temple of the Lord (Eph. 2:18–22) and bestows on each member special gifts of grace and power (*charismata*) by which they may enrich and strengthen the church as a whole (1 Cor. 12:7–11).

The New Testament repeatedly and plainly affirms that Jesus Christ was God incarnate. He is set forth as the all-creative Word of God who actually was God (John 1:1–3). He was indeed the "only begotten God" (John 1:18, for according to the oldest and best manuscripts that was the original reading in this verse) rather than "only begotten Son." In John 20:28 the affirmation of the no-longer-doubting Thomas, "My Lord and my God!" is accepted by Christ as His true identity; for He commented: "Have you *believed* because you have seen Me? Blessed are those who have not seen and yet have believed." Believed what? Why, that which Thomas just acknowledged, that Christ is both Lord and *God!*

In the Pauline and General epistles, we find the following clear affirmations of Christ's full and essential deity.

1. Speaking of the Israelites, Paul says, "Of whom [ōn, the participle really demands this rendering; *ho ōn* ('he is') has to be a relative construction modifying *ho Christos* as its antecedent] was Christ according to the flesh [i.e., physically speaking], who is God over all, blessed forever, Amen" (Rom. 9:5).

2. In Titus 2:13 Paul speaks of "looking forward to the glorious appearing [*epiphaneia* is elsewhere used only of the appearance of Christ, never of God the Father] of our great God and Savior, Jesus Christ."

3. Hebrews 1:8 quotes Psalm 45:6–7 as a proof of the deity of Christ, as taught in the Old Testament: "But to the Son he says, 'Thy throne, O God [the Hebrew passage uses *'elōhîm* here], is forever and ever.'"

4. Hebrews 1:10–11, quoting from Psalm 102:25–26, states; "In the beginning, O LORD [this entire psalm is addressed to Yahweh, and so the author inserts the vocative LORD here from the previous context], Thou didst establish the earth, and the heavens are the works of Thy hands. They will perish, but Thou remainest." Here Christ is addressed as the God who always existed, even before Creation, and who will always live, even after the heavens have passed away.

5. In 1 John 5:20 John says, "We are in Him who is true, in His Son Jesus Christ. He [lit., 'this one'] is the true God and eternal life."

So far as Old Testament passages are concerned, the following have a definite bearing on the Trinity.

1. Genesis 1:26 quotes God (*'elōhîm*) as saying, "Let us make man in our image, according to our likeness" (NASB). This first person plural can hardly be a mere editorial or royal plural that refers to the speaker alone, for no such usage is demonstrable anywhere else in biblical Hebrew. Therefore we must face the question of who are included in this "us" and "our." It could hardly include the angels in consultation with God, for nowhere is it ever stated that man was created in the image of angels, only of God. Verse 27 then affirms: "And God [*'elōhîm*]

created man in His own image, in the image of God He created him; male and female He created them" (NASB). God—the same God who spoke of Himself in the plural—now states that He created man in His image. In other words, the plural equals the singular. This can only be understood in terms of the Trinitarian nature of God. The one true God subsists in three Persons, Persons who are able to confer with one another and carry their plans into action together—without ceasing to be one God.

For us who have been created in God's image, this should not be too difficult to grasp; for there is a very definite sense in which we too are trinitarian in nature. First Thessalonians 5:23 indicates this clearly enough: "Now may the God of peace sanctify you wholly, and may your entire *spirit* and *soul* and *body* be preserved without blame at the coming of our Lord Jesus Christ." We often find ourselves engaged in a debate between our spirit, soul, and bodily nature as we grapple with a moral decision and are faced with a choice between the will of God and the desire of our self-seeking, flesh-pleasing nature.

2. Psalm 33:6 reads, "By the Word of Yahweh were the heavens made, and all the host of them by the Spirit [*rûaḥ*] of His mouth." Here again we have the same involvement of all three Persons of the Trinity in the work of creation: the Father decrees, the Son as the Logos brings the Father's decree into operation, and the Spirit imparts His life-giving dynamic to the whole process.

3. Psalm 45:6 has already been quoted in connection with Hebrews 1:8: "Thy throne, O God, is forever and ever; a scepter of righteousness is the scepter of Thy kingdom." But 45:7 brings in the reference to a

God who will bless this God who is the perfect King: "Thou hast loved righteousness, and hated wickedness; therefore God, Thy God, has anointed Thee with the oil of joy above Thy fellows" (NASB). The concept of God blessing God can only be understood in a Trinitarian sense. A unitarian concept would make this passage unintelligible.

4. Isaiah 48:16 sets forth all three Persons in the work of redemptive revelation and action: "Come near to Me, listen to this: From the first I have not spoken in secret; from the time it took place [i.e., the deliverance of God's people from captivity and bondage], I was there. And now the Lord Yahweh has sent Me, and His Spirit." Here we have the God-man Redeemer speaking (the one who has just described Himself in v.12 as "the First and the Last," and in v.13 as the one who "founded the earth and spread out the heavens." He now says here in v.16 that He has been sent by the Lord Yahweh (which in this case must refer to God the Father) and also by His Spirit (the Third Person of the Trinity). Conceivably "and His Spirit" could be linked up with "Me" as the object of "has sent," but in the context of the Hebrew original here it gives the impression that His *rûah* ("Spirit") is linked up with *'adōnay YHWH* ("Lord Yahweh") as an added subject rather than an added object. At any rate, the Third Person is distinguished from either the First or the Second, so far as these verses are concerned.

In addition to the examples given above of Old Testament verses that cannot be made sense of except through the Trinitarian nature of the Godhead, there are repeated instances of the activity of the "Angel of Yahweh" who becomes equated with Yahweh Himself. Consider the following passages:

1. Genesis 22:11 describes the most dramatic moment of Abraham's experience on Mount Moriah, as he was about to sacrifice Isaac: "But the Angel of Yahweh called to him from heaven, and said, 'Abraham, Abraham!'" The next verse proceeds to equate that Angel with God Himself: "For now I know that you fear God, since you have not withheld your son, your only son, from Me." Then in vv.16–17 the Angel declares, "'By Myself I have sworn,' declares Yahweh, 'because you have done this thing, and have not withheld your son ... indeed I will greatly bless you.'" Very clearly the Angel of Yahweh here is Yahweh Himself. "Yahweh" is the covenant name of the Trinitarian God, and the Angel of that God is also Himself God. That is to say, we can identify the Angel of Yahweh in passages like these as the preincarnate Redeemer, God the Son, already engaged in His redemptive or mediatorial work even prior to His becoming Man in the womb of the Virgin Mary.

2. In Genesis 31:11,13 we have the same phenomenon; the Angel of God turns out to be God Himself: "Then the angel of God said to me in the dream, 'Jacob,' and I said, 'Here I am.... I am the God of Bethel, where you anointed a pillar.'" (NASB).

3. Exodus 3:2 states: "And the angel of Yahweh appeared to him in a blazing fire from the midst of a bush." Then in v.4 we read: "When Yahweh saw that he turned aside to look, God called to him from the midst of the bush." The full self-identification then comes in v.6: "He said also, 'I am the God of your father, the God of Abraham, the

God of Isaac, and the God of Jacob.' Then Moses hid his face, for he was afraid to look at God." Here again the Angel of Yahweh turns out to be Yahweh God Himself.

4. Judges 13:20 states: "For it came about when the flame went up from the altar toward heaven, that the angel of Yahweh ascended in the flame of the altar. When Manoah and his wife saw this, they fell on their faces to the ground." Verses 22-23 complete the identification of the Angel with God: "So Manoah said to his wife, 'We shall surely die, for we have seen God!' But his wife said to him, 'If Yahweh had desired to kill us, He would not have accepted a burnt offering and a grain offering from our hands.'"

From this survey of the biblical evidence, we must conclude that Scripture does indeed teach the doctrine of the Trinity, even though it does not use that precise term. Furthermore, we ought to observe that the concept of God as one in essence but three in centers of consciousness—what the Greek church referred to as three *hypostases* and the Latin church as *personae*—is absolutely unique in the history of human thought. No other culture or philosophical movement ever came up with such an idea of God as this—an idea that remains very difficult for our finite minds to graps. Yet the inability to comprehend fully the richness and fullness of God's nature as embraced in the Trinity should not furnish any solid ground for skepticism as to its truth. For if we are to accept and believe only what we can fully understand, then we are hopelessly beyond redemption. Why so? Because we shall never fully understand how God could love us enough to send His only Son to earth in order to die for our sins and become our Savior. If we cannot accept any idea that we do not completely understand, then how can we believe John 3:16? How can we receive the assurances of the gospel and be saved?

Mark

Who was high priest when David ate the showbread—Abiather or Ahimelech?

Mark 2:26 quotes Jesus as asking His hearers whether they had never read what David did, when he and his men were hungry and entered the sanctuary at Nob to beg for food, in the time of Abiathar the high priest (1 Sam. 21:1–6). As a matter of fact, however, it was with Abiathar's father, Ahimelech, that David had dealings; for Ahimelech was really the high priest at the time of that episode.

Did Jesus err when He referred to the wrong high priest? A careful examination of Mark 2:26 reveals that Christ did not actually imply that Abiathar was already high priest at the time of David's visit. He simply said, *"Epi Abiathar archiereōs,"* which means "in the time of Abiathar the high priest." As things turned out, bloody King Saul soon had Ahimelech and the entire priestly community of Nob massacred by Doeg the Edomite (1 Sam. 22:18–19); and Abiathar the son of Ahimelech was the only one fortunate enough to escape. He fled to join David (v.20) and served as his priest all through David's years of wandering and exile. Naturally he was appointed high priest by David after David became king, and he shared the high priesthood with Zadok, Saul's appointee, until David's death. Under these circumstances it was perfectly proper to refer to Abiathar as the high priest—even though his appointment as such came somewhat later, after the incident at Nob—just as it would be proper to introduce an anecdote by saying, "Now when King David was a shepherd boy," even though David was not actually a king at the time he was a shepherd boy.

According to W.F. Arndt and F.W. Gingrich (*A Greek-English Lexicon of the New Testament* [Chicago: University of Chicago, 1957], p. 286), *epi* with the genitive simply means "in the time of"; and that is the meaning that applies in Mark 2:26 (the same construction as Acts 11:28 ["in the time of Claudius"] and Heb. 1:2 ["in the time of the last of these days" (*ep' eschatou tōn hēmerōn toutōn*)]). The episode did happen "in the time of" Abiathar; he was not only alive but actually present when the event took place, and he very shortly afterward became high priest as a result of Saul's murdering his father, Ahimelech. If Jesus' words are interpreted in the way He meant them, there is absolutely no variance with historical fact.

How can Mark 8:12–13 be reconciled with Matthew 12:38–39, concerning a sign of messiahship for Christ's generation?

Mark 8:11–13 reads: "And the Pharisees came out and began to argue with Him, seeking from Him a sign from heaven, to test Him. And sighing deeply in His spirit, He said, 'Why does this generation seek for a sign? Truly I say to you, no sign shall be given to this generation.' And leaving them, He again embarked and went away to the other side" (NASB). The passage in Matthew 12:38–39 reads as follows: "Then some of the scribes and Pharisees answered Him, saying, 'Teacher, we want to see a sign from You.' But He answered and said to them, 'An evil and adulterous generation craves for a sign; and yet no sign shall be given to it but the sign of Jonah the prophet'" (NASB). (Our Lord then goes on to indicate that Jonah's three days in the belly of the whale were a type of Jesus' three days in the tomb, the interval between His burial and the Easter morning Resurrection.) It should be noted that this particular sign was not something He granted them on that same occasion when they requested it, but it was long deferred until Easter. In effect, therefore, He refused to give them any sign at all, at least at the time of their request.

It is noteworthy that Luke 11:29 repeats substantially the same words as in Matthew 12:39, except that no further elaboration is given of what Jesus meant by the sign of Jonah. Presumably Matthew 12 and Luke 11 are referring to the same episode, except that Matthew gives a little more detail. But it is also significant that even Matthew himself records a different occasion on which the same demand was made for a sign from heaven. In Matthew 16:4 Jesus responds to this demand in largely the same way, ending up as follows: "An evil and adulterous generation seeks after a sign; and a sign will not be given to it, except the sign of Jonah.' And He left them, and went away" (NASB).

From these passages we gather that the demand for a miraculous sign from heaven was made to Jesus more than once. It may be that the Mark 8 episode parallels Matthew 16 rather than Matthew 12. But since Christ did not actually perform a sign before them at that time, it amounted to a refusal to comply with their request, because it was made out of corrupt and unspiritual motives. The only difference, then, between the Matthew 16 passage and the Mark 8 passage is that the reference to Jonah was omitted by Mark. As for the longer or shorter form of Jesus' sayings, there are abundant examples of this throughout the Synoptics. And there is no real discrepancy or contradiction here—any more than there would be if two students took notes of the same lecture in the same class, and one student had fuller notes at some portions of the lecture than the other student. Yet it would be absurd to label this difference an irreconcilable contradiction. The same principle applies here.

At what hour was Christ crucified?

There is an apparent discrepancy between Mark 15:25, which states that Jesus was crucified at the "third" hour on Good Friday, and John 19:14, which indicates that the trial of Jesus was still going on at the "sixth" hour, indicating that the time of His crucifixion was later yet. John 19:14 reads: "And it was the preparation [*paraskeuē*] of the Passover, and it was about the sixth hour, and he [Pilate] says to the Jews, 'Behold your king!'" Obviously one of these Evangelists is in error, or else his text has been miscopied, or else the hours of the day have been numbered by John according to a different system from that followed by Mark.

It should be noted that Matthew and Luke both follow the same system as Mark; for all three indicate that as Jesus hung on the cross, a great and terrible darkness came on the earth at the sixth hour and lasted until the ninth hour, when Jesus breathed His last (Matt. 27:45; Mark 15:33; Luke 23:44). It is universally agreed that in the Synoptics the hours were numbered from sunrise, approximately 6:00 A.M. This would mean that Christ was crucified at 9:00 A.M. and the preternatural darkness lasted from 12:00 A.M. to 3:00 P.M.

This apparent contradiction was unsuccessfully handled by ancient commentators through textual correction. Eusebius pointed out that the numeral "three" was indicated by capital gamma, whereas "six" was indicated by a digamma (a letter resembling our *F*). The copyist thought he saw the extra horizontal stroke and changed "three" to "six." But this does not really solve the problem at all, because John 19:14 does not indicate the time Christ was crucified but only the time of His appearance before Pilate's judgment seat. And so even though many fine scholars have favored this textual-error theory (such as Beza, Bengel, Alford, and Farrar), it is basically unsound—and completely unnecessary.

There is no difficulty at all in the received textual reading, provided we understand that John was following the official numbering system of the Roman civil day. The evidence for a civil day that began numbering the hours right after midnight is quite decisive. Pliny the Elder (*Natural History* 2. 77) makes the following observation: "The day itself has been differently observed in different countries: by the Babylonians between two sunrises; by the Athenians between two sunsets; by the Umbrians from noon to noon; by the Roman priests and those who have defined the civil day, as the Egyptians also and Hipparchus, from midnight to midnight." This is confirmed by Macrobius (*Saturnalia* 1.3): "the day, which the Romans have declared to begin at the sixth hour of the night." (It should be explained that the ancients did not maintain hours of uniform length throughout the year but simply divided the interval between sunrise and sunset into twelve equal parts, known as *horae*—regardless of

the season of the year.) So what would be 6:00 A.M. according to the Roman civil day (and likewise according to our modern practice) would be the first hour according to Athenian and Hebrew practice. Thus it was 9:00 A.M. when Christ's trial was winding up, and He was led away to Golgotha to be crucified. This perception of a differing system of hour numbering removes all discrepancy between John and the Synoptics.

But we may very well ask, Why should John have followed the official Roman system when he had the same cultural background as the Synoptics? The answer lies in the time and location of the composition of John's gospel. As McClellan points out, "St. John wrote his Gospel in Ephesus, the capital of the Roman province of Asia, and therefore in regard to the civil day he would be likely to employ the Roman reckoning. And as a matter of fact, he does employ it, extending his day until midnight—12:1; 20:19" (*Christian Evidences*, 1:741).

The point of the John 20:19 reference is that John reckons Christ's first appearance to the disciples in the house of John Mark as occurring in the latter part (*opsia*) of the *first day* of the week. This proves conclusively that John did not regard the second day of the week as having begun at sunset, as the Palestinian reckoning followed by the other Evangelists would have regarded the late supper hour. (We know from the return of the two disciples from the Emmaus journey at sundown that it was already well past sundown by the time they had delivered their report to the Eleven, and thus before Jesus Himself appeared to them all as a group.) The *fact* that John followed the Roman civil day is thus established; his *reason* for doing so is found in the probable place of composition of his gospel, presumably in Ephesus around A.D. 90 or shortly thereafter.

Luke

Was Luke mistaken about Quirinius and the census?

Luke 2:1 tells of a decree from Caesar Augustus to have the whole "world" (*oikoumenē* actually means all the world under the authority of Rome) enrolled in a census report for taxation purposes. Verse 2 specifies which census taking was involved at the time Joseph and Mary went down to Bethlehem, to fill out the census forms as descendants of the Bethlehemite family of King David. This was the first census undertaken by Quirinius (or "Cyrenius") as governor (or at least as acting governor) of Syria. Josephus mentions no census in the reign of Herod the Great (who died in 4 B.C) but he does mention one taken by "Cyrenius" (*Antiquities* 17.13.5) soon after Herod Archelaus was deposed in A.D. 6: "Cyrenius, one that had been consul, was sent by Caesar to take account of people's effects in Syria, and to sell the house of Archelaus." (Apparently the palace of the deposed king was to be sold and the proceeds turned over to the Roman government.)

If Luke dates the census in 8 or 7 B.C., and if Josephus dates it in A.D. 6 or 7, there appears to be a discrepancy of about fourteen years. Also, since Saturninus (according to Tertullian in *Contra Marcion* 4.19) was legate of Syria from 9 B.C., to 6 B.C., and Quintilius Varus was legate from 7 B.C. to A.D. 4

(note the one-year overlap in these two terms!), there is doubt as to whether Quirinius was ever governor of Syria at all.

By way of solution, let it be noted first of all that Luke says this was a "first" enrollment that took place under Quirinius (*hautē apographē prōtē egeneto*). A "first" surely implies a *second* one sometime later. Luke was therefore well aware of that second census, taken by Quirinius again in A.D. 7, which Josephus alludes to in the passage cited above. We know this because Luke (who lived much closer to the time than Josephus did) also quotes Gamaliel as alluding to the insurrection of Judas of Galilee "in the days of the census taking" (Acts 5:37). The Romans tended to conduct a census every fourteen years, and so this comes out right for a first census in 7 B.C. and a second in A.D. 7.

But was Quirinius (who was called *Kyrēnius* by the Greeks because of the absence of a Q in the Attic alphabet, or else because this proconsul was actually a successful governor of Crete and Cyrene in Egypt around 15 B.C.) actually governor of Syria? The Lucan text here says *hēgemoneuontos tēs Syrias Kyrēniou* ("while Cyrenius was leading —in charge of—Syria"). He is not actually called *legatus* (the official Roman title for the governor of an entire region), but the participle *hēgemoneuontos* is used here, which would be appropriate to a *hēgemōn* like Pontius Pilate (who rated as a *procurator* but not as a *legatus*).

Too much should not be made of the precise official status. But we do know that between 12 B.C. and 2 B.C., Quirinius was engaged in a systematic reduction of rebellious mountaineers in the highlands of Pisidia (Tenney, *Zondervan Pictorial Encyclopedia*, 5:6), and that he was therefore a highly placed military figure in the Near East in the closing years of the reign of Herod the Great. In order to secure efficiency and dispatch, it may well have been that Augustus put Quirinius in charge of the census-enrollment in the region of Syria just at the transition period between the close of Saturninus's administration and the beginning of Varus's term of service in 7 B.C. It was doubtless because of his competent handling of the 7 B.C. census that Augustus later put him in charge of the A.D. 7 census.

As for the lack of secular reference to a general census for the entire Roman Empire at this time, this presents no serious difficulty. Kingsley Davis (*Encyclopaedia Britannica*, 14th ed., 5:168) states: "Every five years the Romans enumerated citizens and their property to determine their liabilities. This practice was extended to include the entire Roman Empire in 5 B.C."

Why is "in spirit" lacking in the Lucan version of the first beatitude?

Matthew 5:3 gives the first beatitude as "Blessed are the poor in spirit, for theirs is the kingdom of heaven." But in the parallel statement of Luke 6:20, Christ simply says, "Blessed are you poor people, for yours is the kingdom of God." Is there a real discrepancy here? Not at all! These are two different speeches, given on two different occasions, in two different settings.

As the term "Sermon on the Mount" implies, Matthew 5–7 was delivered on a mountainside in Galilee. It was ad-

dressed primarily to Jesus' disciples rather than to the multitude as a whole (cf. Matt. 5:1). The setting for the somewhat condensed version of the Beatitudes as recorded in Luke was not on any mountain but on a plain (*epi topou pedinou*—Luke 6:17). It was not addressed to the limited circle of disciples but to a large multitude of disciples and a great throng of people from all parts of Judea, Jerusalem, Tyre, and Sidon—hence a far different audience. Matthew's second beatitude appears in a greatly altered form as Luke's third. Matthew's third does not appear in Luke at all. Matthew's fourth is Luke's second, with the omission of "and thirst for righteousness." Matthew's fifth, sixth, and seventh are missing in Luke altogether; and Matthew's eighth appears as Luke's fourth, in a considerably altered form. Nothing could be clearer than that these were two different messages, delivered at different times. Hence there can be no discrepancy involved here at all.

How can Luke 11:23 be reconciled with Luke 9:50?

Luke 11:23 reads (with Christ speaking): "He that is not with me is against me; and he that gathereth not with me scattereth." Luke 9:50, however, quotes Jesus as saying, "Forbid him not, for he that is not against us is for us." The latter dictum seems much more charitable and kindly than the former.

The difficulty is greatly alleviated by the fact that virtually all the Greek manuscripts that are older than the eighth century A.D. do not read "against us ... for us" (*kath' hēmōn ... hyper hēmōn*) but rather "against you ... for you" (*kath' hymōn ... hyper hymōn*). In other words, prior to that, all available evidence is for the reading "you." (The reason for this confusion is that by the eighth century these two Greek words of such different meaning were pronounced exactly the same—*ēmōn*—and are so pronounced by modern Greeks even to this day. There is a considerable difference between Christ Himself and His disciples, and there is therefore no contradiction whatever between the two statements.

However, it should be noted that even if "us" had been the true, original reading in Luke 9:50, there would have been no true contradiction. The reason for this is that the whole preceding context of Luke 11:23 is a series of hostilities and oppositions: Christ versus Beelzebul (v.15); kingdom against kingdom (v.17); Satan imagined to be in opposition to himself (v.18); a powerful householder set in a posture of defense against a would-be intruder or burglar (v.21). It is against this background that Christ says, "He that is not with me is against me." His hearers (some of whom had suggested that Jesus' healing power came from Satan) needed to be faced with the fateful decision that confronted them as they saw His miracles and heard His teaching. They had to commit themselves either to Christ or to Satan. They needed to understand that unless a person is really on Christ's side, his life leads to dissolution and tragic failure.

In the context of Luke 9:50, however, the question at issue is whether a (presumably sincere) believer not a member of the apostolic band should be allowed to cast out demons from a demoniac in the name of Jesus. Our Lord answered that in such a case, even though the exorcist was not one of the inner circle, he still believed in Christ just about as the twelve disciples; and he was therefore really to be acknowledged and encouraged as one of their own party. From this perspective, then, one who preached or attempted healings in the name of Jesus was *for* them and should not be regarded as against them. Thus there is no contradiction whatever between these two statements when considered in their own contexts—whether we read "for us" or "for you."

How could the dying thief be with Christ in paradise on the day of his death?

Luke 23:43 records Christ's promise to the repentant thief who hung on an adjacent cross: "Truly I say to you, today you will be with Me in paradise." But was it not until the following Monday that Christ rose from the grave and ascended to heaven? If Christ Himself was not in paradise until Sunday, how could the repentant thief have been there with him? The answer lies in the location of "paradise" on Good Friday.

Apparently paradise was not exalted to heaven until Easter Day. Jesus apparently refers to it in the parable of the rich man and Lazarus as "Abraham's Bosom," to which the godly beggar Lazarus was carried by the angels after his decease (Luke 16:19–31). Thus "Abraham's Bosom" referred to the place where the souls of the redeemed waited till the day of Christ's resurrection. Presumably this was the same place as paradise. It was not yet lifted up to heaven but it may well have been a section of hades (Heb. *š'ôl*), reserved for believers who had died in the faith but who would not be admitted into the glorious presence of God in heaven until the price of redemption had been actually paid on Calvary.

Doubtless it was to the infernal paradise that the souls of Jesus and the repentant thief repaired after they each died on Friday afternoon. But then on Easter Sunday, after the risen Christ had first appeared to Mary Magdalene (John 20:17) and her two companions (Matt. 28:9), presumably He then took up with Him to glory all the inhabitants of infernal paradise (including Abraham, Lazarus, and the repentant thief). We read in Ephesians 4:8 concerning Christ: "Ascending on high, He led captivity captive; He gave gifts unto men." Verse 9 continues: "But what does 'He ascended' mean but that He also descended to the lowest parts of the earth?"—i.e., to hades. Verse 10 adds: "He who descended is the same as He who ascended above all the heavens." Presumably He led the whole band of liberated captives from hades (i.e., the whole population of preresurrection paradise) up to the glory of the highest heaven, the abode of the Triune God.

John

How can John 5:28-29 be reconciled with the gospel of grace?

John 5:28-29 reads: "Do not be amazed at this, for a time is coming when all who are in their graves will hear his voice and come out—those who have done good will rise to live, and those who have done evil will rise to be condemned" (NIV). Such a pronouncement as this, when taken out of context, might seem to establish the principle that men are saved by good works, by deeds of the law, rather than by grace through faith. But taken in its own context, it becomes clear that Jesus did not intend to preach salvation through good works, but only to furnish a valid criterion for *saving* faith. In v.24 of the same passage, He had affirmed, "I tell you the truth, whoever hears my word and believes him who sent me has eternal life and will not be condemned; he has crossed over from death to life" (NIV). The requirement for salvation involves careful attention to Christ's word and faith in God, who sent His Son to save sinners from death.

In order to grasp what Jesus meant here by doing good and doing evil, we must remember that it is God's viewpoint rather than man's that finally determines what is good and what is evil. Whatever man does in his own interest or for his own credit or glory is devoid of true goodness in God's eyes, no matter how helpful or admirable it may seem to the human observer. "The carnal mind is enmity against God, for it is not subject to the law of God, neither indeed can be. So then they that are in the flesh cannot please God" (Rom. 8:7-8). From God's standpoint, then, no unconverted person is capable of performing a good work. It is only as the indwelling Spirit of Christ takes control of the heart, head, and hand of the born-again believer that a truly good work is accomplished. And it is good only because God is the one who performs it, working through a yielded human instrument (Rom. 6:12-14).

Yet it should be observed that the fruit of genuine faith is good works, not merit-earning good works, of course, but Christ-expressing and Christ-glorifying good works. As the Epistle of James makes clear, a counterfeit faith is of no value before God; but a true faith will be a working faith. "Faith, if it has no works, is dead, being by itself. But someone may well say, 'You have faith, and I have works; show me your faith without the works, and I will show you my faith by my works" (James 2:17-18, NASB).

This principle pervades Christ's teaching throughout the Gospels. In Matthew 7 the Sermon on the Mount closes with a contrast between the foolish man who heard Christ's teaching but failed to carry it out and the wise man who faithfully obeyed the teaching of his Lord. In the previous

...h Jesus described the sorry ... of those at the final judgment ...o would come before Him and plead their own good works, even though ostensibly performed in Christ's name and service, as a ground for admission to heaven. Because they have not truly done "the will of My Father who is in heaven" (v.21) by sincerely submitting their heart to the Lord, the verdict for them is "I never knew you; depart from Me, you who practice lawlessness" (v.23, NASB). All their ostensibly good works performed in Christ's name go for nothing, because they have been going about to establish their own righteousness (Rom. 10:3) rather than yielding their "members as instruments of righteousness unto God" (6:13).

In other words, the Lord insists that a true and living faith expresses itself in deeds of righteousness and love that are motivated and directed by His Spirit. In the memorable scene described by Jesus in Matthew 25:31–46, He sits as judge over the entire professing church, made up of believers from every nation ("all the nations will be gathered before Him," not, of course, to be judged as national units, but as individual Christians from every nation), and applies the test of godly behavior to gauge the sincerity of faith. All before Him are professing Christians, for they all address Him as "Lord" and suppose that He considers them His own. But only those who have expressed His love and compassion by feeding the hungry, giving drink to the thirsty, welcoming the stranger with hospitality, clothing the naked, and visiting those imprisoned for righteousness' sake (vv.35–36) have displayed a true and living faith. They have shown all these kindnesses as unto the Lord Himself, out of a sincere love for Him. Those who have failed to carry out His will by a life of kindly service to others—and especially to those of the household of faith ("the least of these My brethren") betray a counterfeit faith that is not unto salvation. They are therefore appointed a portion in hell, along with all other hypocrites (cf. Matt. 24:51; 25:46).

From this perspective we are in a better position to understand 2 Corinthians 5:10: "For we must all appear before the judgment seat of Christ, that each one may receive what is due him for the things done while in the body, whether good or bad" (NIV). In this latter passage we are not dealing with counterfeit professors of the faith but rather with the evaluation of the fruitfulness and faithfulness of each born-again believer during his years of stewardship on earth. The appropriate reward and status in heaven will be awarded by Christ to each servant of His according to the measure of the servant's faithfulness and zeal.

The same principle obtains at the judgment of the Great White Throne in Revelation 20:12. The time locus of this judgment is at the close of the Millennium, and so there is a need to pass judgment on those of the newer generations who have grown up during the Millennium itself. While all the earth will be subject to the authority of Christ during that thousand-year period, there will be some who will outwardly conform to the Christian ethic and profess to love the Lord but will never have been truly born again. These will have performed no works recognized by Christ as truly "good." It is for this reason that the heaven-kept books of record will be consulted as each soul comes before the Lord for judgment, not only those books that record the sins of the unsaved, but also "the book of life" (v.12), which contains the names of the sincere believers of the centuries of the Millennium. All will be judged "according to their deeds," to be sure; but only those who are truly regenerate followers of Christ will have any "good deeds" entered on their record, deeds that are genuinely good because they are the works of God performed through His yielded instruments. As Jesus said to the rich young ruler in Matthew 19:17, "There is none good but God." Therefore there are no good works except those that are done by the Lord Himself through truly surrendered believers.

In light of these passages, we must conclude that neither John 5:28–29 nor any other such passage conflicts with the principle of salvation by grace through faith. It is simply a matter of distinguishing between a genuine faith and a counterfeit faith.

How can John 8:11 be reconciled with Romans 13:4 in regard to capital punishment?

In Romans 13:4, the apostle Paul, speaking of the authority of human government, says, "It is a minister of God to you for good. But if you do what is evil, be afraid; for it does not bear the sword for nothing; for it is a minister of God, an avenger who brings wrath upon the one who practices evil" (NASB). This verse makes it perfectly clear that the God-inspired author taught that capital punishment (for the "sword" is not used for imprisonment or for releasing killers on parole) is ordained of God and intended by Him for the protection of human society against those who would unjustly deprive others of their right to life.

Some students of Scripture, however, have found difficulty in reconciling Christ's treatment of the adulterous woman in John 8:3–11 with the imposition of the death penalty for capital crime. To be sure in this particular case the offense was marital infidelity rather than first-degree murder. But adultery was defined by the Mosaic Law as a heinous crime, punishable by death—normally by stoning (Deut. 22:22–24). Nevertheless it has implications for other capital crimes, such as murder and treason. Did Jesus intend to abolish the death penalty altogether by taking this action of releasing the guilty woman in the way He did?

The evidence of the earlier manuscripts of the Gospel of John suggests that this particular passage was not included by John himself in the original text of his gospel. The earliest surviving witness to this episode seems to be the sixth-century Codex Bezae, although it was received into the koiné or Byzantine family of manuscripts, on which the Textus Receptus (and the KJV) are based. Nevertheless it appears to be an authentic account of an episode in Christ's ministry, and it is written in characteristically Johannine style. Therefore it should be reckoned with as an authoritative word of Christ, despite the uncertainty of its relationship to the Gospel in its earliest form.

In this incident Christ is portrayed as responding to a challenge by His adversaries, who wish to catch Him on the horns of a dilemma. If He condemns the adulteress according to the law of Moses, He will tarnish His image as a merciful and kindly messenger of God's love. On the other hand, if He refrains from condemning her to death, He will be open to the charge of annulling or revoking the law of God—contrary to His own affirmation in Matthew 5:17. This was an entrapment device somewhat similar to the question later put to Him concerning the obligation of the Jewish believer to pay tribute to Caesar (Matt. 22:17). Whichever way He answered, He could be chargeable with opposing either the holy law or the duly constituted government of Rome.

At the close of the hearing in this particular case, Jesus found Himself alone with the woman; and He said to her, "Neither do I condemn you; go your way; from now on sin no more" (John 8:11, NASB). What did He mean by this? Did He mean that the woman was not guilty of the offense as charged? Hardly, since the defendant herself made no effort to deny that she had committed adultery and had been caught "in the very act" (v.4). In that sense, of course, the Lord Jesus did condemn her; His words "sin no more" indicate that she was indeed guilty of the capital crime with which she was charged. But the Greek term *katakrinō* ("condemn") carries with it the connotation of imposing a sentence on the defendant with a view of its execution. Compare Mark 14:64: *katekrinan auton enochon einai thanatou* ("They condemned Him as being worthy of death," i.e., speaking of the Sanhedrin's sentencing of Jesus to death on the cross). *Katakrinō* in other contexts might mean only defining the nature or gravity of the offense charged, but in this forensic setting it involved the actual imposition of sentence and the authorizing of her penal death by stoning.

As we analyze the situation faced by Jesus in this particular confrontation with His enemies, we must take into account the special factors that tainted the whole process with illegality. First, the law of Moses required *both* offenders to be dealt with on an equal basis. Leviticus 20:10 states: "If there is a man who commits adultery with another man's wife, . . . the adulterer and the adulteress shall surely be put to death" (NASB). Deuteronomy 22:24 indicates that both of them shall die, the man who lay with the woman, and the woman herself. Thus this entire process in John 8 was legally defective because the woman's accusers had not brought forward her male partner-in-sin. Without him there could be no valid action taken against her.

Second, such an action as this has to be taken before a duly constituted court of law, such as a panel of elders near the gate of the city, whose duty it was to hear cases. What this group of accusers had undertaken was not a lawful court action, therefore, but a lynching. Since Jesus of Nazareth was no official judge in criminal actions, even as He made clear in an attempted civil case (the settling of a probate dispute in Luke 12:14: "Who has appointed Me a judge over you?"), this attempt to remand the case to Him was an obvious farce, devoid of legal justification, and intended only to embarrass the Teacher from Nazareth whom they hoped to discredit.

Third, by their own admission, not even the Sanhedrin had the right under the Roman government to execute the death penalty. While they had authority to impose a sentence, capital punishment could not be carried out except under the authorization of the Roman governor. Thus we read in John 18:31: "Pilate therefore said to them, 'Take Him yourselves, and judge Him according to your law.' The Jews said to him, 'We are not permitted to put any one to death' " (NASB). Therefore it follows that this proposal to Jesus to have the guilty woman stoned to death right there before Him was itself a flagrant violation of the law of Rome. Our Lord would have no part in this. As a law-abiding citizen, Jesus could have no part in such a lynching.

Nevertheless the question raised was whether the woman deserved to die. "Now in the Law Moses commanded us to stone such women; what then do You say?" (John 8:5, NASB). Jesus might have pointed out that they had violated the law of Moses by failing to bring along her male partner. But Jesus pursued another tack because He saw that the accusers themselves needed to realize that they also were very guilty before God, and that they therefore were hardly in a position to carry out the penalty that they demanded of their prisoner. We are told that He stooped down to write on the sand or dust of the ground. What He wrote convicted them of their own sins—sins that they had hoped would remain hidden and unknown to all but themselves. Since He had ruled that the witness who was "without sin" had the responsibility of casting the first stone at the guilty woman, it was essential for at least one of them to have a completely clean conscience before God's law. But not one of them could honestly claim to be free from sin before the Lord, and all the accusers suddenly found themselves accused and guilty. Hence they took their leave, one by one, until not one of them was left.

As we study Jesus' response to this challenge, we must clearly observe that He neither covered over the guilt of the accused (as if adultery was not, after all, really heinous enough to require the death penalty—in that modern-minded, enlightened first century A.D.); nor did He suggest that death by stoning was no longer the proper way to deal with this offense. He plainly implied that the woman was guilty enough to die, and that the legal mode of execution was by stoning. The point He raised was that the accusers of the woman were themselves guilty under the law, and that they were hardly competent to carry out the sentence. Certainly they had all become guilty of an attempted lynching, completely contrary to the law of the Roman government to which they were all subject. Hence the whole process was voided by their incompetence and illegality.

In this episode of the adulterous woman, Jesus was hardly affirming that capital punishment was no longer to be imposed, nor that He was revising the Law of Moses in favor of a new policy of compassion toward those who had incurred the penalty of death. On the contrary, He upheld the continuing sanction of execution for capital crime; but He brought home to His countrymen—and, indeed, to all mankind—the solemn truth that before the Lord every man is guilty of death—eternal death—and that He had come for the express purpose of paying that penalty in the sinner's stead.

What did Jesus mean by saying that men are "gods" (John 10:34)?

John 10:34 reads: "Jesus answered them, 'Is it not written in your Law, "I said, you are gods"?'" This remark came right after the Jews had made preparations to stone the Lord because of His affirmation in v.30: "I and the Father are one." Jesus' audience rightly understood Him as asserting His deity, in terms suggestive of the Trinity. They therefore concluded that He had blasphemed God; for though He was only a man (as they supposed), He was making Himself out to be God (v.33). To counter their hostility and rejection, Jesus quoted from Psalm 82:6, which reads as follows: "I said, 'You are gods, and all of you are sons of the Most High God.'"

In citing Psalm 82:6, Jesus was appealing to a verse from the infallible Scriptures (infallible because they cannot be broken) that attaches the name or title "god" to certain men, not to all men, of course, but only "those to whom the word of God came" (John 10:35). A divine dimension was added to those people who had been especially chosen by God to be bearers of His saving truth and administrators of His holy law. In Psalm 82 God is addressing judges and administrators who have been chosen to serve as His representatives in teaching and enforcing His holy law. To be sure, some of these solemnly commissioned judges exercised their office unjustly and showed partiality to the rich, even though they were in the wrong (v.2). Essentially the psalm expresses a condemnation of these unjust jurists, saying, in effect, "Although you have the status of membership in the family of

God, and although you have been called after His name, nevertheless because of your unfaithfulness to sacred duty you will die like other men and will fall to ruin like one of the princes of the unsaved world."

In using Psalm 82:6 as an *a fortiori* argument for affirming His own unique status as the Son of God, Jesus draws a significant distinction or contrast between Himself and redeemed mankind, saying, in John 10:35-36: "If He called them 'gods,' to whom the word of God came—and the Scripture cannot be broken—do you say of Him whom the Father sanctified and sent into the world, 'You are blaspheming,' because I said I am the Son of God?" (NASB). That is to say, those Old Testament believers who had entered into covenant relationship with God on the basis of His gracious promises had attained the status of membership within the family of God. God the Father had adopted them into His holy family. It was not an essential and eternal status that they possessed by right or by way of reward for their virtue and obedience; it was simply a privilege conferred on them by God's sheer grace. Their sonship was derivative, not inherited. (For other passages in which Old Testament believers under the covenant are called *b̲enê ᵉlōhîm*, cf. Gen. 6:2—which truly refers to believers from the line of Seth rather than to angels, as some have suggested—Deut. 14:1; 32:5; Ps. 73:15 ["your children"]; Hos. 1:10 [Heb. 2:1]).

In John 10:36 Jesus draws a distinction between redeemed sinners under the old covenant and Himself as the Son who ever existed with the Father in glory—the Son who was "sanctified" (or solemnly set apart) for His task as Messiah and Redeemer of the people of God. It was after He had been so sanctified up in heaven that the Father *sent* Him down to earth, into the world lost in sin and in need of a Savior. Throughout the Gospel of John, spe-cial emphasis is laid on Jesus' status as the one sent down from God the Father (John 4:34; 5:23-24,30; 6:38-40,44,57; 7:16,18; 8:16,18; 9:4; 10:36; 11:42; 12:45,49; 14:24; 15:21; 16:5; 17:3,18,21,23,25; 20:21). In this sense He is absolutely unique, for though prophets like John the Baptist might be sent from God to men (John 1:6), they were sent from earth to earth; only Christ was sent from heaven (His proper home) to earth. In that sense He is the Son of God by virtue of His innate status as God; believers are sons of God only by the gracious calling of God and by His act of adoption. By no means, then, does our Lord imply here that we are sons of God just as He is—except for a lower level of holiness and virtue. No misunderstanding could be more wrongheaded than that. But what He does affirm here is that His hearers should not be shocked at His imputing deity to Himself, when even their own Holy Scriptures accord them the status of divinity by the adoption of grace.

One additional observation is in order concerning this occasional employment of Elohim in the Old Testament to refer to believers under the covenant. This seems to operate by the analogy of national designations like *b̲enê Yiśrāʾēl* ("the sons of Israel"), *b̲enê ʿAmmôn* ("the sons of Ammon"), *b̲enê Yᵉhûdāh* ("the sons of Judah"), *b̲enê Bābel* ("the sons of Babylon"), etc. Any or all of these tribes or nations could also be referred to without the *b̲enê* ("sons of"), as *Yiśrāʾēl, ʿAmmôn*, or *Yᵉhûdāh*. By analogy, then, the combination *b̲enê ᵉlōhîm* could be shortened to simple *ᵉlōhîm* alone—i.e., a member of the sons (or people) of God. (Other passages of this class, referring to Israelite rulers and judges as God's representatives on earth, include Exod. 21:6; 22:7-8,27; Pss. 8:5; 82:1; 138:1 [or else "angels"]. Ps. 82:1b [NASB mg: "gods," but "rulers" in the text] belongs to this same category.)

How can Jesus' statement "the Father is greater than I" (John 14:28) be reconciled with the doctrine of the Trinity?

In John 14:28 Jesus says, "If you loved me, you would be glad that I am going to the Father, for the Father is greater than I" (NIV). The Trinity is defined in the Westminster Shorter Catechism (No. 6) as follows: "There are three Persons in the Godhead: the Father, the Son, and the Holy Ghost; and these three are one God, the same in substance, equal in power and glory." How, then, can the Son affirm that the Father is greater (*meizōn*) than He?

Our Lord Jesus Christ was speaking here, not in His Divine nature as God the Son, but in His human nature, as the Son of Man. Christ came to suffer and die, not as God, who can do neither, but as the Second Adam, born of Mary. Only as the Son of Man could He serve as Messiah, or Christ (the Anointed One). Unless He could take to Himself a true and genuine human nature, He could never have represented Adam's race as Sin-Bearer at the Cross. But as the Son of Man, He certainly was lower in station than God the Father. As Isaiah 52:13–53:12 makes clear, He could only become our Savior by becoming the Servant of Yahweh. The servant by definition can never be as great as his master. Hence it was as the death-conquering Redeemer, the God-man, that Jesus would enter into the presence of the Father, who of course would be greater in dignity and station than the Son of Man.

But as for God the Son, apart from the Incarnation, Scripture never suggests any contrast in glory as between the Father and the Son. The following passages make this abundantly clear: John 1:1,18; 8:58; 10:30; 14:9; 17:5; Romans 9:5 ("Christ ... who is God over all"); Colossians 2:2; Titus 2:13; Hebrews 1:8; 1 John 5:20; cf. also Isaiah 9:6 (which affirms that the Virgin-born Immanuel is also the Mighty God—*'ēl gibbôr*).

As for 1 John 5:7—which in KJV reads: "For there are three that bear record in heaven, the Father, the Word, and the Holy Ghost: and these three are one"—the only portion of this verse that appears in any Greek manuscript earlier than the fifteenth century is the first clause only: "For there are three who bear witness"—followed immediately by v.8: "the Spirit and the water and the blood, and these three are in agreement" (lit., "are unto one"). The rest of v.7 appears in Old Latin manuscripts as early as the fifth century but not in Greek until the very late miniscule 635, in the margin. It therefore seems best to omit this verse in the list of attestations of the Trinity, even though it seems to contain excellent theology.

Was Christ crucified on Thursday or Friday?

The uniform impression conveyed by the synoptic Gospels is that the Crucifixion took place on Friday of Holy Week. If it were not for John 19:14, the point would never have come up for debate. But John 19:14 says (according to NASB): "Now it was the day of preparation [*paraskeuē*] for the Passover; it was about the sixth hour. And he [Pilate] said to the Jews, 'Behold, your King!'" The NIV suggests a somewhat less difficult handling of the apparent discrepancy: "It was the day of Preparation of Passover Week, about the sixth hour." This latter translation takes note of two very important matters of usage. First, the word *paraskeuē* had already by the first century A.D. become a technical term for "Friday," since every Friday was the day of preparation for Saturday, that is, the Sabbath. In Modern Greek the word for "Friday" is *paraskeuē*.

Second, the Greek term *tou pascha* (lit., "of the Passover") is taken to be equivalent to the Passover Week. This refers to the seven-day Feast of Unleavened Bread (Heb. *maṣṣôṯ*) that immediately followed the initial slaughtering and eating of the Passover lamb on the evening of the fourteenth day of the month Abib, which by Hebrew reckoning would mean the commencement of the fifteenth day, right after sunset. The week of *maṣṣô-t,* coming right on the heels of Passover itself (during which *maṣṣô-t* were actually eaten, along with the lamb, bitter herbs, etc.) very naturally came to be known as Passover Week (cf. *Encyclopaedia Britannica,* 14th ed., 12: 1041), extending from the fifteenth to the twenty-first of Abib, inclusively. (Arndt and Gingrich [*Greek-English Lexicon,* pp. 638–39] state: "This [i.e., Passover] was followed immediately by the Feast of Unleavened Bread ... on the 15th to the 21st. Popular usage merged the two festivals and treated them as a unity, as they were for practical purposes.") It was unnecessary to insert a specific term for "week" (such as *šā-bûaʻ*) for it to be understood as such. Therefore, that which might be translated literally as "the preparation of the Passover" must in this context be rendered "Friday of Passover Week."

It turns out, therefore, that John affirms just as clearly as the Synoptics that Christ was crucified on Friday and that His sacrificial death represented an antitypical fulfillment of the Passover ordinance itself, which was instituted by God in the days of the Exodus as a means of making Calvary available by faith to the ancient people of God even before the coming of Christ.

Note that in 1 Corinthians 5:7 Jesus is referred to as the Passover Lamb for believers: "Purge out the old leaven, so that you may be a new lump, just as you were unleavened. For Christ our Lamb was sacrificed for us." The statement of E. C. Hoskyns on John 19:14 is very appropriate here: "The hour of double sacrifice is drawing near. It is midday. The Passover lambs are being prepared for sacrifice, and the Lamb of God is likewise sentenced to death" (*The Fourth Gospel* [London: Farber and Farber, 1940], ad loc.). It simply needs to be pointed out that the lambs referred to here are not those that were slaughtered and eaten in private homes—a rite Jesus had already observed with His disciples the night before ("Maundy Thursday")—but the lambs to be offered *on the altar* of the Lord on behalf of the whole nation of Israel. (For the household observance on the evening of the fourteenth of Abib, cf. Exod. 12:6; for the public sacrifice on the altar, cf. Exod. 12:16–17; Lev. 23:4–8; 2 Chron. 30:15–19; 35:11–16. These were all known as Passover sacrifices, since they were presented during Passover week.)

Thus it turns out that there has been a simple misunderstanding of the phrase *paraskeuē tou pascha* that has occasioned such perplexity that even Guthrie (*New Bible Commentary,* p. 964) deduced an original error, for which he had no solution to offer. The various ingenious explantions offered by others, that Christ held His personal Passover a night early, knowing that He would be crucified before the evening of the fourteenth; that Christ and His movement held to a different calendar, reckoning the fourteenth to be a day earlier than the calendar of the official Jerusalem priesthood; or that He was following a revised calendar observed by the Essenes at Qumran—all these theories are quite improbable and altogether unnecessary. There is no contradiction whatever between John and the Synoptics as to the day on which Christ died—it was Friday.

Acts

If Joel's prophecy (2:28–32) was fulfilled at Pentecost (Acts 2:16–21), why were no miraculous signs reported as occurring at that time?

Peter's purpose in citing Joel 2:28–32 (which is the same as chap. 3 in the Hebrew Bible) was to establish the fact that the last days had been ushered in by the advent of Jesus Christ and the charismatic empowerment of His church by the Holy Spirit of God. He declares that Joel 2:28–29 is being fulfilled before the very eyes of the multitude who are witnessing the multilingual presentation of the gospel on the part of the 120 disciples. The Spirit-filled sons and daughters of Israel, the young men, the graybeards, and even the bondslaves, are all telling forth the wonderful works of God as they preach Christ to the assembled worshipers at the Feast of Pentecost.

Acts 2:19–20 includes the concluding verses of the Joel passage, which predicts the occurrence of striking or even catastrophic phenomena in heaven and on earth before the eschatological return of the Lord in judgment. These include a darkening of the sun in the daytime; a bloody hue will be reflected from the moon, and in the atmosphere surrounding the earth will be "blood, and fire, and vapor of smoke." But Peter does not mean to say that such manifestations are occurring right then during the feast. He goes on to quote these last verses of Joel 2:30–32 in order to point out the prophetic scheme that must be completed before the last days will draw to a close and the Lord Jesus Himself will return to earth as sovereign Lord. In other words, Pentecost began the last days; the horrors of Revelation 16–18 will mark the close of these last days before the Lord returns. The drama of human redemption has entered into the last act, from the time of the crucifixion of the Son of God until His enthronement on the seat of David.

Is the reference to Theudas and Judas in Acts 5:36–37 historically accurate?

In Acts 5:36 Paul's former teacher Gamaliel is quoted as citing the unhappy example of Theudas, who led a band of four hundred men against the Roman government, only to be destroyed along with all his followers. This account has been treated with skepticism by some scholars, on the ground that Josephus (*Antiquities* 20.5.1) refers to a Theudas who raised a revolt against the Roman government in A.D. 44 but was caught by the forces of Cuspius Fadius near the banks of the Jordan and thereupon decapitated. But as S. B. Hoenig points out (Buttrick, *Interpreter's Dictionary*, 4:629), the Theudas mentioned by Gamaliel may have been an earlier rebel of the same name (which is probably a short form of *Theodōros*) who raised a futile revolt back in A.D. 6, the year Herod Archelaus was deposed from the throne. (Gamaliel's remarks must have been made around A.D. 31, and therefore could not have referred to the same Theudas as Josephus mentioned.)

In Acts 5:37 Gamaliel also refers to a Judas of Galilee who raised an insurrection during the time of unrest that arose during a general census taking for taxation purposes, ordered by the legate of Syria, P. Sulpicius Quirinius around A.D. 7. This may have been a year later than the revolt of Theudas, just mentioned above. Josephus refers to this Judas several times (*Antiquities* 18.1.1–6; 20.5.2; *War* 2.8.1; 2.17.8–9). Apparently it was he who founded the terrorist order of the Sicarii or Zealots, from which one of Christ's disciples (Simon the Zealot, or the "Canaanite"—from the Hebrew *qānā'*, "be zealous") was recruited. At any rate, he too was killed by the Romans, as we learn from this verse—though Josephus does not mention his death at all.

Neither of these references presents any real discrepancy with the Josephan account. That there should have been more than one Theudas is hardly more surprising than that there was more than one Judas. "Theodorus," after all, was simply the Greek form of the Hebrew "Nathaniel" or possibly "Mattaniah."

Was Abraham only seventy-five when he left Haran? (D*)

In Acts 7:4 Stephen asserts that Abraham did not leave Haran for Canaan until after his father, Terah, was dead. But Terah did not die, according to Genesis 11:32, until the age of 205. That would mean Abraham must have been 135 when he left Haran, since Terah fathered him at the age of 70, according to Genesis 11:26. But Genesis 12:4 states that Abraham was only 75 when he migrated to Canaan.

Therefore Stephen was sixty years off in his statement, and Abraham must have left Haran sixty years before Terah died.

But things are not really as bad for Stephen as the previous paragraph declares, for there is one serious fallacy. Genesis 11:26 records: "And Terah lived seventy years, and became the father of Abram, Nahor and Haran" (NASB). Normally the first named in a list of sons is the oldest, but that rule has its exceptions. Abraham was not Terah's oldest son, even though he was named first. It is far more likely that Haran was Terah's oldest, since he was the first of them to die (Gen. 11:28). Concerning Nahor's death we have no information, except that he outlived Haran, and that his descendants Laban and Rebekah were living up in the region of Haran by the time of Isaac's marriage. But in all probability the reason Abraham was mentioned first was that he was by far the most important of the three brothers. Even though he must have been born when his father was 130—and may therefore have been the youngest of the three—he was the most prominent of them all, so far as historical achievement was concerned.

How many migrated with Jacob to Egypt?

In Acts 7:14 Stephen recalls concerning Joseph in Egypt that he "sent for his father Jacob and his whole family, seventy-five in all." But in Exodus 1:1–5 in the Masoretic text of the Hebrew Old Testament we read: "These are the names of the sons of Israel [the twelve names are given, except for Joseph].... The descendants of Jacob numbered seventy in all; Joseph was already in Egypt." In the face of this apparent discrepancy, we should note that Stephen may have intended to include the expanded number in the Septuagint, which was seventy-five rather than seventy. In fact, the Septuagint gives Exodus 1:5 as follows: "But Joseph was in Egypt. And all the souls from Jacob were seventy-five."

The explanation for this difference in the total is found back in Genesis 46:26–27. The Masoretic Hebrew text says: "All those who went to Egypt with Jacob—those who were his direct descendants, not counting his sons' wives —numbered sixty-six persons. With the *two sons* who had been born to Joseph in Egypt, the members of Jacob's family that went into Egypt, were seventy in all" (italics mine). But the Septuagint contains the following: "And all the souls who came with Jacob into Egypt, who issued from his loins, apart from the wives of the sons of Jacob, were sixty-six persons. And the sons of Joseph who were born to him in Egypt were nine persons. All the souls of the house of Jacob who entered Egypt were seventy-five." In other words, the total of seventy-five arrived at by the LXX included nine descendants of Joseph, rather than just two. Apparently Manasseh and Ephraim had seven sons between them, not by the time of Jacob's migration in 1876 B.C. (when they would hardly have been older than seven and five, respectively), but later on before Jacob actually died in Egypt after a seventeen-year sojourn there. Manasseh would have been twenty-five and Ephraim twenty-two by that date. If they married in their late teens, they might have produced seven children by them.

We therefore conclude that *both totals* are correct, though they were calculated differently. Jacob's own sons numbered twelve; his grandsons by them numbered fifty-two; there were already four great-grandsons born in Canaan by the time of the migration, for a total of sixty-six. Manasseh and Ephraim, born in Egypt, increased the total to sixty-eight; Jacob and his wife (whichever she was) brought it up to seventy. But the Septuagint added the seven grandsons of the prime minister and omitted Jacob and his wife from the tally.

This brings us to the result that Stephen correctly reported the number seventy-five, according to the Septuagint in Genesis 46:27 and Exodus 1:5. Likewise, Genesis 46:27, Exodus 1:5, and Deuteronomy 10:22 in the Masoretic text are correct with their total of seventy. Either figure is correct, depending on whether Joseph's grandchildren are included. (Four great-grandchildren of Jacob were included even in the Masoretic text tally of seventy.)

Wasn't Stephen mistaken about Jacob's plot of land at Shechem as having been bought by Abraham?

In his address to the Sanhedrin in Acts 7, Stephen said, concerning the interment of the bodies of Jacob's sons, "Their bodies were brought back [from Egypt] to Shechem and placed in the tomb that Abraham had bought from the sons of Hamor at Shechem for a certain sum of money" (v.16). In this entire discourse Stephen evidences a thorough knowledge of the Old Testament. How could he have been ignorant of Joshua 24:32, which indicates that the coffin of Joseph was finally laid to rest in a plot of ground that "Jacob had bought from the sons of Hamor." At first glance it looks as if we have a clear contradiction between these two statements. Yet there is a good possibility that what Jacob did when he made that purchase was to obtain once again for his family that which had originally been bought by Abraham.

Quite similar is the case of the well of Beersheba. Originally that well was dug by Abraham's workmen, and he paid for the rights to that property by offering seven lambs to Abimelech, king of Gerar (Gen. 21:27–30). But later on, owing to the nomadic habits of Abraham and his family, the property rights he had legally acquired became ignored; and the tract on which the well was located fell back into the possession of the local inhabitants. It was not until many years later that Isaac, having reopened the well to care for his livestock, found it expedient to secure the ownership by paying for it once more, rather than to assert his legal title to it by means of a range war. He therefore gave an oath of friendship and nonaggression to King Abimelech (probably a son or grandson of the same name as the Abimelech with whom Abraham had dealt many years before) and held a covenant-sealing sacrifice and banquet (Gen. 26:28–31) with him. Here then was a case where both Abraham and his descendant purchased the same ground.

In the case of Shechem, this was the very first location at which Abraham stopped after his migration from Haran, and there he erected his first altar to Yahweh in the Land of Promise (Gen. 12:6–7). There God appeared to him in a vision and confirmed His promise of the land to Abram and his descendants. Under these circumstances it was altogether logical for him to purchase the tract around the Oak of Moreh, where the altar had been erected. Stephen was undoubtedly aware of a reliable oral tradition that Abraham had in fact done so, even though the written record of the Old Testament had omitted this transaction.

In later years, long after Abraham had moved south and Isaac had made Beersheba his headquarters, and after Jacob's twenty-one years in Padan-Aram, the ancestral claim Jacob had to Abraham's plot was quite forgotten by the inhabitants of Shechem. Or else they may have felt that the house of Abraham had really forfeited their rights through the long period of disuse, thereby allowing some local family to take it over and work the land as their own.

When Jacob finally showed up and had settled down in the region of Shechem for an extensive sojourn (until the massacre connected with the rape of Dinah), it was only natural for him to negotiate for the repurchase of Abraham's tract. Genesis 33:18–20 tells how he paid one hundred *qᵉśîṭāh* (a unit of weight in excess of a shekel; the apparently cognate Arabic term *qasiṭatun*, an ancient unit of weight, came to 1,429 grams or 3.15 pounds). It is this sum that is later recalled in Joshua 24:32. (The only other place where *qᵉśîṭāh* is mentioned in the Old Testament is Job 42:11, where it is the amount given to Job by each of his relatives, to help him get started in business again after his recovery from illness.) Undoubtedly this was a much larger price than was originally paid by Abraham, and so it was only natural for Jacob's transaction to be regarded as the firmer basis for Israelite ownership of this land.

One final observation is in order concerning the "tomb" (*mnēma*) Abraham had bought from the sons of Emmor in Shechem. The Old Testament makes no mention of a tomb at Shechem until the burial of Joseph there. Nor does it mention Abraham's buying a tomb anywhere at all—not even when he wanted to bury Sarah in the cave of Machpelah in Hebron. He simply wanted to buy the cave so that he could afterward prepare it as a final resting place for her body. There could have been no confusion in Stephen's mind as to the true location of the resting place Abraham had purchased for Sarah and for himself. Everyone knew that it was the cave of Machpelah, and that Hebron was the city to which that belonged.

We concluded, therefore, that the reference to a *mnēma* ("tomb") in connection with Shechem must either have been proleptic for the later use of that Shechemite tract for Joseph's tomb (i.e., "the tomb that Abraham bought" was intended to imply "the tomb location that Abraham bought"); or else conceivably the dative relative pronoun *hō* was intended elliptically for *en tō topō hō ōnēsato Abraam* ("in the place that Abraham bought") as describing the location of the *mnēma* near the Oak of Moreh right outside Shechem. Normally Greek would have used the relative-locative adverb *hou* to express "in which" or "where"; but this would have left *ōnēsato* ("bought") without an object in its own clause, and so *hō* was much more suitable in this context.

Did not Stephen err in his quotation of Amos 5:26 (Rephan instead of Chiun)?

In Acts 7:43 Stephen quotes Amos 5:26 as referring to a certain idol carried by some of the Israelites of Moses' day in a clandestine cultic practice: "And you took up the tabernacle of Moloch, and the star of the god Rompha." But the Hebrew text reads: "And you carried the booth [or else *sikkût* may represent the name of a heathen god *Sakkût*, an epithet of the Sumerian god NIN-IB] of your king [or your 'king-god'; but Melek may be vowel-pointed as Molek or Molok, which is the way the Septuagint took it] and the shrine of your idols [although *kiyyûn* is a noun found nowhere else in the Old Testament, and may here be intended as the name of a heathen god rather than being a common noun derived from the root *kûn*, "establish, set in place"). The Septuagint reads almost the same as Acts 7:43, except that it has "the star of your god *Raiphan*." In other words, *kiyyûn* is rendered "star," and the spelling *Raiphan* appears instead of *Rompha*. Let us take up each of these variants in order.

First of all, *sikkût* has a very dubious base as a common noun for "shrine." As indicated above, it more probably should be vowel pointed as *Sakkût* (so Millar Burrows, cited in Koehler-

Baumgartner, *Lexicon,* p. 657; cf. E. Schrader, cited in Eissfeldt, *The Old Testament,* p. 507, n.5), an epithet of the star god NIN-IB, which was vocalized as *Ninurta* (René Labat, *Manuel d'épigraphie Akkadienne* [Paris: Imprimerie Nationale, 1948], p. 535); the god of tempest, hunting, and war, and a deity associated with the star Sirius (E. Dhorme, *Les Religions de Babylonie et d'Assyrie* [Paris: Presses Universitaires de France, 1945], p. 81). Hence the rendition *astron* ("star") is appropriate for *Sakkût,* and Stephen quite properly followed the Septuagint at this point.

Second, the Nestle reading (25th ed.) of *Rompha* is based only on Codex Vaticanus; Sinaiticus reads *Romphan;* Beza and the Latin versions favor Rempham. But the reading *Raiphan,* which follows the Septuagint, is supported by the third-century A.D. Bodmer text and the Codex Alexandrinus, and is favored by the *Rephan* of Ephjraimi Rescriptus and the Codex Laudianus; hence it is adopted into the text by the United Bible Societies' edition (Aland, Black, Martini, Metzger, Wikgren) of the Greek NT (also Nestle's 26th ed.). We take it, therefore, that *Raiphan* was the original spelling employed by Stephen (assuming that he addressed the Sanhedrin in Greek—it could have been in Aramaic perhaps, but Stephen seems to follow the Septuagint quite consistently in his quotations from the Old Testament).

If *Raiphan* is the correct reading, we may assume that Stephen used it as it appeared in the Septuagint, which was at that time the only authoritative Greek translation in general use. There was no need at that juncture for him to discuss the earlier spelling of the word back in Amos's text, for it would have served no useful purpose. But it is important to observe that the Septuagint translators may have misread this strange, foreign deity's name because of confusion in regard to similar-appearing letters. During the fifth century B.C., in the Elephantine Papyri composed by a colony of Jews in southern Egypt, the form of the letter kaph (K) was written ל, which resembles the shape of resh (R), written ר. Also, the letter waw (W), written ז, was very similar to the letter pe (P), written ז. Therefore what was written in the Hebrew *Vorlage* as K-Y-W-N might have been misread as R-Y-P-N, which would then be vocalized as *Raipan* or *Raiphan*. In other words ןויכ was copied out as ןפיר.

In a consonantal script like Hebrew, the vowels were only a matter of guesswork in the case of foreign names—though, of course, an accurate oral tradition might have preserved the correct vocalization. In the case of the names of foreign gods, however, the Hebrews had an aversion to pronouncing their names aloud; this militated against any kind of accuracy in the oral tradition of a heathen deity's name. In actuality, the vocalization of the name in the Amos text was probably *Kaywān* rather than *Kiyyûn* (as the Masoretes have vocalized it). By this devious route, then, the original *Kaywān* of Amos ended up as *Raiphan* on the lips of Stephen in Acts 7:43.

Did Paul's companions hear the Voice on the Damascus Road?

An apparent contradiction arises between the first account of Paul's conversion on the Damascus Road (Acts 9:7) and the second account (Acts 22:9) in regard to Paul's companions. Did they hear the Voice from heaven or did they not? Acts 9:7 states: "But the men who were journeying with Paul were standing speechless, hearing the Voice (*akouontes men tēs phōnēs*), but beholding no one." In Acts 22:9, on the other hand, we are told, "And those who were with me beheld the light, but they did not hear the Voice [*tēn de phōnēn ouk ēkousan*] of the one who was talking to me."

In the original Greek, however, there is no real contradiction between these two statements. Greek makes a distinction between hearing a sound as a noise (in which case the verb "to hear" takes the genitive case) and hearing a voice as a thought-conveying message (in which case it takes the accusative). Therefore, as we put the two statements together, we find that Paul's companions heard the Voice as a sound (somewhat like the crowd who heard the sound of the Father talking to the Son in John 12:28, but perceived it only as thunder); but they did not (like Paul) hear the message that it articulated. Paul alone heard it intelligibly (Acts 9:4 says Paul *ēkousen phōnēn* —accusative case); though he, of course, perceived it also as a startling sound at first (Acts 22:7: "I fell to the ground and heard a voice [*ēkousa phōnēs*] saying to me," NASB). But in neither account is it stated that his companions ever heard that Voice in the accusative case.

There is an instructive parallel here between the inability to hear the voice as an articulated message and their inability to see the glory of the risen Lord as anything but a blaze of light. Acts 22:9 says that they saw the light, but Acts 9:7 makes it clear that they did not see the Person who displayed Himself in that light. There is a clear analogy between these differing levels of perception in each case.

(For the technical case-distinction in Greek, cf. W. W. Goodwin and C. B. Gulick, *Greek Grammar* [Boston: Ginn & Co., 1930], #1103: "The partitive genitive is used with verbs signifying to taste, to smell, to hear, to perceive, etc."—with the example from Aristophanes' *Pax: phōnēs akouein moi dokō*—'Methinks I hear a voice.' See also #1104: "Verbs of hearing, learning, etc. may take an accusative of the thing heard etc., and a genitive of the person heard from." This comes very close to the distinction made above, that the accusative indicates the voice as a communicated message or thought, rather than as simply a sound vibrating against the eardrum.)

How long was Paul's ministry at Ephesus, two years or three?

Acts 19:10 states that Paul's teaching at the school of Tyrannus went on for two years, so that all in the province of Asia heard the gospel. But in his charge to the Ephesian elders, as recorded in Acts 20:31, Paul says, "Therefore be on the alert, remembering that night and day for a period of three years I did not cease to admonish each one with tears" (NASB). Which was it, then, two years or three?

As we examine the whole account of Paul's mission to Ephesus in Acts 19, we find that he was there considerably in excess of two years—which was merely the length of his teaching at the school of Tyrannus. But before he ever took up his headquarters there, he performed a good deal of preliminary work among his very first converts. Verses 1-6 relate how he made his first approach to a group of seekers who had already been ministered to by John the Baptist, or at least by converts of John the Baptist (v.3 simply says that they had been baptized into John's baptism—i.e., the "baptism of repentance" [v.4]). Thus he began with twelve converts, all of whom experienced a repetition of Pentecost, speaking in tongues, after Paul had laid his hands on them (v.6). Not until after that did Paul venture into the local synagogue at Ephesus and begin an enlargement of his work there. Doubtless he renewed his contact with those who had showed an interest earlier (cf. Acts 18:19-21), probably in that same synagogue—for a certain period of time not specified but simply hinted at by the clause "for a longer time" (v.20).

At any rate, after Paul's initial phase was over in the development of this smaller group of a dozen or so, he moved into phase two: the ministry to the Jewish community as a whole. Apparently he made a good impression there at first, for they permitted him to carry on a vigorous preaching mission for a good three months (Acts 19:8). But finally there was a determined opposition on the part of the unconverted, and Paul was forced to discontinue his work at the synagogue itself. Yet he had a sizable contingent of followers who left with him, and they apparently hired a meeting room at the school of Tyrannus, which may have been a college of philosophy. It was there that Paul carried on for two more years and managed to reach directly or indirectly all the important population centers of "Asia," which then included the entire west coast of Turkey as far back as the borders of Galatia.

As we total up the preliminary visit of Acts 18:19-21, the initial phase of 19:1-7, and the three months in the synagogue ministry, it becomes apparent that Paul's total time at Ephesus was closer to three years than it was to two. Hence there is no real discrepancy between Acts 20:31 and Acts 19:10—which lists the time at the school of Tyrannus as two years, not the entire time of his sojourn.

Was Paul obedient or disobedient to the Spirit when he went on pilgrimage to Jerusalem?

Acts 20:22-23 expresses Paul's confidence that he is in the will of God as he journeys back to Jerusalem to fulfill his vow as a pilgrim: "And now, behold, bound in spirit [or 'the Spirit'], I am on my way to Jerusalem, not knowing what will happen to me there, except that the Holy Spirit solemnly testifies to me in every city, saying that bonds and afflictions await me" (NASB). But in Acts 21:4 the disciples at Tyre "kept telling Paul through the Spirit not to set foot in Jerusalem" (NASB). Likewise, at the home of Philip the evangelist in Caesarea, the prophet Agabus took Paul's belt from him and symbolically wound it around his own hands and feet, saying, "This is what the Holy Spirit says: 'In this way the Jews at Jerusalem will bind the man who owns this belt and deliver him into the hands of the Gentiles'" (21:11, NASB). After this warning, all the local believers and friends strongly urged Paul to desist from his purpose; but he answered, "What are you doing, weeping and breaking my heart? For I am ready not only to be bound, but even to die at Jerusalem for the name of the Lord Jesus" (v.13, NASB).

It is clear that the Holy Spirit did everything to warn Paul of the danger and suffering that awaited him if he went back to Jerusalem. The statement in 21:4 that the disciples told Paul "through the Spirit (*dia tou pneumatos*) not to set foot in Jerusalem makes it sound as if Paul was acting in disobedience by persisting in the fulfillment of the vow he had taken at Cenchrea (18:18). W.L. Pettingill states his definite opinion that "Paul was forbidden to go to Jerusalem at all. It is therefore evident that he was out of the Lord's will" (*Bible Questions Answered*, ed. R.P. Polcyn, rev. ed. [Grand Rapids: Zondervan, 1979], p. 332). But this is a rather difficult position to maintain in view of God's continued faithfulness to him through all his trials. As Paul stood before the Sanhedrin, before Felix and Festus, and even before Herod Agrippa II, he enjoyed opportunities for witness that would never have come to him had he not become a *cause célèbre*.

If Paul was really out of the will of God, would he have been so marvelously delivered from the violence of the mob at the temple? Would he have been so notably used as a preacher to governors and kings? Back at the time of Paul's conversion, the Lord had told Ananias of Damascus, "Go, for he is a chosen instrument of Mine, to bear My name before the Gentiles and kings and the sons of Israel; for I will show him how much he must suffer for My name's sake" (9:15–16, NASB). It certainly looks as if Paul's arrest and trials at Caesarea, and his later appeal before Nero Caesar at Rome, were God's means of bringing to pass the purpose He announced to Ananias so many years before.

Paul's attitude in regard to the dangers and sufferings awaiting him in Jerusalem is not too dissimilar to that of our Lord Jesus as He too faced the prospect of His last journey to Jerusalem, there to meet His humiliation and death on a cross. There is something almost Christlike about the way Paul spoke of his impending sufferings in the presence of the Ephesian elders: "But I do not consider my life of any account as dear to myself, in order that I may finish my course, and the ministry which I received from the Lord Jesus, to testify solemnly of the gospel of the grace of God" (20:24, NASB). He gladly laid his life on the altar, as one who was completely expendable for the Lord Jesus.

All things considered, then, it seems best to understand Acts 21:4 as conveying, not an absolute prohibition of Paul's journey to Jerusalem, but only a clear, unmistakable warning that he is not to set foot in Jerusalem—if he wants to avoid danger and stay out of serious trouble. But Paul had counted the cost, and he was willing to risk everything in order to fulfill his vow and set an example of fearless courage before the whole church of God. From the sequel it seems quite clear that he was indeed following God's good and acceptable and perfect will for his life.

Romans

Are the unevangelized heathen really lost?

Romans 2:12 (NIV) reads: "All who sin apart from the law will also perish apart from the law, and all who sin under the law will be judged by the law." (Here the reference seems to be to the Mosaic Law, or the Hebrew Scriptures; hence it might be better to capitalize "law" as "Law.") Romans 2:14–15 applies this principle to the Gentiles in contradistinction to the Jews: "Indeed, when Gentiles, who do not have the Law, do by nature the things required by the Law, they are a law for themselves, even though they do not have the Law, since they show that the requirements of the Law are written on their hearts, their consciences also bearing witness, and their thoughts now accusing, now even defending them." With this we should compare Romans 3:19: "Now we know that whatever the Law says, it says to those who are under the Law, so that every mouth may be silenced and the *whole world* held accountable to God."

From these verses we deduce, first, that the Gentiles (and surely Paul includes the unevangelized Gentiles in this group) possess a knowledge of the moral law, an awareness of the difference between right and wrong, that makes them morally responsible before God, even though they have never come in contact with the Bible as such. They show their consciousness of basic moral law by their living in general conformity to it, as though they understood the fundamental principles set forth in the Ten Commandments. There is no organized community on the face of the earth where anyone living in total disregard of all the Ten Commandments would not be considered a lawbreaker and an enemy to society.

Second, the Gentiles "are a law for themselves," that is, they have within their conscience an awareness of a moral standard to which they are accountable, and yet their "thoughts accuse them" (Rom. 2:15). In other words, they realize that even by their own standards of right and wrong they are guilty, for they have not always measured up to those standards. They may "defend themselves" against the accusations of their conscience, but by their resorting to self-defense against the moral law, they impliedly recognize and acknowledge its binding validity and authority over them. Even though they do not have the perfect standard of Holy Scripture and therefore but dimly apprehend their own guilt, they nevertheless are conscious of failures and offenses for which they will have to give an accounting before the powers of heaven—or however they conceive their gods.

Romans 3:19 sums the matter up very clearly: Every mouth is silenced before God, and all the world—both Jew and Gentile—is accountable to Him for sin and guilt. All mankind is lost. All men therefore need a Savior. Without an effectual Redeemer they have no hope of acquittal before the judgment bar of God (or of the powers of heaven). As John 3:18 declares: "Whoever believes in him [Jesus] is not condemned, but whoever does not believe stands *condemned already* because he has not believed in the name of God's one and only Son" (NIV, italics mine).

The sentence of "condemned as charged" has already been passed on the whole human race, and there is no hope for any man except by way of a special pardon from the King. It is highly significant that John 3:18 comes only two verses after John 3:16, which speaks of God's love for the world and His gift of His Son, whose atoning death will prove sufficient to save any and all true believers from the eternal death they deserve. This paragraph in John 3 makes it very clear that apart from Christ there is no salvation. As Jesus Himself said to Thomas, "I am the way and the truth and the life. No one comes to the Father except through Me" (John 14:6).

Sometimes the hope is held out by those who shrink from the concept of the hopeless condition of unevangelized mankind that there may be some second way into heaven other than the way of Christ—"If a pagan who has never had a chance to hear the gospel lives up to the light that has been given him and sincerely seeks after God, then surely he is not condemned to eternal hell for lack of a missionary witness." There are several observations to be made concerning this theory, showing that it cannot be sustained in the light of Scripture.

1. There is an implication in the statement that if the gospel has been presented to one group of people, then God is duty bound to get it out immediately to all the rest of mankind without any kind of human agency. If it came to Christ's disciples or to the Jews in Palestine at Pentecost, then God owed it to the rest of the world without delay. Unless all nations in all parts of the world have equal access at the same time to the Good News of Christ's atoning death, God must be condemned as unfair. This is the necessary implication of the extenuating clause "who has never had a chance to hear the gospel"—with its semi-reproachful innuendo. But this concept must be held up to careful scrutiny.

Is the gospel a matter of grace or a matter of duty on the part of God? The Bible clearly teaches that it is purely a matter of grace. "But God commendeth his love toward us, in that, while we were yet sinners, Christ died for us" (Rom. 5:8). "By grace are ye saved through faith" (Eph. 2:8). If then the gospel is of grace and God owed it to no man (for grace that is owed is no longer grace), then how can it be maintained that God is precluded from telling the Good News of redeeming love to any man unless all men everywhere hear the same message at the same moment all over the earth? Does not the New Testament clearly teach that "everyone who calls on the name of the Lord shall be saved" (Rom. 10:13)? The inescapable logic behind the missionary imperative of the Great Commission continues on as follows: "How, then, can they call upon the one they have not believed in? And how can they believe in the one of whom they have not heard? And how can they hear without someone preaching to them? And how can they preach unless they are sent?" (Rom. 10: 14–15, NIV). If the heathen could actually be saved by living up to the light that has been given them—that is, the light of natural revelation—then this entire line of logic would collapse, and Romans 10 would have to be rejected as false teaching without any authority.

2. If the heathen may be saved by living up to the light that has been given them, then it necessarily follows that men may be saved by their own good works. If that is the case, then Christ died needlessly on the cross; and He was mistaken in saying, "No man comes to the Father but by Me" (John 14:6).

3. If the heathen may be saved by sincerely searching after God the best they know how, this also is simply a specialized form of good works, and grace is rendered unnecessary. But unless the Bible is grievously mistaken, there are no such people as that on the face of the earth. Romans 3:10-11 (quoting Ps. 14: 1-3 and Eccl. 7:20) declares: "There is no one righteous, not even one; there is no one who seeks God." Well then, if there is no one who does sincerely seek God, we do not need to be troubled about the unfairness of barring heaven to those unevangelized heathen who do sincerely seek after God. God Himself says that there just aren't any like that around, nor have there ever been. And even if there were, the good work of seeking God would not avail to save them. Only Jesus can do that.

4. No one is condemned to hell for lack of a missionary witness. He is condemned to hell for his sin. He stands guilty of putting himself before God as the chief concern of his heart—repeating the choice of Eve, who decided to do what was most pleasurable and advantageous for herself and her husband, rather than faithfully doing what God had commanded and putting His will first in her life. Every descendant of hers who has lived to the age of moral decision has followed her in this same choice—all except Jesus! Condemnation results not from failure to hear the gospel but from an utter failure to keep even the first and great commandment: "Thou shalt love the Lord thy God with all thy heart and with all thy soul and with all thy might" (Deut. 6:5; Matt. 22:37).

In the light of the four objections just discussed, we must conclude that either the unevangelized heathen are hopelessly lost, or else the Bible is grievously mistaken and must be corrected by those who have better theological insights than those found in Holy Scripture. There are various passages that have been mistakenly interpreted to mean that there is hope for good pagans who have not heard the message of Scripture—despite what John 3:18; 8:24; 14:6 and Romans 2, 3, and 10 seem to teach. One such verse is Micah 6:8: "He hath showed thee, O man, what is good; and what does the LORD require of thee, but to do justly, and to love mercy, and to walk humbly with thy God?" But in context this is clearly addressed to professing believers who stand in covenant relation to Yahweh (the LORD), the God of the Bible; and it serves to warn them that a credible profession of faith in God must be demonstrated by a godly life. This has no bearing whatever on the unevangelized heathen, who have no knowledge of Yahweh at all, and thereby are precluded from "walking humbly with" Him.

Or again, Malachi 1:11 promises: "'For from the rising of the sun even unto the going down of the same My name shall be great among the Gentiles;... for My name shall be great among the heathen,' saith the LORD of hosts." It goes without saying that such strong emphasis on knowing and honoring Yahweh by name necessarily implies hearing and believing the message of Scripture, without which there is no possibility of knowing that great and redemptive name.

Additionally, consider Peter's statement in the living room of Cornelius: "I now realize how true it is that God does not show favoritism but accepts men from every nation who fear Him and do what is right" (Acts 10:34–35). This declaration is not intended to teach that there are right-minded heathen who are saved by their good works or fine character. It simply indicates Peter's awareness that God has accepted the heathen, equally with the Jews, as candidates for salvation, as they hear and respond to the gospel. Otherwise Peter could have terminated his remarks right at that point and walked out of the room, leaving them all to bask in their new understanding of the blessing of being already saved. On the contrary, Peter proceeded to preach to them about Jesus of Nazareth, His life of love and miracle-working power, and His atoning death and glorious resurrection (vv.36–41).

Peter closed by giving an urgent missionary appeal to his heathen audience, that they should repent of their sins and put their trust in Jesus as their Savior. Here, then, we see Peter using once again the "keys of the kingdom of heaven" (Matt. 16:19) and opening the gateway of salvation to the lost, even as he had done at Pentecost in Acts 2. And by the grace of God, this is what we shall all do, if we sincerely believe what the Bible so clearly teaches, that all men are lost without Christ and that no one has access to Christ except by hearing of Him and believing His words.

(As for children dying in infancy, see the discussion of Rom. 5:14: "those who have not sinned after the similitude of Adam's transgression.")

In Romans 5:14 what is meant by "those who have not sinned after the similitude of Adam's transgression"?

Romans 5:12–14 reads: "Therefore,

just as through one man [Adam] sin entered into the world, and death through sin, and so death spread to all men, because all sinned—for until the Law was given to Israel in the time of Moses] sin was in the world; but sin is not imputed when there is no law. Nevertheless death reigned from Adam until Moses, even over those who had not sinned in the likeness of Adam's offense, who is a type of Him who was to come [namely, Jesus]". ... This passage clearly teaches that (1) in the case of man, created in the image of the immortal God, death was not a necessity of nature but a penalty for sin—that primal sin of disobedience committed by Adam and Eve at the very beginning of the human race; (2) the covenant was made with Adam, not only for himself but for all his descendants, and therefore his sin of partaking of the forbidden fruit involved not only himself but also all his posterity in a state of sin and death; (3) the penal consequences of that primal fall affect all mankind, even before the giving of the law at Mount Sinai, and before the first portion of Holy Scripture was revealed and committed to written form; and (4) because of that primal sin, death struck down all mankind, from the time of Adam down to the time of Moses—even those of Adam's descendants who had not consciously chosen to disobey God as Adam did.

This raises the question, Who of the human race have not like Adam consciously chosen to disobey God? Which of us have not personally repeated Adam's offense, on the basis of our own free will? The answer is, Not a mother's son of us—except for those who died in infancy, without becoming old enough to make a responsible moral decision. It may be arguable how long this state of true innocence continues after a child has been born. All too soon parents come to realize the reality of the rebellious, Adamic nature in their infants; and they find themselves very early in the course of child-rearing speaking of their little ones as being "good" or "naughty" on that particular day. Nevertheless, whether a child may be regarded as culpably sinful when he throws his first tantrum, or whether later, when he enters the toddler stage, his Adamic ancestry is unmistakable. All too soon we recognize ourselves in him—or her!

Be that as it may, it is quite clear that at the very earliest stages of a child's life, he is fully innocent so far as his own moral manifestations are concerned. Nevertheless, as v.14 points out, death—which is for humans a penalty for sin—"reigned" over the whole human race, even including those infants who, dying in infancy, had no opportunity to recapitulate Adam's fall. Yet they are clearly involved in Adam's guilt and in Adam's fall.

This raises the question Why should this be so? How can it be just to condemn a soul that has never personally, consciously sinned? The answer to this difficult question is to be found in the federal headship of Adam and in the foreseen potential of the infant who has been prematurely cut off. Romans 5 sets forth Adam and Christ as the two federal heads (or covenant representatives) of the human race. Adam was appointed the authorized representative of all mankind; Christ was appointed the authorized representative of redeemed mankind. The first representative responded to the covenant of works with an act of God-rejecting disobedience; the second representative responded to that covenant with a God-affirming act of obedience—His voluntary death on the cross as an atonement for the sin of fallen man—as a climax and seal of a perfectly sinless, law-keeping life.

Romans 5 teaches that the moral response of each federal head inured to all those who were embraced within the covenant—by the principle of imputation. Adam's sin was imputed to all his descendants—including infants dying in infancy—just as Christ's sinless obedience was reckoned to all those who by faith belong to Him. All the human race fell into sin and guilt through Adam's fall; but all those who are in Christ are redeemed through His righteousness, which is reckoned to their account by the grace of God, extended to all those who sincerely and savingly believe in His Son, Jesus Christ, as their Lord and Savior. Failure to accept the principle of the federal headship of Adam implies also a rejection of the federal headship of Christ. He who rejects his involvement in original sin (for this is what the federal headship of Adam implies) by the same token rejects the principle of justification by faith in Christ. The same passage teaches both; therefore he who rejects the one by implication rejects the other as well.

But in its application to children dying in infancy, a very serious problem arises in regard to salvation. If the benefits of Calvary are available only to one who repents and believes, what hope is there for an infant who dies before he is capable of repenting and believing? This leads us to the foreseen potential of the dying infant. That is to say, any infant who is permitted to live to the age of accountability will surely repeat the sin of Adam and thus recapitulate his fall on the basis of his own free will and voluntary choice, a choice for which he is fully responsible. But if the child who died in infancy had been permitted to live, he would also have made some kind of response to the gracious offer of the gospel, whether by way of acceptance or rejection. God knows what is in the heart of man even before he is born. God said to Jeremiah, "Before I formed you in the womb I knew you, and before you were born I consecrated you" (Jer. 1:5, NASB). God did not have to wait and see how Jeremiah would respond before He chose him. The same was true of John the Baptist (Luke 1:13–15) and of the messianic Servant of the Lord (Isa. 49:1). If then God knows in advance what each child will do and how he will respond when he reaches the age of moral decision, there is every reason to believe that God knows how every child will respond to His call and whether or not he would embrace His offer of redeeming grace.

Therefore it may be considered a necessary inference (although there may be no explicit teaching in Scripture on this particular point) from God's foreknowledge of the future response of each child that He also knows what would be his response if he were permitted to live long enough to make that response. We therefore conclude that all infants dying in infancy are dealt with in accordance with this principle of the foreseen potential.

We close with an observation about the commonly entertained view that *all* children who die in infancy are automatically saved, since they have not committed any sin. This opinion, however kindly and well-intentioned it may be, suffers from two serious objections. First, it in effect amounts to a rejection of the doctrine of original sin as taught in Romans 5, for it presupposes that we come into the world as sinless and free from guilt as if Adam had never fallen—a clear contradiction of scriptural teaching on this matter. Second, this doctrine of the universal salvation of all children dying in infancy leads to a rather horrifying moral dilemma for every parent. That is to say, if dying in infancy insures the safe passage of one's child to heaven—whereas he might well reject the Lord in later life and thus end up in hell—then it becomes almost obligatory for each parent to strangle his child as soon as it is born—and thus all abortionists are performing a good work! Even though a parent who practices infanticide may be technically guilty of murder, his motive for the deed greatly diminishes (even if it may not altogether elimi-

nate) the guilt that would otherwise attach to that monstrous crime. Is it conceivable that God would so order His moral universe as to furnish a special motive of a most benevolent sort for each parent to slay his infant child before it attains the age of accountability? Yet this is the inescapable consequence of the doctrine of the universal salvation of infants dying in infancy.

In light of all these factors, a far better statement is that found in the Westminster Confession (x.3): "Elect infants, dying in infancy, are regenerated and saved by Christ through the Spirit, who worketh when, and where, and how he pleaseth. So also are all other elect persons, who are incapable of being outwardly called by the ministry of the Word"—that is the mentally incompetent.

Was Pharaoh really responsible for his rebellion against God, according to Romans 9:17?

Romans 9 is largely devoted to a discussion of God's sovereign grace and how it operates in relation to both the elect (i.e., those who are chosen unto salvation) and the nonelect (those who are not thus chosen). This principle of free and sovereign grace is set in contrast to the other principle, that of earning salvation by good works. It first arises in connection with God's choice of Jacob and rejection of Esau even before those twins were born (v.13). Then it arises in connection with the Pharaoh of the Exodus, concerning whom God said, "For this very purpose I raised you up, to demonstrate My power in you, and that My name might be proclaimed throughout the whole earth" (v.17, NASB; a quotation from Exod. 9:16).

At this point Paul raises the familiar objection that has been raised ever since: "You will say to me then, 'Why does He still find fault? For who resists His will?'" (Rom. 9:19, NASB). He then responds to it by adducing two considerations: (1) the finite creature, who has derived all his moral understanding from his infinite Creator, is utterly incompetent to sit in judgment on Him or question His administration of justice (v.20). (2) God knows best how to display His glory in His dealings with both classes of men: "the vessels of wrath" (v.22) and "the vessels of mercy" (v.23). Pharaoh in his arrogant defiance of the God of the Hebrews (Exod. 5:2) represents the vessels of wrath. God endured his defiance, blasphemy, and repeated violations of his promises toward Israel; and God granted him one opportunity after another to let the Hebrews leave Egypt without major loss of life. But finally when His patience was up, and Pharoah had forfeited all right to expect Israel's return to Egypt (after holding a religious celebration away from the land), the Lord poured out His wrath on Pharaoh and the entire nation of the Egyptians. Every firstborn child of every family (even the herds and flocks throughout the domain of Pharaoh)—including the crown prince himself—was taken by death on the night of the first Passover.

As for the "vessels of mercy," these did not comprise "good" people necessarily who earned God's favor by their exemplary lives and virtuous character. On the contrary, these vessels consisted of true believers, both Jew and Gentile, who came to terms with the call of God by their response of repentance and faith (Rom. 9:23–24). Paul finally concludes this topic with the following observation concerning the grace of God: "What shall we say then? That Gentiles, who did not pursue righteousness, attained righteousness, even the righteousness which is by faith; but Israel [by which he means that majority of the Jews, who refused the claims of Christ], pursuing a law of righteousness, did not arrive at that

law. Why? Because they did not pursue it by faith, but as though it were by works" (vv.30–31, NASB).

From the line of teaching in this chapter, we may draw the following answer concerning the ultimate culpability of Pharaoh (who was probably Amenhotep II). From the standpoint of God, Pharaoh's negative response to Moses' plea was completely foreknown by God (Exod. 3:19 contains God's prediction to Moses while still at the burning bush: "But I know that the king of Egypt will not permit you to go, except under compulsion"). Furthermore, in view of that foreseen refusal by Pharaoh, God will "harden his heart" so that he will forbid the Hebrew nation to leave Egypt even for a religious festival out in the wilderness (Exod. 4:21). The apparent purpose of the heart-hardening is to cancel out any obligation on the part of the Israelites to return to Egypt after their festival of worship is over. After the king has broken his word nine times, there will be no moral obligation whatever for them to come back. But then, on the tenth or last of the plagues to be launched against Egypt, God will take the life of Pharaoh's firstborn son.

One important observation remains to be made concerning Pharaoh: the king's heart was not actually hardened by God until after he had hardened his own heart by his first refusal of Moses' petition. "Who is Yahweh that I should obey His voice to let Israel go? I do not know Yahweh, and besides, I will not let Israel go!" (Exod. 5:2). Once he had of his own free will rejected the request of Moses and Aaron, then God began the process of hardening his heart (7:3,13,22; 8:19, etc.), to such an extreme that Pharaoh became almost irrational. Again and again the king besmirched his honor by refusing to keep his word to Moses, as each plague came and went. The sequence of causation here is about the same as that described in Romans 1:19–26. First, mankind received by general revelation a basic knowledge of God's eternal power and divine nature; yet they failed to honor Him as supreme, nor were they grateful to Him (v.21), but became proud of their own wisdom and thus fell into spiritual stupidity (v.22). "Therefore God gave them over in the lusts of their hearts to impurity ... they exchanged the truth of God for a lie, and worshiped and served the creature rather than the Creator" (vv.24-25, NASB). The same hardening befell the heart of the human race in general as is described of Pharaoh in particular.

Returning, then, to Romans 9:17 ("For this very purpose I raised you up, to demonstrate My power in you" [NASB]), we come to God's overriding master plan, by which He not only copes with man's rebellion but turns it into an occasion for the Lord to display both His righteousness and His grace. Pharaoh refused all concessions to the enslaved Hebrews, despite all the promises he made concerning their release. But this intransigence only served to justify a clean-cut break with Egypt; the Egyptian government had no longer any claim on them, and the Israelites were under no moral obligation to return to their bondage after concluding their period of worship out in the wilderness (which was all they originally requested, according to Exod. 5:1). Now they were free to leave for good, with Egypt mourning the loss of their crops, their cattle, and their firstborn sons under the impact of the Ten Plagues. By these dreadful visitations, of which all the surrounding nations received tidings, the dread of the almighty Yahweh was instilled into their hearts; and they took notice of the special status of Israel as a nation in covenant with the one true God—as He revealed Himself to be.

We turn now from this particular example of Pharaoh to the larger questions pertaining to the tension between predestination and free will, between sovereign grace and human responsibility for sin. Divine sovereignty raises an apparent difficulty in regard to the ultimate responsibility for evil. Romans 9:19 puts it quite pointedly: "You will say to me then, 'Why does He still find fault? For who resists His will?'" (NASB). If it is true that God has mercy on whom He wills and hardens whom He wills, must it not follow that man is relieved of final responsibility for his sin? If God chooses to create two kinds of people, the elect and the reprobate, and so programs them that they are free only to respond to the nature with which they have been created—a nature that has been predetermined without any independent choice on their own part—does not the ultimate responsibility for their later sinfulness and failure to repent amount to God's own decision, and therefore His own responsibility? Does this not mean then that God Himself is the author of sin?

Yet this runs counter to the clear teaching of Scripture that asserts: "Thou art not a God that has pleasure in wickedness: neither shall evil dwell with thee" (Ps. 5:4). "Thine eyes are too pure to approve evil, and Thou canst not look on wickedness with favor" (Hab. 1:13, NASB). "Let no one say when he is tempted, 'I am tempted of God'; for God cannot be tempted with evil, nor does He tempt any man. But every one is tempted when he is drawn away of his own lust and enticed" (James 1:13-14). The often-quoted verse in Isaiah 45:7 (which KJV misleadingly renders as "I make peace, and create evil") teaches that God has constructed a moral universe in which punishment follows wrong. The key word here is $rā'$, which covers the whole range of badness, all the way from distressing trials to calamities and disasters that overtake the good and the evil alike, to moral evil as such. But in this context, where there is a preceding pair of antithetical ideas ("light" and "darkness"), it is exegetically certain that *rā'* here is intended as the opposite, not of goodness or virtue, but of *šālôm* ("peace" or "welfare"). Therefore RSV does better in rendering this line "I make weal and create woe"; NASB has "causing well-being and creating calamity"; NIV has "I bring prosperity and create disaster." Hence Isaiah 45:7 furnishes no indication whatever that God is the ultimate author of evil.

Perhaps it should be added here that as the framer of a moral universe, God has created the "possibility" of moral evil. There can be no such thing as moral goodness unless there is also the possibility of moral evil. Without a voluntary choice of what is right, there can be no such thing as virtue; but a freedom to choose good necessarily implies a freedom to choose evil—with all the terrible consequences that ensue from that choice. There can be no possibility of real love without a possibility of rejection and hate. Therefore if God created angels and men for the purpose of loving them and having fellowship with them, they had to have the prerogative of responding to Him in love by their own choice. But unless there is a possibility of refusing love, there is no possibility of affirming love. Without that freedom of choice, there is no morality and no love but only automated, mechnical response. Let this insight serve to answer the oft-repeated questions, Why did God allow there to be such a person as Satan? Why did God allow him to approach Eve through his agent the serpent? Why did not God make Adam and Eve completely good so that they would never yield to temptation? The answer to all of these is, without the possibility of evil, there would be no possibility of good.

There is another important distinctive about man that should not be overlooked. Genesis 1:27 states that God made man in His own image. This means that in his moral and mental construction man was to resemble God—to the extent that the finite can resemble the Infinite. Admittedly God is good, devoid of all evil or deceit. Is He that way because some outside force has so conditioned Him that He could not be anything but good? Or is God good because He chooses to be good and wills to reject evil? One may raise a real question as to whether there could be any moral yardstick outside of God by which His goodness could be measured or evaluated. But surely God's will is unfettered and undetermined by any outside authority or power. May it not be, then, that man too, created in the image of God, has an analogous capacity of original choice—by virtue of which he can be held morally responsible for choosing to put self above God, as all of Adam's race have done (except, of course, for Jesus, whose Father was the Holy Spirit)? We conclude, therefore, that man is totally and ultimately responsible for his own sin, and God bears no responsibility for it in any degree whatever. When God issues a summons to the entire human race that they should repent and turn to Him in faith and total submission (Acts 17: 30–31: "Now he commands all people everywhere to repent. For he has set a day when he will judge the world with justice by the man he has appointed" [NIV]), this is to be considered a sincere offer of forgiveness and new life to all men everywhere—an offer for which they will be fully culpable if they refuse to accept it.

On the other hand, the principle of sovereign grace involves a total rejection of human effort to win salvation or to earn the favor of God. "Grace" means that God does it all, without any help from man. Salvation must come as a free, totally undeserved gift, since man has forfeited all claim to self-justifying merit. "By grace you have been saved, through faith—and this not from yourselves, it is the gift of God—not of works, so that no one can boast" (Eph. 2:8-9, NIV). "He saved us, not by works of righteousness that we have done, but according to his mercy" (Titus 3:5). This means that nothing we can offer God in the way of character, service, or deeds of righteousness contributes any basis whatever for our salvation. Those who are truly saved receive Christ Himself (John 1:12) as Savior and Lord (Rom. 10:9-10); and from the dynamic of His indwelling Spirit (Col. 3:1-4), we will produce works of righteousness and goodness that will manifest the life of Christ within us. ("As the body without the spirit is dead, so faith without works is dead also" [James 2:26].)

However, the work of sanctification carried on in the life of the born-again believer is basically the gracious operation of God Himself (Rom. 8:10-11,14). This transformed life will continually produce the ninefold fruit of the Spirit of God (Gal. 5:22-23), if indeed the surrender of faith is no mere counterfeit or self-deception, and if the true child of God will constantly present his body as a living sacrifice to the God who redeemed him (Rom. 12:1). Thus no longer conforming to this world, he is being transformed by the renewing of his mind through the operation of the indwelling Spirit of Christ (v.2).

Nevertheless it remains true that man contributes nothing substantive toward his salvation—if he is saved at all. Even saving faith is the gift of God, and God receives all the glory for the sinner's conversion (Eph. 2:9). All the unsaved man can do is face up to the claims of Christ and assent to the proffer of His grace. This response of assent bears no resemblance to a work of merit; it is simply the act of a beggar who reaches up his empty hand to receive a gift from his benefactor. Such an act has nothing to do with merit; it

does nothing to make the beggar more deserving than another beggar who keeps his hands folded in his lap. The gift is bestowed out of pity and grace. "God, having out of His mere good pleasure, from all eternity, elected some to everlasting life, did enter into a covenant of grace, to deliver them out of the estate of sin and misery, and to bring them into a state of salvation by a Redeemer" (*Westminster Shorter Confession* 20, as derived from John 17:6; Eph. 1:4; Titus 1:2; 3:7). This statement can hardly be improved on as a classic formulation of the doctrine of grace.

According to these verses God has chosen His redeemed from all eternity, "before the foundation of the world" (Eph. 1:4). This means that He did not have to wait and see; for He who knows all things from beginning to end, knows what each man's response will be to the call of Christ. These true believers, then, who make up Christ's spiritual temple, His mystical body and His beloved bride, are regarded as a love-gift from the Father to the Son (John 17:6: "I have manifested thy name unto the men which thou gavest me out of the world: thine they were, and thou gavest them me").

On what basis has God chosen His elect? It was not on the basis of any merit in them (Eph. 2:8-9), whether their character, their works, or their faith (as a work of merit), but "according as He has chosen us in Him " (Eph. 1:4). This seems to imply that God the Father only chooses those who are *in* the Son, Jesus Christ. Yet there is a mystery about the response of sinners to Christ's call. Obviously we cannot be *in* Christ unless we are united with Him by faith. But what is it that determines that faith? Why is it that when two persons at the same gospel meeting hear the same message from the same preacher, one responds to the invitation and goes forward to receive Christ, while the other remains stubbornly in his seat, clinging faithfully to his sin and self-will? Jesus said in John 6:37, "All that the Father gives Me shall come to Me, and the one who comes to Me I will certainly not cast out" (NASB). This means that there is nothing in the principle of election or predestination that will keep any repentant sinner from coming to Christ and receiving salvation.

In John 6:44, however, Jesus also said, "No one can come to Me, unless the Father who sent Me draws him" (NASB). Those who come to Christ do so as a result of the gracious working of God in their hearts; it is God the Father who draws them to God the Son as their Savior and Lord. This teaches us that we must give to God all the credit and all the glory for the impulse in our heart to respond to Christ's call when the gospel is presented to us. Otherwise we might say to ourselves, "Well, in a way I deserved God's grace, because I responded when He called me—unlike that unrepentant man who sat in the seat next to mine and would not go forward when the invitation was given." No, there is no room for personal merit in the matter of our election. It is all a matter of God's "mere good pleasure," and He receives all the glory when a sinner is saved. Whoever rejects the Lord Jesus must bear all the blame for remaining condemned and lost, but whoever is saved must give to God all the glory and honor for his salvation and his new life in Christ.

To sum up, then, God chooses from all eternity those who will be saved; and the sole basis of His choice is His mere good pleasure, even as the sole basis of acquittal and justification is the merit of Christ's atoning death. Yet God never chooses those who do not and will not believe in Christ; only those that do will He bring to Christ for salvation. But what it is that causes a sinner to open his heart to God's truth and become willing to believe is not really spelled out in Scripture. All we can be sure of is that God, "who is not willing that any should perish, but that all should come to repentance" (2 Peter 3:9), has not made their choice for them. Each man bears full responsibility for his own choice; and as one created in the image of God (and therefore invested with moral responsibility), and as one wrought upon by the Holy Spirit of God (who alone can evoke a true and saving faith), he must decide for himself between life and death, between blessing and cursing— "So choose life, so that you may live!" (Deut. 30:19).

1 Corinthians

Was Eliphaz inspired when he spoke Job 5:13?

In 1 Corinthians 3:19, Paul quotes a statement made by Eliphaz in Job 5:13: "He [God] catches the wise in their own craftiness." This raises an interesting problem, since Job 42:7 quotes Yahweh as saying to Eliphaz, "My wrath is kindled against you and against your two friends, because you have not spoken of Me what is right as My servant Job has." This suggests that the sentiments expressed by Job's "comforters" fall short of trustworthiness in theological teaching. One critic, Dewey Beegle, puts the problem this way: "Traditionally speaking, Eliphaz has never been considered as inspired. Job, so it is claimed, was the inspired one.... Apparently Paul did not care who said it, nor whether he was inspired. The statement was true as far as he was concerned, and so he used it in his argument" (*Scripture, Tradition and Infallibility* [Grand Rapids: Eerdmans, 1973], p. 194).

What this comment fails to reckon with is that Paul really does treat Eliphaz's comment as inspired, for he introduces it with the phrase "It is written." Through the New Testament, Christ, the apostles, and the Evangelists Mark and Luke all use the formula "It is written" to cite authoritative Scripture in proving a point of truth. It is only fair to conclude that in this instance, too, the passage cited is considered inerrantly trustworthy and authoritative. This serves as a reminder that many of the general principles the comforters brought up in their dialogue with Job were quite true in themselves, even though they may not have been appropriate to Job's situation, and may by inference have been grossly unfair to him. But we should remember that Job himself declared to them, "Who does not know such things as these?" (12:3)—i.e., those religious platitudes that they had been preaching to him.

In point of fact, Job in some of his own speeches expresses sentiments very similar to those that the "comforters" had directed at him. Insofar as they recognized the righteousness of God and His willingness to receive the penitent sinner back into His favor, what they spoke was God's truth. But their insistence on the point that God would not possibly allow misfortune to overtake Job unless he had been guilty of some heinous, unconfessed sin was a serious misrepresentation of God's providential dealings. In effect, they demoted Him to their own salvation-by-works mentality, making Him a patron of their own self-justification.

It should also be pointed out that not everything Job said about God in his state of resentment and frustration was true. For instance, in 10:3 Job complains to God, "Does it please you to oppress me, to spurn the work of your hands, while you smile on the schemes

396

of the wicked?" (NIV). Also, in 16:12–13 he accuses God of heartless cruelty toward him. It should also be observed that even a normally uninspired sinner like Caiaphas could on occasion express a sentiment such as John 11:50: "It is expedient for you that one man die for the people, and not that the whole nation should perish." John goes on to comment: "But he did not say this on his own, but rather being high priest that year, he prophesied that Jesus die for the nation" (v.51).

In any book of the Bible, it is necessary to study with discrimination the setting of each statement, to see whether the author himself intends it as authoritative and inspired, or whether it simply gives an accurate report of the uninspired utterances of misguided unbelievers or even of Satan himself. All these distinctions are involved in the doctrine of Inerrancy.

How can 1 Corinthians 7:12 and 7:40 be reconciled with the inerrant authority of Paul's Epistles?

These two verses present a slightly different factor in relationship to Paul's apostolic authority, and therefore they will be treated separately. In the paragraph beginning with v.8, Paul is discussing the question of whether to remain single or to become married. He also alludes to the alternatives facing married couples who prove to be incompatible. In vv.10–11 he cites an express dictum of the Lord Jesus during His earthly ministry (Matt. 5:32; 19:3–9) that forbids a married couple to break up; that is, the wife should not leave her husband, and the husband is not to send his wife away so as to divorce her. (matthew 5:32 allows divorce only on the grounds of unchastity.) Then in 7:12 Paul moves on to the question of whether couples who have thus broken up are free to marry someone else. He takes note of the fact that Jesus never spoke explicitly on

that question (even though the implications of Matt. 5:32 point strongly in the direction of forbidding any such second marriage).

Either because he is simply drawing an inference (albeit an almost unavoidable inference) from Christ's ruling on the matter of divorce, or else because he has received some explicit revelation as to God's will in regard to a special type of marital tension, Paul makes it clear that what he is about to say is not an actual quotation from Jesus' lips. Therefore he says, "But to the rest I say, not the Lord." Jesus never discussed what should be done when one member of the married couple gets saved and the other remains opposed to the gospel; so it was necessary for Paul to make a distinction between the explicit prohibition of divorce (on which Christ had made a definite pronouncement) and a logical and necessary inference that Paul had (under the influence of the Holy Spirit) drawn in regard to the plight of the discordant marriage partners.

There were, of course, many revelations from God contained in Paul's inspired writings; and these often dealt with matters that our Lord never discussed while on earth. But since all of Paul's teaching was given to him by revelation from the risen Christ through the agency of the Holy Spirit, it was as fully authoritative as any of the sayings of Jesus that He uttered during His earthly ministry. In other words, "I say, not the Lord" implies nothing adverse to the binding authority of what Paul taught (either here or anywhere else in his epistles) but only deals with the question of whether he can cite a recorded saying of Christ prior to His resurrection and ascension.

As for 1 Corinthians 7:40, Paul gives his counsel to those who are uncertain as to whether they should get married, and he says, "But in my opinion she [i.e., a woman who has lost her husband through death] is happier if she remains as she is [i.e., in a state of widowhood]; and I think [*dokō*] that I also have the Spirit of God [i.e., as I express this opinion]" (NASB). *Dokō* (from *dokeō*) has the idea of "deem," "suppose," or "be of the opinion that (such and such is the case)." It does not necessarily imply any uncertainty or unsureness on the part of the thinker; it simply emphasizes that that is his personal opinion or conviction. *Dokeō* implies nothing prejudicial to the soundness of the opinion held. For example, in John 5:39 Christ says to His hearers, "Search the Scriptures, for *you think* that in them you have eternal life." The *dokeite* ("you think") certainly does not suggest any uncertainty on Christ's part as to whether eternal life is to be found in the Holy Scriptures, for He unquestionably believed that it was. But He uses *dokeite* to emphasize that they themselves personally believed what was actually true.

Does 1 Corinthians 7:10–16 authorize divorce for desertion?

First Corinthians 7:10–16 deals primarily with the situation arising after one partner in a marriage relationship becomes a convert to the Christian faith but the other does not. Because of the complete change in outlook and ideals on the part of the newly saved spouse, sharp differences of opinion with the unsaved mate are bound to arise. Because of a desire to lead a holy life, the new Christian may be tempted to feel that it would be better to split up with his or her spouse and thus terminate the problems arising from disagreements and misunderstanding that divide the home.

It is in this light that we are to understand vv.10–13, which direct the Christian husband not to send away (*aphienai*) his unconverted wife and the Christian wife not to "leave" (*chōris-thēnai apo*, lit., "be separated from")

her unbelieving husband. In other words, the initiative for separation must always come from the unsaved mate, not from the Christian. The apostle points out that the unbeliever comes under the special influence of the Holy Spirit as long as they both live under the same roof; in that sense the pagan mate is "sanctified" by the Christian partner. First Peter 3:1–2 suggests how this pressure is exerted on the conscience of the unbeliever by the new walk or the transformed life of the believer: "In the same way, you wives, be submissive to your own husbands so that even if any of them are disobedient to the word they may be won without a word by the behavior of their wives, as they observe your chaste and respectful behavior" (NASB).

Second, the apostle points out that if the children of this spiritually divided home have even one parent who is a true believer, they come into a special relationship with God that constitutes them as "holy" (*hagia*), instead of defiled or unclean (*akatharta*), as the children of unbelievers necessarily are (1 Cor. 7:15). In other words, they are eligible to be received into a covenant relationship with God (through dedication or infant baptism) as already belonging to Him. Not that such children are already born again, but they belong to the Lord in the same way that Isaac belonged to the Lord when Abraham had him circumcised one week after he was born (Gen. 17:12; 21:4), (Note that Ishmael also was circumcised as a thirteen year old, but he seems to have wandered away from the Lord when he grew up and may possibly have forfeited the benefits of the covenant; cf. Gen. 16:12).

What 1 Corinthians 7 teaches is that a spiritually divided household is not obliged to remain together under the same roof if there is such alienation or bitterness that the unsaved spouse no longer is willing to stick it out with his

Christian mate. Verse 15 says, "Yet if the unbelieving one leaves, let him leave; the brother or the sister [i.e., the Christian spouse] is not under bondage in such cases, but God has called us to peace" (NASB). In the following verse Paul points out that there is no ironclad guarantee that things will get better if the Christian partner elects to stay on and endure the persecution and abuse of the recalcitrant unbeliever. Even such self-sacrificial devotion may turn out to be completely unavailing, so far as the conversion of the unsaved mate is concerned.

This passage has given rise to much discussion in regard to the matter of divorce. Matthew 5:32 and 19:9 clearly establish "unchastity" (*porneia*) as a valid ground for divorce, for a marrige is dealt a deadly wound by adulterous relations with an outsider. But does 1 Corinthians 7 refer to divorce at all? Apparently not. The Matthew passages speak of remarriage after the original couple has broken up (under the law of Moses, the guilty party in such a case was to be executed by stoning, along with the paramour; cf. Lev. 20:10; Deut. 22:24). But 1 Corinthians 7 makes no reference to a second marriage on the part of the innocent partner. On the contrary, it says quite specifically in v.11: "But if she [the separated wife who is a Christian] does leave, let her *remain unmarried,* or else be reconciled to her husband" (italics mine, NASB). Unquestionably the same would be true of a husband who was compelled by his unconverted wife to leave her.

But the requirement to remain unmarried or to be reconciled to the same spouse again does not amount to a ground for divorce, at least not according to the law of Christ—which is of course final and binding for every practicing Christian. Separation is permitted, if the two cannot live together in harmony; but divorce is

definitely not permitted on the ground of desertion alone. It will normally happen that when such a separation has occurred and continues for a lengthy period of time, the unbelieving mate will obtain some sort of divorce under the provisions of the civil courts and will marry someone else. That, of course, would constitute adultery under the rule of Matthew 5:32 and 19:9; and the innocent party would then be free to marry again. But until that happens, no second marriage is possible without rejection of the authority of Christ. Mere desertion, by itself, is not a ground for divorce.

Two questions remain to be discussed in this connection. Suppose the unconverted spouse goes on for years without sexual involvement with another partner? Must the Christian husband or wife remain in a separated state? Suppose the children are at an age when they very much need a two-parent home in order to develop in a normal and healthy way? Such situations frequently occur, and they raise severe and anguishing problems. Often the option of marrying someone else who will be more congenial, or who is perhaps even a fellow believer, seems to be very attractive. Would it not result in more good than harm to take this easier way out, and thus benefit the children in their growth and development? The answer to this question is the same as in every other situation where it seems easier to solve a problem by doing what any unbeliever would do under the circumstances. The issue of full submission to the revealed will of God and complete trust in the faithfulness of God is really at stake here. Even more important than our achieving and maintaining the so-called happiness that worldlings consider to be the final yardstick of value is the test of faith and faithfulness to our Lord and Savior, Jesus Christ.

God has not called us to be happy,

but He has called us to follow Him, with all integrity and devotion. Hebrews 11:35 honors the memory of those Old Testament believers who "were tortured, not accepting their release, in order that they might obtain a better resurrection." Verses 36–38 refer to the terrible persecution and hardship that they had to endure for the Lord's sake; then v.39 states that "all these gained approval through their faith." None of them enjoyed what the world would call "happiness," but they did obtain something far more important: the "approval" of God. Surely this applies to living with the dismal disappointment and frustration of an unhappy marriage. The husband or wife who makes the best of a single-parent situation may be forfeiting happiness, but the favor and approval of Christ will in the end mean far more both to the believing parent—and even to the children as well—than resorting to a second-marriage alliance without scriptural grounds for divorce.

The second question has to do with a couple who were married and divorced before either came to know the Lord. If the divorce was not on the ground of adultery, or if both of them were involved in violation of their marriage vows, what then? Suppose one—or both—of them gets married to a second partner and then becomes a born-again believer? What should the new convert do? Should he or she endeavor to terminate the second marriage and persuade the original mate to patch up the first marriage once more? Suppose the original spouse will not consent to this, will the new Christian have to remain under a cloud of guilt the rest of his life? Not if he (or she) has made every effort to achieve restitution. (A converted robber would certainly be expected to repay his victim the full amount of his theft; likewise, a slanderer would certainly have to confess his lie and beg the forgiveness of the one he wronged prior to his conversion.)

In some instances, it appears that restitution might result in even greater wrong than the original offense. For example, if children have been born as a result of the second marriage, it would seem to work a grave injustice to them if a reversion to the original marriage partner were attempted. This would surely result in more harm than good. The only honorable option under such circumstances would seem to be faithfulness to the second marriage partner and an honest endeavor to bring up the children of the second marriage in the "nurture and admonition of the Lord." Yet those children would have to be informed sooner or later of the past mistakes of their parents and would need to be carefully instructed in Christ's own standards for marriage.

Even if the second marriage is preserved intact, however, the clear teaching of 1 Timothy 3:2 and 12 is that church officers, such as elders and deacons, must not be chosen from the ranks of believers who do not meet the test of "husband of one wife," for anyone appointed to such an office "must be above reproach." (Of course there is no reproach attached to the widower who marries again, provided he marries a widow or woman who is not divorced. Hence the requirement of being "husband of one wife" must be intended to exclude only men who have been divorced or who are polygamists.) Whereas a sincere Christian believer who has been remarried does not necessarily have a prescriptive right to church office as a minister, elder, or deacon, yet he may have a very worthy role of service to play in other areas of endeavor as a true follower of Christ. Churches or denominations that overlook this restriction (including all the other positive and negative requirements outlined in 1 Tim. 3:2–12) do so in disobedience to the Word of

God and will therefore have to forfeit His favor until the matter is properly rectified.

How can 1 Corinthians 10:8 be reconciled with Exodus 32:28?

First Corinthians 10:8 says, "We should not commit sexual immorality, as some of them did—and in one day twenty-three thousand of them died" (NIV). Exodus 32:28 says, "The Levites did as Moses commanded, and that day about three thousand of the people died." In the preceding verses of Exodus 32, we learn that the Levites had armed themselves to execute all the leaders in the festival of worship of the golden calf; and so Moses had summoned them in v.27, saying, "Go back and forth through the camp from one end to the other, each killing his brother and friend and neighbor." The "three thousand" were slain by the sword in this direct punitive action.

What Paul is referring to is the total number who perished that day, not only from the swords of the avenging Levites, but also from the terrible plague God sent on the camp: "And Yahweh struck the people with a plague because of what they did with the calf Aaron had made" (Exod. 32:35). The Exodus account does not give the number of slain by the plague, but 1 Corinthians 10:8 furnishes us with that total: twenty-three thousand. This presumably includes the three thousand slain by the sword, and leaves the total of twenty thousand for those who died by the plague itself. There is no confusion here with Numbers 25:8, which gives the total of those who died in the plague at Shittim as twenty-four thousand. Since 1 Corinthians 10:7 quotes from Exodus 32:6, there can be no doubt that Paul was referring to the episode of the golden calf, rather than the similar event at Shittim.

In 1 Corinthians 15:29 what is meant by baptism for the dead?

The matter under discussion in 1 Corinthians 15:16–32 is the validity of the Christian hope of the bodily resurrection of all true believers. Current philosophical opinion in intellectual Greek circles as well as among the Jewish Sadducees was that such a reconstitution of bodily form was impossible once physical death had occurred. The appearance of resurrected Old Testament believers in bodily form to many observers in Jerusalem after the death of Jesus on the cross (Matt. 27:52) was apparently dismissed as mere hallucination, spawned of credulous superstition. But throughout this paragraph the apostle shows that the bodily resurrection of believers in the end time is guaranteed by the bodily resurrection of Christ Himself.

It is in this context that Paul moves into a discussion of the personal application of this joyous prospect to the individual believer. As older Christians fell terminally ill and it became apparent that their departure was near, they would summon their loved ones to their bedside and urge those of them who were as yet unconverted to get right with God. "Before long I will have to leave you, my dear ones," the dying saint would say, "but I want to see you all again in heaven. Be sure you meet me there! Remember that no one may come to the Father except through a true and living faith in the Son. Give your heart to Jesus!"

As they would leave that bedside, deeply moved by this earnest admonition, many of those who were still uncommitted to Christ would give serious attention to the gospel invitation and receive Jesus as their Lord and Savior. Mindful of the exhortation of their now-departed loved one, they would prepare themselves for public confession and baptism according to the practice of their local church. As they finally took this fateful step in the presence of witnesses, they would in a very real sense be submitting to baptism "*for the sake of* the dead" (the preposition *hyper* is intended to mean "for the sake of" rather than "on behalf of" in this particular context)—even though their primary motivation would be to get right with God, as sinners in need of a Savior.

No first-century believer reading Paul's epistle could possibly have misinterpreted the expression *hyper tōn nekrōn* ("for the sake of the dead") to mean that the faith of a living believer could possibly be reckoned to the benefit of a dead unbeliever, whether he was genealogically related to him or not. Throughout Scripture it is clear that saving grace is granted to no one except the believer himself, on the basis of his personal faith. Faith can never be imputed from one person to another. But one who has been deeply impressed by the testimony of a dying saint may certainly be moved to join him in repentance, faith, and commitment to the Lord—in the joyous expectation of meeting that loved one in his glorified resurrection body. This, then, is what is implied by v.29:

"For what shall they do who are baptized for the sake of the dead? If dead people are really not raised up, why are they baptized for their sake?" Verse 30 carries on the same thought: "Why are we also subjected to danger every hour?" And then in v.31 he concludes: "If dead people are not raised [bodily from their graves], let us simply eat and drink, for tomorrow we die!"

In other words, if the hope of the bodily resurrection of believers is a delusion, then Christ Himself could not have risen bodily from the grave. And if He never rose from the grave, the entire gospel proclamation is a fraud; and there is no deliverance from sin, death, and hell. "If Christ was not raised, your faith is vain, you are yet in your sins" (v.17). Therefore the doctrine of bodily resurrection is not a matter of option for the Christian; it is the very essence of salvation. But that salvation is available only to those who personally respond with repentance and faith to the Master's call. There is no conversion by proxy. Such a teaching cannot be found in any part of Scripture, and it is completely at variance with what God's Word teaches about salvation.

Galatians

Did Moses receive the law only 430 years after Abraham?

Galatians 3:17 states: "The law, which came 430 years afterward [i.e., after God's covenant promises to Abraham] does not invalidate a covenant previously ratified by God, so as to make the promise void." This is by way of proof that the basis of God's covenant with Abraham and his seed was the promise of grace, not the merit of keeping the Mosaic law—even though the law was added in order to lead all sinners to Christ (vv.22–24). Actually there must have been closer to 645 years intervening between Abraham's migration from Haran at age 75 and the issuing of the Decalogue to Moses and the Israelites at Sinai. This would be 215 years more than the 430 that Paul refers to. Is this a real discrepancy? Not at all! There has simply been a misunderstanding as to the *terminus a quo* that Paul had in mind.

In Galatians 3:16 Paul referred to the promises made to Abraham in Genesis 13:15 (after he had returned from his sojourn in Egypt) and in Genesis 22:18 (after he had returned from Mount Moriah and the near sacrifice of his son Isaac: "And in your seed all the nations of the earth shall be blessed, because you have obeyed My voice" NASB). If Isaac was about twelve at the time of the near sacrifice, this particular renewal of the covenant promise must have occurred when Abraham was 112, or 37 years later than his migration from Haran. This factor makes it untenable to argue, as some have done, that Paul is simply relying on the unreliable Septuagint reading in Exodus 12:40 ("But the sojourn of the sons of Israel that they sojourned in Egypt *and in Canaan* was 430 years"). The insertion of "and in Canaan" takes in the 215 years between Abraham's departure from Haran and Jacob's migration to Egypt in 1876 B.C. Paul had just referred to the "promises," including quite specifically one reaffirmed 37 years later than Abraham's first arrival in Canaan. Hence there would be no way in which the figure 430 would apply.

The real solution is not far to seek. Paul is contrasting the two main stages in the history of Abraham's race: the age of promise and the age of law. The promises of the covenant of grace were repeated several times to Abraham, to Isaac, and to Jacob as well. Essentially these later covenant renewals were identical with the original pronouncements in Genesis 12, with only minor variations from Abraham to Jacob. In fact, the final appearance of God to Jacob in order to reaffirm the Abrahamic promise took place just before Jacob left Canaan for Egypt in 1876 (cf. Gen. 46:2–4). Therefore the total of 430 years was very accurate indeed, and the rendezvous between Israel and Yahweh at Mount Sinai occurred at precisely that interval of time. There is no discrepancy whatever.

Ephesians

Is Ephesians 4:8 a misquotation from Psalm 68:18?

Ephesians 4:8 quotes Psalm 68:18 (19 Heb.) as follows: "Therefore it says: 'Ascending on high, He led captivity captive, He gave [*edōken*] gifts to men.'" But the Hebrew text reads a bit differently: "You did ascend ['*ālîtā*] on high; You did lead captivity captive [*šābîtā šebî*]; you did take/bring/fetch [*lāqaḥtā*] gifts among men." Is this a purposely slanted translation? Was this a deliberate tampering with the Old Testament original in a way incompatible with treating it as inerrant and authoritative? Some have argued that this is the case. But they have not sufficiently considered the context of the Psalms passage, nor have they taken into account the implications of the words interpreted in the New Testament adaptation.

Interestingly enough, Paul is not following the Septuagint rendering here, as if he had not checked with the Hebrew original. On the contrary, the Septuagint quite literally translates *lāqaḥtā* ("You did take") as *elabes*. It is actually the Aramaic Targum, the traditional interpretation of orthodox Jewry, that interprets the Hebrew *lāqaḥtā* as *yᵉhabtā* "You have given"). In other words, the implication of "You have taken-brought" the gifts was in order that they might be conferred on men; not that God was to keep them

for Himself ("as if He needed anything" from men's hands—as Paul pointed out in Acts 17:25), but rather gifts in the hands of the Lord are there for the purpose of bestowal on men. Thus the Targum brings out what is implied by the Hebrew verb, especially in connection with *bā'ādām*, "among men"—i.e., to be bestowed *among* men. This last phrase the Targum interprets as referring to the recipients of these gifts from God and simpllifies the wording as *libᵉnê nāšā'* ("to the sons of men").

Paul also follows the Targum in this—which constitutes significant evidence, by the way, of the antiquity of the interpretative oral tradition that preceded the written form of the Targum (in the third century A.D.). As one trained in the graduate school of Gamaliel, Paul would have been familiar with this Targumic rendition of Psalm 68:18. (Here again, the Septuagint quite literally follows the Masoretic text: *en anthrōpois* ["among men"].) Jamieson, Fausset, and Brown (*Commentary*, ad loc.) make the following comment concerning the Ephesian passage: "That is, Thou hast received gifts to distribute among men—as a conqueror distributes in token of his triumph the spoils of foes as donatives among his people. The impartation of the gifts and graces of the Spirit depended upon Christ's ascension."

We may properly regard this New

Testament quotation from the Hebrew Old Testament as an example of an interpretative rendering that is within the scope of its connotative meaning, drawing out its implications in a way appropriate to the point under discussion in the New Testament context.

Colossians

Does Colossians 1:20 teach that all people will be saved?

Colossians 1:19-20 (NIV) reads: "For God was pleased to have all his fullness dwell in him, and through him [i.e., Jesus Christ] to reconcile to himself all things, whether things on earth or things in heaven, by making peace through his blood, shed on the cross." The question arises, if God was pleased to reconcile all to Himself, both in earth and in heaven, does it not follow that all men without distinction are in fact saved, through the Incarnation and the atoning death of Christ? This is the way it has been interpreted by universalists down through the ages, and it is certainly a question the church has to deal with carefully in the light of all other passages that pertain to the objects of Christ's salvation.

It would immediately follow from the universalist position that if Christ died to save all people without distinction, these consequences would ensue:

1. Faith is completely unnecessary; for Christ's atoning blood would avail for the redemption of all men, whether or not they respond to God's call, whether or not they repent and believe, and whether or not they forsake sin and their loyal service of Satan and all the evil he stands for.

2. Hell never had any occupants in it, has none at present, and never will have; and all Scriptures that speak of unsaved sinners suffering torment in hell are completely mistaken.

3. If the reconciliation spoken of in Colossians 1:20 be understood as guaranteeing the ultimate salvation of everyone, even the unrepentant who die in their sins, whatever punishment there may be in hell amounts to a mere temporary chastisement more or less equivalent to the Roman Catholic purgatory, which purgatory however will give way to a complete emptying of the abode of the damned, all of whom will be transferred to heaven, without any distinction between those who rejected Christ and those who surrendered their heart and life to Him.

4. Thus interpreted, Colossians 1:20 and all similar passages lead to the result that God does not make any permanent difference between good and evil, since no ultimate distinction is made in His actual treatment of those who honor His moral law and those who despise and reject it. This can only mean, then, that there is no genuine difference between right and wrong; and there is no moral dimension to human life or experiences except that which is temporary, illusory, and subjective. Furthermore, there was no necessity for the Bible or for revelation or for the divine offer of

forgiveness and grace. Forgiveness and grace automatically devolve on every living soul, no matter how he may despise them and abhor them, and no matter how cordially he abominates God Himself and everything that is good and holy.

All these consequences unavoidably ensue from such an interpretation of Colossians 1:20. If the sacrifice of Christ means the reconciliation of all moral agents of all ages, whether in heaven or on earth, whether or not they repent and believe, then there is no reality to divine justice (except insofar as Christ suffered for sin on the cross); and heaven will swarm with hate-filled, blaspheming, God-despising, Christ-mocking degenerates, who will condemn as fools all those who in this life ever denied themselves anything that they wanted for themselves, just for the sake of moral scruples. In such a heaven Satan will reign supreme, for his cause will be magnificently vindicated.

To this horrible spectacle of hell in heaven, the traditional universalist will object that he had no such thing in mind. What he meant was that by the temporary sufferings of a transient hell, all the wicked who go there will be transformed into saints. In the excruciating torments of their sojourn in the abode of the damned, they will learn to love God; they will come to a sincere hatred for sin; and they will surrender their hearts to Christ without any admixture of a self-seeking motive (such as a desire to escape the torments of hell). To articulate this idea is to expose its utter absurdity. In this life, for instance, with the constantly available influence of the Holy Spirit, criminals consigned to earthly prisons do not experience a real change of heart through the punishment imposed on them by the courts of this world. Rather, in the end they only come out more hardened in sin and hopeful of escaping future punishment as they continue their lives of crime more cleverly than before. Therefore, what possibility is there that totally without the available influence of the Holy Spirit (who alone can bring about regeneration in sinners' hearts), the wicked serving out their sentence in hell can ever come to a change of heart toward God or toward the moral law?

In Revelation 16:8–10 we read of the true reaction of fallen man toward divine punishment:

> The fourth angel poured out his bowl on the sun, and the sun was given power to scorch people with fire. They were seared by the intense heat and they cursed the name of God, who had control over these plagues, but they refused to repent or glorify him. The fifth angel poured out his bowl on the throne of the beast, and his kingdom was plunged into darkness. Men gnawed their tongues in agony and cursed the God of heaven because of their pains and their sores, but they refused to repent of what they had done (NIV).

If this is the response of the unconverted heart of fallen man while still here on earth, what prospect is there that in the agonies of hell the punishment or suffering will lead to any true repentance or reconciliation with God? None whatever!

No matter how long an unbeliever rots or writhes in hell, he will never come to the breaking point, so far as his opposition to God is concerned. No amount of suffering will ever change his mind or lead to his purification from an evil heart. Hence the entire premise behind a purgatory is false, for it overlooks the incorrigible nature of the hardened, sinful heart. He who has denied and rejected Christ to the end of his earthly life can never learn to love Him and believe in Him in the hate-filled atmosphere of hell, or in the lake of fire that he will share with

Satan as his eternal abode (Rev. 20:10; 21:8).

The Lord Jesus was very clear in His teaching concerning the endless torment of the damned. "Then he will say to those on his left, 'Depart from me, you who are cursed, into the eternal fire prepared for the devil and his angels" (Matt. 25:41, NIV). This chapter closes with the same concept of eternity for both the redeemed and the lost: "Then they will go away to eternal punishment, but the righteous to eternal life" (v.46). Note that the same word *aiōnios* is used for both classes— even as it is used of everlasting life in John 3:16. There is no way of scaling down *aiōnios* to mean something less than endless eternity (as universalists attempt to do) so far as the torment of hell is concerned without also reducing "eternal life" to something temporary and the abode of the redeemed in heaven to something transient.

In other words, Scripture teaches that both the life of Christ in heaven and the torment of the damned in hell are equally "eternal." Jesus said, "I am the first and the last, and the living One; and I was dead, and behold, I am alive forevermore [*eis tous aiōnas tōn aiōnōn*]" (Rev. 1:17–18, NASB). Compare this with Revelation 20:10: "And the devil who deceived them was thrown into the lake of fire and brimstone, where the beast and the false prophet are also; and they will be tormented day and night forever and ever [*eis tous aiōnas tōn aiōnōn*]." This describes the ultimate abode of all the unsaved, according to Revelation 21:8 ("the lake which burns with fire and brimstone, which is the second death"). The endless nature of this damnation completely excludes the theory of universalism and exposes it as a denial of the truth of Scripture.

So far as the moral objection of the universalists to eternal hell is concerned, it is only necessary to point out that once any human being has been created by God, he is created in the *image* of God (Gen. 1:27), a God who never passes away. Therefore, as an ever-existing person, every human being must carry on his conscious existence somewhere in the universe, whether in heaven or in hell (the Bible mentions no other possibility beyond these two abodes). Since the nonelect have misused their free will to remain in a state of rebellion against God and refuse His call to repentance and a new life, there is nothing left for them but endless eternity in the home they have chosen, the abode of Satan himself.

There is no possibility of repentance and change of heart for the sinner in hell; for the Scripture tells us, "It is appointed for men to die once, and after this the judgment" (Heb. 9:27). Once the Lord closed the door on Noah and his family in the safety of the ark (Gen. 7:16), there was no longer any possibility for any of the rest of Noah's generation to enter it and be delivered from the Great Flood. They had scoffed at his warnings for 120 years, while Noah vainly urged them to repent and take refuge in the one way of deliverance that God had provided. Once the door was shut and the skies opened up with their death-dealing rain, it was too late for anyone to change his mind. His doom was unalterably sealed. It could not be otherwise.

Nor is it a valid objection to the goodness of God to raise the common protest, How can a good God condemn anyone to eternal hell? If God is good, He must be on the side of justice, right, and truth. Neither righteousness nor justice could ever allow the guilt of rebellion against an infinite God to be atoned for by a temporary stay in hell, where there is neither repentance nor change of heart (for the reasons that we have considered above), and from which only those could be released who still have hell in their hearts, and who by their presence in heaven would

only turn it into a den of discord and misery. We must therefore reply to the universalist challenge that a good God can do nothing else but condemn the unrepentant who die in their sins to endless confinement in hell. For Him to do anything short of that would put Him on the side of injustice and destroy the sanction of the moral law.

What, then, is the correct interpretation of Colossians 1:20? What is meant by God's reconciling all things to Himself through Christ? In this context it is apparent that alienation and division have taken place between heaven and earth, and the "thrones, dominions, rulers, and authorities" (v.16), both the visible and the invisible, are divided into opposing camps: those who are completely loyal to God and live for His glory, and those not truly submitted to Him. Furthermore, there is a certain hostility between God's angels in heaven and the disobedient, Satan-serving race of Adam on earth. The only way the just demands of the broken law of God can be satisfied is by the shed blood of Jesus on the cross and by His resurrection victory as the covenant Head of a new race, the family of the redeemed. Only through Christ can all these opposing forces be reconciled and brought into harmony with one another, as all bow their knee in submission to Him (Phil. 2:10) in the final day of His coronation in the presence of all the universe, "when every knee shall bow and every tongue confess, that Jesus Christ is Lord, to the glory of God the Father."

It is against this background that we are to understand the phrase *di' autou*

apokatallaxai ta panta eis auton ("through Him to reconcile all things unto Himself"—that is, unto His sovereign authority). In that day Satan's power will be crushed, all resistance from the rebellious world will be completely broken, and all will unite in confessing that Christ is Lord. *Ta panta* implies that all intelligent moral creatures, wherever they live and to whatever realm they belong, will unite in this confession of His absolute sovereignty.

In the case of demonic powers and the denizens of Satan's kingdom, the confession of Christ as Lord will be in the nature of a reluctant admission of fact, rather than a surrender of their heart and life to Him. That is, they will acknowledge that Jesus is the Almighty Sovereign, whether they like it or not (even Satan and his demons acknowledged Jesus' divine messiahship during His earthly ministry). The victory things will be reconciled to God through Christ. The day of opportunity to rebel and defy the Lord will be over. Both the saved and the unsaved will acknowledge themselves to be under His authority and will submit to His power. The angels of heaven will rejoice in perfect harmony with all of God's redeemed from among the human race, all tensions and barriers having been removed by the Cross and the resurrection of the great Mediator, whom God the Father has appointed to be the heir of all things (Heb. 1:2-3). It is in this sense that He will "reconcile to Himself all things . . . on earth and in heaven, by making peace through His blood."

2 Thessalonians

If God condemns all liars to the lake of fire (Rev. 21:8), how was it that He put a lying spirit in the mouths of the prophets of Ahab (1 Kings 22:23) or a deluding influence of men in the last days so that they believe what is false (2 Thess. 2:11)?

The answer to this question is found in the verses preceding, that is, 2 Thessalonians 2:9–10, which speak of the coming of the "lawless one" (i.e., Antichrist) "with all power and signs and false wonders, and with all the deception of wickedness for those who perish, because they did not receive the love of truth so as to be saved" (NASB). In other words, God turns over to the baneful influence of Satan, the Prince of Lies, those who have of their own free will chosen not to listen to the truth but who by preference cleave to error. God furnishes no guarantee that He will disabuse sinners of error if they really prefer error to the truth. There is no reason why He should.

As for the prophets of Ahab who falsely predicted victory for him if he should attempt the recapture of Ramoth-gilead from the Syrians, he fell into this same category. He did not want to know the truth of God; he hated and opposed God's moral law wherever it went counter to his own will. Therefore he could expect no guidance from God in the matter of besieging Ramoth-gilead. Ahab's time had run out. His confiscation of the vineyard of Naboth on the basis of a trumped-up charge for which Naboth was stoned to death was a crime for which he had to pay. Therefore the decision of God and His angels in heavenly conference—as Micaiah plainly told Ahab in the presence of Jehoshaphat—was to send a lying spirit to incline the whole pack of court prophets to give Ahab the same encouragement to march into a battle that would cost him his life (1 Kings 22:18–23).

The faith in a lie that God permitted or even encouraged in each of these cases simply represented the outworking of the moral law. If men refuse the true God, they will have to make do with a false idol of their own devising. If they reject the truth, they must be content to feed on falsehood.

1 Timothy

Does 1 Timothy 2:12 forbid the ordination of women?

First Timothy 2:11-12 lays down this principle: "Let a woman learn in silence [*hēsychia*] with all submission [*hypotagē*]; I do not permit a woman to teach or exercise authority over [*authentein*] a man, but to be in silence [or 'quietness' *hēsychia*]." The reason for the distinction between men and women in the matter of leadership in the church and in the home is then grounded on the relationship between man and woman established at the very beginning (vv.13-14): "For Adam was created first, afterwards [*eita*] Eve. And Adam was not deceived, but the woman, having been quite deceived [*exapatētheisa*] became involved in transgression. But she shall be saved [*sōthēsetai* from *sōzein*, which here implies that woman is saved or redeemed from the disadvantage or reproach of having been the first to succumb to the wiles of Satan's temptation at the Fall] through childbearing, if they [i.e., child-bearing women—or even all women, as potential child-bearers] abide in faith and love and sanctification with sobriety [*sōphrosynē*, which implies 'moderation,' 'good judgment,' 'self-control,' 'chastity,' or 'self-restraint']." (*Sōthēsetai* must not be taken out of context as meaning that a child-bearing woman is saved by her good work of bringing a new life into the world; for her it is just as true as it

is for a man, that salvation from sin and death is bestowed only by grace through faith, as Eph. 2:8-9 clearly teaches.)

Here we have a very clear principle of subordination of woman to man in the structure of the church as an organized body and in the family as a team in a household. God intends that the responsibility of leadership devolve on man rather than woman in both cases. Yet both man and woman are equally precious and worthy before God (Gal. 3:27-28), and the assigned level of responsibility does not give to men any special advantage or any inherently higher status before God than is granted to women.

The following teachings emerge from this passage:

1. There is a distinction between what is permitted for men and what is permitted for women. By implication, since women are expressly forbidden to teach men (i.e., fellow believers in the congregation who are men) in an authoritative way (*didaskein* and *authentein* seem to be intended as a combined concept and describe the function of the teaching elder or minister of the gospel, who instructs and exhorts a congregation from the pulpit), that which is not permitted to women is permitted to men. It seems to this writer that this dictum cannot be re-

worked so as to make it mean that women are granted the same privilege and status as men. (Some of those who attempt to do so are in danger of violating the rights of language and reducing Scripture to a plastic medium that can be interpreted to mean anything the interpreter may choose. Willful manipulation of the plain sense of Scripture must be regarded as tantamount to a denial of the objective authority of Scripture.)

2. On the other hand, this verse does not prohibit women from teaching individual men on a personal basis (as Priscilla—along with her husband Aquila—taught Apollos the way of God more accurately [Acts 18:26]. Nor does it forbid women to "prophesy" in a respectful and submissive manner (symbolized by keeping a covering over their heads in church meetings [1 Cor. 11:5-6]) and to address fellow believers—male and female—to their "edification, exhortation, and comfort" (1 Cor. 14:3 so defines "prophecy").

Indeed, there is a wide scope of opportunity afforded to women who have such a gift; all four daughters of Philip the evangelist were likewise endowed with the *charisma* of prophecy (Acts 21:9). Undoubtedly they spearheaded the Christian outreach to women who could not be contacted in public meeting places but could be evangelized in their homes—along with the younger children, no doubt. An apostolic pattern for Bible study and prayer groups in the home was set by Lydia at Philippi, who was Paul's first European convert. Not only at the "laundromat" by the river but also in her own home she promoted evangelism with all who would consent to enter her house (Acts 16:14,40). And she made the most of Paul's presence in it (along with Silas and his other team members) to introduce her guests to Jesus. Such examples as these show clearly enough that the Lord uses gifted and godly women in the winning of souls and even in the instruction of young and old (males as well as females) in following the way of the Lord. This furnishes ample warrant for that noble army of female missionaries (both the married and the unmarried) whom God has so mightily used in the spread of the gospel in pioneer mission fields all over the world.

3. Nevertheless, it remains a clear mandate in God's Word that in an established church situation women workers, no matter how gifted and talented, are not to have ecclesiastical authority over men. Women are to be helpers in the work of the church, but they are not to have the authority of ordained ministers or pastors in the leadership of the work of the local church. First Timothy 2:12 clearly precludes this, and Christ's example of calling twelve male apostles and sending out seventy others to evangelize the cities of Palestine furnishes a clear and authoritative pattern along this line. This must be observed, even though it is also true that Christ first appeared to Mary Magdalene and her two companions right after His resurrection, before He appeared to any of the men. This distinction must be maintained even though it is true that Paul made very large use of helpers like Lydia (Acts 16), Phoebe (Rom. 16:1-2), Euodia and Syntyche (Phil. 4:2-3), and spoke of their sterling service in terms of highest praise and appreciation. (Some have construed the term *prostatis* applied to Phoebe in Rom. 16:2 as equivalent to "one who presides over an assembly." But no such meaning is demonstrable for New Testament times; rather, it means "helper," "assistant," or "patroness," "protector." Not even the

masculine form *prostatēs* ever means "president" in New Testament usage but only "defender," "guardian," "helper" [cf. Arndt and Gingrich, *Greek-English Lexicon*, p. 726].)

4. In this paragraph a clear correlation is made between woman's subordination in the matter of church order and her subordination to her husband in the home. Even though the wife may be far more gifted and advanced in matters of Scripture teaching and in godliness of life and purpose, nevertheless she has been assigned by God to a subordinate position under the authority of her husband. The husband is invested with the responsibility of ultimate decision in matters of the home (even though he cannot ever usurp the unique authority of Christ in matters of his wife's faith or her personal relationship to God). His authority must be respected at all times, except that he may not set aside the supreme authority of God Himself when he wishes his wife to commit sin or throw off her allegiance to Christ. This last proviso is clearly implied in Ephesians 5:22–24; "Wives, be subject to your own husbands as unto the Lord. For the husband is the head of the wife, as Christ also is the head of the church. . . . But as the church is subject to Christ, so also the wives ought to be to their own husbands in everything."

While it is true that v.21 says, "Be subject to one another in the fear of Christ," this may not be so construed as to negate the teaching of vv.22–24, which spell out the subordinate role of wife to husband. At the same time, v.22 does suggest that there are very important areas in which the husband is to subject himself to his wife, receiving her as a precious treasure from Christ, for which he shall be held strictly accountable. Among these areas—

apart from the obvious commitment to marital fidelity—would be phases of the operation of the household in which he recognizes that her competence is greater than his own, or in which he sees that her involvement is even greater than his own.

It should be pointed out, moreover, that the demand Ephesians 5:25–33 makes on the husband is far greater than that which it makes on the wife. She is to "be subject" (*hypotassesthai* is used of being assigned to a specific post in an army or team, subject to the chain of command by which the whole unit is governed) to her husband, and she is to "reverence" him (*phobeisthai*, lit., "fear"). But the husband is commanded to love her "just as Christ also loved the church [not because it was worthy of Him, satisfied His needs, or appreciated Him enough—but even if it was far from perfect and needed much patience to put up with] and gave Himself up for her" (NASB). That is a far heavier assignment than that of the wife, and no man should ever cite this chapter by way of admonition or rebuke to his wife until he has first made sure to fulfill his own role as it is there set forth. He is to love her as Christ loves His church!

If, then, the subordinate position of woman to man in the economy of the home and the church precludes the ordination of women—as it most certainly does—what can be said of female elders or female deacons? Some have suggested that the reference to *presbyteras* (feminine plural accusative) in 1 Timothy 5:2 points to a woman elder, inasmuch as the masculine form *presbyter* is regularly used for an "elder" in the ecclesiastical sense. But this interpretation cannot be maintained in such a passage as this, which clearly refers to all fellow church members, including older men, older women, younger men, and younger women; the matter at issue is the respectful or brotherly attitude Timothy is to maintain toward each of these groups. This has nothing to do with church officers. The same observation applies to the "widows" (*khērai*) who are spoken of in vv.3–6. These "widows" are unlikely to have had any status as governors of the church. It is simply a matter of what kind of widows are to be put on the relief roll of the church, not all and sundry, but only those who are at least sixty years old, have lived with the same husband until widowhood, have led a life of good works, are avoiding offense in their present conduct, and have no children or grandchildren to support them.

The same applies to the passage in Titus 2, which discusses the role to be played by the young and the old of both sections. The *presbytidas* (feminine plural accusative) referred to in v.3 can hardly be women elders in the ecclesiastical sense, for they are surveyed along with young women (*neās*) and young men (*neōterous*—masculine plural accusative) as to virtues they should especially cultivate and vices they are especially to avoid. There is therefore no real ground for regarding either *presbyterai* or *presbytidas* as women elders.

In the case of deacons, however, there is a good case that can be made out for deaconesses at least, whether or not they were put on the same level as male deacons. It seems quite clear in Romans 16:1 that Paul regarded Phoebe as a *diakonos:* "I commend you to Phoebe our sister, being a servant [or 'deacon'—*diakonon*] of the church in Cenchrea, that you may receive her in the Lord, in a manner worthy of saints, and may assist her in whatever matter she has need of." Arndt and Gingrich (*Greek-English Lexicon,* p. 184) unhesitatingly classify this occurrence as a genuine instance (the only clear

one in the New Testament) of a female deacon. Others are cited in Hermas's *Vision* (2.4.3) and *Similitude* (9.26.2) (second century A.D.).

The ecclesiastical term for deaconess (*diakonissa*) never occurs in the New Testament, and so this single reference to *diakonor* in the feminine is unique in the Greek Scripture. This would indicate that so far as the apostolic church was concerned, a woman deacon was very exceptional, even though allowable. The original seven deacons referred to in Acts 6:5–6 were certainly all men; and they were set apart for their holy office by prayer and the laying on of hands, after they had been elected by the congregation. There is no way of being sure whether Phoebe was thus formally ordained in the same fashion by the Cenchrean church; but if Paul was using the term ecclesiastically (rather than in the general sense of "servant"), she very likely was.

We close with a fine comment from Elisabeth Elliot:

> Supreme authority in both Church and home has been divinely vested in the male as the representative of Christ, who is the Head of the Church. It is in willing and glad submission rather than grudging capitulation that the woman in the Church (whether married or single) and the wife in the home find their fulfillment ("Why I Oppose the Ordination of Women," *Christianity Today* 880 [1975]: 14).

Earlier in that same essay, she made the following significant observation:

> The modern cult of personality makes submission a degrading thing. We are told we cannot be "whole persons" if we submit. Obedience is thought of as restrictive and therefore bad. "Freedom" is defined as the absence of restraint, quite the opposite from the scriptural principle embodied in Jesus' words, "If you continue in my words, then are ye my disciples, and ye shall know the truth,

and the truth shall make you free." Freedom in God's view always lies on the far side of discipline, which means obedience. . . . To attempt to apply democratic ideals to the kingdom of God, which is clearly hierarchical, can result only in a loss of power and ultimately in destruction. Christ Himself, the Servant and Son, accepted limitation and restriction. He subjected Himself. He learned obedience (ibid., p. 13).

2 Timothy

Does 2 Timothy 3:16 really teach that all Scripture is inerrant?

As usually translated, this verse means, "All Scripture *is* inspired by God and is profitable for doctrine, etc." Thus it is rendered by KJV, RSV, NASB, and virtually every other English version except RV and ASV, which render the adjective *theopneustos* ("God-breathed" or "inspired by God") as attributive rather than predicate. Their wording is "Every scripture inspired of God *is* also profitable for teaching, etc." Yet even they supply as a marginal reading "Every scripture *is* inspired of God, and profitable...."

So far as I am aware, no twentieth-century English translation has followed RV and ASV in rendering *theopneustos* as an attributive adjective, whether their translators were liberal or conservative in their theological outlook. The reason for this is that no other instance can be found in New Testament Greek where an attributive adjective is connected with a predicate adjective by means of a *kai* ("and"). The verb "to be" is omitted in this clause; therefore it must be supplied either before or after *theopneustos*. But since *theopneustos* is followed by *kai* and a second adjective, *ōphelimos*, which everyone agrees is predicate, it necessarily follows that *theopneustos* also is predicate. Hence the only legitimate translation is "All Scripture [or

'Every Scripture'] *is* God-breathed and profitable..."

As for the subject of this clause, *pasa graphē*, there is some question as to whether it should be rendered "All Scripture (as KJV, NASB, Williams, Beck, RSV), or whether, because the definite article is lacking, it should be rendered "Every Scripture." Normally the idea of collective inclusion in Greek is conveyed with the definite article (e.g., "all the world" is *pas ho kosmos, ho* being the masculine form of the definite article). Or again, "all the city" would be *pasa hē polis;* whereas *pasa polis* would mean "every city." In this context "Every Scripture" might fit in very well, for the *graphē* follows after a clear reference to the Hebrew Bible in v.15: "From infancy you have known the Holy Writings [*ta hiera grammata*], which are able to make you wise unto salvation through the faith that is in Christ." Then comes our verse: "All/ Every Scripture is God-breathed and profitable."

The important thing to observe is that nowhere throughout the New Testament is *graphē* (whether with or without the definite article) used of uninspired and nonauthoritative writings of any sort. It is specialized in the New Testament to mean either the Hebrew Bible, with its thirty-nine books as we have them today (for copies of all thirty-nine of them survive from Christ's time and from centuries be-

416

fore, and we can be certain of this), or else the New Testament writings like the Epistles of Paul (2 Peter 3:16—*tas loipas graphas*). It would never have occurred to the Greek-speaking recipients of 2 Timothy to suppose that Paul could be referring to any other writings but the inspired and authoritative books of the Hebrew canon. Nor is there the slightest suggestion in any of the recorded utterances of Jesus Christ or His apostles—or indeed in any of the writings of the New Testament authors—that there were any portions of the Hebrew Scriptures that were *not* authoritative and inspired. Therefore we must categorically reject the RV-ASV rendering as inaccurate and misleading, for "Every scripture inspired of God" suggests that there are some portions of the Bible that were not inspired—and that is a view completely foreign to the authors of the New Testament. (For further discussion and evidence on this point, consult the introductory article of this book entitled "The Importance of Biblical Inerrancy" and its subsection "Without Inerrancy the Scriptures Cannot be Infallible.")

One final comment may be made on *theopneustos*, translated "inspired of God," "given by inspiration of God," or "God-breathed." The last of these is of course the most literal. *Theopneustos* is a very strong word for "inspired," for it implies that God in a very personal way controlled and guided the human authors of Scripture in such a way that they wrote down just exactly what God intended them to write. He "breathed" on them, as it were, and they were impelled in the direction He wanted them to go—just as we read in 2 Peter 1:20, that "every prophecy of Scripture" (*pasa prophēteia graphēs*) is not a matter of private or personal interpretation, "for not by the will of man was prophecy ever brought, but being carried along [*pheromenoi* suggests a sailboat driven by the breeze] by the Holy Spirit men spoke from God" (lit. rendering of the Nestle Greek text). Such passages make it clear that the authors of Scripture wrote under the influence, guidance, and control of God Himself. There is therefore no possible way by which error could have crept into the original manuscripts of Holy Writ—unless God Himself was guilty of mistake or deceit (as Satan first claimed in Gen. 3:4-5, when he led our first parents to spiritual death and despair). God breathed it forth and guaranteed it all with His own faithfulness and integrity.

Hebrews

Could Jesus have yielded to temptation to sin?

Hebrews 2:17–18 reads concerning Jesus: "For this reason he had to be made like his brothers in every way [*kata panta*], in order that he might become a merciful and faithful high priest in service to God, and that he might make atonement for the sins of the people. Because he himself suffered when he was tempted, he is able to help those who are being tempted" (NIV). This passage indicates that Jesus really came under temptation in the way that any child of Adam is confronted with temptation, for "he was made like his brothers in every way." He would not have been made like His fellow men if He had not been capable of yielding to the temptation—any more than a hippopotamus can be said to be tempted to fly through the air.

Apart from ability to yield to the temptation to sin, there is no temptation at all. There has to be a deliberate decision to reject what has attractiveness and appeal of some sort to the person attacked by temptation. When man is tempted, he must be confronted by something that requires him to choose between compliance or refusal. Therefore we must conclude that unless Hebrews 2:18 is in error, Jesus Christ had the ability to give in to the temptations that Satan directed against Him. Otherwise He would not have been tempted "like his brothers in *every way*."

A little further on we read in Hebrews 4:15: "For we do not have a high priest who is unable to sympathize with our weaknesses, but we have one who has been tempted in every way, just as we are—yet was without sin" (NIV). The last phrase inserts "was" in order to clarify the obvious intention of the Greek phrase *chōris hamartiās* ("without sin"). KJV omits the "was" and renders the phrase "yet without sin." But even if the "was" is omitted, the basic meaning remains the same; it is no sin to be tempted, but it is sin if we yield to temptation. The consideration added by this last verse is the element of "sympathy," i.e., the ability to understand the feelings of the one tempted and feel compassion toward him during his crisis. If Christ had been utterly incapable of sin, even as the Son of Man, then it is hard to see how He could have felt sympathy for sinners.

On the other hand, there is another sense in which we may say that Christ was incapable of sin, and that is in the psychological sense. When the patriot says, "I could never betray my country to its foes," or "I could never be unfaithful to my dear wife," he is speaking not of a physical inability but of a psychological inability. He has no personal desire to commit the evil he is being solicited to do; in fact, he finds it repellant and distasteful, not so much the act in itself, but the evil consequences that would ensue from that act. Because Jesus was completely in love with His heavenly Father, He could never have brought Himself to grieve Him or go counter to His known will.

Can a born-again believer ever be lost?

Two passages in the Epistle to the Hebrews come up for discussion in connection with this challenge to the doctrine of the preservation of the saints taught in John 10:28; these two passages are Hebrews 6:4-6 and Hebrews 10:26-31. Both teach that a professing believer is capable of turning against the Lord Jesus after he has avowedly taken Him as his Savior. But the question at issue is whether either of these paragraphs has in view a truly regenerate believer.

Hebrews 6:4-6 is well rendered by NIV: "It is impossible for those who have once been enlightened [hapax phōtisthentas], who have tasted the heavenly gift, who have shared [metochous genēthentas] in the Holy Spirit, who have tasted the goodness of the Word of God and the powers of the coming age, if they fall away, to be brought back to repentance, because to their loss they are crucifying the Son of God all over again and subjecting him to public disgrace." Let us examine point by point the description that is given of this apostate.

1. He has been enlightened or illuminated by a clear presentation of the gospel and its invitation to repent and believe. Apparently he has made a profession of faith and has reached out to Christ as his Savior.
2. He has tasted of the heavenly gift (dōrea, which is not the same as charisma, "spiritual gift"); that is, he has had a part in the activity of the church, the joyous fellowship of other Christians in the worship and service of the Lord, and has even seen a response to his testimony and appeal at public meetings.
3. He has tasted the goodness of the Word of God. That is, he has come to a clear understanding of the message of Scripture and has mentally and intellectually approved it and appreciated the faithful and earnest presentation of it on the part of preachers from the pulpit.
4. He has even tasted of the powers of the coming age—just as Judas Iscariot did, when he came back with the other eleven, exuberantly exulting that in the course of their two-by-two evangelistic campaigns even the demons were subject to them as they preached the Lord Jesus (Luke 10:17). Evidently Judas was so completely involved with them in this effort that, even at the eve of Christ's betrayal by him in the Garden of Gethsemane, none of his colleagues suspected the treachery he had in mind during their Passover meal. (We know this because they had to ask one another around the table, "Lord, is it I?" [Mark 14:19]. They could not tell even then whom Jesus had in mind as His betrayer.)

For that matter, all of the first three qualities were true of Judas as well. He had been enlightened and had tasted of the heavenly gift and the goodness of the Word of God as he had sat for three years under the personal teaching of the Lord Jesus. Insofar as he had participated in gospel preaching and the expulsion of demons, he also had been a sharer in the Holy Spirit. But this falls short of becoming indwelt by the Holy Spirit, so that his body was actually taken over to be a holy temple of God. Far from it! Christ could read his heart, and He saw the hypocrisy and treachery within it—as He indicated clearly enough at the last

Passover meal. In the high priestly prayer of John 17, Jesus spoke of Judas as the "son of perdition" (v.12). By no stretch of the imagination could Judas Iscariot have been at any time considered truly born again, no matter how convincing a performance he may have put on before his fellow disciples. Yet all four of the qualities described as marking the apostate were true of Judas.

It is quite clear that all along Judas had been hoping to gain personal advantage from Jesus; perhaps he expected a post of honor in Christ's coming kingdom (which he thought of primarily in a political, earthly dimension). He never seriously took Jesus as Lord of his heart; he never laid his body on the altar of sincere devotion to Christ's will and glory. Judas may have professed such surrender, but he never really meant it. Otherwise, when Jesus made it clear that He had no intention of using His supernatural powers to seize political power, Judas would not have decided to betray Him to the temple authorities for a sum of money. This made it abundantly evident that he had really meant to use Jesus for his own selfish interests rather than giving himself over to be used by Christ for His service and glory.

Eventually a time of testing will come along in the career of every professing believer, who has tried to take Jesus as Savior without also taking Him as Lord—as the one he intends to live for and is willing to die for—and the spuriousness of his "conversion" will become apparent. A truly born-again believer, of the type that will never be plucked out of the Master's hand, is one who has passed through that inward change of heart that centers him on Christ instead of on himself (cf. 2 Cor. 5:14–17). That type of death to the world and to self, that surrender to Jesus as Lord that opens up to the Holy Spirit and lets Him take over the

convert completely, is a kind of regeneration that is both genuine and permanent. Even though he may later backslide for a time and taste once again of his former bondage and shame, he will never be allowed to remain in that state of rebellion and defeat. The Holy Spirit will not leave him alone, but by one means or other He will draw him back to renewed repentance, faith, and surrender.

The second passage in Hebrews that must be considered is 10:26–27: "If we deliberately [*hekousiōs* may also mean 'willingly'] keep on sinning after we have received the knowledge of the truth, no sacrifice for sins is left, but only a fearful expectation of judgment and of raging fire that will consume the enemies of God." Here again there is a prior receiving of the knowledge of the truth as it is in Jesus (similar to the "once enlightened" of 6:4) and a full understanding of the meaning of the Cross. But unfortunately it is possible to grasp the plan of salvation as a concept and communicate it clearly to others as a matter of teaching and yet never really yield to the Lord. The Bible defines true believing as a matter of receiving Christ Himself—not simply the teaching of Christ as a philosophy or a theory—as both Lord and Savior: "As many as *received* him . . . even to those that *believed* in His name" (John 1:12).

The believer who receives Jesus as Lord in all sincerity and truth will never sincerely or willingly go back into the practice of sin, will never "trample on the Son of God" (Heb. 10:29); he will never regard His shed blood as unholy or profane (*koinon*), and will never wantonly insult the Holy Spirit. Anyone who can bring himself around to that kind of ungodliness and contempt toward his divine Savior never gave his heart to Him in the first place. Like Judas, he may have thought that he would just "try Jesus" and see how he liked Him, and whether he would obtain from Him the advantages and blessings he craved for himself and for his own sake. Since he never really faced up to the claims of Christ to total lordship over his life, he was a mere counterfeit Christian right from the start. God is never satisfied with counterfeits. He only accepts the real thing. He can never be deceived, even by the most pious of poses. He reads our hearts.

How can "head of his staff" (Heb. 11:21) be reconciled with "head of the bed" (Gen. 47:31)?

Hebrews 11:21 refers to the dying Jacob as "worshiping on the head of his staff" when he pronounced his blessing on Joseph. But in Genesis 47:31 we read, "Then Israel bowed in worship at the head of the bed" (NASB). Actually the Hebrew text says '*al ham-miṭṭāh* "on the head of the bed"), which perhaps might mean that he leaned his forehead on the headboard of his bed. But this is rather unlikely in view of what he had just been doing, conversing with Joseph, and asking him to place his hand under his thigh as he promised to bury Jacob in Canaan rather than in Egypt. Jacob would have been far more likely to sit on the side of his bed, leaning perhaps on his staff.

Now it so happens that the word for "bed" and the word for "staff" are spelled exactly the same in the Hebrew consonants; only the vowel points (first invented about the eighth century A.D. or a little before) differentiate between the two. But the Septuagint, translated back in the third century B.C., reads *m-ṭ-h* as *maṭṭāh* ("staff"); it was the medieval Jewish Masoretes of the ninth century A.D. who decided it was *miṭṭāh* ("bed"). Hebrews 11:21 follows the earlier vocalization and comes out with the far more likely rendering "on the head of the staff"—like the Septuagint and the Syriac Peshitta. In all probability this was the correct reading, and

the Masoretic pointing ought to be changed accordingly.

How could men like Barak, Jephthah, and Samson be included in the Hebrews 11 roster of honor, which included heroes like Enoch, Abraham, and Moses?

Hebrews 11:32 says very dramatically, "And what more shall I say? For time will fail me if I tell of Gideon, Barak, Samson, Jephthah, of David and Samuel and the prophets" (NASB). The most striking manifestation and proofs of their faith and zeal are listed in vv.33-34, followed by the reference to their willingness to suffer for the sake of the Lord and His holy word (vv.35-38). It cannot be supposed that all the men listed in v.32 exhibited all these characteristics or stood on the same level of consistent holiness. But even in the case of Samson (who was by far the most vulnerable to criticism out of the entire list referred to in all of chap. 11), it was true that he "became mighty in war" and "put foreign armies to flight" (v.34). It is also true that in a sense he ended his earthly career (after a long period of penitence for his previous folly and immorality) by one magnificent "act of righteousness" (v.33), when he pulled down the pillars of the temple of Dagon on the jeering crowd of Philistines, as they derided their blinded captive and his "powerless" God. Samson was willing to give up his own life in the interests of his nation and his Lord—even though part of his motivation was vengeance on his tormentors for putting out his eyes.

As for Barak, it is unclear why his name should be placed in the doubtful column at all. To be sure, he refused to assume leadership in the war of independence against the pagan oppressors of Israel unless the prophetess Deborah would serve as his partner. But under the circumstances this was hardly an unreasonable request on his part. In the case of Jephthah, his willingness to negotiate reasonably with the Ammonite invaders was hardly a reproach to his honor, even though those negotiations proved fruitless in the end (Judg. 11:12–28). Certainly his valor in battle was crowned with success (vv.32–33). As for his surrender of his virgin daugh-

ter for lifelong service at the tabernacle (cf. article on Judg. 11:30–31: "Why did God allow Jephthah's foolish vow to run its course?"), this could scarcely be censured as a failure in his integrity in the performance of his vows. He properly belongs in Hebrews 11:32.

It seems quite
that the passa
sures us tha
in His pr
was co
sin

1 Peter

Is there a second chance after death?

What is the meaning of 1 Peter 3:19, which speaks of Christ's preaching to the spirits in the prison of hades? Did He preach the gospel to them and thus give them a chance to be saved even after they had already died? If we carefully examine this sentence in its entire setting, we shall find that it teaches no such thing—which would be quite contrary to Hebrews 9:27: "It is appointed for men to die once, and after this comes judgment."

In the NASB, 1 Peter 3:18-20 is translated: "For Christ also died for sins once for all, the just for the unjust, in order that He might bring us to God, having been put to death in the flesh, but made alive in the spirit; in which also He went and made proclamation to the spirits now in prison, who once were disobedient, when the patience of God kept waiting in the days of Noah, during the construction of the ark, in which a few, that is, eight persons, were brought safely through the water" (NASB). It will be observed from the above rendering that the verb translated "preached" in the KJV is not the Greek euangelizomai ("to preach or tell the good news"), which would certainly have meant that after His crucifixion Christ really did preach a salvation message to lost souls in Hades; but rather it is ekēryxen, from kērysso ("proclaim a message," from a king or potentate). All that v.19 actually says is that Christ made a proclamation to the souls who are now imprisoned in Sheol (hades).

The contents of that proclamation are not made clear, but there are just two possibilities: (1) the proclamation made by the crucified Christ in Hades to all the souls of the dead may have been to the effect that the price had now been paid for sin, and all those who died in the faith were to get ready for their departure to heaven—shortly to occur on Easter Sunday—or (2) the proclamation may refer to that solemn, urgent warning Noah made to his own generation, that they should take refuge in the ark of safety before the Great Flood would destroy the human race. Of the two options, while the first was undoubtedly a true occurrence (cf. Eph. 4:8), such a proclamation would have been made to all in hades generally, or else to the redeemed in particular. But the second seems to be the proclamation intended here by Peter, since the only audience mentioned is the generation of Noah, which is now imprisoned in Hades, awaiting the final judgment. This verse means, then, that Christ through the Holy Spirit solemnly warned Noah's contemporaries by the mouth of Noah himself (described in 2 Peter 2:5 as "a preacher [or 'herald'] of righteousness." Note that "preacher" in this verse is kēryka, the same root as the ekēryxen referred to above in connection with 1 Peter 3:19).

423

evident, therefore,
under discussion as-
even back in Noah's day,
incarnate state, God the Son
ncerned with the salvation of
rs. Thus the entire transaction
hereby Noah's family was rescued
through the ark was a prophetic event,
pointing forward to the gracious provision of God through the substitutionary
Atonement on a wooden cross—likewise the sole instrument of deliverance
from the flood of divine judgment on
guilty mankind. In both cases only
those who by faith take refuge in God's
means of salvation can be rescued from
destruction.

This relationship of type-antitype is
then spelled out quite explicitly by the
apostle in 1 Peter 3:21: "And corresponding to that [as NASB renders *an-
titypon*], baptism now saves you—not
the removal of dirt from the flesh, but
an appeal [*epērōtēma*] to God for a good
conscience—through the resurrection

of Jesus Christ" (NASB). That is to say,
repentance for sin and a trust in Jesus
alone for salvation on the basis of His
atonement and resurrection are what
furnish deliverance to the guilty sinner
and make it possible for him to obtain
"a good conscience" based on a conviction that all his sins have been paid for
in full by the blood of Jesus.

In view of the focus on the generation of Noah as corresponding to the
lost world of Peter's day (and of every
generation since then, we may be
sure), we are forced to conclude that
the proclamation referred to in v.19
took place, not when Christ descended
into Hades after His death on Calvary,
but by the Spirit who spoke through
the mouth of Noah during the years
while the ark was under construction
(v.20). Therefore v.19 holds out no
hope whatever for a "second chance"
for those who reject Christ during
their lifetime on earth.

2 Peter

Is 2 Peter an authentic work of Peter?

Among nonconservative New Testament critics, it is common to brand 2 Peter as spurious and nothing more than a pious fraud. Yet there is hardly any epistle in the New Testament canon that contains more definite testimonies as to the identity and personal experience of the author than this epistle. Note the following references: (1) The author gives His name (1:1) specifically as *Symeōn*, just as he was referred to by James in the Council of Jerusalem (Acts 15:14). (2) He identifies himself as an "apostle of Jesus Christ" (1:1), a term that generally refers to one of the Twelve. (3) He recalls the overpowering scene of the Transfiguration in the tone of an awed spectator (1:16–18), classifying himself among the eyewitnesses (*epoptai*) and quoting verbatim the divine proclamation "This is My beloved Son, in whom I am well pleased," which he affirms he heard with his own ears while he was on "the holy mount." (4) He plainly alludes to Jesus' prediction made to him in John 21:18 as he says, "Just as our Lord Jesus Christ revealed to me" (1:14).

Other significant internal evidences are (1) his description of this letter as his "second epistle" to them (3:1), which plainly implies that he had already written them an earlier epistle (suggesting 1 Peter); (2) his personal familiarity with and warm regard for the apostle Paul as an inspired author of New Testament Scripture (3:15–16 speaks of "our beloved brother Paul" as likewise writing of "the longsuffering of our Lord" as intended for the "salvation" of many more sinners than a speedier Second Advent would allow for [v.15; cf. Rom. 2:4; 9:22]). Peter classes these letters of Paul as part of the authoritative Word of God, even though there may be some things in them "hard to understand [*dysnoēta*]" (v.16). Rather than an evidence of much later authorship and of composition after the canonicity of Paul's Letters had been finally accepted by the church at large (as some have urged), these cordial and appreciative references to Paul and his writings are altogether what we should expect if Peter made his way to Rome a few years later than Paul did. His Roman readers certainly would expect him to comment on the work and achievement of his predecessor—in just such a way as he does here.

In view of all this explicit evidence from the text itself as to Petrine authorship, we are forced to conclude that the author of this epistle made such a definite claim to being the apostle Peter himself that it would have been grossly fraudulent and deceptive on his part if the epistle were not authentically Petrine. If it was not really by him, it should not be used or respected by the church at all; and it is unwarranted hypocrisy to use it for preaching purposes, for it should be removed from the New Testament altogether as a sheer imposture. It would be hard to conceive of any valid revelation of divine truth as emanating from such a dishonest pen.

There has been much discussion about the resemblances between 2 Peter 2 and the Epistle of Jude. Jude 6 and 2 Peter 2:4 both refer to fallen angels (though in entirely different wording). Jude 9 and 2 Peter 2:11 both speak of the angels as unwilling to bring a railing accusation even against Satan. Jude 17–18 mentions scoffers who carry on in a carnal and ungodly fashion; this bears some resemblance to 2 Peter 3:3–4, which refers to those who will speak scornfully in the last days concerning the Lord's return in judgment (here again without any verbal resemblance between the two). The tone of denunciation is quite similar, but a careful comparison between the two authors offers little support to the theory that one borrowed directly from the other—or even that one influenced the other. In point of fact it is quite possible that both Jude and 2 Peter were composed between A.D. 65 and 67, and both dealt forcibly with the problems raised by ungodly antinomian heretics infiltrating the Christian community and subverting the faith of some.

Much has been made of the contrasts between 1 Peter and 2 Peter in regard to mood and attitude, as if the difference in tone establishes a difference in authorship. But this is a very uncertain criterion to use for demonstrating diverse authorship, for the simple reason that the same author tends to use an entirely different vocabulary and tone when he discusses different subject matter. This is readily demonstrable for all the great authors of world literature who have written on different themes and in different genres. For example, Milton's prose essays bear little resemblance to his pastoral poems (*L'Allegro* and *Il Penseroso*); and those in turn present notable contrasts to his epic poetry, like *Paradise Lost*. Yet these contrasts, which could be supported by long lists of words found in the one composition but not in the other, would hardly suffice to prove a difference in authorship. Everyone knows that Milton wrote them all. So the methodology of these New Testament critics, if applied to Miltonic literature, would lead to completely false results.

So far as 1 Peter is concerned, its purpose was comfort and encouragement to believers suffering from persecution. This requires a quite different style and manner from the theme of 2 Peter, which consists of stern and urgent warning against false teachers and their pernicious doctrines. Considering their diverse themes, it would have been altogether strange if both letters had exhibited striking similarities in vocabulary and tone. In fact, this would be good evidence of deliberate faking, or of a set purpose on the part of a counterfeiter to palm off a specious imitation on the public.

In the matter of idiom and style, however, there are some fairly obvious contrasts. The Greek of 1 Peter runs more idiomatically and smoothly than the rugged, intense diction of 2 Peter, even though J. B. Mayor (*The Epistle of St. Jude and the Second Epistle of St. Peter*, 1907 reprint, [Grand Rapids: Baker, 1965], p. civ), as an advocate of the non-Petrine authorship of 2 Peter, observes: "There is not the chasm between them [i.e., 1 Peter and 2 Peter] which some would try to make out.... The difference of style is less marked than the difference in vocabulary, and that again is less marked than the difference in matter."

Such differences as there are might possibly have derived from the agency of Silvanus, who is referred to in 1 Peter 5:12 as the scribe Peter used in composing his first epistle. NIV renders this verse as follows: "With the help of Silas ['Silvanus,' mg.], whom I regard as a faithful brother, I have written to you briefly, encouraging you and testifying that this is the true grace of God." In all probability this is the same Silas who labored with Paul at Philippi, and he may have been responsible for the simplicity and ease of expression in which 1 Peter was composed. But in the case of 2 Peter, which was probably written by Peter in a Roman jail, without the help of an amanuensis like Silvanus, there is a more intense and rugged style, suitable for matters of such urgent concern as are featured in this epistle.

Nor should the similarities between 1 Peter and 2 Peter be totally ignored in our preoccupation with the contrasts. Both epistles stress (1) the centrality of Christ and the certainty of His second coming; (2) the importance of Noah's ark and the Flood (1 Peter 3:20, with emphasis on God's mercy; and 2 Peter 2:5; 3:6, with emphasis on God's judgment); (3) the pivotal significance of the prophetic word of the Old Testament in a manner reminiscent of Peter's Pentecost sermon (Acts 2:14-36); (4) their common concern with the importance of Christian growth (1 Peter 2:2-3 and 2 Peter 1:5-8; 3:18). Despite the contrast in purpose existing between the two epistles, these common motifs emerge as such significant indicators of a common authorship as to give strong support to the genuineness of the Petrine origin of them both.

We conclude that there is no good ground for denying the authenticity of 2 Peter or for questioning its right to be included in the New Testament canon. The leading critics who have espoused a contrary view have pretty largely operated on the basis of a stereotyped concept of how the Christian religion must have developed as a purely human religious philosophy, along the lines of a Hegelian dialectic. Evangelicals should not be misled into acceptance of critical results stemming from this kind of biased and subjective methodology. (For further study, see the excellent introduction to S.W. Paine's commentary on 2 Peter in Pfeiffer, *Wycliffe Commentary,* pp. 1453-56, to which I acknowledge my personal indebtedness.)

1 John

Does 1 John 3:9 teach sinless perfection?

In KJV 1 John 3:9 is rendered: "Whosoever is born of God doth not commit sin; for his seed remaineth in him: and he cannot commit sin, because he is born of God." In one respect this otherwise adequate translation fails to bring out one very important feature of the *hamartanein* ("to sin") after *ou dynatai* ("not able"): a present infinitive in Greek implies continual or repeated action. (Single action would have been conveyed by the aorist infinitive, *hamartein*.) For this reason some of the more recent translations bring out the true emphasis by rendering it "he cannot go on sinning" (NIV). NASB draws the inference from the present infinitive *hamartanein* that the earlier *poiei* (present indicative) in "doth not commit sin" (KJV) implies "no one who is born of God *practices sin*," since this stands in contrast to the *hamartanein* of the later clause. This is probably justified, even though it would be wrong to say that the Greek present indicative *necessarily* implies continual action (for it often does not do so).

However, it is necessary to study carefully the sense in which this verb is meant, for even the most mature Christian is susceptible to temptation and may fall into sins of various types (even if not the more heinous sins that are considered under human law as amounting to crime). John teaches very clearly in 1:8: "If we say that we have no sin, we deceive ourselves and the truth is not in us." But what he is emphasizing here is the miracle of the new birth (cf. 2 Cor. 5:17), by which the life of Christ takes possession of the believer's heart and draws him into a totally new relationship to God and to God's holy will. Instead of being committed to the old principle of "myself first!" he now comes under the lordship of his Savior and makes it his conscious purpose to please God because he loves Him and completely belongs to Him.

In his new capacity as "one who has been born of God" (*gegennēmenos*—perfect passive participle—*ek tou theou*), the believer has God's holy seed (*sperma*) within him; and this *sperma* develops and enlarges within him like a seed within a flower pot, until it brings forth leaves, flowers, and fruit—all the while occupying more and more of the pot. The dirt in the soil may defile what touches it, but the function of the growing plant is not to soil but develop the new life and beauty that constantly proceeds from the seed. As the believer consciously abides in Christ (v.6, *ho en autō menōn*) and has his gaze fixed on Jesus (Heb. 12:2), he does not fall into sin but runs his race well, to the glory of God.

As for the special force of *hamartia* here, we should pay special attention to v.4: "Everyone who commits/practices [present participle] sin [*hamartian*] also practices lawlessness [*anomian*]." The Devil is then referred to as the archetype, model, and patron of lawlessness (v.8); and it is he (and of course those who are under his control) whose business it is to practice sin as lawlessness. In other words, Scripture is distinguishing between the two great families in the universe: the children of light (1:7) and the children of darkness and disobedience (1:6).

What characterizes a true child of God is wholehearted commitment to the holy will and standard of God; what characterizes the child of this world (whose spiritual father is really Satan, according to John 8:44) is the commitment to self-seeking, self-deification, and transgression of every kind. This principle had to be stressed by the apostle in this letter, because already the antinomian heretics (who taught that a sinful life was quite permissible to the believer, because "grace would cover it all") were confusing his church people; and they were losing their grasp of the holy life as the fruit of a true and living faith. John here

reminds us all that the true believer is committed to a life patterned after Christ, and that as the bearer of the seed of Christ (that is, the Holy Spirit) he will constantly practice righteousness. Only the unconverted and the counterfeit will practice a self-seeking, self-asserting life of sin.

In his *Bible Questions Answered* (pp. 68–72), W.L. Pettingill devotes a very careful and perceptive study to this passage in 1 John 3 and offers this helpful paraphrase of vv.4–10:

> Whosoever commits sin also commits lawlessness, and sin is lawlessness. And you know that He was manifest to take away our sins, and in Him is no lawlessness. Whosoever abides in Him is never lawless: whosoever is lawless has not seen Him nor known Him. . . . He who is lawless is of the devil, for the devil was lawless from the beginning. . . . Whosoever is begotten of God is never lawless, for His seed remains in him; and he cannot be lawless because he is begotten of God. In this the children of God are manifest and the children of the devil.

Jude

Jude 9 and Jude 14 are the passages that raise this question. Verse 9 refers to a controversy between the archangel Michael and the Devil in regard to the disposition of the body of Moses after he had died on Mount Pisgah: "But even the archangel Michael, when he was disputing with the devil about the body of Moses, did not dare to bring a slanderous accusation against him, but said, 'The Lord rebuke you!'" This account is not found in the Old Testament but is thought to have been included in a Christian treatise (now lost) entitled "the Assumption of Moses" (cf. Buttrick, *Interpreter's Dictionary*, 3:450), at least according to Origen (*On the Principles* 3.2.1).

It would be a logical fallacy to argue, however, that an inspired biblical author like Jude was strictly limited to the contents of the canonical Old Testament for all valid information as to the past. Both Stephen (in Acts 7) and the Lord Jesus (in Matt. 23) refer to historical episodes not recorded in the Old Testament. Apparently there was a valid and accurate body of oral tradition available to believers in the New Testament period; and under the guidance of the Holy Spirit, they were perfectly able to report such occurrences in connection with their teaching ministry. We are to deduce from this passage, then, that there was such a contest waged by the representatives of heaven and hell over the body of Moses.

The same observation applies to Jude 14 and the quotation from the antediluvian patriarch Enoch. In this case the pseudepigraphical work has been preserved in which this same quotation is found (though the Book of Enoch is not extant in any translation as old as the time of Jude). Enoch is quoted as predicting: "Behold the Lord has come [probably the Greek aorist *ēlthen* represents a prophetic perfect in Hebrew or Aramaic, and therefore it can be construed as 'shall come'] with His holy myriads, to execute judgment against all and to rebuke all the ungodly for all their deeds of ungodliness that they have perpetrated and for all the cruel things they have said against Him as the ungodly sinners that they are."

Here we have a remarkable example of a powerful prophetic utterance coming down to us from before the time of Noah. The mere fact that Genesis does not include this statement by Enoch furnishes no evidence against his having said it. This by no means demonstrates that everything in the Book of Enoch is historically accurate or theologically valid. Much of Enoch may be quite fictional. But there is no good ground for condemning everything that is written therein as false, simply because the book is noncanonical. Even a pagan work could contain items of truth, as is attested to by Paul when he quoted Aratus's *Phaenomena* 5 to his Athenian audience (Acts 17:28).

Revelation

Who are the seven spirits before God's throne in Revelation 1:4?

Revelation 1:4 reads: "Grace to you and peace, from Him who is and who was and who is to come; and from the seven spirits [Spirits?] who are before His throne" (NASB). Who are these seven spirits? Do they represent the Third Person of the Trinity (God the Father and God the Son are referred to previously in v.2)? Surprisingly enough, the correct answer to this question seems to be yes. (Conceivably they could be seven angels of some sort, but they could hardly be the "angels" of the seven churches of Asia, since those are listed separately in addition to the seven spirits [v.4].)

How could the Holy Spirit be represented as seven rather than one? Well, the first appearance of the sevenfold Holy Spirit occurs in Isaiah 11:2: "And the Spirit of the LORD [1] will rest on Him [the Messiah], the spirit of wisdom [2] and understanding [3], the spirit of counsel [4] and strength [5], the spirit of knowledge [6] and the fear of Yahweh [7]." In biblical symbolism seven is the number of the perfect work of God (cf. Gen. 2:2–3), and so the "rod from the stem of Jesse" (Isa. 11:1) will be endowed with the perfect equipment of the Holy Spirit as He begins His messianic ministry.

The next time the concept of the seven-faceted Spirit occurs is in Zechariah 3:9: "For behold, the stone that I have set before Joshua [the high priest]; on one stone are seven eyes" (NASB). Here we have the perfect oversight, the providential care of God the Holy Spirit represented by the seven eyes engraved on the "stone" (probably a large gemstone) set before the high priest. They appear again in Zechariah 4:10: "For who has despised the day of small things? But these *seven* will be glad when they see the plumb line in the hand of Zerubbabel—these are the eyes of Yahweh which range to and fro throughout the whole earth." The Holy Spirit in His loving providence is promised for the dedication of the second temple, which was coming up in 516 B.C.

But it is in Revelation that the "seven spirits" appear as separate individuals, not only in 1:4, but in 3:1: "He who has the seven spirits of God, and the seven stars, says this: 'I know your deeds'" (NASB); in 4:5: "And there were seven lamps of fire burning before the throne, which are the seven Spirits of God" (NASB); and in 5:6: "And I saw between the throne (with the four living creatures) and the elders a Lamb standing, as if slain, having seven horns and seven eyes, which are the seven Spirits of God, sent out into all the earth" (NASB).

There appears to be a definite connection between the sevenfold Spirit of Isaiah 11:2 and the seven-faceted Spirit of Revelation, who represents Himself in the external guise of seven distinct spirits, appropriate to God's perfect enablement and providential care—the central theme of the Apocalypse. The entire book is full of symbolism; so it should not be considered too surprising that seven should represent one in this striking and impressive way. After all, we have already seen how Christ Himself, who was first represented in His resurrection glory as the white-haired, flaming-eyed Son of Man, wearing a long robe reaching to His burnished-brass feet (1:14–15), is set forth in 5:6 as a Lamb, standing as if it had been slain, having both seven horns and seven eyes. Here again seven represents one, though in this case it is God the Son rather than the Holy Spirit.

Similarly Satan is represented as a red, fire-breathing dragon with seven heads and ten horns (12:3), similar to his viceroy and representative on earth, the Beast with ten horns, ten diadems, and seven heads, resembling a leopard in his overall appearance, but with the feet of a bear and the mouth of a lion (13:2). (In the case of Satan and the final world dictator, the number seven represents a false claim to possessing the perfect power of God.) So also the apostate world church is symbolized as a harlot wearing purple and scarlet and sitting on the scarlet beast (17:3–4). These symbols thus present, not the person or cosmic power in actual appearance, but a symbolic form that is intended to teach the human observer (John on the island of Patmos) something about the qualities and characteristics of the third Person of the Trinity.

A dove represented the Holy Spirit at the time of Christ's baptism (Matt. 3:16), and multiple tongues of fire represented Him at Pentecost, as He empowered and gave utterance to the witnesses of Christ (Acts 2:3). Probably there were 120 such flames, if all 120 disciples from the Upper Room were present at that feast (Acts 1:13,15). Thus we see that the Holy Spirit also is symbolized in many different ways throughout Scripture, always in a guise appropriate to the occasion.

Who are the 144,000 of Revelation 7:3–8 and 14:1?

In Revelation 7:3 a divine command is issued to the four angels who control the winds of destruction on earth, that they should hold back from inflicting havoc until the "servants of God" have been sealed as God's own, with His mark on their foreheads. They constitute a company of 144,000 (vv.5–8), consisting of 12,000 from each of the twelve tribes of Israel. (Notice that the tribe of Dan is omitted altogether— perhaps because some members of that tribe willfully chose a land allotment of their own up to the north of the territory of Asher. Moreover they did so as an act of unprovoked aggression, according to Judges 18:27, and brought with them an idolatrous ephod, which they had taken by force from an Ephraimite (Judg. 18:18–26.) Another interesting feature is that Levi is mentioned as one of the Twelve Tribes, rather than maintaining a special status as a priestly tribe under the old, pre-Crucifixion religious establishment of the Mosaic Law. Ephraim must be equated with "Joseph" in this listing; Manasseh is mentioned separately. Since Ephraim remained on the West Bank entirely whereas Manasseh settled a "half-tribe" on the East Bank, it was reasonable to give to Ephraim the honor of his father's name.

As to the ethnic makeup of these 144,000 saints, it is difficult to suppose that an identical number of converts to Christ would be won during the first half of the final seven years before Armageddon from each of the Twelve Tribes, especially in view of the fact that nearly all modern Jews regard themselves as descended from Judah, except perhaps for the Levines and the Cohens, who claim to be from Levi. It would be reasonable to suppose that even if descendants could somehow be traced back to the other ten tribes, the great preponderance of converts would be from Judah. Even in the first century A.D., this same situation tended to prevail, as a result of the Assyrian deportations of the Ten Tribes in 721 B.C. and thereafter.

As for the twelve groups of 12,000, all Bible scholars recognize its special association with the Old Testament people of God, made up of twelve tribes, and with the New Testament people of God, under the leadership of the twelve apostles. Both divisions seem to be represented by the twenty-four elders who figure so prominently in the scenes of heaven presented in Revelation (4:4; 5:8; 11:16; 19:4). If, then, these two sets of twelve were to multiply each other rather than being added to each other, they would come out to 144 rather than 24. As for the multiplication by 1000, compare Numbers 31:4-6 for the first record of a specially designated army of believers sent out to wage war against the enemies of the Lord. A similar procedure was followed in selecting an army to punish the ungodly tribe of Benjamin back in the days of the Judges (Judg. 20:10). The normal size of a regiment in the armies of Moses' and David's time was 1000.

Putting all these factors together could add up to the result that during the final week (of Daniel's seventy weeks in 9:25) Gentile believers and Jewish believers will work together with such effectiveness and vigor that they will reach that generation for Christ with a tremendously fruitful missionary outreach. Perhaps 144,000 will be the actual number of missionaries involved, and they will constitue regiments of dedicated workers under twelve regional authorities. At any rate, according to Revelation 7:9, they will be amazingly successful; for by their united efforts they will have won to the Lord "a great multitude which no man could number" out of every race and tribe all over the earth. The first three and one-half years of the Seventieth Week will be a time of unprecedented evangelism before the

church has been raptured. (This interpretation assumes, of course, that the Rapture will take place in the middle of the Week. But this view is open to debate and falls short of complete proof.)

As for the 144,000 who appear in Revelation 14:1-5, the identity in number suggests (though it does not necessarily prove) an identity in constituency. In other words, it looks as if these represent the raptured church up in heaven, rejoicing in its personal fellowship with Christ up there. This requires interpreting "Mount Zion" as referring to a heavenly counterpart rather than the earthly citadel of historic Jerusalem. But there certainly was a heavenly Jerusalem (as well as the earthly one) according to Galatians 4:26: "The Jerusalem above is free, she who is your mother." And Hebrews 12:22 speaks of both a Zion, city of the living God, and a "heavenly Jerusalem, and myriads of angels, etc." There is therefore abundant precedent for interpreting this Mount Zion in Revelation 14:1 as a designation of the court of heaven in the presence of the harp-playing angels and the glorified saints.

In this passage special emphasis is laid on the faithfulness and personal purity of these 144,000. They have the name of God inscribed on their brow, having resolutely refused to take the mark of the Beast demanded of them while they were down on earth. Secondly, they are said to be "virgins" (*parthenoi*) because they have not "defiled themselves with women." (This cannot refer to sex relations within the marriage bond, for this would be no defilement at all but rather an honorable act, according to Heb. 13:4. Therefore it must refer to fornication and adultery, such as will run rampant in the corrupt society of the last days.) But the term *parthenos* here undoubtedly extends beyond sexual chastity to an attitude of complete faithfulness and chaste devotion toward the heavenly Bridegroom, whose imminent return they await, for the glad occasion of the marriage supper of the Lamb (Rev. 19:9).

Evangelical commentaries tend to fall into two distinct camps so far as identifying the 144,000 is concerned. In general, J.B. Payne (*Encyclopedia of Biblical Prophecy*, p. 597), Bengel, Alford, Lenski, and Milligan identify them completely with the Christian church, both in chapter 7 and in chapter 14. They have little to say about the specifically named twelve tribes of Israel but simply suggest that the number itself is merely symbolic, reflecting the twelve patriarchs and the twelve apostles. Yet Bengel does make this comment: "Since the Levitical ceremonies have been abandoned, Levi is again found on an equal footing with his brethren" (*Gnomon of the New Testament* [London: Nutt, Williams & Norgate, 1962], ad loc.).

We must, however, take stock of Christ's promise to His disciples in Matthew 19:28: "You also shall sit upon twelve thrones, judging the twelve tribes of Israel" (NASB). This certainly suggests that in the final judgment, the Twelve Tribes will still be around for the purpose of judgment. (Yet, of course, one might construe this to mean that in the Judgment Day the long-deceased members of the Twelve Tribes who actually died back in Old Testament times will be coming before the heavenly tribunal for final adjudication to their eternal retribution or reward.) The division of the territory of the Holy Land during the Millennium will certainly recognize the continuing identity of the Twelve Tribes (at least for the purpose of giving appropriate, historical names to each of the twelve regions.) According to Ezekiel 48 there are going to be seven east-west parallel tracts for seven tribes (Dan [*sic!*], Asher, Naphtali, Manasseh, Ephraim [not Joseph!], Reuben, and Judah). To the south of the city will be the following five tribes: Benjamin, Simeon, Issachar, Zebulun, and Gad. (There will no longer be any tribes on the other side of the Jordan.)

Dispensational scholars construe the 144,000 of Revelation 7 as exclusively Jewish because of the tribe-by-tribe enumeration contained in vv.5–8. Fausset comments: "But of these tribes a believing remnant will be preserved from the judgments that shall destroy all of the anti-Christian Confederacy" (Jamieson-Fausett-Brown, *Commentary*, ad loc.). Harold Lindsell (ed., *Harper Study Bible* [New York: Harper & Row, 1964], p. 1871) takes a mediating view: "The *hundred and forty-four thousand* is hardly to be thought of as an exact number of converted Jews; some have taken it to imply that it represents the complete number of Jews who are the children of Abraham by faith, foreknown and chosen by God, who will turn to Christ during the closing days of the present age" (italics his).

Bibliography

I. *Texts*

Aland, K.; Black, M.; Metzger, B.M.; and Wikgren, A., eds. *The Greek New Testament.* 3rd ed. New York: American Bible Society, 1975.

Crockett, W.D. *A Harmony of Samuel, Kings and Chronicles.* Grand Rapids: Baker, 1959.

Elliger, K., and Rudolph, W., eds. *Bible Hebraica Stuttgartensia.* Stuttgart: Deutsche Bibelstiftung, 1977.

Huck, A.; Leitzmann, H.; and Cross, F.L. *Synopsis of the First Three Gospels.* Oxford: Oxford University, 1949.

Nestle, E., and Aland, K., eds. *Novum Testamentum Graece.* 26th ed. Stuttgart: Württembergische Bibelanstalt, 1979.

Rahlfs, Alfred, ed. *Septuaginta.* 3rd ed. 2 vols. Stuttgart: Württembergische Bibelanstalt, 1949.

II. *Commentaries and Dictionaries*

Buttrick, G. A., ed. *Interpreter's Dictionary of the Bible.* 4 vols. Nashville: Abingdon, 1962.

Gaebelein, Frank E., ed. *Expositor's Bible Commentary.* 12 vols. Grand Rapids: Zondervan, 1976—

Guthrie, D.; Motyer, J.A.; Stibbs, A.M.; and Wiseman, D.J., eds. *The New Bible Commentary: Revised.* London: Inter-Varsity, 1970.

Jamieson, R.; Fausset, A.R.; and Brown, D. *Commentary on the Whole Bible.* 2 vols. Reprint. Grand Rapids: Zondervan, n.d.

Keil, C.F., and Delitzsch, F. *Biblical Commentary on the Old Testament.* 20 vols. Reprint. Grand Rapids: Eerdmans, 1949.

Lange, J.P. *Commentary on the Holy Scriptures.* 25 vols. Reprint. Grand Rapids: Zondervan, n.d.

Pfeiffer, C.F., and Harrison, E.F. *The Wycliffe Bible Commentary.* Chicago: Moody, 1962.

Tenney, M.C., ed. *The Zondervan Pictorial Encyclopedia of the Bible.* 5 vols. Grand Rapids: Zondervan, 1975-76.

Unger, M.F. *Unger's Bible Dictionary.* Chicago: Moody, 1957.

III. *Theologies*

Berkhof, L. *Systematic Theology.* 2nd ed. Grand Rapids: Eerdmans, 1941.

Oehler, G.F. *Theology of the Old Testament.* Reprint. Grand Rapids: Zondervan, n.d.

Strong, A.H. *Systematic Theology.* Reprint (3 vols. in 1). Philadelphia: Judson, 1944.

IV. *Critical Introductions*

Archer, G.L. *A Survey of Old Testament Introduction.* Revised ed. Chicago: Moody, 1974.

Eissfeldt, O. *The Old Testament: An Introduction.* Translated by P.R. Ackroyd. New York: Harper, 1965.

Harrison, E.F. *Introduction to the New Testament.* Grand Rapids: Eerdmans, 1964.

Harrison, R.K. *Introduction to the Old Testament.* Grand Rapids: Eerdmans, 1969.

Pfeiffer, R.H. *Introduction to the Old Testament.* New York: Harper and Brothers, 1948.

V. *General Works*

Finegan, J. *Handbook of Biblical Chronology.* Princeton: Princeton University Press, 1964.

Haley, J.W. *Alleged Discrepancies of the Bible.* Reprint. Nashville: Goodpasture, 1951.

Kitchen, K.A. *Ancient Orient and Old Testament.* Chicago: Inter-Varsity, 1966.

Lyttleton, Lord, and West, Gilbert. *The Conversion of St. Paul; the Resurrection of Jesus Christ.* Reprint. New York: American Tract Society, 1929.

McClellan, J.B. *The New Testament, A New Translation: A Contribution to Christian Evidences.* 2 vols. *The Four Gospels.* Vol. 1. London: Macmillan, 1875.

Montgomery, J.W., ed. *God's Inerrant Word.* Minneapolis: Bethany Fellowship, 1974.

Payne, J.B. *Encyclopedia of Biblical Prophecy.* New York: Harper, 1973.

————, ed. *New Perspectives on the Old Testament.* Waco: Word, 1970.

Pritchard, J.B. *Ancient Near Eastern Texts* (ANET). 3rd ed. Princeton: Princeton University Press, 1969.

Rehwinkel, A.M. *The Flood in the Light of the Bible, Geology, and Archaeology.* St. Louis: Concordia, 1951.

Skilton, J.H., ed. *The Law and the Prophets: Old Testament Studies in Honor of O.T. Allis.* Nutley, N.J.: Presbyterian and Reformed, 1974.

Stonehouse, N.B. *Origins of the Synoptic Gospels.* Grand Rapids: Eerdmans, 1963.

Tuck, Robert. *A Handbook of Biblical Difficulties.* London: Elliot Stock, n.d.

Urquhart, John. *The Wonders of Prophecy.* New York: Christian Alliance, n.d.

Wilson, R.D. *A Scientific Investigation of the Old Testament.* Chicago: Moody, 1959.

Index of Persons

Aaron: descended from Kohath, 220; place of death, 147; pressure on Moses, 135; and revelation of God on Mt. Sinai, 124

Abel: acceptable sacrifice of, 71, 73; and atonement, 76; wife of, 77

Abiathar, the high priest: and David, 77, 362; priesthood of, shared with Zadok, 362

Abigail, sister of David, 175

Abihu: and strong drink, 148

Abijah, son of Samuel, 170

Abijah: victory by, over Jeroboam, 228. *See also* Abijam.

Abijam, son of Rehoboam and Maacah, 185: as Abijah, 317

Abimelech, 94, 95: and Abraham, 90; destruction of Shechem, 195; king of Gerar, 244, paid by Abraham for well of Beersheba, 379–80; in Psalm 34, 243–44; recurrence of names of, 141

Abimelech II: and Isaac, 244

Abinadab, brother of David, 174

Abishag, 123

Abner, general: and David, 175; murder of, 183; and sponsorship of Ish-bosheth, 183

Abraham: and age of law, 403; and age of promise, 403; age of, when he left Haran, 378; and circumcision, 93; defeat of Mesopotamian kings by, 90–91; deceit of, 77, 89–90, 155; fulfillment of promise to, 178; God's promise to, for a king, 170; and heavenly hope, 79; and Keturah, 98; and land of Shechem, 379–81; God's covenant with, 403; and Melchizedek, 91–93; and Mt. Moriah, 360; origin of, 88–89; and polygamy, 121–22; rescue of Lot by, 300; sacrifice of Isaac by, 96; visit of, to Egypt in *Genesis Apocryphon*, 300

Absalom: burial place of, 186; revolt of, and census taking, 186; sons of 184–85; tomb of, 184, 186

Achan: stoning of, 201

Achish, of Gath: and David, 178, 200, 243–44; in Psalm 34, 243–44

Adadizri. *See* Benhadad.

Adah (Basemath), wife of Esau, 99, 100

Adam: and the forbidden tree, 72–74; transgression of, and those who sin after similitude of, 388–90; as type of Christ, 388

Adam and Eve: God's knowledge of disobedience of, 75; as gods, 74–75; historicity of, 22, 25; and necessity of sacrifices, 71; salvation of, 75–76

Adin: sons of, 229

Adonijah, 123: seizing of power from Solomon by, 332

Adonikam: discrepancies in sons of, 229

Adrammelech (idol): and infant sacrifices, 264

Agabus, the prophet: and Paul, 384

Agag: recurrence of name, 140–41; Saul spares, 179

Ahab: and Battle of Karkar, 133; destruction of house of, 207–9; Elijah predicts death of, 201–2; and Jehoram, 204; and Jezebel, 202; lying propets of, 410; and Mt. Carmel, 160; offer to Naboth, 201

Ahaz, king, 132: age of, when Hezekiah begotten, 215; as coregent, 204; father of Hezekiah, 211; and Isaiah and sacrifices on high places, 264, 266–67; and shadow on stairway, 211–12

Ahaziah: beginning of reign of, 206–8; and Elijah, 226; killed by Jehu, 207–8; and building of ships with Jehoshaphat, 202

Ahimelech, 155: and David's deception, 177, 200, 362; massacre of, 181

A-himilki, king of Ashdod, 244

Ahimiti: Aziri replaced by, 244

Ahiram: recurrence of name, 140

Ahmose: Hyksos expelled from Egypt by, 194

Albright, W. F., 91, 196: on historicity of Job, 236; on inscriptions from Serebit el-Khadim, 52

Alcaeus, poet: and Joel, 296

Alexander the Great: and Battle of Gaugamela, 134; conquest of Asia by,

and Book of Joel, 296; Daniel's prediction about, 292; and downfall of Tyre, 276–78; and Egypt, 278; and plunder of Persian royal treasury, 224; submission of Persian Empire to, 87
Alexandrinus: on Gerasa, 325
Alford: on John 19:14, 364; on 144,000 of Revelation, 434
Alleman, H. C., 91, 236
Allis, Oswald T., 13
Amasis, of Egypt, 277
Amaziah: and Azariah (Uzziah), 204; and Jehoash, 208; and punishment of assassins of Joash, 153
Amenemhat III, 95
Amenhotep I, 194
Amenhotep II, 191, 198: birth of, 195; date of reign of, 115; as rebellious Pharaoh, 391
Amenhotep III, 195: and Jericho, 157
Ammon: sins of, 246
Amnon: rape of Tamar by, 185
Amon, son of Manasseh: and idolatry of Judah, 228
Amos: prophecy of, concerning corruption of Jeroboam's reign, 209, 295
Amram, 111
Amraphel, as Hammurabi, 90
Anah, father of Oholibamah, 99, 100
Anak: sons of, 80
Ananias of Damascus: and Paul, 384
Andree, Richard, 84
Anthon, Charles, 134
Antimenidas, brother of Alcaeus, 296
Antiochus Epiphanes: death of, and Daniel, 292; prediction of coming of, 53, 292; reign of, 282
Antiochus III: predicted in Daniel, 292
Apollo: as Phoebus and Pythius, 68
Apollos: taught by Priscilla and Aquila, 412
Aqabah, 137
Aquila: and Apollos, 412; and Isaiah 7:11, 41; and Psalm 90:2, 42
Aquila: Greek translation of, 108, 410
Arah: arrival of, in Judea, 230
Aratus: Paul quotes work of, 430
Araunah. See Ornan.
Archer, Gleason, 134: on pacifism, 220
Arioch, king of Larsa, 90
Ariyuk: reference to, in Mari tablets, 90
Arndt, W. F.: on Mark 2:26, 362; on Passover week, 376
Arrian, on Battle of Gaugamela, 134
Artaxerxes: and Jerusalem, 290; Rehum and Shimshai's letter to, 231
Asa, king: and bribe of Benhadad, 228;

and destruction of cult centers, 160; father of Jehoshaphat, 204; and fortress of Ramah, 225; prayer of, before battle with Zerah, 301; and removal of Maacah as Queen Mother, 185; war of, with Baasha, 225
Asaph, 99
Ashdod, 95
Ashtoreth, of Sidon, wife of Solomon, 251
Ashurbanipal: and Manasseh, 214
Astric, Jean: and understanding of "Yahweh," 66, 67
Athaliah, 226
Athena: as Pallas, 68
Augustus: Cleopatra's navy defeated by, 278
Azariah (Uzziah): as coregent, 204; as father of Jotham, 316; as hostage of Nebuchadnezzar, 214
Azgad: sons of, 230
Aziri (Azuri), king of Ashdod, 244

Baal, idol: as Aliyan, 68; destruction of altar of, at Ophrah, 317; Israelite worshipers of, massacred by Jehu, 207–8; and Jezebel, 160; northern kingdom's worship of, 264, 292; worship of, by Ahaziah, 202
Baalet, Phoenician goddess, 52
Baanah: assassination of Ish-bosheth by, 183
Baasha: date of reign of, 225; Ramah given up by, 228; war of, with Asa, 225
Balaam, 81, 92: and Balak, 140; death of, 142
Balak, of Moab, 81, 140
Baly, Denis, 133: on Paran and Kadesh Barnea, 137; on soil of Israel, 139
Bani: sons of (Binnui), 229
Barabas, Stephen: and Aaron's death, 147
Barak, 105: and defeat of Sisera's army, 163; as man of faith, 421–22; praised as warrior, 344
Barker, Kenneth L.: on Zechariah, 304
Baron, David: on Book of Zechariah, 303
Bartimaeus, son of Timaeus: healing of, 325, 332–33
Basemath. See Adah.
Bathsheba, 97: approach of, to David on Solomon's behalf, 332; death of infant son of, 185–86; sin of, with David, 152–53, 200–201
Baumgartner, Walter, 98, 129
Beegle, Dewey: on Eliphaz, 396
Behemoth: and mythology in Scripture, 239, 240

Beierle: on exposed stratum of Paluxy River, 63

Belshazzar, of Babylon, 210, 285, 286: and writing on the wall, 269, 288, 293

Benhadad: recurrence of name, 140–41

Benhadad, of Damascus, 97: as Adadizri, 133; and Jehu, 208; Asa's bribe of, 228; in Battle of Karkar, 133

Bengel: on John 19:14, 364; on 144,000 in Revelation, 434

Benjamin, tribe of, 183

Berechiah, father of Zechariah, 337–38

Berger, R., 63

Beza: on John 19:14, 364; on Rompha, 381

Bezai: recruited to return to Jerusalem, 229; sons of, 229

Bezalel: and Joshua, 112

Bigvai: sons of, 229

Bildad, 236: God's reproof of, 237–38

Bilhah, 121–22

Bimson, John J.: on date of Exodus, 157, 198

Blair, Hugh J.: on prolonged day in Joshua, 162

Boaz, 150, 107–08

Boice, James Montgomery: and International Council on Biblical Inerrancy, 13

Borchardt, 111

Briggs, C. A., 110, 129

Bright, John, 129

Brill, E. J., 98

Brown, F., 110, 129

Brown-Driver-Briggs: on Deuteronomy 15:4, 150

Burrows, Millar: on Sakkut, 381

Caiaphas, the high priest, 322, 397

Cain: and atonement, 76; unacceptable sacrifice of, 71, 76; wife of, 77

Calcol: as wise sage, 250

Caesar Augustus: and the census, 365

Caesar, Julius, 112, 135

Caleb: and crossing of Jordan, 138

Cambyses, son of Cyrus, 288: annexation of Egypt, 278; and Daniel 11:2, 292; death of, 231

Canaan: curse on, 86–87

Cansdale, G. S., 126

Carson, D. A., 121

Chedorlaomer, king of Elam, 90

Chemosh, god of Moab: Solomon's building of shrine to, 160, 251

Chilion, brother-in-law to Ruth, 167

Chiun, idol Stephen referred to, 381–82

Clark, Austin H.: on missing links, 56

Clark, Robert E. D., 56, 129

Cleopas: Christ's appearance to, 117, 350, 351–52

Cleopatra, 278

Cobb, W. H.: on Nebuchadnezzar as Lucifer, 269

Constantine the Great, 119

Coridethian, on Gergesa, 324

Cornelius, of Caesarea, 341: conversion of, 274; Peter's words to, 388

Crockett, W. D.: on Chronicles, 301; on departure of Elijah, 226

Cross, F. M., 271

Crown, Alan: and soil of Israel, 139

Cush, son of Ham, 86

Cuspius Fadius: capture of Theudas by forces of, 377

Cyrenius. See Quirinius.

Cyrus the Great, 277, 292: and building of second temple, 231; and Daniel, 284; invasion of Babylon, 286; Isaiah predicts his freeing of Hebrew people, 263–64, 265, 270–71; and Sheshbazzar, 217; and vassal kings, 287

Dahood, Mitchell: on author of Ecclesiastes, 257

Damascus road: voice on, 382–83

Daniel, 233: as hostage of Nebuchadnezzar, 214

Darda: as wise sage, 250

Darius, 282, 286: assassination of Gaumata by, 287; and Behistun Rock inscription, 230; and building of second temple, 231; confirmation of existence of, 286–89; and Daniel, 284; and Daniel 11:2, 292; and Darius, son of Hystaspes, 287; as Gubaru, 294; as recurring name in Persia, 244; rise of, 232; search for decree of Cyrus, 231; as temporary appointment, 287; as title, 288

Darius III, 134

Darwin, Charles, 55, 56

David: and amount of gold provided for future temple, 222–24; battle over Hadadezer, 184; brothers of, 174–75; and death of infant son, 98–99; and eating of showbread, 362; faithful ruler, 170; feigning of madness by, 243; and fulfillment of Genesis 15:18–21, 159; and Goliath, 178–79; and heavenly hope, 78; lies of, 155, 175–78, 176–77, 200; as man after God's heart, 200–201; mention of Melchizedek, 92; as musician for Saul, 175; Nathan has Bathsheba approach, on Solomon's behalf, 332; numbering of people by, 186, 220–21;

and polygamy, 121, 122; praised as warrior, 344; receives news of Saul's death, 181; repentance after census taking, 189–90; Saul's recognition of, 175; sin of, with Bathsheba, 152–53, 185–86, 200–201; sisters of, 175; speech of, to Solomon, 301; years of reign in Hebron, 183–84

Davis, Kingsley: on census, 366

Deborah, 105: and Barak, 421; praise of Jael by, 163

Deimel: on Iron Age, 196

Delilah: and Samson, 166

Delitzsch, Franz: on author of Ecclesiastes, 255; on brothers of David, 175; on "curse" in Job, 237; on differentiation between "soul" and "spirit," 260; on 1 Samuel 13:5, 172–73; and numbering during Exodus, 131; on prolonged day in Joshua, 162

DeMille, Cecil B., 191

Deucalion: of the Greeks, 83

Dewar, D., 62

Dhorne, E.: on Sirius, 381

Diblaim, father of Gomer, 294

Dinah: rape of, 380

Dishan: and Dishon in Genesis 36:21, 101

Dishon: and Dishan in Genesis 36:21, 101

Doederlein, J. C.: on Isaiah authorship, 264–65

Doeg, the Edomite: and massacre at Nob, 177, 362

Dougherty, Cecil, 63

Dougherty, Raymond P.: on last king of Babylon, 286

Driver, S. R., 110, 129

Duhm, Bernhard: on Isaiah authorship, 264–65; on Nabonidus, 269

Eglon, king of Moab: death of, 107

Ehud: deliverance of Israel by, 165; and Eglon, 107

Eichhorn, J. G.: on Daniel, 282; on Isaiah authorship, 264; and understanding of "Yahweh," 67; Yahweist-Eloist source division, 66

El, god known as Lutpan, 68

Elah: reign of, 225–26

Eleazar: takes Aaron's place, 147

Elhanan: and Goliath, 178–79; and Lahmi, 178

Eli: and Samuel, 136, 220

Eliab, brother of David, 174, 177

Eliakim: as Jehoiakim, 317

Eliezer, son of Dodavahu: prophet to Jehoshaphat, 202–3

Elihu: and Job, 236–37

Elijah: and death of prophets of Baal, 209; departure of, 226; erection of altar on Mt. Carmel by, 160, 227; and heavenly hope, 79; and letter to Jehoram, 226–27; prediction of Ahab's death by, 201–2; in 2 Kings, 227

Eliot, Elisabeth, 414–15

Eliphaz: and Job, 237–38, 396–97; God's reproof of, 237

Eliphaz, son of Esau, 99

Elisha: and Jehoash, 209; mocked by young men, 205; in 2 Kings, 277; and Syrian troops, 205–6

Elishama, 112

Elizabeth, 247

Elkanah, 233: descended from Kohath, 220; and plural marriages, 123; tribe of, 220

Elohim, 66, 67, 373–74

Emmor: sons of, and Abraham's land purchase, 380

Enoch, 78, 79

Enosh, 78

Ephraim, 103, 106, 379

Ephraimi Rescriptus: on Rompha, 381

Ephron, 97

Eri-aku, god, 90

Erlandsson, Seth: on Nebuchadnezzar as Lucifer in Isaiah, 269

Esau, 242: and Edom, 138; and polygamy, 122; sons of, 100; wives of, 99–101

Essarhadon: and Mitinti, 244

Esther, 234

Ethan: as wise sage, 250

Eusebius: on Matthew, 312; on time of crucifixion, 364

Eve: and tree of knowledge, 72. See also Adam and Eve.

Ezekiel: dates of prophecies of, 204

Ezra, 49: compilation of Chronicles by, 215–16; and Jerusalem, 290; and Jews in Elephantine, 207; and post-exilic Judah, 265

Fah-he: of the Chinese, 83

Farrar: on John 19:14, 364

Faulkner, R. O.: on Hippopotamus, 240

Feinberg, Charles L.: on Zechariah, 304

Felix: Paul before, 384

Festus: and Paul, 341–42, 384

Flack, E. E., 91

Forrer, E., 97

Frada: slain army of, 230

Franken, H. J., 196

Frawartish: army of, 230

Frazer, James, 84
Freedman, D. N., 111

Gad, the prophet: visit of, to David, 189
Gamaliel: and the census, 365; quote of example of Theudas and Judas by, 377–78; teacher of Paul, 404
Garstang, John: on Jericho, 156–57, 195, 196; on "rest" in Judges, 197
Gashmu: opponent of Nehemiah, 233
Gaubarura: and inscriptions of Darius the Great, 288
Gaumata: assassination of, 232
Gaussen, L.: and divine authority of Scripture, 25
Gedaliah: murder of, 277
Geisler, Norman L.: on polygamy, 123–24
Gesenius, H. F. W.: on Isaiah authorship, 264
Gesenius-Buhl: on Deuteronomy 15:4, 150
Geshem, opponent of Nehemiah, 233
Gideon: deliverance of Israel by, 165; as Jerubbaal, 244, 317; and Midianite army, 91; praised as warrior, 344
Gingrich, F. W.: on Mark 2:26, 362
Glueck, Nelson: excavations of Transjordan tells by, 192, 196
God: love of, 309, wrath and justice of, 309
Goliath, 80: David's contest with, 175; sword of, 177; and David's faith, 187; death of, 178–79
Gomer, harlot married to Hosea, 294
Goodall, Jane: on capabilities of animals, 65
Goodwin, W. W.: on Acts 9:7 and 22:9, 382
Green, William Henry, 13
Grimstead, Jay: and International Council on Biblical Inerrancy, 13
Gubaru, governor of Babylon, 288: as Darius the Mede, 288
Guillaume, A.: on Aramaic influence, 236
Gulick, C. B.: on Acts 9:7 and 22:9, 382
Gunkel, H.: on Genesis 14, 91
Gurney, O. R.: on Hittites, 97
Guthrie, D.: on John 19:14, 376

Hadadezer of Zobah: David's battle over, 184
Hadid: discrepancy concerning sons of, in Ezra and Nehemiah, 229
Hagar, 98, 121, 122
Haggai: assisted by Zechariah, 303; directed to rebuild temple, 230; and postexilic Judah, 265
Haldi, god, 68

Haley, J. W., 136
Ham: curse of, 86–87
Haman, 234
Hammurabi, 90
Hamor: Abraham's purchase of land from sons of, 379
Hanani: and Jehoshaphat, 242; as prophet to Asa, 228
Hanani, brother of Nehemiah, 290
Hananiah: as hostage of Nebuchadnezzar, 214
Hannah, 174
Haran, son of Terah, 378
Harding, G. Lankaster, 196
Harmakhis, god, 115
Harpagus, general, 288
Harrison, R. K.: and the Exodus, 192; on Mosaic laws, 149; on statistical numbers, 129
Hashum: sons of, 229
Hathor, Egyptian goddess, 52
Hayes, W. C., 195
Hazael of Damascus: and Jehu, 208
Heidel, Alexander, 84
Heli, father of Mary, 316
Heman: as wise sage, 250
Hendry, G. S.: on author of Ecclesiastes, 255
Hengstenberg: on author of Ecclesiastes, 255–56
Henry, Carl F. H., 13, 57
Hermas: on deaconesses, 414
Herod Agrippa II: Paul before, 384
Herod Antipas: Jesus' withholding of information from, 102
Herod Archelaus: Bible experts of, 320; and the census, 365; close of reign of, 212, 377–78; command of, to kill infants in Bethlehem 317
Herod the Great: and the census, 365
Herod, the Tetrarch: and incest, 168
Herodias: and incest, 168
Herodotus, Greek Historian: and Belshazzar, 286; and Darius the Mede, 287; on fulfillment of Matthew 24:34, 339; on Xerxes, 133–34
Heth: sons of, 96
Hezekiah, king of Judah: as coregent, 204; date of reign of, 207; and date of Sennacherib's invasion, 207, 211; destruction of cult centers by, 160; and embassy from Merodach-baladan of Babylon, 212–13; illness of, 211–12, 227; and Sennacherib, 133
Hiram: recurrence of name, 140
Hiram: and building of temple, 198, 257

Hitler, Adolf, 221

Hoenig, S. B.: on Theudas, 377

Holy Spirit: availability of, 354; Christ instructs disciples to receive, 353; and decree on eating of blood, 85; descension of as fulfillment of Matthew 16:28, 327; function of, 358; influence of, over transmission of texts, 206; outpouring of, on disciples at Pentecost, 117, 273, 327; and Paul's pilgrimage to Jerusalem, 383–84; as permanent indwelling Paraclete, 274; and regeneration, 407; revelation of, to Paul, 397; and Samuel, 180; and Saul, 179; as seven spirits in Revelation, 431; symbolized through Scripture, 431–32

Homer, demigod of Greece, 239

Homer: on fulfillment of Matthew 24:34, 339

Hophra, of Egypt, 277

Hosea, the prophet: analogy to God and Israel, 294; as author, 256; marriage of, to harlot, 294–95; proclamation of judgment on Jehu dynasty by, 208

Hoshea: assassination of Pekah by, 209; and Hezekiah, 211; name changed to Joshua, 137

Hoskyns, E. C.: on John 19:14, 376

Huffmon, H. B., 90

Hupisna: name for neo-Hittite principality, 98

Hystaspes: and Darius, 287

Ikausu, king of Ekron, 244

Irenaeus: on Matthew, 312

Isaac: and Abimelech II, 244; and circumcision, 398; journey of, to Gerar, 95; and Rebecca, 122; and repurchase of well of Beersheba, 380; sacrifice of, at Mt. Moriah, 96, 403

Isaiah: as author, 256; prayer of, for Hezekiah for shadow to retreat, 211

Ish-bosheth, son of Saul: assassination of, 183; reign of, 183–84

Ishmael, 122: and circumcision, 398

Ishtar, god known also as Inanna or Telitum, 68

Ishtunda, neo-Hittite principality, 98

Jabin: Deborah and Barak liberate Israel from, 163

Jacob: deceptions of, 101–2; and head of staff vs. head of bed, 421; loved by God, 242; as Joseph's father, 316; marriages of, 101; migration of, to Egypt, 378–79;

plot of land of, in Shechem, 379–81; and polygamy, 121–22; and twelve tribes of Israel, 103; and witness with Laban, 144

Jael: and murder of Sisera, 163–64

Jalam, son of Esau, 100

James, the apostle: address of, to Peter, 425; and John request to be officials in Jesus' kingdom, 332; on Job, 236; and third postresurrection interview with Christ, 355

Jamieson: on dating of Asa, 225; on humility of Moses, 135; on Levites, 136

Japheth: Noah's blessing of, 87

Jashobeam: enemies slain by, 222

Jeconiah. See Jehoiachin.

Jedidiah. See Solomon.

Jehoahaz: of Israel, 208; as Shallum, 317

Jehoash: and Amaziah, 208; Amaziah taken captive by, 204; beginning of reign, 206; and Syrians, 208

Jehoiachin, son of Jehoiakim, 213–14: age of, at accession, 206–7, 214–15, 226; deported to Babylon, 214; as Jeconiah, 317; in Jeremiah, 275; as senior king of Judah, 204; sons of, 215

Jehoiakim: age of, when Jehoiachin begotten, 215; contradiction with son on throne, 275; and dating of Nebuchadnezzar's invasion, 285; death of, 213–14; as Eliakim, 317; and Nebuchadnezzar, 213–14; son of, 216–17; vs. Zedekiah in Jeremiah 27:1–11, 273

Jehoiada, 337–38

Jehoram: beginning of reign, 204–5, and Edomites, 298; kills brothers, 226; receives letter from Elijah, 226–27

Jehoshaphat: alliance of, with Ahab, 242, 410; commercial venture of, with Ahaziah, 202; as coregent, 204; destruction of cult centers by, 160; fleet of, at Ezion-geber, 202–3

Jehu: and destruction of house of Ahab, 207–9; massacre of Baal worshipers of Israel by, 207–8; shooting of Jehoram by, 207; sons of, rule to fourth generation, 208

Jephthah: as man of faith, 421–22; prediction about, 105; questions Ammonite invaders, 192; praised as warrior, 344; sacrifice of daughter, 96; vow of, 164–65

Jeremiah: abducted to Egypt, 277; as author, 256; chosen by God, 389; and circumcision, 94; prophecy from Zechariah attributed to, 345

Jeroboam: recurrence of name, 140

Jeroboam I: and establishment of temple in Dan, 142; prophet's denunciation of, 301; shrines established by, 159; as supervisor for Solomon, 199

Jeroboam II: and Amos, 297; father of Zechariah, 209; and Jonah, 300; and recapture of Transjordanian tribal territory, 208-9

Jerome: on Matthew, 312; and Psalm 90:2, 42

Jerubbaal. See Gideon.

Jeshua: Jews led back to Jerusalem by, 216; and rebuilding of temple, 230-31

Jeshurun: as Israel in Deuteronomy 32:15, 269

Jesse: sons of, 174, 175

Jesuh, son of Esau, 100

Jesus ben Sirach: on Ecclesiasticus of the Apocrypha, 257

Jesus Christ: acceptance of Jonah as literal, 301-2; atonement and circumcision of, 94; attitude of, toward book of Isaiah, 265, 267; birth of, told to Magi by star, 317-18; and coming of Holy Spirit, 274; as conqueror over Satan, 312-13; as creator, 208; death of, and the centurion, 346-47; as everlasting Father, 268; as God incarnate, 358-59; as head of the church, 261; before Herod Antipas, 102; preaching of, to spirits in hades, 123-24; rejected as Hope of Israel, 118; relationship of, to the Father, 375; Adam's race represented by, 375; as second Adam, 188; as son of God, 373-74; temptations of, 236, 418-19

Jethro, 92

Jezebel, 160, 202: and Athaliah, 226; and blood of God's servants, 207

Jezreel, firstborn of Hosea, 294

Joab: and Absalom, 186; advises against numbering 221; David has, number the people, 186, 187; murder of Abner, 183; report on number in Israel, 189

Joash: age of, at reign, 215; assassination of, 153; end of reign of, 206; order of death of Jehoiada by, 337-38

Joatham, 316

Job: and Eliphaz, 396-97; God's challenge to Satan about, 188; and heavenly hope, 78; historical or fictional, 235-37; as true believer, 92

Joel, son of Samuel, 170, 377

John, the apostle: and James' request to be officials in Christ's kingdom, 332; race of, to tomb of Jesus, 349; and the world, 242; as writer of the Gospel, 311

John the Baptist, 75, 212: chosen by God, 389; conception of, 245; Luke's background for, 313, 330; ministry of, to people at Ephesus, 383

Jonah: accepted by Christ as factual, 21, 25; Christ used, as sign, 363; evidence for, as literal history, 301-2; prediction of recapture of Transjordanian tribal territory by Jeroboam II, 208; and repentance of Nineveh, 81, 134; as type of Christ, 302

Jonathan: exploit of, at Michmash, 172; protection of David by, 176; Saul's anger against, 177

Joseph: and the census, 365; Jesus' genealogy from, 316; and Mary, 268, 316

Joseph of Arimathea, tomb of, 347, 350

Joseph: in Egypt, 193; sends for family, 378-79; receives blessing of Jacob, 421; tribes of, 103

Josephus: and the census, 365; and Hyksos Dynasty, 191; on 1 Samuel 6:19, 169; on Judas of Galilee, 378; on Mt. Nebo, 147; on Nebuchadnezzar's conquest of Egypt, 277; on Theudas, 377

Joshua: altar of, on Mt. Ebal, 159-60; and building of second temple, 230; and crossing of Jordan, 138; and destruction of Jericho, 153, 157-59; directions to, about Book of Law, 45; and Ephraim, 106; Moses changes name of, from Hoshea, 137; and the prolonged day, 161-62; victory of, over Canaanites, 24

Josiah: age of, at accession, 215; destruction of cult centers by, 160; prophet's prediction of coming of, 270-71

Jotham: as coregent, 204; in Matthew's genealogy, 316-17

Judas of Galilee: founder of Zealots, 378; insurrection of, 365; reference to, in Acts, 377-78

Judas Iscariot: as apostate, 419-20; betrayal of Christ by, 188, 344; death of, 344; and satanic influence, 179

Jude: and nonbiblical sources, 430

Judith, wife of Esau, 99

Katuzili (Hattusilis), king of N. Syria of Hittite Empire, 98

Kautzsch, E.: on 1 Samuel 13:1, 172

Keil, C. F.: and amount of gold David gave for temple, 223; numbering of people in wilderness; on prolonged day in Joshua, 162; on 2 Chronicles 16:1, 226; and Sheshbazzar as Zerubbabel, 217

Keil and Delitzsch: on Jephthah's vow, 164–65; on 2 Samuel 8:4, 184

Kenyon, Kathleen: and capture of Jericho, 157; on destruction of City IV, 195; on Roland De Vaux's work, 154

Keturah: and Abraham, 98

Kish: connection of, with Cush, 90

Kitchen, Kenneth: on Battle of Mareshah, 211; on creation order, 68–69; and Egyptian genealogies, 111; and Mosaic Law, 149; on population of Israel, 140; on So, king of Egypt, 211

Kittel, 35

Koehler, Ludwig, 98, 129

Koehler-Baumgartner, 150

Kohath, son of Levi, 220

Konig, F. W.: on discrepancy in Ezra and Nehemiah, 230

Korah, son of Esau, 100

Kothar-wa-Khasis, god also known as Hayyin, 68

Kuizenga, John, 13

Kuwait: Chaldean corsairs from, 89

Kyle, M. G. 136

Laban: deceptions of, 101–2; descendent of Haran, 378; and witness with Jacob, 144

Labarnas, Hittite leader, 97

Labat, René: on Sakkut, 381

Lamech: and polygamy, 122

Lange: on disciples taking staffs on evangelistic tours, 326

Lazarus: Jesus goes to home of, 335

Lazarus: parable of, 98–99, 367

Leah, 101, 121–22

Leakey, L. S. B., 63

Lenski: on 144,000 of Revelation, 434

Leupold: on author of Ecclesiastes, 255

Levi: mentioned by Luke, 314

Liddell, H. G.: on fulfillment of Matthew 24:34, 339

Lindsell, Harold, 13, 20, 434

Linnaeus, 60

Lo-ammi: paternity of, 294

Lod: discrepancy in Ezra and Nehemiah concerning sons of, 229

Lo-rahamah: paternity of, 294

Lot, 88, 206

Louvre: and Nes-Hor Stela, 278

Lubarna (Labarnas), king of N. Syria of Hittite empire, 98

Lucifer: in Isaiah, 268–70. See also Satan.

Luke: associated with Paul, 311; a Gentile, 311; and Quirinius and the census, 365–66

Luther, Martin, 19, 24

Lydia, of Philippi: God's use of, 412

Maacah, 185

Machen, J. Gresham, 13

Machpelah: cave of, 97, 380

Macrobius: on Roman numbering, 364

Mahalath, wife of Esau, 122

Maher-shalal-hash-baz, son of Isaiah: as type of coming Immanuel, 267

Mahlon, husband of Ruth, 167

Malachi: and postexilic Judah, 265

Manabozho, god of the Algonquin: and a flood, 83

Manasseh, son of Joseph, 103, 106, 379

Manasseh: and Ashurbanipal, 214; and moral breakdown of Judah, 271; murders committed by, in Jersualem avenged, 342; release from Babylon, 227; repentance of, 227–28; successor to Hezekiah, 213

Manoah, 361

Manu of the Hindu, 83

Marais, J. I.: on the soul, 259

Marduk: temple of, and Cyrus the Great, 288

Mark, assistant to Peter, 311, 313

Martha, 314, 335

Marti: on Nabonidus, 269

Martyr, Justin, 119

Mary: at annunciation, 247, 313; genealogy of Jesus from, 316; as virgin, 268

Mary, mother (or wife) of James: visit of, to tomb, 347, 350

Mary Magdalene: Christ's appearance to, 117, 347–49, 367, 412

Mary, sister of Martha and Lazarus: Jesus visits home of, 335; mention of, by Luke 313–14

Mattaniah. See Zedekiah.

Matthew: and authority of Scripture, 25; as disciple, 311; as evangelist, 308; mentioned by Luke, 314

Matthiae, P. 134

Maunders, E. W.: on prolonged day in Joshua, 161

Mayor, J. B.: on 2 Peter, 426

McClellan: on why John used Roman numbering, 364

Melchizedek, 48, 91–93, 117

Menahem, father of Pekahiah, 209: defeat of Shallum by, 209; Tiglath-pileser III, bought off by, 211

Mendel, G. J.: and experiments in plant genetics, 56

Mendenhall, G. 129

Merneptah, son of Rameses II, 197
Merodach-baladan, of Babylon: and embassy to Hezekiah, 212-13
Mesha, king of Moab, 208
Micah, the Ephraimite, 105, 141
Micaiah, prophet before Ahab, 410. *See also* Maacah.
Michael, the archangel, 238, 430
Michaelis, J. D.: on David, 282
Milcom, god of Ammon: Solomon's building of shrine for, 160, 251
Milligan: on 144,000 of Revelation, 434
Milton, John, 239, 426
Miriam: pressure of, on Moses, 135
Mishael: as hostage of Nebuchadnezzar, 214
Mithredath, treasurer for Cyrus, 217
Mitinti, king of Askelon, 244
Mixter, R., 57
Mizraim, son of Ham, 86
Molech, god of Ammonites: and infant sacrifices, 96, 264; Solomon's building of shrine for, 251; tabernacle of, and Israelites, 381
Moses: as author of Pentateuch, 153-54; biographer of, 112-13; and burning bush, 22, 308; change of name of Hoshea to Joshua by, 137; Christ's acceptance of, as literal, 25; and circumcision of Gershom, 111; descended from Kohath, 220; education of, 51; and heavenly hope, 79; humility of, questioned, 136-37; and life expectancy, 77; miracles of, before Pharaoh, 113; and obedience for salvation, 71; obituary of, 153-54; and revelation of God on Mt. Sinai, 124; son of blessings, 103-7
Muilenberg, James: on author of Ecclesiastes, 256-57; on Nebuchadnezzar as Lucifer in Isaiah, 269
Mursilis I, 97
Mursilis II, 97
Mutallu (Muwatallis), king of N. Syria of Hittite empire, 98

Naaman: and leprosy, 127
Nabonidus: as king of Babylon, 269, 286
Nabopolassar: and restoration of Babylonian language, 285
Naboth: Ahab's offer to, 201; confiscation of vineyard of, 410; death of, 201
Nabunaid; inscription of, 286
Nadab: and strong drink, 148
Nahor, 88
Nahu, son of Terah, 378
Nathan: Jesus descended from, 316

Nathan, the prophet: request of, to Bathsheba to approach David, 332; visit of, to David, 190, 200
Nathanael: and third postresurrection interview with Christ, 355
Nebuchadnessar, 108
Nebuchadnezzar: Daniel's prediction of insanity of, 282; Daniel's dating of invasion of, 284-85; and downfall of Tyre 276, 278; destruction of Jerusalem/Judah by, 213-14, 263, 342; dream of, 270; and invasion of Egypt, 275, 277; as Lucifer in Isaiah, 269; pursuit of all refugee Jews by, 257; and restoration of Babylonian language, 285; rule of, over Syria, Phoenicia, Samaria, and Judah, 214; taking of treasures of Jerusalem temple by, 214
Necho, Pharaoh: appointment of Jehoiakim as king by, 285; change of Eliakim's name by, 317; and Jehoiakim, 214; overlord of Palestine, 273; victory of, at Megiddo, 273
Nehemiah: and Arab opponent, 233; and Daniel's Seventy Weeks, 290; and Jews in Elephantine, 207; and postexilic Judah, 265; and rebuilding of Jerusalem, 274
Nero Caesar: Paul's appeal to, 384
Nethanel, brother of David, 175
Nicodemus: and burial of Christ, 347
NIN-IB, Sumerian god, 381
Noah: blamelessness of, 65; Christ's preaching to generation of, 423-24; Christ's acceptance of, as factual, 21, 25; corruption at time of, 80; curse of, on Ham, 86-87; and numbering of animals in the ark, 81-82; referred to in Ezekiel, 235; and strong drink, 148; testimony of, 92; as type of Christ, 424
Noiiy, Lecomte de, 58
Nu-u, of the Hawaiians, 83

O'Callaghan, José: on Mark 6:52-53, 346
Ockenga, Harold John, 13
Oholibamah, wife of Esau, 99, 100
Omri, Ahab's father, 202
Ono: discrepancy in Ezra and Nehemiah concerning sons of, 229
Origen: on the devil and the angel Michael, 430; on Matthew, 312
Ornan: threshing floor of, 190
Osiris, of Egypt: various names for, 68
Osorkon I, Pharaoh, 211
Othniel: deliverance of Israel by, 165
Ozem, brother of David, 175
Ozias, 316

Padi, king of Ekron, 244
Paine, S. W.: on 2 Peter authorship, 427
Papias: on Book of Matthew, 312, 346
Parosh: sons of, 229
Patterson, Francine, 65
Paul: appearance of, before Sanhedrin, 341–42, 384; as author, 256; charge of, to elders at Ephesus, 383; commendation of David by, 201; concerning Christ's deity, 358–59; on Damascus road, 382–83; on dates of Exodus to building of temple, 192; and falsehood, 155; instruction of, to Corinthian church, 118; length of ministry of, at Ephesus, 383; on observing Lord's Day, 120; on new covenant, 274–75; pilgrimage of, to Jerusalem, 383–84
Payne, J. B.: on Daniel, 283; on numbering in Chronicles, 222; on 144,000 of Revelation, 434; on "rest" mentioned in Judges, 197
Pedaiah, 217, 218
Pekah, king of Israel: assassinated by Hoshea, 209; assassinates Pekahiah, 209; and Isaiah 7:16, 266; Judean troops slain by, 132; number of years of reign of, in Samaria, 209–10
Pekahiah: assassination of, 209
Pepi I, of Egypt, 133
Peter: Christ's appearance to, after resurrection, 351, 355; Christ's appearance to, 117; Christ's dictum to, 343; Christ's directive to, 355; and Cornelius, 388; denial of Christ by, 75, 188, 339–41; and eating of blood, 85; goes to tomb of Jesus, 349; and Mark, 311; mother-in-law of, cured by Jesus, 321; at Pentecost, 377
Pettingill, W. L.: on 1 John 3:9, 429; on Paul's pilgrimage to Jerusalem, 384
Pharaoh: death of firstborn son of, 115–16; defiance of, against God, 114, 390–95; of the Exodus, 115, 191–98; of the Oppression, 115; and Yahweh, 67
Philcol, a Philistine, 94
Philip: daughters of, 412; and Ethiopian eunuch, 266; home of, and Paul, 384
Phinehas: attack on Midian led by, 142
Phoebe, 412, 414
Pickering: and prolonged day in Joshua, 161
Pilate: inscription of, for Jesus' cross, 345–46; as procurator, 365–66
Pinches: and cuneiform tablet, 277
Pinnock, Clark: on Mark and Jewish religious customs, 313

Plato: portrait of Socrates by, 314
Pliny, the Elder: on Roman numbering, 364
Plutarch: on fulfillment of Matthew 24:35, 339
Porphyry: and Maccabean date of Daniel, 282
Power, W. J. A., 196
Priscilla, 412
Pritchard, James B.: on "archer" 106; on Aziri, 244; and cuneiform tablet discovered by Pinches, 277; and death of a son of Pharaoh, 115; on inscription by Amenhotep, 195, 197; and inscription of Uni, 133; on Jehu, 208; and Mesha stone inscription, 103; and mythology in Scripture, 240; on names of gods, 68
Proksch, O.: on Nebuchadnezzar as Lucifer in Isaiah, 269
Ptolemaeus, Claudias: and weather diary, 132–33
Puah, midwife to Hebrews, 109–10, 131
Publius: fever and dysentery of, 314
Put, son of Ham, 86

Quintilius Varus: as legate of Syria, 365–66
Quirinius: and the census, 365–66
Quirinius, P. Sulpicius: Judas of Galilee's revolt in time of, 378

Rachel, 101–2, 121–22
Raddai, brother of David, 175
Rahab: lie of, 155–56; and mythology in Scripture, 239–40; and Salmon, 156
Raiphan. See Rompha.
Ramm, Bernard: on prolonged day in Joshua, 161
Ramses the Great, 106, 191–98
Ramses II, 97: on Battle of Kadesh, 133; building of, in Goshen, 197; and the Exodus, 191, 193; and genealogy, 111; and victory over sea peoples, 95
Ramses III: campaigns of, 197; Tjeker subdued by, 197
Rebecca (Rebekah): descendent of Haran, 378; as virgin, 268; wife of Isaac, 122
Rechab, assassination of Ish-bosheth by, 183
Rehoboam: and Maacah, 185
Rehum: interference from, in building of second temple, 231–32
Rehwinkel, A. M.: on the Flood, 82–83
Remaliah, father of Pekah, 209
Rephan, idol Stephen referred to, 381–82
Reuben: in census, 129
Reuel, son of Esau and Basemath, 100

Rezin, of Damascus, 266
Rimmer, Harry: on prolonged day in Joshua, 161
Robertson, A. T., 30
Robinson, George L.: on Zechariah, 303
Rompha, god, 381
Rosenmueller, E. F. K.: on authorship of Isaiah, 264
Ruckstuhl, Suzanne, 134
Rufus, 313
Rukibtu, of Askelon, 244
Ruth, the Moabitess: spelling of name of, 174

Sais, city of Egypt, 210–11
Salmon: marriage of, to Rahab, 156
Salome: visit of, to tomb of Christ, 347, 350
Salitis, first king of Egypt, 193
Samson: of Dan, 141; as man of faith, 421–22; marriage of, to unbeliever, 166; as Nazirite, 165; praised as warrior, 344; prank of, at Timnah, 166; prediction about, 105; and romance with Philistine, 165, 166
Samuel: king of Israel chosen by, 170; and falsehoods, 175–78; praised as warrior, 344; sons of, 170; temple work of, 136; tribe of father of, 220; warning of, to Israel about king, 171
Sapalulme (Suppiluliumas), king of N. Syria of Hittite empire, 98
Sarah, wife of Abraham, 97, 98, 121, 122, 380
Sargon II: and Aziri, 244; and captives from Samaria, 133; and Hittites and Horites of, 210
Satan (Lucifer): before God, 238–39; final state of, 73–74; inciting of David to number people by, 186; and king of Babylon, 270; as Lucifer in Isaiah, 269; and magicians of Egypt, 113; rebellion of, 66; represented in Revelation, 432; revolt of, against God, 74; sphere of action of, 239; and temptation of Christ, 320–21; temptation of Eve by, 70, 72; temptation of David by, 221; and war, 219; words to, about Job, 237
Saturninus: as legate of Syria, 365–66
Saul: and Agag, 140–41; age of, when became king, 171–72; anointing of, 171; and battle of Mt. Gilboa, 297; chosen from Benjamin, 107; death of, 181–82; effectiveness of, 173; and evil spirit, 179–80; failure of, to exterminate Amalekites, 173; first ruler of Judah, 170; and Gibeonites, 153, 161; God's sorrow that he was king, 173–74; lifting of siege of Jabesh-gilead by, 171; massacre of priests of Nob, 200, 362; promised eternal kingdom, 173; prophesying of, while naked, 180; punishment on grandchildren of, 153; pursuit of David by, to Ramah, 180; wives of, and David, 121
Schaeffer, Francis, 13
Schoville, K. N.: on Absalom's tomb, 184
Schrader, E.: on Sakkut, 381
Scott, D. D., 25
Scott, R.: on fulfillment of Matthew 24:34, 339
Seele, K. C., 97
Seleucus III: death of, 292; predicted in Daniel, 290
Semkowski, L., 150
Senaah: sons of, 229
Sennacherib, of Assyria: assassination of, 227; date of invasion of Judah by, 207, 211; and Hezekiah, 133; record of, in Taylor Prism, 211; retreat of, from Judah to Nineveh, 212; and Padi of Ekron, 244
Servetus, Michael, 19
Seth, son of Adam and Eve, 77, 78
Seth, patron god of Hyksos, 194
Seti, 106, 194, 197
Shallum: as Jehoahaz, 317; murder of Zechariah by, 209
Shalmaneser: and Battle of Karkar, 133; and Jehu, 208
Shamash-shumukin, of Babylon, 183, 285
Shammah, brother of David, 174
Sharruludari, of Askelon, 244
Shealtiel: as governor of Jewish colony, 217–18; with Sheshbazzar and Zerubbabel, 216–19
Shear-jashub, firstborn of Isaiah, 263, 267
Sheshbazzar: and Cyrus of Persia, 217; with Shealtiel and Zerubbabel, 216–18; and temple treasures, 217
Sheshonq, of Egypt (Shishak), 211
Shethar-bozenai: interference from, in building of second temple, 231
Shewell-Cooper, W. E.: on mustard seed, 329
Shimea. See Shammah.
Shimshai: interference from, in building of second temple, 231, 232
Shinuktu, neo-Hittite principality, 98
Shiphrah, midwife to the Hebrew people, 109–10, 131
Shishak. See Sheshonq.
Sidon: and Jehu, 208

Sidqui, king of Ashkelon, 244
Siebenthal, Heinrich von, 134
Silas. *See* Silvanus.
Sillibel, king of Gaza, 244
Silvanus, scribe for Peter, 426-27
Simeon: prophecy of, recorded by Luke, 313
Simon of Cyrene, 313
Simpson, G. G.: and missing links, 56
Sinaiticus Codex: on Gergesa, 324; on Rompha, 381
Sisera: death of, 163-64
Smick, Elmer, 136
Smith, Wilbur, 13
So, king of Egypt, 210
Socinus, 19
Socrates, 314
Solomon: and Adonijah, 123; as author of Ecclesiastes, 255-58; beginning of reign of, 115; building of shrines for foreign gods by, 160, 251; and forced labor, 199-200; as Jedidiah, 244; Jesus descended from, 316; and materialism, 295; name of daughter of, 99; and Neo-Hittites, 97; and number of stalls for cavalry, 221-22; romance of, with country girl, 261-62; and the temple, 186, 191, 222, 231; trade of, at Ophir, 202; as writer of Proverbs, 250-52, 254
Steindorff, G., 97
Stephen: address of, to Sanhedrin, 379; on age of Abraham when he left Haran, 378; concerning idol carried by Israelites, 381-82; on Jacob's plot of land in Shechem, 379-81; on number in migration with Jacob to Egypt, 378-79; reference of, to history not in Old Testament, 430
Stonehouse, N. B.: on rich young ruler, 329
Sutekh. *See* Seth.
Symmachus: Greek translation of Genesis by, 49:10, 108; and Isaiah 7:11, 41; and Psalm 90:2, 42

Talmon, S., 271
Tamar, daughter of Absalom, 184
Tamar, sister to Absalom, 185
Tartarus: and mythology in Scripture, 239
Tatian: on four Gospels, 315
Tattenai, interference from, in building of temple, 231
Taylor, Vincent, 30
Tefnakht, king of Egypt, 211
Tenney, Merrill C., 97, 119
Terah: Abraham's departure from Haran after death of, 378

Tertullian: and legates of Syria, 365; on the Sabbath, 119
Tezpi, of the Mexican Indians, 83
Theodotion: and Isaiah 7:11, 41
Theophilus: Luke's writing to, 313
Theudas, leader against Rome, 377-78
Thiele, Edwin: on accession of Hezekiah, 212
Thirtle, J. W.: on titles of Psalms, 243
Thomas: and postresurrection visit of Christ, 117, 354, 355
Thutmose III: on Battle of Megiddo, 133; as pharaoh of the Exodus, 198; as pharaoh of the Oppression, 194-95
Thutmose IV, 115, 198
Tiglath-pileser III: annexation of Issachar by, 104; bought off by Menahem, 209; pillage of Damascus by, 267
Timna, daughter of Seir, 100
Titus: and destruction of Jerusalem, 327; and Seventy Weeks of Daniel, 291
Totten, C. A.: on prolonged day in Joshua, 161
Trever, J. C.: on mustard seed, 329
Tudkhaliya: and Abraham, 90
Tunna, neo-Hittite principality, 98
Tuwana, neo-Hittite principality, 98

Uahib-Ra, on invasion of Nile Valley, 278
Ugbaru, general of Persians, 288
Unger, Merrill F.: on Sheshbazzar as Zerubbabel, 218
Uriah, 97, 153, 200
Uriel of Gibeah, husband to Tamar, 185
Ushtani, governor of Babylon, 288
Utnapishtim, of the Babylonians, 83
Uzzah: and Ark of Covenant, 169
Uzziah, 127, 204, 316-17

Vaux, Roland de, 154
Vergil, demigod of Greece, 239
Verhoef, P. A.: on Aaron's death, 147
Vos, H. F., 95, 97

Washingtonensis: on Matthew 8:28, 325
Waterman, Henry, 119
Weidner, F. F.: on Greek coins, 296
Wellhausen: and Amarna Tablets, 52; and JEDP theory, 46
Whitcomb, J. C.: on Darius the Mede, 288
Whitefield, George, 180
Wiener, Harold W.: on alleged conflicting Mosaic laws, 149
Wilson, Robert D., 13, 161, 285
Wood, Leon: and Daniel 11, 292; on date of Exodus, 198; on dates of kings, 225

Wright, G. E., 111
Wurthwein, Ernst, 30, 44

Xenophon, greek historian, 112, 287, 314
Xerxes, king of Persia, 133-34: army of, defeated by Greeks, 303; collapse of attempt of to conquer Greece, 296; and Daniel 11:2, 292; and Esther, 234

Yahweh, 59, 66, 67
Yamauchi, Edwin, 196, 296
Young, Davis, A., 63
Young, E. J.: on author of Ecclesiastes, 255; on Masoretic textual error, 211

Zacchaeus: Jesus' contact with, 332; mentioned by Luke, 314
Zattu: arrival of, in Judea, 30; sons of, 229
Zechariah: and postexilic Judah, 265; prophecies of, 334, 345; and Zerubbabel, 217

Zechariah, king of Israel: murder of, 209
Zechariah, son of Berechiah or Jehoiada, 337-38
Zedekiah, 204: as Mattaniah, 244, 317;
Zerah, the Ethiopian, 132, 134, 210, 211
Zerubbabel: governor of Judah, 217; Jews led back to Jerusalem by, 216; and rebuilding of temple, 230-32; as Shealtiel or Sheshbazzar, 216-19; as son of Shealtiel, 217; sons of, 217
Zeruiah, sister of David, 175
Zeus: as Kronion and Olympius, 68
Zibean, mother of Oholibamah, 99, 100
Zilpay, 121-22
Zipporah, 111
Ziusidru, of the Sumerians, 83
Zoeckler: on author of Ecclesiastes, 255-56
Zohar, 97
Zophar: God's reproof of, 237-38
Zorell, F., on "curse" in Job, 237; on Deuteronomy 15:4, 150

Index of Subjects

Abortion, 246–49
Abraham's bosom, 72, 367
Accession-year system, 206
"Accuser," the, 238
Achor, Valley of: Achan stoned at, 201
Achshaph: destruction of, 158
Actium, Battle of, 278
Adam: water of Jordan dammed up at, 156
Adam's race: represented by Christ, 375; rescue of, 323
Adulteress: Jesus' dealing with, 371–73
Adultery: and Mosaic Law, 371
Agate Spring, Nebraska: and flood evidence, 83
Ai: defenders of, repulse Israelites, 139; destruction of, 158; discovery of, as Et-Tell, 196
Alexandrian War, The (Caesar), 136
Algonquin flood saga, 83
Alleged Discrepancies (Haley), 136
Altamira cave paintings, 63
Amada stela: and campaign of Amenhotep, 198
Amalekite: tells of Saul's death, 181
Amalekites: and David's faith, 187; David's raids on, 178; extermination of, ordered, 121; royal title of, 140; Saul's effectiveness over, 173; Saul's failure to exterminate, 173
Amarna tablets, 52
Ammonites: invasion of Gad by, 105; and Jephthah, 164; Saul's effectiveness over, 173
Anabasis (Xenophon), 112
Anathoth, Jeremiah purchases field in, 345
Ancient Orient (Kitchen), 90, 111, 149
Angel of Yahweh, 360–61
Angels: as sons of God, 79–80; surrounding God's throne, 74; at tomb of Jesus, 348
Animals: having spirits, 258–60; unclean, 126
Annual of Leeds University: on Aramaic influence, 236
Antediluvian geneology, 77–78
Ante-Nicene Fathers, 119

Anthropomorphic language applied to God in Psalms, 244–45
Antichrist, 410
Antioch Pisidiae: congregation at, 201
Antiquities (Josephus): on the census, 365; conquest of Egypt, 277; on 1 Samuel 6:19, 169; on Judas of Galilee, 378; at Mt. Nebo, 147; on Nebuchadnezzar's conquest of Egypt, 277; on Theudas, 377
Apocalypse: central theme of, 431–32
Apostasy: at Baal-peor, 141; of golden calf, 141
Apostles: definition of, 419; and outpouring of Holy Spirit, 273
Apparel: guidelines for, 150–51
Arabah Road. *See* King's Highway.
Aramaic Targum: and Isaiah 9:2, 33; and Psalm 68:18, 404; and Psalm 90:2, 42
Ararat, Mt., 82, 83
Archaeology in Bible Times (Vos), 95, 97
Archaeology and the Dead Sea Scrolls (de Vaux), 154
"Archers": in prediction concerning Joseph, 106
Ark of the Covenant: carried over Jordan, 156; glory cloud over, 125; and sacrilege of Bethshemesh, 169, 222; and Uzzah, 169
Armageddon, Battle of, 292, 432; and Seventy Weeks of Daniel, 293
Armenia, 70
Ascension of Christ, 314
Asher, tribe of, 105, 183
Ashkelon: Samson's attack on young men at, 165
"Assumption of Moses, the," 430
Assyria: Ashurbanipal imprisons Manasseh, 214; Babylonian vassal of, 212; invaders of, destroy Samaria, 266; Isaiah's prediction of destruction of, 269; Sargon II of, 210; Tiglath-pileser III bought off by Menahem, 209
Astrology: condemned in Bible, 317–18; used by Magi, 317–18
Atheism and evolution, 55–56

Atonement: brought by faith, 71; of Christ, 70, 71, 117, 242; day of, 35, 127; the Savior's, and sacrifice of animals, 280; teaching of, to Adam and Eve, 75–76
Authority, of man, 413
Auvergne, France, 83

Baal-hamon: Solomon's estate at, 262
Babel, tower of, 88
Babylon: Belshazzar of, 210; and embassy from Merodach-baladan, 212–13; fall of, 264, 265, 270, 282, 284; invasion of Egypt by, spoken of by Jeremiah, 275; last king of, 286; Manasseh imprisoned at, 214; prediction of destruction of, 54; return from, and Levitical service, 136
Babylonian captivity, 53
Babylonian flood saga, 83
Babylonian exile: Chronicles compiled after, 216; God's promises to Israel during, 274; and Job, 235; and polygamy, 123; setting prior to, 263
Babylonian cuneiform: recent discoveries, 277
Baptism: and circumcision, 94; (commanded, 357); of the dead, 401–2
Barnabas, Epistle of, 119
Battle for the Bible (Lindsell), 20
Beast, the, or Antichrist, 292
Beatitudes, Mount of, 334
Beatitudes: differences between Luke's and Matthew's accounts, 366
Beauty contests, 234
Bedouin mentality: and destruction of Jericho, 158
Beersheba, well of, 94–95, 379–80
Behistun Rock inscription, 30, 133, 230, 287
Bel, of Babylon, 68
Belikh River, 88
Benjamin, tribe of: Moses' prediction about, 106–7; not numbered, 189
Benjamites of Gibeah: destruction of, 158
Berlin Execration texts: on Job, 236
Berlin genealogy, 111
Bethany: Jesus' journey to, 335
Bethel: Jeroboam's sanctuary in, 270; as religious center, 205
Bethlehem: David's home in, 175; house of Ephrathah, 318–19; predicted as birthplace of Christ, 271; Samuel goes to, 176
Bethesda, Pool of, 202
Beth-shean: archers of, 106
Beth-shan: Abner forces Philistines back from, 183
Bethshemesh: and Ark of the Covenant,

169; Battle of, 208; judgment of, 169; number slain in plague at, 222; population of, 169
Bethel: Saul's revival experience at, 180
Beza codex: on Mark 16:2, 347
Bible and the Ancient Near East, The (ed., Wright), 111
Bible Dictionary: on Zerubbabel as Sheshbazzar, 218
Bible Geography (Baly): on Paran and Kadesh Barnea, 137; on soil of Israel, 139
Bible in Its World, The (Kitchen): on population of Israel, 140
Bible Questions Answered (ed., Polcyn): on 1 John 3:9, 429; on Paul's pilgrimage to Jerusalem, 384
Biblical Archaeology Review, 88
Biblical Archaeologist, The, 134
Biblical Archaeology in Focus (Schoville): on Absalom's tomb, 184
Billy Graham Evangelistic Association, 11
Black Obelisk of Shalmaneser III, 208
Blind men: number of, Jesus healed when entering Jericho, 332–33
Blood: eating of, forbidden, 84–86
Blood sacrifice, 75–76
Bloodshed: and remission of sins, 121
Bodmer text: on Rompha, 381
Boghazkoy. See Hattusas.
Bohairic Coptic: on Gergesa, 324–25
Book of the Dead, 89
Book of Isaiah (Young): New International Commentary: on Masoretic textual error, 211
Brontosaurus, 63
Brutality in Psalms, 245–46
Bulletin of the American School of Oriental Research: on author of Ecclesiastes, 256–57
Bulletin of the Near Eastern Archaeology Society, 222
Burden of Babylon, The (Erlandsson): on Nebuchadnezzar as Lucifer in Isaiah, 269
burning bush, 32
Byblos, city of: and Jehu, 208

Caesarea Philippi: Christ's prediction of His resurrection at, 348
Caesarea: Paul's arrest at, 384
Cairo Genizah: early Hebrew manuscript from, 42
Cambrian period: and animal life, 62
Canaan: a more fertile time, 133
Canaanites: oppose Israelites, 139–40
Capital punishment, 341–44, 371–73

Capernaum: centurion's servant healed at, 321–22; Jesus' journey to, 321

Canons of textual criticism, 42–44

Canticles. *See* Song of Solomon.

Carchemish: Battle of, 285; Nebuchadnezzar's victory at, 273

Carmel, Mt.: altar erected on, by Elijah, 160; and death of prophets of Baal, 209

Cenchrea: church at, 414; Paul's vow at, 384

Census taking: by David, 186–88; by Moses, 187; reliability of, in Numbers, 129

Centurion: healing of servant of, 321–22; words of, at Jesus' crucifixion, 346–47

Chaldean domination of Egypt, 277

Chaldean soldiers: brutality of, 245

Chaldeans: as soothsayers, 285–86

Cherethites, 96

Children: of believers and Proverbs 22:6, 252–53; and death, 185

Chinese flood saga, 83

Christian Evidences (McClellan): on why John used Roman numbering, 364

Christian View of Science and Scripture (Ramm), 161

Chronicles (Keil and Delitzsch): and amount of gold David gave for temple, 223; on brothers of David, 175; on 2 Chronicles 16:1, 226

Chronicles: portions of as midrashic, 300–301

Chronology of Hebrew Kings (Thiele): on accession of Hezekiah, 212

Church: apostate, represented in Revelation, 432

Circumcision: of Gersham, 111; God's command for, 93–94

City IV and Jericho, 156–57, 195

Civil Wars (Caesar), 112

Classical Dictionary, Containing an Account of the Principal Proper Names Mentioned in Ancient Authors (Anthon), 134

Codex Alexendrinus: on Rompha, 381

Codex Bezae: and John 8:11, 371

Codex Laudianus: on Rompha, 381

Codex Vaticanus: on Rompha, 381

Commandment: fourth and evidence for Sunday worship, 62, 116–21, 119–20; second and ornamentation in tabernacle and temple, 116; seventh and multiple marriages, 121–24; sixth, and killing in the Bible, 121; tenth and variation in word order, 147

Commentary on Daniel, A (Wood), 292

"Comus": and mythology in Scripture, 239

Contra Marcion (Tertullian): and legates of Syria, 365

"Conversation of a Gorilla," 65

Corner Gate: rebuilding of, 274

Corpus Inscriptionum Semiticarum I, 140

Covenant: God's, with Abraham, 403; in Jeremiah, 273–75

Creation and the Flood and Theistic Evolution (Young), 63

Creation: account of, suggests God as three, 357; and dating methods, 64; discrepancies between Genesis 1 and 2, 69; order of, 68–69; orderly and systematic, 60–63; in six days, 59–60

Cross: inscription on, 345–46

Crucifixion: darkness at, 363–64; day of, 327–29, 375–76; hour of, 363–64; predicted in Daniel, 291; Satan's part in, 188

Cult worship in Judah, 160

"Curse": in Job, 237

Cush, country of: and Garden of Eden, 70

Dagon, temple of: collapsed by Samson, 166

Damascus: threat to Judah, 266

Dan, tribe of: Moses' prediction about, 105; numbering of, 189; settlement of, 141–42; in vassalage to Philistines, 165

Daniel, Book of: dating of, 282–84; 292–93; and Seventy Weeks, 291–92

Danites: abduction of Levite 141–42

Darwin, Before and After (Clark), 56

Dating of the human race, 63–65

Davidic Dynasty: and Jehoiakim, 275

De Oratione (Tertullian), 119

Deacons: and deaconesses, 414

"Dead bury their dead": meaning of, 324

Dead Sea Cave literature: and Daniel, 283

Dead Sea Scrolls. and Isaiah 26:3, 35

Death: eternal, 73–74; penalty of, 96, 143–45, 388; physical, 72; second, 73; spiritual, 72–73; true meaning of, 185

Debir: archaeological evidence from, 191–92, 195; destruction of, 158

Decalogue, 146: given to Moses, 401. *See also* Commandment.

Deistic movement, 19

Desert wanderings: graves of Israelites during, 138; Israelites miraculously provided for during, 130; punishment for eating of quail, 136–37

Deutero-Isaiah theory: destruction of, 264

"Deuteronomic school," 53

Deuteronomy: purpose of, 146

Devil: as archetype, 429

Dialogue With Trypho (Justin Martyr), 119

Diatessaron (Tatian): on the four Gospels, 315

Didache 14:1, 119

Die Flutsagen ethnographisch Betrachtet (Andree), 84

Die koniglichen Tontafelarchive von Tell Mardikh-Ebla (von Siebenthal), 134

Disciples: Jesus' postresurrection appearances to, 352-56

Dispersion Jews: and Mark, 313

Dittography, 33-34

Divorce: and desertion, 398-401; God speaks against, in Malachi, 305-6; and Mosaic Law, 151-52; teachings of Jesus and Paul on, 151-52

Docetic error, 323

Documentarian criticism: and Mosaic Law, 149

Document P, 49, 50

Documentary (JEDP) school: and date of Pentateuch, 48; and understanding of Yahweh, 67

Documentary Hypothesis, 46, 51-54: and names of kings of Mesopotamia, 90-91; reasons for abandonment, 49

Dodanium: race of, in Genesis 10:4, 37

Dothan: and Elisha and Syrian troops, 205

Dream Stela: on evidence for tenth plague, 115, 198

Earth: meaning of, in Genesis, 65-66

Earthquake: on resurrection morning, 348

Ebal, Mt., 45: Joshua's altar on, 159-60

Ebla documents: and Mesopotamian kings, 191

Ebla: excavations at, 134, 140

Ebla tablets, 88, 95

Ecbatana: Cyrus' decree discovered at, 231

Ecclesiastes: argument against authenticity of, 256; author of, 255-58; validity of, as canonical, 254-55

Ecclesiasticus of Apocrypha, 257

Eden, Garden of: and eating of forbidden fruit, 74; location of, 69-70

Edom: Israelites passing of, under Moses, 138-40; join Ammonite and Moabites in attack on Jerusalem, 299; pillage of Jerusalem by, 298

Eglon: destruction of, 158

Egypt: Abraham in, 89-90; annexed by Cambyses, 278; Babylonian invasion of, spoken by Ezekiel, 277-78; Babylonian invasion of, spoken by Jeremiah, 275-76; Hebrew deliverance from, 24; Israelites' sojourn in, 111-12; Jacob's migration to, 378-79; recurrence of names in, 141; So, king of, 210; as symbol of wickedness, 295; Tefnakht, king of, 211

Egyptians: and Yahweh, 67

Eighteenth Dynasty, 11, 115, 191

El-laser, god, 90

El Shaddai, 67

Elath: Israelites pass away from, 138

Elath, port of, 137

Elders: and revelation of God on Mt. Sinai, 124; seventy, elected by Moses, 137

Elephantine: Jewish settlers on, 207

Elephantine Papyri, 38: on letter Kaph, 382; and transmissional errors, 222

Elymais: Antiochus's attempts to raid temple at, 292

Emergent evolution, 58

Emmaus: disciples on road to, 314; 350, 351-52

Encyclopedia of Biblical Prophecy (Payne), on 144,000 of Revelation, 434

Encyclopedia Britannica: on census, 366; on Hittites, 97; on Midrash, 301; on Passover week, 376; on Philistines, 95

Enoch, Book of, 430

Ephesus: apostle John in, 346; length of Paul's ministry at, 383

Ephraim, 141, 200: after Mt. Gilboa, 183; attack against Bethel, 106; forest of, 186; not to return to Egypt, 295

Ephraim, Mt.: Elkanah from, 220

Ephraimite: and Samuel's father, 220

Ephrathah: as land of Judah, 318

The Epistle of St. Jude and the Second Epistle of St. Peter (Mayor), 426

Esdraelon range: and Ahab's army, 202

Esdraelon, valley of: Abner forces Philistines from, 183

"Essays on Pentateuchal Criticism," 149

Essenes at Qumran: calendar of, 376

Etam, Rock of: and destruction of Philistines, 166

Ethics: Alternatives and Issues (Geisler), 123-24

Ethiopian eunuch: and Isaiah, 265-66

Euphrates River, 70, 88

Evangelicals: and Deutero-Isaiah theory, 266

Everest, Mt.: and the Flood, 82

Evil: and God, 179

Evil spirit: and Saul, 179-80

Evolution and atheism, 55-56

Evolution and Christian Thought Today (Mixter), 57

Exile: those who remained in, 216

Exodus, the: date of, 191; Hebrew plunder of Egyptians, 110-11

"Exploring 1,750,000 Years Into Man's Past," 63

Expositor's Bible Commentary (ed., Gaebelein), vol. 7: on Zechariah, 304

Ezekiel, Book of: reference to Canaan, 138; writings accepted as canonical, 276–78

Ezion-geber: Israelites pass away from, 138; Jehosaphat's fleet at, 202–3

Ezra, Nehemiah, Esther (Keil and Delitzsch): on Sheshbazzar as Zerubbabel, 217

Ezra, Book of: discrepancies of, with Nehemiah, 229–31

Fall, the: and longevity, 77

Fallen angels, 426

False Prophet, 113

Family 1 of minuscules: on Gergesa, 324–25

Family 13: on Matthew 8:28, 325

Famine: and prophecy of Amos, 297; years of, during David's reign, 189–90

Father, God the: function of, 358

Feast of Pentecost, 118, 377

Feast of Tabernacles, 49, 120

Feast of Unleavened Bread, 120

Feast of Weeks, 117, 328–29

Fertile Crescent, 88

Fig tree: cursing of, 320, 334–35

First Apology (Justin Martyr), 119

Firstborn of Israel: numbering of, 130–31

Fission: and scribal error, 36

Flood, The (Rehwinkel), 82–83

Flood, 77: and the breath of life, 258; Christ's acceptance of, as factual, 21; and geographical evidence, 82–84; judgment of, 81; loss of life in, 158; racial differentiations after, 88

Flood sagas, 83

Folklore in the Old Testament (Frazer), 84

Forgiveness of sins: and Adam and Eve, 75–76; disciples' ability of, 354

Fossil strata: and Genesis 1, 58–65

Fourth Gospel, The: on John 19:14, 376

Foxes: Samson's catching of three hundred, 166

Free will: and tension with predestination, 392–95

From Sabbath to Lord's Day (ed., Carson), 121

Fundamentalists and inerrancy, 19

Fusion: and scribal error, 34–35

Gad, tribe of: conquered by Moab, 208; Ish-bosheth in, 183; Moses' prediction about, 105

Gadara, maniacs of: and maniacs of Gerasa, 324–25, 333

Galeed (Gilead): as rockpile of witness, 103. *See also* Gilead.

Gallic Wars (Caesar), 112

Gareb, Hill of, 274

Gath-helper: Jonah from, 300

Gaugamela, battle of, 134

Gaza, 95

Gebel Barkal Stela: and creation order, 68

Genesis Apocryphon, 283: as midrashic, 300

Gennesaret: shore of, 324

genealogy: of Christ, 78, 218, 316; listing of time in Egypt, 111–12; and moral law, 385; reasons for, in 1 and 2 Chronicles, 216; and righteousness, 391

Geochronology: fallacy of, 63, 64

Geographical location: as symbol of wickedness, 295

Geography of the Bible (Baly), 133

Gerar: and Abraham, 90

Gerasa: location of, 324; maniacs of Gadara, 324–25, 333

Gergesa. *See* Gadara.

Gerizim, Mt., 45

Gesenius' Hebrew Grammar: on 1 Samuel 13:1, 172

Geshurites: David's raids on, 178

Gethsemane, Garden of: Christ's suffering in, 314; young man runs from scene of, 311

Gezer: dowry for Pharaoh's daughter to Solomon, 199; fortification for, 199

Gibeah: Benjamite atrocity at, 107

Gibeon: deception of Israelites by, 160–61; Israel's covenant with, 160–61; sanctuary at, 160; Saul breaks covenant with, 161

Gibralter, Rock of, 83

Gihon River: disappearance of, 70

Gilboa, Mt.: Israel's disaster at, 183; Saul and Battle of, 297; Saul fatally wounded at Battle of, 181

Gilead: Ammon's sins against, 246; and forest of Ephraim, 186; Pekah's headquarters in, 209

Gilgal: Gibeonites arrive at, 161; Israelite camping at, 156; sanctuary at, 160; Samuel and Saul at, 180; Saul intrudes on priest's rights at, 173

Gilgamesh Epic, 83, 84

Gilgamesh Epic and Old Testament Parallels (Heidel), 84

Girzites: David's raids on, 180

Gizeh: pyramids of, 195

Gnomon of The New Testament (Bengel): on 144,000 of Revelation, 434

Gnostics, 19

God Remembers: Studies in Zechariah (Feinberg), 304

Gods: men as, in John 10:34, 373–74; names of, 68

Golden calf: and death of Israelites who worshiped, 401

Golden Rule, 336

Golgotha, 73, 291

Gomorrah, 91, 95: annihilation of, 158; archaeological denial of, 210

Goshen, land of: 114, 191. *See also* Wadi Tumilat.

Grace: gospel of, 369–71; 386; sovereign, and God's elect, 390

Graves of Greed, the, 136

Great Awakening in 1740, 180

Great Commission, 159, 312, 353, 356, 386

Great White Throne: judgment of, 370

Greece and Babylon (Yamauchi), 296

Greek-English Lexicon, A (Lidell and Scott): on fulfillment of Matthew 24:34, 339

Greek-English Lexicon of the New Testament, A (Arndt and Gingrich), on Mark 2:26, 362; on Passover week, 376; on Romans 16:1, 414; on Romans 16:2, 413

Greek flood saga, 83

Greeks, mentioned in Joel, 296

Habiru: tribes of Joseph defend themselves against, 106

Hades: Christ's rest in, 328

Hallelujah Chorus, 243

Hamath: David's victory near, 184; king of, 133

Hammurabi, Code of, 149

Hananel: rebuilding tower of, 274

Hansen's disease. *See* Leprosy.

Haplography: and scribal error, 34, 35–36

Har Ramon, 137

Haran: Abraham's migration to, 88–89

Hasmonean manuscript, 37

Hasmoneans: as kings in Jerusalem, 275

Hattusas (Boghazkoy): capital of Hittite power, 96

Havilah River, 70

Hawaiian flood saga, 83

Hazor: archaeological evidence from, 191–92, 195; destruction of, 158; fortification for, 199

Heathen: unevangelized, 385–88

Heavenly hope: of Old Testament people, 78–79

Hebraisches und aramaisches Handworterbuch (Gesenius-Buhl): on Deuteronomy 15:4, 150

Hebrew and English Lexicon of the Old Testament (Brown, Driver, and Briggs), 150, 237, 241, 285: on *'elep*, 129; and Exodus 3:22, 110

Hebrews: use of Septuagint in, 308

Hebron, 47, 96, 319: David's reign in, 183–84

Hegelian dialectic, 427

Heliopolis: erection of obelisk by Thutmose III at, 194

Hell: reason people are condemned to, 387; and the universalist, 406–9

Hellenistic times: and Absalom's tomb, 184

Hexapla (Origen), 40

Hieroglyphics: Egyptian and recent discoveries, 277

High priestly prayer, 420

Hindu flood saga, 83

Hinnom: Valley of, and infant sacrifices, 264

Historia 7 (Herodotus), 133–37

History of Israel (Bright), 129

Hittite Code: and death penalty, 143

Hittites: in Battle of Kadesh, 133; denial of, through archaeology, 210; in Palestine, 96–98

Hobah: Abraham's return from, 91

Holy Seed: prediction of, 263

Homoeoarkton: and scribal error, 39–40

Homoeoteleuton: and scribal error, 39

Homophony: and scribal error, 36–37

Hor, Mt.: as Aaron's place of death, 147

Horites: denial of, through archaeology, 210

Horse Gate: rebuilding of, 274

Horsemen: number of, in David's battle over Hadadezer, 184

Human Destiny (de Noüy), 58

Human life: taking of, 247–49

Hyksos: Dynasty of, 191; expelled from Egypt, 194

Idolatry: current vice in Israel at Isaiah's writing, 264; not practiced in post-exilic Judah, 265; and the second commandment, 116

Idols: stolen from Laban, 101–2

Idumea: and Edomites, 299

Ikhernofer Stela: and titles of gods, 68

Il Penseroso (Milton), 426

Image of God: man created in, 359

Immanuel, 266

"Immoral Bible," 29

Immortality: in the Old Testament, 98–99

Incarnation of Christ, 323

Incest: and Boaz and Ruth, 167–68; and Herod the Tetrarch, 168

Incestuous marriages, 77

Inerrancy: doctrine of, 397; of Scripture and 2 Timothy 3:16, 416–17

Inerrant authority: of Paul's epistles, 397–98

Infallibility, 23, 29

Infancy: children dying in, 388–90

Infanticide: condemned by God, 185; in Egypt, 109–10, 194

International Council on Biblical Inerrancy, 11, 13

International Standard Bible Encyclopedia: on Moses, 135; on the soul, 259

Interpreter's Dictionary (Buttrick): on the "Assumption of Moses"

Introduction à l'Ancien Testament (Archer), 134

Introduction to the Textual Criticism of the New Testament (Robertson), 30

Iron Age: and the fall of Jericho, 196

Isaiah, Book of: evidence against postexilic composition of, 264–65; evidence for unity of, 263–65; and sixth-century date, 270–71

Israel: discrepancy in population of, 188–89; restoration of, after Babylonian captivity, 273–74

Israel's History (Wood): on dates of kings, 225

Israel Stela: and devastating invasion in land of Hittites, 197

Issachar, tribe of, 104–5, 183

Jebel Madurah: as site of Aaron's death, 147

Jebel Neby Harun: as site of Aaron's death, 147

JEDP theory, 46

Jegarsahadutha ("rockpile of witness"); 103

Jerahmeelites: and David, 178

Jeremiah, Book of: reference to Canaan in, 138

Jericho, 121, 143: capture of, 156–57; dating of fall of, 195; extermination of people of, 157–59; Jesus heals blind men outside of, 332–33; judgment on, 219; and Rahab, 155–56

Jeroboam: sanctuary of, in Bethel, 270

Jerome's Latin Vulgate: on "Shiloh," 108

Jerusalem: Council of, 38, 85, 425; David establishes himself at, 192; destruction of, in A.D. 70 as fulfillment of Matthew 16:28, 327; destruction of, pronounced by God 227; fall of, in 597 B.C., 214, 245, 263, 265; heavenly city, 433; lack of mention of, in Pentateuch, 48; number of those who arrived in, after captivity, 229; Paul's pilgrimage to, 383–84; pools of, 202; rebuilding of, 290; spoliation of by Jehoash, 208

Jerusalem Bible: and 1 Chronicles 3:4, 183

Jesaja I, Kommentar zum Alten Testament (Proksch): on Nebuchadnezzer as Lucifer in Isaiah, 269

Jewish War, The (Josephus): on Judas of Galilee, 378

Jezreel: Elijah predicts Ahab's death at, 201–2; Jehu's race toward, 207; Pool of, 202

Jezreel, Valley of, 104–5

Job, Book of: postexilic date of, 235

Job, on "curse," 237

Joel, Book of: dating of, 296

Jonah: as midrashic in nature, 300–301

Jordan: crossing of, 138, 156

Jordan Valley: vegetation of, 47

Joseph: tribes of, 106, 200

Joshua, Book of: reference to Canaan in, 138

Joshua, Judges, Ruth (Keil and Delitzsch), 162, 164, 165

Journal of Biblical Literature: on Nebuchadnezzar as Lucifer in Isaiah, 269

Journal of the Transactions of the Victoria Institute (Clark): on censuses in Numbers, 129

Judah: discrepancy in population of, 188–89; Moses' prediction about, 104; numbering of, 189; prediction of total devastation of, 263; threatened by Samaria and Damascus, 266; throne reserved for, 173

Judas of Galilee, 378

Judean Christians: relief for, and Sunday worship, 118

Judge: Jesus as, 370

Judges, Book of: failure of, to mention Egyptian invasions, 192, 197

Justness of God: and 70,000 of Israel killed, 220–21

Kabbath Ammon: Uriah killed at, 200

Kadesh Barnea, 137, 138

Kadesh, Battle of, 133

Kaphtorim: as group of Philistines, 96

Karkar, Battle of, 133

Karnak Poetical Stela of Thutmose III: and creation order, 68

Kassite dynasty, 89

Keys of the kingdom: 322, 354, 388

Kidron: wadi of, 274

Kidron Valley: Absalom's tomb in, 184, 186

Kierkegaardian alternative, 19

King: Israelite request for, 170

"Kingdom of heaven": and Matthew, 312

Kings: rules set for, 170–71

King's Highway, 132, 138

King's Pool: location of, 202

King's Valley: pillar set up in, by Absalom, 184

Kiriath-Jearim, 141

Kirjath-arba: founding of, 47
Kultepe: cuneiform tablets of, 97
Kythera, Island of, 83

LXX. *See* Septuagint.
Labor: forced by King Solomon, 199–200
Lachish: archaeological evidence from, 191–92, 195; city of, 319; destruction of, 158
Lachish Ostraca period, 38
Laish: Danites settle in, 141–42
Lake of fire: and liars, 410
L'Allegro (Milton), 426
Languages: division of, 87–88
Larsa, king of, 90
Last Days: and Daniel, 282
Latin Vulgate: on Isaiah 14:12, 268; and Metathesis, 34
Law: Moses receives, 403
Lawless one: coming of, 410
Legal matters: differences on, between Exodus and Deuteronomy, 149
Lepers, the ten, 314
Leprosy: and clothing, 126–27; and Phagedenic ulcer, 127; and walls, 126–27
Les Religions de Babylonie et d'Assyrie (Dhorme): on Sirius, 381
Levi, tribe of, 103: Moses' prediction about, 104; not numbered, 189
Leviathan, 239–40
Levirate marriage: and Boaz and Ruth, 167–68; and Pedaiah and Sheiltiel, 218; and Sheshbazzar as Shealtiel, 218
Levite: abduction of, 141–42; and Samuel's father, 220
Levites: age of, at entry into service, 134–35; work of, 130–31
Lexicon in Verteris Testament Libros (Koehler-Baumgartner), 98, 129, 150, 381
Lexicon Hebraicum et Aramaicum Veteris Testamenti (ed. Zorell and Semkowski): on "curse" in Job, 237; on Deuteronomy 15:4, 150
Liars: condemned to lake of fire, 410
Libyan Dynasty: Pharaoh Osokon I of, 211
Lies: of David, 175–78; of Samuel, 175–78
"Life and Death at Gombe" (*National Geographic*), 65
Linnaeus: and ruminants, 126
Liquor: and New Testament, 148–49; Old Testament teaching on use of, 147–49
Little Horn: and Seventy Weeks of Daniel, 291
Longevity: in Old Testament, 77
Lord: Jesus as, 420
Lord's Day, the: how to observe, 119–21

Lucifer: in Isaiah, 269
Luke, Gospel of: departure of, from chronological order, 321; emphasis of, 313–14
Lying wonders: Samuel's appearance to Saul, 180–81

Maccabean dating of Daniel, 282, 286–87
Macedonia: Paul's first journey to, 311
Madon: destruction of, 158
Magi: use of star by, to find the Christ, 317
Magicians of Egypt, 113
Mahanaim Abner's headquarters at, 183
Makkedah: destruction of, 158
Malachi, Book of: reasons for differences in English translations, 305–6
Malta, Island of, 33: shipwreck at, 314
Manasseh: after Mt. Gilboa, 183; conquered by Moab, 208; as house of Joseph, 200
Manna: Jesus' acceptance of, as historical, 21, 25
Manumission: grounds for, 149
Mareshah, Battle of, 132, 211
Mari documents: on Job, 236
Mari tablets: and names of Mesopotamian kings, 90
Mark: and Dispersion Jews, 313; emphasis of, 312–13
Marriage: between believers and unbelievers, 80; as paradigm of love between Savior and redeemed, 261; and Paul, 397–98
Martyrs: Zechariah as last of, 337–38
Masorites: and use of vowel indicators, 40
Masoretic Hebrew Text, 30, 31, 32, 33, 79; on Deuteronomy 10:22, 379; on Exodus 1:1–5, 378; and 1 Chronicles 22:14, 223; on 1 Samuel 13:1, 171–72; on 1 Samuel 13:5, 173; and fusion, 35; on Genesis 46:26–27, 379; and Isaiah 26:3, 35–36; on Jeremiah 27:1–11, 273; and Matthew, 311; and Matthew 2:6, 318; on Psalm 30, 243; and Psalm 68:18, 404; and 2 Samuel 21:19, 178; and 2 Samuel 23:8, 222; on Sennacherib's invasion of Judah, 211
Materialism: in Tyre, 279–80
Matthew: composed in Aramaic, 346; emphasis of, 311; and law of Moses, 312; and Sermon on the Mount, 312; use of Septuagint in, 308
Maundy Thursday, 376
Medes and Persians: deal of, with Babylonians, 245
Mediator, Christ as, 409
Megiddo: Battle of, 133; fortification for, 199; Pharaoh Necho's victory at, 273

Melchizedek fragment, 92
Memphis: birthplace of Amenhotep II, 195
Memphis Stela: and campaign of Amenhotep, 198
Mendelian limits, 58
Mesha Stone: and tribe of Reuben, 103
Mesopotamian kings: Abraham's defeat of, 90–91
Messiah: coming of Shiloh, 104, 107–8; coming predicted in Daniel's Seventy Weeks, 291; Jesus' task as, 374; type of, 92
Messiahship, sign of: discrepancy between Matthew and Mark, 362–63
Metathesis: and scribal error, 34
Mexican Indian flood saga, 83
Michmash: chariots at, 172–73; Jonathan's exploit at, 172
Midian: destruction of, 142–43
Midwives of Hebrews, 109–10
Military service: and the Christian, 343
Millennium, 237: and division of territory of Holy Land, 434
Millo: fortified by Solomon, 199
Minoan Crete, 96
Mizpah: Samuel calls national assembly at, 171
Mizpah benediction, 102–3
Moab: Israelite passing of, 138–39; people of, not allowed in assembly of God, 167–68; Ruth of, 167
Money changers: expelled from temple, 334–35
Moon god: Sin and Nanna, 68
Moreh, oak of: Abraham's purchase of land near, 380
Moriah, Mt., 48: and Abraham, 360, 403; chosen for temple, 188, 199; David's acquisition of, 186, 190
Mosaic authorship of Pentateuch: Christ and apostles witness to, 46; evidence for, 45; and military prowess, 50; and Scripture references, 46
Mosaic Code: alleged conflicting laws, 149; and sacrificial regulations, 272
Mosaic Law: and clothing, 151; and divorce, 151–52; and forbidden food, 85; and mixed marriages, 166; referred to in Romans, 385; and sabbatical year, 149; and sacrificial animals, 128
Moserah: as Aaron's place of death, 147
Most Holy One: in Daniel's Seventy Weeks, 289
Most Holy Sanctuary, 289
Mustard seed, 329

Mycenean type sherds in Jericho, 195
Mythology in Scripture, 239–40

Nabatean Arabs: God brings, against Edomites, 299
Nabonidus and Belshazzar (Dougherty), 286
Nahal Paran: and wilderness of Paran, 137
Nain, widow of: raising of son of, from the dead, 313
Naioth in Ramah: Saul goes to, 180
Names of God: in Genesis 1 and 2, 66–68
Names: recurence of, in family lines, 219
Naphtali, tribe of: Moses' prediction about, 105–6, 183
Natural History (Pliny the Elder): on Roman numbering, 364
Nazareth: Jesus' visit to, 321
Nazi, 220
Nazirite: Samson as, 165
Neanderthal cave man, 63
Nebo, Mt., 147
Nebuchadnezzar: as Lucifer in Isaiah, 269
Necromancy: condemned by God, 181
Negeb: tribesmen of David's raids, 178
Negev: cities of, destroyed, 158
Nehemiah, Book of: discrepancies of, with Ezra, 229–31
Neoorthodoxy: and interpretation of Adam, 58
Nes-Hor stela: and invasion of Nile Valley, 278
Nethinim: lack of mention of, in Pentateuch, 49
New birth, 243, 428
New Evolution, The (Clark), 56
New Perspectives (Payne): on Daniel, 283–84
New Testament: Old Testament quotations in, 307–9; picture of God in, 309–10
Nile Valley, 114: invasion of, 278
Nineveh: and Jonah, 301; population of, 134; repentance of, 81
Nisir, Mt., 83
Nob: David eats showbread at, 362; David flees to, 177; massacre of priests at, 177, 181, 200
Nonaccession-year system, 206
North Arabian Nabateans, 236
Numbers: discrepancies between Samuel, Kings, and Chronicles, 221–22; meaning of, in Revelation, 432–34; reliability of, in Old Testament, 129–34
Numerical error: in 1 Samuel 6:19, 169

Odessa: flood evidence in, 83
Og: Mosaic conquest of, 192

Old Testament Introduction (Harrison), 129

Old Testament picture of God, 309–10

Old Testament Commentary (Alleman and Flack), 91, 236

Olduvai Gorge: and dating of human race, 63

Olives, Mt. of: Christ's ascension from, 314, 356

Olivet Discourse: by Christ and Daniel, 284; and Matthew, 312, 339; and parable of wedding feast, 343

On Idolatry (Tertullian), 119

On the Principles (Origen): on Michael and devil, 430

One hundred and forty-four thousand, 434

Ophir: Jehoshaphat's trade at, 202

Ophrah: Gideon destroys altar of Baal at, 317

Ordination of women: and 1 Timothy 2:12, 411–15

Origin of Species, The (Darwin), 55

Original sin, 388–90

Pacifism, 219, 220, 341–44

Padan Aram: Abraham settles in, 88; Jacob leaves, 102; Jacob's time in, 380

Pahath-moab: differences concerning, in Ezra and Nehemiah, 229

Paleozoic era: fossil-bearing strata of, 62

Palestine: David's conquest of, 187

Palestinian customs: interpreted by Mark, 330

Palm Sunday: and number of donkeys, 333–34

Paradise: location of, 367; thief with Christ in, 367–68

Paradise Lost, (Milton) 426

Paran, 137

Partial inerrancy: advocates of, 25–26

Passion Week: Mark's emphasis on, 313; occurrences of, predicted in Old Testament, 353

Passover: blood of, 115; ordinances for, 272; preparation day for, and crucifixion day, 375; sacrifices for, 376

Pelethites: as group of Philistines, 96

Pentateuch: and lack of mention of "Yahweh of Hosts," 49; Philistine references in, 96; pointing to Christ, 353; reference in, to Canaan, 138

Pentateuch (Keil and Delitzsch), 131

Pentateuchal code: and Israel's longing for a king, 170

"Pentateuchal Studies," 149

Pentecost: disciples wait for, 356; Feast of, and Holy Spirit's coming, 211, 327; and Joel's prophecy, 377; signs from heaven, 318

Perfection: and 1 John 3:9, 428–29

Persecution: God's and Satan's involvement in, 188

Persian period: and Book of Daniel, 283

Perwennefer: Amenhotep's estates at, 195

Peshitta Syriac: on Luke 18:29, 331

Pestilence: 70,000 of Israel destroyed by, because of David, 220–21

Peter, Books of: Petrine authorship of 2 Peter, 425–27; purpose of 1 Peter, 426; purpose of 2 Peter, 426

Petito Principii, 53

Phaenomena 5 (Aratus): Paul quotes, to Athenians, 430

Phagedenic ulcer, 127

Pharisaical hypocrisy: and Matthew, 312

Pharisees: Christ's discussion with, on Psalm 110:1, 308

Philistines: in Abraham's time, 94–95; arrow of, fatally wounding King Saul, 181; and chariots at Michmash, 172–73; David in camp of, 178; and Samson, 165–66; Saul's effectiveness over, 173

Phoenicia: Danites' search to, 141; David's conquest of, 187; goddess Baalet of, 52; inscriptions of, and name of Agag, 140

Pi: value for, in 1 Kings, 198–99

Pisgah, Mt.: Moses' death on, 430

Pishon river: disappearance of, 70

Pisidia: rebellious mountaineers of, 366

Plagues: of Egypt, 28, 110, 391, 392; evidence for tenth plague, 113–14, 115–16; exclusion of Israelites from, 114–15, 197; of Israel, 188

Pleistocene animals: and the Flood, 82

"Plunder" of Egypt: by Hebrews, 110–11

Polygamy: and adultery, 123; and Ten Commandments, 121–24

Poor in the land, 150

Potter's field: and fulfillment of prophecy, 345; purchased of, by Judas, 345

Predestination: tension with free will, 392–95

Preservation of the saints, 419–21

Pride: of David and Israel, 221

Priestly Code, 45, 49, 53

Prince of Evil, 239

Prolonged day in Joshua, 161–62

Promised Land, 95, 220

Prophets: pointing to Christ, 353

Protestant Reformation, 19

Proto-Sinaitic Inscriptions and Their Decipherment, The (Albright), 52
Proto-Theodotin, Greek translation: Matthew quotes from, in 2:6, 318
Psalms: pointing to Christ, 353
Psoriasis, 127
Ptolemaic Dynasty, 278, 292
Punon: and Kadesh Barnea, 137
Purgatory, 406
Purification rite: for leprosy, 127

Quail: Israel's eating, and punishment for greed, 135–36
Qumran and the History of the Biblical Text (Cross and Talmon), 271
Qumran Caves, 30
Qumran Cave Four: and Deuteronomy 32:43, fragments of Ecclesiastes found in, 256–57; Micah found in, 271
Qumran literature: and Daniel, 283
Qumran Sectarian Documents, 283

Rabbit, 126
Ramah: Samuel's city, 171
Ramathaim-Zophim: and Elkanah, 220, 235
Ramoth-gilead: Ahab seeks to recapture, 410; Ahab's disaster at, 202; Jehu races from, 207
Ramath-lehi: Philistine destruction at, 166
Ras es-Shamra: discovery of clay tablets in, 52
Rationalism, 19
Rationalist approach, 53
Rationalistic modern critics, 46
Received Text: discrepancy in, 225
Redating the Exodus and the Conquest (Bimson), 157, 198
Redeemer: in Job, 241; Jesus as, 374; man's need for, 386; as true man and God, 323
Redemption, 79
Red Sea, crossing of, 131–32
Relief und Inschrift des Königs Dareios I am Felsen von Bagistan, 230
Remarriage: Paul on, 397–98
Repentance: of God, 80–81
Resurrection: bodily, 78; of Christ, 59, 159; of good and evil persons, 72
Resurrection: body, in Job, 240–41; Christian hope of bodily, 401; discrepancies between four narratives of Christ's 347–56; historicity of Christ's, 347–56
Reuben: conquered by Moab, 208
Reuben: Moses' prediction about tribe of, 103–4
Revelation, Book of: as midrashic, 300

Revenge: in Psalms, 245–46
Revisionist Evangelicals: and teaching ministry of Holy Spirit, 23–24
Revisionist movement, 19, 22
Rich young ruler: discrepancies about, in Gospels, 329–32
Rivista degli Studi Orientali, 134
Rodanim, race of in 1 Chronicles 1:7, 37
Royal Archives of Tell Mardikh-Ebla, 134
Ruminants, 126

Sabbath commandment: difference in Exodus and Deuteronomy, 146
Sabbatical year guidelines, 149
Sacrifices: animal, and renewal of spoken of, in Ezekiel, 280–81; first, by Adam and Eve, 73; of God's Son for judgment, 245–46; human, 96, 164
Sacrificial ordinances in Jeremiah, 272–73
Sadducees: and resurrection, 401
Sakkut, 381
Salem, 47, 91–93
Salvation, 386; of Adam and Eve, 75–76; of all men, 406–9; in Old Testament, 70–72; and obedience, 70–71; requirement for, 369
Samaria: and decapitation of Ahab's sons, 207; Elisha leads Syrian troops to, 205; Pekah's rule in, 209–10; threatens Judah, 266
Samaria, Pool of: and Ahab's death, 201–2
Samaritans: Jesus' concern for, 314
Samuel (Keil and Delitzsch), 172–73, 184
Sanctification: work of, 394
Sanhedrin: Paul appears before, 341–42, 384; Stephen's address to, 379
Satanic influence: and Judas Iscariot, 179; and Saul, 179
Satanic powers: and Samuel's appearance to Saul, 180–81
Saturnalia (Macrobius): on Roman numbering, 364
Savior: announcement of coming of, 76; conqueror of death, 185
Scapegoat: meaning of, 127–28
Scepter of Egypt, The (Hayes), 195
Schweich Lectures, 154
Scribal error: and ages of Ahaziah and Jehoiachin at reigns, 206–7; and 1 Samuel 16:9, 174; and 2 Samuel 8:4, 184; and Luke, 8:28, 325; and the message of the Bible, 29–30; and omission of words, 40; and story of rich young ruler, 331
Scripture, Tradition and Infallibility (Beegle): on Eliphaz and Job, 396

Second Adam, 78

Second Advent, 377: disciples ask about, 356; signs of, 318, 326-27, 338-39

Second chance: for salvation, 423-24

Seleucid empire: confronts Ptolemaic empire, 282; and Daniel, 292

Self-defense: in Scripture, 219

Self-love, 335-37

Septuagint, 100, 273: on Acts 7:43, 381; apostolic use of, 308; and Exodus 1:1-5, 378-79; and Exodus 12:40, 403; on 1 Samuel 13:5, 175; and Genesis 47:31, 421; and Isaiah 9:2, 33; on Isaiah 14:12, 268, 269-70; and Isaiah 26:3, 36; and length of sojourn in Egypt, 112; and Leviticus 16:8, 35; and noninerrancy, 30-32; and Psalm 68:18, 404; and *pneuma*, 259; on population of Betheshemesh in 1 Samuel 6:19, 169; quotations in New Testament, 307; on the scapegoat, 128

Serabit el-Khadim: alphabetic inscriptions from, 52

Sermon on the Mount: 334, 366: and love of God the Father, 309; and Matthew, 312; and pacifism, 341

Seventy Weeks, 282, 289-92

Shechem: congregation of Israel outside of, 45; Jacob's plot of land in, 379

Sheol, 78: Samuel in, 181

Shephelah: cities of, destroyed, 158

Shiloh: as Messiah, 104, 107-8. *See also* Messiah.

Shiloh, Pool of: location of, 202

Shiloh: sanctuary at, 160

Shimron: destruction of, 158

Shittim, Plains of, 139: plague at, 401

Shunem in Isaachar: girl from, whom Solomon loved, 261

Sicarii. *See* Zealot.

Sihon: Mosaic conquest of, 192

Siloam, Pool of: location of, 202

Simeon, tribe of: Moses' prediction concerning, 104; numbering of, 189

Similitude (Hermas): and deaconesses, 414

Sinai, Mt: giving of the law at, 388; revelation of God at, 124

Sins: of fathers visited on children, 152-53

Sirius (star), 381

Sixth Dynasty: inscription of Uni, 133

Slavery: status of, in ancient times, 86-87

Sleep: of God, 244-45

Sodom, 91, 95: annihilation of, 158; archaeological denial of, 210; as symbol of wickedness, 295

Sodomites: blindness put on, 205-6

Soldier: as honorable, 220

Son, God the: function of, 358

Son of Man: Jesus' reference to Himself as, 322-24

Song of Solomon: validity of, as part of the Bible, 261-62

Sons of God, 79-80, 238-39

Sopherim scribes: and dittography, 34

Sopherim Text. *See* Masoretic Hebrew Text.

Soul: differentiated from spirit, 259-60

Sphinx: at Gizeh, 115

Spies: twelve Israelite, sent to Canaan, 96, 137-38

Spirit: differentiated from "soul," 259-60

Spirits: seven before God's throne, 431-32

Staff: disciples to carry, 326

Star: as announcement of Christ's birth, 317, 318

Stoning: of astrologers, 317

Strong's Concordance: on "curse" in Job, 237

Studies in the Book of Daniel (Wilson): on use of "Chaldeans" in Daniel, 285

Submission: of women, 411

Sumerian flood saga, 83

Sumerian god NIN-IB, 381

Summit Conference of the International Council on Biblical Inerrancy, 11, 13

Sunday: as day of worship, 117-21

Supreme Court: and abortion, 246

Survey of Israel's History (Wood): on date of Exodus, 198

Survey of Old Testament Introduction (Archer), 30, 63, 198, 211, 303

Survival of the fittest, 56

Synoptic Gospels: differences in, 311-15

Synoptic Gospels (Stonehouse): on rich young ruler, 329

Syria: David's conquest of, 187

Syriac Peshitta: on *ben,* 100; on 1 Chronicles 2:13 and 1 Samuel 16:9, 174; on Genesis 47:31, 421; on Gerasa, 325; and Isaiah 9:2, 33; on Isaiah 14:12, 268; on Matthew 24:34, 339; and Psalm 22:17, 37

Syrian troops: and Elisha, 205-6

Syrians: and Jehoash, 208

System of Biblical Psychology, A (Delitzsch): on differences between "soul" and "spirit," 259-60

Tabae: place of Antiochus's death, 292

Tabernacle: dedication of, 125; ornamentation in, 116

Tabor, Mt., 105: as place where Jesus appeared to five hundred, 355

Tahpanhos: Nebuchadnezzar's tracking of Jews down in, 277

Tale of Sinuhe, 30

Tanis: built up by Ramses, 191

Tarshish, ships of: and Jehoshaphat, 202

Taylor Prism: Sennacherib's record in, 211

Teaching of the Apostles, The, 119

Tell el-Amarna: correspondence of, 106; discovery of clay tablets in, 52; on Job, 236

Tell el-Sultan, 201: archaeological investigation at, 156–57

Tema: and Nabonidus, 286

Temple: David's donation of gold for, 222–23, labor for, 199; ornamentation in, 116; predicted on Mt. Moriah, 278; reason for delay in building of second, 231–32; significance of, in Ezekiel's prophecy, 280–81; Solomon's, established, 159–60

Tempo and Mode in Evolution (Simpson), 56

Temptation of Christ, 188, 320–21, 322, 418–19

Ten Commandments: differences in, between Exodus and Deuteronomy, 148–49

Text of the New Testament, The (Taylor), 30

Text of the Old Testament, The (Würthwein), 30, 44

Textus Receptus, 371

Textual error: and age of Jehoiachin, 214–15; concerning Berechiah as father of Zecheriah, 338; on John 19:14, 364

Third Intermediate Period in Egypt (Kitchen): on Mareshah, Battle of, 211

Thebes: capital of Egypt, 191

Theistic evolution: and Genesis 1, 57; meaning of, 55

Theophany: on Mt. Sinai, 124

Theopneustia: The Bible, Its Divine Origin and Inspiration (Gaussen), 25

Thief on the cross, 314, 367–68

Threshing floor of Ornan: David's purchase of, 190

Thutmose IV: Dream Stela of, 115

Tigris River, 70

Timnah: and Samson, 166

Tirzah: Menahem invades Samaria from 209

The Titles of The Psalms, Their Meaning and Nature Explained (Thirtle), 243

Torah, 35

Transfiguration of Christ: as fulfillment of Matthew 16:28, 326; Mountain of, 322; Peter speaks of, 425

Transmissional error: in Samuel, Kings, and Chronicles, 222

Tree of knowledge of good and evil, 72

Trinity, 74: Old Testament passages on, 359–61; teaching of, 357–61

Troas, 118

Twelfth Dynasty Egyptian kings, 95

Twelve Minor Prophets, The (Robinson): on Zechariah, 303

Twelve tribes, 103, 122: downfall of, 159; named in Revelation, 433–34; numbering of, 130; represented in Revelation, 432

Tyrannosaurus Rex, 63

Tyrannus: Paul teaches at school of, 383

Tyre: disciples at and Paul, 383–84; downfall of, predicted by Ezekiel, 276, 278–79; during Hellenistic period, 277; prince of and Satan, 278–80

Ugarit: clay tablets found at, 52

"Under the sun," 255

Uni: inscription of, 133

Unitarians: and infallibility, 19

Universalists: and Colossians 1:20, 406–7

Unleavened Bread, Feast of, 376

Unscientific terms in Bible, 93

Ur of the Chaldeas: as Abraham's home, 88–89; excavations at, and last king of Babylon, 286

Urartu: royal inscriptions from, 68

Urim and Thummin, 39

Valley of the Giants (Dougherty), 63

"Virgin" in Isaiah, 267–68

Virgin birth of Christ: prophesied in Isaiah, 266–68

Vision (Hermas): and deaconesses, 414

Visions and Prophecies of Zechariah (Baron), 303

Vorlage: on discrepancies between Ezra and Nehemiah, 230; on 1 Samuel 6:19, 169; on 2 Chronicles 15:19, 226

Vulgate: and Leviticus 16:8, 35

Wadi Qilt, 201

Wadi Tumilat: archaeological data from, 197

War: by the Lord's people in the Old Testament, 219–20

Warfare: chariots at Michmash, 172–73

Wedding feast: parable of, 343

Wellhausen hypothesis, 49: explanation of, for tabernacle, 47

Westminster Confession: on those dying in infancy, 390

Westminster Shorter Catechism: on gift of faith, 394; observance of Sunday, 120; on Trinity, 373

When Egypt Ruled the East (Seele), 97

Widow, duty to, 167–68

Wisdom: and Solomon, 251–52

Witch of Endor: and Samuel's appearance to Saul, 180–81

Witchcraft: condemned by God, 181

Witness: meaning of, 143–45

Yom Kippur, 127

Zealots, 378

Zebulon, tribe of: Moses' prediction about, 104

Zechariah, Book of: evidence for single author of, 303–4

Zerah: Asa's prayer before battle of, 301

Ziklag: David hears of Saul's death at, 182; David sets up headquarters at, 178; David's raids from, 200

Zinjanthropus: of Tanganykia, 63, 64

Zion, Mt.: and temple building, 199

Zoar, city of, 91

Zobah: Hadadezer of, 184

Index of Scripture References

Genesis

1	.68–69
1:1	.65–66
1:2	.65
1:1–3	.357
1:2–5	.61
1:5	.61
1:6–8	.61
1:9–13	.61
1:10	.65
1:12, 18, 25, 31	.65
1:11–12:21	.58
1:14–19	.61
1:14	.77
1:20–23	.62
1:24–26	.62
1:26	.74, 359
1:26–27	.357, 260
1:27	.22, 59, 60, 64, 359, 393, 408
1:28	.77
1:31	.179
2	.59, 68–69
2–3	.58
2:2–3	.62, 431
2:5–9	.65
2:7	.64
2:10–14	.69–70
2:14	.62
2:15	.59
2:17	.70, 72
2:18	.59
2:19	.60
2:20	.60
2:23–24	.122
2:24	.22, 152, 306
3	.22, 70
3–4	.88
3:1	.74
3:4	.72
3:4–5	.336, 417
3:5	.74
3:8	.72
3:8–19	.72
3:9	.75
3:9–21	.75
3:10	.72–73
3:11, 13	.75
3:14–19	.75
3:15	.73, 76, 353, 403

3:16	.403
3:16–19, 23–24	.73
3:17	.403
3:19	.70
3:22	.74
4:1	.67
4:3	.76
4:4	.76
4:5	.76
4:18–24	.76
4:23–24	.122
4:26	.78
5	.78
5:3–5	.76
5:4	.77
5:5	.72, 77
5:24	.78
6:1–2, 4	.80
6:1–2	.79
6:2	.76, 79, 374
6:4	.84
6:5	.80, 158
6:7	.80, 81
6:9	.81–82, 65
6:17	.258
7–8	.82, 84
7:2	.81–82
7:11	.82
7:16	.408
7:19	.82
7:20	.82
7:21	.78
7:22	.256
8:6–9	.83
8:20	.82
9:1–16	.84
9:6	.121, 247, 342
9:20–21	.148
9:24–28	.86–87
9:25	.86, 87
9:27	.87
10:4	.37
10:5, 20, 31	.87–88
10:6	.86
11:1	.88
11:26	.378
11:28	.88–89, 378
11:32	.378
12	.403
12:1	.88

12:4	.88, 378
12:6–7	.380
12:10–20	.89
12:10	.89
12:11–19	.298
12:12–19	.155
12:13	.77
12:16	.89
13:2	.89
13:10	.47
14	.48, 90–91, 93, 300
14:8–10	.91
14:15	.91
14:18–20	.91–92
15:6	.71, 93
15:16	.158
15:17	.93
15:18–21	.159, 178
16:12	.396
17	.93–94
17:6	.170
17:12	.111, 398
17:17	.98
17:23–24	.93
18–19	.95
18:25	.180
19:11	.206
19:23	.93
19:24–25	.158
19:36–38	.247
20	.90, 94
20:1–18	.89
20:2	.244
20:11	.90
20:12	.77, 90
21	.94
21:4	.398
21:12–14	.122
21:27–30	.379–80
21:32	.95
21:32, 34	.95
22	.96
22:2	.96
22:12	.96
22:11	.360
22:16–17	.360
22:18	.403
23	.96
23:1	.98
24:16	.267

24:43 268
24:60 237
25:1 98
25:6 98
25:8 ....72, 98–99
25:26 95
26:1 ....95, 244
26:28–31 380
26:34 ....99, 122
28:9 122
28:15 102
29:27 101
30 101
30:25–32 101
31:1 102
31:11, 13 360
31:12 101
31:22–48 102
31:31 102
31:38 101
31:41, 42 101
31:46–9 144
31:47 236
31:49 102–3
31:52 103
32:1 237
33:18 47
33:18–20 380
35:16–19 101
36 99
36:2 100
36:4 99
36:9, 43 100
36:12, 22 100
36:14 100
36:21 101
36:25 100
36:34 99
36:40 100
43:32 193
46:2–4 403
46:26–27 379
46:34 193
47:10 235
47:31 419
48:22 103
49 103–7
49:8–10 174
49:10 ....107–8, 170, 108,
                173–74, 353

Exodus
1:1–5 378–80
1:5 379
1:8–12 194
1:11 ....191, 193
1:15 131
1:16 109
1:19 109
1:22 198
2 198
2:11–15 115
2:18 100

2:23 198
3:2 360
3:2–6 125
3:4 360
3:6 ....22, 32, 308, 360–61
3:19 391
3:22 110–11
4:19 198
4:21 391
4:24 111
5:1 392
5:2 ....67, 391
6:3 ....66, 67
6:6 323
6:7 67
6:14–27 112–13
6:16–20 111–12
6:26–7 ....54, 112–13
7:3 391
7:11, 22 113
7:13, 22 391
7:17–25 114
7:21 114
8:1–14 114
8:4 114
8:7 113
8:16 114–15
8:16–19 114
8:19 ....113, 391
8:21 114
8:22 197
9:4 114
9:6 114
9:11 114
9:16 390
9:22 114–15
9:25–26 ....114, 197
9:31–32 46
10:22–3 115
10:23 197
11:2 110
12 272
12:6 376
12:16–7 376
12:29 115–16
12:29–30 .....113–14, 115
12:33 110
12:35 110
12:37 130
12:38 114
12:40 ......112, 191, 403
13:3 146
13:17 95
14:4 67
14:21–24 131
15:3 219–20
15:13 321
15:14 95
16:33–36 112–13
17:9 137
17:14 45
19:5 ....70, 71, 272

19:12–13 124
20:2 65
20:2–17 146–47
20:4–5 116
20:9–10 119
20:13 121
20:14 121
20:24 ....71, 272–73
20:24–25 160
21:2–7 87
21:6 374
21:12 121
21:22–25 247
21:23 143
21:26 149
22:2 247
22:7–8, 27 374
22:13 144
22:14 110
22:18 181
23:10–11 149
23:24 50
23:28 197
23:31 95
24:1 124
24:4 45
24:9–11 124
24:12 124
24:13 137
25–27 116
25:18, 20 116
29:40 147–49
31:2–11 112
32:3 141
32:6 ....141, 401–2
32:27 401
32:35 401
32:38 401
33:11 124–5
33:18 125
33:20 124–25
33:23 125
34:6–7 125
34:12–16 251
34:13 50
34:16 305
34:27 45
38:8 165
40:34–35 125

Leviticus
5:1 144
10:8–9 147–49
11 46
11:1–45 85
11:5 126
11:6 126
11:16 47
13:2–42 126–27
13:47–59 126–27
14:33–57 126–27
16 127–28

16:8 35
16:21 128
17:10-11 84-5
18 96
18:16 167-68
18:21 ....96, 164, 185
19:11 155
19:18 335
19:26, 31 181
20 96
20:2 96
20:2-5 164
20:2-5, 14, 20, 27 248
20:6, 27 181
20:10 .....153, 372, 399
20:17 77
23:3 120
23:4-8 376
23:10-11 117
24:15-17 ,,,,,,,,,,,246
25:25 107
25:25 ....167, 323
25:48 323
26 ....53, 371
26:40-45 271
26:41 94

Numbers

1-4 129
1:1 130
1:2-3 187
1:10 112
1:21 129
1:23 104
2:3-31 132
2:32 130
3:27-28 111
3:39 130
3:42-43 130
4:3 134-35
7:10 250
8:24 135
10:29 100
11:4-9 135
11:16 136
11:31-34 135-36
12:1-2 134
12:3 136-37
13 137-38
13:3 137
13:16 137
13:22 47
13:26 137
13:16 137
13:22 47
13:26 137
13:29 96
13:32 ....137, 138
14:34-35 138
20:1 137
20:14-21 .....138, 139-40
20:27 147

20:28 147
21 192
22:13 140
22:17-23 140
22:33 140
22:35 43
23:19 81
24:7 140
25:1-8 141
25:1-9 142
25:8 401
25:9 141
26 ....129, 139
26:2 187
26:28-34 111
26:42 141
28:9-10 120
31 142-43
31:4-6 433
33:1-2 45
33:38 147
35:6 220
35:19 323
35:30 143-45
35:31 143
35:31, 33 342
35:33 143

Deuteronomy

1 192
2:4-7 138
2:8 138
4:24 310
5:5 146
5:6-21 146-47
6:4 357
6:5 387
7:3-4 305
7:5 50
7:8 309
7:20 197
10:6 147
10:16 94
10:22 379
12:2-14 ....159, 160
12:2-3 50
12:5-18 48
12:10-14 250
12:31 ....164, 185
12:31-32 164
13 160
13:1-5, 15 248
13:2-11 50
13:12-17 50
14 46
14:1 ....79, 374
14:3-21 85
14:5 47
14:26 147-49
15:1-11 149
15:4 150
15:11 150

15:12-18 149
17:2-7 248
17:6 143
17:14-20 170-71
17:16 295
17:16-17 251
18:2 275
18:9-12 181
18:10 164
18:10-12 164
18:15 46
18:15-18 353
19:15 143
19:21 143
20 219-20
20:5 252
20:5-7 20
20:14 220
21:3-8 143
22:5 150-51
22:22-24 ....248, 371, 372
22:24 399
23:3 107-00
24:1-4 151-52
24:16 152-53
25:5 218
25:5-10 167-68
27-28 46
28 ....53, 271
28:68 54
30:19 395
31:9 45
32:5 ....79, 374
32:15 ....108, 269
32:43 79
33 103-7
33:5, 26 269
34 ....136, 153-54

Joshua

1:8 45
2:4-5 155
2:11-12 155
3:16 156
3:17 156
4:4, 10-11 156
6 156
6:17-25 156
6:21 ....143, 157
6:22-23 157
6:24 196
7 ....139-40, 196
7:24 201
8:17 196
8:18-26 158
8:30 159-60
8:30-35 160
8:32-34 45
9 160-61
9:1-2 97
9:3-15 153
10:12-14 161-62

10:28 158
10:32, 35, 39, 40 158
11:3 97
11:11-14 158
17:15-18 106
19:40-46 141
22:6 237
24:12 197
24:25-26 144
24:32 ....379, 380

Judges
1:22-25 106
2:1-3, 10-15, 19-23 ...159
2:2-3, 11-15 220
3:15-30 107
4:12 105
4:21 163-64
5:15 105
5:24-27 163-64
6:32 ....244, 317
7:1 ....244, 317
7:19-22 91
8:29 317
11 96
11:12-28 422
11:26 192
11:30-31 ....164, 422
11:31 96
11:32-33 422
11:37-38 165
11:39 165
12:4-6 105
13:20 361
13:22-23 361
14:3 166
14:4 165-66
14:19 165
15 166
15:6-8 166
15:14-17 166
16:30 166
17:6 212
18 ....105, 141
18:1 212
18:18-26 432
18:27 432
19:1 212
19:22-30 158
20 107
20:10 433
20:13 36
20:43-48 158

Ruth
3:13 323
4:3-8 167-68

1 Samuel
1:1 ....220, 235
1:20 174
1:24, 28 220

1:27 174
2:11 220
2:22 165
3:1 135
6:19 ....169, 222
8:5 170
8:7-9 169-71
8:11-18 170
9-10 107
9, 10, 12 171
9:5 171
10:1 171
10:5-6, 10 180
10:17-24 171
10:19, 21 319
11:2-3 220
11:15 171
13:1 ....40, 171-72
13:5 172-73
13:12-13 179
13:13 173
13:14 ....159, 202
14:41 39
14:52 175
15 173
15:7-8 182
15:8 140
15:11 173-74
15:17-35 180
15:20-23 179
15:29 174
16, 20, 21, 27 ...175-78
16:2 176-77
16:9 174
16:10-11 174
16:14-23 180
16:18 175
16:19-21 175
17:57 178
17:55 175
17:58 175
18:1 175
18:8 179
18:10 179-80
18:10-11 180
19:6 176
19:9 180
19:23-24 180
19:24 180
20 176
20:33 177
21 177
21-22 200
21:1-6 362
21:2 155
21:13 241
21:13-16 178
22:11-19 181
22:18-19 ....177, 362
22:20 362
22:22 177
23:23 319

27:8-12 ....178, 200
28:6 297
28:8-16 180-81
30 182
30:1-2 220
30:12 328
30:13 328
31 181-82

2 Samuel
1 181-2
1:16 182
2:10 183
2:11 183
3:27 183
4:5-6 183
5:2 319-20
5:5 183
6:6-8 169
8:4 184
8:7-13 224
10:18 172
11 202
11:11 97
12:7-8 121
12:7-10 202
12:15-18 152-53
12:15-23 185-86
12:23 ....72, 98, 185
12:25 244
12:31 178
13:25 237
14:27 184-85
17:18 186
18:18 ......184-85, 186
21:1 153
21:1-14 161
21:19 ....178, 179
21:21 174
23:1 49
23:8 ....221, 222
24 188-89
24:1 ....186, 221
24:9b 221
24:9 188-89
24:13 189-90
24:15 188
24:18 188
24:24 190

1 Kings
1:11-21 332
1:22-27 332
2:3 46
2:22 123
2:51 219
3:3 250
3:9 250
3:16-28 250
4:15 99
4:26 .....221, 223, 295
4:29 250

4:33 250
5:13 199
6–7 280
6:1–38 116
6:1 ......115, 157, 191–98
7:13–51 116
7:20b 221
7:23 198–99
8 160
8:9 169
8:63 252
8:66 237
9:15 199
9:22 199–200
9:23 222
9:28 202
10:17 223
10:26 172
11 251
11:1 97
11:4 200–201
11:5 160
11:28 199
12:30 142
13 301
13:2 270
15:2 185
15:3 200–201
15:9–24 228
15:10 225
15:10–13 185
15:12–14 160
16:8 225–26
18:4, 13 210
19:19–21 227
21:2–3 201
21:10, 13 237
21:19 201
22 202–3
22:18–23 410
22:19 74
22:23 410
22:34–35 204
22:37–38 201
22:38 202
22:48 202–3

2 Kings
1:1 219
1:3–16 226
1:17 ....204, 219
2:1–11 227
2:11 227
2:23–24 205
3:1 204
3:11–13 205
4:3 110
5 127
5:2 65
6:5 110
6:19 205–6

7:6 98
8:16 ....219, 227
8:20 296
8:24 211
8:25 ....206, 219
8:26 ......206–7, 215, 226
9:6–10 207–9
9:29 206
10:1–10 207
10:18–27 207–8
10:29 208
10:30 207–9
10:33 208
11:21 215
11:43 98–99
13:1–3 208
13:1–4 208
13:11 209
13:14–19 209
13:19 208
13:25–27 208
14:6 ....46, 153
14:13 208
14:23 209
14:25 ....209, 300
15:1–7 316
15:5 127
15:8–16 209
15:10 209
15:19 209
15:27 209–10
15:29 104
15:32, 34 316
16:2 215
17 210–11
17:6 105
18 207
18:1 211
18:1, 9, 10 211
18:2 ....212, 215
18:4 160
18:13 ....16, 207, 211,
        222, 226
19:37 227
20:10 211
20:12–15 212–13
21 227
21:1 213
21:6 264
21:16 342
22:1 215
23:4–8 160
23:8 160
23:15 270–71
23:21 317
23:34 317
23:36 215
24:6 ....213, 275
24:8 .....206–7, 214, 215,
     217, 222, 226
24:13 214

24:14 214
24:17 244
29:8–11 211–12

1 Chronicles
1:7 37
1:32 98
2:1, 4–5, 9, 18–20 ...112
2:13 174
2:13–15 174
2:16 175
3:4 183
3:5 316
3:10 317
3:12 316
3:15 317
3:16–19 216–17
3:19 218
5:22 219–20
6:16, 22–28 220
7:22–27 112
7:25 111–12
11:11 221
17:14 225
18:4 184
20:5 ....178, 179
21 ....188–89, 220–21
21:1 221
21:1–2 186
21:3 187
21:5 188–89
21:5b 221
21:6 189
21:11–12 189–90
21:25 190
22:14 222–24
25 49
27:16 104
28 301
29:3–5 186
29:4 222–23

2 Chronicles
1:1 225
3:16 221
7:5 252
8:10 221
9:16 223
9:25 222–23
11:17 225
11:20–22 185
12:3 172
12:16 317
13:1 185
13:2–20 228
14:3 160
14:8–12 132
14:9 134
14:9–15 .....210–11, 228
14:11 301
15:16 185

15:19 225-26
16:1 225-26
16:7-9 228
17:6 160
19:2 242
20 202-3
20:30 225
20:35-36 202-3
20:37 203
21:4 226
21:12-15 226-27
21:16-17 298
22:2 ....206-7, 226
24:20-22 338
26:1-23 316
26:19-20 127
27:2 316
28:1 215
28:3 185
28:6-8 132
29:1 215
30:15-19 376
33:6 264
33:11-12 214
33:13-16 227
35:11-16 376
36:5-8 213-14
36:7 214
36:9 .....214-15, 222, 275
36:9-10 206-7
36:23 290

Ezra
1:8 217
2 ....211, 222
2:1-2 230
2:3-35 229-30
2:12 229
2:14 229
2:15 229
2:19 229
2:21-22 229
2:28 229
2:35 229
2:36-39 136
2:40 135
2:58 49
3:2 217
3:8 ....134-35, 217
3:8-13 231
4:4 231
4:7-23 231
4:24 231
5:2 217
5:3-17 232
5:13-17 231
5:14 217
5:16 218
6:1-12 232
6:3-12 231
6:15 232

6:18 46
7:6 290
7:10 290
9:9 ....232, 290

Nehemiah
1:3 290
1:1-4 290
2:5-8 290
2:8 290
2:19 233
3:1, 24, 28 274
6:6 233
7 ....211, 222
7:7 230
7:8-38 229-30
7:13 229
7:17 229
7:19 229
7:20 229
7:22 229
7:26 229
7:32 229
7:38 229
7:43 136
7:60 49
8 45
9:35 225
12:1 217
31:1 46

Esther
1:2 ....212, 225
1:14 225
2:8 234
4:16 234
5:1 225

Job
1:1 235
1:5 237
1:6 ....74, 79, 238
1:11 237
2:1 ....74, 79
2:1-2 238-39
2:5, 9 237
2:9 237
2:49 237
2:51 237
5:13 ....237, 396-7
10:3 396-7
11:15 241
12:3 396
16:12-13 397
19:25 78
19:25-27 240-1
19:26 ....78, 240
22:14 93
26:12 240
32-37 236
38:6 74

38:7 238
38:8-11 240
40:15 ....239, 240
41 240
41:1 239
42:3 237
42:7 ....237, 396
42:11 380

Psalms
1:5 78
2:1-2 25
2:7 356
2:9 41
5:4 392
5:4-6 242
5:5 242-43
8:5 374
10:3 237
11:5 242-43
14:1-3, ...387
16:9 259
16:10 ....25, 78, 353
16:11 78
16:10, 11 99
19:14 323
22 ....42, 353
22:16 43
22:17 37
23 34
29 243
29:1 ....74, 79
30 243
32 200
33:6 359
34 243-44
35:23 245
45:6 359
45:7 359-60
45:6-7 359
49:10-14 78
49:15 ....72, 78, 99
51:3-5 200
51:5 73
60:3 148
63:1 259
68:18 404-5
73:15 ....79, 374
73:20 244-45
73:24 ....72, 78, 99
74:14 240
75:8 148
82:1 374
82:1b 374
82:2 373
82:6 373
84 259
84:4 240
84:7 72
89:1 79
89:6 ....74, 79

90 356
90:2 42
90:10 77
96:4-5 357
97:7 ....74, 79
102:25-26 359
103:13 309
103:17 309
104:26 240
105 24
106 24
106:15 136
110:1 ....32, 308
110:4 92
121:3-4 244-45
136 309
137:8-9 245-46
138:1 374
139:2-3 75
139:13 246
145 39

Proverbs
1:7 251
1:33 241
8:27 93
12:22 155
15:3 75
20:1 147-49
22:6 252-53
22:15 253
23:29-35 147-49
31:4-7 147-49

Ecclesiastes
1:1 255-58
1:2 254
1:6 256
2:2-8 254
2:3 256
2:7 256
2:8 256
2:9 254
2:10 251
2:10-11 255
2:22-24 254
3:20 258
3:21 ....72, 258-60
6:12 254
7:15-16 254
7:20 387
8:12 255
9:4-5 254
9:5 255
12:1 255
12:6-7 255
12:8 255
12:13 ....252, 255
12:14 155

Song of Songs
1:6 262
2:3-6 262
4:1-5 262
5:10-16 262
6:13 261
7:1-9 262
8:7 262
8:11 262

Isaiah
1:1 316
1:9-10 295
1:11-17 273
1:12 43
1:15 264
1:19-20 71
1:29 264
2:20 36
4:4-6 39
6:1 316
6:1-3 74
6:9-10 266
6:11-13 263-64
6:13 216
7:1 316
7:3 263
7:4-6 266
7:11 41
7:14 266-68
7:14-9:6 353
7:15, 22 267
7:16 266-68
7:21 267
8:3 266-68
8:4 267
8:8 267
9 37
9:1 104
9:2 33
9:5 41
9:5-6 34
9:6 267-68
9:7 ....265, 375
10:1-2 264
11:1 431
11:2 431
11:12 93
13:19-20 54
14:4-23 269
14:10-14 66
14:12 268-70
14:12-15 74
14:13 269
14:13-14 269
14:14 66
14:21 270
14:24-27 269
25:8 ....72, 78-9
26:3 35

26:19 ....72, 79, 99
27 239
27:1 239
28:1-8 148
28:21 24
29:13 264
30:7 ....239, 240
30:30 34
31:1 213
32:19 34
33:13 37
36:1 ....207, 211
37:38 212
38:1 212
38:7-8 211
38:8 211-12
39:9 213
40-66 ......53, 264, 265
40:3 ......265, 320, 345
40:3-5 265
40:22 93
41:19 265
41:26 75
42:1 265
42:5 61
42:9, 23 75
43:1 323
43:9 75
44 271
44:2 269
44:7-8 75
44:14 265
44:28 270-71
45 271
45:1 270-71
45:7 ....179, 392, 393
45:22 357
48:12 360
48:13 360
48:16 360
49:1 ....247, 390
52:13-53:12 .....353, 375
53 313
53:1 266
53:6 ....128, 242
53:6, 10 358
53:7-8 265
53:11-12 291
54:4-6 261
56:7 335
57:4-5 264
57:5 185
57:7 264
58:2, 4 264
58:13-14 120
59:3, 7 264
59:4-9 264
61:1 36
65:1 266
65:2-4 264-65

Jeremiah

1:5	246, 380
4:4	94
7:22-23	272-73
13:12-14	148
17:9	251, 336
18:2	345
19:2	345
19:2, 11	320
19:4-7	185
19:11	345
22:11	317
22:18-19	214
25:15-18	148
26:1	273
27:1-11	273
27:9-10	181
31:3	309
31:29-30	153
31:31	273-75
31:31-33	273
31:33	274
31:38-40	274
32:6-9	320, 345
36:30	275
43:7-13	275
44:30	275
45:48	241
46:2	285

Ezekiel

14:14	235
18:1-20	153
21:27	108
21:28	289
26	275
26:3-5, 12-14	278
26:3-14	276-78
26:6-11	278
26:15-21	278
27	278
28	278-80
28:2	278-79
28:12-15	279
29:3-5	240
29:8-16	277
29:15	278
29:17-20	277
29:18	276
36:24-28	274
40-44	280-81
40-48	278
42:16	34
43:18-27	280-81
48:16	33

Daniel

1:1	284-85
1:7	217
2	286, 289, 293

2:2	285
2:35	270
2-7	283
3:5	284
3:8	285
4	282
5	282, 286, 288
5:28	293
5:30	270, 285
5:31	244, 286, 287
6:1	244
6:25	288
7	282, 293
7:1-2, 15, 28	284
7:13	322, 324
7:13-14	322
7:25	291
8:1, 15, 27	284
9	282
9:1	244, 287-88, 290
9:2, 21-22	284
9:11-13	46
9:24-27	54, 101, 289
9:25	291, 433
9:26	291, 292
9:27	284, 291
10:1-2	284
11	282, 292
11:31	284
12:2	72, 79
12:5	284
12:7	291
12:11	284
12:13	79

Hosea

1:2	294
1:3-4	294
1:4	209-11
1:10	79
2:2-3	294
3	294
5:13	269
8:11-13	295
8:13	295
10:6	269
11:5	295
13:14	72

Joel

2:28-29	353
2:28-32	274, 318, 377
2:30-32	377
3:6	296

Amos

1:13	246
2:6-16	209
4:1	209
5:5-13	209

5:21-26	273
5:26	38, 381-82
6:1-8	209
6:12	34-5
8:11-12	297
9:11-12	38

Obadiah

13	298-99

Micah

1:15	37
5:1	41
5:2	271, 318-20
6:8	387

Haggai

1:1	217
1:2	231
1:3-4	230
1:13	392
1:14	230
1:15	230
2:1	230
2:9	230
2:10	230
2:15	231
2:18	231

Zechariah

1:1	338
3:1	238
3:9	431
4:6-9	217
4:10	431
9:9	334
9:13	303
11:12-13	320, 345
12:10	37-8, 275
14:4	356

Malachi

1:2-3	242
1:11	387
2:10	305
2:11	305
2:12-13	305
2:14	305
2:15	305-6
3:1	320, 345
4:4	46

Matthew

1:1-16	316
1:5-6	156
1:9	316-17
1:12	218, 275
1:16	316
1:22	25
1:22-23	267

1:24–25 268
2:1–12 312
2:2 317–18
2:5, 15, 23 25
2:6 ....41, 318–20
2:9 318
2:16 317
2:22 212
3:1 212
3:3 265
3:16 432
4 ....236, 239, 300
4:5–10 320
5–7 366
5:1 366
5:3 366
5:16 341
5:17 371
5:18 37
5:25 341
5:32 ....397, 399
5:39 ....341, 342
7 369
7:12 336
7:16 70
7:21 370
7:23 370
8:5–13 321–22
8:5 220
8:10 343
8:20 322
8:22 324
8:28–34 324–25
8:38 333
10:5 312
10:9–10 326
10:10 ....320, 326
10:26 255
10:37 324
11:11 247
12:3–4 177–78
12:11–12 120
12:17–18 265
12:28 312
12:38–39 362–63
12:39 363
12:40 ..21, 25, 301, 327–28
12:41 25
13:1–52 312
13:31–32 328
13:35 25
15:24 312
16:4 363
16:13 322
16:19 ....354, 388
16:26 255
16:27 326
16:28 326–27
17:1–8 326
19:1–9 152
19:3–9 397

19:5 ....22, 25
19:5–6 123
19:8 123
19:9 ....121–22, 152, 399
19:16–30 329–31
19:17 371
19:24 ....59, 312
19:28 434
19:29 331
20:20 332
20:29 332–33
20:30 ....325, 333
20:33 333
20:34 333
21:2 333
21:4 25
21:5 334
21:7 334
21:12–17 334–35
21:13 335
21:18–19 ....320, 334
21:20–22 335
21:31, 43 312
21:43 312
22:17 371
22:32 ......22, 25, 32, 308
22:37 387
22:39 335–37
22:43–45 32
22:45 308
23 ....312, 430
23:2 312
23:34–35 337–38
24 312
24:2 327
24:5–7 343
24:5–14 356
24:9–22 338
24:15 284
24:23–29 338
24:24 113
24:30 ....318, 338
24:34 338–39
24:38–39 25
24:51 370
25 312
25:31–46 370
25:31 343
25:41 408
25:46 ....79, 408
26:11 150
26:33–35 75
26:52 ....341, 343
26:64 322
27:3 346
27:3–10 344
27:9 ....25, 245
27:9–10 ....318, 345
27:43 42
27:45 ....344, 363
27:51 344

27:52 ....79, 401
27:54 346–47
28:1 ....117, 347
28:2–4 348
28:5 348
28:6 348
28:7–10 117
28:7 348
28:8 348
28:9 ....350, 367
28:10 355
28:16–19 312
28:16 ....355, 356
28:19–20 356
28:19 357
28:20 356

Mark
1:2–3 ....320, 345
1:11 322
2:26 362
3:11 322
3:17 312
5:1–20 324–25
5:41 313
6:7–9 326
6:8 ....320, 326
6:52–53 344
7 312
7:3 313
7:34 313
8:11–13 362–63
8:12–13 362–63
9:7 322
10:2–12 151–52
10:17–31 329–32
10:29 331
10:30 331
10:35 332
10:46 ......325, 332, 333
10:46–47 332–33
10:47–48 333
11:2 333
11:11–19 334–35
11:12–14 334
11:12–21 320
11:17 335
11:20–25 335
12:29 357
13 312
13:2 327
13:7–8 343
14:19 419
14:30 339–41
14:64 372
14:67 340
14:68 340
14:69 340
14:70 340
14:71 340
15:25 363

15:26 346
15:33 363
15:34 313
15:39 346–47
16:1 347
16:2 ....117, 347
16:3–4 348
16:5, 6, 8 346
16:7 355

Luke
1:1–4 311
1:5 235
1:13–15 389
1:15 247
1:35 247
1:41, 44 247
2:1 365
3:4 265
3:14 220
3:23–38 316
3:27–28 218
3:27–31 218
3:31 316
3:36–38 78
4 ....236, 239, 313
4:1–13 321
4:3 320
4:5–12 320
4:14–15 321
4:23 321
4:31–32 321
4:33–37 321
4:38–39 321
4:38 314
6:17–49 312
6:17 366
6:20–49 334
6:20 366
6:46 71
7:2–11 321–22
7:11–17 313
8:26–39 324–25
9:3 326
9:30 320
9:31 326
9:50 366–67
9:60 324
10 326
10:17 419
10:18 207
11:15 367
11:17 367
11:18 367
11:21 367
11:23 366–67
11:29 363
12:14 372
14:31 343
16:19–31 ....99, 367
16:22–26 328

16:22 ....72, 98, 99
17:11–19 314
18:18–30 329–32
18:29 331
18:30 331
18:35 ....325, 332
18:36 332
18:38 332
18:39 333
18:40 332
19:27 342
19:30 333
19:43–44 327
19:45–46 334–35
20:14–16 342
21 312
22:30 331
22:31–32 188
22:34 339–41
22:44 314
22:56 340
22:57 340
22:58 340
22:59 340
22:60–61 75
22:61 340
23:9 102
23:27–31 314
23:38 346
23:39–43 314
23:43 ....328, 369–70
23:44 363
23:47 346–47
23:54 327
24:1 ....117, 347
24:2–3 348
24:4 350
24:5–7 348
24:6–7 348
24:18 352
24:19 352
24:22 351
24:32 452
24:34 ....117, 351
24:36–39 314
24:36 352
24:38 353
24:39–40 353
24:42–43 353
24:44–46 353
24:49 356
24:50–53 314
24:50 356

John
1:1, 18 375
1:1–3 358
1:3 ....268, 357–58
1:6 374
1:9 358
1:12–13 358

1:12 ....394, 420
1:14 323
1:18 ....124, 358
2:13–17 335
2:19 59
2:21 59
3:5–6 358
3:16 ....28, 65, 309, 358,
             361, 386, 408
3:18 ....74, 386, 387
3:36 ....74, 309, 324
4:24 64
4:34 374
5:2 346
5:23–24, 30 374
5:24 369
5:28–29 ......72, 369–71
5:39 398
5:46–47 46
6:37 ....358, 395
6:38–40, 44, 57 374
6:44 395
6:49 ....21, 25
6:53–58 86
7:16, 18 374
7:19 46
8:4 372
8:5 372
8:11 ....145, 371–73
8:12 358
8:16, 18 374
8:24 387
8:44 429
8:56 79
8:58 375
9:4 374
10:28 419
10:30 ....373, 375
10:33 373
10:34 373–74
10:35 373
10:36 374
10:35, 36 374
11:26 185
11:42 374
11:50 397
11:51 397
12:28 382
12:38–41 266
12:45, 49 374
13:2 179
13:27 188
14:6 ....354, 386–87
14:9 375
14:17 274
14:18 327
14:23 327
14:24 374
14:26 358
14:28 375
15:21 374

15:26 358
16:5 374
16:7 274
16:14 358
17:3, 18, 21, 23, 25 374
17:5 375
17:6 394
17:12 420
18:15-16 340-41
18:17 340
18:25 340
18:31 372
18:36 343
19:14 ...363, 364, 375, 376
19:13, 17 346
19:19 346
19:20 346
20:1 ....117, 347
20:2 348
20:3-4 349
20:5 349
20:6-7 349
20:11-18 117
20:11 349
20:12 349
20:15 350
20:16 346
20:17 ....350, 367
20:18 351
20:20 353
20:21 374
20:22 353
20:23 354
20:25 354
20:28 ....355, 358
21:7 355
21:14 354
21:18-19 355
21:18 425

Acts

1:3 355
1:4 356
1:7-8 356
1:9-11 314
1:9 355
1:13, 15 432
1:15 356
1:18 344
2 388
2:2-4 327
2:3 432
2:14-36 427
2:16-21 377
2:18 358
2:19-20 318
2:27, 31 78
2:30-31 25
2:32 117
2:33, 38, 43 358
3:22 46
4:24-26 25

5:36-37 377-78
5:37 365
6:5-6 414
7 ....379-81, 430
7:4 378
7:14 378-79
7:16 379
7:22 51
7:43 ....38, 381
8:28 265
9:4 382
9:7 382-83
9:15-16 384
10:1-6, 34-35 220
10:10-15 85
10:34-35 388
10:36-41 388
10:47-48 343
11:28 362
13:19-20 192
13:21 172
13:22 ......159, 200-201
15:14 425
15:17 38
15:18 75
15:19-20 85
15:28-29 85
16:10 311
16:14, 40 412
17:25 404
17:28 430
17:30-31 393
18:18 384
18:19-21 383
18:26 412
19 383
19:1-7 383
19:8 383
19:10 383
20:5-12 118
20:22-23 383-84
20:24 384
20:31 383
21:4 383-84
21:9 412
21:11 384
21:13 384
22:9 382-83
25:11 341-42
28 314

Romans

1:18 309
1:19-26 391-92
2 387
2:4 425
2:5-6 309
2:12 385
2:14-15 385
2:15 385
2:16 255
2:28-29 274

3 387
3:10-11 387
3:19 385-86
3:26 243
4:5 323
4:9-10 93
4:11 93
4:13 71
5:8 386
5:12-21 ....22, 64
5:14 388-90
6:11-12, 17-18 ...71-72
6:12-14 369
6:13 ....159, 370
8:5-8 73
8:7-8 369
8:10-11, 14 394
8:31-38 309
8:33 337
9:5 ....358, 375
9:13 390
9:17 390-95
9:19 ....390-91, 392
9:20 391
9:21 392
9:22 ......391, 392, 425
9:23 391
9:23-24 391
9:30-31 391
9:24-25 392
10 387
10:3 370
10:5 46
10:9-10 394
10:13 386
10:14-15 386
10:20 266
11:25-27 274
12:1 ....71, 165
12:1, 2 394
12:17 341
13 341
13:1, 3, 4 341
13:4 371-73
14:21 148
15:4 297
16:1 414
16:1-2 ....412, 414
16:13 313

1 Corinthians

2:10 358
2:13 358
2:14-15 260
3:16 358
3:19 ....237, 238, 396
5:7 376
6:19 ...159, 274, 337, 358
7:8 397
7:10-16 ..151-52, 398-401
7:10-11 397
7:12 397-98

7:21 87
7:40 397-98
8 85
8:5-6 357
8:6 358
9:7 343
10 302
10:7 401
10:8 ....141, 401
10:27-28 86
11:5-6 412
11:24-26 280
11:30 72
12:7-11 358
14:3 412
15:4 328
15:5 351
15:6 ....355, 356
15:17 402
15:29 401-2
15:30, 31 402
15:44, 46 260
15:51 72
15:54-56 185
16:2 118

2 Corinthians
5:10 370
5:14-15 337
5:14-17 420
5:17 428
5:19-20 337
10:4-5 ....159, 341
11:5 135
12:2 239
12:11-12 135

Galatians
1:12 22
3:7, 29 274
3:16 403
3:17 403
3:22-24 403
3:27-28 411
5:22-23 394

Ephesians
1:3-4 337
1:4 394
1:17 358
2:1 324
2:1-3 73
2:2 238
2:3 73
2:8 ....71, 386
2:8-9 ....358, 393-94,
                    394, 411
2:9 394
2:18-22 358
3:18-19 261
4:6 357
4:8 ....79, 367-68,
                404-5, 423

4:9 368
4:10 368
4:25 155
5:21-27 261
5:21 413
5:22-24 413
5:23 122
5:25-33 413
6:4 253
6:5-8 87
6:11-17 220

Philippians
1:23 72
2:10 409
4:2-3 412

Colossians
1:16 409
1:19-20 406
1:20 406-9
2:2 375
2:11-13 94
2:16, 17 120
3:1-4 394
4:11, 14 311

1 Thessalonians
4:14 72
5:10 72
5:23 ....259, 359

2 Thessalonians
1:6-9 309
2:9-10 410
2:11 410
2:9 ....113, 181

1 Timothy
2:9 151
2:11-12 411-15
2:13-14 ....22, 58, 411
3:2 400
3:2-12 400
3:12 400
5:2 413
5:3-6 414
6:16 125

2 Timothy
1:10 185
2:3-4 343
2:4 220
3:1-3 336
3:16 416-17
3:16-17 15

Titus
1:2 394
2 414
2:9 148
3:1-2 398

2:3 414
2:13 ....358, 375
3:5 394
3:7 394

Hebrews
1:2 362
1:2-3 ....358, 409
1:3 358
1:6 79
1:8 ....359, 375
1:10-11 359
1:14 79
2:17-18 418
4:1-11 62
4:15 418
6:4-6 419
6:4 420
7:1-2 92
7:3 92
7:22-24 92
8:6-13 274
8:9 273
9:11-12 71
9:22 121
9:27 ....408, 423
10:4 71
10:11-14 280
10:26-31 419
10:26-27 420
10:29 420
11 ....165, 421-22
11:4 ....71, 76
11:5 78
11:10 79
11:21 421
11:31 156
11:32-34 344
11:32 421
11:33-34 421
11:35-38 421
11:35 400
11:36-38 400
11:39 400
11:39-40 79
12:1 148
12:2 ....29, 428
12:22 433
12:29 310
13:4 433

James
1:13-14 392
1:13 179
1:14-15 171
2:17-18 369
2:25 158
2:26 394
5:11 236

1 Peter
2:2-3 427
2:5 274

3:18-20 423-24
3:19 423-24
3:20 427
3:21 424
4:13-14 188
4:19 188
5:8 188
5:12 426-27

2 Peter
1:1 425
1:5-8 427
1:14 425
1:16-18 425
1:20 417
1:21 358
2:4 .... 66, 74-75, 238,
            239, 426
2:5 .... 423, 427
2:11 426
3:1 425
3:3-4 426
3:6 427
3:9 395
3:15-16 425
3:16 417
3:18 427

1 John
1:6 429
1:7 429

1:8 428
2:15 .... 65, 242
3:4 428
3:6 428
3:8 429
3:9 428-29
5:7 375
5:8 375
5:20 .... 359, 375

Jude
6 426
9 .... 238, 426, 430
14 430
17-18 426

Revelation
1:2 431
1:4 431-32
1:10 118
1:14-15 432
1:17-18 408
2:27 41
3:1 431
3:20 327
4:4 433
4:5 431
5:6 .... 431, 432
5:8 433
6:10 246
6:15-17 309-10

7:3-8 432-34
7:5-8 .... 432, 434
7:9 433
11:16 433
12:3 432
12:5 41
12:10 238
13:2 432
13:8 75
13:13 113
14:1-5 433
14:1 432
14:8 270
14:9-11 310
14:10 148
14:11 73
14:13 185
16-18 377
16:8-10 407
17:3-4 432
18 278
19:4 433
19:9 434
20:2 270
20:2-3 239
20:7-10 239
20:10 ...... 74, 280, 407-8
20:12 370
20:14 73
21:8 ... 74, 239, 407-8, 409
21:27 237